The Notebooks for A Raw Youth

A pencil drawing of Dostoevsky by I. A. Sharleman, made in 1924

The Notebooks for

A Raw Youth

Fyodor Dostoevsky

Edited and with an Introduction by Edward Wasiolek

Translated by Victor Terras

The University of Chicago Press
CHICAGO & LONDON

Standard Book Number: 226–15965–5
Library of Congress Catalog Number: 75-84588

The translation is based upon the Russian edition of *F. M. Dostoevsky at Work on His Novel "A Raw Youth,"* edited by A. S. Dolinin (Moscow, 1965), vol. 77 of *Literaturnoe Nasledstvo,* edited by I. I. Anisimov *et al.*

The University of Chicago Press, Chicago 60637
The University of Chicago Press, Ltd., London

Published 1969. Printed in the United States of America

Contents

Illustrations

Introduction

I

There are admirers of Dostoevsky who look upon *Crime and Punishment* as Dostoevsky's greatest novel, and just as many who would choose *The Idiot* or *The Possessed,* and many more who would choose *The Brothers Karamazov*. Each of the four great novels can in its own way support the burden of greatness. But *A Raw Youth* cannot. Perhaps it shines less because it lies in the midst of such brilliance, but it still shines dully, and no amount of explanation or justification will make it shine more. For Dostoevsky *A Raw Youth* is a failure.

And yet there was no reason for *A Raw Youth* to be a failure. Dostoevsky was at the height of his creative powers, and *The Brothers Karamazov* was to follow it as definitive sign that *A Raw Youth* did not signal a general decline of talent. The conditions for work were never better. Dostoevsky was back in his native Russia after four years of pining, and from 1871 on he was once again in touch with the contemporary and living life he missed in writing *The Idiot* and much of *The Possessed*. His financial affairs—though far from happy—were better than they had ever been, thanks to the ingenuity and tireless efforts of his efficient wife. His home life, too, was peaceful and happy. He was more sure of what he wanted to write about than he had been when he wrote *The Idiot* and *The Possessed*. There is none of the agonizing search for a subject that we have in the notebooks for *The Idiot* and none of the conflict of wanting to write one thing and finding himself writing something else that we find in the notebooks for *The Possessed*. He knew from the very beginning that he was going to write a novel about disorder in contemporary society and the search of the younger generation for order. He was less haunted, too, at this time by ghosts from the past, less intolerant of "socialists," "nihilists," and "liberals." It is true that these were the years when he was working for the reactionary newspaper *The Citizen,* and the years when, immediately before and after the writing of *A Raw Youth* (1875), he was writing articles on frankly chauvinistic and reactionary themes. But it is also true that he chafed at his cooperation with the unsavory publisher Meshchersky, jeopardized the status of the journal more than once with government censors because of his liberal views, and severed his relationship with the journal because he was unable to live with the reactionary demands of its publisher.

Dostoevsky was beginning to listen to the other side, in a way he had done only reluctantly before this. He had always shown an impatience in his created works with the "other case," and only a tough artistic integrity had held in check a propagandistic impulse in his character. He was a little too eager to establish Sonia's influence and Raskolnikov's conversion in *Crime and Punishment;* his expression of nihilist vulgarity is too enthusiastically put forth in the Burdovsky episode in *The Idiot,* and his portrayal of the socialists and liberal elements in *The Possessed* is gleefully destructive. Such literary executions and easy caricatures as we find in *The Possessed* are lacking in *A Raw Youth,* and the explanation seems to be that Dostoevsky was feeling something of that spirit of reconciliation that he was to express so eloquently in his Pushkin speech in 1880.

Dostoevsky had gone out of his way to break his association with Katkov and the conservative *The Russian Messenger,* where he had published his great novels, in order to place *A Raw Youth* in the liberal journal *The Fatherland Notes* under the editorship of Nekrasov. The overture to publish his next novel there had come from the journal itself, and Dostoevsky took more than six months before he gave his final answer; yet the fact that he agreed to place his new novel there can be explained only by some change in his mental and emotional horizon. It was not a change in political orientation as Soviet critics sometimes hopefully explain. Rather, it was a new eagerness to listen to the new Russia, which fascinated and troubled him. The long years of self-exile abroad had convinced him that he had become out of touch with new realities, and it was toward these new realities that he tried to turn. He was as convinced as ever that socialism, nihilism, and liberalism were wrong, but he seemed readier than ever to believe that they were sincere.

His new temper led him to Nekrasov's journal and also to the Dolgushintsy conspiracy. The Dolgushintsy, who are represented under the name of Dergachev in the novel, constituted a conspiratorial group that called upon the people, and especially the peasants, to overthrow the landowners and the Tsar with the view of distributing the land to the people, replacing the permanent army with a militia, abolishing the passport, and instituting a popularly elected government. Dostoevsky followed very closely the trial of the Dolgushintsy in July of 1874, and a trace of his interest is retained in the Dergachev subplot in the novel. Although the Dergachev subplot figures importantly in the notes, it leads nowhere in the novel. Dostoevsky treats the radical group more gently than he would have earlier, but the subversive group finds no place in his interest and it finds no place in the structure of the novel. A broader and more lasting effect of his desire to keep in touch with liberal currents lay in his attempt to describe a society that was obsessed by money and self-gain and devoid of living beliefs—and against this background to dramatize the search for ideals on the part of the Youth. His intention to do this is voiced in letters and notes; yet no general picture of social disorder emerges in the novel. Something deeper in talent and view militated against what intention decreed.

Dostoevsky had always placed a great stress on contemporary events and went to great pains to ferret out his chronicles of social horrors. They may have had less effect upon his work than is commonly thought. The contemporary events he painstakingly collected from newspapers and courtrooms often languished in the notebooks and letters, that is, in intention. When he used them in the works themselves, they were either so reconceived as to have lost any specific correspondence to the life situation from which they had been collected, or they refused to live in his works, as did the Dolgushintsy-Dergachev subplot, and appeared as artistic blemishes. There is finally very little of the Olga Umetskaia case left in the actions and situation of Nastasya Filiplovna, although there is a great deal of her in the notebooks. Soviet, and occasionally American scholars, have been fond of showing us how much of *A Raw Youth* has been based on factual events. They are right: the Tambovo-Kozlovsky forgery lies at the base of the Stebelkov blackmail of Prince Sergei, the Dolgushintsy conspiracy at the base of the Dergachev subplot, and a newspaper campaign against gambling at the base of the Youth's gambling sprees. Hertsen may be a prototype for Versilov; and the names of public figures, both domestic and foreign, play either spoken or unspoken roles in the novel. Yet it is remarkable how little of contemporary life makes it from the notebooks to the novel. The notebooks are dotted with references to public figures, ministers, engineers, newspaper articles, political events, crimes, and campaigns, the vast majority of which never leave the world of the notebooks for the fictive world of the novel.

I don't believe Dostoevsky himself realized how often his novels rejected his attempts to import the facts of life into them. The impulses of his creativity were not to be found in his researching into and chronicling of the events and horrors of the time, which he was so proud to cite as proofs of his realism. At best these were corroborating instances of what he had already imagined and created. His creative world is an intense subjectivity, as indeed its individual characters are. Dostoevsky's great personalities do not have "prototypes" in the world, nor do his great situations have casual analogues in the real world. They are very special cases, or in Dostoevsky's words "typical exceptions", and they do not live as any conceivable prototypes would live in the real world. They are intensely one kind of thing, and by a special kind of magnetism they attract to themselves only situations, people, and events of a similar kind and by a special antimagnetism repel everything else. Dostoevsky's great novels are built on his great characters, and his great characters almost always remind us of self-enclosed worlds with magnetic cores of their own. *The Possessed* is largely composed of worlds that the intense subjectivity of Peter, Kirilov, Shatov, and Stavrogin bring into being. Dostoevsky's great characters are not created by situations either in or outside the novel, but they themselves create situations and draw to them—as Peter does consummately—others who are like them in some essential sense.

When Dostoevsky attempts to give us a "social panorama," as he tried to do in the middle chapters of *The Idiot,* the novel loses much of its intensity and disperses into minor "subjectivities" and confusion. Characters crowd the stage, situations multiply, and no special magnetism welds the characters and situations into any kind of unity. Dostoevsky's attempt, or at least his desire, to give us a picture of disorder in society in *A Raw Youth,* was doomed to failure by the very nature of his talent. He can give us magnificent portrayals of individual disorder, but unconvincing pictures of general disorder. Lacking the magnetism of the great characters, *A Raw Youth* disperses into plottings, confusions, melodrama, contrivances, and repetitions. Some of the compositional disorder of the novel came about, I am convinced, because there was no great character to impose order by his will and personality. The triangle of Nastasya Fillipovna, and Myshkin, and Rogozhin is powerful enough to command the most dispersed elements into relevance, and Peter and Stavrogin are powerful enough to draw into obedience the satellite worlds of the other important characters. But *A Raw Youth* has no such center. Versilov is almost such a center, and might have become one, but Dostoevsky fought against Versilov's domination of the novel. He wanted to write a novel about general social disorder and about a young man's sufferings and successes in such a world. He was unfortunately able to do largely what he set out to do.

Versilov alone raises the novel above confusion and melodrama, and to the level of tragedy and intensity that is embodied in Stavrogin, Kirilov, Raskolnikov, and Myshkin. Dostoevsky told himself again and again in the notes that Versilov was not the hero, and that the Youth was the hero. But despite his words, Versilov dominates the novel in his person and the intensity of his character. Alfred Kazin was right when he said "Versilov is the true 'hero' of *A Raw Youth,*" and that "those who hate him cannot free themselves from him; those who love him cannot reach him."

Everyone feels his effect, but no one knows who he is. He is mystery to everyone, but everyone needs him. His son needs him, suffers for him, feels his humiliations, and lives for his love, or perhaps only for the sign of his love. Versilov expects love from everyone, but gives love to no one; expects the service of everyone, but serves no one. They all wait on him and he waits on no one. He is quiet, self-contained, confident, sure of his effect on others and of their response to him. He is like a medieval lord who commands fealty without asking for it. He has no position, no money, and no title, but by some inner force exercises an irresistible power over those about him. One of the tasks for the critic of the novel is to discern what the source of that effect is and how Dostoevsky was able to communicate the effect.

The effect seems unlikely, since Versilov has been built of old characters, remnants and snatches of motifs used before. He is, in his sponging and his disregard of his son, something like Stepan Trofimovich Verkhovensky in his Gallicisms, his forgetting of moral obligations, his European "uprootedness." He is a serious Stepan Trofimovich. He is a Shatov in his messianic belief in the superiority of the Russian over other European nationalities, as he is a Shatov in his inability to believe in God. He is an Ivan Karamazov in his adoration of European culture, and an Underground Man in his pervasive nihilism. He is Stavrogin in the dark and mysterious past, the slap in the face he suffers, his inconsequent actions, and most of all, of course, the Stavrogin of the suppressed chapters of the red beetle, the raped girl, and the dream of the golden age. He has elements of the Underground Man, Raskolnikov, Stavrogin, Stepan Trofimovich, Dmitri Karamazov, and surely Ivan Karamazov. Somewhere during the process of writing *A Raw Youth* Dostoevsky found who Versilov was, and the notes are the history of his transformation from a patchwork of motifs to one of Dostoevsky's great characters. Had he permitted Versilov to take command of the novel, as Versilov tries to do throughout the notes, Dostoevsky might have achieved the greatness that *A Raw Youth* promised but never realized. The notes are largely a record of the development and refinement of Versilov's character, not a record of the development of the Youth, Dostoevsky's statements notwithstanding. Versilov dominates the notes and he should have dominated the novel.

II

The Versilov we have in the final version and the Versilov we meet in the early notes are very far apart. The Versilov of the early notes is cruel, passionate, predatory, bored, and indifferent to the sufferings of others. He seduces a young girl and laughs at her when she hangs herself, and in one version seduces a stepdaughter and plots with her to poison the wife and mother. He is ruthless in action and in opinion. He says, "Why should I do good? Why should I love anybody?" and, "Why shouldn't I live to take care of my own arse, what else is there to do? Worry about the common good, make your contribution to the happiness of future generations? To hell with them, what the devil do I care? Let them tell me something more serious to support such notion." He is a Predatory Type and it is by this name that we know him in the early notes.

The Versilov of the late notes and of the final version seduces no girls, and he voices no sentiments of cynical nihilism. On the contrary, he does good deeds; he takes care of the seduced girl of Prince Sergei, then takes care of the orphaned offspring, and he magnanimously gives up an inheritance that is legally his, though not morally his. In opinion, he is a cultured and refined humanist who loves civilization, adores its culture, and is sentimentally attached to the passing of Christianity. He conveys the impression of tolerance, wisdom, culture, and refinement. He seems to be remote from the coarseness of action and the cynicism of opinion of the Predatory Type, but the history of change which is traced in these notes shows us that the Predatory Type continues to live in the cultured humanist.

Between the early notes and the late notes there is a progressive and gradual shift in the portraiture of Versilov from "acts" to "ideas." Philosophical premises take the place of rapacious acts and nihilistic thought. The actor becomes the talker, and the cynic the philosopher. In the final version we are not sure about Versilov. Many of his ideas would be championed by Dostoevsky himself, and many of his acts, despite his aloofness, are admirable or at least morally ambiguous. But whatever he is in appearance and conscious intention, Katerina

Nikolaevna destroys. By her intention to marry Bioring, she turns Versilov into a humble penitent and then raving madman. From olympic calm and philosophical vision Versilov falls into rage, plot, collusion with Lambert, and finally to near-murder.

Katerina Nikolaevna causes Versilov's downfall in the novel, but she does more in the notes. She explains it. Versilov's fall indicates that there is something wrong with his calm, his "idea," and with his views of life. But the "something wrong" is left ambiguous in the novel. The notes tell us what is wrong and why he is wrong. And what is wrong has to do with what is wrong with his idea. We are never quite told what Versilov's idea is in the novel, although we assume that the idea has animated his wanderings and his opinions on Europe, Russia, and the destiny of man. The notes tell us what the idea is:

> I conceived, at that time, my original idea: seek to perfect yourself, try to break your own resistance as your conscience and your faith will tell you, to the best of your ability, and, once having conquered yourself, you may perhaps also find the ultimate idea, your own solution "what to do?" and "what to preach?" I passionately clung to this idea. You were all laughing at my chains. Why? I was actually wearing them, but you didn't know what was going on in my *soul*. Yes, it may be that, finally, I did persuade myself that mine was the right way, but then you appeared before me, and I suddenly realized that without you I am nothing, and my idea unrealizable.

These are Versilov's own words and his own analysis of his idea. Late in the novel Dostoevsky gives us a starker, more explicit, and less flattering analysis of the idea:

> 1) Versilov is convinced of the loss and of the stupidity of every ideal, as well as of the curse of stagnation on that has hit the whole moral world.
>
> 2) For a while he forced himself to believe in Christ.
>
> 3) But his whole faith went to pieces. There remained only a moral feeling of duty ~~as such~~ telling him to strive for self perfection and good <deeds> *under any circumstances* (i.e., regardless of any loss of faith, or any kind of moral despair), owing to his own con-

scious will, a certain uncompromising despair). "Though my ideal may be lost and I may not know good from evil, still, I shall follow my conscience and, gropingly, seek to perfect myself—and I shall get somewhere." Having lost his faith he decides instead of succumbing to despair, to start straight from himself, and he believes that he will get somewhere, and that something will be revealed to him along the way (the chains).

Versilov and Dostoevsky tell us what the idea is, and Katerina Nikolaevna tells us what is wrong with the idea:

> She to Him: When falling in love with me, you were falling in love with no one but yourself and, besides, you certainly couldn't have forgiven me that confession which you made before me, for you saw it as a humiliation. You vain man, you couldn't even stand *that*. How then was I going to help laughing at you?

And with a vigor she does not manifest in the novel, she continues:

> *She:* ("Lack of all form") I have seen your pride, which consists of the idea that, inasmuch as I have learned about your thoughts and you have exposed your soul before me (you have deigned to open it to me, I should therefore value this very highly. I have seen this in every movement of yours, and I've made a point of ceasing to value it. quite on the contrary, I've been often laughing at it. This alone is utterly disgraceful.

Katerina Nikolaevna saw only "the falsity of the idealist, the stiltedness, the affectation" in the idea, and in the man "I have seen your moral disorder."

Katerina Nikolaevna tells us that Versilov is a product of moral disorder and that his idea is the product of affectation, pride, artificiality. But she does not tell us why this is so. We receive judgment and not explanation from her. The intent of the idea seems admirable: by denial, discipline, and the conquering of the self, Versilov would find his faith. Versilov has lost his faith, but not his desire for faith, and he attempts to create with his will what his spirit has lost.

But for Dostoevsky the effort of will is the work of pride. What looks like self-sacrifice and self-command are really self-indulgence and self-satisfaction. Versilov's idea is the ultimate refinement of the self-contained mind which seeks to make God and salvation the products of the will, an effort which is caricatured in Stepan Trofimovich Verkhovensky's explanation of his belief in God as a "Being who is conscious of Himself in me only."

Something of the ambiguity of Versilov's character and actions in the final version are cleared up when we realize, as the notes tell us explicitly, that he does not believe in God, that his faith is a subtle effort to make himself creator as well as believer of the faith, that the delicate scaffolding of culture, refinement, and civilization is vanity and self-love. More than one critic has been swept away with the "sincere" sentiments of Versilov's love of humanity, his nostalgia for Christianity, and the beatific vision of the golden age. The scaffolding collapses so suddenly and so fully when he is touched by Katerina Nikolaevna's rejection, because it was built of vanity and pride. In the notes—much more so than in the novel—Versilov vacillates from adoration to revilement of Katerina Nikolaevna. She is either the worst of women or the best of women, and, of course, vanity would dictate one or the other. If she loves Versilov, she must be the best of women; and if she rejects him she must be the worst of women. We can understand, too, why he turns in the notes to Lidiia after he is rejected by Katerina Nikolaevna. Shame, anger, and humiliation turn him to her; he must reassert his control over another human being, albeit a half-wit and a cripple. As in many other instances in the novel this fact is deliberately obscured and mixed with what seem to be good motives. In the novel he "magnanimously" offers marriage to the seduced and abandoned Lidiia, and after her death "magnanimously" takes care of Prince Sergei's bastard offspring.

And yet it is perhaps too simple to see only vanity and pride beneath the culture and civilized exterior. The relationship is more complex and more subtle. Versilov's vanity is modified by suffering and some sincere desire to give substance to the appearance of nobility and wisdom. The notes make clear that he did not believe in God, that he loved only himself, and that his faith was a faith created to honor him. They show us—as Katerina Nikolaevna says in a half-dozen ways—a false Versilov, and the false Versilov remains in the novel, but this is not the same thing as a "hypocritical" Versilov. Versilov is false and vain despite himself. He would like to believe, to be magnanimous, to love sincerely. He is not a hypocrite when he tells Arkady that he has come to love only his mother. But he cannot be any of these things, because he does not believe in God, and as Dostoevsky showed so many times before and shows here once again, when one ceases to believe in God, one can believe in oneself alone, and when one believes only in oneself, self-interest will corrupt the best of intentions.

It is this special and ambiguous moral nature of sincere intentions and necessary self-interest that contributes both to the ambiguity we feel about Versilov's moral nature and to the moral force and charm he commands over the other characters. We like what he says, and we often like what he does. We like particularly, I think, the self-containment and indifference on his part to what moves others. It has the sign of a man who has come to terms with himself and with circumstances about him. It is the sign of someone who has found in himself what everyone else seems to be looking for. This is a society obsessed by money: Prince Sergei has bartered his honor for it, Katerina Nikolaevna has promised to dishonor her father for it, Arkady has conceived of a program of life in acquiring it, but Versilov magnimously and almost disdainfully "gives up" what others are ready to ravage for. There is a touch of moral superiority in the gesture. Versilov seems beyond the grubby pursuits, passions, and words of the frantic world that surrounds him. He seems, in short, to be beyond the turbulence that touches everyone else. Yet in both novel and notes he is touched coarsely and suddenly by his passion for Katerina Nikolaevna. This is so because the moral superiority, the calm, the indifference, and the sense of a world under his command are such only in appearance. Dostoevsky is telling us that culture, wisdom, refinement, and the acquirements of the best of Russia and the best of Europe are no armor against the ravages of the self. They can refine the predatory character, but they cannot dispel it. This is the tragedy of Versilov, for the Predatory Type of the early notes continues to live in the ambiguous and moral predatoriness of the Versilov of the final version.

III

Throughout a significant portion of the notes Dostoevsky carries on a dialogue with himself about the relative advantages of the first- or third-person point of view. Both have their advantages and their disadvantages. He tells us the following in one of his deliberations: "Think over the possibility of a *first-person* narrative. Many advantages; much freshness, the figure of the Youth would emerge more typical, nicer. I'll be able to cope better with the character, with the personality, with the essence of that personality." On the other hand he realizes that in giving the point of view to the Youth he will not be able to express certain important thoughts and feelings of others: "NOTE. The Youth, due to his tender age, has no access to the events, facts which comprise the plot of the novel. And so he makes his own *conjectures* and *masters* them by himself. Which circumstance is reflected in the whole manner of his narrative (to give the reader some surprises)."

Dostoevsky's dialogue with himself about the mode of narration goes on for a good part of these notes, but throughout the dialogue and long before he cries out "In *the first person,* in *the first person,* in *the first person*" the reader is convinced that Dostoevsky has committed himself to first-person narration almost from the very beginning, at least from that point in the notes when he asserts forcefully that the Youth and not "He" will be the hero of the novel. Dostoevsky needed first-person narration as a device by which he hoped to invite sympathy and love of the reader for the Youth. If we are forced to share with Arkady his confusions, enthusiasms, fumblings, angers, loves, and hates, we might be won over to the beauty of his soul.

I am not sure that Dostoevsky gained this for the Youth. The Youth is too much a "recorder" of what happens and too little the sufferer and undergoer. So much happens, so quickly and so implausibly, that we lose some sense of the seriousness of what is going on. More than once *A Raw Youth* borders on comedy, as indeed melodrama, through the multiplication of implausibilities, always borders on comedy. If we felt that the Youth were suffering, the first-person narration might intensify the suffering and our love, but instead the narration simply magnifies the confusions and the implausibilities. Dostoevsky made a mistake, I think, in giving the point of view to Arkady, and he might have done better in opting for the solution he came to in *Crime and Punishment,* where he toyed with the same alternative narrative modes. As there, he might have centered his narrative on the Youth while keeping the control of the narrative away from the Youth.

There is, however, one advantage Dostoevsky derived from giving the point of view to the Youth: the ambiguity and mystery of Versilov's character is compounded by the confusions and emotional turbulence of the Youth. In the notes Versilov is analyzed directly and the effect is very much different from the effect in the novel. The paradoxical, enigmatic, and mysterious Versilov in the novel is partly the creation of the Youth's feverish and distorting thoughts and emotions. In the notes Versilov is unrefracted; he is presented directly and his motives are analyzed directly.

It seems quite clear from the notes, and it should be noted here, that Dostoevsky very deliberately marshaled his technical equipment to increase the moral ambiguity and the mystery of Versilov. The notes make it quite clear that he knew that Versilov was in a very real sense "false" and very much the predatory type he started with, though softened by culture, suffering, and good intention. But Dostoevsky deliberately manipulates mystery and ambiguity for technical reasons. I bring this up only because it is often asserted today that the conjunction of technique and matter does not occur so deliberately and mechanically. Technique, when it is not an end in itself, is usually put forth as "heuristic," that is, as the means by which an author finds his ideas. It may very well happen that way in some works, but seldom in Dostoevsky's creative world, and never in the notebooks for *A Raw Youth.*

Whereas Versilov undergoes a progressive and important change in the course of the notes, the Youth changes very little and is in essential respects no different in the notes from the way he is presented in the novel. He is at the end what Dostoevsky made him at the beginning, a fact that might testify to the firmness of intention and the imperviousness of the Youth and Dostoevsky to creative change. There is perhaps one exception: the Youth's libidinous desires for Katerina Nikolaevna (the Princess) are expressed openly and frequently in the notes, and even coarsely, but they are veiled and fragmentary in the novel, appearing only in hint and dream. Both father and son know, in the notes, that they are engaged in sexual rivalry, but neither knows it in the final version. Long before Freud, Dostoevsky knew and expressed the concept that the love of the Youth veiled its hostilities, and that both the love and hostility had something of sexual origin. But the sexual rivalry went the way of the frequent obscene words in the notes, and hardly a hint of either is to be found in the final version. If there are those who deny the influence of society on art, the notebooks for *A Raw Youth* offer testimony to that influence.

The object of that sexual rivalry, and in the novel the object of Arkady's and Versilov's sublimated passions should have been a great character. She is, after all, the provoker of passion and destruction. Versilov's "salvation" is ruined by her smile. Yet she hardly seems adequate, in her desire for peace and social security, to the passions and disturbances she provokes. The notes tell us something of the changes in the character of Katerina Nikolaevna, but very little about why she is not more complex and more adequate to the tasks that Versilov and the novel impose on her.

In the early notes she, like Versilov himself, is passionate, cruel, and even depraved: in some of the versions, for instance, she seduces the Youth. Dostoevsky had, in his early design, the intention of making her something of a double to Versilov: "What is going on between Him and the Princess is not passion, but a duel of pride. Yes, the Princess is that kind of person herself." In the final version Katerina Nikolaevna resists the obeisance Versilov exacts from nearly everyone else; she refuses to be touched, and she recoils from his complications. But she recoils not from principle or force of character, but from the desire to lead a simple and peaceful life. She is mystery without substance, a provoker of passions without passion. Versilov's predatory qualities are softened to subtleties, but her predatory traits are softened to innocuousness. She seems at the end like a very ordinary woman of society, who wants in almost a vulgar way the security of position and money.

IV

Horst-Jurgen Gerigk has written two hundred pages of analysis and charts describing the refinements of structure in *A Raw Youth,* but the book will convince only those who want to be convinced. There is plotting and contriving in *A Raw Youth,* but very little structure, if by that we mean the marshaling of all the elements of the novel for a unified effect. Dostoevsky himself was aware that he could wander, and in one passage of the notes he affirmed his intention of not wandering again:

> *1st rule* Avoid the mistake, made in *The Idiot* and in *The Possessed,* of describing (many of the) secondary events in a fragmentary, insinuated, romance-like manner, and dragging them out over a lengthy extension <of the novel>, both in the narrated action as well as in individual scenes, yet without giving any explanations at all, just guesses and hints, instead of *explaining the truth directly.* Being mere secondary episodes, they weren't worth such concentrated attention on the part of the reader, rather on the contrary, they actually tended to obscure, rather than to clarify, the principle objective, precisely because the reader, diverted to a side road, could very well lose the main road and get all confused in his attention.

Dostoevsky was not able to do what he wanted, but as disappointed readers we cannot help speculating on what the novel could have become if he had been able to stem the profusion of secondary characters and situation and if he had found his way to social disorder by way of great and intensely personal embodiments of order and disorder.

What would the novel have been if Dostoevsky had given up the idea of drawing for us a general picture of social disorder and had pruned away the Dergachev episodes, the Stebelkovs and the counterfeiting, many of the inanities of the old Prince, and some of the inanities of the young Prince? Suppose, too, he had done away with the tiresome documents, the eavesdropping, the coincidences, and the melodramatic contrivances. Suppose he had written on what he tells us in the notes the novel is all about: "All in all, the whole novel is a poem of the Youth's love for Him." Suppose he had written about the son's love for a father with all its bruising complexity and its defeats and its minor but precious triumphs, and had permitted both the Youth and Versilov to take command of the novel. Dostoevsky would have had his picture of social disorder without disordering his novel. There was disorder and complexity enough, of the truest kind, in the scattered notes we have of the love the youth bore for his father and both bore for the Princess.

The Youth loves and hates the Princess (Katerina Nikolaevna), because he loves and hates his father. He feels shame and mortification because his father is lusting after the Princess, and greater shame and mortification because he himself is lusting after her, and the greatest shame because he is his father's rival, while loving him. Arkady needs his father and realizes that his father needs him, and he rushes to the defense of Versilov against the "depraved" woman even to the point of casting away his ideas so as to protect his father by vilifying her. The notes give us the embryo of one of Dostoevsky's great triangles, a situation of mortifying and ambiguous love. Most of it is not present in the novel, and if present, it is so veiled by prudence and so confused by the endless plotting and so fixed in contrivance and implausibility as to lose the serious and even tragic character that much of it has in the remarks in the notebooks.

One is amazed that *The Idiot* could have arisen from notes of such uncertain intention, and that Stavrogin could have come from notes of a garrulous and romantic Prince, or that Kirilov could have grown to such proportions from the brief references to him in the notes of *The Possessed.* But far more is promised in the notes for *A Raw Youth* than is realized in the novel. The promise is fulfilled in Dostoevsky's next novel, *The Brothers Karamazov,* where he was to write of the love-hate of father and sons. There he was to give the love Arkady bore for his father to Alyosha, the passion he felt to Dmitri; and he was to give Versilov's predatory qualities to Fyodor, and his intellectual predatoriness to Ivan. Smerdyakov was to be the shadow of them all. The notebooks that follow are as much a preparation for *The Brothers Karamazov* as they are for *A Raw Youth.*

V

One cannot leave a discussion of the notebooks for *A Raw Youth* without calling attention to some remarkable pages in the last section of the notes in which Dostoevsky contrasts his work with that of Tolstoy and defends and defines his "Underground" type. There are enough references to Tolstoy, explicit and implicit, in the notes to indicate that Dostoevsky was thinking of his great Russian fellow writer while he was writing *A Raw Youth.* Dostoevsky probably had Tolstoy's youthful narrator from *Childhood* in mind when he was creating Arkady, and the example of Tolstoy's "normal" family was uppermost in his thoughts as a contrast to his "accidental" family. Dostoevsky had more humility than Tolstoy when assessing his talent and place in Russian letters, but there is something like irritated pride and a sense of being unappreciated in these pages in the sixth section of these notes, where he defends his conception of the underground type against his critics and against the normal type as created by Goncharov and Tolstoy. He says: "'Tolstoy, Goncharov, thought that they were describing the life of the majority;—in my opinion, what they were describing were the lives of some exceptions. Quite to the contrary, their life is the life of some exceptions, while mine is the life of the general rule. Future generations will find that out, as they will be more objective, and the truth will be on my side. In this I believe." Dostoevsky was right about this, of course, but he was even more right and remarkably acute in his definition of the underground type: "I have been the only one to bring out the tragedy of the underground, which consists of suffering, self-laceration, an awareness of a better <life> coupled with the impossibility of attaining it, and, most important of all, a strong conviction on the part of these unfortunate people that everybody else is like them and that it is, therefore, not worth while to improve oneself. What can sustain those who do try to improve themselves? A reward, faith? Nobody is offering any reward, and in whom could one have faith? Another step from this position and you have extreme depravity, crime (murder). A mystery."

Tolstoy's psychology strikes him as unreal and naïve. He says in self-justification and bitter satisfaction: "Bolkonsky reforms as he sees Anatole's leg being cut off, and we've all been shedding tears over it, but a genuine underground man wouldn't have reformed." Dostoevsky was always more generous than Tolstoy in his estimation of others, but his bitterness in these notes may have stemmed from a consciousness of how far *A Raw Youth* was from the quality of Tolstoy's work. Yet the shadow of the great works he had written before *A Raw Youth* and that of his greatest work *The Brothers Karamazov* was present in these notebooks, and it is perhaps both pride and disappointment that feed the feeling that his great counterpart had been too much appreciated and he too little. History has redressed the balance and confirmed what he believed when he said that he was writing about the majority in what seemed to his contemporaries to be the life of exceptions. What better characterization do we have of the "raw youths" of today than "the tragedy of the underground which consists of suffering, self-laceration, an awareness of a better <life> coupled with the impossibility of attaining it . . ."?

VI

This edition is a translation of *F. M. Dostoevsky at Work on His Novel "A Raw Youth,"* edited by A. S. Dolinin (Moscow, 1965), volume 77 of *Literaturnoe Nasledstvo*. The Russian edition has been followed in all substantial respects, and I am indebted to Dolinin's careful and extensive references in the appendix. The notes have been divided into six sections, as in the Russian edition, and I have added a short introduction to each section.

These editorial devices have been used in the preparation of the manuscript: crossed-out words are crossed out in the text; notes written in the margins, between and above lines and in different ink, are enclosed in square brackets; insertions by the editor and translator are enclosed in angle brackets; and incomplete words or sentences are followed by three spaced dots in angle brackets. Italics, capitalizations, parentheses, and unspaced dots are Dostoevsky's. Names have been spelled out in full, and obvious oversights such as the failure to supply end parentheses have been rectified. Dates with a slanted line between the two sets of numbers, as "June 18/30," refer to the twelve-day difference in time between the nineteenth-century Russian calendar and the Western calendar. Punctuation has been altered to conform to English convention. Every effort has been made to retain significant departures from normal usage.

As editor I have supervised the translation and preparation of the manuscript, compiled the sequentially numbered footnotes, and written the introduction and the six chapter introductions. Victor Terras has done the translation (his notes are indicated by asterisks) and compiled the index.

EDWARD WASIOLEK

I

Initial Sketches toward the Novel

February–July, 1874

This is the first part of the notes, and in many respects the sketchiest. As is familiar in many of the notebooks, Dostoevsky is in search of a unifying idea. The germs of situations, plots, and characters appear in profusion. The earliest notes are occupied with a novel about children, duplicating with slight variation the notes to "The Life of a Great Sinner" and anticipating the early notes to *The Brothers Karamazov.* The children are waifs, shift for themselves, and constitute some kind of social unit. But the notes quickly give ground to a consideration of a school teacher by the name of Fyodor Fyodorovich, who loves children, believes in communism, and is something of an idealist. He looks back in certain traits to Prince Myshkin and forward to Alyosha of *The Brothers Karamazov.* He is once called "idiot," as are Prince Myshkin in *The Idiot* and Alyosha in the notes to *The Brothers Karamazov.*

Fyodor Fyodorovich gives ground quickly to two other characters, a younger and an older brother, the prototypes for the "Youth" Arkady and for Versilov of the final version. The older brother, called throughout "the Predatory Type" or simply "He," is a cynical, skeptical, and morally indifferent cultured landowner. He is cruel, predatory, egotistical, bored, indifferent to the sufferings of others, enigmatic, and atheistical. But he is something of a double character, and Dostoevsky speaks of his "bright side." In some of the notes he is courageous and heroic and does good deeds in secret.

The portrait lacks cohesion and is a pastiche of old, new, and future traits of many Dostoevsky characters. Something of Stavrogin, the Underground man, Stepan Trofimovich Verkhovensky, Dmitri Karamazov, as well as of Versilov, characterize his actions. Like Stavrogin of the suppressed chapter of *The Possessed* the Predatory Type seduces a young girl, who hangs herself while he laughs at her; like

Stavrogin, too, he is "seeking a burden"; like the Underground Man he has dreams of the adoration his presence will arouse in others; like Svidrigaylov and Ippolit he does good deeds in secret; and like Peter Verkhovensky he considers everyone to be a scoundrel and implies that there are only stupid and clever scoundrels. His boredom, cleverness, and moral exhaustion, as well as such specific actions as preaching Christianity and breaking the icons, look forward to Versilov.

The Youth arises from the plot about the children that Dostoevsky starts with, then becomes "His" younger brother, and finally his son. As in the novel the Youth's feelings about the Predatory Type are ambivalent: he admires "Him" and looks to him for guidance, but he also hates and is disenchanted with "Him." Despite the fact that midway through these notes Dostoevsky announces in capital letters that "The boy and not he is the Hero," the characterization of the boy is less full than that of his older brother. The boy is naïve, impulsive, sexually hungry, and something of an idealist about women. He is already possessed by his idea to become a Rothschild, and he timidly tells the Predatory Type about the idea. The Predatory Type criticizes and then ironically approves of the idea.

Katerina Nikolaevna Akhmakova is faintly present as the Princess, who is the niece of the old Prince and has an affair with the Predatory Type. Many of Katerina Nikolaevna's traits are present in the portrait of "His" wife, who is compassionate but somewhat predatory. She is totally devoted to the Predatory Type, but cannot forgive him his anarchical convictions. Whereas in the later notes and the final version the Princess is a source of calm and solace for Versilov in her patient suffering, she is crushed, here, by the Predatory Type's disorder, and she herself becomes disturbed and almost loses her mind.

Liza is already present, but Dostoevsky questions whether she is needed. She is seduced by the Predatory Type and kills herself. Lambert appears in substantially the way he will later: cruel, self-seeking, and morally heartless. We are told: "Lambert says that his greatest pleasure, when he is rich, will be to feed dogs with bread and meat, while the children of the poor are starving to death. And when they are without firewood, he is going to buy a whole wood-yard, put all the wood in one pile, and burn it all up for nothing, in the frost, without giving a single log to the poor. 'Let them call me names, it will only make me get a better charge out of it.' " Lambert is already sketchily at work in using a promissory note against the Princess, and as in the final version both the Youth and the Predatory Type are involved in his plot.

Something of the main idea of the final version is apparent in the old Prince's characterization of the Predatory Type as someone who suffers from inner chaos. "And this inner chaos finds expression in external disorders, i.e., his quitting the service, garrulity, restlessness, his odd behavior with his wife; in a word, *disorder,* as if he were trying to dissuade himself, increased preaching of Christianity (the relics)." This quotation points already to the important structural characteristic of the final version, in which Versilov's "Christianity" is an attempt to impose order upon himself, that is, an attempt to find faith rather than an example of acting from faith. Dostoevsky is clear about the Predatory Type's lack of faith, although this is made somewhat ambiguous in the portraiture of the later Versilov. Dostoevsky says: "NOTE. This is the image of an ATHEIST. This is the main idea of the drama (that is, the main essence of His character)." The Predatory Type's doubleness is a psychological lack of cohesion and proceeds from the conflict of inner need and outer behavior.

Tolstoy must have been on Dostoevsky's mind in writing these notes, for there are several rather forthright analogies between what is said in these notes and what is said by several of Tolstoy's characters. Like Prince Andrey in *War and Peace,* the Predatory Type says that he is opposed to any increase in the level of education because "any increase in the level of education is at the same time an increase in the level of suffering." And in an argument against the existence of God, the old Prince says, as does Daddy Eroshka in *The Cossacks* in fairly similar words, "Simply the grass grows everywhere, as it always has grown, and that's all there is to it."

One should point out, finally, Dostoevsky's frankness on sexual matters in these early notes, and his reticence in the novel. In the notes Lambert's plan is scurrilously frank in the payment he expects to derive from the Princess for the letter; the Youth has a session with a whore; and the Predatory Type seduces his stepdaughter, which in the novel, by the process of displacement, becomes the seduction of Liza by the young Prince Sergei.

A schoolteacher, a novel (description of the effect which the reading of Gogol's works, <and especially> *Taras Bul'ba,* has on him). Enemies, the village clerk (a correspondence leads to their approval).

A Christian Hamlet.[1]

A tale about a humble Russian peasant, Ivan Matveevich Prokhodimov.

An apocryphal gospel[2] (N.B. Temptation by the Devil,[3] a clay bird before those poor in spirit. Socialists and nationalists in Jerusalem. Women. Children.)[4]

Children. A mother who has remarried.[5] A group of orphans. Step-brothers and step-sisters. A fighter for justice. Worn out, the mother dies. The children protest. Run away? They go out into the street. The fighter is alone. Wanderings, etc.

A fantastic *poem-in-the-form-of-a-novel:* society of the future, com-

---

[1] Probably a first reference to the future Versilov. Versilov will have an overdeveloped sense of analysis, which paralyzes his capacity for action. This corresponds to Turgenev's depiction of Hamlet in *Gamlet i Don Kikhot* (1860), a work that had broad influence during these years. It is possible, too, that the school teacher mentioned in the first lines was to be contrasted with Versilov, along lines of Turgenev's contrasting of Hamlet, the thinker, with Don Quixote, the believer.

[2] The "Apocryphal Gospel" consisted of early Christian legends uncertified by the church. They were widely disseminated during the early years of Christianity.

[3] The theme of the temptation by the devil will figure importantly in "The Legend of the Grand Inquisitor" and is apparently on Dostoevsky's mind at this early date. A short time later, in January, 1876, in *The Diary of a Writer,* Dostoevsky will address himself to the question of what is meant by one of the devil's temptations, "turning stones into bread."

[4] See Part III, "The Life of the Great Sinner," of *The Notebook for "The Possessed"* (Chicago: University of Chicago Press, 1968), pp. 52–68, for an extended sketch of children and their fortunes.

[5] Possibly a first reference to the Youth's mother, Sofia Andreevna, who leaves her husband, Makar Dolguruky, to live with Versilov.

mune,[6] uprising in Paris, victory, 200 million heads,[7] *terrible sores,* depravity, extermination of the arts, of libraries, a child tortured to death. Quarrels, lawlessness. Death.

A man who shot himself,[8] and a devil somewhat like Faust. Can be combined with the *poem-in-the-form-of-a-novel,* etc.

A NOVEL ABOUT CHILDREN, SOLELY ABOUT CHILDREN, AND ABOUT A BOY-HERO (N.B. They save a suffering child, stratagems, etc.).

They find an abandoned child.

Fyodor Petrovich (a man who loves children, and the nurse).

Fyodor Petrovich, addressing the children upon completion of their commissions, says: "Gentlemen, I have taken care of your business and hasten to render an account to you." Or: "Gentlemen, I have finished reading such-and-such book," and suddenly he tells them about Schiller or about politics, etc. (N.B. He is himself a grown-up child, only imbued with a very strong, and vivid, and long-suffering feeling of love for children).

Man, in his higher specimens and in his higher manifestations, does nothing *simply:* he does not even shoot himself simply, but religiously.

Moskovskie vedomosti, February 26, 1874, <the item> from Bakhmut, about the wife as a trace-horse.[9]

One man wanted to give the other 100,000, but does not know how to offer it to him.

The Parsons (a sketch). "Meat croquettes,* the devil take it," the Little Priest and the Student, etc.

---

* *Kohlety,* apparently a jargon variant of *kotlety,* "cutlets, croquettes."

6 Reference to the revolutionary government established in Paris from May 18 to May 27, 1871. In Part III, Chapter 7:2, Versilov refers to the burning of the Tuileries, a reference to the burning of the Tuileries palace during the last battles between the forces of the Commune and loyal government forces. The "Communards" were blamed for the fire and Dostoevsky—in his frequent reference to this event in his works—accepts this version, and uses the fire as a symbol of the disorder and destruction that ensues from liberalism and radicalism.

7 In Part II, Chapter 7, of *The Possessed* the lame man and Peter Verkhovensky discuss the advisability of cutting off 100,000 heads.

8 This is probably the first reference to Kraft, who shoots himself because he can't stand the idea of Russia's being a second-rate nation.

9 This refers to an item about a peasant wife who ran away to her mother because her husband beat her. Her mother would not take her in, and she then went to a girl friend. Her husband found her there, and with the help of two friends tied her to the shaft and dragged her along by horses; they would stop from time to time to drink at inns and then resume beating and torturing her.

The children plot to establish their own *children's empire.* The children argue about having a republic or a monarchy. The children establish contact with juvenile criminals locked up in prison. Juvenile arsonists and train wreckers. The children make a believer out of the Devil. Juvenile profligates and atheists. Lambert. Andrieux. Children who kill their father (*Moskovskie vedomosti.* No. 89, April 12).[10]

A government clerk, his wedding, a child left at his door: he starts an orphanage, accepts charitable contributions, quits the government service.

Also, another government clerk (on the back), himself a child, etc.

A moment. A rapid encounter of the young man (the ideal of struggle) with a former friend of his who has made up his mind to shoot himself. A day with him. The other man shoots himself.

A magician. At Dussot's, or in Maly Iaroslavets. Turning heads, etc. (The boy who is a liar tells about it and says: "I saw it myself.")

The predatory type (analysis of Prince Danilo by Avseenko).[11] Why is that *fool,* Prince Danilo, deserving of my attention? Confrontation, by Avseenko, of a man who is simply ambitious and who would have absolutely returned to Petersburg for the celebration, and Prince Danilo who, quite to the contrary, failed to return, due to his unbridled nature; for he is passionate, he marries Milusha, and wants to be free in his passion. And yet, later, he whimpers: "Why didn't I go back?" N.B. That's because he is, what's most important, a *fool.* A truly predatory man would have married Milusha by all means, and then he would have returned. It would have been immoral, but a full-fledged predator might have actually felt remorse and would yet have persevered in his sins and passions.

They do not comprehend *the predatory type.*

N.B. N.B. Bear in mind the real predatory type in my novel for of 1875.

This will be This will be already a genuine heroic type, above the

---

[10] This refers to an item about the murder of a father by his children in a small town near Vienna. Three children aged 8–10 decide to murder their father because their mother has run away and they miss her. They do the murder with two chisels. It is possible that this item is an adumbration of the father-murder in *The Brothers Karamazov.*

[11] Refers to the review by the critic V. G. Avseenko of the historical novel of Evgeny Salias, *Pugachev's Followers,* published in *The Russian Messenger* in April, 1874.

public and its everyday life,* and for this very reason will please it without fail. (Whereas Prince Danilo, for example, has nothing to please the public with.)

The predatory type (of 1875).

Passion and immense *breadth of character.* The meanest coarseness along with the most refined generosity. And meanwhile, *the very strength* of this character *lies in the fact* that he can easily support this infinite breadth, so much so that, finally, he is looking in vain for a burden heavy enough for him. Both charming and repulsive (the little red beetle,[12] Stavrogin).

N.B. THINK ABOUT THIS TYPE. May 4, 1874 [A new month has just begun]

Himself He bears a slap in the face, takes vengeance in secret, disgraces the other man, receives powerful impressions.[13]

PUNCTUALITY—*c'est la politesse des rois.*[14] "Come on, you are not a king."

When the Predatory Type meets the Princess, he sacrifices his position with the Prince and is rude to her, which makes her like him.

Once he thought of joining the Skoptsy[15] (money).

A puny little Polish lawyer, Żeromski, is busy all the time. The portrait (he transfers the power of attorney to the lawyer of the other party).

The foundations of society are cracking under the pressure of the revolution brought about by the reforms. The sea has become troubled. The borderlines of good and evil have disappeared and *become obliterated. N. V. D——ko* and *Żeromski.* You can't make an honest living these days. Characters of the milieu, of the trend.

---

* *Zhivaia zhizn',* literally, "living life." Could also mean "true life."

[12] This phrase will be repeated often in the notes, and is an image apparently of the bite of repentance. Stavrogin in the "suppressed" chapter of *The Possessed* looks at a little red spider on a geranium leaf while Matryosha hangs herself, and he sees the same spider when he awakens from his dream about the "golden age."

[13] A repeated gesture in these notes, as well as in the notebooks for *The Idiot* and *The Possessed.* In *The Possessed* Shatov hits Stavrogin in the face, and Stavrogin publicly "bears" the pain as a test of his will. In *A Raw Youth* Prince Sergei gives Versilov a public slap and Versilov does not call him out. This is the "cause" of Versilov's exclusion from society.

[14] French: "It is the politeness of kings."

[15] The "Skoptsy" were a religious sect that arose in the 1770's. A separation from the "Khlysty," their main belief consisted in the doctrine that the only way to salvation was through battle with the flesh and through emasculation.

Vecherom means only "in the evening," while *vechor* means "last night."

"Meanwhile, it seems that you counted on *living off* my lawsuit for a while." Or: "Lived off him for a while."

[Staraia Russa.] The young man (N.B. the great sinner), after a series of progressive falls, all of a sudden reaches the greatest heights of spirit, willpower, enlightenment, and consciousness. (Do not explain it to the reader, simply all of a sudden. What it amounts to is that all the elements of a moral regeneration were already given in his character which, for that very reason, did not succumb to evil naïvely, but rather from conscious evil thoughts, etc.)

You could see him, at our place, like the new moon: he'd show up and immediately disappear again.*

[Ems] Think about the *predatory type*. As much consciousness as possible in the evil he does. "I know that it is evil, and I feel remorse, but I still do it right along with my noblest transports." Might do it this way: *two lines of action* at one and the same time; in one of these (with one group of people) he is a great righteous man who, with all his heart, lives to the exaltation of his spirit and surveys his activities with the most joyful and tender emotions. In his other activities, he is a terrible criminal, a liar and a profligate (with other people). But when alone with himself, he views both kinds of activities with arrogance and despondency, postpones a decision, is ready to give up. He is carried away by passion. *Here,* a passion which he cannot and does not want to resist. *There,* an ideal which purifies him, a heartwarming exploit, and an activity which gives rise to the most tender emotions. Both of these sides, as well as the people involved in them, meet toward the end of the novel. He is angry with his great gift of surviving amidst unbelief, baseness, and vanity.

!?! A task. Combine the novel *Children* with This one. More natural.

This Predatory Type is a great skeptic. The people around him have some social ideas at which he sneers. He unmercifully demolishes the ideals of others (a young boy) and derives pleasure from it.

A trait. He is very kind and polite with everybody, in spite of his crimes. He does evil calmly and even good-naturedly, as he casts a friendly and benevolent glance at a person whom he has ruined and

---

* The Russian phrase is untranslatable, since *mesiats,* "moon," is masculine, which allows a zeugma of "he" and "the new moon."

who has perished through him: "My friend, why did you have to come my way? I needed to satisfy my whim, and I am not going to sacrifice even my slightest whim for your sake."

N.B. But then, sometimes, he would sacrifice everything to somebody else's small whim.

His is a firm conviction (though not a theory): "There is no other life, I am on earth for a brief moment only, so why stand upon ceremony? However, inasmuch as certain conditions of community life have been established by society as a sort of contract, do your cheating in secret, violate your contract in secret, and if this might disturb the harmony of, or introduce a dissonance into, the society of the future, as for this, what do I care if the earth will open and swallow it up, not only in the future but this very moment and me along with the rest of them, *après moi le déluge*. A parallel: just as our indifference to the exhaustion of our soil and to the destruction of our forests. (But not because of any theory about there being no future life, does all this happen. And he laughs himself at the idea that his character might be such as a result of any theory. But he is wrong there: not because of any theory, but because of a feeling of that theory, for he is an atheist not only by conviction, but with his whole being.) He even has this tendency of thought: "We have here a beautiful vision and impression. So let's stifle them as quickly as possible: all of this will exist only for a moment, and in that case it would be better for that thing of beauty not to have existed in the first place."

N.B. A woman becomes passionately enamored of him. (A young man of 20 falls in love with her.) Either she, or the other woman, his wife, has children. His feud with the children (he seduces one little girl who betrays the gang of children and her mother; the mother dies). The mother is jealous of the child, her own little girl. But right in the middle of a fit of jealousy, the mother, while trying to get some answers from her by force ~~torturing her~~, also covers her with kisses. But the girl remains haughtily and warily cold toward her. The mother makes a lot of fuss, whimpering: "Why don't you love me?" ~~The mother~~ The little girl is sick, and delirious. Her mother standing over her. The mother dies. The little girl almost goes out of her mind from remorse. She reproaches him ~~with~~ (he has grown cool toward her and laughs). Strange and fantastic reproaches, though they are *brief*. The little girls hangs herself. Her mother, before her death, falls in love with the Prince.

N.B. The mother's social background is a good one, higher than

His. N.B. Something like Countess V—a Dashkova marrying a doctor. That's why she meets the Prince, having connections with those social circles.

He abandons the child, ~~she~~ the little girl hangs herself. *The little Beetle.* Irresistibility of remorse and impossibility to live after "the little beetle." And this along with an ability to do evil consciously. He is done in at once and quite irretrievably by a subconscious, vital* impression of pity, and he perishes, like a fly.

Embryo of a plan. A wife with stepchildren, a righteous woman, a victim of his diabolic schemes, who has sacrificed everything for his sake and who ruins Prince G<olitsy>n for his sake as well (story of the latter's death), who has surrendered her heart and soul to her tormentor. He tortures her diabolically, solely for the pleasure he derives from her torments.

A band of children and their plot. The traitress is a little girl, the daughter of his wife, his stepdaughter. The child's precocious love. After her mother's death she hangs herself (that's where "the little beetle" enters the picture).

The mother and her little daughter are jealous of each other. (The band of children has a counselor and leader in Fyodor Fyodorovich, an idiot.)

This is *His* dark side. The bright one lies in his love for a young girl, or somebody else's wife. (It is precisely her jealousy of the other woman that kills *his* wife, the mother of <his> stepdaughter.) There, with the other woman, in that other environment, he is affectionate, generous, and heroic.

!?! N.B. He *secretly* does good deeds and pays visits to the needy. The band of children ("the empire") finds out about it. Here, a boy who, like him, is a hero *reveals himself* to him. The boy is fascinated by Him, admires Him, abandons the gang and joins Him, becoming an admirer of His. His relationship with the gang. But still another heroic boy, the leader of the gang, their Emperor ("an empire or a republic?"—arguments), refuses to yield to Him and intensifies their feud. He had always been a rival and enemy of the renegade boy, though secretly his friend. When the other boy changes sides, he suffers, suffers to the point of suicide.

N.B. He does not feel too sorry for his stepdaughter after she has

---

* *Zhiznennyi,* which I have translated literally; perhaps Dostoevsky means "animal," or "living."

hanged herself; much more so (and in spite of himself) he is overcome by pity for his deceased wife. (N.B. N.B. The boy slaps his face.) He marries, or is going to marry, the girl who admires him (the righteous one). And here, suddenly, "the little beetle." The children's republic disintegrates by itself.

Note. This is the image of an ATHEIST. This is the main idea of the drama (that is, the main essence of His character).

But *absolutely introduce** several real, everyday characters (such as the Governor in *The Possessed*)[16] so as to create a more vivid picture.

His social position: a former landowner living off redemption payments (but this is doubtful, think it over).

IN ORDER TO WRITE A NOVEL, ONE MUST ACQUIRE, FIRST OF ALL, ONE OR SEVERAL STRONG IMPRESSIONS ACTUALLY EXPERIENCED BY THE AUTHOR'S HEART. THIS IS THE POET'S JOB. <FROM> THIS IMPRESSION THERE ARE DEVELOPED A THEME, A PLAN, A HARMONIOUS WHOLE. THIS IS ALREADY THE ARTIST'S JOB, ALTHOUGH ARTIST AND POET HELP EACH OTHER IN ONE THING AS WELL AS THE OTHER, IN BOTH INSTANCES.

N.B. *He* is an idle person (a former landowner, redemption money, abroad), and his enemies (and both wives) charge that he is an idle person. And suddenly by accident some area of activity opens itself to him (invent something); and he turns out to be a man who gets everything done in outstanding fashion, while those who had been accusing him and had sneered at him accomplish nothing.

Fyodor Fyodorovich, like Baranov; at the office of some Bashmakov and knows his business exceedingly well.

~~The government official~~ Fyodor Fyodorovich is getting married. (An abandoned child.) The wedding does not come off. Supporting a wife. Children. This is a subconscious passion for children. He offers an explanation to his wife, with whom things have gone awry, as if from a *book* (altogether, he talks as from a book, establishes relations with her, and she gets to like him awfully much).

!?! Perhaps, this wife of Fyodor Fyodorovich's is precisely that other man's wife with whom His righteous feat is accomplished.

Or perhaps, her sister.

---

* "Absolutely" is underlined three times.

16 This is possibly a reaction to N. K.Mikhaylovsky's review of *The Possessed* in which he singles out the governor Lembke as a particularly well-made character. The review is in *The Fatherland Notes,* vol. II (1873).

Fyodor Fyodorovich has given his estate to another brother[17] (couldn't He be actually his brother?). In that case, he does love his brother and is unfailingly affectionate toward him; yet, when the situation demands it he tells him outright that he is a villain, but does so without despising him in the least, but simply stating it as a fact, and continues to be affectionate. An active personage, but in the main part only in connection with the children.

There are some ideas in which he believes unfailingly and blindly. Some social ideas, among others. He does not, however, believe in communism.

Regarding *narodnost'*:* "The precise reason why I am perfectly *narodnyi*** is that I am perfectly Russian. However, it is all the same to me." And to be sure, he cares very little whether he is *narodnyi* or not. But what is strange: the people, whenever they come in contact with him (N.B. present an instance of such an encounter in the novel) absolutely and *directly* recognize him as one of them.

(The children curse classicism. A plot against Katkov.[18] But Fyodor Fyodorovich demolishes their arguments, and they remain admirers of Katkov.)

N.B. Fyodor Fyodorovich marries neither for passion nor for love, but according to certain family arrangements. The bride is terribly cold toward him (before the marriage is broken because of the abandoned child). Fyodor Fyodorovich is from a good family (declining families).

N.B. Should one introduce the fool in the railway carriage? (God's fool) (also in the bath-house—the leg) and the young man? (The young man could be His rival.) It is *he* who is the lover of another man's wife (a righteous feat), and the other man's wife is the former bride of Fyodor Fyodorovich.

---

* Untranslatable: derived from *narod,* "the people, the Russian people, or nation"; it could be translated by "nationalism" or "populism," but neither is adequate.

** Adjective to *narod.*

17 In the final version Versilov does something of this kind when he refuses to accept the estate he has won from Prince Sokolsky.

18 Mikhail Katkov was the editor of *The Russian Messenger,* where most of Dostoevsky's novels were published. He was an extreme conservative. The reference to classicism concerns the edict of July 31, 1871, of the ministry of education, in which it is declared that only students who finish a classical course of studies in a Gymnasium may enroll at a university. Katkov championed this view eagerly and vigorously.

A conversation with Fyodor Fyodorovich:

She (annoyed): "Well, let me tell you one thing, you *are* pleased with yourself."

Fyodor Fyodorovich: "I agree that this is a very bad shortcoming of mine." (N.B. Though he had never thought of having this shortcoming before.)

She: "For another thing, it certainly isn't easy to catch you with your guard down."

Fyodor Fyodorovich (somewhat taken aback): "Were you really trying to catch me? And I was thinking that you were speaking *simply.*"

She. She feels drawn to Fyodor Fyodorovich, talks to him, finds him very much to her liking, but deep inside she says to herself directly: "No, he is impossible!" (That is, as a husband, *as a male.*)

N.B. Fyodor Fyodorovich's (apparent) arrogance and calmness were actually the cause of her hatred for him and set the stage after for the break between them after the incident with the abandoned child.

She (and many other people) consider Fyodor Fyodorovich to be a child understanding nothing about life and people, and suddenly, when the time has come (but quite unintentionally and without having given any thought to setting the stage for it), Fyodor Fyodorovich explains to her the entire psychology of her soul, to a depth which frightens her, yet does it calmly and almost coolly. "But if you have penetrated so deep into people and if you know all these things about them, how can you remain so cool and calm?" she exclaims.

"But I am really neither cool nor calm," he replies, but coolly and calmly *as if* he had not understood her remark.

The solution of the riddle lies in the fact that he is a man with an *idea fixa,* and such people are all calm, even when headed to their own execution.

He is ~~40~~ *forty years old,* and Fyodor Fyodorovich, His younger brother (or even better, his stepbrother) is *twenty-seven.*

A stepbrother. (Give this some thought.)

He experiences an unexpected (and, what is most important, unexpected *for him*) fit of jealousy for his much abused wife, to whom he has been unfaithful himself. He tries to laugh it off, taking it for a fit of vanity, yet this passion weighs on him. (A Dream. Gol<itsyn>)[19]—

---

[19] The first husband of the Predatory Type's wife. A prototype of Makar Dolgoruky.

a duel, the thought of his murder under *her* eyes, and "what is she going to say?" Her love for ~~him~~ (G<o>li<tsyn>. His passionate love for her. The crime.

He is from an obscure family, the son of some kind of government clerk, but his education has made him a *superior* and a *well-known* man. Perhaps he is ashamed of his obscure lineage, and suffers from it. (N.B. His brother says about him, or to him: "Admit that you are ashamed of not being an aristocrat.")

N.B. A candidate for a post in the judiciary. (Couldn't he be the oldest brother in an impoverished family, a righteous man and a stay-at-home?) Before his marriage, he had his face slapped (story and setting), which is why she married him in the first place, but later she keeps reproaching him for that very thing. (~~In her~~ when "my Prince," etc.) *The whole vileness of his fall* is combined in him with all the sensations of an exalted mind. "The whole vileness of my fall is with me" (secret vices). A young boy working for the Count is his brother. (Perhaps, a sermon on Christ and God, whereas he is an atheist.) He chops up some icons.

The children's empire.

(No need of a noble exploit *à part,* as a separate episode.)

N.B. Straighten out and focus (realize) this character more strongly. Make him more attractive. (A depraved man. Depravity.)

N.B.! ! ! He is tired and indifferent, and suddenly (often) he has a quick impulse to do something (and, for the most part, something depraved and frightful), often enough something noble (but he would invariably drag it down into the mud and eventually wind up doing something depraved, secret, and frightful).

He is a preacher of the Christian religion, and this is why the Princess left her high society and followed him. And then ~~when she is dying~~ he smashes an icon (before or after her death, better before). "I am a depraved man, I am an atheist."

~~Or~~ What is most important, he is ~~always~~ sometimes loftily sincere, which is why he fascinates people.

It is *He* who is the head manager of the Count's affairs, who has a liaison with his wife,* he has also written for his brother and made him his assistant (also in the office). It is he who is the central figure in the incident involving Lambert.

---

* The Russian phrase is ambiguous, just as is my translation.

N.B. (N.B. His marriage to the widowed Princess has somewhat improved his financial condition. But the Princess has only a small fortune of her own.)

A PROBLEM: SHOULD ONE GET THE CHILDREN MIXED UP IN THIS?

Fyodor Fyodorovich has a winning lottery ticket, but he does not consider it his own, since he bought it from a certain government clerk. His fiancée and her family are clamoring against his intention to return the ticket. He says nothing and returns the ticket, which becomes known on his wedding day. But the bride still thinks that he has returned only a part and does not learn that everything has been returned until after the ceremony. And here, suddenly, the abandoned child. Everybody leaves.

N.B. The thing is that the friend to whom he returned the winnings from that ticket did not give him a penny. Fyodor Fyodorovich (as usual) finds this neither good nor bad, and accepts it as a fact. "Why, in today's society no phenomena other than of this kind, nor people other than of this type, can be expected to exist."

Nothing can disturb him, not even blatant justifications brought forth in favor of the matricides, much to the satisfaction of the elder brother: "May everything come tumbling down!" And Fyodor Fyodorovich views him with strange curiosity and answers: "Yes, you are so right, may everything come tumbling down, the sooner the better." *He* has said it in the sense that everything should go to the devil, while Fyodor Fyodorovich meant that the new society should come as soon as possible.

Fyodor Fyodorovich is a socialist and a fanatic, but somehow cold and calculating, whereas the older brother is a skeptic and believes in nothing. Fyodor Fyodorovich is all faith, while He is all despair.

Regarding Christ, Fyodor Fyodorovich states that much about him was rational, that he was a democrat, that he had firm convictions, and that some of his articles of truth were correct. But not all.

The elder brother (He), in the presence of his wife and his younger brother, proves to Fyodor Fyodorovich that Christ had founded society on freedom, and that there could be no other freedom, ~~except~~ but in Christ ~~Fyodor Fyodorovich is put out~~. And that he, the communist Fyodor Fyodorovich, is founding his on slavery and idiocy. Fyodor Fyodorovich is put out as far as his arguments are concerned, but not in his feelings. "All right then, so let us accept Christ's system," he says, "only let's straighten out a few things about it." "Why, in that case nothing will be left of Christ," says his brother. "I have to admit that, I am not going to argue," says Fyodor Fyodorovich, for "these are only words," and all this is irrelevant to the real thing. And he quits the debate, remaining calm.

But suddenly he is struck by one thing: the abandoned child. And he *spontaneously* becomes a lover of children and a Christian. He is told that, in the new society, children will have no fathers, for there will be no family ("family, that's as good as private property"). He says that, probably, it won't be that way, if this be natural.* "How is it possible not to love children?" "You see, their fathers and mothers have deserted them, but then, don't I love them? There will always be people like myself." "Oh yes! And they will be a thousand times better than ourselves, for everything will be love and concord! All will be fathers and mothers, and then we won't need to have natural fathers, which, by the way, is almost tantamount to monopoly."

Inflames the children with the doctrines of communism.

"Thou art not far from the kingdom of God," somebody tells him.[20] "You have gotten Christianity mixed up with communism." Even now there are many who prepare this incompatible mixture. But in the meantime, blood and incendiarism (the treasures of the Tuileries).

But blood and incendiarism do not disturb Fyodor Fyodorovich. And there are going to be better treasures, a thousand times superior. "Of course, it might be a good thing to save from the coming conflagration a few of the very greatest items (the Sistine Madonna, the Venus of Milos), for the sake of their past glory and in the spirit of conciliation. But unfortunately this is impossible; it is precisely these things that must be the first to go. I presume that those who will be burning them will do so with their hearts bleeding."

"Quite the contrary, quite the contrary," they shout back. "A right to be dishonorable, much rather than tears. They are happy with it. For these people are all nothing but the vile average. They are the ones who even burn things without an idea. It is only we who understand the essence of the idea, of the brains which direct these vile hands."

"Well, there you see it, you have said it yourself, that it is the average, and that's where you are right. Which means that it couldn't be different at all, and so what are you complaining about?"

---

* Unclear phrase.

[20] Mark 12 : 34.

"And you remain calm!" He exclaims. "It isn't a matter of complaining or rebelling, it means to let it be damned. If the world is moving in this direction, with this vile business taking over and replacing the bright cause, I'd rather see everything come tumbling down: I am not accepting this kind of a world," He says.

His whole misfortune lies in the fact that He is an atheist and does not believe in *resurrection,* whereas Fyodor Fyodorovich believes in the message of communism.

Later, Fyodor Fyodorovich discusses the subject of children with his future wife: "Come on, you don't resemble a *book* at all. Look how you have become all living emotion, all a single sensation," his wife tells him. "But prior to that, you were no more than a book. What would a woman mean to you?"

"Oh, if you only knew how much a woman could mean to me!"

"Really? have you ever loved a woman? do you love one now?!"

"Yes" (when he says this, it comes quite unexpected to the reader).

"Whom then?"

["I love *you,*" etc.]

"Oh, you don't know how I have been loving you."*

"Really?"

"And I still love you, I love you even more than I did then."

(The stage is set for a graceful relationship between husband and wife. Yet they don't get together: *"He is impossible."*) (In her presence, he draws milk from the wet-nurse's breasts and drinks it. Yellow diapers.) This wife of Fyodor Fyodorovich's is in touch with (Him), but it isn't a liaison. His wife is jealous. His liaison with the Count's wife. (An old gentleman, the portrait.)

And so, one brother is an atheist. Despair. The other is a thorough going fanatic. The third represents the new generation, a living force, new people. He was able to withstand Lambert. (And the children, as the youngest generation.)

Most important. The idea of disintegration is present everywhere, for everything is falling *apart,* and there are no remaining ties not only in the Russian family, but even simply between people in general. Even children are apart.

[*Disintegration is the principal visible idea of the novel.*]

"The tower of Babel," he says. "Here we are, for example, a Rus-

---

* The gender of the Russian phrase suggests that it is "He" who says these words.

sian family. ~~he says~~ We speak different languages and cannot understand each other. Society is chemically disintegrating."

"But not the people."

"The people, too."

"But families do exist, and there's an awesome multitude of them."

"This awesome multitude is a sorry phantom," he replies, "it is all nothing but average, run-of-the-mill, people without ideas. It's we who really matter. We are the people who have ideas, and everybody is going to follow us. Belinsky was all by himself when he hit upon his idea of change, after his article on "The Anniversary of Borodino,"[21] and look what happened: everybody followed him. His idea prevailed everywhere. Even the run-of-the-mill keep babbling it, without understanding him. It is going to be the same thing now, all these families and all this *narodnost'** will disintegrate, not even a bare outline will be left of them."

"You are so right saying, 'without understanding.' "

"Yet doing it his way, like everyone else."

"Isn't it you who said that they are only too happy to have been given the right to be dishonorable?"

"This means nothing at all: they are happy to have acquired the right to be dishonorable, others are happy about something else. It's the others who will prevail."

Fyodor Fyodorovich is in favor of a classical education, and defends this view when asked by the children, though he admits that he is at a loss for an answer. He asserts that the classical corresponds more to our goals, and wonders why the liberals have rejected it.

Fyodor Fyodorovich hesitated for a long time how to explain it to the children, [told them] that he wasn't ready to answer the question; finally, he did some research and prepared an answer.

Though the office is located in the Count's house, he has some associates in the business: a certain Count Poletika, two Yids, and a Russian capitalist (railroad).

[3d part] An image of the Earth covered with snow in 100,000 years. The stupidity of creation. "What is most stupid of all is that you will be given proof that it isn't stupid at all, but merely a fact,

---

* See n. (*), p. 32, above.

[21] A work by V. Zhukovskii, "Borodinskaia godovshchina," published in *The Fatherland Notes* in 1839 and reviewed by Belinsky in the same year. Belinsky gives an extended definition and explanation of the meaning of *narodnost'* in this article, and it is to this concept that Dostoevsky refers.

whereas I certainly know, for some reason or other, that it is stupid (that deserted, cold globes be whirling through space). Gambling in Monaco is incomparably higher than anything else in existence."

"What do you care about it?"

"Well, ~~it's a shame~~ nothing."

The old Prince says:

"Listen—oh, my dear, what does it matter to you, let them whirl through space (the globes, that is)."

The story about the slap in the face; bearing the slap in the face. His wife is greatly afraid that there may be a duel. His wife congratulates him on his strength of mind, yet he knows that she despises him. (He had earned the slap in the face earlier, at the time when he was torturing his wife.)

She is aware of his secret debauchery (she follows him one night, and exposes him).

Her love grows more and more, until she meets the Prince. She is 30, she had her first child (a girl) when she was 17.

Prince (G<olitsyn> is ~~26~~ 24 years old.

He speaks about St. Theodosius.[22]

A trait. He is terribly inquisitive, and likes to hear gossip: "What have you got coming up there?" He is too proud to ask himself and waits until somebody would report it to him.

Frequently, he is overwhelmed by remorse, and in tears, on which occasions he simple-heartedly prostrates himself before her, telling her everything. "I'll torture you to death," he tells his wife, "but when you die, I won't be able to stand you. . ."

He poisons her. Or she is simply hit by a fever ~~and he drives a nail into her~~. For she cannot herself endure the strain resulting from her relationship with the Prince, and he regrets not having strangled her.

He is a coward, but in this case he is willing to run the danger.

"I haven't got any money, Madam."

Quêteuse.[23] "I am no philanthropist, Madam."

"I have no love for the poor, Madam."

"I am no philanthropist, Madam."

"I have money, Madam, and I hope to spend it without the help of other people."

---

[22] A monk in Kiev who died in 1074 and who was renowned for his spiritual feats. In the February, 1876, issue of *The Diary of a Writer* Dostoevsky speaks of him with admiration, as the embodiment of the ideas of the people.

[23] French: "alms collector."

?N.B. He has money, and hopes to spend it *without the help of other people.*

? START THE NOVEL: ~~He still is~~ Her conversation with <her> brother, the Count. The Count is a General. He is a superior man, and clever, "I like him very much, but he is stupid, and I dislike him a good deal." He still resigns his commission. She defends him with ardor. But at home she attacks him for having resigned his commission. [about his family] ["You have changed your social circle. Princess *Mimi* <?> He is admitted immediately."] She is also ridiculous, and sickly. They talk about the lawsuit. Her lawsuit about an inheritance. "All our hopes rest here," he says; the money belongs to the children.

A young boy, brother, informs her that he is given to debauchery at night. She chases him out, refusing to believe it. An older boy is being rude to her. Liza. Preparations for the wedding of Fyodor Fyodorovich's middle brother. The younger <brother> goes out and meets Lambert, tells him about his family.

"Is there a Devil?" the third brother asks the eldest brother. Meanwhile, rebellion of the children.

The stage is being set for the incident with the slap in the face. Prince G<olitsyn> (in the matter of the inheritance).

[3d part] "I can't help agreeing with this (i.e., that this is all the same and that it is nobody's fault), but ~~in that case, two shopkeepers playing checkers,~~ having a rational mind, I can't help acknowledging that this is frightfully stupid, no matter how innocent it might be, and a game of checkers, played by two shopkeepers, contains infinitely more wisdom and makes infinitely more sense that all of being and the universe."

"This is to say that you don't believe in God after all, or are you just talking that way?"

"I ~~am saying this~~ am coming to this conclusion in case God does not exist."

"And *in case* he does?"

"In that *case:* eternity exists for me, too, and then, immediately, everything takes on a colossal and a grandiose aspect, and infinite dimensions, worthy of man and of being. Everything becomes rational and makes sense."

Wisdom stifles the human mind, yet man is in constant search of it.

Being must be absolute and in any case superior to the human mind.

The teaching that the human mind is the limiting boundary of the universe is as stupid as the most stupid thing you might think of, and therefore infinitely more stupid than a game of checkers played by two shopkeepers.

July 6.

Shouldn't it begin with Him being mainly a preacher of the Christian religion: set it up accordingly. (Secretly, an atheist.) A young boy, <his?> brother.

Her conversation with <his?> brother, the General (who is ill).

"Before, He was a clever, and even a useful man . . . He wants to turn himself into a saint, and that his relics would perform miracles; a joke! After all, this is the kind of idea one feels strange discussing even hypothetically. A man of the world, used to wear the same clothes we do, well, and the rest, and there, suddenly, his relics . . . *Une supposition!* I am not saying a thing, naturally, this is all sacred. But there, suddenly, his relics. It actually seems somehow improper, for a man of the world, to have his relics perform miracles later."

He, to her: "Let us part, I am going to torture you to death, I am a hard man. Your children annoy me. They look at me as if I were a dragon." A quarrel with the oldest boy. "Either he or I." They are separated.

(Fasting.) The little girl comes to tell him that he is a villain. He moves to an apartment. *Crapule,*[24] suddenly, after the fasting.* The younger brother.

N. B. HE IS TERRIBLY JEALOUS.

"Suddenly, I hold a position in society, and suddenly, tomorrow my relics perform a miracle. This is altogether unbecoming. If it were to happen to me somehow, or if somebody would offer me heavenly powers by any chance, I would decline, I wouldn't want it. *Une supposition* . . . for, perhaps there is really such a thing as relics, and perhaps they do indeed make miraculous appearances of some sort, and the whole thing isn't such a *préjugé* at all, you never can tell, and finally, nobody knows a thing about all this. *C'est de l'inconnu.*"[25]

The *predatory type,* as if it weren't enough that he is seeking for a burden, as if it weren't enough that he is seeking a faith, is *actually* seeking the *despair of utter unbelief,* and cynicism, so as to come to rest at least there. "Otherwise, I believe in nothing at all, and at the

---

* *Posty,* plural of *post* ("fast").

[24] French: "scoundrel."

[25] French: "it's unknown."

same time, I believe in the great idea ("the great idea" is his own private technical term; settle this point with the reader). "What then, is the essence of this *great idea* of mine? ~~In~~ What's both ridiculous and absurd about it is that *it has not been formulated.* The moment I have formulated it to any extent, I'm the first to find it ridiculous myself. No, it manifests itself as an emotion, as an impression. You live, going your way, and suddenly you say: 'this is good'—that's precisely what is not good."

N.B. Though *He* says himself that he is an ignoramus and knows very little, it is necessary to let the reader know that, as a matter of fact, he knows a good deal. He has a synthesis, a whole archive of experience, he *has* feelings in which he firmly believes. (N.B. It is feelings that were his undoing: he couldn't stand "the little beetle.")

He tells his wife: "I am going to torture you to death, nor do I feel sorry for you, as long as you are with me; but after you'll have died, I know for sure that I'm going to kill myself by self-condemnation."

"If at least I were a weak-willed nonentity," he says, "and could suffer with that consciousness, from the lofty heights and the low envy of that consciousness! But now I do know that I am infinitely strong; 'strong with what?' you may think. Well, with that immediate strength of vitality and adaptability, with those (good) feelings, exactly, which right now make me say: 'this is good.' These are of course good feelings, but . . . you understand that there is a *but.* This is to say that I love life."

"It is a base thing, for a man like myself, to love life. Could it be really true that the Earth exists only for men like myself? Most probably this is true. (Whereas saints are either stoned by other people, or burn themselves to death.)"

"Nothing can destroy me, and what is the vilest thing of all, nothing can perturb me either. I am continuously without shame. I am capable of feeling two contrary feelings at the same time. Which is dishonorable, and actually against my own will. But imagine, I even don't know whether this is good or bad."

"I am dishonorable almost to the limit, and what's even more important, I'm glad that I am. ~~I am sh<ameless>~~ My name is shameless,"* and nothing else."

---

* The Russian word *sramnik* is a noun.

A *big* N.B. (for the plan). "Whereas the Krafts hang themselves. To be sure, the Krafts are stupid, whereas we are clever."

"I very nearly was glad that, for as long as about 15 years now, every intelligent element in our country has, as a consequence of Russia's requirements, embraced realism and taken to specialization, and in this particular sense, I swear that I am actually opposed to any kind of ~~reform~~ school reform, to any increase in the level of education. In our dear fatherland, things have quite naturally worked out the way that any increase in the level of education is at the same time an increase in the level of suffering."

"So really, it is even better if they do specialize; to increase the level of education means to increase the level of *suffering*."

The young boy, <his> brother (the one who is with Lambert, and everything), slaps <his?> elder brother's face. After this has happened, he runs away from his family. Later, he makes friends with <his?> elder brother, *with reserve,* but *irrepressibly*. He does not want to show him any respect—and listens to him with terrible curiosity. *He* listens to him, finding him somewhat entertaining. In the end He is done in by "the little beetle," while the younger brother is resurrected to a superior exploit. Get both of them mixed up in the same intrigue (with the Princess). The Y<oung> Man paralyzes* his crimes.

For a while, He associates with Lambert.

He asserts that he is a product of Russia, and typical of her people as they all are at the given moment. He supports the idea that they are all such (scoundrels) as he is, provided only that they are clever. They don't know if this is to be a joke, or not. (N.B. He does not mean it as a joke.) And when they tell him: "So everybody is such a scoundrel?" he answers: "It isn't only that we are scoundrels, we are, besides, the only bearers of a higher idea."

"Yes, but as skeptics, without suffering," his wife, or somebody, tells him. "What you need is suffering."—~~You~~ "We have not reached the maturity of suffering, for only a heart that has not been corrupted is worthy of suffering."

"I am praying for suffering."

Suffering ("the little beetle"), once it has made its appearance, is crushing him, like a cockroach.

"What is he up to? Was he simply chatting with me? As if he had

---

* Perhaps Dostoevsky means "neutralizes."

no one else to chat with. I noticed that there was something wrong, yet at the same time, there was so much strained and spent suffering about every one of his escapades, no matter how contrived <?>, that I simply couldn't leave him or remain indifferent to him. On the contrary, I was becoming more attached to him every day."

"And besides, I always suspected that, perhaps, He was merely talking that way, driven either by spite or by his suffering, but that secretly, with himself, He was actually the fanatical adherent of some higher idea, so that in effect he continued to appear before my eyes covered with an aura of mystery."

Liza hangs herself because she ~~says~~ has broken with her mother, and says: "I have hurt my mother." She hangs herself at a time when her mother is with the Prince. He is glad that she has hanged herself, and feels nothing. A colossal impression upon her mother. She suddenly recovers from her infatuation with the Prince, and dies of a broken heart. He has two deaths on his conscience. However, "the little beetle" that tortures him to death is not the one that reminds him of *his wife,* but the one which reminds him of *Liza* (the little beetle of *disorder*). On the last day, flight of the child (the boy, Liza's brother).

N.B. N.B. N.B. Scenes and excitement in the family on account of the dismissal of a housemaid. A picture of everyday life.

!N.B.! He feels no passion for the Princess, but simply vexation, intrigue, spite, and hurt vanity. That's where he makes up his mind to ruin the Princess.

[For the plan.] He *simply* is the Princess's lover *without loving her.* He is looking for money. The younger brother proves to her that he wants to rob her. The Princess breaks with him and throws him out. She has never *belonged* to him. That's the time when He gets involved with Lambert.

"If for no other reason, I am a typical *Russian* nobleman," he says, "because I am dishonorable to a very high degree. During the past 20 years, dishonor and the right to be dishonorable have become the highest quality of the Russian soul."

"No, it really seems that I am a genius," he says, "yes, indeed. Any other, average person would have been finished a long time ago, but I have that accursed gift of vitality. No, I am not going to shoot myself."

The boy (<his> brother), instead of him, begins to pursue the course of righteousness.

A story, a story is what is needed! An entertaining plan.

Revenge suffered by the Princess.

The scene with the housemaid (his sordid cohabitation <with her> is exposed). He falsely accuses the housemaid of theft. The boy is terribly indignant about this and reproaches him. He then *takes* his brother *in hand,* going even further in his unbelief than the latter. On the contrary, in his belief in crime <. . .>.

Secretly, he does good deeds, but after "the little beetle" he becomes indifferent and *abandons the recipients of his beneficence.*

He does not esteem his wife as his spouse, though, in his words, it isn't exactly that he wouldn't recognize marriage, but he is simply indifferent. But the moment it is he who is affected he goes into a fit (when she goes to the Prince).

After having had his face slapped he is surprised that he feels no anger. He chuckles to himself and says, for everyone to hear, that probably the reason why he isn't angry is that he actually deserved to be slapped.

"I AM BORED," he says.

"But aren't you an intrigant, a petty gossip," the *boy* tells him, "how is it that you are bored?"

"I do not know, I am an intrigant and a petty gossip, but I am still bored."

July 23/11.

The BOY, and not HE is the HERO.

The story of the boy, how he arrives, whom he happens to meet, under whose care he is put. He falls into the habit of seeing the professor; he dreams of the university; also, the idea to get rich.

He, on the other hand, is only an accessory, but what an accessory!!

THE YOUTH*

The boy has failed an examination in the classics. They had actually written him that there was *a job* waiting for him in Petersburg, ostensibly he was to replace his older brother, who had gotten married and who was therefore lost to the family. Furthermore, they are actually stepbrothers, and those relatives are his aunts, and close relations, while being virtually unrelated to the other brother. So the boy drops a hint to the effect that he feels they brought him in so they'd have somebody to take care of the aunts. He is told, by the family, that

* *Podrostok,* "youth" or "adolescent," which is also the title of the novel.

as of now it is he who is being taken care of, and, in a word, they cut him down in every possible way. He arrives having already conceived the idea of becoming a Rothschild.

The "despot" brother (i.e., He) whom he had taken for a pompous despot impresses him with his cynical simplicity; for instance, he frankly tells him himself that He is uneducated, etc. He corrupts him. Infinite vanity.

The boy becomes friends with Liza. He foresees [*sic*] all His relations with Liza and breaks with Him, since he despises Him. Makes a direct turn <back> to the right way. He won't forgive him Liza.

The young man arrives smarting from an insult, thirsting for revenge. Colossal vanity, a plan <to become> a Rothschild (his secret). Organize the theme: Liza isn't needed.

Decide? His wife's age. Is there a need for the Prince and jealousy, or isn't there? Liza alone, or Children and their flight after their mother's funeral?

The old Prince, the Princess's husband (who has made a will and is being cheated). An old chatterbox. Used to be a dandy and with the horse guards. (A capitalist.) Now he likes to come up with an occasional bon mot, and will point out to an unsuspecting party, with childish (however, quite innocent, cheerful) vanity, that he has done just that, come up with a bon mot. To make up for it, those who want to win his favor make a point of taking notice of his bons mots, and to them he is awfully grateful, and willing to do anything for them.

[February] Both good nature and egoism. Fits of stinginess. The strange view (the only serious trait in him) that now, *in our age,* honors, nobility (all in the sense of rank) mean nothing, so that money is the best thing of all. He states this idea with sadness. He has also preserved some noble traits. He does not suspect his wife, for reason of his indolence (or egoism, wishing to avert an unpleasant dénouement), which he states openly and for which he really gets it from the Princess, who has a most severe influence on him. A strange trait: he actually boasts of this severe influence, he likes to let everybody know that he is being ruled with a rod of iron, so as to appear to be such a gay blade and rake, such a naughty boy who would take to carousing the moment she'd look the other way.

It is he who speaks of the "relics."

It is a remarkable fact that 10 to 20 years ago he was a more serious person and actually performed meritoriously in an important government appointment. A man with taste. He dearly loves a scabrous anecdote and is bored when nobody will turn the conversation that way. They arranged for him to see Mlle Andrieux, but he returned embarrassed, he didn't like it at all, not the right thing, unaesthetic. He is greatly interested in *the new woman*. So they arrange for a visit with a *new* woman. He is even more embarrassed. He is getting ready to die and <tells them> what they should bury him in, and he seriously expects ~~to him~~ to die, and *blague*. (He has had a vision.) He makes a break for <Mlle> Andrieux, in spite of the fact that he is prepared to die, and suddenly dies. He is a capitalist, and a shareholder in a number of companies.

Once, the Prince began to talk like a nihilist, and promptly made a fool of himself. Deny everything (he is a Senator, or a member of the State Council).

As for the Princess, he married her 10 years ago (he is 62), out of vanity, so that people would say: "Look what an attractive young wife he has got." This he tells her himself, trying to appear frivolous.

He makes fun of human nature and points out, in himself as well as in others, various psychological traits that are comical or trivial: "You can't cover those with any uniform," he says. A good deal of wit, here.

The Prince has been listening to various atheists for a long time and has become an atheist himself: "And so, there just isn't anything of that kind (i.e., God)," he says. "I must admit that I always suspected it to be so," he says. And he immediately proceeds to ramble along, arguing that *this* (i.e., God) would actually be indecorous.

"I don't know how to express it, but, in my opinion, it is actually trivial. As if somebody were always ready to give me a spanking—*une idée*. I am a General, and there . . . 'he's realized the vanity of earthly existence.' All right, he's a general, let him be a general, yet we are still wetting our pants,* still being the same naughty little boys."

"And finally, if it is really as you say, then prove it to me, so I can see it, or as they say, have a sensation of it. All right if He (God) exists in person (and not in the form of an effusion of spirit or something, for I must admit, that is even more difficult to understand), then what does he wear? How tall is he? Don't be angry, my dear, naturally, I have a right to ask this question, for if he is God, a personal God, i.e., a person, then how tall is he, *et enfin,* where does he

---

* *Sikaem,* a nursery word the basic meaning of which is "to squirt"; another slang meaning is "to drink (vodka)."

live? This is an important question, where does he live, a most important question. I am not talking of His having a passport or anything of the kind, of course. As for a rational spirit, that's nonsense as far as I can see. This is nothing but clouding ~~the issue~~ the idea. Well, and still, *un domicile,* that adds authority to the idea of order and, so-to-speak, decorum. An effusion? Well, what could that be, some kind of water or what? Yet in my opinion, there hasn't ever been any effusion at all, but simply the grass grows everywhere, as it has always grown, and that's all there is to it. I always suspected it to be that way, I always did."

The old Prince is critical of Him all the time and, behind his back, likes to crack jokes at his expense, but to his face he is for some reason afraid of him. *The other man* is confident that he can turn him around in any direction of his own choice. So he turns him against the Princess.

~~They are married to two sisters.~~

He says to his wife: "I never loved her (i.e., the Princess). It was only vanity on my part, only envy, perhaps."

"But why were you tempted by Liza?"

"Liza was my enemy from the very beginning, I needed her submission. It flattered me."

The boy (Liza's brother) was sick, a kind of God's fool. He loved Liza. *He* was the boy's enemy. While his wife was still alive he would really rip his mouth apart.* When everybody was dead, he wanted to make friends with the boy. He goes with him. The boy runs away.

The boy (the youth) passionately dreams of how he will save a lot of money, but he does not tell anybody; in his dreams he shines shoes, etc.

N.B. *Important.* Not a word about Lambert until he appears on the scene (everything in the narrative).

About the ideas which interest the Youth (except Rothschild). Also, everything at the proper time, for instance, the image of the Earth all covered with ice. Here, suddenly, his remarks, showing that he has already been thinking, experienced certain emotions, and felt excited about things.

(Women, the desire for a woman which agitates him), his scene with Mlle Andrieux, and later, how he had a whore.

---

* *Razryval rot,* obviously a slang expression; I did not find it in the dictionaries and had to guess its meaning.

He arrives in town and locates Vitia, who brings him together with a high school boy. Together, they plan to *run away* to America. About God, with Vitia: "There's one more thing which I forgot to tell you," etc.

His first night at the house, after his return from Vitia's place. The chambermaid. His daydreams about himself (about Rothschild). He counts his money before going to bed.

Next morning he is at the office (with the old Prince). There, a conversation between the old Prince and His wife, also about "relics." The boy bursts out laughing. He gets to talk with the Prince.

At home, he runs into a scene involving the chambermaid. A scene about the children. He quarrels with <his> brother (with Him). He tells him that he was brought there to take care of his aunts.

He picks up a letter at the office and learns the secret of the Princess.

Slaps His face.

The boy gets to know Him more closely on account of the slap in the face (inimically, at first). His wife makes scenes to Him, on account of <her> jealousy. His last tryst with the Princess. <He> learns the whole truth. The Princess has insulted him *by failing to take notice* of him. He vows vengeance.

The little Prince appears on the scene. ~~K~~

Lambert appears on the scene.

?N.B. Perhaps there is no need at all to have Liza. She is 24 at the time, and she is with the Prince.

~~?N.B. She is 26 and has two children, 8 and 7.~~

Perhaps he has made a will, and he scares her by letting her know that the will is as good as worthless (5 percent and on the security of the estates), and that ~~he~~ the Prince is not going to make out a new one, especially if he will show the old Prince those love notes.

? The young Prince, of whom he is jealous (the old man's nephew and legal heir), never had anything to do with the Princess (something strange did happen, deceiving Him), but suddenly his wife falls in love with the Prince. Then, he becomes jealous of his wife and, together with Lambert, plans to ruin the Princess.

?N.B. Couldn't Liza be her stepdaughter? Liza's strange friendship with her. Liza wouldn't allow her to marry Him. From the very beginning she is his outspoken enemy. She stands up for her little brother (stepbrother) at the house, creating a turmoil. She incites <her> stepmother against Him (13 years <old>). And suddenly ~~her~~ love for him. ~~The stepmother is thunderstruck. Liza's death.~~ He seduces her. Liza (in her innocence) thinks that she has reached the utter limit of vileness (she marries him). She hangs herself. <His> wife (<her> stepmother) is thunderstruck.

N.B. The old Prince laughs at His cuckoldry. He proves to the old Prince, while in a fit of temper, that he, too, is a cuckold, and that it is, again, the Prince who is responsible for it. With this in mind, he launches the <love> note picked up by the Youth.

It is also Lambert who works out a plan according to which she'd have to give 20,000 plus herself, for that note.* The Youth saves her.

The Stepmother's love for the little Prince borders on insanity.

EVERYTHING CAN BE FIXED BY MAKING IT SO THAT HE and the old Prince are NOT married to two natural sisters. On the contrary, the Stepmother (His wife) is a distant [(or even a close)] relative (a niece) of the old Prince's. *The old Prince* incessantly criticizes his late brother, the freethinker, who is the father of the Princess, his niece, i.e., His wife. He died a Collegiate Registrar, in poverty and while awaiting criminal trial. And always an enemy of the Princess's, but *she* used to play with the little Prince in their childhood. And therefore, when *she*** (i.e., the Stepmother) hears about the little Prince, she remembers this and tells her husband and the Prince the delicate story of how she and the Prince were engaged when they were children (a love between two children, with the little Prince a year younger than herself). On this occasion she recalls and tells them one anecdote after another about the terrible character of the little Prince (even when he was still a child), who had fascinated her with his utter fearlessness. Inasmuch as she keeps reminiscing and talking <about him> for several days in a row, and with her cheeks burning, He has the impression that there may be something behind it.

N.B. Later, after having been "engaged" as children, they had not met at all until *the very eve* of her wedding to the late General. The little Prince had just received his <first> commission and offered to elope with her. She tells Him this with an air of profound mystery which actually surprises Him. "And I had seen him for all of one hour, though we were still calling each other by our first names," she says. Now the little Prince has returned from his exile (for a duel)

---

* *Chtob ona dala i dala 20,000;* in Russian *dat'* ("to give") is routinely *double entendre.*

** Underlined twice.

and taken to carousing about Petersburg. The Wife (the Stepmother) suddenly goes to see him, particularly since she has heard *that he is the* Princess's *lover.*

She (the Wife, the Stepmother) is all aroused when she hears that the little Prince is supposed to be the Princess's lover. Whereas the little Prince is perhaps indeed the lover of both women (both the Princess, and the Stepmother).

Two infuriated women.

The young Prince is a most open-hearted and delightfully charming person (overcome this difficulty).

The Stepmother seems to be out of her mind. She tells Him outright that she was infatuated with Him in a morbid way, but that she never loved him. That she had taken a similar fancy to her late husband, the General. She is amorous, like Don Juan, but a female Don Juan. She is all *compassion:* she loved the General, who had squandered her dowry, out of compassion, for his defenselessness, she also <loves> Him out of compassion. She also loves the little Prince like a mother. "But only now have I learned what bliss is!" she exclaims. "Now I live only for myself, I myself am cruel!" This statement, that she is "cruel," shows of course that she is all compassion, just as before. The death of Liza, of whom she had been jealous, leaves her thunderstruck. "She died," etc., etc.

A TYPE which should be given more finish along with <that of> the LITTLE PRINCE.

WHAT IS MOST IMPORTANT. Before her death (of moral disorder and exhaustion) she says: "How terrible all this is, suddenly! What a disorder, suddenly! No, I am no predatory woman. Rather, I have been a poor victim all my life. How hard it is to weather this storm." She cannot stand Liza. Him either.

Had He been the type of a superior and righteous man, she would have obeyed him and been an exemplary wife.

"All my life, it seems, I'v been looking for somebody whom I could obey," she says. But he disturbed her soul and crushed her peace of mind with HIS anarchic spirit. He disturbed her. He transmitted his own disturbed condition to her. This is why she suffered together with him. She took care of Him like a nurse, she would forgive Him everything, every admission of His <guilt>, every villainy. But she would not forgive Him his anarchic convictions. Seeing what an influence he had on her, He arrogantly increased his influence, and her confusion. Toward the end she seemed to be going out of her mind. He finally reached the point where he would regularly make full <drunken> confessions to her. That's where she threw herself on the Prince.

It is she who says as she lies dying, with a wistful smile, that she had been looking all her life for somebody she could have obeyed.

N.B. Moral admonition. N.B.

Create (*créer*) an extraordinarily novel and graceful type of woman and wife.

!? N.B. More than to anything else in this novel, pay attention to the element of confession, to his erotic influence on her through disturbing her mind and frightening her soul. A cat playing with its victim. But then, how very angry does He get when somebody takes her away from him (the little Prince). When this happens he immediately gives up his affair with the Princess, and the whole business, forgetting about it and quitting having any feelings about this business, for he realizes that he needs his *wife,* whom somebody is trying to take away from him. A sign that he had nothing going with the Princess.

A LARGER ROLE FOR THE YOUTH.

He himself explains this whole THEORY (i.e., *his influence on his wife*) while the affair is taking its course and *expounds* the whole idea of the novel to the reader, ~~what his sensations are~~ and how this idea actually has to do with Him. And let this rule be valid for the entire novel, so that the characters would themselves explain <their actions> and so that IT WOULD BE MORE READILY UNDERSTOOD.

THE LITTLE BEETLE—not Liza, but she, his wife. He recalls her wretched clothes and predatory type. ~~He~~ She was crushed by compassion. Tenderness for the persecuted child. He ran away. The boy with the birdie.

"How could you have gotten together with Him then?" the old Prince asks her (the Stepmother). N.B. At this point her story is to be told.

"I thought that I was [such] a great man, but <it turns out that> I'm such a small one," (the Stepmother) says of Him.

July 24/12.

TRY THE CHILDREN TOMORROW, NOTHING BUT THE CHILDREN.

Make it so that the Youth, toward the end, inadvertently reveals his main idea (about Rothschild) to Him. This happens at a time when he is himself beginning to lose faith in his idea. Yet he expounds it to Him with *intense* ardor and *irritated* presumption. The other man listens to him very carefully, is apparently impressed, and asks: "How much money have you saved so far?" And he ironically approves of the idea. (N.B. The Youth explains, for instance, how one can make money through stock transactions. *Get the details from Anna Grigorievna.* The idea of buying stock apparently fascinates him and renews his faith in his idea about Rothschild.)

But the Youth sees clearly that He is making fun of him, and does not want to tell him what he thinks.* And therefore he is pestering Him (with adolescent awkwardness, rashness, and angularity) to point out a better ideal to him: how <else> could he become a free man? The other man does not give him an answer and finally says: "Why should I care about all of you? (His wife has just left him) I am living for my own sake, I don't care if you all go to hell. [Let each live his own life."] And, among other things, he reminds the Youth of a recent episode involving his aunt, a squeamish old spinster, who had managed to make the Youth (in the generosity of his heart) beg her forgiveness, pay court to her, a spiteful, dried-up squeamish and demanding sort, and spend some money in the process. "With impulses such as this," He ironically tells the Youth, "you will never become a Rothschild; much rather, you'll become a good-natured milksop of a government clerk." But the Youth replies to him that this has been the last time and that he has even made an entry in his diary saying that this is the last time, and that from now on he is going to be businesslike and cruel. "You will see, you'll hear soon enough," the Youth tells Him, hinting at Lambert. And it is this promise, made *on a dare* and out of pride, which is in part responsible for the fact that he agrees with Lambert's plan to rape her, and to take from her a promissory note for 30,000 and 10,000 in cash.

?N.B. The Youth, incidentally, makes friends with the children who want to murder and rob their father, or he sees those children immediately after they have killed their father, at the house where he has got his flat, and is strongly impressed by this scene, yet he still joins Lambert. What is most important to the Youth is also the fact that the Princess has "insulted him," the way he sees things. Getting ready to rape her, he is still confused and embarrassed, which he communicates to Lambert, who can't even understand him. *The Youth does not know* until the very last hour, that He is involved in

* The Russian phrase is just as ambiguous as this translation; either the Youth or He could be the subject.

this affair along with Lambert. It is Lambert himself who lets him know about it at the very last moment. Which causes an outburst of indignation on his part.

What matters most to the Youth is to be free, and he is willing to achieve his goal of becoming a Rothschild even by way of committing crimes. *"And do good deeds once you have achieved it,"* says He. The Youth blushes, and it is at this point that he pesters him with his question: "what is freedom?"

And what is MOST remarkable here is the fact that at this point the Youth's cycle of ideas about Rothschild, so silly yet so passionate, suddenly acquires a broad new dimension for Him, and that He sees, with astonishment, the tremendous depth of this idea; much that is based on *actual experience,* something one could have hardly expected from him; *emotions and thoughts* which were already *his own**, and acquired from life itself, something quite unexpected at his age. *He* lets him know about all this.

HERE a huge *nota bene:* that He systematically, out of spiteful irony and satanic destructiveness, and under the guise of his usual querulousness, *skillfully flatters and admires*** the Youth, in order to turn his head, throw him off course, and sneer at his downfall caused by <his> pride. All of this *He* tells either the Youth, or his wife, who warns the Youth to be more cautious with Him. On this occasion, the Youth tells Her that he is wondering how she can love such a base character as *Him.* That's where she tells him this: "He has really subjugated us both, hasn't he?" At any rate, the reader should be made aware of His plan of action, i.e., corruption of the Youth out of malice.

Once, the Youth angrily says to him: "You simply haven't accomplished anything and this is why you're envious of everybody." He says the same thing to his wife. He makes Him very angry by saying this, particularly since it is unfair to Him.

From the very beginning, *Liza* is hostile to the Youth, she makes fun of him, and toward the end she almost hates him. Yet before she hangs herself, she leaves a letter for him in which she chooses him ~~to whom to reveal~~ to be the sole executor of her last will. In her letter she begs him (without giving the slightest reason why she has chosen him alone, and no one else) to defend her before her mother,

* Underlined twice.

** Underlined three times.

to implore her to forgive her, and to reveal her sin to her (she says in her letter that *she surrendered herself* to Him, that "she got married to him," but he proves quite clearly that Liza, being a child, had no understanding as yet of the meaning of the word *to surrender,* and had thought that she had surrendered *everything,* i.e., her virginity). She leaves him one of her dresses as a keepsake, the one in which he saw her for the last time, but asks to be buried in the dress which she was wearing when she hanged herself. Finally, she solemnly asks <him> to forget her altogether. This letter leaves a strong impression on the Youth, but what is *particularly remarkable* is the fact that he is not at all surprised that Liza addressed herself to him. And still, the fact that she did address herself to him is one of the stronger reasons for his moral turnabout. "It must be that I am capable of doing something good, if she chose me to be the executor of her last will," he thinks.

Lambert, among other things, tells him the story of how he was being detained in the provinces and how he *had* Viktoriia, having scared her with his threats to tell her mother. The Kirghiz coachman. He tells this story without the slightest embarrassment, but on the contrary, is actually boasting of this despicable action. Make it clear to the reader that this successful precedent with Viktoriia may have perhaps caused him to believe that he could do the same thing with the Princess. *It is amazing* that Lambert failed to tell the Youth that he would be asking the princess for *that very special favor.** But it turns out that he did tell Him. He does not believe that they will succeed in obtaining *that other favor,* and actually advises against trying for it. He does, however, agree with the scheme, figuring that, "well, the devil knows, perhaps she will after all." But he does believe that they will get that promissory note. Incidentally, it is neither the promissory note nor *that other favor* which are important to Him, but rather, it is the scandal which he is sure will come out of it, due to the imprudence of the two youths, while He himself would, in any case, stay out of it.

After *everything is over,*** when the Princess has already made peace with the Youth, and the latter says to her, full of remorse:

---

* *Prosit' u kniagini i klubnichki,* literally, "ask the Princess for some strawberries, too," where *klubnichki* has an obscene connotation similar to that of "cherry" in English slang.

** Underlined three times.

"Where is there an honest man, show me an honest man" (this is when Lambert is lying there, unconscious), the Princess tells him, pointing at him: "Here you have an honest man."

With Liza, the Youth has several scenes even before that, a whole long story. Create one. Liza, like a princess in a fairy tale, sets him various tasks. He fulfills them. Liza only laughs at him. The Youth vows eternal vengeance. ~~The Youth~~ *On one occasion they have a fight* (absolutely), and have to be parted. The Youth is deeply humiliated, but refuses to beg Liza's forgiveness. Liza sees to it that this scuffle, *instead of being seen as a mere joke,* is turned into a *hyperbolically serious* and scandalous incident, derogatory to the Youth.

In Liza's suicide note to him there is not a single word addressed *to him personally;* for an explanation: why was it he whom she selected, why did she turn to him, and why did she always respect him, and love him?*

no { couldn't there have been an English atheist in Moscow, who converted the Youth to atheism?
shouldn't the entire biography be written in his childhood?

In the beginning of the novel, He must *absolutely* be a preacher of Christianity. Relics. Which is what elicits the Youth's indignation more than anything else. The Youth hears the old Prince's opinion regarding *relics* and laughs heartily, thus earning the old Prince's benevolent attention, as the latter is *flattered* that his witticism has produced such an effect (even if it be only upon a mere youth!). The same episode also seems to bring the Youth closer to the old Prince, since prior to it the Youth had already been thinking of leaving the office, and not without kicking up a big row. But now his pride is vanquished quickly, and he and the old Prince seem to become friends through this incident, so much so that the old Prince actually takes lessons in nihilism from the Youth. And altogether, this will be the beginning of a series of comical scenes, characteristic of the relationship between the Youth and the old Prince.

Yet toward the end He must absolutely *chop up some icons* (this takes place at the time of the final catastrophe), and do it when He sees that his slavishly devoted wife is awfully attracted by the young Prince, but still before she definitely breaks with her husband and *runs away* to the young Prince.

---

* Unclear and somewhat ungrammatical phrase.

N.*Bene*. What is important here is that He, in preaching Christianity with all his might, as well as freedom (in Christ, as opposed to the social theory of crime) and a future life, makes it quite plain that the life of a man, and of mankind, is quite *unthinkable* without Christ (Orthodox) and Christianity, because life *is not worth* living *otherwise* (i.e., for a moment, shopkeepers and checkers, icy rocks for planets, etc.). *So that* when he chops up those icons, it turns out that he never did believe anything of what he had been saying, having always been at heart, and *even as long as* he had been alive, an inveterate atheist, which was also the cause of his torments.

"Now I can understand his sufferings," says the Youth. "Really, he can't have been faking when he was preaching Christ so *zealously;* on the contrary, he must have been extremely sincere about it. He was trying to convince himself that he *believed*. He was trying to prove to himself that there could be *faith,* he was struggling with the monster of his doubts, trying to strangle it, but the monster finally ~~realized~~ devoured him."

[February] Conversations with the boy, for instance, about crime and ~~theoretically~~ his theories, or about the workingman's struggle with the bulldog. "Here I am, Sir!" Even in Europe they (the *bourgeoisie*) want to stop this fourth estate by force. We have already seen the prelude. *You* (i.e., the young people) must get ready, for you are going to be participants, the time is near, and precisely when things look so solid (armies a million strong, explosive shells). All this power, built up to defend civilization, will fall upon civilization and will swallow it. The Youth is listening to such talk with a sinking heart. (Also, about classical education.)

The Youth is *of amorous disposition,* a scene with various young ladies, he lost his virginity to a whore, and sheds tears about his lost innocence.

A similar scene with Mme Andrieux. Lambert tells him, "Fuck her," and ~~he~~ leaves the two of them alone, but something strange happens. Mme Andrieux starts by making love to him in a superficial way, but then she bursts into tears about her hard lot and about the insults she has suffered. The Youth has a good cry together with her and leaves, having done nothing. [February (In the 4th part.)]

Conversation about the hunchback baron and about the island in the Baltic Sea.

Important nota bene. At the beginning of the novel He has already quit the service and abandoned his career as a man of affairs. He quit when he received the inheritance. Even the old Prince blames him:

"He could have been a man of affairs, had he only wanted." "And altogether," says the old Prince, "I see him as some kind of a poet; up to now he has been restraining himself, but now his true nature has come to the surface and He has revealed his true self."

It was exactly as the old Prince had said. It was exactly at the point where the novel begins that His inner chaos and conflict with himself (unbelief, etc.) had grown altogether ripe. The claims of his conscience had grown more persistent, etc. And this inner chaos finds expression in external disorders, i.e., his quitting the service, garrulity, restlessness, his odd behavior with his wife; in a word, *disorder,* and as if he were trying to dissuade himself, increased preaching of Christianity (the relics).

Let the reader know about this at the very beginning of the novel, explaining to him that <He,> a man of orderly habits, of moderation, and of action is, to everybody's surprise, beginning *to go off his head,* which poses a problem to his friends and family, though his aunts actually find it charming and are delighted with his new direction. But all the others are saying: "Why, he even used to be a progressive."

July 18/30.

An idea. Shouldn't one let Him embrace Pietism, absolutely and totally, with fanaticism, so that he has fully convinced himself, made himself believe in it, that he is preaching it (*trembling* for his faith, i.e., seeking to protect it), doing great deeds, thwarting the plans of other people, and all of a sudden chops up some icons (only not immediately after his wife has left him).

The old Prince calls him *the bishop,* but listens to him, and is afraid of him. *He* takes charge of all <his> affairs, gets his wife mixed up <in this>, <. . .> etc.

The pedagogue, on children: "You know, here we are, bringing them up, but what a pity it is, really, that they will grow up to be schemers and boors, whereas right now they are so simple-hearted and so charming. They are scheming and lying even now; and they are fighting with each other, but all this is so simple-hearted."

"We are infinitely more evil than they are," he runs to the janitor.

"I am humanizing them, and they are humanizing me. There are things which I'd have never understood without them."

[February] He says about Lambert, having heard everything from his younger brother: "That is good."

"What is so good about Lambert?"

"An integral idea." Apparently, he did not care to finish <his

thought> and fell to thinking in an absentminded way. The young man did not want to be inquisitive either, and also got lost in his thoughts. The young man says: "I would also like to represent an integral idea, but I wouldn't like to be Lambert."

?! An idea. Shouldn't they have a sister who, having been the purest of maidens, suddenly becomes a whore.

Make up some French phrases for Mme Andrieux (like Guizot).

"Eh, may the devil take them!"

"A fine wish."

"By the way, I'm ready to join them."

"I cannot understand the ~~human~~ character of Satan, yet every man has some of it. I could understand the irony, the arrogance, and the dejection of a conscious spirit, if there be existence, but no God. But Satan knows God; how then, can he deny Him?"

The ideals of both sides { Satan—peace in nothingness, in eternal death.
God—~~rest~~ peace in eternal life.

"Look for the man with the deepest gaze and approach <him> boldly, for it is he."

Write my "bibliography."

We have withstood the Tartar invasion, then two centuries of slavery. Now we must withstand freedom. Will we succeed, or will we stumble?

[Here.] Perhaps railroads have done Russia more bad than good. And anyway, everything has been going that way with us, ever since Peter the Great, always at one gulp and unnaturally. Our present time is the [time] reign of the golden mean, of semi-enlightenment, ignorance, laziness, inefficiency, of claims for satisfaction of one's demands without contributing anything oneself, etc.

Three blackguards of shopkeepers are beating up an honest woman on a boulevard (perhaps Lambert is telling this story). The police are egging them on. (Lambert the fool answers, when asked by Perchatkin the fool: "Why are the police egging them on?"—"Because they are afraid that, if they won't allow it, somebody might take to things political, and so, with this in mind, they are actually egging them on.") Perchatkin says: "Aha!"

A tirade about the clergy who are doing nothing.

Elpidiforova (Aleksandrova). *A cosmopolitan.* The story of how she broke her jaw.

The bath-house. An Apollinian leg. "Why should you take a wife? You could become a kept man."

Lambert says that his greatest pleasure, when he is rich, will be to feed dogs with bread and meat, while the children of the poor are starving to death. And when they are without firewood, he is going to buy a whole wood-yard, put all the wood in one pile, and burn it all up for nothing, in the frost, without giving a single log to the poor. "Let them call me names, it will only make me get a better charge out of it."* (N.B. His phantasies are all of this type.)

A phantasy about an island in the Gulf of Botnia, and the prison there, etc.

<Absolute> *being* certainly must be reality, and in any case it must transcend human reason, so that man will be searching all his life. And this is not enough; [it is absolutely necessary] ~~and everything~~ that he *never find it:* that's more decent. There's a philosopher for you. [Come on . . . quite ordinary] Come on, it's not the philosopher's fault. This is something <quite ordinary?>

Regarding the order in which the various creatures appeared ~~the Book of Genesis.~~ Who taught them when there was no science? (An Egyptian papyrus.)

He thinks to himself: "And still, I am an ignorant dolt, even though I am a clever man."

His explanation: the temptation of Christ, 40 days in the desert. (A chapter.)

"Well, after all, it isn't so one feels insulted by what just anybody may say."

A GENUINELY PREDATORY TYPE (see p. 3 of the plans).

Description how he is looking for some money. (Baseness and breadth of character.) He is admitting it to himself and is surprised at himself. *He does call himself a predatory type.* (See to it that all is explained to the reader.) *He is searching for a load to carry, he is searching for faith;* but the "little beetle" crushes him.

He talks about those 40 days in the desert, but what is most important, *he does not believe.* He puts this question to himself: "Well, what if I did believe? Surely, after everything I've said, I would have left for the desert right away."

Finally, he breaks down and chops up those icons.

The man who hanged himself.**

[A man with hopes.] [with Kraft]

---

* . . . *U menia ot etogo stoiat' budet luchshe, literally,* "mine will stand up better for it" (obscene).

** *Udavivshiisia,* literally, "suicide by hanging."

"The deforestation of Russia is taking its course, her soil is being exhausted, transformed into a steppe, and prepared for a takeover by the Kalmucks. Who is doing it? The merchants who buy up the land, and the ancient nobility, the landowners, who formerly would have fought for the land, until the abolition of serfage. Let a new, young landowner with some hopes come and plant a tree, why, everybody will laugh at him: "Do you really think you'll live to see it grow up?" On the other side, well-meaning people are talking about what's going to happen a thousand years hence. The idea of raising children, the idea of patriotism, the idea of integrity, of a future ideal—all of these ideas no longer exist; they have been broken up, undermined, sneered at, justified by the lawlessness which has come after the abolition of serfage.* They have destroyed the nobility, yet they demand a renaissance and a regeneration from it, they want it to act as the guardian of Russia, as the bearer of some higher idea, they address their manifestoes on the education <of the Russian people> to it.[26] But a man who is abusing his soil, thinking 'What do I care what happens after me,' has lost his spirituality and his higher idea. It may be that he has altogether ceased to exist."

"Well, what about your idea of Russia, and your despair at her being second-rate? Doesn't that look 1,000 years ahead?"

"This, this is the most topical question of all. A basic fact. The truth ~~is~~ that, if out of 100,000, there is just one bearer of the higher idea, everything is saved. But is there even one for every 100,000? That's the question."

Answer: "He exists, he is sitting right before me and talking."

[Vitia.] *He* bends down and whispers into his ear: "He is lying."

The boy's bons mots: "I don't want to be Schiller."
"Why not?"
"Because it is too vile." } with Lambert.

How he studies nihilism and other things, learning what is good and what is evil, etc.

"I don't want to love [act] gratis, like Christ," He says.

"Are you looking for a reward?" asks the [Youth] boy.

"Yes, a reward. What did you think?"

---

* The last part of the sentence is unclear in the original, too.

[26] A reference to the Tsar's public letter of December 25, 1873, addressed to the nobility and appealing to it to act as a guardian of the education of the people.

"What kind of a reward?"

"That's precisely the point: I don't know. That's the point, I want something really special. That everybody should love me. Imagine me walking down the street: 'This is he,' people whisper. Let me do something: 'This is he, our benefactor.' They applaud me, a commune, a monument even while I'm still living. A maiden, dreaming of her beloved, would be thinking of me. By the way, they'd all have to be in love with me, etc. The Czar will learn about me, and make me a Czar too." (Brazen, ironic, comical presentation of *Everyman's* dream of happiness.)

The Youth smiles and says: "No, perhaps you don't need a reward, and you are making fun of me." The other man replies, laughing:

"How do you know, perhaps I need it very much, and precisely in that form."

After three days he couldn't stand it anymore; if it were in that form, it would bore him to death.

"You'll get bored without fail: you are no MacMahon."[27]

"What three days, I couldn't stand it for three hours!"

"A university student," who shouts obscenities at women at night (reportage in *Russkii mir,* around July 10, 1874).[28]

---

[27] A marshal of France (1808–93). He distinguished himself in the Crimean war and was governor general of Algeria from 1864 to 1870. He suffered a crushing defeat in the war of 1870 and later became president of the republic from 1873 to 1879. Dostoevsky satirized him in *The Citizen,* September 17, 1873.

[28] Printed actually in *The Russian World (Russkii mir),* July 12, 1874. It is an account of how a writer, accompanying a lady, is molested by a drunk, who turns out to be a university student. The narrator appeals for help from a policeman, but the policeman shakes the hand of the drunken student and permits him to continue abusing women in the street.

ВОСКРЕСЕНЬЕ, 17 (29) ФЕВРАЛЯ 1874 — № 48 — ГОДЪ ДВѢНАДЦАТЫЙ — № 48 — ВОСКРЕСЕНЬЕ, 17 (29) ФЕВРАЛЯ 1874

ГОЛОСЪ

ГАЗЕТА ПОЛИТИЧЕСКАЯ и ЛИТЕРАТУРНАЯ

ЕЖЕДНЕВНОЕ ИЗДАНІЕ

Masthead for the newspaper Voice *of February 17, 1874. Dostoevsky read about the trial concerning counterfeit shares for the Tambovsko-Kozlovsky railways. Dostoevsky drew upon the facts of this affair for his narration of Stebelkov's manipulations and Prince Sergey's unwitting participation.*

СУДЕБНАЯ ХРОНИКА.

Дѣло Колосова и Ярошевича о поддѣлкѣ акцій тамбовско-козловской желѣзной дороги.

Засѣданіе санктпетербургскаго окружнаго суда, по 1-му отдѣленію, съ участіемъ присяжныхъ засѣдателей, 15-го февраля.

(*Продолженіе* *).

Свидѣтель полковникъ Жевановъ показалъ, что въ правленіе общества тамбовско-козловской желѣзной дороги прибылъ судебный слѣдователь по особо важнымъ дѣламъ, привезъ съ собою двѣ акціи этого общества, о которыхъ просилъ сказать, настоящія онѣ или нѣтъ. По первому впечатлѣнію нельзя было придти къ окончательному выводу и находившіеся въ правленіи члены приняли ихъ за настоящія, тѣмъ болѣе, что подпись бухгалтера сдѣлана на акціяхъ до того хорошо, что самъ онъ не могъ дать утвердительнаго отвѣта— его ли подпись или нѣтъ. Потомъ предложено было судебному слѣдователю доставить всѣ находящіяся у него акціи, въ количествѣ 259 штукъ, при сличеніи которыхъ съ настоящими оказалось, что онѣ поддѣльныя; для болѣе точнаго разрѣшенія вопроса были приглашены эксперты, которые, при тщательномъ разсмотрѣніи, открыли въ представленныхъ акціяхъ большую массу подробностей подлога.

На вопросъ прокурора, Жевановъ объяснилъ, что акцій тамбовско-козловской желѣзной дороги было выпущено 35,960 штукъ; когда обнаружилось, что есть подложныя акціи, правленіе общества обратилось съ ходатайствомъ въ министерство финансовъ и выхлопотало разрѣшеніе о замѣнѣ акцій стараго образца акціями новаго образца и въ настоящее время акціи общества почти всѣ обмѣнены.

Прокуроръ. Акціи, представленныя вамъ, въ продажѣ не оставляли никакого сомнѣнія въ томъ, что онѣ настоящія?

Жевановъ. Навѣрно не было никакого сомнѣнія потому что я весьма близко стоящій на

A clipping from Voice *concerning the trial of those arraigned for counterfeiting railway shares. The text of the clipping is about the discovery and determination of the counterfeit shares and the subsequent issue of new shares.*

II

The First Period of Work on the Plot

August–September, 1874

The plot of the boys and the abstract idealism of Fyodor Pyotrovich are missing from these notes, as they will be throughout the notes. Dostoevsky has settled on the Youth and the Predatory Type, now son and father, as the focus and center of the novel; and the characterization of each and the relations between them dominate these notes. As in the novel the Youth is ambivalent in his attitudes toward his father. He loves and hates him, and seeks and does not find the guide to life that he looks for. He does not know how to judge his father, and the reader, too, is ambivalent and unsure of how to judge him. The father—now called occasionally Brusilov—is less mysterious, more talkative, and more revealing in these notes, but the revelations bring complexities and not illuminations. He is in love with the Princess, but intent upon wreaking revenge upon her; and in love with his wife, to whom he looks for purity and salvation, but he drives her out of her mind by his affair with Liza, the stepdaughter. He is cynical and impassioned, an intriguer and a recluse, charming and cold and spiteful.

Versilov preaches Christianity so eloquently that the Princess almost takes the veil under his influence, but he attempts to seduce her and provokes her hate and disgust. Whether his preaching of Christianity comes from mocking contempt or a searching heart is a question that the Youth—and even Dostoevsky—agonizes over. The Youth asks himself, "Is he religious, or is He an atheist?" And Dostoevsky says of the Youth's quandary: "In connection with this, his passionate sermons on Christianity (and this is MOST IMPORTANT) are particularly characteristic, so that the Youth can never, in the course of the entire novel, make sure if he is saying these things *in earnest,* or not." Near the end of the section, the following dialogue takes place between the Youth and Versilov:

> "But what about Christianity?"
> *He:* "Why, I really never believed in it."
> "So, you were playing a role?"
> *He:* "How could I have played a role? I believed because I was afraid that I didn't. And now I've realized that I really didn't believe in anything at all. Only now have I discovered that everything is disorder, that everything is cursed."

But this dialogue is not the last word on the matter.

Dostoevsky experiments with many dialogues between the Youth and the father and many monologues in which Versilov's enigmatic views are put forth. The Youth hates and loves his father, and Versilov looks on the Youth with amusement, indifference, and occasionally with tolerant interest. There is something static and immovable about these conversations, as if Dostoevsky were seeking some lever to move them. They are often repetitious, and they return again and again to a few insistent motifs. In many respects these motifs are not different from those we find in the final version. The Youth is seeking an ideal, some guide to life, but his thoughts and his actions are contradictory, naïve, and even vile. Versilov is and is not a worthy guide, and both substance and void are concealed behind his mysterious words and actions.

Dostoevsky is not sure what Versilov is supposed to stand for. In some of the notes he is tormented by a great idea, despite his weaknesses:

> BUT WHAT IS MOST IMPORTANT, retain throughout the entire narrative a tone of His unchallenged superiority over the Youth and everybody else, all His comical traits and all His weaknesses notwithstanding: let the reader feel all along that, at the end of the novel, He is tormented by a great idea. And motivate the reality of His suffering.

But Dostoevsky also says of him: "Simply: an amoral man, a man who has failed to develop a moral principle. A purely Russian, universal type." And Versilov says of himself: "But so long as I still have my two rubles, I want to live all by myself and do nothing." And—anticipating Ivan Karamazov—"Why should I do good? Why should I love anybody?" Even more emphatically: "Why shouldn't I live to take care of my own arse, what else is there to do? Worry about the common good, make your contribution to the happiness of future generations? To hell with them, what the devil do I care? Let them tell me something more serious to support such notions!"

Dostoevsky seems more sure of what the Youth is to stand for, and it does not differ greatly from what he embodies in the novel:

> *Finale.* And altogether, this is an epic poem about how *the Youth* made his debut in the world. This is the story of his searchings, hopes, disappointments, corruption, rebirth, education—the story of a most attractive, of a very nice person. And it is life itself that teaches him, yet it is he, the Youth, who learns his lesson, for some other person might not have learned it.

Dostoevsky is sure that the main idea concerns the Youth:

> THE MAIN IDEA. Though the Youth arrives with a ready idea in his mind, the whole idea of the novel is that he is searching for a guideline to direct his actions, for good and evil; he is thirsting for something that is lacking in our society, is intuitively searching for it, and this is what the novel is all about.

But the essence of the novel also concerns Versilov:

> *The essence of the novel is this:* His untidy love for Liza and the sufferings from it. His love and admiration for His wife, and their mutually inflicted suffering. Yet they are hiding the secret from each other. His love-hatred for the Princess.

The situation that Dostoevsky returns to again and again is the plot of revenge upon the Princess. As in the novel the Youth and the father, as well as Lambert and Liza, participate in the plot. The Youth conceives of the plot to humiliate her and in some of the notes plans to exploit her sexually. The device to humiliate here is a secret letter that the Youth comes across in various ways. There is talk of two letters: one in which the Princess declares her love for the young Prince, and more insistently a letter in which she recommends that the old Prince (here her husband) be incarcerated in an insane asylum.

Sexual complications appear clearly and insistently in these notes but are muted in the novel itself. Both father and son seek sexual revenge upon the Princess and both have affairs with Liza, who is, apparently, stepdaughter and stepsister to them. Dostoevsky says: "Liza has enthralled the Youth, making him fall madly in love with her. He is aware of it, and is jealous (but he does not believe Liza altogether). In the meantime, Liza is complaining to the Youth that He is trying to seduce her (this, after she has already slept with Him). The Youth begins to hate Him." And: "On one occasion Liza enticed the Youth and surrendered herself to him he actually sensing beforehand the Youth's horror after the act. She laughs at his horror."

Throughout the section Dostoevsky vacillates between narrating the novel from the "Youth's point of view," that is, in the "I" form, and from the third-person point of view, closely centered on the youth. In dozens of comments he weighs the advantages and disadvantages of both modes of narration. The narration from the Youth's point of view will express well the searching, naïve quality of the Youth; it will endear the reader to him and will even permit "Him" to appear in a more mysterious light. Dostoevsky details the advantages for himself:

> Think over the possibility of a *first-person narrative*. Many advantages; much freshness, the figure of the Youth would emerge more typical. Nicer, I'll be able to cope better with the character, with the personality, with the essence of that personality.

But Dostoevsky fears some of the limitations of this mode of narration: the reader may become bored and it may not be possible to narrate convincingly everything that must be said from the youth's point of view. He worries about whether certain intimate thoughts and experiences of Versilov will be known by the Youth:

> NOTE. The Youth, due to his tender age, has no access to the events, the facts <which form> the plot of the novel. And so he makes his own *conjectures* and *masters* them by himself. Which circumstance is reflected in the whole manner of his narrative (to give the reader some surprises).

The "I" point of view will be used in the final version, with questionable results. Versilov's enigmatic character will be retained with magnificent results. The sexual rivalry over the Princess will be muted into insignificance and the sexual rivalry over Liza will disappear entirely. In the private world of his notes Dostoevsky could play with what modern psychology has come to consider as one of the elements of the struggle of the generations, but in the public world of Russian convention, the struggle had to take place on an ideal plane.

August 1.

*An idea.** Couldn't He be a contemporary father, and the Youth His son? *(Think it over.)*

At first sight, one might think that He is merely a vile creature and a sackful of shit *(which is what he likes to pretend to be)*. Regarding his duties as a father, he says: "Leave me alone." He preaches Christianity in a mocking way (but it turns out that this mockery is full of bitterness). But later it turns out that He is very serious, and that he suffers from his unbelief and the sensation of *vitality* which accompanies it and which he considers base (hence depravity and cynicism).

He has suffered an insult and there has been a severe rupture between him and the Prince and Princess, with whom he is still at odds at the beginning of the novel.

AS EARLY AS IN THE MIDDLE OF THE NOVEL HE RETURNS THE ESTATE, IN A WAY THAT MAKES IT COME UNEXPECTED, AND AGAINST ALL EXPECTATIONS COMING FROM HIM.

---

* Underlined twice.

If He is *a father,* in that case the Youth is summoned <by the family> (already after his decision to return the estate), but only after he has quit Moscow University of his own accord. His wife (the Princess-Stepmother) is very glad that he is returning what is actually her own estate.

The estate is returned *in the middle,* strangely, inadvertently, and against everybody's expectations. The Youth is not being told about it. He is staying with his aunts who are resentful of His marriage. Also, these aunts had been bringing up and supporting the Youth even before, since he does not remember his mother. The Youth learns about the return of the estate by himself, and what is most important, from <overhearing> conversations between the old Prince and his Stepmother. As for his aunts, they do not consider it necessary to discuss serious subjects with him.

But he has come to rebel.

Later, when he asks his father and stepmother what they are going to live on, he receives practically no answer: "Well, somehow we'll manage."

The family to whom the money was returned. Etc.

The old Prince is wondering why He quit his position with him. He, on the other hand, explains *a parte* that to remain with the old Prince would have meant for him to pander to the liaison and plans of the young Princess and the young Prince (Gol<itsyn>). But this is a lie, and He is simply in love with and jealous of the Princess, and in his *desperation* actually ventured to proposition her most audaciously, threatening to tell the old Prince. She had shown him the door. He is out to get even with the Princess, and finds Lambert most welcome.

His wife is jealous of him. But when she gets involved with Golitsyn, he gets rid of the Princess and makes furious attempts to get his wife back (in a word, his biography is full of base actions). He never gave up any of his passions.

N.B. Meeting between father and son, the latter having arrived from Moscow to join his family, after he failed an examination in the classics. The father laughs boisterously, calls his son a "darkie,"* sneers at classicism, teaches him some scandalous things, etc. The son despises his father.

---

* *Chumka,* "blackie, darkie," not necessarily literal, since it might be an allusion to his son's classical studies; the classics were often associated with obscurantism.

An idea (something quite different). At a time when everybody is holding Him in contempt for His meekness (including even his wife), He comes up with an exploit (an act of martial heroism, almost) and puts up with a slap in the face. But his exploit is divulged. Think up something.

There is a rumor that He will perform a miracle, lots of people, some of them from far away, are coming to see it.[1]

On the three temptations by the Devil.

[?February,? 3d part.] *More intelligibly.* His main desire is to explain to people that vice is not repugnant at all. *He* hates those *Genevan ideas*[2] (i.e., love of man, i.e., virtue without Christ) and refuses to recognize that there is anything natural about virtue. The Youth is taken aback, but his aunts tell him that this is an argument *e contrario* and that it must be taken in the opposite sense, that he merely wants to carry <the argument> *ad absurda.* But the Youth has a hunch that he is saying it quite naturally and that there is nothing absurd about it. *(He meddles in the Princess's affairs out of fanaticism.)*

He is talking about Ungern-Shternberg and suddenly chops up some icons. After the icons, he wants to shoot himself, but there his wife's affair with the Prince comes up. Death of his wife. His suicide. The Youth takes over his place on Earth.

The Youth says: "I want to be kind simply because I like it."

The Youth has this word to say about Him *en lieu* of a funeral oration: "He was too conscientious."

[February, 3d part.] "If I were a government official or a bourgeois," He says, "I'd wish for order, peace, so that (1) I myself, and (2) (for humanitarian reasons) other people as well might live as

---

[1] This incident may be an anticipation of the scene in which father Zossima talks to the peasant women: Part I, Chapter 4, of *The Brothers Karamazov.* It may also be an anticipation of the miracle expected at his death. This is one of frequent references to themes and details that Dostoevsky will use in *The Brothers Karamazov.*

[2] Dostoevsky had in mind Rousseau's ideas and the fund of egotism that he saw in the doctrine of natural virtue. More immediately, however, he probably had in mind French utopian socialism, which incorporated much of Rousseau's belief in the natural "goodness" of man and the corruption of his institutions, and especially Russian utopian socialism, which Dostoevsky had direct contact with and against which—after a period of ambivalent attraction in the forties— he fought a lifelong battle. Perhaps, also, Dostoevsky had in mind the revolutionary ideas he heard at "The International Peace Congress," which was held in Geneva in 1867.

comfortably as possible (and with atheism, too!). Moreover, I would be supporting law and order myself. But inasmuch as I am an honest and conscientious man, I sincerely favor (under the conditions of atheism) crime and destruction, nor have I any use for those Genevan ideas." But he could not overcome crime, and his conscience killed him.

Staraia Russa, August 4

The Youth believes that money will make him a conqueror, allowing him to face the future proudly and without fear, like a perennial conquerer... But He scares him with a description of the petroleum of the future.*

In Him, who is a predatory type, there lives a passionate and *indefatigable* drive to enjoy life, *real life,* but from the whole breadth of life he would like to pick not too spectacular a lot (such as Napoleon's). "You're too much in the limelight, you must play a role too often, *create an image of yourself* and pose. Every man to his taste, for myself I prefer freedom. And in particular, I like secrecy. ~~The role~~ The lot of Ungern-Shternberg[3] is better than that of Napoleon."

Like Rousseau, who derived pleasure from revealing his innermost secrets, so He, too, would derive a perverse pleasure** from baring his innermost secrets before the Youth, actually corrupting him by his frank revelations. He enjoys the Youth's puzzlement and astonishment. Yet he is passionately religious, even though he is suffering from that sore of atheism and eventually *is consumed* by it, when he chops up those icons.

He is consumed by fire, consumed by fire.

THE YOUTH is astonished and asks himself: "Is he religious, or is He an atheist?"

When the Youth challenges Him, asking how He could be a religious man and reconcile Christ with secret debauchery, he says: "Well, so what if I am base and repulsive; the truth is the truth even *without me.*"

[February, 3d part.] "No, it cannot *without you,* if you only *be-*

---

* Unclear phrase.

** *Sladostrastnoe naslazhdenie,* literally, "voluptuous enjoyment," but *sladostrastnyi* tends to be negative in Russian, so that "perverse" seems in order.

[3] He was a pioneer in railway building in the south of Russia. His methods were the occasion of political polemics in the sixties, and articles on this subject appeared in journals that Dostoevsky edited (*Vremia,* April, 1863, and *Epoch,* 1864).

lieve. That's right, it cannot *without you,*—that's the way you must reason. You must quit everything and become an ascetic."

"I shall certainly do this, I certainly will. This is what I'm thirsting for, this is what I need, for right now I'm only playing with the Devil, though he is not going to get me."

And here then, a lecture on willpower and how to strengthen it, and on the freedom of a hermit (but not for pride, but for Christ).

It is He himself who tells the Youth about *baring one's innermost secrets.** His wife, too, knows everything, he had been baring his secrets to her, before he did so to the Youth.

But in the end he is consumed by <his own> fire, and chops up those icons, commits a crime, not being able to endure "the little red beetle."

200,000, and he returned it (Shchelkov), and he is vexed by the fact that he has done a good deed.

When he has destroyed those icons: "There is no good and no evil, I want to live thinking of my own arse only." And "the little beetle" tortures him to death.

He explains himself what a *predatory type* and a *flabby type* are.**

A Russian type, an artistic strain about his desire to express himself, total ignorance, an interest in a great idea, a story about the plain young Russian who got the better of a German engineer, as he dumped the <huge> rock by Pavlovsk Barracks into a hole he had dug, how he was talking to the then Governor General, Prince Suvorov, and how he told him the anecdote about the crow who had lived in this world for three years, when the Prince had shown too little understanding for the overwhelming simplicity of certain ideas. Oh, without a doubt, Suvorov found it so very funny and later told the anecdote to the Czar. So they got to question the man why he wasn't in the government service: "Well, Sir, I have a small capital." So he was given a post—and then he really got going...what a career he made! Yet he was just knocking about the world until he came to Petersburg and came across that rock.[4]

Christ was on trial in England.

[Perhaps for the story <which I promised> to Kozlov. February.]

---

* The Russian word *zagalivanie,* "laying oneself bare," is used by Dostoevsky rather as a "technical term," meaning "baring one's innermost secrets."

** *Babii tip,* from *baba,* "(old) woman," thus "effeminate," "weak," "flabby."

4 This anecdote appears in the final version in Part II, Chapter 1:2.

Opposed to this type, there is another insupportable type, a real nemesis to those artistic ones, a type of people who are just as uneducated and ill-informed as the "artistic ones," but make up for it by being extraordinarily *exact.* What does he care for the poetic aspect of the story, in fact he won't even notice it, that bear of a Sobakevich, he won't become emotional about it, the scoundrel, no he won't; but he won't let you get away with any nonsense either and will surely take you up on some detail: "where, when, and in what year, and, come on, there wasn't any Suvorov around at that time, and besides, that couldn't have been Aleksandr Ivanovich, it must have been Pavel Ignatievich, but he wasn't even in the service that year, but was rather managing some salt-mines," etc.

He is not a general manager of the Prince's affairs, but had been something of that sort before; but then, like Shchelkov, he wins a fortune (unfairly) and lives the life of a man of means, gets married—and suddenly he returns everything, including a secret document pertaining to this affair. Could be that Fyodor Fyodorovich insisted that he do that and forced him to take this step.

Though the Youth meets Vitia occasionally and visited all of his *old friends* upon his arrival, he thinks very little of their projects (America, anonymous letters), *having his own idea,* and is told by the others that he has changed, and betrayed his former convictions. But the Youth reveals his secret (to become a Rothschild) to none of them. Which immediately makes the reader see him in an aura of mystery and enigma (he keeps counting his money, frequents the money-changers, the flea-market, looks for ways to increase his capital, asks questions, sniffs around, skimps).

Stepson and stepfather. An artistic nature. A charming character (he refuses the inheritance). To bare one's innermost secrets. He fascinates him (literally so). It turns out that he is involved in some frightfully base actions, very nearly a plot, against the Princess (think up something). The young man turns away from him and leaves him (secret debauchery). He chops up some icons (it turns out that everything about him is serious). For his wife. "The little beetle" (his wife). Those Genevan ideas were his ruin. The Youth turns honest. [Nota bene.] In the meantime, the Youth's friends get caught. Episode with the aunt. (N.B. This is a poetic treatment of early youth.) He talks with his stepfather about how much of an education he might need, and how to conduct himself. He is angry with himself for having opened his heart to his father. Meanwhile the action rolls on all by itself, as the plot of the novel runs its course. The Youth himself, having found the letter, thinks up a scheme how to put the Princess into a tight spot, and explains his idea to Lambert who has recently arrived. ~~He~~ He is scared by the way in which Lambert accepts this idea. About how he got together with <Mme> Andrieux. About Liza. And all along, about the fascination which He exerts upon him. In a word, don't leave the Youth for a single moment, the fragrance of early youth, a poem.

Better if he is his natural FATHER.

Liza must absolutely be (a stepdaughter), the General's children. The poor sick boy. He left after his mother's death. (Or killed himself. The little birdie.) His stepfather persecuted him in a morbid way.

Later, in the end, when his wife has died, Liza hangs herself, and the boy runs away: He makes a confession to his son, saying that he cannot stand *the icons;* he tells him everything, how he used to bare his innermost secrets (terrible simple-heartedness, Valikhanov,[5] fascination), how he used to torture his wife, <their> child, Liza—he shoots himself.

The boy, for a moment, is in a tight spot together with Lambert. But he is rescued by the Princess, and finds his father already in a state of desperation (he has been an aggressive atheist all the time;* the depth of his suffering now becomes evident).

Nota bene. GOOD! August 7/8.

(N.B. On the absence of ideas in society, and on the lack of family ties, His theory, etc.)

He is just as fascinatingly simple-hearted with his wife, when they are having their quarrels, and the Youth tries to reconcile them.

BUT WHAT IS MOST IMPORTANT, retain throughout the entire narrative a tone of His unchallenged superiority over the Youth and everybody else, all His comical traits and all His weaknesses notwithstanding; let the reader feel all along that, at the end of the novel,

---

* *Ateist so svistom vse vremia,* literally, "an atheist with a whistle all the time."

5 Dostoevsky became acquainted with him in Omsk. He was attracted to his good-hearted simplicity, and referred very positively to him on more than one occasion in his letters. On December 14, 1856, Dostoevsky wrote to Valikhanov: "I never felt such an attraction to anyone, including my brother, such as I feel to you" (*Letters,* I, 200–202). And on October 31, 1859, he wrote the following to Baron Vrangel: "Valikhanov is a dear and most remarkable man. I like him very much and I'm very interested in him" (*Letters,* I, 279).

He is tormented by a great idea. And motivate the reality of His suffering.*

Thus, for instance, he is an atheist, yet suddenly he is explaining the sermon of the mount to the Youth, though it comes to no decision.

Or, the advent of communism. ("What will save the world?—Beauty." But always with a sneer.) Perhaps, he is chopping up those icons, while saying, "I want to live thinking of my own rear-end only," and as for having returned the estate, he says: *"c'était <une> bêtise."*[6]

"Will Russia stand her ground? (against communism)," asks the Youth. He cursorily points out some signs showing that Russia has her own idea, *but* ~~in time~~ concludes with a sneer: "I am not educated nor an expert, who am I to decide it?"

N.B. To motivate the fact that he shoots himself, an example—on account of the idea that Russia is a second-rate nation and merely serves as raw material.

We haven't got a single idea in Russia that might guide us. Example: the role of the nobility, the principle has been lost, an abstract idea high up in the air, on the tip of a needle, it just won't stay up there.

FOR EXAMPLE. The scene with the chambermaid at the house, almost on the very first day after the arrival of the Youth. The sick child tells <him?> about the chambermaid.** Hatred, they force the child to admit that he had been lying, etc.

Therefore the Youth, *having a father,* starts to save money and begins to dream about <becoming a> Rothschild, the reason for it being that He (his father) has been treating him more than casually for a long time, which the young man has also recognized a long time ago (facts).

"I cannot understand the idea of being useful to society," He explains. "To what end? Why? One must believe in and love that desire to be useful, and I neither love it nor believe in it. What is society to me? I can't stand that trite idea.*** I may yet find myself

---

* Unclear sentence, not quite grammatical.

** Might also be: "The sick child tells on the chambermaid."

*** *Kazennyi,* "trite," "banal," has a connotation of something imposed by the government.

[6] French: "It was nonsense."

something to do, but not in order to be useful, but merely for the salary, if I really were in great need of the money. But so long as I still have my two rubles, I want to live all by myself and do nothing. At least this gives one the satisfaction of doing nothing at all, so that one can say with a clear conscience that one isn't involved in anything."

He is deeply *impressed* by the Youth's idea to start saving money (though he laughs at him). "This is a most profound idea and a most profound inclination," He says. "A most remarkable trait of yours."

N.B. Think over the plot (Lambert, Andrieux, the Princess *et al.*) <to make it> BETTER, deeper, BROADER AND MORE SERIOUS. About the Princess, etc.

N.B. There must absolutely be a rupture between him and the Princess, so that he would be burning with vengeance. Which circumstance greatly surprises the Youth later on, when he learns about it, namely that He, being such a skeptic and recluse, is also an intrigant ~~and~~ a passionate one at that...* and that, with all his charm, he is so cold and spiteful.

For instance, *He* makes the Youth tell him, right off the bat, that he has had some dealings with the Princess and traps him into admitting that he is enthralled by her. The Youth is frantic, while He suddenly turns malicious, cold, and superciliously casual.

He tells the Youth: "Assuming I'll be aware of all the inventions of the exact sciences and, through them, get a multitude of things to increase my comfort, <like> now I am sitting on thick cloth, and then *everybody* will be sitting on velvet, and what of it?** The question still remains: what shall we be doing then? With all that comfort and velvet—~~what to do?~~ what will we actually be living for, what goal will we have? Mankind will be thirsting for a great idea."[7]

"I agree that to feed humanity, and to distribute food among it, is at the given moment a great idea also, for it implies a goal. But it is a secondary and a subordinate idea, for the moment man is fed, he is certainly going to ask: 'What am I living for?' "

---

* Or "is also a passionate intrigant."

** The whole sentence is slightly ungrammatical.

[7] This refers to one of Dostoevsky's many formulations about the fact that comfort alone will not satisfy man. This is fairly close to what the Underground Man says in his argument against the crystal palace, and what Lebedev has to say in *The Idiot*. The Grand Inquisitor, however, argues the opposite point in *The Brothers Karamazov*.

"So that all of these *secondary* goals, which mankind sets itself, appear to be mere diversions from the great main idea: 'Here, my good little child, keep yourself occupied and relax, don't give any thought to the great idea.' And believe me, the moment there will be enough food for everybody, people will immediately think up some other, also secondary, idea, to keep them busy for the time being and to divert their attention from the great idea. Mankind has been doing this as long as it has existed."

(To the Youth:) "There you are, saving money and wanting to become a Rothschild. Don't tell me this is for velvet, for tasty dinners, or is it? On the contrary, it is for pride. You'd rather eat dry bread, than pie, just to attain your goal."

"And your goal is not material wealth, but power."

An IDEA: "FATHERS and CHILDREN"—CHILDREN and FATHERS. For the son who wants to become Rothschild is essentially an *idealist,* i.e., a new phenomenon, an unexpected consequence of nihilism.[8]

With regard to the Youth, He displays a condescending air of mockery throughout: he would invariably conclude (as if he had had an afterthought) even the most pathetic exchanges with a gibe and a negation (but condescendingly, *casually,* as if in passing, *lazily,* without warmth and without effort).

A tyrant and a despot at all times. Likes to parade his egoism. Even in his worst moments of petty baseness and weakness of character, as when he is ripping apart the mouth of the <little> boy. Even then the Youth cannot get a grip on Him, for in the very last resort he would *catch himself* and expose his own shame <for everyone> to see.[9]

In connection with this, his passionate sermons on Christianity (and this is MOST IMPORTANT) are particularly characteristic, so that the Youth can never, in the course of the entire novel, make sure if he is saying these things *in earnest,* or not. Until the very moment when he chops up those icons; he makes an effort to start laughing imme-

---

[8] Idealism is a trait that Dostoevsky studiously avoided attributing to nihilists, but near the end of his life he was tempted by the idea that Russian atheists and liberals were really "believers" who had gone astray. He voiced this sentiment in his Pushkin speech of 1880. It is possible that Dostoevsky's restraint in his criticism of them in his later years contributed to the seriousness with which he deals with a version of the "atheist as believer" in the figure of the Grand Inquisitor.

[9] This reminds one of Lebedev's frequent parading of his shame in *The Idiot.*

diately after he has done it, but it is a wry smile. The Youth realizes that this is very serious.

PLOT! PLOT!

ABSOLUTELY. From the very beginning, every independent effort of the Youth to make a penny must be included in the novel: the flea-market, auctions, sale, purchase, successes and failures, i.e., profit and loss. In the end result, <let him> absolutely make a profit, to his great satisfaction. Daydreams about shining shoes, etc. *Daydreams about inventions.* But the Youth finally decides that he despises inventions. What gives him most comfort about his system of gaining wealth is that it requires absolutely no talent. Precisely the fact that one doesn't need genius, wisdom, education, and in the end one is still a big man, a king to each and everybody, and one can *get even* with all those who had at one time insulted one (list them, starting with the Moscow professor, and down to his aunts, the Princess, the Prince, and that officer who shoved him in the street). Get even, or do <them> an infinite amount of good. "When I'm that far, I'll do as I please; what matters <now> is to attain freedom and independent power." His system is this: saving, willpower, character, seclusion, and secrecy. The idea of joining a company does not appeal to him. He is fascinated by his being so alone, poor, ragged, and wretched. "Nobody wants to pay attention to me, they walk by haughtily, and whenever they do address me, it is invariably with condescension or even with contempt that they do. Oh, if they only knew that I am already a power, that given a little more time, I shall suddenly make my appearance, that I could do it even right now."

He counts his years, figuring when exactly he will have a capital of so-and-so-much, and by what year, approximately, he will have become a Rothschild. He knows some anecdotes, like the one about Rothschild making millions by having learned, a few hours before everyone else, that the Duc de Berry had been assassinated,[10] etc. N.B. He is fascinated by <the report about> a beggar who had 200,000 hidden in the lining of his coat. *I am satisfied with this knowledge.** (N.B. *Pick up some anecdotes.*)

---

* A quotation from Pushkin's "Covetous Knight."

10 Duc de Berry was the second son of Charles X, pretender to the French throne. He was assassinated in 1820, but Dostoevsky was wrong about Rothschild's profiting from his knowledge of this fact. Rather, Rothschild learned of Napoleon's defeat at Waterloo early and profited from this fact.

He actually likes the idea of being uneducated; however, he changes his mind regarding this idea and decides to acquire knowledge and learning, so he could astound everybody when the time would come for him to make his appearance.[11]

He asks questions about socialism: he is particularly impressed by the abolition of private property, his very first conversation with Vitia has to do with this. Vitia isn't able to explain anything to him, and so he introduces him to somebody like Dolgushin,[12] a group of people who carry on discussions about "normal man" (they are later arrested). He does not agree with socialism: it is against nature.

But *He* gives answers to many of his questions. When He demonstrates the unnaturalness of socialism to the Youth, the latter is so delighted he must laugh. Seeing this, He immediately confuses him again by pointing out the grandeur of the idea of socialism. For a while, the Youth is actually carried away.

WHAT IS MOST IMPORTANT. The Youth's whole idea about saving money is also a great and a poetic idea in his daydreams.

In order to avoid making the novel too abstract, it might be necessary to introduce a few visiting Zemstvo workers. His anecdote about how he was, at one time, working very hard for his Zemstvo and how an allotment of 10 rubles was made, and how, when everybody had voiced his agreement, only three got up.* (Inquire with Father Ivan.)[13]

(August 12) AN IMPORTANT SOLUTION OF THE PROBLEM. Write *in the first person*. Start with the Word: *I*.

"Confession of a great sinner, for himself."

"I am nineteen years old [nineteen going on twenty], and I am already a great sinner. After the catastrophe which has hit me, I want

---

* The story is not clear in the original either.

[11] This is a variation of a common idea in Dostoevsky's works. The Underground Man tells how while at school he tried to intimidate his schoolmates with his learning. He also has fantasies about impressing Zverkov and company with his superior knowledge. In the notes for *The Idiot* this is a frequent refrain.

[12] He is called Dergachev in the novel. The "Dolgushintsy" were a conspiratorial group which called for revolt against the Tsar, extermination of the bourgeois, division of the land among workers, substitution of a militia for the army, the building of schools, and the abolition of the passport. Their slogan was "life according to nature and truth" and their aim was equality and brotherhood.

[13] Reference to Ivan Rumiantsev, priest in *Staraia Russa*. Dostoevsky became friends with him and rented an apartment from him. His relations with Dostoevsky are narrated in A. G. Dostoevsky's *Vospominaniia*.

to put it all down. For myself, later, many years hence (for I shall have a long life), I shall understand all these facts much better, but this manuscript will even then help me to know myself better," etc.

Start directly and *concisely:* how and why he decided to get rich; and when that idea was conceived. While taking an examination with a professor. (Anecdote.) And only *later,* that he has a father in Petersburg, and who his father is, and how he went there. ?N.B. He left without saying good-bye to Lambert. (In the railway carriage, a fool—30,000).

(N.B. Or, that story about how Lambert went there later, and though he didn't witness anything personally, he still tells the story *as if he had been there,* having warned the reader that it is based on hearsay and on facts gathered by him.) These advertisements are very naïve: "I am now presenting my story according to facts which I have gathered, even though I wasn't there myself."

"I am writing this without paying attention to style," or: "Naturally, I am writing this without paying any attention to style, but just for myself," or something of that sort. This is in the middle. The confession is extraordinarily concise (learn from Pushkin). A lot of things that remain unsaid. His own peculiar manner: for instance, he is on his way to join his father, but the facts concerning the latter are given only after he has already arrived, and his father's biography even later.

MORE CONCISELY, AS CONCISELY AS POSSIBLE. The story how he had a fight with Liza—more naïvely. "I could have omitted this trivial detail, but I am putting it down for myself."

On chambermaids, on women's derrières. Frou-Frou, derrières and trains arouse his indignation. Trains which raise a lot of dust make him particularly angry, and how he *used to get even,* either by using bad language, or by quickly crossing over to the other side.

About how, on the night before his departure, he and *the university student* were walking up and down the boulevards saying obscenities to respectable women (more concisely).[14] Here, a very slight and insignificant recollection about Lambert.

AGAIN, A SOLUTION. The fool is in a railway carriage *together with Him,* when he is on his way, but Lambert arrives later, telling him about the fool as if it had been an encounter which he, Lambert, handled in his own way<and already> in Petersburg.

---

[14] See note 28 of Part I.

?About this: "Is there a Devil?" He shoots himself and summons the Devil.[15]

About a duel he fought.

About *Kraft* who shot himself because Russia is <so> worthless (theory of the worthlessness of Russia). He used to know Kraft only superficially, and Kraft appears (before the reader and before him) only after the catastrophe, i.e., after his suicide.

A lot of interlinked and characteristic events, even though they may be episodic and do not pertain directly to the novel, create *a strong impression on him at the time of their occurrence*—for realism, vividness, and plausibility.

But then, *plot, plot!,* which should be developed awfully concisely, consistently, and unpredictably.

In the end of the novel (of the confession), the idea is that he is thunderstruck, crushed, <yet> plucks up his spirit, gets his mind set, and prepares to start a new and different life. A hymn to every blade of grass and to the Sun (the concluding lines). And he quits accumulating wealth.

And so, the type of a youth *emerges* all by itself (also, through the *awkwardness of the narrative,* and in the fact that "life is so beautiful," and in his extraordinarily serious character. A high artistic quality must help out. But just as in *The Tales of Belkin*[16] it is Belkin himself who matters the most, so here, too, it is the primary objective to delineate the <character of the> Youth.)

The character of his father, before whom he stands in awe all along, also stands out better <this way>, for the Youth's superstitiously cowed attitude toward Him makes him appear in a more fantastic and, one might say, in a Bengal illumination. Yet the idea of the novel (and the plot) *motivate the fact that* the Youth is concentrating so much on his father.

About women and about <Mme> Andrieux. A few exceedingly frivolous, yet bright, cheerful (the joy of having begun one's life), and childlike deviations on the part of the Youth, compared to the seriousness of the main events.

???Only one QUESTION—regarding His torments upon the death of

---

[15] This is possibly an anticipation of Ivan's dilemma in *The Brothers Karamazov.*

[16] A collection of five short stories by Pushkin written in 1830 and published anonymously the following year.

his wife, the flight of <his> child, etc. And, what is most important, about "the little beetle." Would a narrative from a third party be natural here? However, *the father* might tell this to the Youth himself, shortly before his suicide.

A happy day spent *together* on the eve of His suicide.

MOST IMPORTANT. There prevails, in the narrative of the Youth, in many instances a most cheerful and even joyous tone, which would then quickly change into a severe or into a suffering tone in the following chapter, in accordance with the event described.

The problem of ARTISTIC QUALITY.

Full title of the novel:

THE YOUTH. CONFESSION OF A GREAT SINNER,
WRITTEN FOR HIMSELF.

NOTE. The Youth, owing to his tender age, has no access to the events, the facts <which constitute> the plot of the novel. And so he makes his own *conjectures* and *masters* them by himself. Which circumstance is reflected in the whole manner of his narrative (to give the reader some surprises).

[For the story <I promised> Kozlov. February.]

!A CHARACTER: (a type). A *dreamer* who dreams that he is riding in a railway carriage, talking, and with all the ladies thanking him. Or, how he would act if his wife were unfaithful to him. Invariably it turns out, after terrible cruelties, that he is forgiving everybody, and that everybody is happy. A Field Marshal, Ungern-Shternberg[17] (describe in great detail).

Perhaps it is, again, He himself.

N.B. MOST IMPORTANT. This character ought to be introduced only as something that is organically connected with the novel.

[February, 4th part.] *Note:* about how it is the Youth himself who is the first to think up an idea how to ruin the Princess—the basest, the meanest <idea>, but audacious and bold, and he becomes fascinated by it. *Here you have a plot.* So that the Youth was almost the cause of a terrible misfortune.

The psychology behind this: it is precisely the monstrosity, the fearful audacity and enormity of the scheme which exerts an irresistible fascination on the Youth, something like arson on children. He is quivering ~~is quivering~~ with nervousness and can no longer abandon his project which is now irrevocable. He no longer has any willpower,

---

[17] See note 3 of this section.

the only thing in his mind is *to set the fire* as soon as possible, to get it done with. He is not deterred by the moral hurt to his dignity, nor by the prospect of committing a low-down action.

He has visions of Ungern-Shternberg.

What is particularly *strange from a psychological point of view is* the fact that when his FATHER accepts this idea, the Youth all too clearly sees his father's baseness, and turns his heart away from him on account of his baseness.

"Isn't it strange that I was condemning my father, with repulsion, for the very same low-down action I was about to commit myself?" In the meantime, *He* actually does listen, vilely, to what the Youth has to say; though, without saying a word himself, being afraid to compromise himself; he manages to change the subject with a cheap sneer and some clowning; and later, he bypasses the Youth and *behind his back* allies himself with Lambert in this matter.

As for Lambert, he immediately ~~appalls~~ repels and appalls the Youth with the insufferable coarseness and frivolity of his version of the idea.

(N.B. The new generation is involved here. Lambert and the Youth, in contrast to Him, who is infinitely better educated, has so much more understanding, and is so much more sophisticated than they are.)

Also, the psychology of *material fascination,* of a crime against a young soul—*through audacity. And in everything,* the absence and loss of a general idea during the present reign, as a consequence of the reforms. Everything apart.

["I am a cosmopolitan."] [Of reconciliation and happiness, universal man, youthfulness of the heart, Don Juan.]

His father tells him about Liza himself, *in the beginning,* immediately after her death (he comes to see the Youth), and *later,* after "the little beetle." On this occasion he amazes the Youth with his amazing frankness and his almost incredible sincerity. N.B. The Youth had thought that He was much *more severe and harder.*

Besides: The Youth realizes that he means a lot more to his father than he had wanted, that there isn't and never was any haughtiness about Him, but on the contrary, some kind of strange, easygoing familiarity and urge to communicate, yet one that is not founded on any strong feeling, or, *perhaps,* not on any feeling at all. (Predatory type.)

Absolutely pay attention to the question what He was doing before (i.e., all his life, His biography), i.e., whether he was in the government service, or was a landowner, whether he was an active man or a do-nothing.

Work it out accurately and definitively.

A biographic sketch. A landowner and son of a landowner, but not a grandson. Studied at Russian and German universities. Married very young (the facts about his first wife are lost). Served in the Army during the Crimean campaign, but not very long, and never saw action. Resigned his commission. District Commissioner <in the administration of the agrarian reform>* of the first call-up, resigned. Traveled aimlessly abroad. Married a widow, a Princess. They suddenly made an inheritance (the Princess did). The company of the <old> Prince. Stockholder and society figure. Return the inheritance. Takes the money, 200,000, and returns it. The Princess is the Prince's <. . .> The end. (N.B. He always acted in a sensible and businesslike way, in a word, he was showing certain abilities.)

SAVING <money>—MERELY A POETIC IDEA.

HE IS DRINKING CHAMPAGNE *à la* HERZEN. Remembers Herzen, used to know Belinsky.

The Youth is amazed how He, with all his charm, is so cold and spiteful (Liza, the Princess his wife, the sick boy, etc.) (he is guilty of a lie—the chambermaid, which he subsequently admits to his son *in a most ingenuous manner*). *The basic traits of a predatory type.* He admits to his stepson that he is capable of any low-down action. He used to tell the Youth about "the secrets of his married life," <and> that he wasn't admitting any aesthetic principle. And yet, in spite of all this degradation and his weaknesses, he UNQUESTIONABLY retains his authority over his son. Sometimes he is terribly reserved and unsociable. (For there is *a secret*. He is his own secret.)

Characterization of the student who is telling obscenities on the boulevard. How this student got involved with a lackey, drinking vodka <with him>. (No, he has no goal.)

Railway station, they've arrived, an idea—how much, he will find, is going on there, yet, in all probability, nobody has any real business going.

QUESTION. Absolutely to be solved. Was he fanatically religious and was he actually preaching the Gospel when the Youth arrived (as the old Prince and the aunts were claiming)? If so, the Youth is hostile, and ready to have a fight with him, when they first meet.

---

* *Mirovoi posrednik,* an office Leo Tolstoy held for a while.

The Youth arrives on the very day when the aunts (two months after they had buried the head of the family) were about to leave; they sit down, have a good cry, and decide to stay at the flat (the Andreevs).

August 15.

Best of all, make it so that he did his preaching before taking this fancy (even though his wife would be saying, while conversing with the old Prince: "This is not it," or "There's something wrong here"), and that's the stage at which the Youth meets him. And there, right in the middle of his sermonizing, and with extraordinary sincerity (or after having continued his preaching for some time), he becomes frivolous, and depraved, and spiteful, and broadminded, yet always clever and witty. The Youth is amazed, and reproaches him for his debauchery (develop this).

Perhaps the Youth gives up on him, thinking that "there's *a smart man* for you, and *an artist*" (this is before the icons). DEVELOP THIS.

When the Youth arrives in town, it is a full two weeks since the lawsuit has been definitively won. The late Andreev had handed Him a note, according to which the 200,000 thus won were not His.

It is also at the moment of the Youth's arrival that the fate of the money is decided. The old Prince is indignant, the Princess thunderstruck. But the Youth ~~learns~~ learns only later, from *strangers,* and after he has already ~~become intimate~~ become intimate with his father, that the money has been handed over.

Couldn't it have been the family of the *young Prince* that was carrying on the lawsuit about those 200,000?

THE MAIN IDEA. Though the Youth arrives with a ready idea in his mind, the whole idea of the novel is that he is searching for a guideline to direct his actions, for good and evil; he is thirsting for something that is lacking in our society, is intuitively searching for it, and this is what the novel is all about.

Apparently, he sometimes feels sorry for him and wants to lead him away from evil, and actually points out to him what is good and what is evil. (In connection with the plot against the Princess, after He has himself approved it; on the following day.) This is why he bypasses the Youth and allies himself with Lambert.

?The Youth has found a note written by the Princess, but what kind of a note? (determine that) (that's where you have the plot).

An idea. ~~Liza is an adult, 18 years old, and secretly in love with Him. *La haine dans l'amour.* It is she who gives the Youth the idea to ensnare the Princess. She is also in on the plot, along with Lambert.~~

~~She is jealous of the Princess because of Him. There is no stepmother, everything takes place in the aunts' house.~~

Theme. NN is considered to be the greatest scoundrel; all the evidence is against him. He is held in such contempt that everyone whom he loves renounces him, his wife leaves him for another man; he cannot prove his innocence, nor does he want to compromise *a certain person.* His son, the new generation, *children.* It turns out that he is innocent. *The Youth.* Only one of the children had blind faith in him. Here, intrigues on the part of Liza may play a role.

Or: Liza and Lambert. Liza incites Lambert to blackmail the Princess, joining into a conspiracy with him. Also, she tortures her mother, making her jealous of Him ~~inadvertently~~. *He* realizes all too well what is going on, and that Liza is in love with him. His character; besides, *the Youth.**

There is an accidental yet inevitable showdown between Him and Liza, *he has had her.* Liza wants to get rid of her stepmother. (The Stepmother and the Prince. The Stepmother's death. Liza hangs herself. The Youth goes his own way. Lambert and the document received from Andreev. The Youth is in love with the Princess. Fascinated by Liza. *He* is not in love with the Princess, but is terribly, with all his heart and soul, interested in her opinion. Vanity, amorousness, and hurt pride *to the point of madness.* Moreover, <he feels> insulted. Playing the insulted lover. Everything turns out to have been nothing, when his wife betrays him. It turns out that who was really dear to him was his wife. It is she who is also "the little beetle."

There's your plot. It contains *the net* in which *the Youth* is immediately caught. The characters are the same.

The tone of the whole. All the time, he is preoccupied with his higher idea (disintegration), his *loss of a goal,* and his own *chemical* decomposition. And therefore, *as long as the affair was still in progress,* he treated everything *with condescension.* ~~But when~~ His debauchery wouldn't let him take the affair into his own hands, as he should have. In the end, when he has done in his wife, and all has come to an end, "the little beetle" comes into its own and defeats everything.

He *has feelings.* "I should have rebuffed Liza *from the outset,* I should quit torturing my wife, turn honest, work hard, do my duty."

But the main question is: *to whom?* United to nature, to the predatory type, to a call to *disorder and adventure.*

---

* Unclear phrase.

N.B. The whole question is: is this a true character and has it taken a firm shape in the author's mind? All of his former qualities: mystery, seriousness, frivolity, no effort whatsoever to improve himself, motivated by a rejection of principles, and a charming simple-heartedness which delights Liza, and his wife, and the Youth, and the Princess.

There are some attempts: he returned those 200,000, etc. But all this means nothing, and even makes him angry, since it suggests that he still believes in something after all. His preaching of religion *is there,* even fanatically so, once he warms up to it, yet casually, jerkily: "Don't interfere, I have business to do." Whenever he gets willy-nilly carried away by his own preaching he gets angry with himself, which fact is noticed by the Youth (who lets the reader know about it).

"A MEMBER OF THE OLD GENERATION. I AM ONE OF THE MEN OF THE OLD GENERATION, and as for the new, I do not see any; and what I do see is nothing serious," *He* says, treating everything with supercilious condescension.

He also sees the new in the men of the new generation, i.e., their *lack of principle,* their rejection of duty, or simply their ignorance of duty without an actual rejection of it, and as a result of this, no fear of crime, egoism.

The belief in one idea only, a thirst for material pleasures, <and> on the other hand, abstract ~~materialism~~ idealism (the Dolgushins).

[February, 3d part.] "These are the fruits of the bankruptcy of the old generation," He says. "We have transmitted nothing to the new generation that might have served their edification or guidance, not a single firm or important idea. And yet, all our lives *we have suffered* from our thirst for great ideas."

~~Well~~ "Well, what could *I* have transmitted?" *He* says, "I am myself a beggar. All my life I have been believing that I am a rich man and that 'I shall not want'; and there, in my approaching old age, I must beg my bread, there is nothing in me, nor was there ever."

When he had had Liza: "I had her whom I hate most," He said.

When he had had Liza, they parted as enemies, not telling each other, though (traces left by the crime).

They embraced, and they parted, and suddenly she ran up to him, in a fit of rage: "Look out, *I shall kill* you."

[February, 3d part.] *He says:* "In reality, we were the nihilists, we, the eternal seekers for a higher idea."

"Whereas now, we have either ~~uneducated dullards~~ *indifferent* dullards, or monks; the former *mean business* and often shoot themselves, the latter are communists, such as Dolgushin, and their followers."

"There is a third category—[thoroughgoing] *scoundrels,* but this ~~always~~ category is the same always and everywhere."

He is always much, much too frank with his son, the Youth. It is not only the immeasurable *charm* of his simple-heartedness which wouldn't let one despise Him *too much** for his frivolity. It is just that, in the course of the novel, the Youth will begin to lose his respect for Him, on account of that simple-heartedness, and it is then that something unexpected, mysterious, new will immediately appear about Him, something the Youth had never even suspected about him. *Toward the end* the Youth is quite firmly convinced that he knows Him only from a single, almost a superficial and minor side, and that there exists a great multitude of unknown and secret facts about Him, facts which *He* (so the Youth suspects) is never going to reveal to him. So that, toward the end, the Youth is taking great pains to penetrate and to get to know this character, and does so because he is fascinated by Him and because he loves Him.

[February, 3d part.] What also *amazes* the Youth, in the course of the novel, is the fact that all His sincerity and all his simple-heartedness somehow do not seem to come from the heart, that they are not based upon a strong feeling of friendship or a ~~need~~ warm need to confide in somebody. On the contrary, they do appear heartless (the predatory type). Except for religion! (and this terribly stuns the Youth). He sometimes discusses religion with inspiration, even though later he won't forgive it to himself. (The Youth makes all these observations in his confession *to the reader,* and equally notes the preceding point—about the impenetrable mystery of his character.)

The Youth is asking himself a thousand times: "What is it that entertains Him, that interests Him? Could it really be ruling the roost with <a bunch of> women, or idle chatter à la Herzen to a bottle of champagne, etc.?" He is asking himself this question, and there, suddenly, He gives away 200,000, etc., and once again the Youth does not know where he stands.

In the very end, the Youth is quite confused by the fact that He, though suffering very much and ready to shoot himself, has no particular regrets about anything, not his wife, nor the Princess, nor

* Underlined three times.

Liza, though perhaps some about the boy. And yet his sufferings are intense and he dies in severe torments. But he very nearly went mad from the pain he suffered on account of "the little beetle" (i.e., the boy). Yet he won't recognize even this pain as HIS VERY OWN essence, or as that OF HIS VERY OWN suffering. (Irregularity, not knowing what to believe in, "What is the sense of all this?")

At this point, Kraft shoots himself. They receive his suicide *note*. He becomes very much interested in the motive of Kraft's suicide. "Kraft was devoured by an idea in which he happened to believe, whereas+I suffer the same fate having lost every single idea which I could have believed in," He says.

And thus, the Youth and the young generation are *victorious*.* The concluding idea is formulated by the Youth in the end of the novel, thusly: "Only he can be saved who already in his youth manages to work out for himself that strong moral sensation (feeling) which is called a conviction. The formula of a conviction can change in the course of one's life, but the moral sensation of this feeling ought to remain unchanged all one's life. He who possesses it will survive." (He may have said this to the Youth before His suicide.)

Here is what he says about his suffering on account of the boy: "Could it be that I have found the essence of the emotion, that immediate sensation of pain, which I have been pursuing all my life?"

Simply: an amoral man, a man who has failed to develop a moral principle. A purely Russian, universal type.

If this is a purely Russian and a universal type, why doesn't everyone suffer and kill himself?

Answer: because the spirit of analysis and conscientiousness is not developed in every person, as it is in Him.

"Because the fools [the brutes] are many, and the wise [men] few," He says. "The wise men [brutes] depart, and the fools [men] are left."

"I might have left my life untouched**, to the very end, I would have found myself some duty to follow, ~~deception~~ I would have found a way to deceive myself, all but for this boy ("the little beetle")."

"Why is it that *I* feel sorry for nothing, except this one boy? Why is it that my entire self-judgment is formulated in connection with this one boy?"

---

* Underlined twice.

** *Ia b i ostavil zhizn'* is ambiguous, since *ostavit'* means both "to leave," "to depart," as well as "to retain." Specifically, *ostavit' zhizn'* can also mean "to die (voluntarily)."

"~~Why~~ What made *me* marry my wife? Because I feel terribly sorry for her. Yet it is I who am torturing her. And besides, I have made her my nurse. Really, isn't she my nurse now?"

?Important question. Should it be that the Stepmother falls in love with the Prince? Shouldn't one get rid of the Prince altogether?

???! Shouldn't one confine oneself to letting the Stepmother learn about Liza's liaison with Him, which causes her *to break down.*

And shouldn't one let Liza fall in love with the Prince and advertise her liaison with him? "I am a predatory type," says Liza, "when I go, I go all the way." And so she gets even with the family in a big way, and makes fun of Him spectacularly and *in public.* So He gets mad and calls out the Prince on account of Liza.

~~Liza~~ dies in the arms of <her> Stepmother, but strangely.

??? Liza Couldn't it be that Liza already has a liaison going with Him when the Youth appears on the scene? However, He reveals it to the Youth ~~only~~ in the middle of the novel. But when he makes this revelation, he does not know as yet whether Liza loves Him, or whether she continues to hate him (for she keeps smearing Him before <her> mother just as before, carries on her intrigues against him, and makes fun of him).

But *He* is captivated by Liza and tells the Youth that he is beginning to fall in love with her precisely because she continues to hate him, even though she has slept with him.

He has been begging Liza for more and more love trysts. Those trysts are characteristic; every time <they make love> with hatred.

Finally, witnessing her attempt to poison her mother, He is terribly shaken.

Absolutely this way. Liza won't sleep with him at any of these trysts, but rather teases him, driving him to a frenzy.[18]

He is amazed at her intellectual depravity *in spite of her innocence.*

"What a predatory type you are," she says.

"Let's poison <her> and run away."

"Where to?" She is willing to follow him anywhere.

"Doesn't matter."

"I'll fall out of love with you."

---

18 This theme is to be found in *The Gambler,* which is based in part on Paulina Suslova's sexual teasing of Dostoevsky. Paulina Suslova left a record of her relations with Dostoevsky in a diary which was published in 1928 under the title *Moi gody blizosti s Dostoevskim,* ed. A. S. Dolinin.

"I don't care, just leave me in the gutter."*

And suddenly, at the very moment when <her> mother has learned the whole truth, Liza surrenders herself *to the Prince.* Fanatically, so it seems, yet she does not love the Prince (to be sure, she did get carried away, and so she made up a story about *"her Prince";* the Prince, to be sure, takes advantage of her, but in a most casual way). She surrenders herself to the Prince to make Him insanely jealous. (Not so: as far as Liza is concerned, it is simply a game. "Though <he> isn't worth a penny, I'll still get <him>." She wants to torment <Him.>)

Most important. Liza sees through His character: i.e., disintegration and no integrity, yet she is in love (His simple-heartedness has enthralled her). *Instinctively and unaccountably* she wants to make Him jealous. As for the Princess, she wants to ruin her entirely because she is jealous of Him. Then, when everything fails, she hangs herself in a latrine.

(The moment when *They* were alone the mother wasn't there. "The little beetle.")

The mother couldn't stand it, broke down, went out of her mind, and died.

Then the boy (that's the way!)

Liza with Lambert, lying in wait, and with the Princess. The Youth is captivated by Liza. Yet he saves the Princess.

Most important. N.B. The youth tells the story in the first person: I, I.

So then, the Youth does meet Him right in the middle of a stormy affair with Liza, but without passion on His part. On the contrary, everything is but fiction and fancy.

He calls out the Prince to a duel on account of Liza.

The problem is solved! August 20, just after midnight.

N.B. It is Liza who found out about the chambermaid.

August 26.

[3d part. February.] [Another novel.]

He sees in Liza another *case of disorder,* i.e., a person who has lost her goal who, in spite of the presence in her of the most powerful passions, is apparently rushing about aimlessly in a general chaos.

"She does not love me," He says, "she is doing it just so, though it may not be worth a penny, just to have it her own way... A game

---

* Literally, "at the crossroads."

born of desperation (if one were to translate it into conscious terms, it would be a game born of desperation, even though there is no such consciousness in her)."

An adventure of the Youth's, theft of a bracelet. The boy is loyal. The Youth is in possession of an important secret. The temptation.

He chops up those icons when, after the first time (of possessing her), Liza drives him to a frenzy by her refusal and mockery. He is madly in love with her. He walks along with the Youth: "All this is nonsense, all this morality, shopkeepers and games of chess." He fights a duel with the Prince. And when it is all over, he realizes that HE NEVER LOVED LIZA at all and that *there really was nothing!* At this point, self-judgment and suffering.

An idea. The Youth, then, projects all of His frenzy upon himself, and comes up with Lambert. (Which means that he is not in love with the Princess, though Liza is jealous of her.) He is NOT in love, but he still joins Lambert.

N.B. The role of the Youth? N.B.

An idea. The role of the Youth.

Liza has enthralled the Youth, making him fall madly in love with her. He is aware of it, and is jealous (but he does not believe Liza altogether). In the meantime, Liza is complaining to the Youth that He is trying to seduce her (this, after she has already slept with Him). The Youth begins to hate Him. But not for long, for he can't hate him, because he adores Him so much. Finally, each confides his secrets to the other.

The Youth ardently thirsts for the good and does not know what to think of his father, whereas Liza is a demon. (She slanders (?) him to those who have been arrested, telling them that it was he who betrayed them.)

Liza is only teasing Him with the Youth. She assures the Youth that He is in love with the Princess. He swears that this isn't so, and thinks up a plan how to bring ~~her~~ the Princess to her knees. Liza encourages him, with much enthusiasm, to proceed with this plan.

The idea of the novel. The predatory type is a female, Liza, and not *He*. Liza appears simple, very frank, as if bornée, somewhat crazy. And suddenly she displays, in her mocking remarks, a terrible depth of thought and of development. She convinces Him that he has corrupted her with his own *disorder*. She adores <her> mother quite sincerely. She ~~writes~~ proves to Him that he is not worth being loved. She has a great weakness for the Youth.

Liza and the Youth are traveling from Moscow to Petersburg by railway together. She is telling him about Him (she knew him even before and fell in love with Him before her mother's wedding). The Youth tells her about his plan of getting rich.

Liza had been visiting in Moscow and accidentally meets the Youth.

He is afraid of Lambert's plot against the Princess; however, the idea to bring the Princess to her knees does tempt His craven spirit also. He does *not,* however, *know* that Liza is the principal leader of the plot. Since it is the Youth who first thought of this plan against the Princess, He believes that the Youth and Lambert are acting all by themselves. Later on, as we already know, He gets so carried away by this idea that he seeks out Lambert, while bypassing the Youth. Had He known that Liza was involved in the scheme, He would not have participated in it, but would have rather counteracted it and, very definitely, he would have gotten cold feet. But Liza has learned (from the Youth and from Lambert) that *indirectly* He, too, has joined the plot, and she is laughing in her sleeve *spitefully:* for she realizes that He has joined the plot driven by jealous and haughty vengefulness against the Princess, which would mean that *he is still interested** in the Princess, that he is trying to take his vengeance on her, and that he consequently <still> loves the Princess. (N.B. Even before, and what is worse, in the presence of the Youth and her mother, Liza had been teasing him by telling Him to his face that the Princess had shown Him the door, on which occasion the Stepmother had taken His side, and heatedly so; and, as a result, Liza and <her> mother were at odds for some time.) Neither He nor the Youth are aware of the full extent of Lambert's (and really, Liza's) villainous schemes against the Princess.

[February, 3d part.] Otherwise, ~~even He~~ the Youth would have desisted, while He would have gotten cold feet. Yet the psychology lies in the fact that even the Youth, and certainly He, both have a foreboding of Lambert's terrible role and that, in spite of this, both rather relish the idea, whereas if it were a matter not of foreboding but of direct knowledge, they surely would have protested against it. (N.B. This is a valuable psychological observation and a *new bit of information* concerning human nature.) This also explains why He and Liza, who in a certain sense are enemies, get together and participate in the same scheme, whereas if He had known that Liza is taking part in

* Underlined twice.

it, nothing in the world could have made Him join forces with her. Liza is laughing to herself and is annoyed by the thought that, to come right down to it, she is once again making a fool out of Him, while He is caught in a mess not even of his own making,* being unable to withstand his petty idea of haughty vengeance. Yet, and I repeat, He, too, causes Liza great suffering in that, though she is gloating on account of having made a fool out of Him, the whole thing is yet another proof of the fact that He is [interested] in the Princess, that he has been interested in her, and that he will remain interested in her. (N.B. In the novel, express all of these considerations *in words,* so the reader will be more clearly aware of them.)

The predatory type, passion and breadth of character, the vilest crudity, along with the most refined generosity. He comes to see the Youth, sometimes being delighted with Liza, then sad again, skeptical and spiteful, then again desperate. One notices a streak of petty boasting of <His> successes with Liza (and with women in general), this in front of the Youth. He awakens in him an enthusiasm for a great idea and a thirst for education. The Youth witnesses how he helps a certain poor family. Right along with passionate faith, derisive skepticism (this is before he breaks those icons). He tells the Youth outright: "If I had no faith, how could I go on living?" And he goes on to explain all that has been said before about those two shopkeepers.

N.B. The main questions. The difficulty of the beginning of a novel. The Youth's actions at the flea-market, in the family, at Dolgushin's, at Vitia's, etc. Write it in the first person, or in the third person.** The role of the aunts.

It is a quality of the aunts (the Andreevs) that they actually brought ~~him~~ up the Youth since he was a small child, and he finds out, to his surprise when he arrives in Petersburg that He had never contributed anything toward his upbringing, but that Andreev had been paying for it all along. On account of this latter circumstance, the Youth does not want to see Him; but the aunts shout: "Come on now, come on, he will give you a job." From this, the Youth draws the conclusion that he was sent for to take care of the aunts, which is quite a surprise, and starts counting his money.

The fact that they simply sent for him by sending him the money

---

* *Popalsia kak kur vo shchi,* literally, "got caught like a cock in some cabbage soup," the point being that cocks are not used in cabbage soup.

** Literally, "from the author."

to Moscow, the aunts say, is to be explained by his being only 19 years old: no sense in being fussy about that, nothing worth mentioning even. They scold him for having traveled second class, rather than third. (Explain that through Liza?)

The Youth (in either case, whether he is the first-person narrator, or tells this to Liza) expresses this idea: take that Petersburg man traveling from the capital to that village of Moscow, and yet he'll be immediately taken aback by something there; and by the same token, a man who travels from Moscow to Petersburg will immediately run into some people who are a lot more clever than he is.

In the railway carriage, Liza and the fool. He tells Liza about Lambert. She is more reticent, yet she tells him about <his> father, etc.

In case the Youth is not the first-person narrator (I), do it in such a manner that the narrative would cling to the Youth, as its hero, and never let go of him through the entire beginning of the novel, so that, for instance, the Princess, and He, and the situation of the aunts, and the Dolgushins, and everything, is all described only *insofar as it gradually involves the Youth* (it goes without saying that this pertains to the initial stages only) . *This might produce excellent results.*

Important question: does he or doesn't he tell Liza, in the railway carriage, about his plan to get rich? (He definitely does, but under a seal of deep secrecy.)

?N.B. Without knowing it himself, the Youth acts as Liza's spy at the Princess's.

In the railway carriage, the Youth only gradually becomes acquainted with Liza, giving her his name, and she hers to him. However, having learned his name, though she is surprised (for she has heard a little about His son, in passing), she first subjects him to a thorough examination and finds out everything that the Youth could possibly know, and only then, at Malaia Vishera, tells him that they are from the same family, which comes as a terrible surprise to the Youth, though he is delighted; but for all his delight, he does, however, realize that this young lady is nobody's fool and has a strong character. At the same time, he is very indignant with himself for having told her about his idea. Whereas she starts making fun of his idea, after <the train has stopped at> Liuban', and laughs at him very loud and in a shameless fashion. He is furious. When they are approaching Petersburg she suddenly makes up with him, swearing solemnly that she will never tell anybody about his idea. The Youth melts once again. In this way, Liza has succeeded in *subjecting him to a thorough interrogation* and has *felt him out* very substantially.

And yet the Youth, even though he did melt, is still full of bitter misgivings regarding Liza's perfidy, as well as, more than anything else, <regrets> his own blundering. But Liza fully sets his mind at rest even on that score, saying: "I was spying you out on purpose, yes, I did stoop to that. But it was only because I am so unhappy and so defenseless. I need a protector, a helper, and I have been looking for one for a long time. You are pure, truthful, and clever. Oh, very soon I'll be coming to you begging you to protect me. I'll tell you later about my grief, and about my needs, we haven't time now; and even if we had time, I wouldn't tell you now, on the contrary, I want you to survey everything with your own eyes, impartially, for if *I* were to tell you, you would, generous as you are, see it willy-nilly through my eyes, which would be too bad, because, who knows, I may be wrong myself. But you, a new man, will be a judge of my position, you will decide my fate and tell me everything."

Having arrived in Petersburg, she continues to ~~remain silent~~ remain silent, nor does she visit him. A week goes by, another week; on the contrary, she even starts making fun of him <again>. This leaves the Youth confused, and hurt in his pride; but his pride won't allow him to mention anything to her.

For the first few days he is still in love with Liza, but later he thinks of her with contempt, treating her as if she were a vaudeville "soubrette." It is only later that Liza, suddenly, again casts her spell over him, leaving him confused, telling him about the young Prince, telling him that she is in love with him, that she is jealous of the Princess, setting the Youth against the Princess, etc.

In general, treat Liza *lightly* throughout the narrative (in accordance with the Youth's attitude toward her) ~~and only later~~, though she ought to be presented to the reader as an invariably mysterious character. And only later, in the course of the novel (and again in accordance with the Youth's attitude), portray Liza as a giantess, a Satan<ic woman>, who crushes the Youth. And then, her tragic death and her affair with the young Prince will crush the reader also. It was a genuine infatuation that made her run away to the Prince's, and this is the tragedy about it. Liza's end must be solemn and terrible, like the ringing of a bell.

A thirst for truth and simplicity in Him discovered what was false, immediately asked for an ideal, and accused Him, i.e., the first comer. She did not want to wait.

In the railway carriage, she took her seat in the following way: on one bench, Liza and the seminarian, and across from them, the fool and the Youth. Liza was frequently interrupting the Youth at the most pathetic junctures (for instance, right after he had revealed his idea to her), and immediately says, without giving him an answer: "Let's not listen to them (i.e., to the fool)."

The Youth is stunned by such heartlessness every time: he develops the notion that this is always the rule in high society. Having finished listening to him, Liza immediately addresses the Youth and starts discussing his idea with so much apparent interest that all his doubts are immediately dispelled.

And yet he says to himself: "A high society serpent." At this point, explain his attitude toward women, disdain, frou-frou, trains, and chastity.

On the occasion of ~~one~~ one of Liza's *slights* he reasons thus: "I'll never marry, down with women, let me be alone with my idea," etc. (N.B. However, toward the end, develop this idea from a comic and childish thing into something that would strike the reader as both powerful and poetic. Everything gradually.)

?N.B. The seminarian on that trip: no sooner has he walked away from the fool having been accused of the theft of 10 roubles when he stumbles across that incident with the lady. N.B. N.B. Shouldn't these personages later reappear in the novel?

[February, third part] N.B. The theft of some diamonds. He was, if not accused outright, so certainly under a strong suspicion at the Prince's house. The Prince hurriedly hushed up the affair; the Princess blushed. Later, they found the diamonds under the ~~Prince~~ old Prince.* There wasn't much of an apology extended to the Youth, which offends him greatly (for he is already in love with the Princess); and so the Youth, having been so unfairly accused, retreats into his shell and forms terrible plans about becoming a gloomy money-grubber. But when he finds it impossible to save, he wants to become a thief. He prays. On the next day, he saves a pair of earrings after they have been recovered. He is surprised at how quickly this whole mood of his has passed.

Set fire to everything. A night in the streets, the dark image of Our Lady of the Miracle.

Though Liza is telling him (later, when she is frank with him) that she is in love with the Prince, she still makes him (i.e., the Youth)

* *Sic.*

fall in love with her by pretending that she is attracted by him also. This is still before He admits his relationship with Liza to the Youth. The Youth even admits to Him (upon His questioning) that he loves Liza, and He frowns. The Youth is trying to talk Liza into loving Him, and into being more just and more affectionate toward Him.

It affects him so much *more strongly* when he learns from Him that Liza loves Him.

The Youth is very much impressed by and sympathetically attracted to the Stepmother (especially when she stands up for the child). And altogether, the Stepmother's beauty presents itself primarily through the Youth's impressions of her.

The action in Petersburg starts with a quarrel between the Youth and the aunts [on the very first day.] during the first few days of his stay there; he announces to them that he has been sent for to take care of them, they cut him down, and He reconciles them. He very nearly asks the Youth, during the latter's quarrel with the aunts, to move in with him. The Youth does move, and is stunned at His house by the Stepmother, and the relationship with Liza, and the chambermaid, and the sick boy, and the argument about Christianity.

After <the incident with> the boy, he winds up quarreling with Him, and leaving Him. It is during the same days that he enters the employ of the old Prince, and frequents the flea-market, and meets Vitia, and runs into Kraft. He feels that he needs to have his own flat, a place of his own. A discussion of this topic. He tells this to the communists.

The old Prince actually does have three grown-up daughters and a ward.

Explain the fool and the widow Mrs. Perchatkin (develop).

~~You~~ Returning home one night on one of his first days, the Youth ~~walks~~ has some melancholy thoughts: Petersburg, its influence, poverty, looking for a flat, the flea-market, the Dolgushins, thirst of Christ (that same night, an argument about Christianity). And in general, more poetry in his impressions.

That very same night, the boy with his mouth ripped open.

And altogether, there will be plenty to keep the Youth busy before <the arrival of> Lambert. More poetically.

Evil passions, depravity, cynicism, His example (when he learns about Liza) have their effect upon the Youth, and, from pride and spite (as well as from a taste for destruction*), and also due to the fact

* Literally, "conflagration."

that his nerves are in disorder. As a result of this general confusion, he comes up with the plot against the Princess.

N.B. And altogether, express the whole warmth and humanity of the novel in the person of the Youth, all those affectionate spots (Ivan Petrovich Belkin); make the reader love him. Then the Stepmother, He.

It ends with the Youth asking: "Where is justice in life?" (which is what he is looking for throughout the entire novel). And on the last page, after he has buried Him, paid a visit to Dolgushin, etc., this melancholy and solemn thought: "I am embarking upon my life." A hymn to being a just man. "I know, I have found out what is good and what is evil," he says.

Work out this last page. Make it more meaningful and more poetic.

N.B. Do NOT FORGET. About how the young Prince "insults" the Youth, how he decides to take vengeance on him, how he goes to see him, how the young Prince receives him most elegantly, reconciling and delighting him. Passionate love for the young Prince. But soon, a disappointment: all these predatory high society types, dead-wood. And it turns out that He alone remains as having a warm and soothing heart for the Youth (but still, there remains a problem up to the point where (He) begins to suffer; here, the Youth is all melting with compassion for Him.)

And altogether, a thirst for <more> heart, compassion, for a great idea (He gives it to him, but there is always some doubt). So that on one occasion, ~~torturing~~ being tormented by the aridity of life, he is tempted by one of the squeamish aunts, but what he gets out of it is nothing but compassion for her, and this conviction: if you really go to the root of a person's life, or soul, you will find depth even in a person whom you detest (the aunt).

Having quarreled with Him ~~he rented~~ (in the beginning, when he is renting a flat and does not know Him yet), he talks the sick child into joining him. But the child begs to be sent home; here He looks him up and acts in a conciliatory way.

And altogether, the whole novel through the person of the Youth who is seeking the truth of life (Gil Blas and Don Quijote), could be most attractive.[19]

---

[19] Alain René Lesage (1668–1747) is the author of *Gil Blas de Santilane* (1714–35). Dostoevsky probably refers to this novel because he sees a relationship between the way the hero of Lesage's novel hunts for truth through various strata of society and the way the youth searches for truth in an unbelieving world. In intention at least Dostoevsky wanted to make the Youth a good-hearted idealist (like Cervantes' hero).

Don't forget the last lines of the novel: "Now I know; I have found what I was looking for, what is good and what is evil; I shall never stray again."

Finale. And altogether, this is an epic poem about how *the Youth* made his debut in the world. This is the story of his searchings, hopes, disappointments, corruption, rebirth, education—the story of a most attractive, of a very nice person. And it is life itself that teaches him, yet it is he, the Youth, who learns his lesson, for some other person might not have learned it.

À propos N.B. Do not forget about how He gradually develops a respect for the Youth, marveling at his heart, his sweet sympathy, and the depth of his ideas, in spite of so little of an education. On one occasion he actually expresses all this to the Youth. And altogether, arrange things so that the reader would understand that He is, throughout the novel, observing the Youth with the greatest attention, which fact presents Him in a most attractive light, and as having great depth of soul, as well.

Do NOT FORGET. At Dolgushin's, too, he was very nearly taken for a spy, but it turned out that it was somebody else. And yet the Youth felt offended by such a suspicion, and with his soul receiving hurts from every side, he did not know where to turn. (Torments.)

N.B. Once he went to see Nadezhda Prokofievna,[20] having remembered her for her sympathetic glance. He spent the evening sitting with her. She was keeping busy, left <the room>: "Never, never shall I renounce this bright idea." So much power, and all so one-sidedly concentrated! Yet the Youth leaves deeply touched.

By no means forget THE MOST IMPORTANT. Do not forget the Youth's friendship with the poor boy: he has not forgotten him even after he had lured him away from Him. He is taking an interest in him throughout the novel. Secret meetings with the boy, but without any big words (7 or 8 years old, create the character of the boy). Liza, on the contrary, has no sympathy whatsoever for her brother, is actually hostile to him. But when the Youth is arrested in connection with the Dolgushin affair, the boy runs away. ~~TONE~~ The Youth is terribly stunned.

And again, in the course of the novel (and more and more often

[20] The sister of Apollinaria Suslova. Dostoevsky knew and liked the sister very much. On April 19, 1865, he wrote to her: "I value you very highly; you are one of the rare beings that I have met in life, and I do not want to lose your affection. I value very highly your view of me and your memory of me."

toward the end), leave the Youth and devote *single chapters* to other characters, conducting the narrative in the author's name. It is in this way that the episode of the boy's suicide and the birdie will be unveiled. In these single chapters presented by the author (i.e., leaving the Youth <out of sight>), the author will always inform the reader beforehand, for instance, in this fashion: "But in order to explain the meaning of this, and to show what had happened ~~with~~ (i.e., in the preceding chapter, to the Youth), let us find out what happened to so-and-so or there-and-there, or let us step into a small, country type cottage on the Petersburg side," etc., etc.

!N.B! SHOULDN'T THE TITLE BE (THE BEGINNING OF A CAREER), a novel, etc.

Another title: DISORDER (August 26).

Another title: A DETAILED STORY.

Or: ONE DETAILED STORY.

In the railway carriage, when the Youth has been developing his theory of accumulation of wealth and Liza cuts him short in order to listen to the fool, the Youth frowns and gives a lot of thought to frou-frou and to the wickedness of women in general. But when Liza suddenly turns back to him and continues the discussion about the accumulation of wealth at the very point he had left off, and does so with the greatest sympathy, the adverse impression received by the Youth is dissipated in a jiffy, and he suddenly begins to tell her about his own coarseness, ignorance, and impatience: "Why, really, how petty of me; of course, it is all on account of my crudeness, but also because I do not know life; so different people have different habits, and so what? really, cutting short a conversation and turning to someone else, why, this is only a habit, isn't it?" etc. And in the same breath he admits that he hates women, as well as frou-frou, and so on.

Absolutely. He first loses his innocence in a vile house, and with a very vile woman. Impressions. That creature. His pity, etc. Here is another occasion to show his compassionate and kindly character.

When He starts chopping up those icons, the sick boy is at first stunned by fear, but then suddenly he falls headlong on the sofa and starts sobbing *inaudibly.*

He says, on the eve of his suicide: "But whoso shall offend one of these little ones, shall not be forgiven, neither in this world, neither in the world to come."*

---

* Seems to be a contamination of Matt. 18: 6 and Matt. 12: 32. It does, however, render the meaning of Matt. 18: 6 correctly.

King Louis XVII, a shoemaker,[21] they decide at Dolgushin's that they are right, reading Victor Hugo.[22] But someone by the name of N who has remained silent until then (a young man of 24, and a rabid socialist) (later, at the trial, it turns out that he has been the ringleader and the guiltiest of all) gets up and suggests that he moral question rests with the fact that it won't matter if even all of France were to perish, and that millions of people won't matter either, etc. Dolgushin and the rest won't agree with him. This young man impresses the Youth as the most beautiful <soul of them all> and when he is in a sad mood, and looking for sympathy, he pays him a visit. (Description of the visit.) Later, he drops in on him again, but N finds his presence trying and tells the Youth frankly, kindly, yet firmly: "You have grown fond of me, you are looking for sympathy, but I have no time and, inasmuch as you are not one of us, let us part," etc.

N.B. (All the personages, images, portraits.)

Kraft is one of them, but he refuses to "join the people"* with them; he drily and abruptly states a part of his theory, and later shoots himself.

Liza owes nobody a thing, everybody owes her. (I refuse to live other than in uninterrupted happiness.) A predatory type.

Vasin (an ideal nihilist) is a paragon of reason and logic (as well as heart) amidst stubborn folly. The Youth arranges for a meeting between him and his father.

Vasin says: "Although the revolution will serve no useful purpose in this country, it is still *necessary,* in view of the fact that there is nothing else to do, to engage in revolutionary activity. There is no immediate advantage, except perhaps the fact that the *idea* is thus being kept alive, examples are being established, and [a continuity of] experience sustained for the benefit of future revolutionaries. This is in itself enough reason not to abandon the idea. Nothing will happen at once; unfortunately, I am apparently the only one of our group who recognizes this notion, for everybody else seems to believe that, once a society has been formed, it ought to achieve all of its objectives immediately; and they actually believe this to be true, so

---

* *Idti v narod,* the term applied to the activities of the Russian populists among the Russian people.

21 The second son of Louis XVI. He was arrested with his father, but afterwards was released, separated from his mother, and sent to be apprenticed to a shoemaker. He was later reimprisoned and died in 1795.

22 Reference to Victor Hugo's novel *Quatre-Vingt-Treize* (1874).

much so that if they did not have their faith, they wouldn't have ever started this thing, even though there are some fine people among them. I haven't got faith, but I am still <with those who are> starting it. I believe in the future. And anyway, what else is there to do, except the revolution; really, what else is there?"

The Youth: "It seems to me that one can simply be a citizen, meaning well. For example, teach, work with the health department, engage in scientific work, etc.—all of which serves the common good, little bit by little bit, just as in an ant heap, and eventually there will be a whole large heap."

Vasin: "This is absolutely impossible, I am sorry to say. You see, imagine that we have an extraordinarily large machine, made of steel, cast iron, lumber, etc. Now imagine that all the parts of this machine, instead of being connected by strong joints, screws, etc., as should be the case considering how heavy and complex it is, are kept together by some sort of paste or string, that is, for no more than a second or so: a gust of wind, and everything will fall apart. As for myself, I would be very glad to accept any kind of a job with that machine, working on any one of its particular parts, but if I am absolutely sure that the whole thing will fall apart in no time, tell me, will I really care to take the job, and where will I find the enthusiasm for it? Except, perhaps, if I work for the money. But that would be like that District Commissioner* about whom I read in the papers and who was saying openly and ~~himself~~ to show off before the people of his district, and quite loudly too: 'I am holding on to the job because I need the salary, however, I am not going to do anything at all while I am on the job.' I approve of this Commissioner from every possible point of view. Low-down, but right. No, I'd rather work to help the machine fall apart faster. Well, and then we'll start our own, and that will be a strong one." (N.B. However, Vasin does not talk much.)

He does not counter Vasin's arguments.

"I did not respond to Vasin," writes the Youth, "but I liked the way he was talking to me, not in the least arrogantly, he, such a learned man, talking to such a young and insignificant person as myself, and what more, not knowing either me or my ideas at all, and being convinced of only one thing—that I wouldn't inform on him."

N.B. Among the members of the young generation, do not forget that young man, a wealthy landowner, who apprenticed himself as a

---

* See n. (*), p. 84, above.

laborer at a German-owned factory, an engineering plant. (Persistence.) *Grazhdanin* <"The Citizen">, August 19, A——r (Poretsky's) letters. He is present at one of the meetings at Dolgushin's house. In part <he resembles> Speshnev.[23]

"Gentlemen, I suggest that you turn your attention to technology and do something in the technical field."

"Serve the machine?"

"No, gentlemen, but if only the technical field got a good start all over Russia, there already would be an upheaval (a revolution), and one that would be immeasurably stronger and more successful than all of your appeals to the people."

In the railway carriage, the Youth initially says that his father is private secretary to a minister, "allow me not to identify who in particular" (the Princess is the wife of a minister).

The tone of a little fop (Pasha).[24] Childhood and adolescence. The poet of petty self-love.[25] Liza brushes literature aside. But Liza's charm causes the Youth to change his tone quickly, and he changes into the simple-hearted, high-minded, and funny child that he is.

Later, when they learn each other's names (after Liza has found out from him everything she wanted), the Youth is awfully embarrassed about having told these lies and having promoted the old Prince to the rank of a minister.

Liza, on the other hand, enhances his sufferings by insisting, *most naïvely* (i.e., purposely), *specifically,* and *lengthily,* that the old Prince is very far from being a minister, and, as if this weren't enough, that he is in a bad mess right now, and practically under the guardianship (of his family, with whom the Princess is carrying on litigation). And altogether, she establishes the actual insignificance of the <old> Prince, which is also quite useful for the reader to know.

The Youth, in the meantime, is trying to wiggle loose, is very much

---

[23] Nikolai Aleksandrovich Speshnev (1821–82), a revolutionary, atheist, and member of the Petrashevsky Circle, in which Dostoevsky participated in the late 1840's. He was condemned to ten years of prison.

[24] Dostoevsky's stepson, Pavel Aleksandrovich Isaev. Dostoevsky writes to him a number of times in his letters, usually lecturing him about leading a more disciplined life. Pasha was something of a dandy and amounted to very little.

[25] These early works by Tolstoy (*Childhood* and *Boyhood*) are narrated from the "I" point of view, as are Rousseau's *Les Confessions* and Lesage's *Gil Blas.* All four had some influence on Dostoevsky's considerations and his adoption of the first-person narration.

ashamed, and finally just barely manages to induce Liza to let go of the minister; he is glad that Liza, at least, has not noticed that he told his lie to show off before her and in this particular instance in an extremely petty and ridiculous way.

But when they reach Liuban' and quarrel, Liza tells him to his face that he told her a lie, just to show off. "Secretary to a minister! No, sir, it is you who is 'a poet of petty self-love,' and not Count Tolstoi" (yet, the bird-cherry tree).

N.B. Important. Judging from part one, it is quite impossible to recognize in Liza *the person* she becomes toward the end. But it is absolutely necessary to convey the notion of the predatory, animal <strain in her>, and a foreboding of *something* very deep.

When the Youth has told Liza (in the railway carriage) about his idea to become a Rothschild, he suddenly becomes sad: "Why aren't you saying anything? Why won't you at least laugh at my stupidity in telling you about it?" he says. "I didn't know how to express myself, and I can see that what I've just said must look stupid to you, very plain and childish. But my feeling for it is quite different, a lot more clever."

~~Liza does not say a word. This annoys him even more. "Why aren't you saying anything?"—"I.e., I was feeling" "You say"~~

"Do you really feel that it is more clever?"

"Listen, you are awfully clever," says the Youth.

"Really, I've noticed, all you have to do is express yourself, and you suddenly realize the absurdity <of what you have just said>."

"A thought once expressed is a lie."[26]

N.B. Liza lets him talk away till he is sick of it all the way till <he gets to the subject of> Baron Ungern-Shternberg.

August 26.

An idea.

He, a young wife, love, jealousy, disorder, he is being unfaithful himself, he tortures his wife, betrays <her?>, Liza, the boy, the Youth, the young Prince, etc.

Or: the husband betrays his wife* and attends their meetings.

[February—3 and 4] Regarding the meeting of Vasin, Him, and the Youth. They discuss suicide. The Youth asks this question: "What is it that makes practically every one of them (or at least very many of

---

* *Prodaet zhenu,* literally, "sells his wife."

[26] A quotation from Tiutchev's poem "Silentium."

them) write *confessions* during their very last moments (N.B. so that, if all of them had the means to do it, perhaps all of them would be writing confessions). Self-love, petty vanity. In fact, there are some suicides which are caused entirely by vanity. (Unbelief?) (The absence of a universal, guiding idea, which might affect <people of> all levels of education and all stages of development, for instance, that cook who hanged herself having lost 5 roubles belonging to her mistress.) And this universal trait belongs to our age only, for it certainly cannot be said that even before the promulgation <of the emancipation> suicides were as numerous, and of the same type, as today. The contrary is true. It is precisely in our day that they have increased, and this is specifically a trait of our age. A link has been lost, a guideline, a certain something that was holding up everything."

"Well then, tell me, what is it that got lost? Do you really think it is the serf's dependence on his master?"

"No, not only that."

"What then?"

"There has been a loss of order in general."

"You mean to say that now we have disorder, in a general way?"

"Precisely. I am not praising whatever has gotten lost. It was a bad order, but good or bad, at least it was some order. Whereas now, it's good, but we have disorder."

"Rather, you want to say, it's bad, and we have disorder."

"Have it your way, I'm not arguing."

People destroy themselves for many different reasons, they also write confessions for multiple reasons, and ~~though it is possible~~ not from vanity alone. Yet one can also find some common traits, for instance, the fact that, at a moment like this, everyone has an urge to write. *Golos:** a man who cut his throat with a knife, in a tavern <wrote>: "The image of dear K. is always before my eyes." Well, in this case, we can hardly speak of vanity, and besides, who is going to cut his throat with a blunt knife, just from vanity? And yet, there is again a common trait: right there, in his suicide note (*in spite of dear K.* whose image, *quite surely,* was giving him no rest, in case he did cut his throat because of her), there is this comment: "My head is surprisingly empty; I would have thought that, at such a moment, some special thoughts would come to one." I don't know whether

* *The Voice,* a contemporary Russian newspaper.

this remark was clever or stupid, but what matters is the fact that they are all looking for something, that they are all asking a certain question, to which they are not getting any answer, that they are interested in something which has nothing to do with their personal interests. Something universal and eternal, even in spite of the image of dear K. which, without any doubt, could have dispelled any universal idea as well as any urge for a deeper realization of oneself, and transformed the action into an *absolutely* personal affair.

Garibaldi's[27] *Notes.* "Gentlemen," he says to the governments and monarchs <of Europe>, "you are the creators of the Internationale and of the revolution, for you are opposed to the truth and to the brotherhood of men." Garibaldi's economic system boils down to the following: "How shall we avoid this danger? Nothing is easier than that: those who are now consuming ~~not~~ the share of fifty people will consume no more than if there were only twenty-five of them."

A man of such convictions has it easy in this world of ours. You can establish as many economic rules of this kind as you want, but how are you going to fulfill them? This latter question never enters the minds of people like Garibaldi. So simple-mindedly do they believe in such absolute nonsense that one is surprised at seeing them with this much influence.

"By virtue of their pure and great character.* By virtue of having served as the heralds of a great idea."

Thus, when relinquishing <his position>, Garibaldi, as against all other revolutionaries, had not made a fortune and rejected the millions [hundreds of thousands, 600,000] offered him by the Italian government! And yet you'd have to agree that this brave general and honest man *is no great mind.***

An accident.

"~~By virtue of this~~ He was the defender of a great idea all his life."

"You see, sir; these people find it easy to keep their faith, and that's why theirs is an easy life."

"And what about their great deeds?"

"Great deeds come easily to those who have such simple minds."

---

* Or "Purely by virtue of their great character."

** *Mysliiu ne orel,* literally, "is no eagle, as far as his mind is concerned."

27 Giuseppe Garibaldi (1807–82) led a series of efforts to unify Italy in the 1850's and 1860's. He became something of a symbol for democratic elements throughout Europe.

Note. N.B. The Youth's conversations with Him, in the beginning, sometimes proceed as follows:

"And what do you think of Garibaldi?"

"And what do you think of women in general?"

"And what do you think of future life?" etc.

I.e., all kinds of disconnected questions, asked quickly and suddenly (similarly also with Vitia at their first meeting). It appears as if the Youth is hurrying his questions so as not to forget to ask them, questions to which he *must have given a lot of thought before,* and which interest him very much.

Ice-covered rocks.

The Youth: "Perhaps there is intelligent life on the planets."

He: "Science denies it."

The Youth: "Perhaps there is something even higher than intelligent life?"

He: "Science doubly denies it."

"What use is it then to do good?"

"Just so as to get along <with other people> for such a short time?"

"Yes, if such be the law of nature, if you are doing it because you cannot help doing it."

He: "Is it really true that I couldn't have kept those 200,000?"

The Youth: "No, you could not."

He: "But somebody else could have, what do you think?"

The Youth: "Yes, somebody else could have."

He: "Which means that there is no such thing as universal good. A man holds sacred whatever he does."

The Youth: "No, universal good is the thing. Toward the end of its life, mankind will finally realize that everybody must keep returning 200,000, and that this is to his better advantage, and thus general well-being will become a fact."

He: "Yes, for two weeks! No, better let me indulge in my fancy during those two weeks, and tell me, what will be so wrong about my doing so?"

The railway carriage and Liza.

At first he just looks and blushes, puffy, he was innocent in the literal sense of that word.

About the boulevard. ("You find that women are unfair? Frou-frou is unfair.")

His own idea, he was daydreaming and suffering: there were minutes <when he> suffered a lot. ~~Thus~~ Newspaper, all nonsense, one must stick to the golden mean.

"Let's listen to the fool."

And the Youth thought: ("This is characteristic of high society.")

"Who is your father?" (He started lying: "A minister.")

"~~Finds out that Liza~~ You have such a good heart." (He beams with joy, indulges in confidences.)

She starts making caustic remarks. (He falls asleep for a while, wakes up red-faced.) She taunts him mercilessly. At first, not about his family name.

"I was sent for to take care of my aunts. I decided not to go to the university on principle. I don't want to feel obligated to my father."

They make up <when the train pulls out> after the last stop. She tells him that she is going to need him. She finds out his family name.

"But I didn't tell her about my idea."

~~But~~ Liza *didn't tell him either who she was, or did she?* So that he is stunned when he meets <her> at his father's.

The moment he hits the whirl of the big city,* he abandons his idea.

N.B. Keep reiterating that he has got an idea.

In the railway carriage: That he is an illegitimate son. "I am proud of it." She does not say a word. "You are a young girl, it wouldn't be polite to explain this to you." (The girl laughs.)

N.B. When he suddenly blushes and starts pouting: "I am begging no one to talk to me."

The fool at first makes the Youth indignant, and he stands up <for him?>, but then suddenly he bursts into loud laughter.

And still he says to her: *"I have my own idea."* Both the night before (she remains silent), and in the morning. In the morning, Liza takes up the subject and starts discussing his idea. Venomous taunts. Quarrel. Liza: "You look puffy." He wanted to strike her. Suddenly he confesses *his shame,* i.e., that he wanted to strike her. He concludes: "You are a mocker; generosity and a sense of justice have moved me to make this admission. Go ahead and laugh. I despise your laughter." At this point, Liza <says these things> about his heart and about his mind. They have gotten up and, already on their way out, he says to himself: "Still, she cannot despise me, for I didn't tell her about my idea."

---

* Literally, "he steps on the pavement."

While leaving the railway carriage, he is sad, "I have abased myself."

Mistrustful, gloomy. *To seclude himself.* An argument with a cabman (he flings a twenty-kopek piece to the ground, but picks it up). "No, to seclude myself, 'puffy.' " Daydreams about how clever he is, alone. "This ~~puffy man~~ man was a misanthrope." Liza. A hussar. "Cut <them> down with my sabre." The outlook of cutting <somebody> down with his sabre already consoles him.

Author's comment. One acts that way when one is 15, but this one is 19, sitting in a corner all by himself, and thinking.

N.B. Absolutely, right in the middle of a caricature-like discourse, a few *very clever* remarks on the part of the Youth. Liza, when she is making up with him at Kolpino, deftly uses these phrases to prove that she respects his wit. The Youth is delighted.

At the aunts'. "You fool, I am your godmother; if you don't care to be affectionate, you could be polite, at least."

N.B. The aunt: "You could be helping us now. You haven't got a heart."

"So you are my godmother~~—about this~~ is that so?"

"Christian religion is meaningless."

"Good Lord, how do you mean, 'meaningless?' "

"Just so, meaningless."

"Come on, Marfa Petrovna, you can see that he is a nihilist."

"I respect Christ as a <historical> figure and generally as a person, but I don't believe in all the rest, because it is stupid."[28]

"My father is a hypocrite and a hanger-on."

"Oh you whelp, you." (N.B. What made me so angry was the fact that I had made up my mind to maintain a proud silence, but the moment I was touched to the quick, I couldn't restrain myself and told everything.)

When I returned home that night: "Auntie, I was joking when I said that I don't believe in Christ. I do. You may, of course, consider my admission despicable; however, I am saying this not to ingratiate myself to you, or to do you a favor, but simply because I did wrong, and lied, and my conscience tells me that, shameful as it may be, I have to admit it."

---

[28] A variation of the belief of many liberal Russian intellectuals. The Petrashevtsy were bitterly anti-religious and looked upon Christ as a historical figure and person.

"Well, never mind," says the aunt. "You know, he (Christ) is like that. Right now he is glad about you, and if he were here, he'd call you and give you a kiss. If a man has blasphemy in his heart,* why, that's different; Christ does not forgive that."

"That I know. I can understand that this is indeed so. The spirit is the spirit of glory and of freedom, things which man (at least man of the European type) will never again abandon, as well as of a harmony which extends to the whole of society, and which will create a rational society, founded on rational principles."

"You talk very subtly; but that doesn't matter. That's one way to do it."

A pillow was in his way, he placed the package with the documents under <it?>.

A letter: to her grace, the Princess, under the icons.

About Christ: "When I blurted that out."

If in the first person, ~~the scene~~ use this form for the passage about Brusilov:

I was crying, crying, crying, crying. I had been all alone for 5 years. Really, I didn't want to <do it?> at all, yet irrepressibly.** I told him about Souchard (all in answer to his questions). He is feeling sincere pity. Embraces Him, as his father. About the island, high school, the tattle-tale, *he always kept apart.* <His> theory – didn't want to tell about it. Explained it. He leaves, *skeptically* impressed. ~~The Youth~~ I was left alone. I had a strange feeling. I was embracing my father. I had finally found <him?>. That's how it is. I loved <him?>. Oh, for nothing in the world did I want to talk <about it>. But the idea—*had lost some of its lustre.* I crossed myself.

Even in the 2d part, a tingle of revulsion. He loves and doesn't love his father. "It started somehow strangely," he casually tells him about family life in general (all a lot like frou-frou).

After the discourse *on the spirit* <of Christianity>, he gets up at night to kiss her hand. But his aunt is asleep. Nightcap, drooping lip (Leo Tolstoi).

Frou-frou throughout the novel, including part two.

"But that would be too smart on her part. ~~All this is happening.~~ Moves which are too smart usually fail. Exceedingly subtle and delicate affairs always require that a touch of stupidity be added to their execution; otherwise they would fail."

---

* Literally, "in his spirit."

** Incomplete phrase and unclear.

"People do not like ~~too~~ things that are clever beyond any doubt, and remain cool to them. Smart guys who are a little on the stupid side are more to people's liking. The more stupid, the closer. So that the smart guys who are on the stupid side are perhaps, in effect, smarter than those undoubtedly smart guys."

In a third-class railway carriage. A soldier's head in the window. April. Why didn't he take a third-class seat, but a second-class one?

~~At the ticket office~~ "I felt it would be mean to hide, and so I took <. . .> (at the ticket office, encounter with Liza).

He and his wife. "We get together and shame (upbraid) each other."

He, cursorily and suddenly, takes the Youth aback by such frequent statements:

"Why should I do good? Why should I love anybody?"[29]

"Really, one loves just so, not for any particular reason."

"Really, this is stupid. What sort of a system is this? 100,000 years of love, and then everything turns into an <ice-covered> rock. So much for human society in general. And as far as I am concerned, it is much closer than that."

"And still, you love."

"And still, this is stupid."

"All right, believe then."

"I do believe, I do believe with all my heart, I do believe precisely because it is impossible not to believe."

So then, it is almost unnatural to have so little control over oneself as He does, to be so subservient to one's passions as He is, and to work so little on oneself <as is true in His case>. Everybody says that he used to be a man of action, that he used to have goals which he actually pursued. And suddenly he is preaching Christianity! But if it is to be Christianity, where then are his feats? He's got a goal, he's got love. Why doesn't he do anything for it?"

"What an ardent, what a vigorous character," thinks the Youth (as he observes some of His strivings), "and what a flabby old woman he is at other times!"

When I saw Him at Souchard's, when he came to see me there, He appeared exceptionally beautiful and brilliant to me. When I met him in Petersburg, he looked entirely different (balding and gone to seed).

---

[29] This is the question that Ivan Karamazov will pose in the meeting in Father Zossima's cell, at least hypothetically.

He comes to see the Youth and starts accusing himself: "I am a conglomerate of petty vanities," etc.

Once, *He* does not visit the Youth for a long time, after a dishonorable action. The Youth runs into him: "Why don't you ever come to see me?"

"Why, I was afraid of you, I really was. This is all so dishonorable that I thought that you were going to scold me a good deal, so I wouldn't even dare to face you."

All this fascinates the Youth, and *yet, though he is admitting his own dishonor,* he never expresses remorse: on the contrary, he is skeptical. However, it appears that he suffers. But what? The Youth is preoccupied with these questions.

When the Youth has already found out about His liaison with Liza, *He* comes to see him being terribly worried about what he should buy her (the Stepmother) for her name-day.

In a fit of passion He says to the Youth about Liza: "*I* am going to hang *her* with my own hands."

In the railway carriage. "No, I have seen the Vestal (the statue), she is covered from head to foot, that's more decent (there is the Bourbon museum, Naples)—simply a statue."

The Youth's own idea [His own idea.]. "I have power, and I am calm. I know that I want to eat well, and I can, whenever I want. Well, enough of that. I would eat a piece of bread and ham, and I'd be satisfied with the knowledge. High rank, the title of a Baron, women. I do not want to torture anybody, nor am I going to. But I know that if I wanted to have somebody tortured I could do it. Enough of that. I am poorly dressed. A learned man, a Galileo, whereas I am an ignoramus. But I know that I am stronger. And enough. Actually, I find it rather agreeable that I am so ignorant, and that's why I didn't go to the university and was a poor student in my last year <in high school>."

"Won't it be boring to accumulate wealth?"

"No."

"Yes. Patience, constant calculating, perpetual waiting, a full life, very good" (says He). "How did you come up with this idea?" (he gives the Youth a long, strange look).

Le ris tenta le rat. Le rat tata le ris.[30]

---

30 French: "The bait tempted the rat. The rat touched the meat (bait)."

He says to Liza, during their first tryst: "I do not understand you."

"Why then did you come here, if you don't? I have ~~called~~ come to tell you that I hate you. You are torturing my mother. You love the Princess."

N.B. He tells all this to his stepson. His scene with her is not described.

"Poison her? Come on, *I* won't exchange her for 1,000 the likes of you."

"Then I shall poison myself."

"Then poison yourself."

Just sitting there. Not saying a word.

Liza: "I want *you** to embrace and to kiss me right away."

The Youth to Him: "Why, it is quite impossible that she (Liza) should have a passion for you. You are an old man." And He feels as if something stabbed him.

Note (if in the third person). The *finale* of the novel. Everybody is dead. The Youth is left all by himself. Melancholy. Three days, just sitting around. He leaves his flat in the evening. The idea of acquiring wealth is fading away. The sun is setting above the Neva. "I want to live." ~~He prays~~ Every blade of grass prays. The Youth's prayer: "Save me, oh Lord, and I thank you that I want to live. And what will be, will be."

The young generation, entering life.

N.B. After Souchard,[31] as well as at Souchard's, the Youth initially made an effort to study very hard (he read Karamzin), but precisely with the idea of *withdrawing* <into himself> *and gathering strength.* And so it went on, starting from his first years at high school, even though he was being considered a dull boy who was getting where he did by his assiduousness only. "Let them," he thought, "it's just my looks that hurt me. I am liked by no one, [*His own idea.*] but later, in Paris, I will <make up for it>." Daydreams of a fourth grade high school student, how he <will> later <write> a dissertation and prove that his teacher didn't know a thing. He then goes to Paris, publishes in Paris, everybody takes him for a scholar. He is invited to come to Russia. I am not coming. I'll crush all those professors and academicians; I'll tell them that they are fools. And, having told them off, I'll stay there, rejecting all offers. I'll withdraw from the world.

---

* She is using the intimate form *ty* ('thou").

31 Nikolay I. Souchard, Dostoevsky's childhood French teacher.

They'll get even angrier and will start trying to prove that I am but an insignificant pygmy. They'll prove it. I'll wait on purpose for a long time, so that even the public will get to believe them, and so that I'll be completely forgotten and it will be considered disgraceful to have a high opinion of me. Then suddenly, after three or four years of silence, I <bring out> another book, in Paris and in French, with a preface saying that it is impossible to have it published in Russian. And again, Europe will raise a howl. And again they will be crushed. And so all my life. I'll make a point of never discussing any learned things, just trivialities, with learned Russians. (N.B. In his daydreams he always considered himself to be a great man.)[32]

(For Christ's sake, repent, miracles, coming from Kharkov, Eilekon,* the academy.)

Ungern-Shternberg.[33] (Two heads come down.)

Ruler of a deserted island. Since he was in the fifth grade of high school, the idea about <becoming a> Rothschild began to occupy him. "Shouldn't I become a mean character? Let them detest me, as long as I am powerful." Though he continued to be an excellent student, it was only due to the force of habit. But in the last grade he quit being a good student, on account of his idea of the triumph of the golden mean.

He tells him, in the middle of his confession: "I see that you always placed yourself first and foremost. [*His own idea.*] And this (uneducated) *golden mean* is nothing but that same pride. It is an excellent practical idea. To spend all one's life nursing one's pride and vanity. That is a tremendous job, and one can lead a full life with it and spend a pleasant life. And be not such a bad person on top of it."

He, inveighing against Souchard: "Tell me, what were you daydreaming about, in that corner of yours, my boy? (and I wasn't even aware of it)."

"This is what I was dreaming about," the Youth began, with his eyes flashing...—i.e., *under no circumstances* did he want to tell about it, but as his mood changed, he revealed everything.

And when he had left, he became *sad,* not because he had told about the island, but because he had betrayed his idea <to him>. It

---

* I am not familiar with this obviously foreign name. Therefore, I just transliterated it.

[32] These daydreams remind one of the Underground Man's daydreams of glory, as well as those of Ippolit in *The Idiot.*

[33] See note 3 of this section.

was only the idea that was shaken. As for his confession, he wasn't ashamed of it in his thoughts. Nor was the idea shaken because He had failed to approve of it. On the contrary, He had listened to it very seriously and had said something mysterious. But it was shaken because he had told somebody else about it. "I did not explain it too well," he thought as he was falling asleep. Later, he became very much excited and confused on account of <some> social ideas.

"Come on, what could I pass on to the young generation?" He says. "I am a beggar myself. All my life I believed that I was a rich man who would never come to grief, and there, on the threshold of my old age, I find myself a beggar. There is nothing in me; ~~not that there ever was~~ it won't matter that there isn't, that I could bear. What's so sad [What really hurts] is that there never was."

He says: "Who were the nihilists? Essentially ~~we~~ we were, we, the perennial seekers of a higher idea. What you've got now are either indifferent dullards or monks. The former (they are the "men of action") are the ones who, incidentally, happen to shoot themselves not infrequently, all their businesslike attitude notwithstanding. As for the monks, they are socialists, believers to the point of madness, and they never shoot themselves."

"Come on, you don't say that nihilists never shoot themselves?"

"Only those who have become nihilists by mistake. Nihilism without socialism is a mere repulsive nihilistics,* and certainly not nihilism. That's a good name for it: 'nihilistics.' What you have got there is stupidity, or swindling, or being glad to have the right to be dishonorable, but certainly not nihilism. But most often it is being glad to have the right to be dishonorable. Genuine nihilism, true and pure, is based on socialism. Here, everybody is a monk. A veritable monastery, boundless, mad faith. That's why they reject everything else ~~the whole world~~, <just> because it is against socialism, <just> because they are believers. Everything that isn't of their faith is rejected. And what is against their faith? This whole world of ours. And so this world of ours is being rejected."

The Youth: "Are there any other categories, or are there just these two?"

"There is a third category, thoroughgoing scoundrels of various kinds, but these are the same at any time and any place, so there isn't any use to talk about them."

---

* *Nigiliatina,* with a pejorative suffix difficult to duplicate in English.

Liza: "I have been blaming *the first comer* for not being the ideal <man>, but who are you in my life, but <such> first comer?"

I would call him a youth, if he hadn't passed 19. In fact, does one grow after 19?* If not physically, so at least morally.

Not a grain of truth.

About the drunken student. All this, he tells ~~her~~ to Liza.

This *Geschichte.***

In our society things are quite confused.

"A genuine nihilist cannot, must not, dare not become reconciled to any part of the existing <order>. Under no condition should he dare to make deals <with it>. And he knows only too well that any such deal is decidedly out of the question."

"Absolutely no moral ideas exist today," (He says) "suddenly, there isn't a single one left; and above all, it looks as if there hadn't ever been any."

"Well, and before?"

"I don't know anything about what was before. I only know that I looked around me and found nothing. Idealism."

"Were you already 40 years old when you looked around?"

"*Le temps n'y fait rien.*[34] However, let it be 40."

He has "an insatiable appetite for life."

"He also talks in a taciturn way (Vasin)."

"How is that, 'he talks in a taciturn way'? What sort of an expression is that?"

"Well, there are people who even talk as if they weren't saying a word. It is a good expression."

The Youth: "Now, that I know that I won't ever become a serious person, I have decided," etc.

To write in so much detail—that means that my whole life will have as many volumes as a code of laws.

He is explaining poetry to the Youth—"sweet lemonade." " 'Songs of the Western Slavs'—that is, sweet lemonade."

Nervous behavior.

According to a remark by Ivan Ivanovich Dmitriev, Derzhavin had two <participants> in Pugachev's rebellion hanged solely out of poetic curiosity.

---

* Russian *podrostok,* "youth," is derived from *podrasti,* "to grow up. "
** *Geshikhta,* the Russian form of the German word meaning "story."
34 French: "Time has nothing to do with it."

When Vasin left Him and the Youth, He tells the Youth: "He didn't say a word all the time, and the two of us did all the talking, making fools of ourselves." (Petty vanity. But here the Youth adds a note in the novel, saying that "to remain silent is good, beautiful, and safe," and how nice it would be to take advantage of this <maxim>.)

The Youth: "You are a stern judge of yourself."

He: "I have no use for this remark. Let me tell you that I shall never allow anybody to judge me. But so long as I still have a couple of rubles, I want to live in seclusion and do nothing. At least this gives me the satisfaction that I am not involved in anything; I have a clear conscience, since I am not participating in anything, not doing any damage, making no mischief, not dirtying myself along with them."

"Wagons that are hauling grain to mankind.[35] This is a lofty idea, yet a secondary one, and one that is great at a given moment only. For I know that, the moment I shall have changed stones into bread and feed mankind, man will immediately ask: 'All right then, I have satisfied my hunger; what shall we do now?' "

"Mankind has always acted that way: it would thirst for a great idea, yet couldn't stand the thought of it and, the moment it arose, men would invariably sneer at it and spit upon it, trying to see it as something below them. Just so they wouldn't have to give any thought to the great idea, (I presume that, even if you do not understand what I mean by 'that great idea,' you at least have a presentiment of it) they invariably come up with, always have come up with some secondary idea, *to divert their attention,* just so they wouldn't have to think of the great idea."

"Father, this sounds vague. What do you call 'a great idea'?"

He: "I don't know what. I know that it is [always] the thing from which *real life** springs, immediate, and not cerebral, manufactured, ~~fabricated~~ fabricated life."

The Youth: "What is real life?"

He: "Real life ought to be something terribly simple, something one meets every day, something that strikes the eye, something that

---

* *Zhivaia zhizn',* literally, "living life."

[35] Compare this phrase with the words of Lebedev in *The Idiot:* "Vile as I am, I do not believe in the carts bring bread to humanity. For the carts bringing bread to humanity, without a moral basis to the act, may quite cold-bloodedly exclude a considerable part of mankind from the enjoyment of what is brought, which has already occurred" (Part III, Chapter 4).

is so simple we just don't want to believe that it could be that simple, and pass by without even noticing it, *not to speak* of recognizing it."

"The consequence of nihilism will be idealism," says the Youth.

"Not true," He retorts, "on the contrary, the most salutary and the most sobering positivism, for nihilism is itself, perhaps, *practically the last stage of idealism.*"

He: "I never judge anybody, and this is why I never make any definitive conclusions either" (answering the Youth's reproof), "this is because I do not want to judge anybody."

The Youth: "Why so?"

He: "Because I wouldn't dare."

The Youth: "But why so?"

He: "I don't know why, but this is what my conscience tells me. A certain wise person (the Princess) [my wife] says: because I do not know how to suffer. In order to become a judge, she says, it is necessary to acquire the right to judge through suffering. This sounds [a little grandiloquent,] but perhaps it is the truth."

"A Russian atheist, if only he has brains and a heart, is always inclined to show some affection for God, because he is a kind person and immeasurably pleased to be an atheist. Atheism is for him a source of pleasure, and not of suffering."

The Youth: "You always talk in an awfully, awfully abstract way."

He: "Don't you pick on me."

The railway station—they've arrived. "Why, it could be that nobody around here has anything to do, and that this is true of everybody."

He: "Before, a long time before, I used to think: 'The moment they emancipate the peasants they (the liberals) will immediately become terribly unhappy [here]. What will they have to talk about then?' But I was wrong. They recovered quickly: they immediately began to write *again*—and they still are shouting and writing about it—that the peasants must be emancipated."

The Youth: "Come on now, show me where."

He: "~~I assure you~~ At least they haven't come up with anything new."

The Youth calls him "daddy," sometimes "father," and on one occasion they keep calling each other *"father"* and *"sonny"** all evening,

---

* *Batiushka,* which I have translated as "daddy," is both respectful and affectionate; *synok* ("sonny") is also very affectionate, but more formal and dignified than "sonny."

and *emphatically so*. But on the very next morning He is already frowning and no longer says "sonny," and another day later he asks the Youth to never again repeat this foolishness.

Being guided by a single idea.

"He has gorged himself with nihilistics, he has stuffed himself with nihilistics."

"Who are they to negate things? With them, even the negation of religion has been converted into a religion. ~~Idealists~~ These people are perpetually prayerful. Of course, I am not talking of the scoundrels and fools. There are an awful lot of scoundrels and schemers among them, though even more fools. Nihilistics. That's Lambert."

"Isn't that also a moral idea?"

"God knows. Let's change the subject."

"Thoroughgoing scoundrels."

A conversation at the nihilists' (he is delighted): *"Quae medicamenta non sanant,"*[36] etc., and then set fire to all the cities ~~villages~~ and villages all over the land, make that the beginning. "That's how I understand it." (It is the spy who says this; some others argue with him.)

The two late Rothschilds, and how much of a fortune they left, etc. (The Youth, making money, his idea.)

New.

According to the new plan of August 26.

Title of the novel: "Disorder."

The whole idea of the novel is to demonstrate that we have now general disorder, disorder everywhere and wherever you go, in society, in business, in guiding ideas (of which, [for that very reason,] there aren't any), in <our> convictions (which ,[for the same reason,] we don't have), in the disintegration of the family unit.

"If there are any passionate convictions, they are all destructive (socialism). There aren't any moral ideas; suddenly not a single one is left, and above all," *He* ~~the Youth~~ says, "one has the impression that there never were any."

"Well, after all, you, for instance, are a religious man."

---

[36] Latin: "What medicine does not cure." In the final version, someone cries out the following when the Raw Youth enters the Dergachev apartment: *Quae medicamenta non sanant—ferrum sanat, quae ferrum non sanat—ignis sanat!"* ("What medicine does not cure, iron will cure; what iron does not cure, fire will cure.") (Part I, Chapter 3:3.) Quotation from Hippocrates. The quotation is used by Dostoevsky as a call for revolution.

268

О МУЧЕНИКѢ НИКОЛАѢ

И КАКЪ ДОЛЖЕНЪ ЖИТЬ ЧЕЛОВѢКЪ ПО ЗАКОНУ ПРАВДЫ И ПРИРОДЫ.

Въ память мученика Николая, и чтобы въ народѣ жило и славилось его имя, идите въ народъ и говорите ему правду. Говорите народу, какъ онъ жилъ и какой онъ былъ святой человѣкъ, и какъ его царскіе чиновники, злодѣи и взяточники мучили, тиранили и били до безпамятства, какъ они его въ цѣпи ковали и пытками пытали. Раскажите народу всю правду до послѣдняго слова, и какъ человѣкъ долженъ жить по закону природы.

По закону природы всѣ люди равны. Смотрите развѣ одинъ человѣкъ родится въ золотѣ и бархатѣ, а другой въ изгребной тряпкѣ. Всѣ родятся голые, всѣ родятся такими же малыми и слабыми; ни одинъ новорожденный ни говорить, ни читать, ни писать не умѣетъ и всѣ они похожи другъ на друга. Ростутъ люди одинаково: нѣтъ человѣка, который былъ бы въ два вершка, а другаго, который былъ бы въ пять саженъ. Есть собаки малые и большіе, есть змѣи малые и большіе, а людей малыхъ и большихъ нѣтъ. Тутъ законъ прямо виденъ, между людьми должно быть больше равенства чѣмъ между собаками и змѣями. Но развѣ есть собаки бѣдные и богатые, развѣ есть змѣи бѣдные и богатые; какъ же между людьми, которые болѣе равны другъ другу могутъ быть бѣдные и богатые. Дѣ-

This is one of the proclamations composed by the conspiratorial group, the Dolgushintsy, who are referred to in the notes. The title reads: "About the Martyrdom of Nikolay and how man should live according to the law of truth and nature." The text concerns itself with the fact that all men are born equal and consequently should be equal in society.

"All I need is to lose that, too."

[February, 3d part.] "You, for instance," he says to the Youth, "have chosen the idea of <becoming a> Rothschild. This idea is another bit of evidence concerning our moral disorders. You want to withdraw into *your own* burrow and shun everybody, and you are taking action to make this possible."

Liza is an example of complete moral disorder; she refuses to live without happiness.

The Dolgushins are another instance of moral disorder.

"Let *them* be wrong," says the Youth, "yet *their* convictions imply honor and duty, and consequently there can be no talk of disorder in this instance."

"Convictions implying honor and duty, and aimed at universal destruction; that's some fine order for you; however, *I* don't want to argue with you," He says.

The Youth is convinced, up to about the middle of the novel, that He has married her for her money. And there, suddenly, he returns 200,000.

<His> Stepmother is very young, 24 years old. Toward the end, absolutely the young Prince. *He* takes his vengeance. "For everything."

Liza makes the Youth believe that He is selling his wife to the young Prince, (or that the Stepmother is being supported by the old Prince).

The Stepmother suspects that He has a liaison with Liza and, having discovered that this is indeed so, she surrenders herself to the Prince, but not for revenge, but from despondency: "I am a predatory type myself."

The Stepmother dies insane ~~and embraces~~. Even before, when she had surrendered herself to the young Prince, she embraces Him and says: "What will become of you?"

He says to the Youth: "Live to the moment. I do not believe in a future life; consequently, there is no need to engage in *moralizing*."

"Is that why you keep immoralizing?"* says the Youth.

"No, not just because of that; I am generally a scoundrel, but that's all right that way" (this is already after the icons).

Toward the end: ("Faith in duty, and convictions—that is happiness.")

The Princess hates Him, in addition to other reasons, because she suspects that He is ready to sell his wife to the old Prince. (The Stepmother is a relative of the old Prince's.) (Perhaps this is slander on the part of Liza, but perhaps it is true.)

?He married a girl who was being supported by the Prince (i.e., the Stepmother was said to be supported <by the old Prince>, until she inherited 200,000 herself).

---

* Nravstvennichat' ("engage in moralizing") and *beznravstvennichaete* "you keep immoralizing" are neologisms formed *ad hoc* and difficult to translate.

A will in favor of the Stepmother.

He is scheming, among other things, <to show> that the Princess is in possession of a forged will.* (The plot!)

The Youth realizes immediately that the Stepmother *cannot be sold* (for reason of her exalted character), but it is true that she and the old Prince are friends, since they are distant relatives. She respects the old Prince as the benefactor of her family (Al. Alekseevich). However, as far as He is concerned, it is still true that He has received a good deal of money from the Prince to cover his own expenses (pocket money, and some secret <expenditures>). And suddenly the Youth learns that this man, who had married a girl for her money, has returned 200,000, and even without making any fuss about it.

His is "an insatiable appetite for life."

A tormentor of his wife. ~~1~~

[February, 3d part.] "Is this also a part of your appetite?" (i.e., torturing his wife) asks the Youth.

"Certainly," He replies.

The Princess is convinced that the Youth belongs to His gang in the affair of the will. (Think it all over.)

(N.B. Shorten the railway journey.)

Liza says: "If I had lived in the 16th century, I would have been a poisoner."

"I like disorder," (Liza suddenly says).

He is in love (with the Princess, after a fashion).

"You are an old goat, that's what you are."**

[February, 3d part.] "Why shouldn't I be one, why shouldn't I live to take care of my own arse, what else is there to do? Worry about the common good, make your contribution to the happiness of future generations? To hell with them, what the devil do I care? Let them tell me something more serious to support such notions!"

"Well, this is a moral feeling, a striving to do one's duty, a thirst for harmony."

He comes back with the shopkeepers. "No, my friend, it couldn't be that things rest upon a sense of duty and of harmony; it must be something natural. ~~pressure~~ A natural pressure, like that which makes a tree produce fruit, or a bird build a nest and hatch its eggs. The pressure of nature."

---

* The Russian sentence is not quite grammatical and is unclear.

** *Vy myshinyi zherebchik,* literally, "you are a grey stallion,"where *zherebchik* is literally, "a little stallion." Disparaging and slightly obscene.

"All right, let it be that way."

"Oh no, nobody ever consulted me about this arrangement of things, so why should I submit to it, if, perhaps, I mustn't?"

"But if you have no will, if you can't help submitting?"

"Well, didn't I say *perhaps?* But for the time being, I don't know, and I am going to try it out."

"Why, this is atheism!"

He: "I was just making fun."

Vasin was not saying anything, stood up silently, and left.

N.B. This conversation took place at Vasin's flat. Vasin had come to see him having learned that he had returned 200,000. However, only He and the Youth did any talking, while Vasin was listening all the time. So that later He is embarrassed and angry that He talked so much.

He actually *had lived* with Liza. In the end, <her> Mother found out about it. Liza alternately enthralls Him during their trysts, and tortures him the rest of the time. Liza once made an attempt to enthrall the young Prince, but he rejected her. An insult. After her stepmother goes mad and dies, Liza hangs herself.

The essence of the Novel is this: His untidy love for Liza and the sufferings from it. His love and admiration for His wife, and their mutually inflicted sufferings. Yet they are hiding the secret from each other. His love-hatred for the Princess.

On one occasion Liza enticed the Youth and surrendered herself to him, ~~He~~ actually sensing beforehand the Youth's horror after the act. She laughs at his horror.

Vasin suddenly tells Him: "You were compromised in connection with such-and-such-affair," he says.

"No, I was not."

"You participated in such-and-such."

"The proof is in the fact that I am here, talking to you."

"However, you were compromised," Vasin remarked in his taciturn way.

"To make money is dishonorable," *He* tells him. "Well, you buy cheaper, you sell at a higher price—you've cheated twice."

The Youth gets to think.

"There must be a line," he says. "Nobody would have given this soldier more, this is a market."

"You think a little, and you'll see that there is no line."

Conversation with Him, but already a long time after he has revealed the secret about Rothschild, and somehow by accident. As a result of this conversation, the Youth begins to waver, but there is a moment when he would rather be a crook, but with money.

"If I renounce this idea," the Youth thinks, "what is there left for me to do? There is nothing for me to do then: it is very stupid to live that way. Unless one decides to enjoy life the way my father does.* I do not believe in socialism. If <one believes> in religion, one ought to go all the way and become a monk. What shall one believe?"

And very soon after this conversation, He suddenly bursts out laughing:

"Has this really discouraged you so much? The devil take it, haven't you ever come to think of this yourself? Why, you knew all along what you were up to and, as it appears to me, you are no simpleton: you keep asking questions, and looking for the answers."

"I have been thinking of that even before," the Youth said gloomily.

[February, 3d part.] "But before, until somebody else told you the same thing, you didn't believe in what had occurred to you? That makes sense, that's what always happens to people. However, I certainly did not say this to dissuade you from your idea. Frankly, your idea is a good one, and is worth as much as any other idea. Keeping busy in life <leads to?> the destruction of ideas."

The Youth frequently regrets** that he is never going to be a serious person.

?N.B. Vasin's father, who has sold his wife, goes to see ~~him~~ Him because he thinks that He, too, has sold his wife.

Though Vasin is a senior member of the secret society, all the other members disagree with him on many points, and some are his enemies and actually look at him with suspicion.

The Youth *must* witness, in the course of the novel, a number of exceedingly craven acts on His part. He must be coming to see the Youth *all excited,* to tell him that nobody in His family respects him, that they refuse to consider Him the head of the family, etc.

When the Stepmother has surrendered herself to the young Prince, the young Prince suggests that He sell <him> his wife.

A NEW TRAIT: *He* absolutely must be jealous of his wife even before <her affair with> the young Prince. He (the father) is mistrustful. He

---

* *V klubniku pustit'sia,* literally, "to go into plucking strawberries." See n. (*), p. 55, above.

** *Plachet,* literally, "cries."

keeps looking under beds,[37] <lies awake> at night listening. Liza takes notice of all this and subsequently exposes it. In the beginning the Youth suspects nothing, he just sees that something is wrong in the house. One day they're like turtle doves, the next day there is a hysterical scene, and suddenly He takes the Youth aback by *informing* him that his wife is having an affair with so-and-so. The Youth refuses to believe it, but He insists that it is true, and the Youth is almost made to believe it.

The affair ends with Him put to shame. Contempt, Liza's jeers on account of this affair,* yet it had been Liza herself who, to some extent, had been egging him on. All this happens *before* the Youth learns about His liaison with Liza, or about His love for the Princess, about which he is also told by Liza.

N.B. The Stepmother, on the other hand, is jealous of a chambermaid; then again of certain other trivial involvements, but most of all of the Princess. Liza is also trying to fan this jealousy of hers for the Princess. Being aware of it all, He is furious. The torments inflicted on his wife ~~Altogether the Youth~~ are organized. "He needs a nurse," etc.

Altogether, the Youth is amazed at the contrast between His definitive, severe, and exaltedly fascinating convictions (or reversed convictions) and the surprisingly unfinished state of his character in real life. He is easily swayed, he is a slave of his impressions.

"What have you found in Him?" the Youth asks Liza indignantly.

"He has debauched me, and must belong to me," Liza replies, "because I can't stand him, and because I despise him." (That He has debauched her is a lie.)

N.B. Liza *absolutely* suggests to Him that he must poison his wife, threatening that she is going to tell ~~her~~ <her> mother everything. But she finds out by herself. The Stepmother finally guesses what is going on, mainly as a result of some amazing scenes between Liza and Him.

These scenes are arranged as follows. In the beginning, the <Step> mother ~~was scolding on account of them~~ was angry with Liza for being so insolent to Him. Then later, she got curious and began to take a closer look at what was going on. Finally, his cowardly behavior before Liza, a number of careless actions on Liza's part, and

* Or: "Liza's contempt and jeers on account of this affair."

[37] Dostoevsky's father was supposed to have looked under his daughters' beds in search of suitors.

several slips on his, made her suspicious. When she first became suspicious, she initially experienced a jealous animal curiosity, later a boundless sadness, and an exaltation of her own character. She made an attempt to get something out of the Youth, as she came to see him and cried (a scene, more gracefully). Finally, in a violent scene, Liza tells her everything herself. A scene.

Then, the Stepmother all of a sudden surrenders herself to the Prince. Liza accuses her vehemently. "You were a saint. Why did you deprive me of yourself?" Liza's fury ~~she hangs herself~~. The Stepmother's madness. Liza hangs herself.

"You can't love me, having noticed so many funny traits about me," He says to Liza.

TWO IDEAS. *Definitively*.

Liza never submitted to Him, but she is carrying on a love affair with Him, and goes on rendezvous' with Him. She tortures Him by leaving him uncertain. Does she love Him, or does she hate Him? She offers to poison her <Step>mother. "You are mad," He says. Perhaps Liza herself does not know whether she loves or hates Him. Leave it that way, don't ever clarify it.

In a mad fit of passion, Liza surrenders herself to the young Prince (earlier, she has been inciting His jealousy of her mother and the young Prince). She causes Him terrible suffering by her admission: "Why, I have been his mistress for a long time," i.e., the young Prince's (she is lying). ~~He goes into a mad frenzy as a result of this, chops up some icons, a duel.~~

The Stepmother, having found out about it from Liza, dies, having lost her mind. Liza suddenly becomes utterly devoted to her dying Stepmother. She abandons the young Prince, as they part enemies (she sneers at him, drives him to a frenzy, spits on him as he is groveling at her feet). And when her Stepmother dies, she hangs herself.

N.B. NOT NECESSARY THAT THE STEPMOTHER SUBMIT TO THE YOUNG PRINCE.

It is not necessary that Liza *submit to Him even once*. Love without it.

Or thus: ~~Liza, in order to drive him to a frenzy, surrenders herself to the Prince. He chops up some icons and leaves the house to challenge the Prince to a duel. Then the Stepmother, fearing <that> the challenge <might be accepted>, rushes to see the young Prince begging him not to accept the challenge. "You have promised to be my friend," she says. "Save Him, save Liza. Save me from these disorders, from this terror. I always used to love you a little, ever since~~

~~we were children. Please, give me back my peace of mind" (at this point, dreams of the past, of an ideal). She dies in a feverish state, in a frenzy.~~

~~N.B. So that, though the Stepmother did rush to see the Prince, *nothing* at all ever happened between them.~~ [Think over the pro and contra. A task]

The death of his wife brings Him back to his senses, he is stunned, there is no duel. After his wife's death, hatred for Liza, she hangs herself on the day of <her Stepmother's> funeral.

But what does this *domestic** disorder mean, and what is its role as far as the whole poem is concerned?

The idea is that, theoretically, He has worked out a rule according to which nothing on earth has any value. Yet in practice He is fully devoted to <life on> earth. He is ashamed to live, yet in fact he has great vitality.

He who denies everything and is desperate about not having anything to cling to is at the same time attached *to everything*.

Think over the possibility of a *first-person* narrative. Many advantages; much freshness, the figure of the Youth would emerge more typical. Nicer. I'll be able to cope better with the character, with the personality, with the essence of that personality. It is all written while he is under arrest, for the second time, in connection with the Lambert affair and the murder of Perchatkin.

It will be easier to describe as something typical *the passion of arson,* i.e., the passion to set fires (comparing the plot against the Princess with incendiarism). His and Liza's characters will take shape in a more typical fashion, and more gradually.

A task.

Finally, descriptions could proceed more rapidly and more concisely. Instances of naïveté. Make the reader develop a liking for the Youth. They'll get to like him, and then they'll read the novel to the end. If the Youth as a character should turn out a failure, the whole novel will.

August 27.

Give it a good deal of thought. Color. Will I succeed in giving life to this character? If I write the novel in the *first person,* this will

* Or: "family," "familial."

undoubtedly give it more unity, and less of *that* what Strakhov[38] has been criticizing me for, i.e., too large a number of characters and subjects.[39] But what about the style and the tone of the Youth<'s narrative>? This style and tone may help the reader in anticipating the dénouement.

The plot against the Princess (details).

About a year and a half prior to the beginning of the novel He married the widow of a General, who is a former ward and a very distant relative of the old Prince. She was then 24 years old. But before that, He had for some time made a strong impression upon the Princess (the Princess, a young society lady, 26 years old, is the old Prince's second or third wife). The Princess has a rather somber and most impressionable character, though not without an occasional, exceedingly bright flash of light. A society lady's presumption, insufferable arrogance, the stubbornness and punctiliousness of an Englishwoman (the wife of <Lord> Byron),[40] petty vanity—this is her high society aspect. On the other hand, she shows flashes of true generosity, flashes of genuine philanthropy, mystic inclinations (which is how He gained influence on her, i.e., through religion, preaching) and, of late, an inclination toward socialism (perhaps it could be arranged so that Vasin might have some influence on her). As for His influence of a year and a half earlier, it undoubtedly existed, and even not without an element of budding love. It was the Princess who had declared herself, a fact she is forever ashamed of, and most painfully so. There also had been a rendezvous, at some sort of a dive, something like a tavern, where they had suddenly quarrelled. The principal reason for their quarrel at the tavern may have been his crude seminarian* blundering in selecting the place of their rendezvous, as well as the obviousness, bordering on coarse and comical blatancy, with which he had made his preparations for a certain triumph.

---

* Untranslatable: Russian seminarians were notorious for semiliteracy, crudity, and clumsy manners, coupled with "intellectual" presumption.

38 Nikolay Nikolaevich Strakhov (1828–96), critic and philosopher, conservative in view. He cultivated the friendship of both Tolstoy and Dostoevsky and was biographer and critic of both. Dostoevsky took very seriously his criticism of *The Idiot.*

39 Translation of the word *"siuzhet."* This word in Dostoevsky's time meant "theme" as a structural element.

40 Dostoevsky was perhaps familiar with Macaulay's biography of Byron in which the domestic crisis of Lord Byron's life is treated.

Absolutely include in the Youth's narrative a description of this rendezvous and its setting, with details à la L<eo> T<olstoi>. (N.B. In his narrative, it might come out even more concise, more naked, leaving more things unsaid.)

Silver and gold.

They parted as enemies, and yet His sudden marriage to the Stepmother terribly angers the Princess. Without spreading any slanderous rumors, she was sincerely convinced that He had married a woman kept by the old Prince, and that his function was that of a paid, dummy husband. He feels very much insulted by this, and greatly resents being so affronted by the Princess, but most of all <he suffers from> the memory of the rendezvous. The Princess is a seeker of *the serious;* a puritan, with sudden flashes of extraordinary femininity, gracefulness, and *joie de vivre.*

Of late, i.e., immediately after Him, the young Prince, too, has had some influence on her. There is really some love here; however, it is a kind of motherly adoration, so that she even forgives him his betrayals, for instance, *en haut lieu*[41] (there is only one betrayal which she does not forgive him—it is his affection, a pure one as it turns out, for the Stepmother). Actually she had quarreled with Him, a year and a half earlier, because He had started to preach to her about her being an adulteress, even if she was only mentally unfaithful to her husband; whereas she had, on that occasion, freely confessed to him her motherly affection for the young Prince.

Then, a strange game had developed. Up to that point she had been sincerely impressed by His preaching, but now she suddenly noticed that there was hidden, behind his sermon to her: "Do not commit adultery," His own jealousy toward the young Prince, and a desire to lure her over to himself, i.e., "commit adultery not with him, but with me." This is where she exposed Him (at a point where she was already beginning to love Him, yet with her inner self seeking convulsively to escape from this love, which seemed repulsive to her), and this was also the theme of their rendezvous at the wretched tavern so *inappropriately selected* by him.

During that year and a half of separation He had to bear a good deal of scorn and contemptuous opinions from her, but it was precisely this very fact that elicited in Him some sort of inexplicable passion and desire for the Princess, a love of pride, *la haine dans*

---

41 French: "In high places."

l'amour,[42] etc. As for real love, perhaps there actually wasn't any. But He always assumed that there might be a little bit of that same *haine dans l'amour* in the Princess, too, and was still dreaming of regaining her heart. However, of late He was almost forced to abandon such hope, on account of her terribly contemptuous attitude toward Him.

This is already after the novel has started, and it will be *necessary* to invent such a scene (perhaps the theft of those diamonds). On which occasion He intercedes for ~~the boy~~ <his> son. It's the Princess who has made the Prince believe that He is preaching *l'evangile*, and about those relics. And it is Vasin who converts the old Prince to atheism.

Furthermore, about two years earlier the old Prince had had an attack of softening of the brain (Lamansky).[43] That's when he lost his positions. It was at that time that the Princess, in her efforts to intervene in favor of the young Prince, her husband's <legal> heir, wrote a letter to Andreev telling him that the old Prince had made a will leaving his entire capital to the Stepmother (a fiction, but where did it originate?).

N.B. She also told Him about it, not knowing yet of his impending marriage to that very same Stepmother, and so she was quite stunned when she suddenly heard (already after their rendezvous at the tavern) that He was going to marry that *kept woman*.

N.B. In the course of the novel, the Princess is stunned by the fact that He returns 200,000; also, He proves to the Princess that there is nothing in the will about leaving anything to the Stepmother; so that there takes place (already in the novel) an attempt at a reconciliation between the Princess and Him; however, it ends in another quarrel and contempt.

And so, when the old Prince was suffering from softening of the brain, the Princess wrote a letter to Andreev concerning how the old Prince might be declared insane and the will which he had just then made, invalid (she trusted Andreev as she would herself). Also, a letter to Andreev about the young Prince (in reply to old Andreev's suspicion that she was in love with the young Prince) <somehow> turned up, and this letter, too, could, *if necessary*, compromise her.

---

[42] French: "Hate in love."

[43] Porfiry Ivanovich Lamansky (1824–75), a government official with whom Dostoevsky was slightly acquainted, and who committed suicide from a deranged mind. Dostoevsky wrote to his wife on February 6, 1875: "Imagine Porfiry Lamansky died from a dagger struck in his heart!"

Still in Andreev's lifetime the Princess had once, all of a sudden, asked him to return those letters to her, and he had replied that he had destroyed them (burned them) immediately. Which was not true.

After Andreev's death, the Princess, fearing an intrigue on His part, i.e., a denunciation to the Prince, a denunciation on His part, with the aim of having her excluded from the will ~~(for he is young)~~, goes to see one of the aunts with whom she had been on friendly terms before, begging her to let her have those letters, but the aunt says that she hasn't found anything of the kind.

This scene: the Youth was asleep behind a screen, and the aunt didn't know it. The Youth woke up and involuntarily, as well as voluntarily, listened in to her confession about the letters, concluding, though not quite clearly, that the Princess was afraid of those letters. At this point he got up, stepped out from behind the screen, much to the Princess's embarrassment. Then he realized that, from there on, the Princess was going to be afraid of him. (N.B. He hates the Princess, i.e., he loves her passionately, which he has confessed to the reader *beforehand.*) But she gets to be even more contemptuous and rude toward him; at this point the insult <which the Youth suffers at the hands> of the young Prince, and the scene with the theft of the diamonds.

During a night of despair, when the Youth is aimlessly walking around the city, the thought of the letters suddenly occurs to him. [Or simply, he accidentally finds a package of Andreev's correspondence.] He recalls that there is a package of letters at the flat. (N.B. He has already *learned* from Him that these letters have great importance.) And there, without any previous intention or plan to take vengeance <on her>, he starts looking for these letters and finds them.

Having found them, he has an idea which begins to torment him. (N.B. Perhaps he is no longer working for the Prince by that time.) From some conversations with Him, very cleverly conducted by the Youth, he sees that the Princess is quite vulnerable to pressure. *At first* he isn't after the money, nor does he want *to have* the Princess, but simply wants to triumph, to show them, to be a success (at first he had been daydreaming of shooting somebody).

(Fantasy about Ungern-Shternberg.)[44] This fantasy is related by *a dreamer,* a most kindly person (couldn't he be Vasin's brother?). Now, *as is* generally *the case with* adolescent *passion for incendiarism,* he is

---

[44] See note 3 of this section.

seized by a feeling of his own power. He does not tell Him that he has found those letters.

Finally, he reveals to Him a plan, still remote and vague, how to violate her.* He consults with Him. The other man is amazed, then falls to thinking, and is stunned. He says nothing. Apparently he doesn't want to say what he is thinking, or give advice. But the idea obviously appeals to Him.

What is *most characteristic* about it all is the fact that the Youth, when telling Him about those letters, gives him nothing really definite, i.e., that he has actually discovered that correspondence, but merely makes a supposition to the effect that if one could find these letters, such-and-such might be done.

When the Youth is discussing that [fantastic] letter to the Princess, meant to lure her to an appointment, He gives him this bit of advice: the letter of invitation ought to contain one or two characteristic expressions quoted from her correspondence with Andreev—"I bet you that'll scare her." "If I had those letters in my hands, I'd know what expressions precisely," He says, but the Youth remains silent. (N.B. The Youth deeply despises Him for the very thing he had himself wanted to do.)

He comes to see him several days later, looking positively alarmed, in order to talk him out of it, and indirectly advises him not to go through with it, i.e., he says that any such idea, if there actually were a person who had such an idea, would amount to a low-down trick. On the occasion of this visit He inadvertently reveals his thoughts to the Youth by asking one *careless* question, which he doesn't notice himself, something like: "Well, what about that business with the letters?" etc. Which suggests to the Youth that he has taken it all seriously, that he is awaiting the effect <of the plot>, that he wishes it to materialize, but by someone else's hands, and that, morally, he is seeking to detach himself even in the eyes of the Youth.

But at this time the Youth is overcome by a feeling of disappointment. He views the idea with the letters with hatred; quarrels and exchanges angry words with Him.

But the thing gives Him no rest. He tells Liza about the letters, though in a roundabout way. Liza has some caustic comments on the baseness of His thinking, as well as regarding the fact that he, apparently, is still interested in the Princess, as a result of which He aban-

---

* *Plan nasiliia,* literally, "a plan of violence."

dons the idea altogether and becomes even more spiteful than before. But then Liza, having won this victory, proceeds to use her charms on the Youth and finds out about the letters from him. The Youth is stunned by the fact that Liza knows <about the letters>, and since no one except He could have told her, he now for the first time begins to suspect that they are in liaison. Friendship, and almost love, between the Youth and Liza (<initially> Liza is putting him on, but later she is very nearly carried away by love herself, for hers is such a nature that a planned game of love, once it has taken possession of her, will rapidly turn into real love, even though it will last only as long as *the game*). It is Liza who concocts the whole scheme. She incites the Youth, arranging for him to be insulted by the Princess again, etc.

They are working on it, but He meets her on the occasion of returning those 200,000 (through Vasin, maybe). The Princess makes an attempt ~~concerning the letters~~ to determine whether the letters might be in His hands, while He, seeing this, and becoming convinced (falsely) that the Princess had sent for him and was trying to effect a reconciliation merely in order to find out about those letters, makes a rude insinuation to this effect. She turns pale and asks Him to leave. He feels insulted, even though he had behaved in a dignified way. He immediately goes to see the Youth and now asks him directly whether or not he has found those letters. (But no more than that, without making any mention of the chance <that he might now be willing to go along> with his plan.) The Youth answers that he hasn't, but tells Liza that He has been asking him. This gives Liza another occasion to make fun of Him: how He is being abused by the Princess, how she has once more shown him the door, etc. But what is most important, He is stunned by the fact that the Youth has told Liza (for who else could have?), and deduces from it that there actually must be a letter. Nevertheless, having discovered that Liza is involved in the affair, He again seeks to dissuade the Youth, and in a (tumultuous) scene swears that he will warn the Princess.

At this point Lambert suddenly <enters the scene>. Liza now joins Lambert and tries to talk the Youth into abandoning <his scheme>. But Lambert is being careless and lets the Youth know about it (thus betraying Liza), for he needs some material help from the Youth.

But having learned from the Youth that He has perhaps already informed the Princess <. . .> (N.B. When He threatened to inform the Princess, the Youth failed to pass this phrase on to Liza, ~~wishing~~ since he was himself struggling with his noble<r> feelings, which he did not expect Liza to have. But then Lambert again made him change his mind.) Lambert comes to see him, asks some direct questions, and even tells him what to do. (He was ill at the time—from <the incident with> the Princess, from Liza's surrender to the little Prince, from the flight of his own wife, etc.) Having analyzed Lambert and realized that this thing is really going to be a scandal (the violation), He agrees <to join in> and says that he has not warned <the Princess>. His struggle with himself: should he warn her or not? All of which He later ~~admits~~ tells the Youth in his confession.

But the Youth relates this to the reader even before the confession.

At this point, a scene with the Princess, the Youth gives Lambert a surprise. Lambert gets up and leaves.

They lure her to the aunt's flat. They know for sure that she doesn't know the aunt's hand. The aunts had left on a pilgrimage. Liza is hiding there, etc.

A note, August 31.

The Youth writes that, in explaining his facts he must inevitably make mistakes, and this is why, if ever possible, only the bare facts will be given.

N.B. August 31. A factual presentation in *the first person,* by the Youth, will undoubtedly reduce the length of the novel, *if I succeed.*

August 31.

Absolutely. Draw attention to the extraordinary amount of disharmony and *nervous tension* in His family, including the Stepmother and Liza: to perpetual grumbling, suffering, and pain which, as far as He is concerned, ~~sometimes~~ almost invariably end right there. Tragic as things may have looked, they come to an *abrupt* end in forgiveness and reconciliation, as he cheerfully forgets everything. But they never end that way for the Stepmother, who always forgives everything but in whose heart the pain keeps lingering and growing. (Liza is there, too.) When he feels the pain growing within, he sometimes awakens the Stepmother at night. Explain her eventual rebellion and flight to the Prince as a result of her derangement: "I am myself a predatory type."

The psychology lies in the fact that she is stunned by Liza's action. She may have suspected for a long time that Liza was living with Him; but though she was suspecting it, she always refused to believe it. On the contrary, some terrible things were happening to her: self-accusations, self-*derision.* On one occasion she actually makes an attempt to confess the *"baseness"* of her suspicions to Him and to Liza, and she tells <them> of her dream (which she had really dreamt) about Liza's liaison with *Him.* But in the end she cannot stand <the

thought of> that dream; she bursts into tears and begs Liza's and His forgiveness on her knees (the Youth is a witness of that scene).

But then, having learned that Liza has been seeing the Prince, and when *He and Liza give themselves away* in her presence (the icons), she is so thunderstruck that she goes out of her mind.

When she leaves <her husband> for the Prince she is already mad, and moreover, in so doing she is following Liza's example. The Prince shows Liza the door. This is where He makes an effort to challenge the Prince to a duel, *but not on account of Liza, but on account of the Stepmother.* The Stepmother dies having been unable to stand these disorders.

August 31.

EXCEEDINGLY IMPORTANT. The first idea of violating the Princess belongs to the Youth, not to Lambert. As for Lambert, he only wants 30,000 (and actually thinks of killing her). In this "idea" there lies "the terrible crime of the Youth."

N.B. "I would have never dared to even open my mouth to say such a thing to the Princess," *writes* the Youth. "I would have started, and then my voice would have failed me. I was imagining it a thousand times, as I was roaming the streets of the city. And yet I decided that I would absolutely bring off the rendezvous. And that's why I was trying not to think of how badly I would be scared, and if I was imagining anything at all, I was imagining only the moments of triumph which were to follow. I was seeking to reassure myself by thinking how *base they were.*"

August 31.

Think over part one, i.e., already the details of details.

TASK. That the reader have, toward the end of part one, a presentiment of the importance of the ending (of the idea) and of a further development of the idea of the novel. A plot. Conclude part one at the most interesting spot.

Another most important note. The Youth must write (the whole novel) in the same unexpected and original fashion as <the episode about> frou-frou.

September 1.

A doubt resolved.

There is nothing pathetic or sympathetic about the novel.

"What do you like yourself?"

The novel is going to be a failure and will turn out *artificial and forced* if it doesn't have the following: the character of the Youth, tortured, overwrought, suffering, and gloomy, with flashes of light and of joy, who has retreated into his somber idea and who, in his clashes with the outside world, sees the problems, the tasks, the horror <of life>. So that only then can one see how the Youth could have come up with such a somber idea.

1st, the childhood of the Youth (absolutely), in a number of fragments throughout the novel, cursorily, how they used to beat him at the boarding school. For instance, when he defends the sick child. His long-suffering late mother, his first friendship, Lambert, etc.—all cursorily.

Sufferings of the Youth at the boarding school, *absolutely* in a cursory manner, and how they nicknamed him *the barn-owl*. Not only cursorily, but even *as if he didn't want to tell about it*. A good many *things that remain unsaid*, but this will make it all the clearer to the reader. On one occasion he tells Lambert about his sufferings at the boarding school (and at high school)—only 6 lines. On another occasion he recalls Brusilov. Later, about how the idea of alienation was conceived by him early, to be precise, when he was dreaming of becoming king of an island known to no one, near the Pole, or in the middle of a lake in Central Africa.

Couldn't he be Brusilov?

He is Brusilov, which he mentions only once in his notes (Lambert is the son of Souchard; that's where they became friends). He never told Him about it, never complained, <being> proud.

"At times I thought that I might take my revenge on Souchard, even burn his house; I was giving it a good deal of thought, but couldn't make up my mind. Neither could I make up my mind to run away. (I am a coward.)"

His character is gloomy, hypochondriac, nervous, suspicious. But <occasionally> a ray of light <would break> through the clouds. Youth. And, finally, the great idea wins out. But he has terrible pride, so that he does not complain to anybody. The tone of his notes is somber and naïve. Sometimes naïvely ironic, but sincerely so. A seeker and a wanderer. His father was then a Brusilov, a grand seigneur (of the middle bracket). *Il faut le rosser.*[45]

He is also the one who dreams about Ungern-Shternberg.[46]

"I must admit that I am a terrible dreamer and a coward; I am admitting this *before myself*. If I had to admit it before other people,

---

[45] French: "You have to beat him."

[46] See note 3 of this section.

I'd rather die. I could never imagine myself in my thoughts as anything but the head man, as a hero. I could never accept a secondary role. And therefore, when it comes to making a fortune, it must absolutely be a million."

He is from a very good family and not a government official, nor a lawyer, but a wanderer all his life, who has spent two average fortunes in his lifetime. Never managed to make a career. To be sure, he did manage to start a law practice.

See the biography. Combine with the inheritances and with Brusilov.

His aunt removed him from Souchard's <boarding school> and placed him in a high school (cursorily). In high school, they used to beat him up. Tattle-tale. Barn-owl. Lambert. Souchard has died, and Lambert only has his mother.

The Youth is both petty and profound; he knows a lot, and is naïve; and gloomy. Overwrought. But resurrection and light in the end. *And do not* explain why light and resurrection.

The Youth has his own flat. A doorman in a government building. An unctuous fellow. (It is this doorman who takes the kidnaped boy over to His place.) The boy was with the doorman's sick daughter. The boy was later begging to be taken to that girl, and the Youth used to take him there. Death of the little girl, who insists that the boy say good-bye to her. The Youth relates in detail and with severe seriousness how he arranged for that last meeting between the two children. This is how He and the doorman became acquainted.

The doorman is an unctuous fellow, not too talkative. The Youth respects and loves him and only with him alone is he completely sincere. The doorman has a frequent visitor, a certain lieutenant who keeps begging people for 20 kopeks ~~and he once~~. This lieutenant tells the story about ~~the laborer~~ that boat in England, about that rock, etc. The doorman has a wife, a woman of easy virtue. After the death of their daughter, he burns her to death on her kitchen stove.

After the boy has run <away> for the last time, he is on his way to drown himself and drops in on the doorman, thinking that he might find the Youth there. He finds nothing at the doorman's flat. The Youth collects the boy's <tales of his> wanderings.*

---

* The whole paragraph is quite awkward in the original.

The Youth NEVER* was in prison, and was only superficially connected with the Lambert affair.

The Youth. Notes. In the railway carriage. "It appears to me that what I was saying to her was pretty stupid. It is a strange thing; I still don't know how to talk to women, whereas I can say clever things when talking to men. But in a woman's presence I always get mad at something right in the very beginning, and then I go on to talk a lot of nonsense. This must be corrected. But this is of course what was causing my hatred for <all> women. And altogether, I am terribly vain. I am vain and give myself away in trivial things, but I know how to keep <my> great idea a secret."

When I met this character for the first time ~~Liza~~ (Liza)—that was a long time ago, almost six months now.

Make sure to insert the phrase "[to be sure,] I have read a lot."

The Youth HAS GRADUATED FROM HIGH SCHOOL, but he does not want to go to the university, because Andreev who had been supporting him had died and he did not want to be supported by Him, while the aunts had written him to Moscow that they could not send him any money. Secondly, he failed to enroll in the university (even gladly so) because he wanted *to tackle his idea* as soon as possible.

The Youth was among the best students through all the grades of high school, except the last, where he barely passed his examinations. (Purposely. *The golden mean.*) But he did pass.

He won't talk to the Stepmother for three days at a time, while having the intention not to talk to her for 10 days (he comes running to the Youth, telling him everything). Or else, he would wake her up in the middle of night to lecture to her (while she is sick).

(N.B. The Stepmother is so intelligent that she can understand this psychology perfectly well.)

September 1.

PLAN OF THE FIRST CHAPTERS.

N.B.! Be aware of the main point in each chapter and stick to it. Leaving things unsaid.

The railway carriage, Liza, arrival in Petersburg, etc.

Reception at the aunts'. He goes to see Him, but He isn't in, <only> the Stepmother and Liza.

Goes to see Vitia, Vasin, goes back to see Him in the evening, embarrassed because it is so late. A comical situation because of its

* Underlined three times.

being so late, and because of how it is settled (the Youth does some pouting).

He returns home to the aunts. *The letters.* Staying for the night. The aunts give him a tongue-lashing. He decides to rent himself a flat.

On the next morning, a flat. The flea-market. *Make money.*

He (the day before): "Come and have dinner with us." He comes—*they are quarreling,* no dinner. "Let's go to a tavern."

At the tavern, they become acquainted. *He* is showing off.

Returning home. The chambermaid has already been fired. Liza. On the child. The Youth leaves ~~for his own flat with a strange feeling~~.

The Prince and the Princess (riddles everywhere). He listens in on the conversation about those relics and makes friends with the Prince.

Insults on the Princess's part ~~he is young~~.

Again at Dolgushin's. They talk<ed> about the young Prince.

He stays for the night at the aunts'. The Princess's visit. He comes out from behind the screen.

At His place. The scene with the child. He rents a flat. He takes the child with him. The child is taken back.

He is convinced that He married her for her money and that his wife is being supported by the old Prince. "What business is this of mine?"

He gets together with Him and ~~terribly would like to~~ reproaches him for letting the Stepmother be supported by the old Prince. His aunt chases him out of her house for that.

At this point he learns that He has returned 200,000. (N.B. This happens early.)

Feeling insulted and sad, having quarreled with Him and insulted the Stepmother, he <sulks> in his corner.

~~About Souchard, about his daydreams. Statement of his idea.~~ He comes to see him. He ~~Liza comes to see him~~, who had insulted *Him,* tells Him everything: about Souchard, about Brusilov, and about his idea. A fascinating evening. At this point he asks Him about Vasin.

On that fascinating evening, he asks Him about Vasin, for the theories of those people, while they haven't shaken *his own idea,* still are causing him some anxiety and doubt.

What is most important, on that fascinating evening the Youth is impressed by the fact that He is not treating him with condescension, that He won't brush off his questions with biting remarks, but answers them all, even his question~~s~~ about petroleum, etc.

(N.B. *A task.* But how to coordinate "a boy <who feels> insulted" with "a fascinating evening"? *Answer.* By letting Him ask the boy's forgiveness, so that the latter cautiously embraces Him, by then letting Him confess all his weaknesses to the Youth and, finally, by letting the Youth make him promise, upon leaving, to take good care of the boy.)

Meeting with *the fool* at the Princess's (still in part one). The Fool used to visit the Youth. The Youth tells Him about the Fool. They both laugh. They see the Fool.

2d part.

Development of His boy. The Dolgushins. Vasin. He almost abandons his idea. He quits respecting Him, but is still interested in Him. With Liza. Women are whores. The Princess. The diamonds. Rejected. 200,000. At this point, Lambert. A meeting. For the first time, the idea of *revenge* occurs to him. He puts his own idea aside for the time being.

N.B. Only *in the beginning* does he ardently adhere to *his own idea;* later he puts it off, *being busy with other things. It comes back to him* during <the incident with> the diamonds. He is cheated at an auction. A popular scene. However, though he has abandoned the practical pursuit of his idea, he continues to defend it theoretically, before Vasin and everyone else.

The unctuous doorman teaches the Youth to disdain wealth and great intellect, pointing out the happiness and freedom offered by the possession of a firm will. "Pray!" (A great character.) And yet he, who possesses willpower, burns his own wife to death on her kitchen stove.

~~In the 2d part~~ (1st part. The Youth confesses his idea, and later is sad *that he has told it;* conclude it with some characteristic items from his biography. High school. The desert island, etc. <He has had> the idea for three years.)

In the first part, absolutely include also some highly spectacular action. Rude behavior at the Prince's. Insults at the hands of the Princess. The young Prince (give a beating.) Vasin. He steals a child. Tells his father that he is married to a kept woman. Reconciliation. He reveals his plan of getting rich. His sadness about having revealed an idea which he had been keeping himself for three years. *He* leaves having said nothing. Conclude with his biography.

[Andreev's letter.]

In the 2d part, the Princess. Meetings with Him. His family life. Liza's rude behavior. *He* disenchants him regarding Rothschild, also Vasin. But the Princess detests him, a real clash with the young Prince. The diamonds. He says something impertinent about her depravity—something frightfully rude. He is shown the door. Nights. Revenge. "Let me become an enemy of humanity."

[The boy is in his care all along.]

An unctuous soldier. The diamonds are found on the following morning. But he has behaved so rudely that he leaves. (N.B. He was threatening the Princess about his knowledge of Andreev's letter. He had learned about this letter from Him.) (N.B. Suddenly he finds out about His liaison with Liza. Liza tells about the letter while they are at his place. The beginnings of a plot. A rupture. He withdraws from everybody. Wanderings. "I'll shoot myself." Lambert.)

[Meeting with the little girl. Death of the little girl.]

September 2.

Two questions. If told *in the third person,* will it be interesting? If the Youth tells the story (*in the first person*), that alone will make it interesting. And more original. Also, it shows the character better. *In the first,* or in the third person? (in *the first person* is better even as far as Brusilov is concerned, more original).

N.B. The arrangement of the narrative would be more original with the Youth telling the story. Jumping from one detail to the other. Such arrangement is revealing of his own character, *but as for the chapter arrangement* <. . .>

In *the first person* it would be so much more original, and show more love; also, it would require more artistic skill, and would be terribly bold, and shorter, easier to arrange; moreover, it would make the character of *the Youth* as the main figure of the novel so much clearer, and the meaning of the idea as the cause upon which the novel hinges more obvious. But won't this originality bore the reader? Will the reader be able to stand this *first person* through 35 quires? And what is most important, can the basic ideas of this novel be fully and naturally expressed by a twenty-year-old writer?

~~N.B.? The Youth is writing four years after the event, which explains how he has managed to comprehend Him, His ideas, etc.~~

The Youth brings Vasin together with his friend Shveitsarov,* and what do you know, Shveitsarov is in complete accord with his doctrine, except one point, "that everything should be broken to pieces": "It will go to pieces all by itself." "Either he didn't under-

* This name is derived from *shveitsar,* "doorman," which connects this character with the nameless doorman of a few pages back.

stand a word of what I said, or he understands more than I do," Vasin remarked to the Youth. "At any rate, he has got some sort of an idea of his own. These are the most dangerous people." (?) [*Idée*]

[Idea] The young Prince, instead of responding to His challenge, offers to buy His wife from him.

If *in the first person,* it will become necessary to go less into the development of various ideas which the Youth could not naturally transmit in the form in which they were uttered, and to let him transmit only the heart of the matter.

A narrative *in the first person* is more original by virtue of the fact that the Youth may very well keep skipping, in ultra-naïve fashion, <from the main line of the narrative> to all kinds of anecdotes and details, proper to his development and immaturity, but ~~quite~~ impossible for an author conducting his narrative in regular fashion.

The Youth's feelings for Him can be more direct, and expressed more clearly and more simply (*and more unexpectedly*), if the narrative is conducted in *the first person;* for instance, suddenly and unexpectedly: "I was grieving bitterly about His being so frivolous," and later: "This is where I realized that he was being consumed by some idea ~~which~~ and that he wasn't so frivolous at all, but what precisely was it?"

And in the end: "Disorder of the soul as a result of unbelief" (as a result of atheism). "Strange words! I would not have understood them, or would have considered them meaningless, hadn't I seen in Him a living example."

The Youth to himself, in the end: "I simply believe in life, I want to live with all my might. But what ought one to do as one lives?—that's the problem. That's something I don't know. Could it be no more than making a living? That's not enough. Simply love everybody, and inasmuch as I don't know how to do that, but want to, to spend one's whole life learning how to love, and then—well, I don't know what then, I am still too young."

"And first of all, I think, I'll go to the university . . ."

~~He~~ If in the third person, draw <your characters> in a detached way, as if concealing your sympathy, restraining yourself, with as much originality as ever possible both in the tone of the narrative as well as in the *arrangement of the order* of the scenes and subjects to be described.

(N.B. It was the Stepmother who placed him with the old Prince.

The latter had long been asking to have a young secretary.) The Old Prince had actually told the Stepmother: "Why won't you find a young secretary for me?"

He told the Youth that the Prince was in his second childhood.

~~In the first part~~ In any case, pay attention to His character in the first part. (Insofar as He is not as yet expressing himself either through Christianity, or through any intrigues.)

One ought to plant something *dazzling* and *mysterious* about Him in the first part.

A valuable note. This is already in the first part, when He fails to visit the Youth for fear "that he might give Him a scolding" (a trait which *touches* the Youth by its simple-heartedness).

Also in the first part, the Youth tells Him that He is an old man and that He was more dazzling before, when he saw Him the last time. "You were still walking with a limp." ~~*Il faut le r*~~

"Yes, my dear, I still loved you."

"You said to Souchard: *"Il faut le rosser."*[47]

The Youth steals the letter from Andreev's package. The Princess had said to the aunt: "My entire fate depends on that letter. He is going to show it to my husband, who will deprive me of everything. He is capable of doing it. (Can't you find it somewhere? Couldn't it be among some slips of papers?)." Here, about being a kept <woman?>. The aunt takes her part. The Princess tells the aunt outright that she had suggested that the Prince be placed in an insane asylum. Her husband would never forgive that. The Youth recalls having seen a package behind the icons. He tells Him about it. He explains to Him what it is the Princess is afraid of, and He is terribly interested in the whole thing.

"Are you really in love with her?"

However, the Youth does not tell Him that he has got the letter.

AN IDEA. Couldn't it be Vasin to whom he tells the story of his childhood (when the child has fallen asleep)? "I shall never tell my father?" But he does not tell Vasin about his idea. But he does tell his father about it. And when He has left, the idea has lost some of its lustre. But to make up for that: "*I* told <him> nothing about Brusilov."

The character will turn out more genuine. And only toward the end of the novel He tells him: "Vasin told me everything, everything

---

[47] French: "You have to beat him."

(about Brusilov), on the very next day, asking me to save you from getting into trouble. This is how I've been saving you" (i.e., He has himself led him on to commit a crime).

He tells Vasin <his story> in this form: first, about Brusilov, with restrained irony, but everything. And then, how he used to withdraw into himself, how he used to daydream (here one might let the Youth devote a separate chapter to his daydreaming, but let him address it to the reader, rather than to Vasin). He tells Vasin only about Brusilov. Vasin is feeling him out: withdrawn, wouldn't he make a good socialist and conspirator?

"Too bad you haven't met any people. Nor have you read any good books. Nor developed a good idea."

"I've got an idea."

"Which is?"

"I'll tell you later. Only it isn't any of yours."

"Well, it is time to go to bed," says Vasin (white nights).

When He comes to see the Youth (this is when, for several days, He is very tender to him), He suddenly says: "I know, Vasin has told me about you."

He flushes: "I didn't want to tell him. I don't want to beg for anybody's pity. Why, and you weren't such an old man either." And he suddenly bursts into tears.

An idea: "Vasin has told me about <your> idea, and about all of your ideas. Don't you worry, you've been trying to withdraw from people. I understand, I am not laughing." He confides his idea <to Him>.

When he has left, he feels sorry that he has told him about his idea. "Why did Vasin tell him about me? At least it wasn't *I*. But I did start crying. That's bad. But what was bothering me most of all was the fact that I had told him about my idea. Eh, too bad I did tell him."

And later, in the 2d part, many times about the idea (raising it to the level of a poetic idea in the reader's mind).

Then, Lambert. *Finale.* The idea has lost its lustre.

But as far as *He* is concerned, he tells him, prior to the confession and to <the meeting with> Vasin, only about: *"Il faut le rosser."*[48]

"This was a kindly, a most kindly Frenchman."

"Yes, kindly."

"You seem to disagree."

---

[48] French: "You have to beat him."

"Not at all."

"That's why I placed you with him, because he was a kind man."

In *the first person,* the Youth ~~can~~ says: "I am of course incapable of stating all these ideas as they were expressed." And later: Even in a *first person* narrative he can write as if he were writing *in the third person,* describing scenes that occurred before his arrival, and scenes which he did not himself witness. For instance, in this fashion: "What had happened was this: Vasin went to see Dolgushin and told him." Or, "once, the Princess entered her husband's <study>, saying," etc.

If the novel is to be told in the *first person,* the whole poem lies in this: how I fell, and how I was saved.

I have called it: Disorder. This is His word. *He* used this word more often than any other.

If the novel is to be told in the third person, something everybody *is sick and tired of;* and the narrative devices, too, are available in literature; besides, it will be more difficult to make the Youth look original, i.e., to explain why he has been selected.

About the letter, there absolutely ought to be some casual mention of it in part one.

It could be done so that he has already stolen the letter and doesn't feel in the least guilty about it; only much later his conscience begins to bother him.

[668] But there should absolutely be something about the letter in part one.

Basic and most important. When He learns that Vasin has told <his father> about Souchard, He feels hurt.* "I couldn't have thought of any pain that could have stung me harder. I had been left with only one thing: the pride of knowing that I had suffered. But I don't say a word, nor am I reproaching Him, and suddenly everything is gone. ~~I cried~~ I began to cry (from being deeply moved, but also from anger. Father). Then I got mad and in a fit of temper told him about my idea. When he had left, I was feeling sad. There's your father, yet . . . and angrily—and I dropped off to a heavy sleep. An evil spirit was already hovering above me."

N.B. "I was in a somber and excited mood, and how could I do

---

* The Youth seems to be the subject of this sentence even though "He" is capitalized.

these foolish things—the old Prince's visit at <Mme.> Andrieux's."* This helps to draw the character of the Youth. Also how he went with that wench.

BUT THE TONE** [Here] of the narrative shows that all this happened *a year ago,* i.e., he is now, a year later, in a way still a youth, yet he looks down upon the youth of a year ago.

N.B. He can make this remark himself (write it down), in his notes.

He—after having revealed <to the Youth> that Vasin has told *Him:*

"My friend, I am ready to ask your forgiveness 1,000 times, but what will come of that? You are such a..." (Yet it was He who had been looking for me.)

He: "At any rate, you can be sure that now..."

My eyes went flashing: "I want nothing... to hell with Vasin, I had this one thing left." And I began to cry, and cried, and cried.

"I have yet to meet a man whom I didn't hurt in some way!"

"I want to become a Rothschild."

He: "Well, so what? ~~or perhaps your plan~~ That isn't at all new, or perhaps it is your method that makes your plan <a novelty>."

The Youth: "No, there isn't anything special about my methods either."

He: "Well, and then, having grown rich, you will live in luxury and—be happy?"

[February] "Not at all, I'll be wearing sackcloth. (Women.) I'll never touch a woman."

N.B. Very true psychologically that after having cried, and cried he begins to explain his plan *for spite,* and is being ~~somber~~ abrupt, frowning, insolent. But when He leaves, they embrace and both begin to cry.

What is most important, He begins to cry walking down the back staircase.

I fell asleep with mixed feelings. But on the very next day, toward nightfall, my *mixed feelings* turned into being angry with myself about having cried; also about having told him about my idea, and angry with Vasin. And if there had been any chance at all for me to go away somewhere, away from them all, and as fast as possible, to

* Ungrammatical and unclear.
** Underlined twice.

leave Petersburg in a hurry, I would have left for some faraway place and would have stayed there all by myself, without them, forever. But already there was something (~~attracting~~ i.e., the Princess) attracting me.

And then the next chapter immediately in the following fashion: "How curious that I was ashamed about having cried, but not ashamed about having, already then, committed a villainy (the letter)."

Also in the first part, <present> Him in a most impressive and mysterious fashion.

Most important: Between the scenes with the child, He comes to see the Youth merely to let him know that He has learned *everything* from Vasin. Between those two times, during a period of several days, he <once> met ~~Him~~ the Youth, looking angry and frowning, and said in passing: "You are seeking solitude."

The Youth was struck by the fact that these were Vasin's words. And suddenly it becomes clear that Vasin has told Him everything. But the reason why He comes to see him is that He wants to tell him about Liza, about the family; the Youth asks to be spared <these details>, and that's when He lets him know that Vasin has told him.

(Ideas.) (Plans.)

Absolutely. N.B.? After this has happened, the Youth immediately writes Him a letter saying that he wishes to have nothing to do with him. ~~Absolutely put this in, but not after the meetings when He asks: "Seeking solitude, eh?"~~ On the *very* next day after he had told *him about his idea.* And all the next day he is worrying: "Why did I tell him about my idea?"

He is a most depraved man who has factually had Liza.

He is terribly religious, which he shows most specifically in one chapter. (N.B. The Youth hears <Him?> read <the passage> about <Christ's> temptation by the Devil. It leaves him stunned. He goes to see Him to have a talk about Christianity.

(A *passionate* chapter.)

Finale. "The main point is that I haven't held a single conviction in all my life. Not just the fact that I haven't had any convictions; this in itself isn't so bad, but rather the fact that I have become convinced that I could never have had any, and what is even worse: that I can never have any <in the future> either. There's an idea for you. It is hard to bear."

Already, in the first part, the Princess insults him. "Oh, how I hated her. I felt like jumping up and striking her. But since no one will ever see these notes, I am putting down the fact that at that very moment a strange sensation passed through my heart: I would like to have jumped up and started kissing the spot where she had been sitting. I wouldn't have told this even to my confessor... Well, let me then put down everything: that's what I did."

September 4.

THE MANUSCRIPT IS FOUND AT A HOSPITAL, AFTER THE WRITER'S DEATH.

If it is in the first person, a most original (the more original and uncontrolled, the better) *conciseness,* as well as the whole WAYWARDNESS OF THE NOTES will be preserved.

If in the first person: "I have now outgrown all these things, and so I must not be ashamed (but there are some memories of which I am very much ashamed)."

The notes <are written> a year later, at a hospital.

"I'll recover and start a new life."

Vasin and Dolgushin have been arrested. *He* has lost stature in his eyes, and when Lambert tackles the idea head-on, yet on an enormous scale, the Youth: "Eh, come what may!" "Disorder has overtaken me." And what is most important, he *triumphs* over the Princess.

At the end of part one. "I cried and cried, but He left. Why did I tell Him? In all my life I wasn't going to tell Him, and be proud. I had been dreaming about how I was going to be proud."

[See 668] "Now, a year later, when I have *perhaps* become an entirely different person, even now the thought that I have revealed to my father that proud anguish of mine (about Brusilov) keeps lacerating me and ~~decided~~ decidedly fills me with shame. Shame about not having been able to hold back. Could it be that this shame is lingering to this day because I feel, even now, that I might perhaps not be able to restrain myself either in this <kind of a situation>, or in any other, weak-willed youth that I am? No, a good deal of hard work still lies ahead for me, if I want to become a man of willpower and fortitude."

"Now, when I may perhaps decide to abandon my idea, I still feel sorry that I revealed it on that occasion. I almost stooped to where I was seeking praise <from Him>, although I was of course seeking only advice, just seeking to make a check of myself. I did not, however, tell Vasin about it, but rather Him, even though I trusted Vasin more at the time ~~in spite of which He~~. To be sure, He, too, was then beginning to impress me greatly. But the most curious thing for me now is the fact that I was then fretting about my weakness, considering it a low-down action, while having actually committed a truly despicable action (the letter), yet never giving it a single remorseful thought."

"When He listened to my idea, there was no derision or condescension in his attitude. But still, He isn't my brother. There was a feeling that He, too, had *his* idea, which He would never express, but to which He was so devoted that he would consider everything that is transitory, including my confession, the trivia as well as the tragedies of life, to be secondary while holding *it** to be the most important. Yet at the same time, wasn't He plunging into this life, even to the point that one couldn't help calling him a petty man, and a gossip?"

He, in a conversation with Vasin: "There are, however, some inexplicable things..." And at this point, <Christ's> temptation by the Devil from the Gospels. This is already in a conversation with Vasin which takes place in the presence of the Youth, who can't help thinking to himself: "He won't talk to me that way, but he will with Vasin, because he is more clever than I am."

[For part two.] Vasin responds with silence. The Youth notices, furthermore, that though He does produce some evidence to prove the supernatural origin of Christianity, he does so in passing, not in any great haste, or excessive zeal, to propagate <his idea>, but merely in the course of conversation: "Take it into consideration, or leave it; personally, I really don't care what you do." I.e., He always acts that way, though in this particular case he got somewhat carried away, and later felt hurt about it: "There, the two of us were jabbering away, while he kept silent all the time."

I: "Why do they keep silent? Because they're dull or because they are very clever?"

He: "It's because they have nothing to talk about. They know everything and have every decision made for many thousands of years ahead. What's the use of talking, if this is so?"

The Youth is so pleased that he laughs when He has thus put down socialism. But He comes back to see him and again says: "The great idea is at hand, <it is> at the door."

"And still, He <is saying it> just so," the Youth remarks. But since he is interested in the matter himself and, besides, is anxious to find out definitively what His convictions really are, the Youth keeps pestering Him with questions about Christianity. *He* responds with the <two> shopkeepers. But still in the same, unhurried way, cursorily

---

* Translator's italics.

and abruptly, as if He were going to say: "Why won't you leave me alone!" "He does not, of course, have any passion for propaganda," the Youth observes in his notes, "but He himself is of course being burnt out and tormented by these ideas."

By the way: The Youth, too, puts down these observations in his notes as if it were in passing; for example, he mentions this not immediately after the chapter about the <two> shopkeepers (which he breaks off without making any conclusions), but somewhere else, two or three chapters later.

He, about Belinsky[49].... "And most of all, self-adoration. Most of all, the fact that science had not even started in our country then."

He comes to see the Youth one day and talks about the French and about the coming of socialism. "It is at hand; it is at the door. You must all be ready for it."

The icons. When the Youth enters the room for the first time, he notices a magnificent icon-case. He assumes that it is the Stepmother's. Learns that it is His. It was this particular icon-case that got chopped up later.

Absolutely include something about a poor family, or something of that order, which He is secretly helping, being angry with himself for having done it.

After all this heartbreak He suddenly disappears in the finale. The Youth learns that he has gone to a monastery. A month later hangs himself in the monastery.

He brings 25,000 to the Youth. He won't take the money. Or does he return it later? THINK ABOUT IT. Or (He) gives it to the aunt suspecting that the Youth might, conceivably, "accomplish" the stupidity of refusing it.

September 6.

Definitively: *in the first person.*

SOMETHING VERY IMPORTANT. Never in the whole course of the novel does the Youth totally relinquish his idea about Rothschild.

---

[49] Vissarion G. Belinsky (1811–48), the most important Russian critic in the nineteenth century. He was largely responsible for the reputations of Dostoevsky, Gogol, Lermontov, the later Pushkin, Turgenev, and others. He was an immense presence in Russian criticism and literature, and his influence may be compared to that of Dr. Johnson in English literature and Sainte-Beuve in French literature. In his later years Dostoevsky nurtured bitter feeling toward Belinsky and wrote disparagingly of him. He held him responsible for having led him on wrong paths during Dostoevsky's early years.

This *idea fixa* is his *solution* of *everything,* of all problems and difficulties. It is based upon his feeling of pride, which has taken shape in <his> idea of withdrawal <from society>. [*He* says that to the Youth.]

[February, 3d and 4th part.]

Arrange the whole novel so that this idea would be of *outstanding* importance in the novel. Outstanding precisely for the reason that it never leaves the Youth, having a firm grip on him: shall he perish or shan't he? This is why he suffers so much from his doubts in the course of the novel, first on account of Vasin's arguments, then again on account of His <arguments>. And this is why, occasionally, the Youth will suddenly forsake the most curious events which he is in the process of relating and in which he is himself very much interested, and will begin, most emphatically, (though, apparently, for no good reason at all) to state his doubts:

"If I cheated that soldier, buying from him and selling to someone else, as He is telling me—why, this is a paradox, for doesn't the whole world live and cheat that way? But then, is the whole world an authority <for me>? It suffices that I have become aware of the fact that I have cheated. That means that one must abandon everything, walk around clothed in rags, keep working without even asking for higher pay. Surely so, for one must be true to an idea which one has conceived. But if this is so, why doesn't He go to a monastery or accomplish feats, once he believes in Christianity? Why are all socialists such skinflints (here, give some examples)?"

~~No~~ *He,* to the Youth: "Probably according to the principle that now, in our present society, no different life is possible, for it is society that is at fault. But when society is rebuilt, we shall all be living differently."

"So then, I am not guilty of a dishonorable deed; it is society that is guilty. This is why Vasin plans to destroy it. Vasin, incidentally, is sacrificing everything *to his idea;* why, he could be sitting around idly, too, saying that 'it is all the fault of society.' No, apparently that is no excuse. And, incidentally, is it dishonorable, and is there indeed something dishonorable about my idea?"

And later: "I asked Him (as late as in the *finale,* at a time when He was in a depressed state), and received the answer that it won't pay to be honorable for a time, in view of <the fact that all planets eventually become> ice-covered rocks. How terribly does the thought of those ice-covered rocks torment Him!"

~~What do you care for those rocks the Youth~~

Very necessary. The Youth communicates His idea about the ice-covered rocks to the old Prince. The latter replies: *"Mon cher,* I have always thought so, *c'est une idée.* But why does he ~~forget~~ worry about it? Let them fly through space, let them fly. I won't be around, and none of us will. Should we really worry about what's going to happen in tens of thousands of years, while dinner is just being served? Why, our dinner may get cold!" The Youth quotes these words to Him, and He laughs a lot, and says: "This old arsehole has naturally solved all the problems, but the thing is that not everybody has an appetite for dinner under these circumstances." ~~Yet it is funny that I can't solve them, i.e., that I am not willing to live under these conditions.~~

He tells the Youth in the *finale,* in a depressed mood, that his idea of withdrawal <from society> is inferior for its *pride,* full forgiveness, renunciation of vengeance.* Besides <the idea of becoming a> Rothschild contains a rather contemptible element of petty concern with one's own material security.

The Youth, to Him: "Does it really pay to be honest, or even proud? And what about those ice-covered rocks? Isn't it better to live thinking about one's own arse only?"

"And what do you do with your heart?" He says.

"You're right, I've overlooked that! We are really in a fix, aren't we?"

And once he is alone, the Youth says: "I want to live, but how? Is it worth it to be honest? Will my idea really prevent me from doing good? Is it really harmful to other people? Of course, society is at fault, but... I still don't know if I am going to accept those 25,000."

He is walking along, and <then,> the embankment, the setting sun, ecstasy.

"If you are saying that it isn't worth while to love mankind for a short moment (ice-covered rocks), you have no real love of mankind."

"I have been told that before. I have heard that. Only, you see, a natural inclination to love mankind and any other great idea is of course an unchallenged fact, much as such natural functions as sneezing, shitting, eating; yet, in view of the fateful inevitability of the prospect of ice-covered rocks, such love of mankind resembles a con-

---

* Not quite clear in the original. The Russian text does not allow a translation ". . . inferior . . . to full forgiveness, renunciation of vengeance."

dition of bondage and gives me no satisfaction. So that, perhaps, I may decide in favor of rebellion rather than love."

"I deny everything," He says, "and I am desperate about not having anything to cling to, yet at the same time I am <so> attached to everything. 'Ashamed to be alive, yet in fact full of vitality.' "

"You are lying: a fresh young girl smells of apples" (somebody tells the Youth).

Frou-frou, he used to spit on it, or avoid it. Stooped to such pettiness. Anger at <such> injustice.

In the railway carriage. Liza. "I quit talking with Liza. I sat down and fell to thinking *about my idea."*

Or: "I used to run up and down the boulevard with that student, because I considered all this to be infinitely inferior to my idea, and consequently, something irrelevant, something that didn't really seem to pertain to me. Here I want to note that this daydreaming about my idea had, already for a long time, caused me to be somehow distrait and just barely in touch with the world, as if it were in passing only. I was actually addressing myself to many things with a strange condescension; even to many things that should have, on the contrary, deserved my full attention, being in effect of the most immediate concern to me."

"My idea, or my plan, made me take a train and change my whole life without a bit of excitement. As I was approaching Petersburg I was thinking rather about how I would begin to apply my idea, than about how I was going to meet *them all,* and what I was going to tell them. ~~Strange~~ The moment I found myself in the streets of Petersburg the question how I would meet them became first and foremost in my mind. I am mentioning this fact because it was so strange and because my meeting with them and, most important, with Him was the beginning of a new life for me, and the object of my fantasies during my entire life even since my earliest childhood."

"Oh, how I had fancied what I would say to my father at our first meeting! I had been daydreaming about that even while I was still in the first grade of high school. But I said nothing and was very pleased ~~with it~~ <with myself> that I had behaved so proudly." (N.B. This ought to come in definitely still in part one.) At the end of part one, possibly about the idea, about Souchard and Brusilov.

In the railway carriage. "I am yielding and petty in trivia, but when it comes to essentials I never give in. I remember very well what I was thinking to myself as I was looking at Liza (with the train approaching Petersburg): 'And yet I haven't told you about my idea.' I was awfully pleased with that thought, so much so that all my rather petty anger at ~~Liza~~ that young girl, which I had been feeling, suddenly evaporated. Later on I became convinced that my anger hadn't been so petty after all, and <that> I had been right. Anger at what? At her sitting there? Both at the fact that she was a lady and that she looked so unapproachable; in a word, I was rebelling against tyranny and injustice. For, if you take a broad enough view of it, that's what it amounts to.'"

"This is Pavel Fyodorovich Fyodorov. He has graduated from high school, but has decided against going to the university" (this is how He introduces the Youth to the Stepmother).

"My friend, I am ready to support you. But you have rejected my help."

"But haven't my aunts been supporting me?"

"Come to think of it, it's true, right from the time you were at Souchard's. That Souchard, he was a kind man, wasn't he?"

"The further I went in explaining my idea to Him, the more it seemed to me that I was betraying something, betraying my idea, and the further I was getting in developing it, the more I was losing my faith in it. When he had left, I returned sad, almost jaded."

He tells the Youth, in his own *uncontrolled* confessions: "Oh, in those moments, how I wish to catch a serious fever, or just any fever: I'd be lying there, and they'd be pacing the room at my bedside, suffering the pangs of a guilty conscience, trembling and moaning with fear and remorse, crushed and punished. But the Lord isn't sending me either any serious fever, or even the merest *febris catarhalis*, since I am healthy as a bull!"

In the railway carriage:

I—and suddenly I blurted out, I don't myself know why: "You had recognized me, of course."

Liza: "Since I am not talking to you and don't even want to look at you, you naturally had to get the clever idea that I had recognized you."

A bag has been stolen. (The fool.) Everybody is looking around. Liza sits down. ~~Liza sits down~~ A small bag, it has been stolen.

To Liza: "Pardon me, it seems that I put it <somewhere>. There it is! How did it get here?"

Liza: "If you're saying that you put it there."

"Yes, but how did it get behind you?"

"Why, if you're saying that you put it there."

"Could be, but... it is behind you."

"I sat down not noticing it... It is so small."

"Not noticing it? That's strange."

"You are a fool." It made no impression, but he gave me a look.

The Fool: "Ahem...How can that be... Ahem. There were some silver things in there, but they're still there. Look: this is silver."

"Look, you have been told once."

Liza: "Let him."

"I didn't mean to. I was just saying that to lose things... you must agree... there's some silver here... and I could think." He stopped. He was talking not only as if he had been dissuaded but also a little as if he were convinced that she had actually stolen <the bag>.

September 6. N.B.

N.B. Tomorrow think it over on the train, and gather your notes.* "Why, and the phrases, too, were conventional, *heard from someone else."*

He: "That means, *chacun chez soi, chacun pour soi,*[50] and whatever will come of it, will be."

[February, 3d part.] Socialism consists of ~~having destroyed~~ leaving the confines of Christian civilization, which implies its destruction, and creating one's own, based on a denial of <the existence of> the kingdom of heaven, and limiting oneself to mere earthly <concerns>. An outright Antichrist.

The Youth is familiar with some poets, writers; he has read some books, though in haphazard fashion. None of his schoolmates ever took an interest in these things. He knows physics very well. He is very good at mathematics. [101X]

On the boulevard, with Liza, obscenities. "This was a swinish trick" (comments the author).

In the first part there isn't any preaching of Christianity; yet, only the Youth accuses Him to his face that He is a Jesuit. Whereupon He asks the Youth: "Who told you that I preach?"

"I heard that still in Moscow."

But it would be good to bring out some brief, yet weighty flashes of a forced Christianity.

"Petersburg. What good is Petersburg to me?" Contempt for Petersburg. (This is when he is leaving the station.)

---

* Unclear in the original. Perhaps: "On the next day, think over what had happened on the train . . ."

[50] French: "Everyone at home, everyone for himself."

"I heard that still in Moscow," <says the Youth> but He asks some more questions, and there remains no doubt that it was the Princess who told him. He is visibly impressed by this circumstance, so much so that the Stepmother is all flushed and it looks as if there is going to be a scene. Liza immediately injects some more poison, as she ~~remarks about the Princess~~ mentions some (very accurate) facts, drily and concisely, concerning what the Princess is saying about him right now, what she used to say before, what she plans to say in the future, and what further steps she is probably going to take. A terrible quarrel. The boy. Reminding <Him> of the chambermaid (who was chased from the house the day before, or two days ago). A scandal. Liza ~~to them~~ purposely addresses the Youth, telling him <about that incident>, thus making the Stepmother relate <her version of the story>, too. The Youth, somberly and abruptly, asks not to be made a party <to this argument>. Suddenly, a scene with the child. The Youth is in a frenzy (mouth is ripped open). A terrible quarrel, in the course of which the Youth tells Him everything. When he is about to leave—in a dark corner, the weeping boy. He immediately talks him into leaving with him. Only when they are out in the street together, the question: "Where am I going to put him? It won't go with the aunts, it's impossible with Vitia. With Vasin?" He goes looking for Vasin, though he doesn't have his exact address, leading the boy by his hand. Vasin is willing to take him.

He took him over to Vasin's solely because he had taken a liking for him, for he had never exchanged a word with him yet, but had just heard him talk at the Dolgushins. An adventurous night, they try to cheer up the boy who suddenly, <though> noiselessly, as if he were afraid to show himself ungrateful, starts to cry for his mother. They promise him that tomorow they'll bring back his mother, and that his mother will actually be living at their place. He spends the night at Vasin's. He returns to the aunts only in the morning.

They charge into him. (They have heard about the kidnaping. He throws himself on his aunt's neck and kisses her.) He rents his own flat. He lets the mother know; she is at Vasin's. He takes the boy over to *his own* flat, as the boy begs him hysterically not to leave him, but the boy's mother insists that he should stay with the aunts. The boy is with the aunts. *He* begs the boy to forgive him. *It is through this incident, too, that He hears about Vasin.* (N.B. At Vasin's, that night, they talk about fundamental questions, but Vasin is reluctant to talk—etc.)

~~*He*, to the Youth: "It all happened on account of the Princess.~~

~~Why did you bring it up?" And He tells him what the Princess is afraid of, also asking the Youth what it is the Princess is saying about Him. The Youth reacts with haughty irony. Deep contempt. *He* coolly takes his leave. About the "kept woman." [The Youth is already in love with the Princess.]~~

~~In the morning there is a big commotion at the aunts':~~ He has returned the 200,000. The Youth is thunderstruck: only the day before he had charged Him with letting himself be supported. The Youth rushes over to Vasin's; the latter listens to his story with great interest, but in the end asks him not to visit him anymore.

The Youth, in a scene of reconciliation. Champagne. About the Princess. He is complaining about his wife, makes some equivocal statements about Liza, speaks convulsively of his own character (but without remorse).

Then, ~~the scene with the Youth's confession~~ Liza in a frenzy, awaiting Him. An ecstatic exchange of words. The Youth is stunned: "What kind of a relationship is this?"

He won't come. The Youth goes to see him. He tells him: "I was afraid to come. I thought you'd be angry with me." A meeting at the Youth's flat. The Youth's confession, Souchard. The idea. "But what is my father really like?"

In the 2d part, too, it is further developed "what his father might be like"; Liza's liaison. The Youth is a confidant of the whole affair. Liza violates him (after her own fashion), *la haine l'amour*[51] <*sic*> toward the Princess, diamonds, a quarrel, the found letter, etc.

N.B.! ~~The Youth~~ *Most important* (*psychologically*). The Youth, besides being crushed by the <fact that He has returned those> 200,000, is also crushed by the thought that he has stolen the letter. That's why both <his> hysterics and his confession: ~~as <He> leaves~~ as he says good-bye to Him, he feels, for a moment, like showing Him the letter, but he holds himself back. ["Won't go? Too early for the letter?"] When he is left alone, he has mixed feelings <about it all>. "I had expressed my idea poorly. Did I really love Him? But on the other hand, I hadn't told Him about the letter. Amazing: I suddenly felt satisfied that I hadn't told Him about the letter (i.e., 'you see how I can be firm and keep a secret—that means I'll be able to handle my idea, too'). But what about Him?"

~~"There's nothing dishonorable about my holding on to the letter.~~

---

[51] French: "Hate, love."

~~So I do have a father. But do I love Him? How touchingly did He say the other day that 'you'd be angry with me.' "~~

~~Last idea: the boy. One great idea—saves and recovers the whole mood, reconciles everything, he falls to thinking about the boy. He falls fast asleep.~~

~~He finds the letter after the <incident with the> diamonds.~~

September 7.

Passionate love for Liza, when the Youth arrives it is already there.

That's how it goes. Having married, after long <years of> wandering (legend has it that He was just about to enter a monastery when He suddenly got married) <. . .> Having married, He actually did preach Christianity, but was somber, moody, capricious, both cheerful and hypochondriac, both petty and generous, both great idea and cynicism.* *All this* from *inner* dissatisfaction with his own convictions, secret atheism which remains hidden even to himself, doubts concerning the truth of Christianity, etc., i.e., from inner disorder. [N.B. He is one of those noble natures who, if they believe in an idea, devote themselves to it body and soul, but who perish if they have nothing to believe in. (N.B. He himself says this to the Youth.)]

In his family life He is now capricious, with everybody acting as his nurse, then again (very rarely) patient as an angel. At times He hates his stepchildren, then again He loves them passionately. Liza has grown to hate Him.

"I've come to love Him out of hatred," she says, "I've come to love Him so I could destroy Him" (this is her innermost passionate desire). At the same time, she is herself a predatory character and pursues her passion with a savage vehemence. She really does have a passion for Him, but not in order to make Him happy, but in order to destroy Him; she looks at Him like a crocodile wanting to swallow its prey alive.

It is remarkable that she is telling Him all this right to his face, without trying to conceal it at all. This is precisely what intoxicates Him, this is what drives Him mad; he madly falls in love with her and *desires* her terribly. It is in such a state that the Youth finds Him when he arrives. Their love affair has already begun, and there have been several meetings. But Liza refuses to submit to him. "I am walking around like a man who has been bitten by a rabid dog," He says to the Youth.

---

* Ungrammatical.

It is remarkable that, during the last five years of his life, He had seemingly turned from a highly frivolous (though always deeply thinking) man into a quietly and calmly religious one. A quiet love made Him marry that "beautiful angel of God," the Stepmother.

"I grew restless," He says, because I felt, in the presence of that angel (my wife), the whole extent of my own moral inadequacy, as well as that of my convictions and, what is most important, <the shortcomings> in my cultivation of my inner self. What hit me *harder* than anything else was the fact that instead of actually beginning to perfect myself, I had suddenly begun to yield to an irrepressible urge to view everything with haughty condescension. From so much inner dissatisfaction and disorder, I became capricious: 'What I need is a good thrashing, and not such perfection <of all virtues> as is seen in this woman.' I even got to be jealous (and of the young Prince, of all people, on account of what she had been telling me about him), and at times I was beginning to hate my stepchildren." It is at this point that Liza turned her attention to Him. *"I felt the devil in you,"* she used to say later.

N.B. All of this He tells Liza in a passionate, troubled, and tragic manner, during their meetings.

It was precisely this anxiety, caused by his failure of self-perfection and by his realization that He was essentially a predatory type, that was pursuing Him. And the secret idea: "Why strive for self-perfection?" (predatory type). This is precisely what Liza sensed, i.e., <that he, too, was a> predatory type.

Liza starts being violently and irrepressibly jealous of Him, on account of the Princess, for example. (It is a remarkable fact that she is not jealous of her mother.) "You love only yourself," she tells Him, "and so there really isn't any reason to be jealous."* And yet she is terribly jealous of the Princess, and the longer the affair lasts, the more jealous.

In the meantime, His relationship with the Princess, *in reality,* amounts to the following. He had given a warm and ardent answer to the Princess when she, having the greatest respect for Him, had opened her soul to Him and laid bare before Him the whole horror of her condition as the wife of the old Prince. This woman is a pas-

* Literally, "and so there really is no one on whose account one ought to be jealous of you."

sionately ideal<istic> person, thirsting and searching for what is true and good (later she even listens to what the nihilists have to say).

Yet in this capacity of <being> the Princess's spiritual guide and confidant, which continues for a whole year, and through preaching Christianity to her, <He gets her> to where she almost decides to take the veil. (N.B. The old Prince says: "He has conditioned her for the monastery; she has been asking me for a divorce, so that, imagine that, I would have had to become a monk, too, to keep her company. Imagine only what a fine monk I'd make. Though, on second thought, I might make a good monk, and, you know what, I like this costume of theirs.") (And altogether, this whole year which he spent with the Princess must be included as *a separate episode),* with this relationship going on, and He her spiritual guide and saint, the predatory type is suddenly awakened in Him, and He begins to seduce her. She sees through it and ignominiously chases Him out, moved by *the indignation of outraged innocence.*

N.B. However It is precisely this indignation of outraged innocence, without any admixture of Christian forbearance (as seen, for instance, in the Stepmother), this boundless pride of <triumphant> virtue, that cuts Him to the quick even then.

He denies her charges, but she contemptuously refuses to answer him. Then He confesses <his guilt>, writing her a passionate letter; but she contemptuously returns the letter.

And so, from then on, *two* feelings remain forever present in his soul.

1) Terrible pangs of conscience on account of having wanted to corrupt <her> innocence. "This was my worst and dirtiest action ever." From then on, he is lacerated by the thought of the ungovernability and lack of discipline in his character in the face of any sort of convictions. He gets married solely because he hopes that he will succeed, under this angel's wings, in restraining his nature through a pure life and in bending it to the good <in Him>.

2) A very high respect for the Princess, her opinions, and <yet> with a hidden hatred for such exceedingly lofty nobility of spirit.

It is clear that He does not love her anymore; however, under Liza's influence there is awakened in Him a seed, concealed so far, of hatred for the Princess, her purity and her virtue.

"Eh, spit on everything, break up everything," just as He breaks the icons.

This was a concealed hatred, but He obviously still wanted to meet her, and returned those 200,000 *for the Princess's sake,* so she would change her mind about Him. But having been bitten by that rabid dog, He suddenly develops (as He now consciously realizes) a hatred for the Princess's perfect purity. It is Liza's "inner disorder," a desire to see everybody as being just as impure as Himself, <His> skepticism, etc. (here, psychology) that make Him become an involuntary, impersonal participant in Lambert's and Liza's plot, for He knows that Liza is involved (though he once makes an attempt to divert the Youth <from going along with them>).

Meanwhile Liza is giving Him more and more trouble and has brought Him to the point where he thinks of escaping <with her> and of poisoning <His wife>. *He* rejects it. But he does chop up those icons, and his wife guesses what is going on. His wife flees to join the young Prince. Her death, and Liza says that it is all His fault. She hangs herself. (She cannot stand <her> mother's death and His loathing, or the vileness of her own conduct.) But what is most interesting is that she says that it is all His fault. "You corrupted me."

In the frenzy of the *finale* He says to the Youth: "You know, this kind of dullness is really attractive erotically. 'A foolish woman is good also,' says Iaichnitsa.* Admitted, this isn't quite the same thing, but still there are times when the most depraved creature seems more attractive than any angel. And the more so if she is dim-witted and unfair. I am depraved to the bones."

"But what about Christianity?"

He: "Why, I really never believed in it."

"So you were playing a role?"

He: "How could I have played a role? I believed because I was afraid that I didn't. And now I've realized that I really didn't believe in anything at all. Only now have I discovered that everything is disorder, that everything is cursed."

Ergo. His character cannot be that of a frivolous, playful, effeminate, jovial fellow, or "an old goat."**

He is passionate, morose, a skeptic, restrained, and it is rarely that his heart would reveal itself impetuously. He *cannot* be proud of his erotic triumphs over women, <including> Liza, or frivolously and playfully tell the Youth about it.

---

*Literally, "Mr. Scrambledeggs," a character in Gogol's play "The Marriage."

** See n. (**), p. 123, above. Dostoevsky uses *zherebchik,* "young stallion," in the first instance and *zherebenok,* "colt," here.

Most important. All the time, He has been bitten by that rabid dog.

Now, it turns out, we're facing the question of form!

September 7.

N.B. As regards His preaching of Christianity; the Youth meets Him when <everything> has been decided: abrupt, skeptical, brushing <him> off; but so much stranger is the one *chapter* (only) containing a passionate confession.

The letter written by the Princess from the country, in which she was suggesting that the Prince be placed in an insane asylum, was inspired by Him (as He was seeking to corrupt her). "I began to corrupt her consciously and step by step." Yet later on, after He had quarreled with the Princess, He was mean enough to threaten her with that very letter. Eventually He wrote her a letter in which He confessed everything. Including that He was trying to corrupt her. This letter in part Contempt on her part. Yet he inquires with Andreev about that letter. Andreev, smart man, won't give it to Him. But after Andreev has died, He makes further inquiries (for He is already itching to have his revenge. But it is the Youth who finds it.)

N.B. We are facing, then, the question of form:

How will the Youth describe, *in the first person,* those psychological explanations involving Liza and the *antécédents* of His relationship with the Princess, even if it be in quoting His words?

But then again, if it is going to be *the third person,* won't this make the Youth a secondary figure, and Him the main character?

If it is going to be the third person, the role of the Youth disappears entirely.

Liza used to visit the Youth from the very beginning (feeling that she could use him, and having explained the whole thing to him briefly).

The Youth despises Him. After various peripeties He explains to the Youth what had really happened, also describing their meetings: "I was sitting there, she was sitting there, with downcast eyes. 'You have corrupted me.' " ~~N.B. the aunt~~ And later He drops in on the Youth to tell him even about the poison.

Moreover: the Aunt admits to the Youth that the Princess has been His mistress. Also, that she has got the letter (the aunt, that is; the Youth then steals it from her). Liza also asserts that He has been living with the Princess. But she chased <Him> out. Thereupon, He dissuades him from believing this. That's the kind of form it is going to be in.

As far as the Princess is concerned, He confesses to the Youth that he has only feelings of the deepest respect and reverence for her, but that He has quit loving her a long time ago. (And there, suddenly, the Youth learns that He <has allied himself> with Lambert.) It's the same thing as when He is being so very sincere and keeps dropping in on the Youth, making a display of His simple-heartedness: His need of having a confidant, and showing His love for the Youth, all of which doesn't fail to move the Youth. However, the Youth notices that even while He is trying to be on such familiar terms with him He is still maintaining His independence (an air of mystery), meaning that he, the Youth, does not satisfy Him.

By the way, He *started* dropping in on the Youth only when He began seeing some advantage in so doing. Until then, He had been keeping much more aloof from him.

(N.B. He *absolutely* wanted to get even with the Princess, in the literal sense of that word. A predatory type.)

He has an irrepressible desire to find out about the Princess. In the beginning, Liza practically convinces the Youth that He has sent for him only to have him do *some finding out about the Princess* (*sic,* and most important).

And later: He starts dropping in on the Youth when He finds out that Liza has been seeing the Youth. As a result the Youth finds himself right in the middle of a developing intrigue.

In the beginning He wouldn't tell him everything, but later He was feeling an irrepressible urge to express himself.

"How then, are you going to act?" the Youth says to Him (about Liza). "I don't know," says He, and the Youth is appalled.

"You come to see me only because you need me," says the Youth.

N.B. Most important. The Youth *never admits* to Him that he is in love with the Princess, and is angry at His bilious and derisory insinuations. He even breaks off relations with him.

But His ultimate confession to the Youth comes in the finale.

So then, it is *the first person* after all.

Always follow this *last* plan of September 7.

"I have no convictions or rules, and I almost became your undoing," He says to the Youth in the finale. "Your idea—remain true *to your idea,* or are you wavering?"

"I have left 25,000 with your aunt, to get you going in life."

The Youth may have been in possession of His posthumous memoirs and may be quoting from same directly.

His memoirs. "Now, when everything is over (a year later), I have

His notebook. It seems to me that this was written down *after everything had happened* (i.e., in the *Finale*). It presents in no way a whole, but only scenes—with Liza, for example—and cursory notes of His, all quite disconnected. But *this particular* meeting (with Liza, the one about which he writes in his confession, is described in its entirety, and this is how it was)."

"But what is so very sincere about this?"

III

Second Period of Work on the Plot

September 8–November, 1874

Late in this section of notes Dostoevsky reminds himself of the following:

> *1st rule.* Avoid the mistake, made in *The Idiot* and in *The Possessed,* of describing (many of the) secondary events in a fragmentary, insinuated, romance-like manner, and dragging them out over a lengthy extension <of the novel>, both in the narrated action as well as in individual scenes, yet without giving any explanations at all, just guesses and hints, instead of *explaining the truth directly.* Being mere secondary episodes, they weren't worth such concentrated attention on the part of the reader; rather on the contrary, they actually tended to obscure, rather than to clarify, the principal objective, precisely because the reader, diverted to a side road, could very well lose the main road and get all confused in his attention.

Yet, whatever the difficulties in *The Idiot* and *The Possessed,* they do not compare with the proliferation of diverting detail in *The Raw Youth.* Dostoevsky's imagination always teemed with more life than his organizational ability could encompass, but in *The Idiot* and *The Possessed* great characters and great passions, like magnets, were able to give order to a world that always seems to be on the verge of dispersing in chaos. There is not enough of great character or great passion to force chaos into order in *The Raw Youth;* yet when the notes are placed beside the novel one has some idea of how much order Dostoevsky was able finally to impose and how great his accomplishment was.

The rummaging for situations, details, and lines of development in these notes seems ceaseless and often seemingly profitless. The notes do not move forward as much as they move in a circle. Everything seems possible, nothing seems settled, and every tentative solution seems to give birth to three other possibilities. In the novel the Youth has the letter and he doesn't know whether he will use it or how he will use it. In these notes Dostoevsky is not even sure of who has the letter: the Youth has it most frequently, but sometimes Lambert has it, and sometimes no one has it. Lambert thinks of extorting money from the Princess; the Youth thinks up the idea; and in other notes Versilov thinks of it. Sometimes Versilov is part of the plot to humiliate the Princess, and sometimes he is the dissuader. The plot is put into action and consummated in some of the notes, and sometimes it is not. When it is effected, the Youth saves the Princess or he doesn't save her. In some of the notes he kills Lambert, and in one note he kills his father. The Princess is engaged to the young Prince, is married to him, or has no relations at all with him. There is doubtlessly something instructive in Dostoevsky's willingness—even his insistence—on entertaining every variant of a situation, but it is difficult to imagine what. Life seems to move in every direction and to include every complication for Dostoevsky, and it is only the agony of deadlines that forces him to choose.

Still, some things are fixed and some situations are immovable. Above all the Youth's character seems to be fixed. Here, as in the earlier notes, the Youth continues to be naïve, good-hearted; tempted by disorder and thirsting for order; loving and hating the Princess and his father; talking of ideals and imagining debaucheries: "Besides, they both *hated* the Princess. The Youth got to hate her even more when he realized that He, in spite of his ostensible hatred, was more in love with her than ever. And suddenly he the Youth feels that he is himself in love; he spits with disgust. Chastity, and the hideous thought that he is his father's rival." Above all, Dostoevsky clings relentlessly to the belief that the Youth is the center of the novel: "The Youth is <the> hero in every respect. He is both with the old Prince (a duel), and with his father, and at his own flat with the government clerk, and with Vasin about his idea. The latter hands him his papers. He is also aware of Liza's romance. He also loves the little child, is close to his mother, greatly impressed by Makar Ivanov. N.B. It might be that Lambert, in particular, fascinates him."

For many readers of these notes, as has been the case for many readers of the novel, Versilov will be the hero of the novel, dominating the Youth and all about him and dominating the dramatic interest. The portraiture of Versilov (called variously "He," Brusilov, and Versilov here) is in some respects similar to that of the early notes and in other respects very different. Versilov continues to preach Christianity; he loves and hates the Princess, breaks the icon, returns a large sum of money, and teaches the Youth while mocking him. At one point in the notes, Dostoevsky says to himself, with something of amazement and something of weariness, "HE ONCE MORE?" and proceeds to give us a long analysis of Versilov:

> A landowner, a despot, a strong intellect, critical enough not to become either a Slavophile or a Westernizer. He becomes a profound egoist. An egoist from despotism. He is, though, a despot to the bone; a true despot must place himself so highly that he actually treats people unctuously, without anger, for to him they are mice, moles. They must be given help and encouragement. The fact that everybody is in love with Him he must accept as something necessary. And this is why he cannot understand how the Princess *is not in love* with him. He refuses to believe that he is in love, and is embarrassed when he must finally prove it to himself, and he gets to think. He thinks that he wants only to save the Princess. Everything is solved by his passion. This passion ~~crushes,~~ his admission that he is capable of *sinking* to the level of passion, leaves him completely crushed. A despot to the bone. He admits himself that he is an atheist—ruins the Youth, is running the risk of ruining him, changes his mind and comes to talk him out of going along with the plot.

The characterization is negative and bitter, but not as negative and bitter as in the earlier sections. He no longer has an affair with a young girl who hangs herself, nor with his stepdaughter, nor does he consider poisoning the mother. He is still the Predatory Type, but the predatoriness is becoming more subtle. In small steps Dostoevsky seems to be moving toward the enigmatic, cultured, and weary aristocrat, who is too withdrawn from life to commit the atrocities of the early pages. Dostoevsky burdens him more and more with "ideas," often of a predatory nature. He is as self-interested as in the earlier notes, where he had said, "Why shouldn't I live to take care of my own arse, what else is there to do?" But here he says, in an argument against socialism reminiscent of the Underground Man's argument against socialism:

> My God, what a miscalculation on your part: when did man ever do what was to his advantage? On the contrary, hasn't man always done what he liked to do, rather than what was to his advantage, and not infrequently knowing full well that it was to his disadvantage? For man has an innate tendency to consider as *advantageous to himself,* in almost any calculation that he may undertake, that which pleases him, and nothing else.

His self-interest is becoming abstract, as it will be in the final version. Philosophical premise and principle are beginning to take the place of naked will, but for Dostoevsky an idea hides but does not replace an act of will. Indeed, Dostoevsky has begun to do what is so much in evidence in the final version and what contributes so much to the mystery and enigmatic evil of Versilov: to give him "good" ideas and even—from Dostoevsky's own point of view—correct and precious ideas. Dostoevsky would agree with his argument against socialism quoted above, and he would most certainly agree with these words of Versilov:

> If only Christ would not die in the hearts of the Russian people, then, even though there were night ~~all~~ around us, it would still be possible to strive for that bright dot <of light> with everything one has got. That is, it would be a joy to be alive, provided the idea does not die. You see, if the idea itself should die, and the European idea become accepted, an idea of mechanical and not of inner equality, everything would be lost.

It may seem strange for Dostoevsky to give to Versilov some of his precious ideas, but here—at least in germ—and in the final version, Dostoevsky shows us how "truths" can become "errors" in the words of Versilov. Versilov often has the right ideas, but always the wrong movement of his heart, or no movement at all. He is laden with the best, which has somehow become the worst. Versilov cannot teach and he cannot love, because he cannot believe. For Dostoevsky it is an article of faith that when a man ceases to believe in God he believes in no one else and indeed finally not even in himself. Dostoevsky has begun to understand his character and the following quotation is astonishingly close to the kind of assessment that one can make of the final Versilov:

> Besides catholic narrow-mindedness, despotism, and intolerance, besides contempt for one's own land, there is also present <in his character> such a thing as a stubborn, almost enthusiastic pursuit of an idea, of a world view, etc. Besides extreme and diabolic pride ("no one can be my judge") there also are present extraordinary, harsh demands directed at <him>self, "though under the condition that I be responsible to no one." A most elegant, polished exterior: an apparent ingenuousness, an affability, an apparent tolerance, an absence of any purely personal ambition. And yet all this is only the result of a haughty view of the world, an incredibly exalted position which He has arbitrarily assumed opposite the whole world.

One of the values of these notes, surely, is the harsher and more direct light Dostoevsky throws on Versilov. Once Dostoevsky has seen him—and he takes a long time seeing him—he dims the light, until in the final version it takes strong seeing to discern the despot and the rapacious ego through the mist of elegance, refinement, culture, and "right" ideas.

The problem of Versilov's progressive alienation from active cruelty and toward "rootless" cruelty comes from how we see him, and Dostoevsky spends in this section as in others many pages thinking about the implications of narration from the Youth's point of view. He has finally decided to give the narration to the Youth, but he busies himself justifying his decision. In one excited note he cries out: "In *the first person,* in *the first person,* in *the first person.*" But when he thinks about "why," his arguments seem more intent on shoring up the Youth as the central character than in seeing the advantages it will give him in expressing the character of Versilov. He is quite right that in giving the Youth the point of view he will dramatize the naïve, questioning, sifting, misunderstanding, fumbling and questing spirit of the Youth.

Dostoevsky believed that in centering the story in the consciousness of someone other than the Youth he would be taking something away from the picture of the Youth. He did not want a picture of the Youth; he wanted the Youth picturing. He was equally intent on tempering the immediacy by the remove of time. He wanted the Youth's assessment of the events after the events had taken place, and he experiments in this section with having the Youth narrate the events one year after they have taken place, five years, and even eight years. Five years, he tells us, will not do:

> *Can't make it* 5 years. The reader will be left with the crude, rather comical idea that "there's that young adolescent now grown up, and perhaps holding a Master's degree, and a jurist, describing with great condescension (the devil only knows why) how foolish he used to be before," etc. And thus the whole naïvete of the narrative is destroyed. And therefore, better let it be a year. In the tone of the narrative, the whole impact of a recent shock would still be apparent, and a good many things would still remain unclear, yet at the same time there would be this first line: "A year, what a tremendous interval of time!"

Dostoevsky knows, too, that by giving the point of view to the Youth he will gain some advantage in the portraiture of Versilov. At least in section two of the notes he makes reference to this. But in this implication is firm in his mind, there is very little reference to it in these notes. Giving the point of view to the Youth has an important effect on the dimensions and obscurity of Versilov's character. Versilov is one person in the notes and in essential respects someone very different in the novel itself. As we have seen, Dostoevsky moves in his conception of Versilov toward a more subtle evil by changing "acts" to "ideas." In the notes Versilov is often analyzed flatly and the effect is sharp and clear. The enigmatic, paradoxical, and mysterious Versilov of the novel is largely the creation of the Youth's ignorance, naïvete, and obfuscating emotions. In the novel we see Versilov reflected in the passionate and distorting mind of the son. Even when Versilov emerges into sunlight and tells us himself what he believes in, we have been prepared, by the many Versilovs that have succeeded themselves in Arkady's mind—to look on this as another Versilov.

Makar Ivanov.

STINKING LIZAVETA.

The aunts are not his aunts, but distant relatives of His.

A lawyer is a hired conscience.

God has already forgiven him, he's dead.

They interpret <the scriptures?> allegorically and in a derivative way (metaphorically. N.B.), in a spiritual sense. And thus dumbfound ignorant people. Worrying about one thing only, how to get any kind of an interpretation out of it, even if it be a silly one, so long as it is their own.

Enoch is natural law, Elias is written law, and John is the law of grace (the doctrine of the Bespopovtsy).*

Comfort in my sorrows which have afflicted me gravely.

Holy inviolate relics, a great fragrance.

He will save me by willing what He himself knows well.**

This arrow has pierced my heart.

Being most ignorant myself, how can I teach another, knowing nothing myself.

O bitter delusion! O great madness!

Receive me, oh Lord, as you once received Paul, accursed that I am, like (some) wicked sinner.

And <I> used to have as many as four thousand books of my own.

P. 30.

[In sweet scriptural style.] The soul inside me is one only; if I lose it, I cannot find another one. Also, if I shall spend my time without profit to my soul, I shall not be able to return that time.

Be zealous in your service of the Holy Church, and if the time should come and you be called, die for it, as you would die for Christ. ["Yet they are only servants, and not gods, and thus servile, and curious."]

---

* Literally, "the priestless ones," name of a sect.

** This and the following sentence are apparently a scripture quotations.

"Occupy till I come." (Luke 19:13)

And many elders bearing God <in their hearts>.

They read and discuss, yet they all remain in bewilderment, nor can they solve <the mystery>.

For though I have studied it according to the scriptures, the Holy Scriptures are an unplumbed depth.

Queen of Heavens! For what great authority does she have with her son Jesus Christ, our Lord!

And hardened worse than a stone.

Another would be satisfied to have his own.

Do not tempt me, your aren't my enemy yet (the Devil).

There was sincere love between them, and as if their two bodies had only one soul.

Stinking Lizaveta. "Do not send me, the stinking one, to your bright paradise, but send me into utter darkness, so that even there, in fire and in pain, I could raise my voice to Thee: 'Holy, holy art Thou, and I have no other love.' "

"My dear Lizavetushka, my Lizanka, calm down."

"Stretch out your little hand, once every year, [at least once every thousand years, for I love you and I shall kiss you."]

" 'Shut up, Lizaveta you fool, I know that you love me, shut up.' And I to him: 'I'm not going to shut up, I want to keep raising my voice until even the devils will believe in you.' "

" 'Keep quiet, you happy-go-lucky one!' " (Before her Holy Communion: "I am not begging to be in eternal pain." "Keep quiet, you happy-go-lucky one!" And she took fright, and partook of the sacraments, and went on to die.)

And so we went to do some work for our Lord.

And he is talking such nonsense that it's not worth listening to.

And as for the books, he had picked out nothing but the prettiest flowers, and even those at his own discretion.

They don't know themselves where they are going.

For a mystery such as transcends all human reason has been revealed (to her, to him, to us).

Nor did he want to commit himself to marriage. (To take a wife.)*

Delivered us to be trampled upon by all men.

We want no part of alien (wickedness).

But to live without God is sheer torture.

---

* The expression in the original is typically biblical.

Save us from the machinations of the Devil.

Because of envy.

And he got to love our Lord Jesus Christ so much that he didn't want to leave him in his thoughts even for a little while.

And he obtained the gift of clairvoyance.

Everyone is lost, it is only that everyone is boasting of his own ruination, never even thinking of reverting to the Truth.

And observing his youth *with apprehension.*

Whatever sanctifies us we curse, without being aware of this ourselves. Do what you have to do step by step, without flinging yourself forward, or rushing ahead.

For they are not gods, but men like ourselves, and apprehensive of us.*

May the Lord not leave unrewarded my sorrows and my (your) pilgrimage (we are praying for that, that is).

He (i.e., a contemporary member of the upper classes) is like the prodigal son, having squandered his patrimony. (They did in fact receive two ten-kopek pieces, but had to pay a hundred rubles of their own [money] for it.) Let him return [(to the people),] and a fatted calf will be killed for him.

Laymen are tied down by their families, and by worldly concerns.

And without ever getting satisfaction, they are gathering (perishable) wealth.

And they are living in obedience and having completely cast off their own will (and so much firmer they are <in their faith>).

And found peace from worldly concerns for his feelings.

[Get to know Christ, <and you shall know> that you have not accomplished anything.] See p. 253.

So that the world become the most beautiful and happy abode, replete with every kind of joy.

And to leave all this behind is no small cross, nor is it a light grief.

He would give his life for his wife, and almost everybody would be willing to suffer and die for his children's sake.

For a wife to be left behind, alone like a homeless swallow, after the loss of her husband (it is hard, that is).

For he owes them this debt by nature (i.e., he must love them).

Into a quiet and mute refuge.

**Podobostrastnye,* literally, "servile," "obsequious"; however, the speaker here tends to use book words in meanings that are a little off the target.

He was tossing about and suffering anguish, like a fish pulled out of the water.

I say this is an impious thought.

Don't you *give up* (don't break off) your enterprise on account of any kind of faint-heartedness.

They are all so intemperate, each of them is out to surprise the whole world.

How he could surprise the world.

But you are standing before him shifting from one foot to the other, refusing to stand still, rushing about(as if he were worth it).

Crone, jade, <scare> crow.*

And he also said that one should not smoke tobacco, which point he sought to impress upon <his audience> at length, with sorrowful mien and with many a sigh.

All you [he] care about is to have a good laugh at your own joke.

A military force.**

As they say around our place: take some nice yellow sand, strew it on some nice little rocks (cover some nice little rocks with it), and when the yellow sand begins to sprout from those rocks, your dreams will come true.

He would get drunk, of his own free will, and then cry: "Oh mother dear, why did you ever bear me, sorry drunkard that I am? Rather, you should have crushed the life out of me at birth, than let me into this world (the way I am)." (He is coming from the tavern stark naked, yet reciting his lamentations.) (He is coming from the tavern, naked as his mother bore him.) They made up such a song, there is such a song.

And he forfeited*** some of his own capital.

Yet you are more 'xhausted (exhausted) than he. An exhausted soul. Exhausted people.****

Drinking up and eating up his soldier's pay.

Where will a poor soldier go, a soldier must take orders, that's what a soldier is for.

And now I am going to tell you that there is a little child.

Stinking Lizaveta. "Do not forgive me, Christ, let me be the only

---

* *Karga-zagumennaia, vorona,* literally, "Crone behind-the-barn, crow."

** The expression in the original is typically biblical.

****Istomchivyi,* a dialect word, from *istoma,* "weariness."

**** *Reshilsia.* This particular meaning is dialectal.

one whom you won't forgive, but let me go down to Hell. They'll be burning me, and I'll be praising you, I'll be loving you. I can't live without suffering. Let me suffer some; give me the gift of suffering."

Lizaveta, don't ~~thou tempt~~ you tempt me with words, or with pies, or I'll burn your town, so I may again suffer.

It is envy, envy that kills a man altogether; envy is followed by death.

Even God's angels are imperfect; only our Lord Jesus Christ is perfect and free of sin; that's why the angels serve him.

And you will come to your grave in your old age, like an ear of corn to the sheaf, all in their own time.

It has been said: "The words of a desperate man are blown away by the wind."

We have all only come yesterday, and we haven't had time to find out anything yet.

It has been said: "The hope of a hypocrite shall perish, and his safety is that of a spider's house."*

+ Man has been deprived even of his right to complain, for he actually cannot even point a finger at whomever he is complaining against, man being surrounded by mystery. What will it help me if I shall complain? For as I will be complaining, I shall know that I speak as a man who lacks any sense and that my tongue is turning in vain, because I really know nothing, and so haven't the power to point my finger at anyone.

So then, is it possible at all for an atheist to remain calm and not kill himself? Only he can live who believes that God is always right (and that it couldn't be any different), even though it might appear to him all the time that injustice rules the world. Take it for a temptation, and believe.

And you shall become immersed in such filth "that your own clothes will begin to loathe you," that's what it says.**

Liza: "At least you might help her (mother), why are you just sitting around there?"

"Right away, my dear, forgive me." Makar got up, staggered, and fell down (his feet were swollen).

"It's my feet are swollen," he smiled, as if he were guilty. "E—eh!"

---

* I have translated literally: *dom pauka* is "a spider's house"; "a spider's web" is *pautina,* of course.

** Inexact quote from Job 9: 31.

Liza was embarrassed. And later she stepped up to Makar.

"O that ye would altogether hold your peace! and it should be your wisdom." (Job 13:5)

"Your remembrances are like mounds of clay." (Ibid., 12)*

"The first thing for you is your ambition: 'What do you know, what is it you could know?' is your very first question."

An intemperate and corrupt man, "drinking lawlessness, like water."

But in your hearts, thoughts are hovering about.

Your fame will be scattered, like the wind, and your happiness will pass, like a cloud. (There he is, fortunate and redoubtable, high in rank, covered with decorations, but he will die—and where will he be? Who will remember him?)

The remembrance of an undistinguished man is less than fifty years.

And they die (blissfully and quietly), full of days.**

Impenetrable fog. Impenetrable grief.

Full of the sweetness of learning.

Makar: "Get to know Christ and preach him, and provide an example by your deeds, and nothing will shake you. And thus you will serve even the whole world."

"True," says Versilov, "Europe is expecting Christ from us. They gave us science, and we shall give them Christ (this is Russia's whole mission)."

Makar: "I used to be hard and cruel. I would impose burdens and demand service." The story of the hermit and the child. " 'Why, these are cherubs!' I didn't believe it: why was the hermit doing my pleasure? (I fell to my knees before him. Departed in anger. 'I knew that you would come.')"

"Stinking Lizaveta, why are you struggling so hard, poor sinner?"

"Because I do not want to be saved, my dear; I want to go to hell, darling, right to where the devils are . . ."

"Why is it you don't want to be saved, you madwoman?"

"Because I want to suffer the torments of hell, that's why . . ."

"But I'll be shouting 'Holy-Holy' all the time, so all those devils will get tired of it. They will be burning me, and tearing off my skin, and I'll still keep shouting: 'Holy-Holy.' "

---

* Quoted incompletely in the text.

** Quote from Gen. 35: 29.

"Christ, in my sleep: 'Shut up, stupid . . . what are you doing, Lizanka?' This is exactly how he called me: 'Lizanka.' "

She was about to give up the ghost: "I am guilty more than anyone else, I am guilty of my disorders."

This happened in the town of Afimevsk. I spent a long time there on account of having fallen ill . . .

"A boy with a canary drowned himself. But why are you telling these stories? Why are you gloating? It's all disorder, and you are still speaking of order: you are speaking up against yourself."

"I am not gloating, my dear, yet one must accept everything with a trembling heart. You see something that is good—so you are full of joy; you see evil—and you begin to weep in your soul. One as well as the other is good and profitable for your soul. The Creator is great in one as well as in the other. And how do you know his ways so well?"

"Be firm, man, don't let anything disturb you."

". . . That things are changing for the worse. [Though] this may be true, and has been so prophesied for those last days, do not believe it in the least, but act as if <things> were going just fine. Preach Christ by your words, and even more so by your deeds. Be firm, man, and calm, do not let anything trouble you. And your life shall be to the glory of God."

"Most of all, serve by your own works. There is nothing stronger than the example of your own works; and don't let it trouble you that you have not completed everything, or that you have done but little, for it will all contribute to the general good order of things."

"Will it really?"

"Why won't it? How does a man live but by good examples?"

Makar: "Sanctify yourself, and you will serve everybody: by being a light to the world."

["Why, <I> have been speaking of the godless all the time. What godless people are they, really? That's asking too much of them. And besides."]

The hour destined to <end> my life is come.*

"Do not rejoice over another man's grief. (Do not injure the Church of God.)"

[Every] "Man cannot exist without bowing before something. Without it, no man could stand himself, ~~such~~ no man could, and not

* Apparently a variation on John 17: 1.

just simply so, but he has been created that way. Let him reject God, and he will bow before an idol made of silver [stone], or of gold, or one that is in his mind. That's the kind of godless people they all [these all] are! They are idolaters, that's what they are, and not godless. [And all who are living in this world."]

"So there is no such thing as godless people?"

"There must be, my dear, there must be, but I've never met any."

"His soul is like a wild forest, and there is no peace in it. All his life. Such is his lot. There are people who are given this." ~~This~~

"So it is given?"

"Yes; beauty-in-God (i.e., a feeling for beauty-in-God)."*

"And so, as far as I have been able to notice, all people lead dull lives everywhere."

"If all people would be like Christ, could there be any hunger?"

"And all this kind of people, they're all untidy, all of them."

Stinking Lizaveta: "Forgive all of hell, and take all the sinners up to you, and leave me there alone to suffer. And <he> will leave me there alone (for love). Isn't that enough bliss for you? Satan will give in."

"I am not afraid of Satan."

"All right, Lizanka, go and suffer all you want."

There was a man, "I am not asking (<him to repay his?> debt), because he loves, and a man won't know what makes him insist on his own opinion."**

And <I> have heard that one ~~sinner~~ ancient saint said: "The nearer we come to God in our love, the more sinful we feel." And believe me, my friend, that the reverse of this [undoubtedly] must consequently [must properly] be true also: the further we are from God with our hearts and with our minds, the more righteous we consider ourselves to be.

"Whosoever does not want to work, may he not eat either," has been said before (Nil Sorsky).

Lizaveta: "I am not eating either; I'm not eating."

"Forgive me, as the son of God, king of all ages."

About Lambert's character.

Makar Ivanovich has some touching recollections about Versilov's

---

* *Blagolepie,* a Church Slavonic word, literally means "good beauty," i.e., a beauty or an order agreeable to God.

** Quite unclear and apparently ungrammatical in the original.

childhood, about how he used to teach *mamma* how to walk, how he would carry her into the forest.

Stinking Lizaveta. "Shut up, you strange woman, you."

They also put her in an insane asylum once. Her relative, a merchant, gave her a beating—and she kissed his foot.

She lies on prickly straw.

"Lizanka, my Lizanka, there is none fouler than you."

And they sure beat her a lot, the poor dear.

She would be sitting there, pricking her shirt with some straw, then suddenly she would have a fit and start screaming.

"Here then, the temperature of my head went down a bit" (he became sober).*

September 8.

Special plan.

[to remember] The Youth is from Moscow. He sees the whole family: mother, elder brother prior to <illegible>, Olia, and the small boy. They are all illegitimate, and <his> father, at 50, married a young relation of the old Prince's. Scenes with the child at the old Prince's, the aunts, etc. A showdown with <his> father, the diamonds. It is He who makes inquiries about the Princess. *He* got married in a provincial town, but when he met the Princess again he was once more seized by passion and vindictiveness. Olia surrenders herself to the young Prince. The Princess fears Him: the document. His wife, having learned of His passion for the Princess, leaves Him. The Youth and Lambert, and the plot against the Princess. The Youth goes to see his father and puts him to shame. He affects his reconciliation with <His> wife. The young Prince marries Liza. The Youth abandons his idea. The Youth who is running errands for his father and acts as a spy at the Princess's falls in love with her.

A NEW STORY.

Makar Ivanov [an old-time house serf] is dead. ~~However~~ He lived a pious life. After February 19 <1861> he spent his time collecting funds to build churches. He had come back to Petersburg to die and died at the family residence. The family <consists> of his wife, 37 years old (N.B. She was a beauty all along, until 8 years ago, when she ~~rapidly~~ suddenly got all doubled up from the birth of her last child, a small and sickly boy); Olia, 17 years old; and the eight-year-old,

* Literally, "Here then, those degrees went out of my head a bit."

sickly boy. They are all *His children,* Makar Ivanov being ostensibly the husband.

The Youth had been brought up by the aunts. Later he was attending high school, <then> quit; *his own idea.*

The old Prince is altogether under His influence and fears Him.

He is a gentleman from a good family, who has squandered his fortune (Brusilov).

The Youth knows his story and travels to Petersburg with hidden anger in his heart—to get even <with Him> with the aid of his idea.

He has some poor female relatives (~~aunts~~ the so-called aunts of the Youth). They have lost Andreev. They respect Him very much (they are doing some sewing <for a living>, and are not being supported by Him). Tender, yet cautious and, so it appears, for some reason timid relations with Makar Ivanov's family.

~~The Princess~~ The General's wife—<rather,> the widow of a General, and the Prince's daughter, 26 years old.

The young Prince (not a relative), 28 years old (Golitsyn).

About half a year earlier, *He* apparently had a strange influence on that cold idealist ~~the Princess~~, the General's <widow>. N.B. The old Prince might marry.

Having recognized His intention to marry her, she chases Him out with ignominy.

He suddenly lets the family join him, coming from Luga (a little later, Makar Ivanov shows up quite unexpectedly and dies). The Youth meets with <His> despotic rule over the family, <witnesses how He> rips open the <little boy's> mouth, etc. But the family trembles <before Him> all the time. Only the Youth rebels and takes his little brother away.

He had been patient, but now he no longer could, and suddenly went into a rage hearing that the General's widow was going to marry the Prince.

Meanwhile he returns those 200,000.

[He finds out that the Princess has been visiting the family.]

The Youth gets to hate the Princess, is insulted by the young Prince. The diamonds.

The Princess fears the document. The Youth has found the document. ~~He sends her the document.~~

[He chops up those icons.]

~~The last rendezvous. At first *He* threatens her, document in hand; then he tears up the document; then wants to rape her. The Youth saves both Him and the Princess. Meanwhile Liza surrenders herself~~

~~to the young Prince. She drowns herself. *He* is desperate, while the General's widow breaks with the Prince. The little boy can't endure Liza's death and drowns himself. *He* wants to marry Makar's widow, but she refuses. (N.B. It is remarkable that Makar's wife had been His friend and advisor.) Makar's widow suddenly dies. (The Youth is arrested.) The little boy stays with Him and drowns himself. (To Liza.) *He* hangs himself in a monastery.~~

Note. Work out the episode of the rape. This is how it happens: after the return of those 200,000, etc., the Princess is cool <toward Him>. Thereupon He threatens her with the letter, for that letter has been found. The Princess responds by <seeing to it> that the old Prince dismisses Him. Marriage to the young Prince. *He* is furious at such a show of contempt and (psychology) asks Makar's widow to marry him. She refuses (she used to be his advisor). On that day, He chops up those icons. In the meantime Liza's romance takes its course, without anyone being aware of it. The young Prince doesn't know who she is? Desperate as a result of his comic situation, He allies himself with Lambert. The Youth saves Him.

He is crushed by his own baseness. At this point Olia's romance comes to light. (The Youth is arrested.) His mother dies of a broken heart. The Princess breaks off her wedding. *He* is left alone with the little boy, broken-hearted. The boy drowns himself.

He reasons this way: "She is afraid that the old Prince might disinherit her, for she herself is penniless. Then, the young Prince will abandon her." Besides, she is sure that the document has been destroyed. She is sure of that mostly because He has told the old Prince about the document and about the lunatic asylum. But the old Prince asked to see the document and when He replied that <the document> had been lost at Andreev's, he showed Him the door. It is after having committed this low-down act that He proposes to his wife. (N. B. He is suddenly convinced that the Princess is passionately, madly in love with the young Prince. At last His eyes are opened. Up to that time He had had a theory according to which it had been a mere case of *la haine dans l'amour.*[1] The Youth, in spite of the fact that he is his mother's son, is very much under His influence, i.e., they have become *that close* friends. At times he finds Him repulsive, then again he is attracted to Him.) After this, He chops up those icons. (Liza's romance, without anyone being aware of it.)

---

1 French: "Hate in love."

Lambert finds out about the existence of the document from the Youth and tells Him about it. *He* reasons like this... (and wants to take vengeance on her by violence and scandal just before her wedding). Then the Youth sees how far things are gone, and he saves the Princess. But he does it on an impulse, for he was himself in on the plot, though with trepidation. [Though in love himself, he would spit with disgust, a misogynist.] The thing is that <while> he *hated* the Princess, *had suffered insults* from the young Prince, he still loved even though he despised Him and looked down <on Him>, for he forgave <Him> (after the scene with Souchard).*

Besides, they both *hated* the Princess. The Youth got to hate her even more when he realized that He, in spite of his ostensible hatred, was more in love with her than ever. And suddenly ~~he~~ the Youth feels that he is himself in love; he spits with disgust. Chastity [and the hideous thought that he is his father's rival.]

When the Youth finds the letter, he experiences a sensation <as if he were an> Ungern-Shternberg.[2] He now wants to put the screws on her, then to send her the letter; then again, considering this to be base (for he senses that he is yielding to his love for her), to give the letter to Him. But it is too late for that, for he is frightened by the news that He has already reported the matter to the old Prince, and was shown the door <by the latter>.

[The old Prince] *He* later tried to convince the Youth that, had she only been shown the document, she'd have been licking their boots. Incidentally, He also told the Youth that He wouldn't have married her in any case, aside from the fact that it was impossible now.

(N.B. Having learned about Liza's romance, he tells her about it. He gets mocking remarks in return, and the date for the wedding is set.) Then He suggests to Lambert, having learned from him that the letter does exist, that he make a copy of its content and mail it from the aunt's, thus joining the plot. (Rape her on the eve of her wedding day.)

Lambert tries to tempt the Youth with an offer of 30,000 and "fuck." The Youth is excited both by the thought of revenge, and by <his> love <for her>. But having learned the whole extent of the scheme, and also (from Lambert) that He had asked Lambert not to tell him, the Youth, that He is involved in the plot, he becomes

* Ungrammatical and unclear in the original.
2 See note three of part II.

scared, realizes how base it is. And yet he is drawn to it, like <an arsonist is drawn> to set fire to a village. *He* wanted to see with his own eyes the vileness of the Princess, the vileness of the aristocracy.

But he saves the Princess, for she conducts herself splendidly. (N.B. Here the crime and the cynicism of the Youth and, incidentally, also his thirst for power. The document being a temptation to apply his power. As for the 30 thousand, he wanted to let Lambert keep them, and without a moment's hesitation. As for fucking her, the thought never entered his mind, not even for a moment, nor would he let Lambert do it.) ~~However~~ The Princess fell ill after that; but, having learned about Liza's death from the Youth, seeing the young Prince's despair, and realizing that he would be forcing himself to marry her, she proudly broke off their engagement.

[N.B. Olia's romance absolutely must take place *after* Lambert's plot.

Lambert is terribly frank, the peculiar and unusual *ingenuousness* of a crook, who doesn't even suspect that there might be some honest people, too.]

Characters.

The old Prince. A year and a half earlier he had been suffering from softening of the brain. He has gotten well again, but has not fully recovered. He feels terribly insulted whenever someone suspects that he is in a state of imbecility. This is why he would have cursed his daughter if he had learned that she was going to place him in an insane asylum. He has lost his official positions. He has invested his capital in some business transactions (which gave the Princess reason to say that He is stealing <from her father>).

Then there is He, an old-fashioned type of gentleman. The precious traits of skepticism, generosity, unbelief, [idle] atheism, laziness, liberalism, despotism. Above all, passion, a predatory type. But passion <which has taken?> refuge in Christianity ("It's his third year of preaching the Gospel," says the old Prince). N.B. (The old Prince has become terribly witty precisely since the time when he was suffering from softening of the brain.) Hidden atheism and despotism in the family. Almost the same as in *the earlier novel.* This is how *the Youth finds it* when he arrives on the scene.

Olia is an angelic type. The intimidated ones. She got frightened when the young Prince proposed to her. But she felt terribly flattered and was very happy. She turned him down, drowned herself. ["One could get married, <but> he won't love me. Surely, he would never give me a word of reproach, and <yet> he would regret it all his life."]

The mother. A Russian type (a tremendous character). They are both downtrodden, and humble, and firm, like saints.

Makar Ivanov. (A Russian type.) He wonders.

The Youth as before.

Dolgushin *et al.* Vasin—very cursorily.

He'll need his own flat, I suppose.

However, *his own idea* is just too persistent.

Only this problem: who is the hero? The Youth or He?

The young Prince Golitsyn, charming, also 24 years old.

N.B. More strongly about his own idea—and more strongly on Christianity as preached by Him.

Olia is a frightened <soul>, because He had frightened her in her childhood, which is also why He <later> surrounded her with care. He hired a Swiss governess for her. They used to travel abroad. Venice, cathedrals. Cathedrals scared her.

A legend. In Luga there is living an old lady, a relative of the old Prince's; not wealthy, but independent. It is under her patronage that Makar's family was living <in Luga> in seclusion. In Luga, the young Prince also met Olia. (But he didn't find out whose daughter she was.) Meeting her in Petersburg he asks her directly: "So you are here?" (N.B. The young Prince is poor himself, but is having success in Petersburg.) They become acquainted. For a long time he *has pity* on her, and finally she becomes pregnant.

~~He finds out about that pregnancy (by challenging the young Prince to a duel, for no particular reason, just being mad about the Princess; the challenge is ridiculous, <in view of> the difference in years; by this time the Prince already knew (through the aunts) all the secrets of Makar's family; the Prince refuses to fight a duel and admits to Him that he is guilty before His daughter).~~

Thereupon He is fired by a decision to force the young Prince to marry Olia. ~~On account of this, his first rupture with the old Prince. But He has accomplished his end: the General's widow is mortally hurt. But He is not doing it for her sake.~~ *He* is doing it for his daughter's sake. ~~It is precisely at this point that Makar shows up and dies.~~ Olia meets the young Prince. She asks him about the Princess: "Do you love her?"* The young Prince cannot possibly marry her, but

* Olia is using the obsequious plural, literally, "Do you love them?"

he does feel awfully sorry for her. Olia drowns herself (after having seen the Princess and *set her mind at rest*). The Princess breaks with the young Prince. The young Prince himself breaks off his engagement with the Princess. The mother dies of a broken heart. The Youth is arrested, but soon released. The little boy drowns himself.

Fussing around with father, etc.*

Makar still in the beginning. After Makar<'s death> offers to marry her. On the same day—[~~Makar still in the beginning~~ He chops up those icons. It was at this time that Lambert's plot materialized. The Princess is ill. But He challenges the young Prince in a fit of fury. The young Prince, dumbfounded, tells Him about Olia. It is at this point that He finds out about Olia, *not* any *earlier*.

The young Prince had stolen some icons, was tried and then pardoned. Later he rose in the service thanks to the efforts of a young General.

He has squandered his own 70 souls.

Bon jour, papa le grand.[3]

He has been at Souchard's only as an adult.

During their first meeting the Youth asks the young Prince about Souchard. The young Prince doesn't understand and forgets about it. Sincerely. Traveling by train. Tells his story to <his> aunt. "I hate!"]

That's how it was: Olia used to go with the young Prince until she found out that he was engaged to the General's widow. Then she broke off their relationship, without anger: ["Maybe you couldn't help it at all."] She used to go to Kazan Cathedral. <Then> she began staying at home, afraid to make a move, to see the Prince. Meanwhile the young Prince was pleading, fretting, visiting the aunts' place, writing letters. Having found out whose daughter she was, he refuses to accept His challenge, issued in a fit of madness (a long time prior to the scene with Lambert). The Youth arrives just at the time when Liza has become pregnant. Scene between him and the young Prince. The young Prince is actually making up to him. A strange impression. On her own part, the General's widow is miserable and jealous, as she sees the change in the young Prince, who is displaying alternate fits of love and an almost timid aloofness. The Princess finds out about Liza from the young Prince himself. After the scene with Lambert,

---

* Impossible to determine whether the subject is masculine or feminine.

3 French: "Good day, great papa."

rupture with the young Prince, while *He* learns that Liza is pregnant. He wants to kill the young Prince. But Liza drowns herself, etc. In the meantime, Makar. *His* proposal to <Makar's> wife. He chops up the icons. [The mother had known for a long time that Liza was pregnant.]

Form, form! (plain narrative à la Pushkin).

N.B. Makar.

Makar shocks everybody by his appearance: the Youth, the family, but especially Him. He has a nervous breakdown and suddenly offers to marry <Makar's> wife. Thereafter, he chops up those icons.

N.B. The Fool is staying at the same place where the Youth has rented a flat.

N.B. N.B. First make an outline of <the Youth's> own idea, as well as of the characters <of the novel>; then work out the plan of the entire novel, event after event.

September 9.

Tentative plan of part one alone.

In the railway carriage. The aunt and the Youth. N.B. The Youth had met his aunt casually before, and they run into each other at the railway ticket office. If Lambert, then the Fool is right there, too. [The aunt talks to the Fool, mentioning that she knows the Princess.] In the railway carriage the Youth and his aunt discuss and argue about Christ, about frou-frou, about "I am proud <that I am an illegitimate son?>," about his running around with a student of the university. [He surprises the aunt by his familiarity with the old Prince, about the General's widow, except that it is all distorted. Somber, but his age (he is 20) shows.] [He feels very sorry that he was so outspoken with the aunt.]

His own idea. About who Brusilov is, the soldier in the railway carriage, April 25. Doubts, about <his> mother. "Your mother, she has seen you, hasn't she?"

They arrive at the aunts' place. "I don't want to <stay> with my mother," while she is right there. Scenes.

Should he or shouldn't he be introduced to Him?

But he goes away to see Vitia, <or> to the market, <or> to Dolgushin's. Vasin. [At Vitia's he must absolutely <say something> about Lambert. Lambert worries him.]

He comes home at 8 o'clock. [*He* won't pay proper attention to the Youth.] A scene. He is being rude. The ripping of <the little boy's> mouth. [He chases him out of the house.] He is leaving of his own accord. The little boy, frightened, has already run out into the street.

He takes him over to Vasin's place. [Even glad to do it, wanting to take his revenge. "No, I had only one feeling, that of compassion! *We both wanted to run away.*"]

At Vasin's. He tells Vasin everything, whole confession, but not about his idea. (The little boy has fallen asleep, as he keeps asking for Olia.) The Youth falls asleep also. Vasin sends word to his family. His mother comes.

The Youth goes out to rent himself a flat. [Vasin asks him not to come anymore.] He goes to the aunts' place. In a dark room. Overhears a conversation in spite of himself. (The General's widow has come to see the aunt.) Letters. The aunt is perturbed by the fact that he has heard what was said. He asks the aunt to tell Him to please stay away from him, and that he won't need that job either. He goes to see his mother *to pay a visit to the child.* Liza. Now *they* will forgive everything.

[After <Vasin's> request not to come to his place anymore he goes to the aunts' place where he starts a letter to his father asking that they sever all connections. Enter the Princess. He eavesdrops in spite of himself. The letters.]

He returns home (an incident with a wench, something that happens in the street). At home, he finds Him waiting, engaged in a conversation with his landlord. A showdown. *He* charms him. Besides, the Youth is considerably shaken and exhausted. About Vasin (about socialism). He learns that Vasin has told <Him> the story of his <the Youth's> childhood. Ardently <expounds> his idea. *Ce n'est pas si bête.*[4]

They had promised to visit the General's widow. Captivated by her. ~~He doesn't know yet that his father is a villain.~~ He leaves, pensive and crushed.

The Youth ~~writes a letter in the morning, goes to see~~ falls asleep cursing himself for having told him about his idea.

[He curses and tears up. <. . .> A villainy. The curse. He goes home. Alone. His own idea. En route, the incident with the wench. He is shaken.]

First Part

All of this had a very strong effect on the Youth (He is talkative). But prior to this conversation, coming home one day, he found Him

---

[4] French: "This isn't so foolish."

with a government clerk <talking> about that <huge> rock,[5] and was surprised at such triviality.

He has mixed feelings. But he wakes up and proceeds to the Prince's house.

Second Part

On the next day I went to see the Prince, the Prince and the General's widow. But *jeune homme,*[6] toward the end of the conversation (about how the old Prince ought to get married) <. . .> The young Prince insults him ("I could not restrain myself, went up to him: 'Weren't you a friend of Lambert's?' "). The Princess whispered something about him to the old Prince and left, chuckling. The Youth returns in order to quit everything and leave. He meets Liza in the street. A brief meeting. [A ray of sunshine. For the first time, he recognizes the real Liza. N.B. Compose a scene.] The General's widow, stepping out of her carriage. A strange sensation. He swears revenge.

He returns home, knowing that He is going to question him regarding the General's widow. But He does not. [He announces that he is not going to <work for> the old Prince. At this point, <the scene> at the Liar's flat. The Youth is surprised that He, such a somber person, diverts himself with such trivialities. Spending time on bagatelles. He challenges Him fiercely on account of this.] The Youth is irritated by the idea of Christianity, so, exactly at this point, a sermon on Christianity and about his own idea. About Vasin, about socialism. The future, about Vasin and about his own idea. He hasn't seen his mother. Full of sorrow. ["Let's go, and the devil may care!" In his fall, he has visions of Liza.] A scene at his flat, involving the landlord and landlady.

On the third day he wants to challenge him to a duel. An insolent refusal. The diamonds. She accuses <him>. He leaves. Was about to give himself up for lost. Got home late. He finds the young Prince already waiting to tell him that the incident with the diamonds has been taken care of, and that he has already received a challenge from Him. He had asked the <Youth> to come to see Him. He is at home. ("You don't know!" i.e., about Liza.) He blushes. He doesn't want to

---

[5] The anecdote about how a huge rock is disposed of by digging a hole beside it is narrated by the Youth's landlord in Part II, Chapter 1, of the final version.

[6] French: "Young man."

give any answer, is somber and irritated. He says that he has seen the old Prince and has settled the business with the diamonds.

Makar arrives. The whole story of Makar. His death. (The Youth is terribly impressed.) After Makar's death He comes with a new confession, with tenderness, imprecations, about the Princess, about passion, about the letters (at Andreev's). [The idea about Andreev's letter,] the letter. Meanwhile the old Prince is very much upset. An incident with the landlord—death of the small child. The Youth's agony at seeing that the letter has this effect on him. He realizes that he is in love; he kisses the Princess's tracks.

A meeting with Vasin. Vasin about Him. They get together and have a talk.

His mother comes: "Why aren't you coming to see your brother, he is calling for you." His mother is very sad.

~~Liza suddenly comes to see the Youth and asks him if it is true that he loves the Princess.~~

The young Prince says that Liza doesn't want to marry him. She wants to break with him.

N.B. The Youth is aware of Liza's romance a long time before He is. He does not tell Him. At first he was going to tear the young Prince to pieces, but the latter bends him to his will. He grows more somber, finds that the whole thing is base.

The Youth had learned the facts about his father, about the General's widow, and about the old Prince from Lambert who at one time had been drinking together with ~~the old~~ the young Prince.

Absolutely in *the first person,* it is more naïve and more charming, though it would lack any moral.

A story.

September 10!

The aunt tells the Youth about the death of his mother after he is released from arrest. Absolutely make it so the Youth is *not* present at his mother's death.

Or make it so his mother dies in his presence.

He is arrested, and returning four days later, on the day of the funeral, he discovers that the little boy has disappeared. They find the boy. The aunt suggests that he use those 25,000 to buy a place in the country and take both of them there. The Youth would like to get an education. ~~A year later~~ the little boy makes friends with the Idiot. They spend their time together. Leave the city and go to the country!

N.B. He, as well as Vasin, brings up the subject of <the Youth's>

continuing his education many times throughout the novel. They decide that he will get his education.

He has mixed feelings about things. "I don't want to see anybody." The aunt, He, and the little boy. "I did, however, pass the examination." A ray of sunshine. "Oh my dear, you have such a long life ahead of you!" (the aunt says).

If in *the first person,* then, provided it is close <to the event> (3 months), the manuscript must bear the traces of a certain lack of purpose. <But> if the Youth has already overcome this period, the resulting conscious purpose of his narrative will cause it to lose its naïveté.

In *the first person* it would be more naïve, incomparably more original, and, in its deviations from a smooth and systematic narrative, even more delightful.

The young Prince as he appears in the Youth's judgment and all the scenes with Liza will come out more original from the Youth's pen. In *the first person,* in *the first person,* in *the first person!*

But if the third person were used, it would be extremely difficult to give the reader a sound reason why the Youth should be the hero, and to justify such <choice>.

Start without any kind of introduction—more original that way, and only in some other place, later, in the following chapters: All this happened a year ago, of course I am a different person now, etc.

[Also in the first chapter: ~~the reader~~ One might think that what I'm writing is all nonsense, but it is really very serious and, what is most important, I'm writing nothing that isn't necessary, everything is quite important—even that Fool, for the time will come when he will begin to play a role.]

But in the finale: A detailed description of how he was saving the child,* with all the horrors of it, and later, how he is dying, without the slightest hint regarding the meaning of life, etc.

[In *the first person,* it's definite now. No matter what happens. But he is writing it a year after <the event>. Keep this in mind in every line.]

"We are living *in seclusion*"—two aunts. To see the mother's grave. "I think that your aunt is right, suggesting that you enroll in the university." 25,000.

---

* *Spasal rebenka.* The Russian form is ambiguous, since it could mean "saved" or "was trying to save."

A ray. Everything casually and significantly. "But now I shall stop, for I have [other things to do. My idea.] [September 12 I drove to <the Cathedral of> the Savior.] Or should I rather not take those 25,000? In that case, I'll join the civil service."

The Youth makes his way into real life from a sea of idealism *(his own idea).* He is suddenly surrounded by all the different elements of our society at once.

His own idea failed to stand the test and at once began to waver. Hence his depressed state. [An idea. Convey this mood to the reader more clearly.] But being the gloomy misanthrope he is, he won't concede defeat, but keeps viewing the world with arrogance. He accuses everybody and decides to go against every law. (N.B. When Makar is dying, he sheds tears and kisses his hand; and in a scene with his mother and Liza, he accuses them of servility.)

Now he is really in a whirl. Scene with the Princess. Somber scene involving Lambert's leg. His arrest. The scenes after his arrest are already in a different mood.

The novel contains all the elements <of our society>. Civilized and desperate, idle and skeptical, of the higher intelligentsia—that's He.

Ancient Holy Russia—Makar's family.

What is holy, good about new Russia—the aunts.

A <great> family gone to seed—the young Prince (a skeptic, etc.)

High society—the funny and the abstractly ideal type.

The young generation—the Youth, all instinct, knows nothing.

Vasin—hopelessly ideal.

Lambert—flesh, matter, horror—etc.

"I can see that my idea has not been realized; however, the idea still stands. Having made this statement I conclude by saying that I won't write anymore for at least five years. I shall devote this time to my studies. And then, after five years, I may reread what I have written <and> check myself. In 5 years the status of my idea will become more definite also."

Perhaps [unnecessary].

DEFINITIVELY. Better *without even the slightest* comments or reservations, just say that it happened a year ago.

N.B. In the finale. "I wanted to say that <we> shouldn't take any money from the Prince, but said nothing. <My> aunt only gave me a look."

About frou-frou. I was in that kind of a mood *then.*

DEFINITIVE.

All the elements of our society were present, and it appeared to me that we were like mummers, refusing to understand each other; yet we speak the same language, we belong to the same country and even to the same family. (N.B. That's it. And the transition to the next chapter. Finish it abruptly. Write more abruptly all along.)

Disorder.

In *the first person,* in *the first person*—September 12.

The Youth is amazed at the baseness <of the world> and curses the whole world. He is himself in agony about his idea concerning the letters. Vasin and the landlord. The Youth is thinking of suicide. Kraft shoots himself (while Vasin comes suddenly to return the papers). Everybody has been arrested. Lambert talks him into it. The letter. His father reports to the old Prince about the letter. He <the father> is shown the door. He proposes to <Makar's> wife, chops up some icons. The next day he tells the Youth that, if he only had the document, she'd be licking his boots. He wants to get even with her. "I would have never married her." [Lambert's story left out. Death of the old Prince left out.] He doesn't say himself that he is out to get even with her, but the Youth can see it. The Youth about his father: "Quite decidedly, he had become attached to me." The Youth is terribly excited. His landlord has burned his wife. Lambert and Andrieux. The old Prince to Andrieux. [They both start crying. A disgusting, nerve-wracking scene. Nothing comes of it. Lambert says that nothing will come of this idiot.] ~~The Youth~~ "What is this whole world good for?" exclaims the Youth. The Youth reveals the secret of the letter to Lambert. Liza. Some kind of desperate scene [between him, his mother, and Liza.] The mother: "Bear it." The Youth: "Eh, to hell with it all!" Power, start a conflagration, he suddenly learns that He is in on the plot with Lambert. The scene of the violation, kills Lambert, the Princess. The Princess has already learned about Liza's romance. The Youth finds out about it. Back home, Liza drowns herself. She leaves a letter. (N.B. The Youth hears the story of Liza's romance either from the Prince, through the latter's incidental remarks, or <from> Liza: "Farewell, my darling.") Liza's body recovered from the water. *He,* <her> mother. The Youth is arrested.

~~The Youth is under arrest for a short time only, a week or so; upon his return he finds his mother dying.~~ Returning from prison. ~~The aunt tells him. He goes there. The little boy.~~ The little boy has disappeared. The Youth rushes to find him. He is found (to Liza). He brings the boy. He, the aunts, and the boy. "Live for their sake. Forget about my own idea." Three months later the boy laughs, embraces Him. He is an idiot. Cries.

[25,000, get an education. The Princess has gone abroad and has taken the old Prince with her. The young Prince is living somewhere in the country.]

N.B. À propos the novel. The Youth is <the> hero in every respect. He is with the old Prince, and with the young Prince (a duel), and with his father, and at his own flat with the government clerk, and with Vasin about his idea.* The latter hands him his papers. He is also aware of Liza's romance. He also loves the little child, is close to his mother, is greatly impressed by Makar Ivanov. N.B. It might be that Lambert, in particular, fascinates him.

"To hell with everything. Leave everything and run." He cannot see any sense in Him, though He is dear to him, and so he argues with Him all the time. Also, the meekness at home doesn't make sense to him. Neither can he understand the meaning of his budding love for the Princess. Even his own idea seems senseless and shaky, which makes him feel terribly giddy. And Vasin, too, seems senseless. And Liza's romance is terrifying. And what good is justice? ~~And he would like to~~

He is terribly impressed by Makar Ivanov. He would like both to see an aristocrat humiliated and, tempted by Lambert, to get all that money. But he loves his little brother to the point where it hurts.

THE YOUTH GROWS MORE AND MORE UNSOCIABLE AND SOMBER.

~~A dreamer, the [thought] of suicide.~~ Especially after [Makar and the icons.]

~~Young~~ The Youth was turning somber and taciturn. [It might go even without Lambert.]

Lambert (without the Fool). "You ask for 30,000 and a fuck." He is thinking about the idea of fucking <her>. And altogether, he is thinking of the entire scene of <her> humiliation; he has an urge to start a conflagration—to get even <with them> for everything; as for those 30 thousand, he haughtily dreams of leaving them to Lambert. An urge to set a fire. He** penetrates the conspiracy at the very last moment. Perhaps, only Lambert and he, without Him, though He knows about everything.

[Incidentally, the Fool is needed. Lambert kills him.]

---

* Ungrammatical in the original.

** Apparently "He" is meant.

[Think, but the 1st part is good.]

~~Shouldn't it be <written> in *the first person?*~~

The tone is such. For instance, the story of His relationship with the Princess... They parted as enemies and this is the state of affairs when the Youth arrives on the scene, etc.; etc. *à la Pouchkine*—the story of each character being a *secondary* one, with only the Youth being dealt with *primarily,* i.e., the poem is devoted to him. He is the hero.

All this had a terrifying and a somber effect on him. It led him all the way to falling in love with the Princess (without his father being aware of it) and to crime. *Idea.* I.e., the Youth despised them all for their guilt, and became *guilty himself. He is saved* from having to stand trial.

Perhaps the little boy didn't drown <after all>. The Youth finds him. He drags him from the water. He stays with the little boy and with his deranged father.

"For the time being I shall be working to support these two; there's a job for me. I'll be a bourgeois."

The young Prince himself breaks off <his engagement> with the Princess. He has 200,000 which He has conceded to him. The Princess has a passion for the young Prince. He says: "A widow, an old woman, madness."

September 13.

Adjustment in the plan (complication of the *sujet*). He has summoned <his> family to have a moral (refuge), i.e., the devil only knows why. I.e., precisely because of his excited state and his strained psychic condition. Rejected the year before by that proud idealist, the Princess, merely because of her suspicion that He does not love her for her own sake, disinterestedly, but rather intends to better his financial position through this marriage, He marries the Prince's stepdaughter, an orphan. [(N.B. Upon the old Prince's own suggestion.)]

The General's widow is afraid of a will, but succeeds in making the Prince reserve for her another huge dowry (the first had been dissipated by her late husband, the General).

[She fears the letter for the reason that the document concerning those 200,000 had been found at Andreev's, so why not also the letter?]

She is engaged to the young Prince. *He* denounces <the marriage> of a 26-year-old "old woman" to a 27-year-old <man>; furthermore, he, i.e., the young Prince, is not serving anywhere, etc. [Passion, he had been charged with <the desecration? of> some icons.]

Nevertheless, he returns those 200,000 (in the beginning of the novel. The report of this event exceedingly impresses the Youth, who has just arrived from Moscow.) However, the return of those 200,000 makes no impression whatsoever on the Princess, except sneers. [The Princess is laughing at his having returned the 200,000, and she lets the aunt and ~~stepdaughter~~ her father the Prince know how she feels. The latter is amused *by it*. The Youth communicates this conversation to Him.] *He* is bitter about it.

Simultaneously, the Princess lets the old Prince and his stepdaughter know about *the existence* of Makar's family. He ~~they are assuming that it is the Princess who has been tattling~~ knows that it is the Princess who has been tattling. Which makes him even madder. He challenges the young Prince to a duel, but the latter won't accept the challenge (after the return of those 200,000). The challenge brings Him and the Youth closer together, on account of the fact that he had offered 50,000.*

Makar dies. The young Prince loves Liza, but isn't, God knows why, attracted by Liza. The Princess finds out about this. She forgives the young ~~suspect~~ Prince. But she keeps suspecting Him [and (in a fit of passion) accuses Him of wanting to make the Prince marry Liza, and of buying the Prince <for> 200,000,] whereas He doesn't even know about Liza at this point. [This is why her hatred against him has grown.] [She demands that the young Prince return those 200,000. He does not want to.]

Suddenly Lambert appears on the scene. He has documents to prove that the Prince has committed forgery. [He wants] to suggest that either the Prince or the Princess buy them from him. *He* <the father> gets together with Lambert and buys the document. He sends it over to the Princess. ~~rendezvous She~~ On account of the Princess, His rupture with the old Prince and his stepdaughter. *He* offers to marry <Makar's> wife and chops up those icons. He goes to see the old Prince and denounces her to him, saying that she wanted to have him declared insane (thus casting prudence to the winds). He is shown the door. The letter is found. With the Youth. Shows it to Lambert. *He* wants to wheedle it out of him. The scene with the violation, etc. *He* is indirectly involved in the plot.

The Princess insults Liza.

[Makar Ivanov. The diamonds. The Youth finds out about Liza.] [From Lambert or from the Princess. She tells him about Him—that

---

* Not quite clear in the original.

He wanted ~~to sell~~ to buy the Prince for Liza.] [N.B. A showdown between the Youth and the Princess, during which she treats him casually, insulting him. ~~Revenge~~ At first he is charmed, but then he finds reason to feel insulted] and joins the conspiracy. The Princess has obtained all the information for the Youth and subsequently <says> to him: "What is it you were going to say?"

Meanwhile Lambert has arrived in town. He has taken 5,000 rubles from the Princess for a compromising document. *He* tells Lambert that he is a fool, that even the young Prince himself now has a fortune of nearly 200,000, and that he could have gotten 10,000 from the young Prince and the Princess for this kind of document. But Lambert hadn't known that the young Prince owned 200,000 (on this occasion, he expresses his surprise that He has returned those 200,000) and tells him that he had negotiated the deal with the Princess who, upon having bought the document, had begged him not to tell the young Prince about the document. But as for herself, she felt that these were trifles. "She wants to reproach the young Prince for it, she wants to nag him with this document, and hold him firmly in her hands besides," says He. (N.B. When the Youth asks the Prince, "Are you acquainted with one Lambert?" the Prince gets angry, but later tries to make up to him, though in a condescending manner, just barely receiving him at his house. Then, the theft of the diamonds, etc.)

He tells Lambert outright that he is a fool—why didn't he give that document to Him? And states, in this connection: "If I only had that letter!"

[The old Prince, [Mme] Andrieux. A pathetic scene.]

The Youth tells Lambert that he has got the letter. ~~The Youth~~ Lambert communicates this information to Him. But the Youth won't let him have the note, even though Lambert offers him money; but he is willing to go along with the plan according to which Lambert would rape her, take 50,000 from her, "and later you can fuck her, too."

He keeps aloof. He would like to have his revenge. (It is right at this point that the Princess has just insulted Liza and the young Prince has deserted her, even though he had done some crying before the Princess.) *He* finds out that Liza is dishonored. The day before her wedding. Lambert is about to rape her, but the Youth won't let him. Then Lambert, seeing that his scheme has failed, decides ~~momentarily~~ to kill the Fool and to make his escape as fast as possible.

The young Prince ~~would have preferred~~ has a premonition that life with the General's widow is going to be hell. Meanwhile Liza drowns herself. Wedding of the Princess and the young Prince. *He* is put to shame, and stunned. <Makar's> wife dies. *He* suffers very much from the fact that the little boy is afraid of him. The Youth has no end of trouble with both of them. Lambert with his leg. The Youth is arrested. He shows up again 5 days later. The boy has run away.

Couldn't He have sent the compromising document to the young Prince, but *without being rewarded,* etc.? Lambert tells the Youth outright that He is in on the plot, but has told Lambert not to tell him. When Lambert learns that He has turned over the document <to the young Prince> he tears into Him, but ~~He calms him down~~ having learned from Lambert that the letter does exist, <He> explains the whole importance of the letter <to Lambert>, insisting, also, on going through with the rape.* Lambert openly tells everything to the Youth, much to the latter's amazement; he is disturbed by the fact that He is asking <Lambert> to rape her, but it also inflames him. The proud Princess.

After Liza's death the Youth is so depressed that he does not want to take revenge on the Prince. [He is reproaching himself for having forgotten about Liza.]

It is even worse with Him. He is even more crushed. After Liza's death he accuses everybody; the whole family is gathered; the heartbreaking scene of Mother's death. On the day of the funeral the little boy keeps asking for Liza. He <his father> is trying to talk to the boy, but he is afraid of Him, and won't let go of the Youth; but the Youth is arrested, and the little boy runs away to drown himself (to join Liza). They find him.

The whole question about the marriage amounted to this: Would the Prince give (the Princess) another dowry? The old Prince was trying to stand firm (to show his authority, while being afraid of everybody, as He explains to the Youth), but on the day He denounces <her> he gives her 300,000 and chases Him out of his house.

"I do not love her," He says to the Youth, "all I want is that she admit that I am an honest man, that's all."

"And a great man?"

"What do you mean?"

"An honest and a great man," the Youth repeats.

---

* Ungrammatical and not quite clear in the original.

"Mon cher, vos sarcasmes <. . .>"[7] (They quarrel, but later He still comes back to see ~~him~~ the Youth.)

In the beginning he says this about the Princess: "I am very glad that she is so smitten with the little Prince. ~~Both she and he~~ God is punishing them both, [and him even more so, for] she will at least be holding her own" (however, in reality he isn't glad at all, but on the contrary, opposes <this match> with everything he's got). Toward the end.

Absolutely, a scene showing a rendezvous between Him [and] the Princess, a meeting He has extorted from her. [The scene featuring insincere emotions <on His part> and his insincere position after the return of the forged promissory note is unmercifully exposed by the Princess. However, He does return the document.] It all ends in sarcasms and sneers. (This scene takes place *in the Youth's presence,* perhaps purposely so). "What do you want from me?" says the Princess, "I agree that you are a great man."

After this scene He offers to marry <Makar's> wife, then chops up those icons, and tells the Prince that the Princess had wanted to place him in an insane asylum.

Though the old Prince does not make much fuss when told that Makar's family is at his place ("I always suspected that there was something of that kind going on at his place"), and actually wants to meet the family, but when he denounces the Princess, He shows Him the door and refuses his stepdaughter permission to marry Him.* Though she had already turned him down earlier.

Having learned from Lambert that the letter exists, ~~He~~ he asks to have it, in order to show it to the old Prince, but Lambert says that <this way> they wouldn't get any money, and so it is decided that ~~it is the money~~ she should be asked for some money, and raped. Lambert wants to ask for 100,000. He suggests 25, then decides that she may, perhaps, give 50,000—and rape her.** In a word, He is *blinded* and lost himself, but is counting on Lambert, <and> figures that, at any rate, there is going to be a scandal.

He suspects (even before Lambert) that the Youth has got the document and makes an attempt to wheedle it out of him. But he simply tells Him that he hasn't found a thing.

---

* The translation duplicates the anacoluthon found in the original.

** Ungrammatical in the original.

[7] French: "My dear, your sarcasms."

The Prince's stepdaughter is a passive creature.*

With all these scenes, notes, and violating going on, He knows nothing about Liza's romance. When he finally finds out, he is crushed.

During their meeting, the Princess makes some strange mocking insinuations regarding Liza. ~~But seeing that He does not know yet... she remains silent~~ This is where he hears about Liza<'s affair> for the first time.

~~A challenge to the Prince, who refuses to accept it,~~ disgrace. [There had been an earlier challenge.] He rushes home, makes a scene to Liza, offers to marry <Makar's> wife, so as to break all ties, and rise above <the Princess>. (The proposal is made in front of everybody; on the next day, the icons.) [N.B. The proposal to <Makar's> wife is completely unprovoked.] He goes to see the old Prince, who shows him the door. *He* is acting as if he were mad. The letter and the rape. When he returns home after the scene of the rape Liza has drowned herself.

Question: When does the Youth find out about those 200,000? ~~On the train, from the aunt. And when the aunts~~ From his mother, when she comes to pick up the little boy, and from Vasin. The Youth is surprised that Vasin knows about it.

With private *explanations* in the chapters <written> by the Youth. For instance, "He did not know about Liza at the time. The Prince was told about Liza by . . . How could I know that the first hint that the letter existed would have such a painful effect upon him? But I was purposely teasing him with my hint... and only a hint, no more." Later, the Youth makes a point of revealing nothing about the letter, as He sinks lower and lower in his opinion. "I was going to do the very same thing, yet I wouldn't allow Him to do it, and was condemning Him with loathing."

Important note. Since the whole thing has happened four years earlier, all these digressions and explanations on the part of the Youth are actually indispensable. HOWEVER, WATCH OUT THAT THE NARRATIVE DOESN'T LOSE ITS NAÏVETÉ.

PLAN. *September 14.*

~~Only~~ All this happened [over] 4 years ago. [Over] 4 years. What a terribly long time. [Everybody was calling me "a youth" then.] However, in order not to write anything that isn't necessary, I find it to

* *Podushka,* literally, "a pillow."

~~make~~ appropriate to make a short introduction. As I am describing the first steps [of my career] in Petersburg, I don't want to make this a Code of Law.

I am the illegitimate son of a gentleman. From Makar, and who Makar is. I saw my father once. At the aunts'. The family. [I'll tell about him later.] Mother, in passing. In Luga. I am at Souchard's, later in high school, a German. I was absorbed in my idea. But there will be many pages about me later on.

Who is my father? <Went through> several fortunes, of a good family, worked as a District Commissioner (his biography in a few lines). Well educated. Religiousness. ~~During~~ A year prior to the beginning of my notes, <affair> with the Princess. Daughter of the old Prince. About the old Prince, *bon mot*. Ideally cold, how they got together, and how they parted. The Princess openly said that <He was> after her fortune, thus cruelly insulting him. He could never forget the insult. Enemies. [The letter and Andreev.]

He had the urge to see her acknowledge that he was a great man. Cruel sarcasms. She drove him to that state of frenzy in which I found him when I arrived.

The old Prince was afraid of both. Drive both of them mad.

[The inheritance.] [A claimant (the young Prince, to the inheritance).]

About how the family moved from Luga. The father. Did he want to retire from all the noise <of the world>, and to the bosom <of mother Russia>? He had always respected Mother, though it is hard to imagine how it could have been otherwise. ~~I began to~~ He continued to run the Prince's affairs. I have no idea who was the first to think of the Stepdaughter. A passive creature* out of finishing school. The Prince *makes it his concern*. Father, in order to show that he wasn't thinking of her anymore. Alas! He thought to the end that it was only *la haine dans l'amour*.[8] At least that's what I think.

Meanwhile, there's that claimant, the young Prince, in Petersburg. Father finds out that he is her protegé. About her several unfortunate protegés; at first she almost married a wretch of a Frenchman, <later> her General <husband> who gambled away her dowry (150,000), then later her own father became a protegé of hers, for he was suffering from the pangs of conscience, finally the young Prince and family.

---

* *Ibid.*

8 French: "Hate in love."

Who the young Prince is. His trial. Acquitted. "Where do you put him?" However, I think that there was some passion in it also, for he had charm. Casually, [with a crook,] Lambert. [The Princess has spread the rumor that by marrying that passive creature <the Prince's stepdaughter> he is in effect becoming a kept man.] That's when Father is driven to a frenzy. What, then, did he do?

The document <left> after Andreev's death. Returns 200,000. I wasn't yet aware of the return of those 200,000 when I first met my father, etc. [The return of this money had a great effect. But the Princess got a scare on account of <the other> document.]

But as for my having been called <to Petersburg>, the fact was that I had done poorly during my last year in high school (my own idea). *I was stuck with that idea.* Failed to pass my examination. My father called me. I do not know if he wanted to return <. . .>, break with everything, start a new life. He was sickly then, many sensations, <in a> daze, and disorder.

But this is how it came out: The Princess, having learned that the matter involving "that passive creature" had been decided (the Prince was under the thumb of both of them, and would try to play one against the other, but would, in special cases, also seek the support of one against the other. He liked to show off his independence, which is why he came up with the passive creature without asking for anyone's advice, i.e., without having asked the Princess). She then told him about Makar's family, and the Prince found it amusing: "*Cher,* you have a son, but where is he?"

"He has failed his examination [every time]. He writes me that he wants to earn his living."

"You see, I can use a young man; he could learn some manners."

"He is a nihilist." (It ought to be mentioned that I was not a nihilist at all, just had my own ideas.)

"So much the better."

And for three full days he was nursing this idea, pestering people with it. Then he almost forgot it. The Princess was showing her disdain by silence. My father chose to play it defiantly:

"As your secretary? But he would be nothing but a spy!"

They were expecting the Prince from Moscow. My father was furious. But playing it defiantly. I think that he was expecting me with some anxiety, to see for himself what kind of an impression I would make. But the Prince was insisting <that I come immediately>. And so I went. [The night before,<the episode> with the university student.]

And so, 5 years ago exactly, I came to the Moscow railway ticket office, etc.

[And later, explanations concerning how this all came about, how he himself became involved, and Liza, and Christianity, Vasin, <my> idea, and 200,000. Makar Ivanov.]

The end of the novel: He and the infant. A ray. We find <?> a cheap flat, then I enroll in the university. [It turns out we have some money, father had some. ~~The aunt says: I took 25,000.]~~

And so the decision to write in *the first person* has come all by itself.

September 14.

The old Prince has left the Youth 10,000. Whereas the fact that the young Prince had made an attempt to return 50,000 to Him, in the beginning of the novel, had caused Him to challenge the Prince to a duel.

The Youth is summoned on account of Liza.* At this point, a meeting, and showdown, with the young Prince.

Insert this in the first part: Arrival of "that passive creature" and a fleeting glance at Liza, when he enters the aunt's flat one evening in order to write Him a letter. This is also when he overhears the General's widow in spite of himself. He is struggling hard with himself, whether he should come out or not, finally comes out, and like a fool, too ("spy!"). Then he goes home to his own flat. (No need of the wench here. The wench will come up in part two, during his wanderings after the incident with the diamonds.)

September 18.

Can't make it 5 years. The reader will be left with the crude, rather comical idea that "there's that young adolescent now grown up, and perhaps holding a Master's degree, and a jurist, describing with great condescension (the devil only knows why) how foolish he used to be before," etc. And thus the whole naïveté of the narrative is destroyed. And therefore, better let it be a year. In the tone of the narrative, the whole impact of a recent shock would still be apparent, and a good many things would still remain unclear, yet at the same time there would be this first line: "A year, what a tremendous interval of time!" Toward the end of his notes—"our means," etc. And suddenly, these final lines: "If ever these lines should happen to get into the Princess's hands, let her see how unmercifully ~~etc.~~ I have drawn her character, etc. However, nobody will read them, of course: I am going to seal

* Might also mean: "The Youth's challenge on account of Liza."

them and look through them in about five years." (N.B. He is still undecided about the university, his own idea is still weighing on him.) And there is one *last* and very important note: "Alas, my idea has diverted me from my feelings for Liza, for my mother; it has not allowed me to make <my life> meaningful, and still doesn't," etc.

N.B. *For myself*. The introduction must be written cleverly. If it is a success, everything will be.

The young Prince used to live in Luga, having been exiled* to that town. He has come to Moscow for two weeks only, to visit with his family. And suddenly he receives a cable from the Princess, informing him that the document has been found.

He, to the Youth regarding the Princess: "A woman is capable of any cruelty, any Jesuitism." The Youth fully agrees with this statement.

Suddenly, a letter from "that passive creature" to Him, in the 2d part, completely unmotivated.

September 19.

The young Prince finds out about the existence of her letter to Andreev, a letter which would cause the old Prince to disinherit her. Without a moment's thought he gets a hold on "that passive creature" (who will be given some money). It is at this point that the Princess pounces upon the document.

He would have liked even to return her the letter as a noble gesture.

The young Prince, to Him after the challenge: "Why won't you yield 'that passive creature' to me? Of course I could get by even without you, but you do have some influence on the old Prince." He shows the young Prince the door, but when the old Prince has chased Him out, it immediately develops that the young Prince will marry "that passive creature." (Lambert has convinced the young Prince of the existence of that document.)

He had been trying to get the document in order to give it to her, but was vacillating himself. Whereas the Youth and Lambert would not surrender the document. "All right then, so fuck <her>," He thinks.

The Princess, having received the document, takes it straight to the old Prince, and he leaves his whole fortune to her. At the same time,

---

* Not to be taken literally; the meaning seems to be "having been drummed out from his regiment and forced to leave the capital."

he does not allow "that passive creature" to marry the young Prince. As a consequence the latter takes to carousing with Lambert. Loses 200,000 to Nekrasov; he and Lambert together kill the Fool. The young Prince to Liza: "Liza, give those 25,000 back to me," and she immediately lets him have the money.

The young Prince is 26 years old. Earlier (4 years ago) the young Prince had stolen some diamonds; He was a juror <at his trial?>. Now he's gotten to be very proud, wants to restore the <honor of his> family. Treats Him haughtily on account of those 50,000. Used to have Liza in Petersburg, whenever he wanted. Somehow the Princess finds out about it. She demands that he break with her. He gives 10,000. The Youth demands an explanation. (The affair with the diamonds is solved by the young Prince purposely in favor of the Youth.) He explains <the whole thing> in a condescending manner. The Youth expresses *his idea* of getting rich before his mother and Liza. In a frenzy, he is drawn into a mad whirl. Liza always feared the Prince and loved him with a strange love. Finally, he personally sends Liza on her way. After Liza has left, almost glad, she is suddenly seized by a fit of melancholy. (Even the Princess had found it beyond her powers to insult her.) The Youth is amazed at such base humbleness. She means to go and watch the wedding. Drowns herself. It is at this point that He learns everything, whereas the Youth had known about it earlier.

The young Prince tries to arrange a match between Liza and some young man. Not knowing what is going on, He approves of it. Liza comes to see him and explains everything. The liberal young man feels a little hurt. He admits the liberal young man in the very beginning, not knowing that he has been sent by the young Prince. So he is an early acquaintance. *Work on this character.*

Liza: "I shall enter a convent."

In the beginning Liza is willing to listen to his proposal, but then she suddenly turns him down. This is the cause of her (last) meeting with the Prince.

The young man is quite persistently trying to make friends with the Youth. Finally, he gains recognition as a suitor, but when Liza's heart begins to ache she turns him down.

Wandering around (with her fiancé) she drops in on the young Prince. "Let's go to Luga, let's live far away from here..." (a touching exchange). Then she collects herself: "Oh God, what am I talking about!"—and leaves. Her fiancé feels insulted: "You might have spared my feelings, Lizaveta Makarovna."

"Oh, I don't know... Well, good-bye."

At home: "Oh, it is hard." Mother: "Does it hurt, Liza?" Liza: "It hurts, mamma." "Bear it."

September 20.

Final version.

He knew about the Prince and Liza and when the Youth arrived, *the young man* was, with everybody's consent, expected to make a visit. On the first day the Youth was not aware of that, but just before the scene where <He> rips open <the little boy's> mouth he ran into the young man. The latter leaves, and then the scene where <He> rips open <the little boy's> mouth. 10,000 had been allotted to the young man in the form of a promissory note cosigned by the old Prince. [He is terribly upset about the old Prince's apparent intention to act as a benefactor of His family.]

He was furious that the Princess had a part in this business, but preferred to shrug his shoulders, considering the disposition of his family. Besides, he was finding it to his own advantage to marry off Liza. "That passive creature" also used to come and visit. All of which He later explains to the Youth. However, He does not like the fact that she and the young man are, obviously, creatures of hers.

However, the Youth finds out about that only much later, from the young Prince himself, and already at the time of the <incident with the> diamonds and after His sudden and unmotivated challenge to the young Prince. This is why his challenge, also, seems merely ridiculous and troublesome to the Prince. After the <incident with the> diamonds the young Prince explains the matter to the Youth and, most important, His and Liza's view of it. "Eh, what the devil!" thinks the Youth, and this is the first time that ~~the essence of the matter~~ cynicism finds a way into his heart. Yet He is still trying to save him, is sincere with him, and fascinates him. At this point, Makar Ivanov. Here the Youth inadvertently gets together with Liza [and his mother] and tells them about his idea, upbraiding and condemning them for their meekness, even though Makar Ivanov has left a strong impression on him. As for his father, he speaks of him with contempt, suggesting to them that they should leave Him.

~~After this, a meeting between Him and the Princess at which the Youth is present. Sarcastic statements about Liza.~~ The Youth is so confused he wants to stay away from them all. But there's the letter. *He* again mentions the letter to him after that meeting—again, since he had mentioned it before. The Youth disgustedly insults Him. ~~He~~

Yet the letter is beginning to preoccupy the Youth, and worries him greatly. He is roaming the streets at night!

Offers his hand to <Makar's> wife. Chops up those icons. A nocturnal encounter with him. Again about the letter. The Youth shows Him the door and ~~calls him a scoundrel~~ heaps ridicule on him. [He remains silent (that night).] Encounter with Lambert. Quick influence. The latter surprises the Youth by telling him that he has passed on to Him a forged promissory note of the <young> Prince's.

[Admission of the existence of those letters, but to whom?]

Furthermore, the Youth is present at a meeting between Him and the Princess on the occasion when He hands over the document to her. The Princess heaps sarcasms on Him. She also insults both Liza and the Youth. Both leave. He is in a frenzy. So is Lambert. But Lambert mentions the letter. His advice, etc. On the following day He reveals everything to the old Prince, in a fit of impotent fury. The Prince shows Him the door.

The Youth is convinced that He won't be present at the meeting on account of the letter, but there He suddenly emerges, having killed Lambert;* the Youth runs away, to his own home. As for the Princess, she had come to the meeting because He had made the young Prince believe that the Princess would not be getting much.

In the meantime Liza's romance had taken its course ~~and she drowns herself~~. Liza turns down her suitor. On the following day the Princess sees the Youth.

Lambert recovers.

He suffers a moral breakdown.

Liza drowns herself. She had been insulted by the Princess the day before.

He has a moral breakdown, etc.

I.e., cynicism and all almost to the very end. He both loves and corrupts the Youth. The Youth is beginning to shun society; at one time he is consumed by an urge to break with society altogether, after having humiliated the Princess to his heart's content, <but> he cannot make himself go through with it.

The young man mentions several times, both to the Youth and to Liza, that He is to all appearances about to become a member of a not quite respectable [clean] family. [Meetings with the Princess.]

---

* Though this is the literal translation, it may well be that "emerges and kills Lambert" is what is really meant.

The Princess won't marry the young Prince. "That passive creature."

"Who needs the good; the good is of no use to anybody," He corrupts the Youth after <the scene with> the icons.

He was greatly pained by falsities and failures: i.e., having handed over that 200,000 promissory note, his false position within the family, the refusal of <Makar's> wife to marry him, the icons, the release of the document. [Meetings with the Princess.] <Also,> the challenge to a duel, as well as his last, mad sally when He lets the old Prince know that the letter exists.

"Where then, is that letter?"

"This letter has been purloined by this person" (i.e., the Youth).

But the Youth denies it. (Though Lambert had already admitted it.) N.B. The young Prince needs a personality. Liza has a personality.

The young Prince is also a sickly person, but charming; he would like to rise above his present condition. The Youth sees that he, too, has got *his own idea* and, while hating him, loves him.

"I am a coward," says the Prince to him. The Prince is challenged to a duel. At the duel <he retains his composure> with difficulty. The Princess is stunned.

?
All Questions {
About Dolgushin.
The Fool.
Andrieux.
The old Prince.
The Fool and the Youth are sharing a flat.
The Liar-Windbag is their landlord.

The Youth, in spite of his gloomy airs and tragic moods, is still an adolescent: he loves, he laughs with the old Prince, and later he sympathizes with Liza.

The old Prince suddenly decides to pay a visit to the Youth. Vasin. N.B. *A table*. N.B.!

THE SPIRIT OF THE YOUTH. Vacillation. He seeks a solution from Vasin. Vasin causes him to waver, but his thought does not coincide with his idea [(he cannot comprehend man without property).] He becomes a devotee of his father's (morally) and is tormented by the fact that He is not a good man. Incomprehensible episodes with Makar and his family. The mood he is in prevents him from seeing Liza. Pride, and insults from the Princess and the young Prince. Rivalry with the young Prince. They are arrested. He is quite stunned and withdraws into himself. Wants to kill himself. "No, it is better to live by being base. [People aren't worth a Vasin. How about Christ? When I become powerful, I'll be doing good."] The power of that letter. Ungern-Shternberg.[9] The icons, and <His> whole weakness. Liza's grief, and the family's. Lambert. Fascinates him. The passion to start a conflagration. He comes to his senses. Destruction, is seized along with Lambert, who has told on <Him>. The Princess, who has not married the young Prince, intervenes on <his> behalf. He is released. His little brother and He. He is saved by a strong feeling, and by his aunt.

He is writing his notes in order to send them abroad, to the Princess, who suddenly starts giving him encouragement. (Think this through. About the Princess.)

His own idea. Get an education, but his own idea. His own idea still stands.

The old Prince: ["If I should marry,] of course I wouldn't have any children."

His daughter: "Quite the contrary, ~~you will~~ it's you precisely who is going to have children, if you get married."

The old Prince: "Tiens, c'est un bon mot.[10] ~~And malicious~~ And inasmuch as there is very little wit around these days and wit is in fact shunned, I forgive you your [malicious] *bon mot* from the bottom of my heart, in spite of the biting remark directed against me, which it contained. I was ~~seven~~ two months premature, we were twins and the two of us would have fit on one plate. My brother died when he was two weeks old, while I've been living for better than fifty years now, and ~~even~~ going strong, so it seems."

He was living a reverent life (Makar Ivanov).*

"They are all downtrodden and meek, yet firm as saints."

~~No~~ *Idle atheism* all over.

Olia, frightened: "I love you too," and she put her hand on his elbow.

Frightened by Him.

Later, the Swiss governess. Two years (N.B. He hired the governess because He had frightened her.) Makar. He was living a reverent life. Sanctified by his bonds (that's why he stayed at the flat). Praying

---

* *Zhil pochtitel'no,* literally, "he was living respectfully, he was living reverently," a solecism from the viewpoint of the literary idiom.

9 See note 3 of Part II.

10 French: "Say, that's a clever word."

for the atonement of their sins. Knows everybody by his first name. He would give <alms> all over to help people.*

Mother to Olia: "Bear it!"

In the railway carriage ~~the aunt~~: "I am proud to be a bastard."

The aunt: "Forget the color. You don't have to be proud, nor do you have to feel humiliated."

In the railway carriage: "Eat a bite." The fact that she was a relative had its effect, but he was gloomy and even embarrassed, the more so the closer they were getting to Petersburg.

They are there: "Should I go and see Him, or shouldn't I? Better if he'll come to see me." He tells <the cabman> to take him to His place.

In the railway carriage. The aunt has fallen asleep. The Youth recalls his childhood, his mother and the new hospital; at Andreev's, his stern aunt who was also kind, and now he puts a pillow under her head... [In *the first person.*]

"What are you doing, dear?" She's asleep, a good face, good wrinkles.

"Auntie, I'm just giving you a pillow."

"Thank you, Vasia, thank you."

"Auntie, it isn't that I don't respect *your* Christ" (I couldn't help saying that,) "I respect him very much as a historical figure."

"Well, all right. But watch out, you can't <speak in this way> against the <Holy> Ghost."**

"So why won't you let me sleep."

About Lambert, firm (they've thought up a plan). <His> mother comes <. . .>

He asks his aunt at dawn: "Is that so?" By the time they get to Liuban' he is overcome by mixed emotions.

[April, head, soldier.] Of course, if I were to write down all of these anecdotes I'd get a whole Code of Law.

I am not going to make any more such comments.

In the railway carriage he says to the aunt, after some silence: "I saw my father the last time when <he said> *'il faut le rosser.'* "[11]

"So don't be angry." I was really going to say that to my aunt, but I didn't (when all of a sudden she began to talk to me peaceably and kindly). "So what, it's a good name," said my aunt.

---

* Unclear in the original.

** Allusion to Matt. 12: 31–32.

[11] French: "You have to beat him."

"Makar Ivan<ov>, why has he got that resounding name Dolgoruky? I don't know it, nor do I want to know it." "I understand that you used to like Russian history."

The fact that she was a relative did have an effect.

Father: *"Il faut le rosser."*[12]

At Vasin's. After telling <him> about his dreams.

"It is already three years since I have given this any thought at all."

"I understand, you must have thought up some plan of your own."

~~He was getting ready to be a future citizen~~

~~"You know what, you're telling me this, too, just to make fun of me."~~

~~"Is that what you think? You are being most suspicious <?> with people. However, even if you feel that I am making fun of you, believe me, it isn't so."~~

The Youth, who during his last few years in high school had been rooming with a German, a teacher, gloomily and in alienation from the soil. "They have their own life, in which I did not participate on purpose; I really was glad, for I had my own idea. [And the more you become alienated, the better." This he says to the young Prince's valet.]

Finale of the novel: "That's nothing," says the aunt (i.e., about everything that has happened), "let this be a lesson to you. Why, you still have a long life ahead of you."

But that's exactly how things turned out. Makar Dolgoruky, letters, "tall and upright."[13]

[I was born.] In the railway carriage. In my daydreams about how I was going to deal with people, I would always do the clever thing, whereas in practice it would always come out stupid, for I would invariably give myself away while talking, and was always too much in a hurry. Perhaps I am exactly the same even now, and altogether this self-control is a very bad thing; in fact, sometimes it deserves unqualified contempt.

Makar Ivanov tells about vespers and vigils, take it from Parthenios.

He. The Youth to a lackey. "We haven't got a nobility, and perhaps we never had one."

"Perhaps you actually couldn't have acted otherwise," says Olia to the young Prince when she learns that he is engaged to the Princess.

---

[12] *Ibid.*

[13] Quotation from Nekrasov's "Vlas."

A valuable observation of the Youth's in the middle of the novel, after his landlord has fried his wife: "I could not write about all these things [many things] at all. They are all so secondary! But I was so very much excited by all this!"

(In the first person, or not?)

They say *He* cried terribly on his wife's grave. Yet he calls it "a mausoleum" when talking to the Youth.

The Youth forgives everybody. "My idea."

He is attending the university. "You know what," says his aunt, "they need medical help, and so they need you. And it's also a good thing to get an education. Why won't you stay in Petersburg? And, my dear, what a long life you've still got ahead of you!"

Though I am no "youth," for I was already 19 at the time, I am calling <this novel> "The Youth" because I was being called by that name by quite a few people then (last year). I am writing this manuscript as notes for myself. Here, in this godforsaken place, I have nothing else to do. [It goes without saying that I am writing this after a year's lapse so that I have really outgrown my childhood.] (Exiled by administrative decree.) [I'll be writing down everything, i.e., only what is relevant. If I should slip up here and there, it won't matter, for I am no littérateur.]

Beginning of the novel.

We were buying our tickets at the ticket office. My aunt insulted me by not paying any attention to me. I for my part was displeased with myself in a vague way. With students on a boulevard. Later, after ~~aunt~~ my conversations with my aunt on the train, I got to thinking about frou-frou, trying to find an excuse for myself in my conscience.

Life is great, own idea.

[The aunt. *He* is not very rich.

20 thousand—yes, 20,000.

The Youth: "If I leave, it means that I have a reason why I'm not going to obey you; we are Makar Ivanov's children."

"We are nothing but the children of Makar Ivanov."]

Then, having taken a seat, about the lost bag and about his aunt, etc.

Without *the first person,* a good many subtle and naïve remarks will get lost.

1st aunt: "You'll complete your education, and then you'll see what you'll do."

2d aunt, a silent (character): "And there you'll see what you'll do."

In the railway carriage, his aunt: "You'd be better off continuing your education (at the university)."

The Youth: "I wasn't studying on purpose."

N.B. If the narrative is to be in the third person, there might be some explanation of the Youth's condition and state of mind, such as: "Indeed, a daydreaming idealist, he was suddenly caught in a whirl of *all* the different elements of Russian society" (*all* the elements).

If in the third person, then only the Youth should be presented in a primary role; everyone else in secondary roles.

N.B. The aunt is pestering him throughout the novel about "continuing his education."

And, regarding what has happened: "That's nothing, it is good for seasoning" (in the finale).

Everything has a limit, even our All-Russian stupidity which, [however,] is nevertheless in a way boundless [on <his> own part.]

IMPORTANT N.B. While discussing Ungern-Shternberg,[14] at Vasin's, the Youth suddenly interrupts himself: "I don't remember how I got to explain this to Vasin, or what exactly I was explaining to him, but it is a fact that this used to happen to me during all of those three years; in fact, it is happening to me even now. My daydreams had taken such a hold on me that I could no longer live without my daydream; as a matter of fact, I can't understand how people can survive without daydreaming. I suppose that all people do some daydreaming. And whoever thinks that daydreaming interferes with business just doesn't know business. When I was only 11 years old I used to jump up and smite the Tartars. I never took vengeance on Souchard in my daydreams, but I did become Ungern-Shternberg.[15] Later, a learned academician, an unrecognized professor. When I had finished (I had told Vasin all about my daydreams without being ashamed), he said to me: 'I notice two things—withdrawal and always being first, never being second.' "

The very same thing, but mockingly and skeptically, in a somber sort of way, more genteel. His character.

The Youth: "Why didn't you at least use your influence to dispel some of Mother's prejudices? I, of course, am not saying a word, for I do not pretend I can raise a person from the dead. But there must have been a time when she was alive."

He: "My friend, she never was. You won't believe it... Here—I even don't know what I should say. Here, there was from the very beginning, humility, meekness, gentleness, and at the same time, firm-

---

14 See note 3 of Part II.
15 *Ibid.*

ness, power, real power, [my friend.] For I have seen how she has been nurtured by that power. [To be sure, it isn't worth much.] <But> there where it comes to—I won't say convictions, for there can't be any talk of true convictions in this case—those things that are considered sacred [by those people,] there she is simply ready to stand any torture <in their defense>. [Consequently, what could I have done, if a tormentor couldn't have accomplished a thing?] Decide for yourself if I look like a tormentor. [I preferred to remain silent, and did the right thing.] I have always been humane and liberal, and she has been trembling before me all her life, yet at the same time she has positively refused to succumb to any form of culture. How she has managed to do that, I just don't know. She just won't say a word. ~~What's most important~~ She doesn't say a word all the time, [that's what is most important,] and then, [perhaps, when really pressed for an answer;]—well ~~I must admit~~, you'll see for yourself that there's no sense in even talking about it! Besides, <her> rejoinders will be of an entirely unexpected nature. You are smiling at my saying that I am humane and liberal, for you are thinking of Makar. God is my witness that the whole thing was conducted in a most humane and liberal manner. I summoned Makar, even before having sinned <with his wife> and put it to him squarely, offering a compensation of 3,000. He said nothing. Here I offered, in case he wasn't satisfied with these conditions, to let him state his own wishes without any fear, and to give him his freedom, together with hers, and *they could go anywhere they wanted.* And keep the money, too. We were all such enthusiasts in those days, and in such a mood, all burning with zeal to do some good, to serve our country, great ideas, "everything that was lofty and beautiful," as they used to say in those days. I'm telling you, I had just finished reading "Anton Goremyka" and "Polinka Saks"[16] when I arrived at my country estate. Have you read these books?"

"I don't remember."

"You should have. I admit that I was actually crying when I was

---

[16] D. V. Grigorovich's *Anton Goremyka* appeared in 1847 and had a great influence on the attitudes of Russian liberals toward the lot of the Russian peasant. A. V. Druzhinin's *Polinka Saks,* published in 1847, concerned the "woman question" and treated it in a sentimental manner. The novel shows the influence of George Sand. When the wife of Polinka Saks tells her husband that she is in love with another man, he gives her his blessing. This work undoubtedly influenced Dostoevsky in *The Possessed,* when Virginsky gives his blessing to his wife when she falls in love with Captain Lebiadkin.

saying these things, for I was afraid I might lose her, I loved her so much—*elle était très belle.*[17] Makar just waved his hand and left. ~~I to him~~ [Altogether, it is worst of all when these people say nothing. He is a somber character.] And I had little hope that he would cooperate. Now."

"And you hadn't sinned yet?"

"That is, you see, *mon ami,*[18] there hadn't been any sin between us, but there was love; that is, my friend, this is all relative; in a word, there was love." [the appearance of a gardener.]

"~~and~~ Did he take the money?"—"He left his wife with me ~~and on the third day,~~ a week later and without too many words, or rather, almost without any words at all,* [asking only that she be given her freedom,] just waved his hand. And he himself became a traveling man. [went traveling]. And so, <your> mamma and I did the same . . . we, too, went traveling.** As for the money, it is, maybe, really a strange story. He took 1,000 rubles in cash and gave it all to a monastery; 2,000 on a promissory note. Nine years ago he collected the money from me practically through the courts, because I didn't have any at the time . . . I don't know about this money; perhaps he gave it to the monastery also, and perhaps he is carrying it on his person, though he is walking around in rags and in bast shoes, wandering all over the country and collecting money to build churches. [A very strange character.]

"An did she love you?"

"*Mon cher,*[19] I've spent all my life trying to find out, but in vain. ~~He~~ If she did indeed, then in an exceedingly hushed manner. I only know that she loves me now—and perhaps she is the only one who does in the whole wide world. I don't know what for, that is, perhaps precisely because I am not worthy of her love. [However, if this were so,] she is only following the example of all women."

[With this elegant quip he closed the discussion.]

"Also, she somehow secretly respects Makar Ivanovich. They write each other about every other year, and most reverently. Sending each

---

* Untranslatable: the Russian *bez dal'nikh slov* means, literally, "without long words," but has the meaning "without further ado."

** The Russian verb *stranstvovat',* used here, has a connotation of "pilgrimage."

17 French: "She was very beautiful."

18 French: "My friend."

19 French: "My dear."

other their respects. He has been around once or twice—[but I wasn't there at the time.]

At their ~~1st~~ meeting at night at the flat, when his father comes to see him, and as he is already saying good-bye: "My dear, I am vilely sentimental, but this is because I'm ill."

N.B. *Most important.* Emphasize His preaching of Christianity and make it clear that *It* is actually serious with *Him.*

The old Prince to the Youth: "My friend, you will allow me to call you by your first name, won't you?"*

"Oh, you're so welcome."

"Fits of youth or what, but even though I shouldn't have been in a mood for such things, I used to be naughty with the Prince, told him about the stones, took him over to <Mme> Andrieux."

He: "If there is consciousness, there is also <free> will."

The Youth: "That's not one and the same thing."

He: "On the contrary, it is literally one and the same thing..."

"He is unfamiliar with the progress of science," Vasin says later. The Youth stands up for Him with great ardor: "Oh yes, He is familiar."

"I am surprised not by the fact that you are preaching (that there is no such thing as an individual will), but rather by the cheerful way in which you people are preaching it. If this is so, what are you going to do with freedom, equality, brotherhood? What kind of freedom can you have, if there is no such thing as individual will, what kind of equality without free [will], what kind of brotherhood without either?"

N.B. It is apparent that He is under compulsion. He has torn himself loose from all his grief to talk about these things, even if it be only to spite somebody. Yet by so doing He shows that all these questions have been disturbing and tormenting him, that He is interested in more than just his own self, and that *nihil humanum mi alienum puto.*[20]

In the railway carriage: "I admit that I was traveling (to Petersburg, the Youth) with hidden anger in my heart."

Liza says: "If I hadn't taken that ~~money~~ money (promissory note)

---

* In the original, he is asking for the Youth's permission to say *ty* ("thou"), to him *(tutoyer).*

[20] Latin: "I do not consider anything human foreign to me." From Terence's "Heau ton ti morou menos," Act I, Scene I, line 77.

then, it would have been all the same as if I were reproaching them ~~with it~~ a great deal."

And when she drowned herself, she had those 10,000 sent to the Prince. Or didn't give it any thought at all.

When about to drown herself, she was wandering around aimlessly: she was also at the Youth's.

The young Prince wants to marry her off to a respectable young man. She is bitter about it.

The Liar is telling about the French in 1812, a peasant woman has a goat, "Ah, cossack!"*

"I didn't like her (the Princess) at all; I couldn't understand why I had started that... game."

Vasin to the Youth: "There you are, I have noticed that you like general topics (i.e., generalizations). Imagine then, *a machine* which," etc. (see earlier <note>).

"You little fool, you—you aren't going to make any money," says Makar Ivanov. "You aren't an enterprising man," says Makar Ivanov [Makar].

In the railway carriage, the Youth strikes up a conversation with a lackey. A young man later says to him: "You started a conversation with a lackey."

In the railway carriage. After Christ and the Holy Ghost. "I knew that you are a good boy." Toward morning: "Mad again."

He to him, in part one, in his confession: "Your idea is very good; there is much that is frightening about it. Yet..."

He makes up <with the Youth>, and then: "If you want to, you can quit your job with the old Prince, but do as you please," as a result of which the young man decided to take the job with the Prince. And later, when saying good-bye: "Well, forgive me," and tears; then I cried, and cried.

"Why is it you love me so much," says He. "My dear friend, my situation was so very difficult, but now I'm going to have a new friend."

Last little page.

In his biography, a statement on wealth. About Vasin's opinion, and the entire development *of his own idea,* absolutely from the very beginning.

I, during an exchange with Him: "I want to be rich. I know in

---

* Untranslatable pun: *koza* "goat"; *kozak* "cossack."

what way shares were being underwritten only recently. I know how Rothschild made 50 million in connection with the assassination of the Duc de Berry.[21] I wasn't studying for I was seeking mediocrity."

Write in the right order, more briefly, à la Pushkin.

In the railway carriage: "You are <talking> to a lackey."

The Youth: "I am a democrat." (I was lying. I had a passionate hatred for democracy.)

Vasin tells the Youth about the immorality of the ultimate goal of *his own idea,* gratification of animal drives, etc.

SPb. vedomosti, No. 263.*

"No, no, in my case it isn't gratification of animal drives," writes the Youth.

"He couldn't possibly marry (the Prince, that is, couldn't) that Dolgoruky girl," they are saying about the Prince (during a drinking bout) in the Youth's presence.

"How come? Why couldn't he marry that Dolgoruky girl?" Some people put up an argument. . .

"That document (about those 300,000) has no legal meaning whatever."

"Oh yes, it does, but not enough so, and the Princes S. could of course do nothing at all, even if they had it in their hands; yet, holding that document in my hands, I was morally convinced that they were in the right. . ."

He, about the Princess: "That woman worries me. Once she is in my way, she must follow me.** Nobody stands in my way unpunished."

[February, 3rd and 4th part.] ["That woman has made me *hate* her. Previously, I merely loved no one, now she (i.e., the Princess) has made me hate her."]

He about Christ: "It is impossible to love people the way they are. And yet one *must* love them, for this is what we are ordered to do (by Christianity). And therefore, do good to them, in spite of your feelings, and in particular, holding your nose and, almost always, keeping your eyes closed, and suffer the evil which they do to you, without getting angry at them. Of course, it is your duty to be stern with them. If you feel that yours is the vocation of a pastor, you must be stern. People are base, they like to love and to adore from fear. So they

---

* *St. Petersburg News,* No. 263.

** The statement is just as illogical in the original.

[21] See note 10 of Part II.

will adore you, too. Do not give way to their adulation, do not prove to be petty, but continue to despise people even when they are good, for most often it is precisely then and there that they are wicked, too. Without any doubt, Christ could not have loved them; he suffered them, he forgave them; but of course he also despised them. At least, I, for my part, cannot comprehend his personality otherwise. Love for mankind must be understood as love for a perfected mankind, one that exists so far only as an ideal, and God only knows if it will ever become reality."[22]

Once, a tirade about Christ, an enthusiastic one; but He is taking Christ so seriously that he is even afraid to talk about him.

Only twice in the course of the novel does He speak about religion: once about the rocks, and another time about temptation by the Devil. The first time, unwillingly and skeptically, while it is He himself who comes to see the Youth and tells him about temptation by the Devil, in a separate chapter.

The Youth: "How is it that you, a Christian, have praised *my own idea* for the hatred which it contains, thus encouraging me to persevere in my hatred?"

He: "My friend, you shall learn about my goals later. I am only praising you for having had the strength, in that jelly-like age of ours, to develop a powerful feeling, and besides, to nurture that feeling, to develop it, and to stick to it."

[*I:* "Is this what you call a feeling?"]

"I am glad to have met a man who is deeper than all this dust, <all these> rats and mice. 'To persevere in hatred,' you say; but, my dear, you don't know yet that a good deal of love is hidden in your hatred (just as some people's love is nothing but hidden hatred). You are now in a certain phase of your development; wait a little, you'll enter a different phase, and you'll see things more clearly. I don't want to stop you solely on the basis of the principle: 'Live and work yourself.' But you will not perish, you will find your way, and that's enough. In the meantime, your idea is keeping you occupied; life won't be too boring with it. And, at any rate, I'm not your nursemaid: live as you please, do as you want."

---

[22] In the "Pro and Contra" section of *The Brothers Karamazov* Ivan Karamazov argues against the possibility of loving one's fellowmen as Christ had commanded in terms similar to those used here. Ivan tells Alyosha: "In my opinion Christ's love for humanity is by its nature an impossible miracle on earth." Part II, Chapter 5:4.

A LAST, VALUABLE OBSERVATION.

Prior to the plot, He suddenly drops in on the Youth and says to him: "If you've got the letter, hand it over directly, without any schemes, try to raise yourself above these mice."

My own idea got me all confused; I quit reading in an orderly and sensible fashion.

After their first conversation they (He and the Princess) parted hating each other. I don't know who hated whom, but this passionate thought persevered in my father's mind: that she was continuing to love Him, even adore Him, and that it had all been only a game, coquetry, *la haine dans l'amour.*[23] Incidentally, there will be a lot more said about this later.

He is a misogynist, he hates women. "Women? One must be as polite with them as possible, and show one's affection to them as best one can, and that's all."

Regarding his passionate longing for a meeting with Him, he won't admit it in his notes about his childhood, but <admits it> to Him, during a showdown, with tears.

The Youth: "Would you pronounce yourself infallible?"

He: "Your crude joke has a certain meaning of which you aren't even aware. Let me tell you that I don't fear infallibility, nor would I be ashamed to apply it to myself. I have sinned only in the eyes of my own conscience, and this stays with me and inside me. But as for ~~the fact that~~ the opinion of you people, or of society, I am ready to claim infallibility in many a point, even in everything, though really only on the grounds that none of you will know how to even accuse me. What do you people know of good and of evil? I'll convince any one of you tomorrow, that it is most virtuous, indeed, to become a Rothschild, and that, conversely, it is a great sin to turn the other cheek, and you are all going to believe me."

As he is having that showdown with his father in the final scene of the first part, he almost tearfully declares that he loves him. In <his> convulsive manner, he *inadvertently reveals* that he has been dreaming of this meeting day after day, and then, angry about having let out this secret, starts rapping his father's hand.

"Come on, beat me up, beat me up!" says He.

MOST IMPORTANT. The Youth is particularly surprised by the fact that He is sometimes furious at the Princess for some sally of hers, but would, on some other occasion, be almost delighted about practi-

---

[23] French: "Hate in love."

cally the same words, calling them "the insolence of the enamored." Sometimes he would start by being delighted and end up being mad, or vice versa. His theory about submission to women.

October 2.

MOST IMPORTANT.

1) The Youth notices, however (gradually, in the course of the entire novel), that his father—in spite of the fact that there has been a *reconciliation* between them, and even though He has himself told the Youth that He is more clever and better than all the others—still does not treat him on equal terms with *His own* children, but that He, on the contrary, sacrifices him and all of Makar's <children> (Liza) to His own. Hurt pride (noticed by his father with a smile), and cynicism.

2) Abandoning his duties as a human being, the Youth, in his bitterness and confusion, not only becomes a cynic, but actually preaches *to himself,* in connection with each *adventure* of his, that depravity, even baseness, even banality, even cowardice, are all to the good, and really better for his own idea. Not enough: "A thief is an improvident person." This is true of pickpockets only, whereas the big thieves enjoy the support of all society, and are never caught. *"The golden mean"* is best of all. I.e., *regarding his own idea,* though he still likes the role of the lonely avenger, he is also getting reconciled to all kinds of degradation. And ~~for~~ because of this he forgets about Makar's family, about Liza, and about the child. His cynicism has taken him to the point from which he can see only one aspect of Liza's story, i.e., contempt for the concepts, beliefs, and views of their environment. (N.B. Though Makar Ivanov leaves him stunned and has, apparently, left a *strange* impression on him, the corrupting influence of his environment gains the upper hand.) When the predatory designs on the Princess are about to be realized, he seems to be making a forced effort to rid himself of all positive impressions, though there were those impressions left by his rare (yet remarkable) meetings with Liza, like rays of light, as well as with the child (whom he suddenly gives some candy, right before the *plot*). To be sure, even when surrounded by the full stench <of corruption>, when he was about to shoot himself, he would get to thinking of his responsibilities toward Liza, for example. But: "What can I do about it?" he thought, reassuring himself with this perfectly rational question. But after the *morning with the Princess* he suddenly has a *longing* for home: Liza, the little boy! This is why he is so thunderstruck by Liza's death... [Here]

N.B. Vasin is arrested toward the middle of the novel, during the period of the diamonds, and though he is stunned he says: "It serves him right!" But then, later . . .

After <the incident with> *the diamonds* he is roaming the streets of the city: "I'm responsible for my own humiliation," and there, at night, he meets a fallen woman.

The last. The Princess must absolutely marry the young Prince; she must be passionately, terribly in love with him.

N.B. How can the combination involving the young Prince's marriage proposal be coordinated with the lawful daughter?* Answer: By various phases of love. She loved the Prince, but her pride made her leave him. He ~~in his frivolous way, was her slave~~ did love her, yet *was* also *afraid* of her. But now, after her return, she again attracts him (besides, the young Prince is positively convinced that she is having a liaison with Him). <His> *daughter* immediately sees through this. He could not well reject ~~initially~~ the combination involving marriage. The Princess is a little ashamed even to admit to herself that she loves the Prince.

On a university education.

He: "You don't mean our specialist-professors who are merely becoming stultified from their specialties?"

"Must a professor be an educated person? In Russia, we don't even ask this question; as long as he is a specialist."

He. On environment. *Moskovskie vedomosti,* 74, No. 244, October 1.**

Editorial. Opinion of that fool A. K——rov, to the effect that there are no good and no evil people, only *environment.*

"Lady teacher prepares children for educational institutions, and gives lessons in arithmetic."

He went to see her and wanted to give her *a hundred rubles.* He gave her the money and she hangs herself, or something of this sort. *An episode.* Might also attach Perchatkin to him. ["Oh, I am not blaming her at all," He says.]

He is vain Russian average man, uprooted from everything, and possessed by the idea that He is an undiscovered genius, and not at all average. Christ would save Him owing to the fact that He always imagined ~~in his future Catholicism~~ Him <Christ> as his support. But He turns out to be an atheist.

---

* Unclear in the original.

***Moscow News.*

After having chopped up those icons He comes to see the Youth: "For 8 whole years I imagined that I was a believer," He says.

"How did you suddenly lose your faith?"

"My friend, I always suspected that I wasn't believing in anything." ~~But at least now I can live thinking of nothing but my own arse.~~

"So from now on you'll be living to your own a<rse>."

"No, my friend, but according to my ideal of nobility, which I have myself set up ~~and nothing is going to stop me~~.

"Who then is forcing you?"

"I am forcing myself."

VALUABLE OBSERVATION. When leaving Makar's family, He would sometimes make the sign of the cross over the little boy; if he were asleep, He'd let him sleep; but after having made the sign of the cross, He would never ask him to kiss Him, either His face or His hand—with distaste (and irritation)—not wanting to violate the child's feelings, since it (He sees that) continues to be afraid of Him, the longer, the more.

N.B. *Unsolved question:* How can the Youth, *suspecting* finally, after the proposal, that He is in love with the Princess, join a plot to dishonor her?

N.B. When the Princess learns that it is the Youth who has brought the document concerning those 300,000 (he bragged about it to the old Prince), she makes an attempt to make up to him: hasn't he also got her letter to Andreev? She is trying to charm him. He refuses

October 5.

?SOLUTION OF THE PROBLEM. CHANGE OF PLAN.

All the time, step by step, and the longer he thinks of it the more so, the Youth becomes convinced that He is a victim, persecuted by a Messalina. ~~At the time of his arrival.~~ Even before his arrival, the old Prince had severed his intimate relations with Him on account of a slanderous statement to the effect that his daughter was a whore who would serve the first comer. He is assuring the Youth with ardor that He is being persecuted and a sufferer. Since <his marriage> to "that passive creature" had been planned before this rupture and His ejection from the old Prince's house, the old Prince, seeing that "the passive creature" wants to marry Him anyway, does not veto the marriage, in spite of the rupture. Besides, the rupture is a rather delicate one. Moreover, the Prince does not want to relinquish his idea of a marriage between the young Prince and his lawful daughter (the Prince's ward) either.

But when He obtains 100,000 for the old Prince, in the form of his daughter's dowry, the old Prince heartily approves of it, but still fails to go along. He makes an effort to reconcile Him with the Princess, but she disdainfully rejects his overtures. In a word, by the time of the Youth's arrival, the Princess has gained the upper hand with the old Prince, while the father is in disfavor.

Having gotten together with the Youth, the young Prince tells him (*in a friendly way*) that the Princess is in love with him, that she is after him again, and that he is afraid of that, particularly since she has a liaison going with Him. And that she is having liaisons with God knows whom. When the Youth asks him; *With whom, then?* the young Prince can't give him an answer. There are many facts which make the Youth believe that this thought has been suggested to the young Prince by Him, and that he has been and still is under His influence. Meanwhile the young Prince speaks admiringly of His wisdom and *justice,* and also shows some fear of Him. In his opinion, He can't have told a lie. The Youth is surprised by such frankness and in turn tells the Prince that there isn't any liaison, but that she is a Messalina who wanted to seduce his father.

In the meantime, return of the 300,000. Reconciliation between the old Prince and Him. [The Princess suddenly insults Liza.] Liza's romance is revealed (for the first time, for everybody; nobody knew about it). Meanwhile the Youth has already informed his father that the Princess is after the young Prince again. His challenge to the latter, immediately withdrawn. The young Prince learns through the Youth that the Princess has no dowry. Also, that there is this letter.

In a *first-person* narrative, the Youth has this to say, in one chapter:

"He didn't like to discuss Christianity and, as I noticed, avoided such discussions in a strange manner. Perhaps He wanted to let me experience these things myself. However, when I kept insisting, I remember especially those days following so-and-so and so-and-so, he would sometimes let himself be persuaded to talk about this subject. ~~Thus~~ I recall that we discussed these matters twice or so (once in connection with Vasin, the other time upon my persistent questioning), and here is, more or less, what I have retained in my memory from these discussions:

"Here, about the rocks. On the eternity and relativity of virtue. On <being a> man for two weeks, on virtue for two weeks (the rocks).*

* The allusion is apparently to the notion, repeatedly mentioned before, of the Earth's becoming "an ice-covered piece of rock" like other planets.

On the relationship between socialism and Christianity; about the fact that socialism is trying to conceal, by putting forward a series of Genevan ideas, that its ideal is, in spite of everything, nothing else but material prosperity; on environment, etc. (*Moskovskie vedomosti,** No. 245, from Wiesbaden), etc."

He expresses sympathy with Kraft: "Only, that's a strange idea, for did he really assume that things are better in Europe? However, he may be right in his own way: there really is something about Russia that can make you shoot yourself."

N.B. ABSOLUTELY. In the course of the novel the Youth is wondering: "How could this tolerant man, so firm and possessing such a high ideal of generosity (N.B. His indulgence toward those who had insulted him, the lady school teacher, etc.), rip open the child's mouth?" And so he learns from His own mouth that the child had not been simply irritating Him, but rather, that he child was one of those who refused to worship Him, "and *never will worship* me," (He adds). This is why a temporary fit of frenzy followed. He also hates the Princess because she refuses to worship Him. His passion <for her> was ignited by <her> contrariousness.

Without Lambert. Everything that happened to Lambert happened to the Father. But what could replace Lambert? (N.B. In Lambert's presence, but without him. And, at the very last moment, he goes to <his> father).

N.B. Couldn't it be so that the Youth does not give the letter to Lambert and shows him the door? Then, Lambert again seeks the company of the young Prince, giving him money and encouraging him to take <money> from her. He lets the young Prince know that they've got that letter and that the old Prince won't be giving <her> any money. The Princess quarrels with the young Prince and chases him out of her house. Here, the Youth plans his scheme all by himself, letting his father know about it on the eve <of its execution>. Meanwhile the young Prince has robbed Perchatkin. The plot. Liza. The young Prince shoots himself—suicide note, sympathy. Before his death, the young Prince is with Liza again. Liza shoots herself, having learned of his death.

During a drinking party, the Princess tries to go after the Youth, hoping "Maybe he's got the letter." The Youth is rude to her, refuses,

* *Moscow News.*

but falls in love with her. The diamonds, and that feeling of Ungern-Shternbergian[24] intoxication, "so I can really do you (the Princess) in, if I want." *He* begins to suspect that the Youth might be in love with the Princess, makes fun of him, torturing him as well as Himself. Messalina makes a hint regarding the letter. He finds out that the Youth has been seeing the Princess. The Youth does not realize that He is jealous, and confides everything to Him, except the letter.

"Is it true that you haven't had her? Listen, there is a certain letter! Whoever has that letter could fuck her if he wanted." The Youth is excited—was it intentional on his part, or was it unintentional; does he know, or doesn't He, that the letter is <in the Youth's hands>? ~~Suddenly the Princess insults Liza.~~

Liza insulted by the Princess for the second time. As a result of this, the "lawful daughter" pretends to have heard only just now that the young Prince had anything to do with Liza. Impossible, though they be Dolgorukys, but mainly because the insult inflicted upon Liza by the Princess confirms that the Princess loves the Prince, and that he loves her. "I don't want to." [October 14?]

Yet <she> surprises <her> father with this question: "Does He intend to propose to the Princess?" In that case, she is offering to marry the old Prince... Won't give away those 100,000. ~~When~~ Suddenly ~~refusal~~ a letter from "that passive creature," under the pretext that He loves the Princess. Lambert makes his first appearance. Infuriated by the passion attributed to Him, He demands a showdown with the Princess (she accedes, under the pressure of His threats). He makes her a present of the young Prince's documents, sarcastically remarking that it was for her love of Him, but demands that she dare not seduce the Youth and debauche him, like a Messalina (that's what He is calling her, a Messalina). [February, for part four.] She slaps His face. The old Prince summons Him: He affirms that she had been trying to seduce the Youth, in order to wheedle that letter out of him. The Prince is stunned by <the news about> the letter, calls in the Youth, who refuses to say that such a letter exists. [Here] The Prince calls him a scoundrel. "The passive creature" refuses <to marry him>. A formal proposal to the Princess. Everybody is screaming: "He is out of his mind!" Chopping up those icons, proposal <. . .>

[He says to the Youth: "I really got it for you, you *scoundrel,* but

---

[24] See note 3 of Part II.

you did right] in not giving up the letter." The Youth is furious about His complaining to the Prince that she was corrupting him (the Youth). He meekly admits that he was carried away by His anger and contempt for her, and, "My boy, if you do have that document, be generous and hand it over." Such magnanimous confession leaves the Youth perfectly convinced that He does not love her, [and is suffering an injustice, and a giant among people.] But the Youth is sneered at by her, and by everybody, including the young Prince and the old Prince (try it without Lambert).

At this point, Lambert. Dishonor her. Both agree. The Youth is convinced of his father's absolute hatred for her. On the very eve of the attempt, when he is wavering, Lambert suddenly stuns him with the admission that He knows about the plot also and is approving of it. ["He has just proposed to the Princess."] Upon his repeated questions Lambert does, however, retract what he has just said about Him. He agrees that he hasn't understood him right, but still leaves a lingering suspicion in the Youth's mind. The Youth is convinced that he hates her. (N.B. He never did admit to his father that he was in love; on the contrary, he was always angry that everybody was teasing him about his being in love. He knows himself that he is in love, but is trying to persuade himself that he hates her on account of being in love with her.) [But Lambert, who does not believe the Youth, calls on his father. The latter jumps out <from his hiding place> at the moment when the Youth kills Lambert.]

N.B. *Most important.* ~~The first time he admits his passion for the Princess is when he has already sent her the letter. He comes to see Him and confesses. He says sarcastically: "All right then, rape her." But he is asking for help. *He* shows up and goes mad.~~

The Youth never admits, not even to himself, that he is in love with the Princess, not even when he has found himself kissing her tracks ("How can they be so depraved! so materialistic!"). He begins to hate her for having kissed her tracks. He comes to see his father, telling him that he hates her. Don't want to rape her. "I am afraid to rape her!"

October 6.

Besides catholic narrow-mindedness, despotism, and intolerance, besides contempt for one's own land, there is also present <in his character> such thing as a stubborn, almost enthusiastic pursuit of an idea, of a world view, etc. Besides extreme and diabolic pride ("no one can be my judge") there also are present extraordinary, harsh demands directed at <him>self, "though under the condition that I be responsible to no one." A most elegant, polished exterior: an apparent ingenuousness, affability, an apparent tolerance, an absence of any purely personal ambition. And yet all this is only the result of a haughty view of the world, an incredibly exalted position which He has arbitrarily assumed opposite the whole world. The essence of which is, for example, this: "No one can insult me, for they are all mice <compared to me>. I am guilty, and they've found me guilty, so let them, and may God give them wisdom, at least for a time, for they are so paltry, so very paltry!" [February, for part four.]

"I hate her, yet I am afraid to rape her," says the Youth as he comes to see his father for the last time, and asks him to join the conspiracy.

"Do it, do it," says the Father.

"How?"

"A young man of your age can hardly avoid getting soiled by some woman. So it really does not matter whether it be her, or some streetwalker. But you will see that she will be worse than a streetwalker. You will see tears, and vileness, and deceit. Use her, and throw her pay to her, get even with all of them, son of a whore, Dolgoruky."

The Youth remains silent.

"I knew that you hated her," he says.

"What about you?"

"I hate her more than you do!"

"Listen: simply give it to her, give it to her generously—give it to her without any words, if you can. This will be best of all, and fairest of all. Then, turn your back to her, without asking for a remuneration."

"Would you care to be present?"

["Are you truly ready to hand it over just like that?" "I am and I was actually expecting such advice from you. You hate her so much you surely would have simply handed it to her, crushing her with your magnanimity."]

"You want me to talk to her?"

"No, stay in the next room."

"What for? So I could hear your beautiful speech to her?"

"I am telling you, I fear that I might fail; I am afraid of raping her."

"I'll go." There is hatred written on his face.

(And that's how they decide to act.) (N.B. "I have already sent a letter.")

The young Prince has been behaving badly; he is no longer admitted to society. The Princess has chased him out of her house; he did make a move to win the hand of "that passive creature," but the old Prince, learning of his dishonest action (theft) [a duel], also shows him the door. Then the Prince and Lambert kill and rob Perchatkin. N.B. Lambert is hoping all the time that the young Prince is going to get a lot of money, and has been giving him money himself. Lambert was hoping that he might get money from the Princess, from the old Prince, from "that passive creature." Lambert is thinking that the young Prince failed to get any money from the Princess because, as a result of that letter, she hadn't got and was never going to have any money. And that's why he keeps pestering the Youth: Isn't there a letter somewhere, for she would give a lot for that letter (because the old Prince is furious at Him, and tactfully, in view of the fact that he is getting married himself, has promised to provide her with another dowry). Then, in his opinion, the young Prince and the Princess would make up again and pay him. He has made the young Prince give him a promissory note, which the young Prince promises to honor as soon as he gets 20,000, if only he gets that letter from the Youth. But Lambert has another idea: "I'll make the little Prince pay up on the promissory note, as soon as they make up," he thinks, "but I can still shake her down for 20,000 with that letter." And this is why he is furiously trying to talk the Youth into becoming his partner in the deal, "We'll split the money, and you can fuck her, too." And, strangely enough, though the Youth does not capitulate before Lambert, the latter's passion-laden words—"Let's shake her down, revenge; let's fuck her; it's all a moment's work; one must take advantage"—in spite of their crudeness, have an intoxicating effect on him. "Or don't they?" he asks himself. Finally he decides to go it alone. (While Lambert and the Prince, together, kill Perchatkin.) But at the last moment, two hours or so before the act, he goes to see Him, inviting him <to join the plot>.

As He is rushing about the room, like a beast, the half-dead Princess in his arms, He suddenly and with all his might, after having dropped her on a bed, strikes her face (after kisses) with his fist (he had bared her leg). This is where the Youth kills him.

In the plan for part one.

As the Youth is entering the Brusilov residence, a lady school teacher forces her way in, carrying a letter (and 100 rubles). "Tell this scoundrel," etc. The Youth takes it upon himself to convey <the letter and the money>. He returns <the letter and the money> with some rude and caustic remarks. "That passive creature." Rips open <the little boy's> mouth. The school teacher hangs herself. ~~Her mother.~~ The next day the Youth pays a visit to the school teacher. He is there, too. But the Youth does not exchange a single word wih Him, while they are at the dead school teacher's. <Her> mother exonerates Him. The Youth leaves embarrassed Then, his father comes to see him at his new flat. Among other things, he also mentions the school teacher, but in a quiet, delicate way. (N.B. When the Youth comes <to the aunts' place> to write a letter (and also to pick up his belongings), he makes mention of Andreev's letter which he might hand over to Him; which he does when they become reconciled).

N.B. Important. The aunt, who is the godmother and a very distant relative of the young Prince's, is a ~~very close~~ closer relative of the old Prince's. She is living in Luga, is poor, and the Prince had stayed at her house for some time, while in exile; furthermore, Makar's family was also under her wing.

It was this aunt who had a lawsuit with Him, for 300,000. Having won the 300,000 He promises to return 100,000. But ~~the family~~ the old Prince, to show his tact, since he has suddenly decided to get remarried, promises to take care of the dowry himself. Then, He will give away 100,000 with his daughter, and he deposits <that amount>.

"However, you are not visiting me too often, are you?" says the Youth to Him.

"I haven't time, my friend; I just haven't the time, forgive me; please, don't feel hurt."

He, about Bismarck: "It is bad when a man, or a cause, are easy to understand: it's the first sign that they are worthless. He has united <Germany> mechanically, with iron and sword, while disuniting it morally, as he is sowing the seeds of future religious hatred. Isn't he counting on atheism?"

Nothing durable was ever created by iron and sword.

Prince Bismarck is one of those men who are quickly understood by their environment (there are such poets, public figures, publicists). Theirs is an ephemeral and a foolish fame. [To the lackey, on the train.]

The old Prince: "Imagine, He is jealous of Bismarck's fame; nor will he recognize that he is a great man."

He, about the Princess: "She is modest."

"If she's modest, how can she be a Messalina?"

"You can't understand it."

A letter by the Youth, from Moscow to Petersburg, addressed to a certain unknown "dear Sir," and asking to be left alone; but his aunt appears on the scene and turns everything the other way.

When I let this German know that I didn't intend to enroll in the university, this (Russian) German made a slight effort to make me change my mind, presenting to me the advantages <of a university education>, but I cut him short quickly (my own idea). Then, he let me know that he had informed my family in Petersburg that, in his opinion, everything would of course go the way I wanted it, for though I was still a minor, I already had certain rights (acquired by graduating from high school) and nobody would, of course, force me, except that I would have to bear the unpleasant consequences myself. Let me note that it was the German who was in touch with my "relatives." I never wrote a single letter. Those "relatives" were the Andreevs. But I knew that Andreev had died in Petersburg two months earlier, and that his wife, two of my aunts, and his two unmarried daughters were then in Petersburg. Somehow, my German, through all this time, had shrunk from discussing my relatives with me. But I never wrote them a line, nor did I ever talk about them, though I knew a lot about them. Here's exactly what I knew at the time. This is essential in the presentation of my arrival in Petersburg. I knew it from some German women, from servants.

First, about my father. My father... all the information—with the old Prince. (N.B. What a romantic effect every bit of news about my father had on me!) And here, Father, the old Prince, the Princess ..., etc.

[<My> father's marriage, for <?> the German.

I: "I couldn't care less."]

Most of all, I was worried about the news of my father's marriage, and about Makar's family then staying with him in Petersburg. Then, the aunt shows up. They've found a job for me in Petersburg. I don't have to leave right away. I had a talk with the German—<my job will be> to entertain the old Prince. Then, frou-frou. The university student, and the trip. N.B. Toward the end <of the year> I was in the seventh grade. The story of the little Prince, then a quick encounter with Lambert.

Something remarkable. Or thus: the day before I was going to leave for Moscow,* the German, his wife, and I sat down together in the evening, and here is what I learned. Then, a package of Andreev's

* An obvious slip of the pen; should be "Petersburg."

letters. The German: "I have decided to let you have them." Or else, the German dies and his wife lets me have them. ~~The letter <to> the Youth~~

(October 9.)

"A man of undoubted intellect, but not a very clever man."*

"Listen, Prince, where do you get these things?"

"Mon cher, je sais tout, mais je ne sais rien de bon."[25]

The Prince was happy that I was admiring his wit. But I swear that I had been sincere, not just flattering him. *On the contrary,* I'd been rather laughing at him, being quite sure that he said it without thinking, just by accident. Then the Prince immediately came up with another bon mot, but that second one didn't come off.

Je sais tout, mais je ne sais rien de bon (Faust).[26]

I know everything, but I know nothing right (I have learned everything, but I haven't learned anything right).

[February.] It is the same anxiety which entices a soul thirsting for faith and carries it off to the heavens, ~~the same~~ that also induces the realist to reject faith. Realism and atheism present a tranquillity which is deceptive (for never does atheism capture an indifferent soul). A soul which is trying to calm itself through complete negation may thirst, more than any other, for complete affirmation (for the positive), for complete faith.

But there is "average man," who is glad to have acquired the right to be dishonorable. Our youth doesn't even suspect his existence, or that it is mixing with this dirty mass.

People know nothing about socialism in this country, yet socialist ideas are present everywhere.

We have become Europeans under the absolute condition of losing our self-respect.

[February.] Many things will age before they mature, but society does contain <some> undeniable evil. This is true.

[Worn to rags.] He: "Your mother is the exact contrary to certain Petersburg newspapers in which, 'what's new is bound to be good.' "

"To repent would mean, in my case, to immediately attack some-

---

* The bon mot is more effective in Russian, since *um* ("intellect") and *umnyi* ("clever") are derived from the same root.

25 French: "My dear, I know everything, but I don't know anything good."

body with some accusation." (N.B. He: "Well, so much we know: to repent means, in our country, to immediately attack somebody with some accusation.") Comparison of nihilism to the appearance of the poet Benediktov (He).[27] The old Prince on Versilov's action: "How it cheers one's heart to rejoice at somebody's noble deed!"

Versilov: "The idea of a nobility and of 'better people.' "

Versilov: "The nobles freed the people, while the government officials merely stole their idea."

Versilov: "If we only had enough of that Russian spirit, i.e., of the spirit of Christ, and all this chronological determinism of evil, which you have in Europe, would be unthinkable in Russia (factory-owners, the people <?>), no one would want to abuse his lesser brethren, for *life's happiness,* life's *joy* would be found in something else, i.e., not in gold, but in self-denial."

"Could such a country be for real?"

"If not so, at least its ideal and the striving for it are always possible. If only Christ would not die in the hearts of the Russian people, then, even though there were night ~~all~~ around us, it would still be possible to strive for that bright dot <of light> with everything one has got. That is, it would be a joy to be alive, provided the idea does not die. You see, if the idea itself should die, and the European idea become accepted, <an idea> of mechanical, and not of inner equality, everything would be lost."

Versilov: "We Russians haven't got any honorable memories, and those which we used to have we have lovingly dishonored and rejected."

Versilov: "I am not assuming or allowing that there might be any freely thinking or freely acting people in Russia: everybody is a lackey, you hear, a lackey, not a slave. Russian boldness, if it should show up anywhere, is nothing but a lackey's insolence, and invariably accompanied by a cowardly concern for oneself: 'Watch your step, <careful with> what you're doing.' "

"Those nihilasters have grown old; they've lost their teeth."*

---

* *Nigiliashki,* derived from *nigilist* ("nihilist") with a Russian suffix which suggests contempt.

[27] V. G. Benediktov's first book of poetry was enthusiastically received in 1835 and was praised by Pushkin, Dostoevsky, and Turgenev, among others. Belinsky alone criticized his poetry as empty music and composed of a series of commonplaces. Time quickly showed that Belinsky was right. When his third collection of poetry was published in 1842, the reading public ignored him.

[26] *Ibid.*

Versilov: "Russia is just about getting ready to start living."

"And these preparations will take her a thousand years?"

"A big ship takes more time to get clear. It will take less time to build a Neva river boat of 4 <horse> powers than the frigate *Minin.*"

Makar is glad to hear these words.

Political discussions (about China).

"Not only don't we have well-informed people, we don't even have any honest people. There is almost no such thing in Russia as an honest man."

Our clergy has given us, for the most part, atheists and nihilists (dreamers, as a result of not knowing the world, and practicing discrimination, as a result of their forming a separate estate). In their academies they continue to represent *a separate estate;* one really ought to break it up and make it a part of our universities.

They haven't been participating in our general progress, but have for those past 20 years reacted to every reform with nothing but contemptuous sneers and sullen sniffs.

"My friend, these are all very painful questions, and I am making every effort to avoid them."

To the socialists: "You are hoping to lure people with promises of their own advantage, with rational calculations of their own advantage, and you think that in view of their own "indubitable" advantage they will all join you (so thought Chernyshevsky and Dobroliubov:[28] 'Let me talk to the people through the window for a quarter of an hour, and they'll follow us.') My God, what a miscalculation on your part: when did man ever do what was to his advantage? On the contrary, hasn't man always done what he liked to do, rather than what was to his advantage, and not infrequently knowing full well that it was to his disadvantage? For man has an innate tendency to consider

---

[28] Nikolay Gavrilovich Chernyshevsky (1828–89) was one of the most influential critics and political activists in the nineteenth century. His most important critical work is *Esteticheskie otnosheniia iskusstva k deistvitel'nosti* (1855) (*Aesthetic Relations of Art to Reality*). His novel *Chto delat'* (*What is to Be Done?*) (1862–63) inspired generations of young Russians to revolutionary zeal. Dostoevsky satirized this novel, as well as some of Chernyshevsky's views of man expressed in various essays, in *Notes from the Underground.* Nikolay Alexandrovich Dobrolyubov (1836–61) was an idealogical and political contemporary and a follower of Chernyshevsky. With Chernyshevsky and Pisarev he forms the triad of important and influential radical critics. His most important article is *Chto takoe Oblomovshchina* (*What is Oblomovism?*) (1859).

as *advantageous to himself,* in almost any calculation that he may undertake, that which pleases him, and nothing else. You have forgotten that."[29]

"It isn't your special privilege to be lovers of mankind. On the contrary, quite often you are nothing but petty egoists, thirsting for fame. Socialism means hatred."

Versilov: "<The image of> this planet with a God is contiguous with totality and immortality (the family is being destroyed, and with it one's forebears, and the individual. Only mankind remains; and so, <life> is limited to earthly existence, whereas if <we believe in> resurrection, there is reunion, and revelation)."

The Youth: "It was with this kind of passion-laden words (abrupt, disconnected, yet poetic) that he was stirring my imagination and irresistibly attracting me (I am mentioning these items just to show what kind of phantasies were dwelling in this man's soul)."

Christianity and socialism. Anger and struggle (forward!). Advantage instead of any moral principle. They've gotten their hatred mixed up with love of mankind. The burning down of the Tuileries. Personal responsibility, and there is no such thing as crime (i.e., individuality). They'll surely win. In the end, Christ will be victorious.

"Lord, have mercy, give me some money."

"Lord, have mercy on all men who have no one who will pray for them."

"Lord, make a move."

Lambert is urging the little Prince to collect the 30,000 which He had spent and failed to pay him, and also the 100,000 which the <Prince's> daughter is absolutely refusing to surrender.

The Youth makes up his mind to go through with his scheme all by himself, but learns, on the eve <of its execution>, that He, *after all that has happened,* has proposed to the Princess. The Youth is stunned by this bit of news: "So He is in love!" He goes to see Him, and never before has he heard more insults hurled at "that Messalina" than on this occasion, when He has <just> proposed marriage to her. "I proposed to her out of contempt for her."

He is cited before a Justice of the Peace in connection with his having given 100 rubles to that governess.

A lawsuit on account of the money he has paid short.

---

29 The Underground Man makes similar points in his argument against the Crystal Palace.

The Youth has just arrived, <and> He hastens to ask him questions: "Did the young Prince have a good trip?"

October 14.

The Princess is the old Prince's daughter. The Youth is in love <with her>, though he won't believe that he is in love, and thinks that he hates <her>. However, he *instinctively* hides his feelings for the Princess from Him and everybody else, as he fears to be *shamed* for it. How great then, are his embarrassment and his anger when He takes the liberty to tell the Princess that she is corrupting the Youth by making him fall in love with her, so that he has completely lost his head! The main thing is really that the Youth has been trying, throughout the course of the novel, to conceal his feelings from Him: suspecting, in spite of himself, that He may be in love, even though he has been believing Him when he was saying that He has had nothing but hatred for her in a long time. *His feeling of tact* has prevented him from becoming his father's rival. He is seized by cynicism, a loathing for Him, and even more so, for the Princess. He finally gets to believe that He hates her. It is He himself who suggests that he rape her. Yet he is working on his scheme all by himself, and in deep secrecy. And then, suddenly, practically *the night before,* he learns (from Lambert) that He has proposed to her. [The Youth] goes to see Him.

"How then, could you say that you didn't love her?"

He replies: "My life isn't worth a thing. I can save her."*

"But if she hates you?"

"No, she adores me, though I do not love her."

"But she won't admit it."

"Perhaps she'll be wise enough to admit it."

The result is that the Youth is struggling with himself and, finally, *an hour before* <the act> invites Him over.

October 14.

Absolutely stick to these two rules, throughout the course of the novel.

1st rule. Avoid the mistake, made in *The Idiot* and in *The Possessed,* of describing (many of the) secondary events in a fragmentary, insinuated, romance-like manner, and dragging them out over a lengthy extension <of the novel>, both in the narrated action as well as in individual scenes, yet without giving any explanations at all,

---

* Or: "I can save it." Since *zhizn'* ("life") is a feminine noun in Russian the phrase is ambiguous.

just guesses and hints, instead of *explaining the truth directly.* Being mere secondary episodes, they weren't worth such concentrated attention on the part of the reader; on the contrary, they actually tended to obscure, rather than to clarify, the principal objective, precisely because the reader, diverted to a side road, could very well lose the main road and get all confused in his attention.

Try to avoid secondary details and seek to assign an insignificant place to those <that you do introduce>; present them much more briefly, concentrating the action exclusively around the hero.

The 2d rule lies in the fact that the Youth is the hero of the novel. Everything else is secondary, even He is secondary. The poem is about the Youth and his idea, or better, about the Youth, solely as the bearer and inventor of *his idea.*

The Youth sets out from Moscow, all *imbued* with his idea, and loyal *to it.* He is armed with his idea as he is riding out to battle, and he knows it. He already has sacrificed a few things to his idea: to be precise, three years of alienation, <a good deal of hard work> to strengthen his character, saving money and declining a chance to get a higher education, explicitly on account of his idea. In Petersburg, *his idea* suffers some damage and is shaken by a number of things, to be precise:

1) Meeting people, and the fact that he cannot restrain himself but reveals his idea to other people: *being ashamed of it.*

2) His faith is shaken by socialism: he wants to retain his idea and yet remain a noble human being.

3) His condescending attitude toward the idea: He does approve of it, yet the Youth has the feeling that His idea is higher, more proud and noble ~~than his own~~ than his own. What then is His idea? The Youth is trying to guess it through the entire course of the novel.

4) His clash with life, voluptuousness, ambition, uncongenial company, the young Prince. Cynicism as well as other avenues to brilliance make their appearance. Everything collapses as a result of insults, which return him to his idea—no longer theoretically, but as a genuinely embittered man who is out to take his revenge. Cynicism and daring, Lambert, the young Prince. The plot, money. It is during this period that he has an *attitude of contempt* for Him, having lost his respect and his love for Him, and a desire to get even with Him for what He has meant to him in his life, so decisively and for such a long time. At the same time, a lack of respect for his family. So much more is he <then> affected by his meeting with Liza, the child, etc.

5) His relationship with the Princess, ambition, passion, and the plot. In the very end, it becomes clear what He is. [N.B. However, he decides to join the plot certainly not on account of his idea, but because of his passion <for the Princess>.]

6) Makar Ivanov, and those others. A shattering impact which does not, however, destroy his idea.

3d rule: ~~the young Prince.~~

October 15.

After Souchard, conclude it quickly. [Mother, a meeting.] He withdraws into himself; later, in high school, daydreaming, about his father, about meeting him, his idea, his social position; it actually had an influence upon his decision not to enroll in the university. But do not say that this is so, later, at Vasin's. Then, living with the German, and facts about his father. Andreev's letters, "I've deciphered them, I've learned a few things from these letters;" so he travels <to Petersburg> armed <with these letters>. The aunt shows up: "<You are going> to Petersburg, <where you have a job> with the Prince." The trip, etc. An auction, 10 rubles.

["The German said that 'you like to economize.' "

"Why won't you say, 'a tightwad'?"]

["Why are you doing it?"

I, with a guffaw: "I want to become a Rothschild," etc.]

It is He who tells Vasin about the Youth's *very own idea,* and Vasin unexpectedly comes to see him (right before being arrested) and has a talk with him. He causes the Youth to waver. Question to the Youth: "So he is concerned about me?" And, again because of his pride, he is not too fond of the notion that Vasin knows about <his idea>. But Vasin is arrested. The Youth is stunned.

[October 14.] N.B. Absolutely. Carousing with the young Prince, in good company (hussars), to which the Youth is admitted (he can see, though, that he doesn't belong there). Later, the young Prince's duel. The Prince shows himself a coward at the duel. The Princess summons the Youth and asks him questions about it. The Youth turns away—but after <some affairs with> women, <Mme> Andrieux, the old Prince, playing a hoax on the Fool, etc. He* suddenly withdraws into himself, cynicism, a mad rage at the Princess, "take revenge on them all," the letter, which irritates him, quarrels with his father, of

* "He" is capitalized in the Russian text.

whom he demands an awful lot, and Lambert. ("Alas! The mood I was in didn't let me see Liza." Their romance, separately.)

The day after the attempt <on her honor> the Princess says: "He is honest, noble, ~~but all this affected, bookish, artificial and <a sense of> honor (as in all of our society), I knew it.~~ He was always capable of believing that I would get frightened by that letter. I always, always felt that this might happen. He lacks a great idea."

In his introduction to the Princess: "If I were to explain my idea to you, I would never succeed, nor bring my undertaking to an end, but here is my story. Though it may not have been written for you, it will be completely frank: I thought that some day you might want to read it."

With every line.

Why did I think, not in the least expecting this letter from you?* <. . .>

Here, I want to severely <. . .>

I am not even rereading it, yet I am sending it to you.

Though He has incited everyone else to go ahead with their plot, He is still wavering and ~~almost wanted to~~ would like to make a noble gesture and send the letter. It is with this idea in mind that he takes the final step of trying to filch the letter from them. *But they won't let him.* He comes to see the Youth and, in allegorical language, advises against going through with it ("father's noble feelings flared up for the last time"). But the Youth takes it for a ruse to get the letter from him. Then, He waves his hand and, with a guffaw, decides <to go along with them>.

"I didn't love her (the Princess) at all. I don't know what game I've been playing."

N.B. Carousing with the young Prince. Women. The Youth feels that ~~he is being accepted~~ he *isn't on equal terms* with them, but already he is beginning to be corrupted, already he is getting fond of sweet luxury (Petersburg is having a physical effect on him). Women. ~~He tries it in the streets~~ He is arrested in a secret gambling house, <since> some money <has disappeared> from the table. The little Prince betrays the Youth, when he is under suspicion of having stolen the money. He leaves, night, a wench, he throws himself at the Prince in a mad rage. "I have straightened out that business," says ~~the~~

---

* Unclear in the original.

~~Youth~~ the young Prince to the Youth. "The money has been found." But he has already withdrawn into himself; he is full of hatred.

To Liza, to his mother, to them, about his idea; *they understand nothing*. Dolgushin is arrested. Liza's farewell with the Prince takes place in the Youth's presence. <Her> fiancé reproaches <her>. Liza thanks him. He apologizes. That same night, at home, the scene between Liza and her mother: "Bear it!" ~~The next day she turns down the young man.~~ Here, He and the Youth are also present. As they leave, the Youth says to Him: "Scoundrel!" Yes, that's where <he calls Him?> a scoundrel. Whereupon they meet again as co-conspirators. And then, later that night, the Youth is with his mother. Liza is not at home. Suddenly his mother throws up her hands: "Oh! I feel sick!" She runs out to look for Liza and comes across the people who are bringing her <body>. It is the fiancé who brings her. Immediately following, this description: the mother, back home, dying. He, just barely suppressing his sobs; the little boy, crying for Liza and not letting the Youth go away. Lambert with his <injured> leg. Arrest.

Write more briefly. (Imitate Pushkin.)

The young Prince's proposed marriage to the Princess is far from being official. Nothing has been said in public, and the Princess is *free*. But throughout the novel there are many instances when rumors of an official announcement of the marriage are afloat, and on each of these occasions He gets terribly excited. When the Prince arrives together with the Youth, this is already enough cause for him to get excited. Here, the challenge after <the return of those> 200,000 also takes place. He wonders why the old Prince has become involved in the young Prince's promissory note to Liza, etc., *on this subject*.

[Most important.] N.B. After his arrival, the Prince is seeking to meet Liza, which is why Liza is all smiles (even though she has a suitor). They actually have a rendezvous. The young Prince suggests that the Youth be present, so he can see how *innocent* this all is. And so the Youth is there. This is in part two.

In part one.

The Youth tells Him that, though he hasn't seen Him since his childhood, he has <always> loved Him, 'I don't know <why>' and that he has been always daydreaming about how he was going to tell and show Him all in a general showdown, after which he would be either rejected or forgiven, and that now he was having a hard time, really, realizing that He was no longer quite the fine fellow and dandy, no longer quite so ideally handsome, as He had been when he had visited <his son> at Souchard's.

What is absolutely necessary is a conversation between the old Prince and the Youth about Liza, a conversation which makes certain things considerably clearer to the Youth (i.e., to the reader), specifically, why the old Prince has been helping to provide Liza with a *dowry ("cher enfant, enfin c'est juste").*[30]

It is Makar Ivanov who says "Bear it!" when Liza's mother tells him about it.

When, in the scene of the conspiracy, the Youth has killed Lambert, he says to the Princess: "Do you really think that I would have been afraid to take advantage of you? No, solely in order to show you that I am not afraid of you and how much I despise everything, beginning with you and down to the penalty that is awaiting me, I am telling you this: go, leave, out!" Whereupon the Princess steps closer, opens the door, sees his father who has been hiding there and says, with a smile: "I'm not in the least surprised."

"Go, we are all guilty."

Makar Ivanovich on Peter the Great.

N.B. Makar Ivanov is preaching continence, fasting, pursued with methodical rigor (monasticism), i.e., the exact contrary of the Youth's <own> idea. He overwhelms him with his Christian ways. But he is too busy with other things at the time. Versilov also discusses Christianity.

There is a certain solidity (of intellect, of knowledge, of erudition) about him.

"He is neither this nor that..."*

"He is like a babe: whatever he sees he wants to grab."

"Breathing down my neck."

"Unexpectedly."

"Failed to get a hold on her (his) throat."

"As yet, he couldn't bring himself to do it; he hadn't the heart (to kill <him> with his knife)."

"So as to subject himself to such eternal torments."**

---

* For the next several pages we seem to be dealing mostly with Makar Ivanovich Dolgoruky's stories and words of wisdom. The language is "substandard," which cannot always be rendered in the translation.

** In the original the phrase contains distorted forms of literary phraseology.

[30] French: "Dear child, at last it's just."

"I have lived reverently."

"Little kids will give you small trouble, once they're ready to reap, they'll knock ol' dad off his feet."*

"She helped herself <?> to an egg (a mouse stole it)."

"Our trouble (our grief)."

"Ah, he is in such a bad shape (the sick man), it's just his soul is barely [still] hanging on; he ought to have died a long time ago."

"Live off you for a while."

"One does not take offense at everybody."

"He is like the new moon at this place: he'll just barely show himself, and be gone again."

This is one of those many Russian writers who ~~all~~ don't know why they are writing.

"A soldier is a muzhik turned rotten."

~~Scare Scare over~~ "Render him an example, scare him a bit. Set a good example through him." [for him]

"He used to order even other people's <children> to be flogged in this fashion."

"You are a youth."**

Makar Ivanov: (Peter the Great.) "So you go ahead and get an education, ~~all~~ and don't waste any time. Get to know everything, so that when you run into some ~~mischievous person~~ godless or mischievous person, you can ~~tell him~~ answer him so that he can't smother you with his words. And so that he can't confuse your immature mind."

"I have a backache as bad as if some dogs were chewing it."

"You're a fussy one; you never think ahead."

"It's not for you, fool that you are, to get rich."***

"You ought to be flogged, though you may have risen to officer's rank; yet somebody ought to take off your pants and punish ~~you~~ for an example." ("Makar Ivanovich! I am taking a generous view of your words, and so I am willing to forgive you.")

"And so he is sitting in that tavern, stark naked."

"He is going to give you a lot of trouble (he'll put you into a lot of trouble)."****

---

* Free translation of a doggerel "epigram." The Russian edition has *Detki malen'kie, tak i vedki malen'kie,* where *vedki* is apparently a misprint for *bedki.*

** This sentence and preceding two paragraphs contain distorted forms of literary phraseology in the original.

*** Literally, "to make a kopek."

**** This paragraph and preceding five paragraphs contain distorted forms of literary phraseology in the original.

"But all this is to no avail, there'll be just so many more rumors afloat."

"You'll put it (i.e., a good word of advice) to good use also, if there's anything at all in your soul you can get a solid grip on."

"He's grown up, but still has no sense."

"Look what our degrees are doing" (i.e., how cold it is).

"A man-turned-dog, turned-animal."

"A lawyer is a hired conscience."

"Here, they'll find out everything, down to the last little thing."

"<He> was waiting for him, like a raven for blood."

"Listen, my friend, couldn't ~~you~~ quit this thing?" (in the sense: quit a bad thing one has started).

"In no time he extracted me by the collar, tearing my collar" ("extracted" in the sense: seized and pushed away).*

"They immediately tore off our hands, mine and his" (i.e., stopped them from doing what they were about to do).

"You've lost your measure. Don't ever lose your measure. A man who has lost his measure is in trouble. Such a man is lost."

"So you were thinking."

"You made bold to him."

"You are a captive of your mind, instead of being its master."

"You were thinking! What good is it you were thinking, if you didn't think it through to the end!"

"What do you think you're worth once you have broken your oath?" (i.e., violated).**

"You haven't handed out enough lickings (i.e., beatings). Gave him a good licking (a good beating)."

"Crying bitter tears. Taking out what little he owns (what little is his own)."

~~"Everywhere~~ the little man is shedding tears, shedding tears day and night, shedding tears all over, <for> he's got no bread, he's got no shoes and no clothes to wear, while the big man is eating and drinking more than his fill. And that's how it is going to be all over the world, right till the advent of Christ, always growing and multiplying."

"And they beat her up that time, so badly she almost died."

---

* *Ibid.*

** In the original the phrase contains distorted forms of literary phraseology.

"What does she say? I love her. What, me not love her? I love her day and night—that's how much I love her.."

"Straighten out a warped kopek piece."

"Why, you ought to shape up first, and give some shape to all you're doing. Give it an effort; as is, you're all spread out, nor do you see what your job really is; [nor do you really have a job in front of you] you don't know what you want, and you're no longer aware of yourself (or you've quit being aware of yourself)."

"In the first place, work (on yourself), [for yourself] and just by doing that you'll also work for other people; and start a great feat with<in> yourself, and if God won't forsake you, you'll end up working on a great cause. Each and every one should work on himself, and no one else—no state, and no rule, and no law. You can remain a righteous man even in Sodom, if only you will never cease viewing yourself, and judging yourself with your mental gaze [eye]. Never abandon yourself—this is the first rule. But what about you: not only are you out of hand, but you won't give in to a word either" (i.e., he does not even want to listen when somebody is talking about him).

"I'll make you see the stars."

"He blew into her ear" (whispered into her ear, gave her an earful, taught her).

"A daily day."

"Though money may not be God, it is half a god."

"A soldier is a muzhik turned rotten."

"As was said by you to be your pleasure."

"It is not for you, little fool that you are, to get rich. You're a fussy one, and business likes a cool man."

"Remember throne-and-fatherland."*

"One must also remember throne-and-fatherland" (ex abrupto).

Stinking Lizaveta.

["How Lizaveta, a beggar-woman and a servant <of the Lord>, was elevated—and she had a dream: on the day of judgment Christ calls her, 'there hasn't been anyone more wretched, more evil-smelling than you—so if you'll forgive, I will.' And Lizaveta says: 'They burnt me, and they whipped me—I did not complain, as if I never felt it, nor did I take notice of the insults I was suffering; but now as the time has come where all the guilty are judged, here's what I say: no,

* This paragraph and preceding two paragraphs contain distorted forms of literary phraseology in the original.

I am not forgiving them, many times a sinner that I am <myself>,' and they all perished. And the merchants heard about it, and gave her cotton material, and kvass to drink, and plied her with pies, offered her as much as five rubles in cash—Lizaveta wouldn't take it. Then they gave her a beating and chased her away. She rolled off the stairs, and screamed, screamed for a long time, cursing them."]

Drunken men out in the streets. Nobody wants to work. A high school student killed himself finding studying too hard. A flabby, vile generation. No sense of duty or responsibility.

The aunt, in the railway carriage: "You are acting as if somebody had insulted you, my dear."

"...Here I realized that I was taking a conventional line."

In the provincial town, intimate-polite-commonplace-familiar discussions, in a tone considered best as well as proper:

"Listen, doctor, you've really told us some tall stories in connection with this affair."

The doctor: "Not at all, and to begin with, I'd ask you to address me in a more polite tone."

"I..." etc. (N.B. Yet they don't continue their discussion any more politely, but continue in exactly the same tone.)

In the railway carriage: "I promised myself to never tell Father, or anyone else, about the persecutions I suffered at Souchard's in my childhood—*they aren't worth it.*"

October 15.

Or leave it as before, without shortening the part about his daydreaming, and then at Vasin's about Ungern-Shternberg[31] as well as, in passing, about his own idea—in a mysterious form.

October 23.

"Seeing myself at the height of such power (as a Rothschild), I decidedly fell in love with myself."

October 26.

It isn't that I was a coward, but I was imagining that I was a flunky; well, and if I was a flunky, then I had to be a coward as well, and a thief (I did steal), and so I was taking pleasure in wallowing in this stinking filth. At the same time, another world, the world of books, Walter Scott, daydreaming. Light up (a dream). (N.B. Besides, think up another daydream for this spot.) Think up some noble action. And so, he feels the torture of the noble deed which he has done.

---

[31] See note 3 of Part II.

A visit by his mother.* The aunt, moving to the German's place. Both <of his> lives continue and develop further. A description of his daydreams, and what exactly he dreams. (N.B. Without fail, his father in each of these dreams.) Then, reality, a description of the German, life with him, high school, yet an arid, wretched life. Finally, he has shut himself up in a well-ordered way of life, as in a shell (every single item has its own proper place. A terribly small life, and the smaller, the better). Once, he is torn away from this life by Lambert. After <the episode with> Lambert he withdraws into himself completely. News about his father. He is eagerly gathering them. His heart is palpitating every time he gets such a bit of news. The first signs of sex. Kuznetsky Bridge. A ray <of light>. Suddenly, his own idea. It takes him three years to get his idea organized. Through with high school, a quick change, a letter to Petersburg (he wasn't even told to whom the German had written the letter). The German dies. The package. Information about his relatives. The aunt. Frou-frou and an encounter. With the aunt. The trip.

In the meantime, he had some miserable teachers in high school (examples). "Amazing how little I cared." Examples, anecdotes. It might have seemed that he was all engrossed in that life (a high school student's), yet *this wasn't true at all,* on the contrary, he was just *going through the motions.*

The German used to talk about the boat that went to England, the trial of Christ, etc.

[Cope with this material.] Daydreams. The prophet. <The cap> that makes you invisible. An arrow into Napoleon's eye. A merry tale about a head cut off. How he told it very well. I am telling it at the Countess's. The rout near Moscow, and Ungern-Shternberg.[32] I am describing it step by step, how it all started and how it kept going.

N.B. *He,* to the Youth, at their first showdown: "If you think that I am doing the wrong thing in marrying this woman, tell me—I'll break the engagement; there is still time. To be sure, she is almost officially my fiancée, but there is still time. I have also told your mother what I am telling you now."

"And *your* children?"

"No, I haven't told them: I do not intend to ask them."

In the first person.

His life during his childhood is to be distributed between the

---

* Or: "to his mother." The Russian sentence is ambiguous.

[32] *Ibid.*

various parts of the novel thusly: In the railway carriage—Chatsky; also on the train, about the Prince's lawsuit. At Vasin's, his mother's visit, daydreams, etc. About Lambert, while he is drinking with the Prince. (A word or so can be be dropped earlier.) But it is the Prince himself who tells him about Lambert.

In the railway carriage. "I would ask him about Lambert." "Do you know Mr. Lambert?" The drinking bout should have this scene—he is trying to kiss <him?>, and <he?> grabs <him?> by the hair.

"Drive me to the Princess's, too. She is a rotten one."

October 27.

[February.] He is thrown out of a sled while it is traveling at full speed, and he bears it. Gambling. "I want this man to leave, either he or I will leave." Stolen money. After he has been led out <of the gambling place> he returns and says that it was the Prince who stole the money.

N.B. <The Youth's> story at Vasin's is interrupted either by episodes with the child, or at night, by the episode with the girl who has hanged herself, and who should be living in the same house.

"I didn't have enough character to stand a little suffering, but I could have withstood great suffering; I knew that I could."

Before his departure he talks to N. A., who says to the Youth: "Do you know that there's a wedding coming up between the Prince and your sister?"

"I know even more, there's also my father's wedding."

HE ONCE MORE?

A landowner, a despot, strong intellect, critical enough not to become either a Slavophile or a Westernizer. He becomes a profound egoist. An egoist from despotism. He is, though, a despot to the bone; a true despot must place himself so highly that he actually treats people unctuously, without anger, for to him they are mice, moles. They must be given help and encouragement. The fact that everybody is in love with Him he must accept as something necessary. And this is why he cannot understand how the Princess *is not in love* with him. He refuses to believe that he is in love, and is embarrassed when he must finally prove it to himself, and he gets to thinking. He thinks that he only wants to save the Princess. Everything is solved by his passion. This passion ~~crushes~~, his admission that he is capable of *sinking* to the level of passion leaves him completely crushed. A despot to the bone. He admits himself that he is an atheist—ruins the Youth, is running the risk of ruining him, changes his mind and comes to talk him out of going along with the plot.

N.B. He views Vasin with extreme condescension (i.e., benignly to the point of unctuousness). N.B. The only person he is not treating benignly is the sickly little boy.

"He is really something to look at, so perfect the type of a despot," says Vasin.

Suffering in his egoistic way, He can stand the death of his wife and Liza's suicide. Then he takes the boy away himself and *leaves him out in the street.* Later, when the Youth returns he begins to scream that he has abandoned the child. [Ran away from him.]

Or: The child ran away by himself. Even though he had been taking care of it, entertaining it, and playing with it (the aunt wasn't around), but the child ran away from him, which delivered the final crushing blow to his pride.

October 28.

When the old Prince had shown Him the door for having denounced his daughter (regarding that letter in which she was taking steps to have him declared insane), He went home and wrote a letter to the old Prince, in which He said that he had slandered the Princess under the influence of his own passion for her, etc. ("What if this is the truth?" He says to the Youth, but mockingly.)

His lectures to the Youth concerning depraved creatures, the depravity which reigns in society (in connection with the Princess). He is taking advantage of the Youth's fanatic hatred of the aristocracy, and thus excites him (to play the game). The Youth blindly believes Him to *the last moment.* His game consists of making the Youth fall in love with Him, subject him to His will, take complete possession of him, all with the idea of later abandoning him.

The question regarding his *mother* He presents to the Youth in such a manner that the latter believes that He actually had no chance to act in any other way.

The Youth is outraged by the fact that He pays no attention to Liza's fate. Also, he is having a slight suspicion that He may be too egoistic even with him. But at the last moment when He comes to see the Youth asking him to quit the plot, He is noble and shows him how to give up <his plan> proudly. It is on this occasion, too, that He gives <the Youth> an exalted judgment of <the latter's idea to become a> Rothschild. He invites him to become an ascetic.* The Youth begs Him to come along with him as he hands over the letter.

---

* *na verigi,* literally, "to <wear> chains <worn by ascetics as an act of penance.>"

The Youth to the aunt, in the railway carriage: Information about the story of his father's life, about the old Prince, etc.

"You are quite wrong there," says the aunt.

The Youth likes the way his aunt isn't at all embarrassed by what had happened the day before, but rather adjusts skillfully to everything.

He, to the student: "You are mediocrity itself, you are going to graduate and become the most respectable citizen; even now, as you were shouting obscenities <at that woman>, you were entirely lacking in *any kind of idea of your own.* You don't even understand what I am saying."

"The devil take you, you're a swine, you're the one who forced himself on me."

"And you are what kind of ———"

"And you, you—so much for you, I know."

October 29.

Absolutely. The Youth also reveals his idea to Vasin.

But when Versilov comes to see him at his flat in order to ask his forgiveness, he tells the Youth that now he ought to be in a mood hostile to the whole world, for he had just revealed *his own idea to a stranger* for the first time in his life, and so he actually ought to hate Vasin. The Youth is amazed at His knowledge of people.

"I beg you to never discuss this matter with me."

"Naturally, and I also ascribe your letter asking to be left alone to this very mood of yours."

[Versilov adds: "I am not enticing you with any kind of bourgeois virtue to replace <your> ideals, nor am I saying that happiness is superior to heroism, because, my dear, heroism is superior to any kind of happiness, and I am respecting you for having conceived an idea."]

Versilov tells him a few other things. Touchard is kinder <than you might think>, and there are only few villains <in this world>. People are a lot kinder and more "average" than you might think. You thought that you had found a villain in me, but here now, we've had a heart-to-heart talk and you can see that I am no villain at all, but just <an average person>, and you are angry and even ashamed, seeing that the world is turning out to be different from what you thought it to be like. [Either he or I? You're a fool, she is going to trade you in for him.]

"Right now you'd like very much to set fire to something, smash something to pieces, rise above all of Russia, sweep past like a thunderstorm leaving everybody behind, and then, having thus manifested yourself, disappear in a desert, or in the United States of America, where you'll make another meteoric appearance."

Absolutely. After the Youth had been beaten up (when he was with the young Prince), he did think of fleeing to America.

"A soldier is a muzhik gone rotten."

"That republican chicken, Michelet;[33] hebephrenia in his old age."

[Here] The husband says to his wife who has been away from home: "Don't you know where you have been?"

(To our liberals:) "You are romantics, you are dreamers, you are minor poets."

To strong and *undisputed* recognition of certain writers as being important or even great is in part evidence of the shallowness of these writers, of the fact that they are well within the range of the golden mean. Turgenev.

About Sherstobitov (Putilin).[34] Looks stern, has got canaries singing at his house, plays the guitar himself. Owns a brick house.

They've expressed their affection for God.

N.B. (A marvellous artist. About Turgenev.)

"So that I have decided to conclude the debut of my life" (from a letter left by a nihilist girl who had shot herself).

"Cocklets."*

Don Basilio, chain smokes. Boundless impudence.

"Note that this gentleman is giving himself very portly airs."

"Kind of strange."

The word "abroad" (write it as one noun throughout).**

He is like the new moon (etc.).

Live off you for a while.

It isn't so everybody (every man) can insult one.

Man, ~~from~~ in his higher exemplars and his higher manifestations, does nothing *simply;* and so he won't shoot himself *simply* either, but religiously (even though he be an atheist). But the run-of-the-mill

---

* *Koklety,* apparently a colloquial allomorph of *Kotlety,* "cutlets."

** Russian *zagranitsa* is really *za granitsei,* "across the border."

[33] Jules Michelet (1798–1874). Dostoevsky does not refer to him in any of his works nor in any of his letters; yet it seems clear that he was familiar with Michelet's works, especially with his arguments with Hertsen. Dostoevsky probably knew his *Pologne et Russie* (1852) and his *La Pologne martyre* (1863). Hertsen's famous article "The Russian People and Socialism" was addressed to Michelet. Dostoevsky is probably thinking in this note of his sentimental and rather trite sketches *L'Amour* (1858) and *La Femme* (1860).

[34] The first note of a story that Makar Dolgoruky narrates in Part III, Chapter 3:4 of the final version.

and the ordinary [people,] they are the ones who even shoot themselves in a banal way and without being fully aware of what they're doing, simply ~~but~~ and stupidly. Simple and *simpler,* but more stupid, too.

This turmoil.

Markus, telling how the merchants on that boat gave word to England in three days.[35]

About how they reenacted Christ's trial in England and decided that he was guilty.

About the vision of that Swedish King.

(N.B. They tell the old Prince about *the boat,* and he laughs, then himself tells about Christ's trial in England.)

N.B. "I'd like to have a nice chat; in our country, people always find lofty subjects entertaining. Yet I would also like to communicate it to you to make my audience happy, and moreover, to be myself worthy of all that is beautiful and sublime."*

The hole under the rock (see plan).

And postpones his decision, waving his hand <in a gesture of resignation>.

Whatever he could not understand or value he would sneer at insolently, in particular if he'd ~~see~~ notice that it might be of importance to high-minded people.

With our entire progressive movement of the past 17–18 years we have proved, more than anything else, that we are terribly uneducated.

They were laughing at my better feelings, in those rare moments when I was really ~~entirely~~ sincere. Well, I am glad that I cannot forget this; at least they have rid me of the misfortune to love them.

"You, a future Rothschild," (He says to the Youth). "Of course you are an idealist—and there you have a [new] and unexpected consequence of positivism and nihilistics."**

Having chopped up the icons:

"Haven't I believed in all this [all my life,]" *He* said suddenly, pointing at the fragments, as he was leaving the room together with the Youth.

---

* Purposely awkward in the original.

***Nigiliatina,* formed from *nigilizm* ("nihilism") with the pejorative suffix *-iatina.*

35 Fyodor Antonovich Markus was a steward in the hospital where Dostoevsky's father worked as a surgeon. He lived above the Dostoevskys and visited them often.

"That is, [all your life] you have not believed in all this," said the Youth.

"All right, I haven't believed in it all my life," he repeated, ~~hesitating for a moment~~ breaking off the conversation (with that intonation of his, so well known to the Youth, with which *He* habitually interrupted <their> conversations).

God sends us misfortune. Misfortunes are useful, too, and how! Without misfortunes there wouldn't be any happiness. Without misfortunes, life wouldn't be worth living.

N.B. The tale of St. Paul's conversion, on the road, after the murder of <St.> Stephen. About the temptation in the desert. About the essence of asceticism in monasteries. The freedom of Christ even in communism, the freedom of Christ even in <17>93. All these tales both delight and puzzle the Youth.

He shook the dust off his feet at Dolgushin's, and kissed the threshold.

[Here] Any time your wife is getting too affectionate with you, assume that she is about to take a lover.

[The lackey in the railway carriage] We fools (i.e., husbands) can be always deceived, and how simply and easily at that."

"The reforms launched during the present reign have caused any common idea as well as any common bond to disappear. Previously, there was at least something; now there is nothing at all. Everything has fallen apart. The order that existed before was foul and wretched, but it was order. What we've got now is complete disorder in everything." This is one of His cynical phrases. ~~"Why is this? asks the Youth.~~

"Why is this?" the Youth asks Him.

"The devil only knows, must be because of the reforms. As far as I am concerned, it may all go to hell."

The Youth: "You know what, father, you are a terrible reactionary."

He: ~~Well, I~~ "I don't give a damn, really."

About how the notion of good and evil has become lost.

He: "For goodness's sake, here's what it says, right there, a District Commissioner stated outright: 'I'll take the money, but I won't serve,' and there's that other one who'd simply have the peasants flogged if they bothered him with any official business. (*Golos,** early

* *The Voice.*

August.) Well then, how can we in Petersburg decide if it's good or bad?"

The Youth: "Of course it's a low-down <attitude>."

He: "Hardly. These people will be screaming and writing that it is a low-down <action>, but secretly they'll be glad, for it can only mean that the reforms aren't working, that they aren't taking root, so that things are getting closer to a complete collapse, and thus, to the advent of a new social order. If these people were put in the place of those District Commissioners, they'd certainly act exactly as those did. And so, we really don't know what's good and what's bad."

"These are paradoxes, father."

"Hardly so. For these things have been bothering me all my life."

"I think that all this will happen most simply. People will just refuse to pay their debts in order to get a new deal through universal and solidaristic bankruptcy. I've only presented a tiny part of the whole situation, but isn't this tiny part connected with all the rest, and, so-to-speak, with indissoluble ties?"

"What then, are we to do?"

"What to do? Be honest. In a word, read the ten commandments."

"But this is old, and besides, what am I going to accomplish all by myself?"

"Look, all these questions notwithstanding, do follow the ten commandments, and you'll be a great man. [If you're going to do it in a serious way, then once you are engaged in some serious business, you'll naturally quit asking questions. ~~I have postponed.~~"]

"Unknown to all."

"There is no secret that won't be revealed <some day>."

"You're laughing <at me>?"

That's right, sometimes it would seem to me that he was definitely laughing <at me>, and it made me sad, ~~but~~ sad, for all my life. On the other hand, it still made me think.

[The 10 commandments and, in addition to that, love somebody or something, and you will be <a great man>, and best of all, become a specialist in some field.

I postponed telling him about my idea. It wasn't the proper time. I saw this... Besides, it wasn't the proper time for me either. God knows what kind of a time it was—a time of both exaltation and disgrace.]

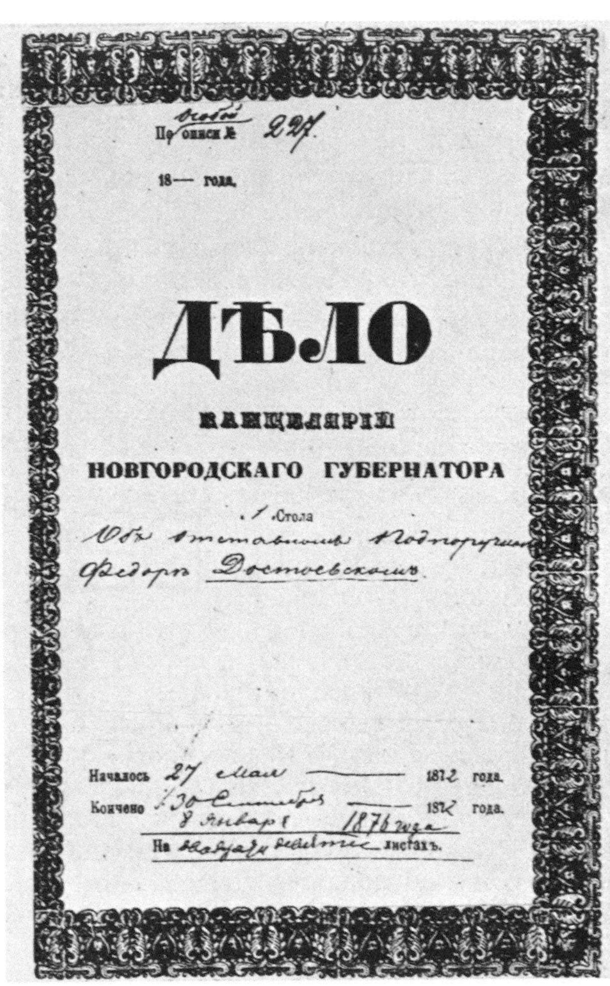

По особой описи № 227

18— года.

ДѢЛО

КАНЦЕЛЯРІИ

НОВГОРОДСКАГО ГУБЕРНАТОРА

1 Стола

Объ отставномъ Подпоручикѣ Федорѣ Достоевскомъ

Началось 27 Мая 1872 года.

Кончено 30 Сентября 1872 года.
8 Января 1876 года

На [illegible] листахъ.

File on surveillance of Dostoevsky in Staraia Russia. The dossier is dated January 8, 1876, and covers the period from May 27, 1872, to September 30, 1872.

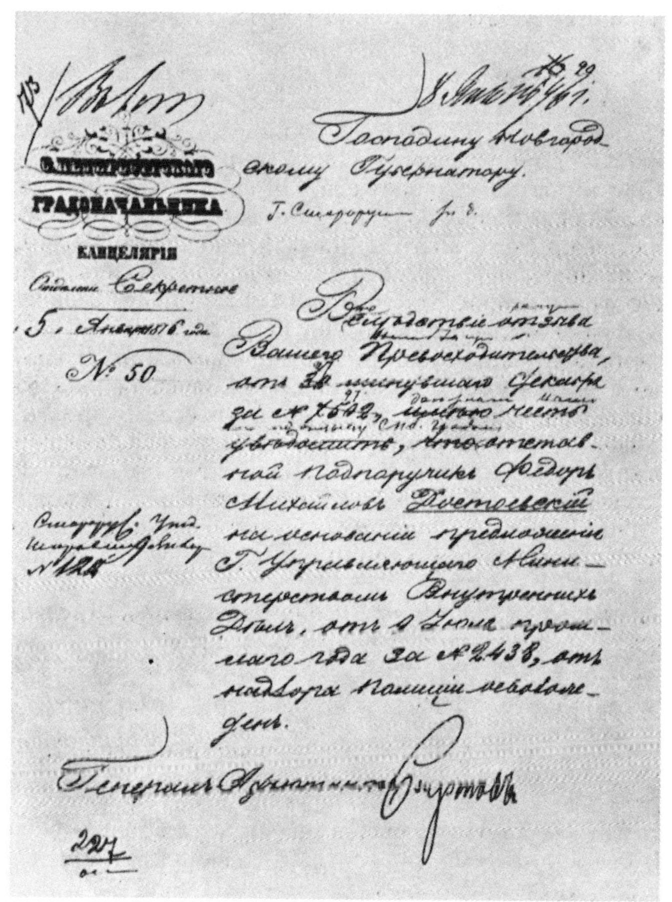

С.ПЕТЕРБУРГСКОГО
ГРАДОНАЧАЛЬНИКА
КАНЦЕЛЯРІЯ

5 Января 1876 г.

№ 50

Господину Новгородскому Губернатору.

Вследствие отзыва Вашего Превосходительства, от 23 минувшего Декабря за № 7542, имею честь уведомить, что отставной подпоручик Федор Михайлович Достоевский на основании предложения Г. Управляющего Министерством Внутренних Дел, от 9 Июня прошлого года за № 2438, от надзора полиции освобожден.

Генерал Адъютант Трепов

Notice of abolishment of police surveillance of Dostoevsky. The notice is from the St. Petersburg head to the governor of Novgorod and is dated January 5, 1876. Dostoevsky was under police surveillance from the time of his release from prison to this date.

IV

Notes to the First Part of the Novel

These notes for the first part of the novel have something of a miscellaneous character, because Dostoevsky ranges over many of the subjects and situations of the first part of the novel, often without transition and often in very abbreviated form. In effect, the writer seems to be grouping elements in summary fashion, and checking out what has been decided and what still needs to be decided. What Dostoevsky still finds unsatisfactory is signaled by his return again and again to the same situations and by his analysis at length of certain scenes and character portraits. From these notes one can see that Dostoevsky is still very much at work attempting to fathom the relations of the Youth to his father, still very much intrigued and challenged by the character of Versilov, vacillating and unsure about the Princess (now called occasionally Akhmakova) character, and in a quandary about how to present the relations between the Princess and Prince Sokolsky.

As before, the Youth's attitude toward his father is one of hate and love, but a hate that is itself a form of love. Dostoevsky says, perhaps more directly and more extremely than before: "And all in all, the whole novel is a poem of the Youth's love for Him." And the Youth himself says, "I was feeling that I could not live without Him, I was full of spite, I was acting like a woman in love." The relations between the two, as well as those of both to the Princess, are still being experimented with. In one version the Youth attempts to kill the Princess with a revolver, and it is Versilov who wrestles the revolver from him and shoots her. In one version Versilov "unmercifully lures him into debauchery and moral degradation" in order to get the document from him.

Such actions are, of course, at odds with the Versilov who moves with sublety and mystery and achieves his effects without direct pressures. Much of the fascination of Versilov in the novel comes from the force he exerts on others without exerting force, and it is something of a surprise to find Dostoevsky still picturing Versilov in some of these notes as coaxing, luring, conniving, antagonizing, and demonstrating. In the novel Versilov is something of a still point in a vortex of action: he "permits" things to happen and they often happen in a way that seems to accord with his intention. Near the end of this section of notes Dostoevsky gives us a long analysis of Versilov's character that is fairly close to the core of Versilov's character as portrayed in the novel. Yet the effect of the analysis is quite different from the effect we receive in the novel:

> In spite of his self-adulation, he is restless, since he is often dissatisfied with himself. He wants the feats of a superior man; He wants chains and sacrifices, but his *attitude of considering people no better than mice* as well as his pride justify Him to His own conscience every time. It is impossible to love people. The idea that he may be in love with the Princess is humiliating to Him [and eventually leads to his ruin.]... Furthermore, he cannot exist without a circle of admirers, starting with poor Sofia. He likes to be adored even in the most petty ways and would be unhappy in a trivial way even if a Tatiana Pavlovna turned away from Him; yet it would never make him lose heart.

The tone of the analysis is too sharp, too critical, and even debasing. Versilov comes out something of a moral scoundrel in such an analysis, and one may legitimately wonder why he is worshipped by all about him, and why the Youth should seek his love so forcefully. It is possible that this consideration leads Dostoevsky to say the following:

> N.B.! In order to elevate the tone of the Youth's worrying and suffering as he is following His every move with deep emotion, tortured by His very person, it is absolutely necessary to also *raise to a more tragic level* the very tone of the events and accusations weighing upon Him on the part of society. Many legends and Catholicism are being

> **charged to Him; *but it is necessary:* to also elevate the person of the Princess. Make her proud and fantastic, too.**

The pride and self-love that Versilov represents must not prevent, artistically, a belief on the part of the reader in the love and attachment that he provokes. The task is delicate and Dostoevsky seems to sense the difficulty, but he will not resolve it in this sections of the notes. Versilov is, in the final analysis morally corrupt; yet he must be, as he is in the novel, someone who commands admiration, respect, and fanatical devotion. He is corrupt, but he must be able to seduce those about him into believing in the sincerity of his "sufferings," in the seriousness of his goals, and in the importance of his gestures. Perhaps more important, he must seduce the reader into believing in these things.

At this point in the elaboration of Versilov's character, Dostoevsky sees the solution to the expression of corruption and admiration in making more tragic Versilov's exclusion from society. In the novel itself the reasons for Versilov's exclusion from society are shrouded in rumor and mystery, and we are given scanty facts and vague speculations. But a good part of these notes, perhaps the major part, are devoted to variations of those events at Ems that led to Versilov's complicated relations with the Princess, the slap in the face that Versilov endures from Prince Sokolsky, and his consequent exclusion from society. At least for a while Dostoevsky evidently contemplated giving these events a much larger part than they have in the final version. The events, as in the novel, concern Prince Sokolsky's fathering of a child by Lidiia, the stepdaughter of Katerina Nikolaevna Akhmakova; Versilov's love affair and proposal to Lidiia; Lidiia's death under ambiguous circumstances. But the relations between Prince Sokolsky and the Princess in these notes are substantially different, for in some of the versions there has been a passionate love affair between the two. It is this love affair that provides the motives for Versilov to attempt in various ways to discredit the Prince in the Princess's eyes and the Prince in Lidiia's eyes.

In the novel the passionate love affair between the Princess and the Prince is reduced to a flirtation, and Versilov's intrigues against

Lidiia, the Prince, and the Princess are either eliminated or clothed in rumor and mystery. Despite Dostoevsky's intention in these notes to elevate the tone of the circumstances of Versilov's exclusion from society, he succeeds only in placing more emphasis on Versilov's intriguing and ruthless character. For in all the versions of the romantic complication Versilov fathers complications and crises by revelations and plots, the whole point of which seems to be to break up the love affair between the Prince and the Princess and, it seems, Lidiia's attachment to the Prince. Dostoevsky understood quite rightly that Versilov needed a stature and a tone that he did not have as a predatory type to explain the silent obeisance of those about him, and to explain also the furious tenderness of his son's love. But he was wrong in believing that an elaboration of the circumstances of Ems would do this.

In the notes up to now Dostoevsky's portraiture of the Princess has taken a course similar to Versilov's development. She has been pictured largely as passionate and in many respects cruel, and in these notes she is spoken of as "a depraved woman-of-the-world." She insults the Youth, plays with him, in some versions seduces him; indeed she abuses the Youth in ways that are similar to those that the father uses. Her portrait has far less body and less coherence than Versilov's, but Dostoevsky seems to have had in mind—to judge from these notes—the idea of creating a woman who in many respects was to be Versilov's female counterpart. In the following note he expresses this directly: "What is going on between Him and the Princess is not passion, but a duel of pride. Yes, the Princess is that kind of person herself."

The subtilizing of Versilov's predatory nature in the course of these notes results in a character of chilling and ambiguous evil, and a certain charm, sincerity, and suffering raise him almost to the tragic tone which Dostoevsky speaks of here as necessary to his character. Whereas the final portrait of Versilov is a monumental achievement, Dostoevsky will not be as successful in his portrait of Katerina Nikolaevna Akhmakova. The same concealment and ambiguity will result in a woman of society who strikes us as inadequate to the passions she provokes. She is in many respects an empty and shallow woman, and yet these notes make it clear that Dostoevsky intended to make her as complex, mysterious, and tragic as he was making Versilov. In the last interview with Versilov she conveys the impression of a passionless, frightened woman looking for peace and security of the most mundane sort.

One must note finally that "the Rothschild motive," which floats idly in the final version, with little connection to other events, receives in these notes substantial elaboration. In one paragraph of notes the Youth describes in some detail his program of privation and hermit-like existence and the happiness they have brought him. Immediately following the description of the program, he asks himself the following: "This was my poem on independence. Why then, that Akhmakov woman, why the document, why did I want to save Versilov from his enemies—by doing all this, I was only betraying my idea." In this quotation the Youth provides us with a motive for connecting the Rothschild theme and the Youth's relations with Versilov. It is love of a particularly brusing and mixed variety that deflects the Youth from the pride, isolation and superiority that he is tempted to practice; but it is love, too, that deflects Versilov from his superior self-sufficiency. Both father and son are challenged by love and love is a contradiction to the ideas of both. Whereas Versilov reacts with rage and frustration against love, the Youth reacts with agony and pain and finally with acceptance.

October 29, 1874.

After <the scene> at Mother's <involving> *"either he or I,"* he throws 100 rubles to the young girl, stamps his foot, and leaves, because: he had felt that he was in the right, and had felt serious and exalted, while it came out stupid and humiliating.

[Either at Vasin's or at Dolgushin's.]

"Under socialism, I lose my property; in a commune I must be together with everyone else, but I don't want to be with everyone else."

"Let's forget it, Vasin, let's forget it."

"Let's forget it..."

Program (in *the first person*) [IN A SPECIAL STYLE, AND MORE

BRIEFLY.] Touchard <?>, Chatsky,[1] Drouchard <?> has a lackey ~~mother~~. Lambert and the young Prince, books, daydreams. ~~Drouchard's death.~~ He cried and cried. Mother. At N. S., high school, in the beginning like everyone else, ~~daydreams~~ Lambert, gets involved in Touchard's prose. Everything was so mean, I was considered a traitor, and I withdrew, and I was having friends. Daydreams, books, garden, ray <of light>, life, daydreaming devoured everything. Daydreams: robbers, a general, a prophet, a scientist who publishes his works in Paris, bow and arrow, Ungern-Shternberg.[2] I am not talking about religion. I am not talking about women, frou-frou. Two ladies. Said it outright. ~~On the boulevard, with the student~~... Later, he once met <a> girl, withdrew into himself even more. For a while, the lady whom he had seen step out of her carriage was exciting his imagination. They'll all be mine: leader of a band of robbers, etc. "But how am I going to get my revenge?" Daydreams about him, news about him. Communicating with Mother, a letter. Suddenly, *his own idea,* it wholly captures him—he'd even be a scoundrel. He quits studying. The money he got for his name-day gift. An encounter with his brother, 25 rubles. <Time> goes by without a word. The last two years without a word from his mother, who had been taken abroad, then to Luga. Rumors about 300,000. Later, about the marriage of the young Prince. The young Prince's story. He knows about his preaching Catholicism. In <illegible> Andreev's death. They send him a letter. 23. He travels there to find out about the job. He returns, his aunt has been there in the meantime, orders to come to Petersburg. He decides to go. Andreev's package. On the train—<meeting> with the young Prince. They arrive, <the Youth> in a most wretched mood as a result of his first clash with reality. He decides to break with everybody, to leave everybody, even to go to America. He meets his mother, brief and forceful <scene>. "Either he or I." He leaves, etc. [At this point, the university student.]

Versilov: "I've brought 100 rubles, why did I do it? I never give anybody a thing."

The Prutkov woman. "Mother, why won't you come closer?"

"Oh, I'm afraid I might do something wrong." (N.B. "Forgive me, Sir, if I'm guilty before you.")

---

[1] Chatsky is one of the protagonists of Griboedov's play *Gore ot uma (Woe from Wit)* (1822–25).

[2] See note 3 of Part II.

He, to Him (in the presence of their family): "Because you are a scamp and a scoundrel!"

Marriage to "that passive creature." "What's the cause of it?" the Youth initially exclaims at N.S.'s, later when he is on the train with the Prutkov woman, and finally, at his mother's. During a showdown with the Youth, He says: "If you want me to, I'll break <the engagement>. But the cause of it will still remain unclarified."

He goes to Moscow to see N. S. and inquire if *that letter* might not be there. But N. S. won't tell him. Yet he told the Youth.

IMPORTANT. Before leaving Moscow. About the fact that Versilov is an extraordinary man. Even when he was only 16, when he got those letters from his mother, and 15 rubles.

In connection with the statement of *his own idea* (general), a tirade on *indefatigability*.

A letter to her, a preface, "an illegitimate son in the highest degree." "I'm in the service, I've got my salary."

"It just so happened that my General had given me a surprise on that very day." Three stories by Lambert—the picture and the student, his own idea.

Relics, Catholicism, about his salary and his official duties, about the fact that he has never had a woman. His attitude toward women, frou-frou, "I hate them, they stir up a lot of dust."

"~~You are idolizing your father, you are dissatisfied with something.~~ I'm glad that you are talking to me so seriously, as If I were a friend. ~~One must be more serious~~ (I am wary of the Princess.) *Entrefilet.*[3] He was a madman. One must be more serious. "I notice that you are amusing yourself and ~~as if~~ as if you were reproaching yourself for something. You idolize your father, you are dissatisfied with something." ~~One must~~ "Why did you show my father the door? I am not staying with you, <I have> my own idea."

[Or "your father" (with tact)] He has broken with everybody, has withdrawn <into> Catholicism—~~the Princess I~~ Suddenly the Versilov woman and "the passive creature" come to see us. [I got up.] [Arrival of the Prince.] Salary, Tatiana, about <my> job—I got it. At that moment, the Princess, Dolgoruky, a lorgnette. I heard it.

[Get some witticisms for the General.]

"Forgive me, my dearest General, it may be that I have to quit your service." I said this quite inadvertently because I had seen that

---

[3] French: "Newspaper item."

Princess (and it is with this day that I am beginning my notes). But this is how it was. Finished, I must break <with him>. My weakness for this man was quite inexcusable. I thought of writing a letter, otherwise it wouldn't have worked out, <but would have been turned> into a joke, or into irony. I am much more serious than I am <*sic*>.

An auction. To Vitia—about Kraft. Dolgushin, Vasin, sister, *quae medicamenta,*[4] conversations, arguments, Lambert. Somebody asks: "Prince Dolgoruky?"—taking my measure. Not my idea, Vasin—a machine, Kraft—Russia, to Kraft. (The latter asks me very urgently to come and see him right away.) Opinion about my father—about Russia. Three lives. Kraft on the Princess's little stepdaughter. The Youth asks the question himself. [Kraft answers politely and readily, yet as if it were costing him an effort.] [He tells him how he attended that auction.]

Back home, at home before father is back, "I said that you had given 117 rubles. Forgive me."* (A tender, and the best, scene with his mother, with his sister about Vasin.) He is terribly rude. He comes home, "we've won <the lawsuit>," money, Tatiana Pavlovna, he is rude about yesterday's announcement, today <he is rude?> to the Princess, a Catholic (he was dreaming). "You've been chased out everywhere, I don't want that job. I bought and resold something *at an auction.*"

Clothes to the tailor. About Touchard. Two lives. "I hate," he has stirred my pity. "I'd give them a whipping."

Motives of the 1st part.

Vitia says that Vasin knows <the Youth's> sister. *Everybody* is telling the Youth that he is somber and secretive. The old Prince used to say it, also Vitia, the people at Dolgushin's, and He. He says: "It looks as if he had something important in mind, two lives, and besides, something else: I've got it, he'd like to become a Rothschild." "All right, so I'll be a Rothschild." I stamped my foot and went upstairs. "He finds that all these words, and steps, are much too petty, relatively speaking, and is actually ashamed of it." The Youth thinks: "It annoys me that everything around here is so lacking in seriousness, <all> this *blague,*[5] and humor. I'd better write Him a letter.

---

* The gender of the verb suggests that this is a woman speaking.

4 Latin: "What medicine . . ." See note 36 of Part II.

5 French: "Joke."

Otherwise, if I do it orally, He'll turn it all around, so it will come out as nothing serious."

"You've got your own idea. I'm sure of that, it has something to do with buying and selling." "I know, he wants to become a Rothschild." I got up and left. I decided to leave, so I sat down to write Him a letter. Suddenly He entered my room. A discussion. Rebellion, "I don't want to, I want to leave. I would like you to be more serious, I have nothing to hide before you." *"Mon enfant,* your mother," discussion about Makar Ivanov. "You are still laughing."*—"You are more clever than I thought" (here, he'll add something) (on flattery) —about Rothschild, in passing, then He left. I was left with the thought that it was my last night there. This is what I was thinking: "I have a serious idea, and I don't want to sacrifice anything to anyone." And at this point, to the reader: "This is what that letter had to say" (I reread it). "But I must say that this letter had been bothering me for three hours already. I got to thinking, 'Really, they'll take over that property, not knowing that...' Eh, to hell with it."

Next morning: Things look a bit different, not "to hell with it"; I went to see the Prince so He wouldn't think that I had really deserted him. But I left early and went to see a lawyer. At the Prince's—politeness, to Vasin, who wasn't home—next door, ~~"I've delivered it"~~ behind the partition: "I've delivered it." I went to Tatiana Pavlovna's place. There, the eavesdropping scene. "You rogue!"—"I couldn't come out." *"Le petit espion."*[6] I left. "Surely she is referring to the letter Kraft was mentioning. To hell with all their intrigues. I'll send it over to her right tomorrow, and as for myself, I'll withdraw into my shell, where I have spent three years of solitude."

[Finish it more spectacularly.]

Returning home I ran into that roomer. She had brought a letter and 50 rubles. Threw them to me. She was ashamed to do it in front of the family. On account of this, an argument: "It is your fault." [Recently, the old Prince had been talking about little girls.] ~~A letter~~ An abandoned infant. Argument. "You're a rich man." "Take one half, and the other half, 40 rubles, for the child. To the orphanage." "You are absolutely right: here is a letter for you. Of course, you are a rich man, and I am going home as my conscience bids me. What do I care? I am sorry that I have to leave Mother. I'll be

---

* Or: "You are laughing all the time."

[6] French: "The little spy."

seeing you, mamma, *but it is either you or I,* we are the children of Makar Ivanov, so why are you here?" Tatiana Pavlovna jumped up: "Yes, I am a swine."

I went to Vasin's. "Yesterday Kraft shot himself." Vasin's story about the young girl and the 50 rubles. Told him everything. Asking to stay the night. Telling him all kinds of things, about my daydreams, really got going, and still more, and more. "I can see that you have pride, and *your own idea.*" "Don't ask what idea." ~~You know, Vasin, but there, screams, she has hanged herself—that <girl> of ours~~ A tirade about how everything serious came out unserious, about character. " 'I am serious about big things and unserious about little things.' (Been dreaming for a long time, that's why such a character)." Vasin has a few words to say about my sister. The package. Vasin's prediction that I wouldn't want to run away from <all those> Counts and Princes. "You'll want to take your revenge."

In the morning, screams, she has hanged herself, Father is dumbfounded, not a word to the Youth. ~~Meets Tatiana~~ Encounter with <my> sister. "Come and apologize." ~~I've come~~ "I was on my way. I am going to make up with everybody, but I'll get my stuff." Returned the money. I was sitting at the ~~Prince's~~ General's when the Prince came in; "imagine, *c'est si noble,*"[7] the young Prince. I came home. Tatiana Pavlovna: "Why, why? You're a righteous man." A scene, a confession, I had decided to break <with them>, that's why I am saying this. Statement of my idea. ~~About the Princess~~ I cried, and cried. [About the Princess as the misfortune of ~~my~~ His life]. That's an idea! And there I am, tied up with them again. There will be a day when I'll be able to prove it—they don't need it, excitement, Kraft, and this death. Ahead, ahead, there is still a lot of time ahead. I am lacking stability.

[?Told <Him?> about the scene at Tatiana Pavlovna's, <as I was listening> behind the door.]

Motives of the 1st part.

Kraft: "Stay around a bit, you are perhaps the last person I'll ever see."

With the Prince, about nakedness, and ~~later, after the boulevard~~ about the foul language used by the punks and by the officers he has been with. "This is true! (I) You are my only friend, my dear boy, my son!"

---

[7] French: "It's so noble."

During the confession upstairs: "The Prince fears nothing so much as to be considered insane. Kraft also used to say that this is why he liked his bons mots so much."

The Prince to him: "You know what, I started in the Guards, and I am now, by appointment of the Czar, a Full Privy Councilor."

"*A propos:* you are probably going to have children *(mais c'est charmant)*[8]."

"You know literature." "I know nothing."

"I can see many strange things about your childhood, you were so lonely. Yes, there are those unhappy children! You aren't angry with me for my calling you by your first name?"*

Initially I had planned to be rude with them, but later <. . .> I was ashamed to ask for money. "Now we're in trouble! We are no longer going to have those discussions."

Order: At first, at the Prince's, about his father, the relics and, after a long conversation: an *entrefilet*[9] about his being deranged. And then, after a lot more talking, take the money. *Entrefilet,* "Tatiana Pavlovna has gotten me this job."

It is necessary <to insert>, as soon as he is leaving with Vasin, or so: "Why not the university?"—"Nineteen years old, I have my own idea." And at night, with his father, again: "You quit the university even though your tuition was being paid, Andreev."

"You have been living off all those people, and still they all adore you. <Like> a Japanese deity."

The old Prince: "I raised the question in my club: Why is it that a soldier is a muzhik gone rotten?"

With the old Prince. About the lawsuit—"they are going to win it." "Is it true that He is in love with your daughter?" "Yes, he has been having influence on women," and later: "She is my brother's stepdaughter, and take note of this phenomenon: she loves Versilov." N.B. *She has somehow* got involved with Versilov.

At the old Prince's. About the Princess. "Why did she quarrel <with Him>?" "Here, *mon cher,*[10] something happened here—there was love..."

I (with my eyes flashing): "But I know for certain that nothing of

---

* Literally: ". . . for my saying *thou* to you?"

8 French: "But this is charming."

9 French: "Newspaper item."

10 French: "My dear."

the kind ever happened, and that she has been the cause of all his suffering!"

"How do you know?"

"And so, my dear, I beg you to leave this. [There are certain limits, don't take it as if I were lecturing to you, but don't get angry with an old man.] You are on his side. I have noticed that he fascinates you. Yes, yes, he fascinates me also, I'll admit that," etc.

["I noticed this trait about the Prince, that he liked <to talk> about girls."]

General.

In the 1st part the Youth is stunned by and interested in the Princess (and show *it in the 1st part*), and it isn't an accident either, but rather, he was so inclined even in Moscow, *in a preparatory way*, as it were. Besides, WOMAN. This feeling for her as a woman is to be expressed in an unnatural and excessive hastiness with which he turns hostile toward her from the very first step. Further along in the novel, let him insult her, which insult he takes for an insult to himself, during a drinking bout, still during his happy period; <then,> precisely when he is about to break with his father, let him clash with the Princess (and the Princess, also, on account of the letter). She has lost her shawl, he takes it, kissing her tracks, he wins 800 rubles, brings home the gold, lies down—passion. He wakes up in the middle of the night, furious at himself, and on the very next day finds a pretext to insult the Princess stupidly and rudely. (In a letter?)* He even has a clash with his father on account of that. Later, during those unhappy days of his carousing, it is already the Princess who insults him —terribly, boundlessly, crushingly. Dreams of revenge (Lambert), arson, dreams in different forms, endless dreams that last for several days (N.B. he thus remains true to his principal character trait, that of a dreamer), finally, even to kill her in the end, with <his> revolver. (N.B. The revolver is taken away from him *on the spot* by Him, who then fires at her also, when their plot is carried out.) (N.B. N.B. About shooting a woman who keeps being recalcitrant, Suvorin's feuilleton, November 3, No. 303).

Motives of part one.

The Youth, at his father's: "I know that the old Prince may, in one of his foolish moods, decide to get married, and that everybody is afraid of that, which is why they are carrying on these intrigues."

---

* Or: "Through that letter?"

The Youth: "I admit, *I was scared* and sitting there, cowering. It didn't seem so terrible to me. I've got my own idea—I just want to be left alone. Society—I want to quit society, I want to use everything and quit. I'll be paying enough, and that's it. [Gentlemen, it takes a long time to present a serious idea. I do not see the slightest reason why I should do anything for others.]"

! Most valuable. The suicide's mother, telling about Versilov's visit, says "*She* said that she took it because Versilov didn't smile even once and was terribly serious, even cool." And later, *Versilov* to the Youth: "It seems to me that I was laughing and looked frivolous, which later affected and irritated her."

Even more valuable. At the old Prince's. "When the Princess appeared I grew pale and wanted to leave without a word of explanation. Later, leaving the auction, I saw a lady and recalled the impression left on me by the Princess. And later that night, at Kraft's, again about the Princess, and then, while going home: "The devil take you all! <Back> into <my> shell!"

The old Prince owns a huge male cat. "My friend, *j'aime le bon dieu*"[11] (and he begins to cry). This is already on the next day, or after the news of the Princess's arrival.

The old Prince liked to arrange matches for young girls; all his life he had been marrying them off.

N.B. Make it so that Kraft, as he is talking to the Youth, would look like a man preparing for suicide.

He said: "This is semi-idea, half-education, half-life, half-health, half-knowledge."

Vasin says that he has read Kraft's manuscript.

The Youth to the old Prince: "But why is he living with our family? Our name is Dolgoruky."

The Prince asks about his sister.

MOST IMPORTANT GENERAL NOTE.

This whole thing is a story about why I got rid of my idea. Because I got carried away by the idea, by a passionate duty to rehabilitate *Him,* being in possession of the document. This, toward the end of part one. (As for the feeling, see that torn sheet). And this is why, in the first part, he is desperate, and in tears, wanting to break off everything. To be sure, he is defending Him with his eyes flashing, but Kraft is pressing him hard with facts, and he returns home as if he were intoxicated.

---

[11] French: "I love the good lord."

Quarrels, but he is blaming himself for those quarrels. To Vasin: "What bothers me most is this: Couldn't it be that I am myself guilty, while accusing others?"

Cynicism and mockery cause the Youth to feel aversion and antagonism, especially in connection with His account of Makar Ivanov.

He breaks <with his father>, but the news of how He has acted in connection with the inheritance, and all the rest, win him back and attract him again <to his father>, then the confession.

The final words of part one: "Why, after He had left, after 'and I cried, and cried,' did I have this thought: 'Are we completely reconciled? Wasn't he acting a role?' and, secondly, 'Probably it was just regret on my part, regret about having revealed *my idea* to him.' And then, these words: 'Rehabilitate Him through the document.' These words: 'The whole story is nothing but an account of how,' " etc.

Motives of part one.

The Youth is at Dolgushin's. "And then, I pay enough to society ~~for~~ in the form of money and taxes for seeing to it that I won't be robbed, or beaten up, or killed, though I want you to note this: Society is taking money from me for this, and a lot of money, too, yet it doesn't guarantee my [absolute] safety at all; it just protects me as best it can. But inasmuch as there is no other order which would allow me to live in safety, nor can there be, I am in favor of the ~~society~~ state, i.e., of society, but this is all the state can expect of me, and not that I go running around embracing everybody, feeling neighborly love and being consumed by tears of tender emotion. No, just leave me alone; it's enough I'm paying my money. [You've been talking of the mankind of the future; what good is it to me?] [and probably stupidity] I had said this nervously and angrily, [but I] I had been silent for three years already, after having come up with this thought, and I had never expressed it to anybody before, which is why I uttered it so angrily, expecting to be contradicted and fearing to be refuted by my audience."

Through the entire novel, develop the notion that the Youth, though emotionally involved in all of these events, isn't seriously affected by them, but just temporarily, just so. He keeps repeating that after every event which leaves him with another failure, or deeply entangled. Even *in his preface* he says: "Let me note that I came to Petersburg a year ago (this is the time at which I begin my notes) while already in possession of *my own idea;* and that, even if I did take part in the life into which I had been [suddenly] thrown ~~and altogether~~ after having emerged from my shell, in which I had been living practically since my childhood, and if I was an active participant in all of the events which I am describing in these notes, I was never serious about it and was doing it 'just so.' I was considering myself a temporary newcomer who due to certain circumstances could not immediately sever his connections entirely, or escape [from them] altogether. The idea was in my mind, and I was awaiting the time when I could turn everything over to someone else, and leave. This impression, which continually accompanied every step of mine during all of last year, was in all probability the cause of many of my imprudent actions; it was certainly the cause of the nasty things, and most likely of the stupidities which I committed in the course of that one year. However, even though I am willing to admit that this was indeed so, I do not feel obliged to either answer or repent it before anyone save myself."

Then, after part one, he is His devoted slave (the feeling on that torn sheet).

He challenges the young Prince to a duel, but, having learned about His challenge and the Prince's refusal to meet it, forgives the young Prince (he and the young Prince have become friends by accident).

Then, "that passive creature": the Youth flushes, but He says to him: "If you don't want me to, I shan't marry her." As a result of which the Youth actually encourages Him.

Then, throughout the novel, the passionate excitement of love. He follows His every step, His meeting with her, etc., demands an explanation, is infinitely sad because He, though boundlessly sincere, still seems to be lying and making fun of him.*

Profound, pure sadness and despair. This feeling is actually one of the reasons why he becomes involved in the game. Each noble, <or> apparently <noble>, step on the part of his father enraptures him, and he is singing his praises to everybody (Makar Ivanov, the introductory episode. The Youth is embarrassed by the fact that his father apparently does not understand him at all).**

Then, after a hellish night, the terrible thought that his father may not have been helping him and that he may have actually turned his back on him. [Roaming the streets that night, an encounter with

---

* Ungrammatical in the original.

** Ambiguous in the original: "him" could be either the Youth or Makar Ivanov or the episode.

a whore.] Liza. Then, a desire to take revenge and to break <with him>. Satanic despair at the realization that his father is corrupting him, that he has apparently gotten wind of the document, and is pushing him into committing a crime.

The crime. Arson, but he can't stand it and in utter despair goes to see his father. And suddenly, the latter: "Forgive, return <the letter> proudly." "You are saving me!" the Youth shouts.

[Lofty and electrifying words about socialism, about Christ, and immediately thereafter, about the fact that these are only ideals, and that one ought to despise people. "And I'm starting right with my own person."] Dénouement.

Liza's death. He and her mother are *at his side,* as he has gone out of his mind. "I am thinking about my idea ~~idea~~."

The last chapter *presents the theory* of the entire idea.

Motives of the 1st part.

The old Prince tells the Youth this about Him: "He is after little girls all the time, unfledged young girls.* There's one instance I know about him, in which..."

N.B! In order to elevate the tone of the Youth's worrying and suffering as he is following His every move with deep emotion, tortured by His very person, it is absolutely necessary to also *raise to a more tragic level* the very tone of the events and accusations weighing upon Him on the part of society. Many legends and Catholicism are being charged to Him; *but it is necessary:* to also elevate the person of the Princess. Make her proud and fantastic, too.** The legend, of which the Youth is already aware, is that He has done something base, ~~from~~ as a result of which society has renounced Him, so that he has been forced to live in seclusion. Another segment of society (Tatiana Pavlovna) is for Him.

There was the following legend: Abroad, there were living the Princess and her late husband, a washed-up General who had gambled away her fortune and was feeling guilty before his wife on account of that. He <Versilov>, too, was then living abroad, being a friend of the family and having an extraordinary influence on the General. He was trying to insinuate to the General that the Princess had become involved with the young Prince, who was there also, but

* I am translating *devochka* once with "little girl," and once with "young girl," since it could mean both and is ambiguous here.

** The whole paragraph is quite awkward in the original.

that it was not, however, a serious affair and that, much rather, they had some secret between them. But *what is most important,* He had an extraordinary influence on the General's 16-year old *daughter,* the Princess's stepdaughter. The legend has it that this stepdaughter apparently fell in love with Him. Then, the Princess, being opposed <to this match>, raised a fuss over it, trying to prevent this marriage by strongly advising both the General and her stepdaughter against it. Then, He made the stepdaughter believe (and what he said to her also reached the General's ears) that the Princess was a Messalina, that she was in love with Him, and that the Prince was merely a dummy who, little fool that he was, would take her coquetry for actual encouragement. The stepdaughter became very excited, wanted to drown herself, got jealous, charging that, on the contrary, He was in love with the Princess, and that the whole thing was merely a clash between two strong characters, *la haine dans l'amour,*[12] whereupon she fell ill and died of a brain fever.

[Now, Maria Ivanovna had told the Youth quite a different story, i.e., that the Princess actually had been in love with him and that she was taking her revenge on him for having been scorned.]

The General, unhappy and ill, who had adored the stepdaughter, couldn't bear her loss, nor his wife's infidelity (in which he did not believe)*, fled, and also died. [A motive for part one.] Whereupon He started to embroil the Princess with her father and with the Prince. This whole story became public knowledge and besides, suddenly, the Prince slapped His face (abroad). He did not challenge him to a duel. Everybody turned his back on Him. His affairs went into a decline, etc., etc.

When the Youth arrived he, too, had heard this legend; it is also explained to him by Kraft, by the old Prince, by Tatiana Pavlovna, and by [the young Prince] (all in part one).

And suddenly dies. Fifty rubles. Thereafter, later, "that passive creature," etc. All this is having a continuous effect on the Youth; *however,* the Princess, too, has a shattering impact upon his curiosity. Already when en route from Moscow he had been thinking of her, thinking of her for a long time. However, she becomes an enemy of his in the course of the novel. It is also against her that the Youth directs his ultimate scheme, thus realizing his ultimate revenge on society.

---

* Ambiguous in the original. Could also mean: "whom he did not believe."

[12] French: "Hate in love."

This is why the search for the Princess's letter to Andreev, i.e., possession of this letter, has such a shattering impact on the Youth.

Having left <the family room> at the end of part one, and gone *upstairs,* just before his father comes to his room and prior to his confession, the Youth reads the letter: "Well, well, we shall see!" He is deeply shaken by the content of the letter, for he sees that the Princess is in his hands and that he is ~~his~~ <her> master. In the meantime, he had already decided to quit everything and withdraw into his shell. He had actually been thinking of giving the letter to Him, and so to put an end to it all; but there He comes in, the confession begins, and when He has left (having told the Youth about the Princess), the Youth is overcome by mixed emotions: he has revealed his idea; he has revealed the secret of his love for Him; he has postponed his withdrawal into his shell and, "still, I didn't give Him that letter! Can it be that I'm involved with them already?" He falls asleep with mixed emotions.

[He read it at Vasin's on the next day, as he was waiting, and overheard <a conversation> behind the wall.]

[D. February.] After Makar Ivanov's death, the Youth says: "... I haven't as yet organized my thoughts and, regarding many things, I am still at a loss for a set opinion. I have left many facts pending; right now I'll just put them down and remember them, and only later on I may, perhaps, learn to judge them. Yet the death of this man, my nominal father, left a very strong impression on me, which I shall in all sincerity admit."

OF FUNDAMENTAL IMPORTANCE. Versilov has returned the money—this has a terrific impact on the Youth, and he decides: "Never, under no circumstances, shall I take advantage of the document against the Princess. THAT WOULD BE BASE!" Also, Makar Ivanov's influence stops him.

This was right at the height of his gambling spree. A sadness that he was gambling, and a desire to win his money back. He didn't even go to the funeral. A momentary winning streak. Get to know Versilov through this document. But there is one temptation—to simply return it to the Princess, without telling Versilov, and thus set her mind at rest.

However, the Princess goes on to insult him, Liza. Night—a temptation to take revenge! Take an honest revenge and then withdraw into his shell. But Versilov corrupts him by pointing out to him that these people aren't deserving of any such good deeds ("Why then, are you *doing* them?"), and then Lambert turns up.

VERSILOV TO THE YOUTH: "I am the same as you, I am the image of you." (Except for his generosity, for it is only pride and a senseless desire to be first.)

THE PRINCE, ABOUT TO MARRY THE VERSILOV WOMAN, intends to make an allotment for his daughter. And this then, would be the fateful moment at which the document would have to be presented.

November 2.

The Youth is hiding the old Prince at his flat, after he has fled there, crazed with fear: "*Mon cher, she* wants to have me declared insane; she wants to have me certified." This develops into a scandal, *new* relations with the Princess for the Youth, and A CHANGE IN THE PLOT OF THE NOVEL.

Motives of part one.

The father's official record.

During the confession, and if possible even earlier, Versilov is surprised that the Youth is so excited about the Princess and speaks of her with such hyperbolic ardor.

Again, this problem—how to account for the possession of the Princess's letter in part one?

Couldn't it be accounted for in the following way: The letter isn't even mentioned in part one, and Kraft hands over only a document pertaining to the lawsuit and some other worthless papers. However, he does mention that such a letter of hers exists, that she is looking for it and actually went to Moscow on account of it.

"So she did go to Moscow?" the Youth asks eagerly, etc.

Then, in his confession, he tells his father about the letter. After the confession, the Youth says these final words: "I had that letter, sewn into my jacket. I got it from N. S."

To his sister Liza, on the first night: "You were mentioned three times today: by the old Prince, by the Princess, and by Vasin." ~~and the Prince~~

The Youth to Kraft, before leaving: on humaneness, wittily.

"I would only like to love one person, no matter whom, and enough." "Why, you do love!" ~~Him~~ I didn't follow it up. Kraft didn't finish his phrase, politeness. With Kraft, on nobility. A booklet of <?>.*

When he learns from the old Prince that *He* has returned the

---

* *St. Knizhku.* The abbreviation "St." could stand for a number of different things.

money and *c'est si noble* <. . .>[13] He starts the chapter *without saying* that he was depressed: "I had decided to break <with my father> anyway. I entered the flat," etc.

After the confession, when the Youth tells Him about the scene behind the door at Tatiana Pavlovna's (about the letter), He says, having listened with rapt attention: "My friend, you are charging me with frivolity, cynicism, and frankness. Do you want me to show you how absolutely frank I am with you: tell me, why are you taking such an interest in the Princess?" (too much, that is).

Bring out the fact that the Youth is an enemy of socialism. He was aware of their ideas; "and though I said those things at Dergachev's merely in order to shine with my wit, I did know it from hearsay, as well as from my discussions with Nikolai Semenovich."

The character of the Princess ought to be set forth more simply, <in a> better <light> (a woman after the straightforward Russian fashion, that's why she could never get together with Versilov). It is necessary that the Youth get to know her from this brighter and more just point of view, and fall to thinking about it. He also must have several clashes with her, in the course of the novel, one of these being a major one. Prince S. also imagines that she is in love with him, and he actually chats about it with the Youth (but even this is not true). *He* once sends the Youth to her on an errand, yet all of the clashes between the Youth and the Princess are in his disfavor, and merely upset him and irritate him, as he gets to thinking that she is looking down on him with disdain. *La haine dans l'amour*.[14] Invent some special details for these scenes in which the Youth clashes with the Princess.

Motives of part one:

During his confession the Youth asks Him if He believes in God?

[See] Vasin says to the Youth: "I have heard of Him. He is a man who may make tremendous demands on himself, yet be accountable to no one," etc. "What about Catholicism?" ~~I've got~~ "I (i.e., Vasin) have got information to the effect that he actually is a Catholic, and a devout one. Yet it is unlikely that he believes in God."

Vasin: "This is a very proud man. You know, very proud. People like to believe in God, especially people who have great contempt for mankind. It is something of a need to bow before someone, yet...

---

[13] French: "It is so noble."
[14] French: "Hate in love."

These people ~~often~~ are deceiving themselves and [in reality] they don't believe at all."

"What a clever man you are, Vasin!"

Important. The moment the Princess shows up: "So there she is! ~~I~~ about whom I've been thinking for a full year, even when still in Moscow."

The old Prince about "that passive creature": "She, [that girl], is not very... brilliantly endowed with qualities of the intellect, though she is an extraordinarily ~~nice~~ kindhearted girl."

The old Prince has the habit of saying about everybody: "Well, he is no genius." About Versilov: "A very witty man, but that wit of his, is it quite regular?" At this point the Youth immediately <inserts a remark> on the Prince's derangement.

Occasionally the Youth <tells> about himself, about his secluded life while in high school, i.e., about details of his surroundings, for of course he could not withdraw from everything at once.

He leaves the auction and decides: "Enough of this for the time being."

The Youth makes a remark concerning the old Prince's wit. Later that night, at home, Versilov observes, regarding "those little girls": "After his illness he has grown very fond of bons mots, and keeps saying that other people are fools." The Youth: "Yes, today he said that your wit is 'an irregular wit.' "

Having learned that the letter concerning the inheritance was produced by the Youth, the Princess falls to thinking: "Maybe he's got the document, too?" (Maria Ivanovna.)

Part one. In the first part, specify more exactly the nature of His exclusion from society. ~~What.~~ What were the actual reasons? What did he actually lose? His official record. (A stockholders' meeting.)

In the meantime, the Daughter is with the old Prince. The Daughter has heard that the Youth has got the document. She is making up to the Youth. But he refuses to talk. Makar Ivanov. Meanwhile the Prince is not too attracted by the Princess. The younger Prince goes on a drinking spree.

[And really, in the end everybody is convinced that He is blindly in love with the Princess. It is the Youth who convinces them of this, while He remains proudly and contemptuously silent.]

There is no young Prince.

November 2–3, at night.

Last transformation. *Fabula.*

The Lawyer had actually told the truth when he said that the

Prince had met his family in Luga. The Prince had returned to Petersburg shortly before the Princess. At the moment when he receives the money, he asks Him this question: "Weren't you the Princess's lover 1½ <years> ago?" And the other man almost answers "Yes." The Prince tells Him that he is lying. He calls him out. The challenge is, however, quickly retracted. The Prince believes <Him>. Here, this psychological angle: the Prince was almost looking for a pretext to break with the Princess, for he had again met Liza, whom he had spared in Luga, and <now> again. [It was He who issued the challenge, the Prince was very glad to reject the challenge, on account of the fact that He is Liza's father.] He finds occasion to make friends with the Youth, introduces him in society. The Youth yields to his influence, drinking bouts and honor. Meanwhile He has moved in with <his> children (after having become engaged), and the Youth has joined his family. Here, arrival of Makar Ivanovich, and his death. Yet the Prince finds occasion to see her: at the family home as well as at the Youth's. Finally, she agrees to a rendezvous with him. He had approached the subject of Liza several times in conversation with the Youth, and had gathered from the latter's words that he was ready to sell <his sister> and to further his designs. But the Youth, though he did have a notion, still didn't quite understand what was going on. At that time, he was befogged by his drinking, and by his pride, continually put on edge and continually insulted, and also by the insults of the Princess who was taking him for a pandering brother. Meanwhile the Princess insults Liza. The Youth is gambling at the time. He is suffering from the awareness that he has betrayed his idea and is making money the wrong way. He is losing, takes some money from the Prince, who actually encourages him with a sneer: "Take it, take it, that's the only way to get your money back. You'll pay it back later and, besides, have some capital on which to withdraw from society." (The Youth's favorite dream is about that bootblack who later becomes a Lord, etc.) The Prince even suggests to him that the money is really his, the Youth's, for it was he who presented the document. The Youth can clearly see where the error and the falsehood lie, yet he persists, as the game has gotten the better of him. In the meantime he is being rude with the Prince, and also with <some other?> gentlemen. He loses altogether nearly 80,000, and the Prince finally asks him to quit. He walks out into the fresh air, his head burning: to America, or kill himself. He returns, and suddenly some money has disappeared from the gaming table. He is under suspicion, he hits somebody, and is hit back. He is ejected. Night. Vasin has been arrested. Lambert. Turned down at the old Prince's. The Princess is triumphant. Yet He shows complete indifference. Previously, he used to go and see Him, when he was on his drinking spree, when Makar was there, and when he was having <trouble?> with the Princess. *Both the Prince and his father* have been gathering information concerning the Princess from him. The Prince kicks him out. A duel, but where is the money? etc. "You've been pandering your sister for me." The Youth is indignant. Meanwhile the Prince himself has left Liza and in the meantime received once again from the Youth (in some way) a firm statement to the effect that He is lying and that She was not with his father.*

In the meantime, "that passive creature" has turned <Him> down, which proves that she is *pas si bête,*[15] while He has had a rendezvous with the Princess and has proposed marriage to her. Then, he tells the old Prince that she wanted to place him in an insane asylum. He asks for a proof. He writes a letter in which he says that everything he had said was a lie, and he also writes to the Prince that what he had said about <their> affair was a lie also. "That passive creature" turns him down. He moves in with the family, quarrels with the children, especially with <his> daughter. <Then,> he proposes marriage to <Makar's> wife, chops up those icons. He had told the Youth that the Princess was forever in love with him. Boundless pride. But that very night the Youth meets Lambert. Lambert is pushing him to extort some money and flee. The Youth—put the document to work. Conflagration. Set fire. Gain possession (for it would be a terrible thing for the Princess to lose the Prince's favor at this time). He, however, suspecting that the Youth may have the document, has been telling him a 1,000 times that she'd submit to him** immediately, and actually <had repeated this> the night before. The Youth comes, all consumed with passion,*** and ~~calls Him~~ makes a confession to Him. He implores him to be generous and return the document, to remain proud without having said a word. She doesn't want to be saved; let her perish and be happy as before. And suddenly, in a frenzy. But Liza perishes.

Break down the plot into individual parts and collate it with this

---

* Unclear and not quite grammatical in the original.
** The Russian expression is vulgar.
*** Literally, "on fire."
[15] French: "Not so foolish."

plan. N.B. Think up some mysterious, yet striking action for Him, committed during the Youth's drinking spree, which is also the time when *he* is courting "that passive creature." That action must be connected with the Princess. That action must *stun the Youth* and make him think, and (2) all the time the Youth is on his drinking spree and in a frenzy, not knowing at all what he is doing, he must be watching his father passionately and excitedly, get reconciled to him, despair <of him>, live in <with> his character and his perturbations. For his father has captured his imagination once and forever. Meanwhile He is exploiting the Youth, but when the latter has lost all that money gambling, he suddenly begins to preach to him, partly with a wry smile, which always leaves a deep impression on the Youth, his theory of proud solitude, mentioning that people are mice, etc.,* and again scores a strong emotional effect on the Youth. He mentions the girl who hanged herself, saying: "There you have another case of my intervention. I wanted to save the Princess, too. Now I want to make her happy."

Liza *won't submit* to the Prince, begging him not to do it, because it would be blamed on her mother. A simple Russian girl of inexpressible loftiness. There is this particularly spectacular moment when she raises her arms and falls down before him, surrendering herself to him with a smile on her face, and when the Prince (certainly no ideal) acts like a hero, stepping away from her. The Prince is in a frenzy, thinking: "I haven't the strength to marry this perfection for the sole reason that she is a *nobody* by birth." He proposes to her. Liza says: "How could that be possible?" After Liza's death he breaks with the Princess. The Prince, when conversing with the Youth and with Vasin, likes to bring up certain independent and nihilistic ideas. Maybe Liza comes running to Vasin.

An important and decisive N.B. If the novel is to be written in *the first person,* the Youth must describe all the scenes between Liza and the Prince as if this were a third person narrative: "Liza came, Liza left," etc. "She stretched out her hands," and then add: "I knew nothing about it at the time." N.B. Later, he could have heard about it from the despairing Prince, after it is all over.

Do not explain what is going on in his mind when he chops up the icons, or <when he challenges the Prince to a> duel.

---

* As far as I can see, this is not an idiom. Therefore, a literal translation seems to be in order.

?Question: couldn't there be a third boy? One must create one.

Early in the 1st part, when the Youth hasn't gotten to be close to Him as yet, but is about to become close to Him, <there is a scene> where they are joking with each other and the Youth suddenly stops and says: "I don't want any jokes!" He was hesitating whether he shouldn't quit everything and leave, and was finding Him unworthy. His capricious behavior would amaze him time and again. But sometimes, when walking along the boulevard, he would say: "I was feeling that I could not live without Him, I was full of spite, I was acting like a woman in love." And through the whole course of the novel the Youth is tormented by His reserve, His pride, His secretiveness, and His *inhumanity,* His lack of love for people, and for him. The Youth, on one occasion, defines His feelings for himself thus: He may, in a fit of remorse, wish to love ~~and toward this~~ him and is straining all his powers toward this, but he can't, for he is an egoist and a proud man, who loves no one. At the same time *it is quite possible* that he imagines that He has already done a lot and that he has fulfilled his duty, having made some effort to conquer his own nature and force himself to be more attentive and more tender toward the Youth. What is going on between Him and the Princess is not passion, but a duel of pride. Yes, the Princess is that kind of a person herself.

Tone! [Tone!]

[tomorrow] Think over and overcome the difficulty connected with the circumstance that the Youth, being in possession of the document, must feel that he is the master of the Princess's fate. He was exploring the situation and waiting for an opportune moment to give the document to his father, or should he give it to him?* Having it in his hands, he was satisfied just to be holding her fate in his hands. AT NIGHT he would know that he could ruin her, and he would find solace in the fact that he wasn't doing it, this being a feat of his unbeknown to anyone. He spent several nights roaming the streets in this fashion, finally confessed to his father. But then, temptation, and even lust for the woman. Set fire. (Despair about Liza, taking revenge on the Prince).

A reference sheet.

The Youth. Kraft has got the documents.

"Thank you, Kraft. I like you for being a polite person."

"Oh yes?"

---

* Not quite grammatical in the original.

"If I were in your place, having this kind of Russia in my mind, I'd send everybody to the devil: beat it, carry on your intrigues, keep wrangling, or beslobbering each other as you wish, but leave me alone!"

"You've met so few polite people. I have, for a long time—"

"No, it is because I know how to be polite myself, on occasion, and this is why I like polite people. Good-bye, Kraft, may God give you to live to 90, rather than shooting yourself on account of such nonsense."

"If I had three lives, I'd be vary happy to shoot myself three times, if only you would be able to prove to me, with mathematical certainty, that my sadness is all nonsense."

"I can't prove a thing, I merely know that you can give me three lives to live, and it still won't be enough for me; I want to live so much.'"

"And so much material."

"An awful lot of material."

"Your own idea."

"That's right, my own idea."

"You know what, I don't regret that I don't know what it is, for I don't believe in it. Au revoir—may it be a happy one."

Kraft has shot himself.

"It can't be true! You know what, I must have been thinking myself that he was going to shoot himself; I've been dreaming about it all night!"

[The father of the family, suddenly: "He'll live two lives.]"

[The Lawyer: "The Prince used to know your family in Luga. This is irrelevant to our case.]

Points. Look into the documents, hide them at Vasin's. The Prince continues as before. His sister stuns him. Suddenly, the strange news that He is marrying the Stepdaughter. Makar Ivanovich, a frank talk about Liza, the younger Prince.

The old Prince: "She is a stepdaughter of my late brother's deceased wife, and I am responsible for her. She owns a fortune."

As soon as He ~~found it~~ considered <it opportune>, he moved in with his children, having gotten reconciled to them, and "that passive creature" comes visiting in order to get acquainted with his devout family.

A reference sheet.

Points. The Youth is being exploited. ~~Points.~~ He gets his salary. The auction. He goes to see Vitia, the Dolgushins, and Vasin, comes home late. *At home, a quarrel and* <the day> *ends* upstairs with the conversation about Makar. On the following day, at Kraft's. He gets the documents. Meanwhile, the news about the lawsuit. 500 rubles. But the Youth has got that document. At home, scenes again. ~~The Youth~~ His sister. The Princess arrives. The Youth goes to see a lawyer. The Prince. A meeting. A quarrel about the Princess. The Prince, condescendingly. [The Princess is at the aunt's, and something about Liza.] The Youth comes. A quarrel at home. "I don't want that job anymore." Tells Him off about everything, wants to make Him leave, "either He or I." He takes the little boy away with him, shows Him the document. At Vasin's. Death of the young girl, caused by Him. ~~The Youth shows Him the document.~~ The Youth suddenly finds out that He has returned the document. The young girl's death is explained. ~~Confession~~ Reconciliation and the Youth's confession before Him. His own idea. *He* tells him about the Princess. "They are all depraved." *He* appears before him as an ideal. "Why aren't you rich? why are you weak?" The old Prince. [*He,* to the Youth in the course of the confession: "You are everybody's equal."]

[Kraft has shot himself.]

N.B. He is in the old Prince's service since his very arrival. He had gotten the job through the influence of Tatiana Pavlovna, a person highly respected by the whole family. The old Prince is not concealing from him the circumstance that he is afraid of the Princess's arrival, on account of having hired him. The Princess arrives and calls him *le petit espion*.[16] A quarrel with the Princess. Later, at Tatiana Pavlovna's, he learns that the Princess is afraid of that letter. The Youth, having received the money, comes home (for the first time) and says that he is quitting his job, and that he is going to look for a <different> job. But when *le petit espion* <is brought up>, he makes a scene at home, too, insisting that his father leave the house. But after they have made up again he tells Him that the Princess is afraid of that document.

[He has hidden the documents at Vasin's.]

An exception <?> With the Youth about women and the fact that they are all depraved. "Yes, yes! All." And the Youth, excitedly at night, in a hell <of conflicting emotions>, recalling that it isn't she whom he is about to ruin, is true to himself since his very childhood,

---

16 French: "The little spy."

when he was suffering those beatings at Touchard's hands and withdrew into himself.*

Right from the 1st part, a passionate attitude on the part of the Youth toward this creature. The latter, on the other hand, proud man and formidable reader of the human heart that he is, satisfied with his own pride in silence and *without glory,* and <feeling> that people are all mice, has understood from the very first moment that the Youth is in love with Him, accepts this as his *due,* and is merely playing his condescending game with ~~Him~~ him. He also tells him during his confession that He has been reading his feelings for a long time, but has remained silent, just studying him. There was one trait about this proud man (and a proud man he really was), however, which terribly impressed the Youth: that He was a great master of flattery, and that he dearly loved to flatter people. When he told Him about it, He said: "One must handle them, without respecting them (like mice)." Christian love is beyond his understanding.

The time of the Youth's drinking spree coincides with the time of the Youth's disenchantment with Him (because he is about to marry "that passive creature," because he is beginning to suspect <that He is> lying to the Princess). Also Makar, etc., enter the picture. An extremely egoistic attitude on his part toward the *hellish* situation the Youth finds himself in. And all in all, the whole novel is a poem of the Youth's love for Him.

N.B. What is needed is another character who is as strong as the Princess. (There is Liza.)

Perhaps the Princess does not love the Prince, but likewise because of her pride wants to dare him not to love her. In the finale she may admit this before the Youth.

The old Prince has a dream and dies quickly.

Shouldn't Lambert be introduced in connection with the old Prince; at [Mme] Andrieux's it was He who frightened the old Prince.

About how Chernyshev,[17] a Minister of the Czar, was eternally young, how did he do it?

About how, at the wedding, a certain Notary hadn't ever heard

---

* Ungrammatical and unclear in the original.

[17] Aleksandr Ivanovich Chernyshev (1786–1857) participated in the wars of 1805, 1807, and 1812. He was war minister from 1832 to 1852.

of either Victor Hugo or Dumas, and how one of the writers called himself "a proprietor," whereupon the other man began to treat him with a good deal of respect.

In the Senate, he went down on his knees.

Motives of the 2d part of the program of November 1 (in *the first person*). *Autant de gagné*.[18]

[November 2.] He enters the old Prince's <study>. At the very first step he is insulted by both the Princess and the Prince. But suddenly the 2d Prince appears *(Le captif de Luga)*.[19] He is the terror of the family, and especially of his older brother, who is poor but trying to restore the family honor, and boundlessly proud. The 2d Prince is pointedly seeking the Youth's favor. In the beginning debauchery stings his pride. He distinguishes himself in the company of high society playboys, his success being due to the 2d Prince's efforts. (The 2d Prince is making up to the Youth because of Liza. But with that inheritance, toward which he has succeeded in obtaining some money, he has totally fallen for materialism, and that easy Petersburg life, from restaurant to restaurant.) His brother is desperate. A disgrace to the family. The Princess is also desperate (because the older brother is desperate), and they both hate the Youth. Whereupon he makes a point of carousing with even more vigor, to make both of them angry.

At this point, perhaps an *entrefilet*,[20] he couldn't go through with it and discovered that he was the Princess's master. But not quite. *He*, too, was quick to grasp the situation. N.B. *He* hardly tries to stop the Youth, for he is busy with *his own affairs:* a challenge ~~to the Prince~~ to the o<lder> Prince, and the Princess. The Princess insults Liza. The Youth still doesn't know a thing about Liza, and suddenly finds out by himself. He tells the young Prince. The latter promises to marry her. Lambert, a forged promissory note. *He* makes a present of it to the Princess. ~~Meanwhile the Prince has lost all his money gambling and credit~~ (He thinks, as a consequence of a stupid letter which the Youth has sent him, concerning the fact that he has got the document.)* The Princess is indifferent, but has a meeting with the Youth.

---

* Ungrammatical and unclear in the original.

18 French: "So much gained." (The sense is that of being grateful for what one has gained even though it is less than one may have wanted. Perhaps "Better than nothing.")

19 French: "The captive of Luga."

20 French: "Newspaper item."

He restrains himself, she makes fun of him, showing that she isn't afraid of anything, and crushes him terribly with her haughtiness. He has a desire to get some money quickly, to win some money, some money *of his own.* (About the fact that he has departed from *his* idea a long way.) At this point, arrival of Makar Ivanov, and his death. The young Prince has lost all his money gambling and, in his anger, starts insulting the Youth, "for costing him so much." The Youth would like to have some money of his own, so he could win some. The young Prince steals some diamonds. They think that the Youth has done it. The Youth gets a beating. An exchange of vituperations between him and the Princess. The Youth wants to kill himself. Vasin is arrested. ~~He~~ But somehow it comes to light that it is the young Prince who has stolen the diamonds. (N.B. In the meantime, the Youth's relationship with Liza.) At this point, also, the episode when Versilov's daughter wants to marry the old Prince. In one word, when the Youth is *in trouble,* everybody turns his back on him, including Him. Encounter with Lambert. Lambert's ideas. The Youth both rejects them, and is tempted to start a *conflagration.** Meanwhile Liza is insulted again. After a period of mutual coolness, the Youth again gets to be on closer terms with his father. The father proposes marriage; He denounces <the Princess?> to the old Prince. The Youth is surprised. Destroy the Princess, and end it all! A meeting. He. Liza's death. The young Prince and Lambert kill <. . .>. The young Prince shoots himself. The old Prince dies after his engagement <to Versilov's daughter?>. The Princess marries her fiancè. The mother dies. The Youth stands for *his own idea.* (N.B. A scene between the Princess and Him, in which he charges that she is corrupting the Youth.)

But the plot must never deviate from the main idea: the Youth's urge to start a *conflagration,* as a perversion of his idea, and his first unsuccessful step in life. He is fascinated by his father, and He, in his immeasurable pride toward people, is really convinced that they are all "mice" (including the Youth, and everybody—they are all but the pawns of his desires). And so is also convinced that the Princess has been in love with him for three years, while he is merely her brother in Christ, and this until his ultimate state of frenzy in the plot. His indifference toward Liza, and toward the Youth.

---

* Could also be: "and is tempting him to start a *conflagration.*" Ambiguous in the original.

In *autant de gagné*.[21] The Youth, on the other hand, arrives with all those documents, and is crushed by his responsibility. He wants to go to America.

Liza, too, loves the elder Prince, and not the younger.

He went to see Vitia, he also went to see Versilov. At the auction, at Dolgushin's. Again at Versilov's, the young girl and the 100 rubles. He goes home. "That passive creature." He hands over the letter and the 100 rubles in the presence of "that passive creature," knowing full well that it is a mean thing to do. The ripping of <the little boy's> mouth. The quarrel. He takes the child away. At Vasin's. That night, she hangs herself. Morning. The mother; He is present at the suicides' suicide's <flat>. The Youth rents himself a flat. He goes to pick up his belongings. The letter. The Princess, he leaves. He goes home. At home, Versilov. He is sad about his sister, and about everybody, to America, and suddenly, Versilov. A reconciliation. An agreement. Mixed emotions. He is fascinated and depressed by Versilov. The Youth tells him everything. He wants to challenge the Prince, with whom he had quarreled on the train. He goes to see the Prince, meets his sister <there>. He hands over the letter.

The story of how he can't restrain himself and falls into debauchery. Lambert, besides, about his father. (A task: compose it in a more lively way; He discovers that he is the Princess's master.)

Motives of part one.

Most important (the solution).

"My dear, your admission of your innocence has always remained a surprise to me."

The Youth: "That morning I tried to be particularly gentle to him, as I had come with the intention of definitely quitting my job. I knew that it would chagrin him. He liked to talk with me about frou-frou."

Most important. "I saw the Princess. Never in my life shall I forget that moment. I drank in the features of her face."

"I almost took that letter for a joke, since I know that people make jokes in such cases."

The Prince: "*Cher,* I feel sorry for you."

Hatred, frou-frou!

Advice <?>. The story about <the episode on> the boulevard.

---

[21] French: "So much gained." See note 18 of this section.

"*Mais, mon cher,*[22] you've got a sister."

["Imagine, my brother's stepdaughter finds him fascinating and handsome, I wonder where he may have seen her?"]

He appeared fidgety to me, as he was awaiting the Princess, his daughter, whom he feared.

I was getting some money from the old Prince since the very beginning, hence then <our> conversation about my family, about him, and about the Princess. ~~I was feeling that I should better change the subject~~

The relics. "An irregular wit." On the deranged condition of the old man.

On the day I was going to tell him that I was quitting I had planned not to stay long, but he was keeping me there. *"Cher,"* he said to me, "when the Princess comes, *j'aime le bon dieu.*"[23] Change the subject —about how Versilov <likes to be> with young girls. "My fault! I can't talk to you about that, because you don't like to talk about young girls." F<rou>.

<His?> sister and "that passive creature," the Princess has arrived and enters the room. "Good bye, my dear Prince. I'll never come back to you."

He certainly discusses the lawsuit with the old Prince. A N.B. by the Youth: "And imagine, I didn't even know that the case was in court that very day. This is how talkative he was when it came to trivia, and how secretive with regard to things he knew. Everybody would have shared his concern. No heart. And, later that night: 'You concealed the lawsuit.' "

MOTIVES OF PART ONE.

MOST IMPORTANT. During the confession, his father says terribly seriously: "My dear friend, I saw <in you>, from the very beginning, [a whole month] a creature that had come to love me to the point of a sort of passion, though I don't know for what... [And you were thinking that I was laughing at you.] You, my poor boy, dreaming of Ungern,[24] still at Touchard's or later <. . .>."

"How do you know?"

"I went to see Vasin on purpose, to talk to him after you had left, and he passed everything on to me ~~the scoundrel~~. No, he did it, be-

---

[22] French: "But, my dear."
[23] French: "I like the good lord."
[24] See note 3 of Part II.

cause he had taken a strong liking for you. Don't worry, he doesn't trust me either, and values you more highly."

The old Prince. "I am there to entertain him, rheumatism and what not... Besides, I know that many people have deserted him. What with that change in his influence in the line of service, and with his illness, many of his friends, well, it isn't exactly that they have deserted him, but their attitude toward him has changed, and he has been noticing it: they're polite with an ambiguous smile. I wouldn't have been able to stand it: I'd have smashed something, told them to go to hell, and left. But I'll note the most important thing: his fear for his sanity, hypochondria; this old man might fall seriously ill or even die; ~~He~~ incidentally, this proved to be true, but about that, later."

The old Prince about Versilov: "*Cette histoire infâme,*[25] I don't believe it. I never did believe it, but I'm being forced to believe it, I'm being pressured: believe me, believe me!"

The old Prince. He was afraid of the Princess.

This Lambert, who plays a certain role in his notes in his own words.

The document, does it ~~not~~ have any importance? It has no importance, inasmuch as no direct legal application is involved, but it has some indirect importance—which might be great, since it might influence the opinions of the court.

Motives of part one.

The first night at home, upstairs, after his first conversation with his father, about Makar Ivanovich, etc. When he is left alone:

"Why is this man so dear to me? Why am I forcing my love on him? So what if I have been seeing him in my dreams for those past 9 years? I'll leave them all, and be independent. Yet what about the letter concerning the inheritance, which Kraft gave me, what should I do with it? Let me solve this last question, and then good-bye! I am finding him repulsive! Away with everything! Just my idea, and nothing else!"

At Vasin's. The Youth is complaining about Petersburg, says that solitude is much better, <also mentions> his own idea, queer and nasty. Vasin says: "The fact that such minor events have caused you so much excitement indicates that they are too big for you, and that there must be quite a secret here. Secondly, you aren't content with

---

[25] French: "That base story."

solitude; on the contrary, you want to be right in the whirl of things, though on condition of being on top, having your revenge, and dominating. That idea of yours, which you say can be a substitute for everything else, must be very powerful indeed, [if it is to be a substitute for all these passionate impulses of yours."]

He says the same thing after having heard about the Youth's "own idea" during the latter's confession. The difference lies in the circumstance that Vasin immediately begins to discuss the matter pathetically, while He has up to this point approached it in a humorous vein. "I could understand this very well, my friend," He says, "and I could see that you needed the pathetic. How could your ideal behave in such a vaudeville-like and insolent manner, refusing to accept your love, and your friendly assistance! I could see all those things, but I wanted to wait and... to take a closer look at you."

After having eavesdropped at Tatiana Pavlovna's place, the Youth decides to sever relations and rents himself a room; a conversation behind the partition, tragic and terrible, Versilov's name. The mother begins to scream and runs out after her, on the stairs, the Youth <runs into her>. The mother says: "She is going to drown herself." But then, having looked him over attentively, she leaves and locks herself up in her room. In the meantime, the girl went to see her girl friend, at whose place she wrote a letter to Versilov and a note to her mother. The girl, with her letter, and the Youth meet on the stairway of Versilov's house. "Let's go in together."

IMPORTANT SOLUTION OF A PROBLEM. After having seen the lawyer (think up something), the Youth gladly agrees to go and see the Prince. Most important to find out from him personally what his opinion of Versilov might be, and whether or not he had slapped His face. He admits that this is true, and the Youth almost challenges him to a duel. (The Versilovs have been robbed.) It does not come off. And only then, that scene behind the door at Tatiana Pavlovna's and all that follows. Already the night before, having gotten that letter from Kraft, the Youth knew that he was going to meet the Prince on the following day (having met the young Prince on the stairs of the old Prince's house recently one morning, he said to himself: he didn't know we were going to meet the next day). [Motives for part one.] But, having met and challenged him, he becomes even more confused about what he is to do: ~~turn over~~ should he present the letter, or shouldn't he? Present it. And if Versilov is going to hand it over, it will look like his revenge on the Prince, etc.

Versilov denied that the Prince was deranged, and so was I—except, perhaps, for his one strange idea: to remarry after having been a widower for such a long time, and incidentally, rather as a joke.

"For Ivan An——ch has already let me know what he thinks of this matter, as a preventive measure, and anticipating the general contingency of such an event, [as a preventive measure, and foreseeing a certain contingency] and if he were to learn about this letter, I'd really get it <from him>, and perhaps something worse than that could happen."

"I cannot lose my happiness. In particular, I am begging you, in this widowed state <. . .>"

The very first night Versilov asks him about the Stepdaughter ("that passive creature"), whether he hasn't seen "that passive creature"? [In the beginning, at the Prince's.]

I am now writing soberly and rather ~~partly~~ as an outsider. But how could I describe my melancholy mood of those days, so firmly entrenched in my heart, [which I remember] and most of all my excitement which, at times, would reach so confused and feverish a state that I couldn't sleep nights, from so much vexation and so many unsolved riddles, [from my own impatience at the riddles which I had posed for myself.] which then surrounded me and which I was unable to solve. I must note that on September 19 I almost decided to break with them. [That first month was really doing me in. One thing I could not stand was his pride.] "Do what you want, but do it without me! Solve your own problems, I won't be in your way." [waiting for that person]

Absolutely, after the first [introductory] words about the Prince, <tell> how I used to entertain him, even before that, frou-frou and a tirade against women, and only after this: that morning, the money, about Versilov, etc. N.B. Some cute sayings for the Prince.

It (the Prince's marriage) was a threat to his older daughter, the Princess.

"Finally, I have put down this fateful name!"

Here, a chapter.

Used to have to pawn that icon, that's why the salary <. . .>

About the sadness which I carried with me when I joined the old Prince.

I decided to entertain the old man and to forgive him many a thing. I do not think that by making this decision I betrayed my honor in any way.

Catholicism. Heard about it still in Moscow. An idea which I then laughed at, not taking it seriously at all.

At Dolgushin's: "That is, mercy. Satisfying one's own emotions. Whereas this other thing is demanded of you as a duty and a responsibility. I owe nothing and am under no obligation to anyone."

"Only, he's trying to scare you too much when he speaks of the kingdom of heaven, and he likes it."

"And believe me that I wouldn't have taken Mlle Sapozhkov with me to Italy. My attitude was of the holiest."

The Youth to the old Prince: "You know what, it sometimes appears to me that I am a conglomerate of all vanities." Develop paternal relationships. [But I don't want to ask anyone's forgiveness. No one's.]

The old Prince: "*C'est moi, qui connaît les femmes.*[26] The life of a woman is a constant search for someone she could submit to."

AN ATHEIST.

The night he won he sent for champagne.

"The idea that is bothering me most is this: Couldn't it be my fault?—When I am accusing others." (Say that in the first person, at the end of some chapter.)

The very first conversation was, of course, about women (with the old Prince).

He is religious, and used to pray, but then all of a sudden he would say something like this: "But what if nothing of this ~~spirit~~ really exists?" ["The spirit has been poured out."]

The Youth, an *entrefilet*[27] to himself: "What amazed me most, looking at him (the old Prince) at times, was that he had at one time sat in conference somewhere, and acted as a councilor, and it is said in one assignment had displayed much wisdom and done an important service."

The old Prince: "One shouldn't make women into an ideal (<they need> someone they can obey)." The Youth on Othello: "You know, the reason why he killed Desdemona was that he had lost his ideal." And suddenly the Youth looks at the Prince: "You know what, I am partly in the position of an Othello, because I am afraid I might lose an ideal."

"My friend, have you really been in love?"

He hadn't understood a thing, I was speaking of Him. However, I told him about my love. I found it pleasurable myself to let myself be

---

[26] French: "It's I who know women."
[27] French: "Newspaper item."

carried away by funny recollections. Here, ~~he~~ a description of my love, I was entertaining him. He got very interested.

In the beginning, a discussion: pawn the icon. "That she,* the Princess, is the cause of all <our> misfortunes; just listen to the old man." He is a Catholic, God, relics. An atheist. I was looking at him, <thinking that this man had been a member of> the State Council. ~~at women in~~ around young girls. First bits of information about "that passive creature," *c'est moi, qui connaît,*[28] looking for someone she might obey, can't make <them your> ideal. Othello. <About> love, I was entertaining him. Affectionate gesture, "You are my only one. She is coming, oh, she is coming today." And I didn't even know, trouble, a visit. She—I got up and left the room.

COLLATE THIS PROGRAM WITH THE MOTIVES, AND COMPLETE IT.

When <he starts> about women and nakedness, the Prince stops him. About Lambert, "*mon enfant,*[29] yours was a terrible fate! These dear little children, when they grow up," etc.

N.B. To the young Prince, [then] he went to consult the lawyer, to find out a thing or two about that slap in the face.

N.B.2. LAMBERT ABSOLUTELY. He saw Lambert in his dreams (he was frightening a child in that dream).

N.B. VASIN AND <the Youth's> SISTER. That night at Vasin's, the Youth notices that he knows his sister, and that he actually seems to have already discussed some things with her. It seems that Vasin is giving him a hint, that he is reproaching him and advising him to take more interest in his sister.

A precious item. When the Youth is ardently begging Vasin not to ask him about his idea, Vasin agrees too *easily*. This hurts the Youth (secretly).

The Prince has a tendency for fits of limpness.

To start crying. *Je sais tout, mais je ne sais rien de bon.*[30]

"Why, it is Faust who says this."

"Is that so? And yet imagine, it is I who said it."

"But you do know literature."

In the street—an idea—new people.

At Dolgushin's, the Youth meets Kraft.

[Kraft] Take our railroads, every station master <uses> filthy lan-

---

* Literally, "they," but it is apparently a polite plural.

[28] French: "It's I who know."

[29] French: "My child."

[30] French: "I know all, but I don't know anything good."

guage, Columbus's *(columbarum timilorum)*.[31] Clean out the railway carriage because, to tell the truth, Europe and the railroads have caught us without people <who are able to respond to these things>; we are incapable of being people. Some vain nonentity who is sitting in the Petersburg-bound baggage receiving office—that scoundrel can stop the train for a half hour and does so with absolute impunity. And a Justice of the Peace who doesn't know the law gets up, puts on his robe in front of the public, and goes on to "serve mass," fining a poor peasant woman 25 rubles—there you have him, your master, despot, the lord of your fate. Why are people fleeing abroad? It is physically impossible to stay. Absolutely no justice. I am not defending serfage, but before, there existed, *if a bad* <order>, *still an order;* now there is no order at all. District judges do as they please, in a drunken craze—so now there isn't any <order> at all. Things have never been worse than they are now. Yet this would mean absolutely nothing if things could only be straightened out in, say, a hundred years. But the situation is irreparable. Russians are second-rate material. I can't live without being sad."

[Kraft:]" I would like to be an average man."

He and Vasin, in passing, an exchange of words regarding Kraft, by the corpse of the girl who has hanged herself. About Kraft: He had recently made a trip all over Russia.

On the chosen nobility.

~~Tomorrow: Read the copied text and correct whatever is written of the 2d chapter, to get it ready for writing at nigh~~t.

On the boulevard, *c'était ignoble;*[32] I actually told it to start <my> punishment.

"You probably suffered a good deal later." "No, I almost didn't suffer at all. I suffer later. Incidentally, I had a different idea at the time. You know what," I said suddenly, casting a glance at him, "when you are altogether possessed by another idea, your whole life seems to be just so—and many of your actions and many events leave no impression on you. Even your own abominations, of which later."

How badly this fits logically! I had been waiting for a whole month for this door to open and for a certain person to enter the room. And this is why I began to talk about my hatred of women with great frankness and power.

---

[31] Latin: It should read *columbarum timidarum* or *columborum timidorum* (genitive plural of "timid doves").

[32] French: "It was ignoble."

Versilov about Makar: "That is, he was a house serf, but a house serf who was after a certain kind of glory."

Portefeuille: *"Merci, monsieur"* (I was well dressed).

When I had revealed my idea to Versilov: "Now I no longer have an idea of my own; now I am somehow on the same level as the rest of them. I have no fortress to which I can retire."

"Vasin, why should I be honest?" And later, after hearing <his> arguments: "But I still don't know why I should be honest."

Vasin: "There is something here that you can't express, while I am incapable of understanding you."

Versilov's daughter, whispering something to the Prince, while the latter was smiling. I knew for a fact that he was greatly concerned about providing her with a proper and brilliant match.

~~"I know that you would like to marry her off."~~ After Versilov's gesture of returning the money, and after Versilov and the young Prince had become reconciled (after the challenge), the old Prince suddenly conceives the idea to match up Versilov's elder daughter with Prince Sokolsky (so much does he ignore the liaison between the Prince and the Princess).

Vasin, about Versilov: "A proud man."

"What a clever person you are, Vasin."

"Tell me, did I do wrong in telling that I was illegitimate?" I couldn't restrain myself, I melted, I embraced him, I couldn't restrain myself, "my own corner."

"How do you know?"

"Don't think that I am a fool, I was just talking a lot of nonsense, for three years I have <. . .> I thought that they were going to defeat me, and I was afraid; I've got my own idea."

Vasin smiled: "All right, you may come, but I am warning you, I have very little time, good-bye."

"Why are you..."

"Running after me?... Go ahead, say it."

I was walking along with Kraft.

"It is true, I'm going to hang myself. I ought to be more somber. No—people, no matter who they are, I find hard to take."

... and so he chooses God, or rather, it is <his> nature that does the choosing, for his intellect sometimes has no part in it. That isn't so bad at all. These people sometimes have a tremendous amount of faith, i.e., they haven't any faith, but they want to have faith and take that desire for faith itself.

"It seems to me that I can't stay with people and it also seems to me that you were the only one who didn't make fun of me," I suddenly said to Vasin, as I left.

Make an effort to live according to the laws of nature and of justice.

Kraft, an assistant and private secretary. Through court action by Andronikov.

"They're cutting down Russia's forests," i.e., "I am stern, yet I feel sorry for them, too, and I would like to finish things off with a mutual embrace."

I believed, I was being carried away, but <feeling> a secret shame; "I ought to be more somber, while actually I'm squealing, I, who was going to crush them all." But they were remaining silent and were smiling.

... you just follow the course of the people. Don't worry, even while living in Russia you can be of some use to the common cause. You don't absolutely have to go to Germany for that.

[February.] The Prince: "In our days, a new breed of people can be seen walking around, all bearded, and all with that same thought, so that one can judge from their physiognomies: Are they or aren't they readers of 'The Pickwick Club'?"[33]

At Dolgushin's: "Sit down and don't worry; nobody is going to come in here who shouldn't be here."

Still his own idea. Precisely his own idea. "Explain your idea. Any explanation of things is useful." "Join the people."[34] "Why should I be honest?" "Why, this is my main point."

"In that case, mustn't we all be watching our handkerchiefs?"

"Oh, don't worry, I don't pick pockets."

"That's precisely the point, for it means that you, theoreticians, don't transform your ~~cause~~ idea into action, and that all you do is dream. Well Sir, we are men of action."

---

[33] Reference to Dickens's *The Posthumous Papers of the Pickwick Club.* Dostoevsky had great admiration for Dickens. In a letter to S. A. Ivanova on January 1, 1868, when he was beginning to work on *The Idiot,* he compared Pickwick to Don Quixote—he considered them both positive types—and wrote: "There arises sympathy for the ridiculed hero who does not know his own value—and consequently sympathy in the reader."

[34] A reference to the mass social movement in the spring of 1874, nurtured by the Russian populists, when more than 3,000 young intellectuals left their homes to propagate a vague doctrine of socialism and progress among the peasants. The unofficial leader of this movement was Nikolay Konstantinovich Mikhaylovsky (1842–1904), whose ideas and journal *The Fatherland Notes* created the atmosphere from which the movement arose.

Of such a well-fed cow. Vasin. Kraft's idea is <not> magnanimity, it's just perplexity. He definitely has a quarrel with Vasin.

Kraft to the Youth about Dolgushin: "No, I'd like here <. . .> for the last time."

"You won't be going there anymore?"

"No, I won't."

He to the Youth: "But if this is so, the Prince can reward you in his will."

[Very important] If I am describing this in such detail, it is actually <because it is> necessary. In the beginning it may have seemed that this wasn't so, but <those missing items> would be felt in their proper place.

This, after his first sale: "I took this step for a trial, and I am postponing ~~the rest~~ for the time being."

What kind of a "youth" am I? People don't grow any more at nineteen, or do they?

He is leaving the Prince's house, asking himself: "What, *she* has insulted me? No, she hasn't. I almost loved... I'm really glad." A triumphant impression.

Kraft: "Well, good-bye now, I'll be alone from here on. No, from now on I'm not going to see any more people."

Vitia to be his second. "The devil take you. I may agree to load your pistol for you. But I'm not going to go and talk to him. You're such a lofty one."

[February.] Where's the beginning, and where's the end of Versilov? This is not permissible. Versilov is before you, and that's enough. Any critique is unthinkable.

"I don't understand," says Kraft, "how a person who is under the influence of some overwhelming thought, to which his mind and his heart have fully surrendered, how such a person can still live for something else, for something that is beyond this thought. If you believe in God and in the Church, why wouldn't you immediately become a monk; if you live in the 10th century and you are convinced that the Holy Tomb should be freed, quit everything and take the cross."[35]

---

[35] Compare these words to those about Alyosha in *The Brothers Karamazov:* "As soon as he thought seriously about it, he was struck with the conviction that God and immortality exist, and at once he said simply to himself: 'I want to live for immortality, and I will not accept any compromise.' " Part I, Chapter 1:5.

"Do you believe that a person who believes with his whole heart must absolutely become a monk? I heard that thought only today."

"Why do you find it so strange if I, having become convinced of the correctness of my findings, decide to shoot myself?"

"To take the cross or to become a monk are positive ideas, while this thing—why, it isn't even an idea."

"True, but a [full] conviction is a feeling." [And if I've got that feeling, even if it be a feeling of despair <. . .>]

"That's it; that's exactly it! Conviction is a feeling. You know what, today, when I was at Dolgushin's, I was terribly afraid that they might shake me with their sophisms, for I, too, have [my own] conviction, a certain *idea of my own*. But I didn't know nor did I realize that a feeling cannot be shaken by reason, but that one must rather first eradicate the idea which has ensconced itself in one's heart in the form of a feeling, and replace it by a new, by a different feeling—only then might one be shaken. Anyway, what could they ever offer me in a positive way with their stupid little idea of 'joining the people'? Join them with what?"

"So what, I just bought a thing and nothing more. Yet, what this step, this thought, this experiment meant for <me>! But about this, later."

N.B. N.B. N.B. "I'll return it to Versilov. I'll return it to her."

"That is, you'll keep it and think for a long time if you should, and... *you will return it, if <. . .>*"

I blushed and said nothing.

~~"If I'm going to return it, believe me, it will be for nothing."~~

"Well, I don't care."

Kraft: "From a legal point of view, this document, (this letter) isn't worth much. But there is a chance. I haven't been involved in this case; of course, the lawyer of the other party would know what he might do with this kind of a document, whether a lot or a little, or nothing at all."

"What then, should I do?"

"As you please."

Still, it was terribly difficult to make a decision. If I gave it to Versilov, his conscience would bother him. If I gave it to the lawyer, this would mean that Versilov and my mother would be at <his> mercy. If I didn't give it to anyone, but kept it myself—I hadn't even known that this could be so hard."

IN THE LAST CHAPTER OF part one, Versilov says, in response to the Youth's question, casually and while he is already about to leave:

"I've got that letter!" After <an initial> pathetic shock, this affects the Youth as if someone had thrown cold water on him. However, after his despair, the Youth decides to *forgive* Versilov this trick <illegible>. He just makes up his mind to watch Him and to study Him from here on.

VERSILOV TO THE YOUTH: "It was quite unnecessary for you to present yourself as 'illegitimate' all around; you are perfectly 'legitimate,' and you have quite needlessly smeared your mother's honor. Or did you, perhaps, find it unpleasant to admit that you were the son of a petit bourgeois, thinking that to be the illegitimate son of a nobleman was still superior [and more beautiful] than <to be the son> of a petit bourgeois?"

(N.B. I had been aware of all this for a long time myself, and had long been bothered by it.) "Why are you thrusting such a dishonorable thought on me?"

"No, forget it, really, ~~to be~~ to be the offspring of a nobleman, even illegitimately, is more beautiful than to be a petit bourgeois. It is really a matter of taste. It depends on a man's inclinations."

"Why, I am not suffering from it in the least," Versilov tells him in reply to his remark concerning being persecuted by the Princess.

The Youth says: "I don't know how to tell ~~him~~ about my idea; it keeps coming out funny."

"I'll tell it for you," said Versilov and went on to explain to him his very own idea, <its> glitter, <its> tearful nights.

"Yes, yes!" exclaims the Youth, "I am yours."

IMPORTANT. The rupture, when he left for Vasin's, was a consequence of the fact that he was called a spy—by her, also that he was fussing over the letter for days on end, furthermore, as a result of having met the Prince, as well as of a case of <bad> conscience, and, finally, on account of the governess and her letter.* After his father's action <when He> returns the money, he becomes purified and rises in stature (N.B. also, after <meeting> Vasin), and does not want to take advantage of the Princess's letter. "This was the purest minute of my life!" he exclaims on the last line of part one.

He has just entered his mother's <room>. "Did he tell you about that thing?" Versilov: "He has got his own idea, and he is going to surprise us."

I sadly said good bye to Kraft. "What I have learned from you

---

* The sentence is awkward and barely grammatical in the original.

<. . .> I am no believer yet, but I feel that I'm going to make a break. One must start a new life. I'm not going to join Vasin." ~~Blessed he who~~

"So you are hoping to live. Blessed he who has an idea."

"If you only knew what you've just said there. Kraft, I've got my own idea."

I came home in a sad state of mind, and felt irritable.

The Youth, at the end of his first showdown with Versilov: "No, this man must not know that I have suffered so much longing for him. He is not worth my tears."

Versilov counted on stunning him with his coolness and irony. He isn't trying to justify himself (regarding the Princess, regarding the slap in the face), finding it to be below his dignity to make excuses to the Youth. The Youth is indignant, decides to leave.

The Youth ~~argues~~ quarrels with Vasin.

The Youth to Versilov: "Why am I surprised; would it be possible for you to talk other than wittily?"

After the first showdown: A thirst of something higher, dissatisfaction, "I'll break <with them>, take a flat. I'm not going to join Vasin," regarding the document—a sad smile.

A precious item. Suddenly, as he is about to go to bed: "Why is it that I love Vasin less than before? Because I humbled myself too much before him the other day. 'I'm just a punk, and nothing else.' "

The day after his first conversation with Versilov: Finish that thing with the letter. Reasoning thus: *impossible* to go and see a lawyer. To the Prince, to challenge him to a duel—no one to act as a second. Won't go. However... He goes to see Vasin for advice. Vasin in a rooming house. Next door, the governess with her letter. To Tatiana. With the Princess. She insults him terribly (tears). The document in his pocket. "I'll tear it up!" Runs into the governess at the house: away.

THE CHARM OF A DESCRIPTION. More lively and more concise.

"As pertains to generals and such, I was routing [HERE] <. . .>

HERE IS MY IDEA, THE WAY IT APPEARED TO ME THEN.

He fascinated me when I was still a child. Since then, <I'd be dreaming of Him> covering my head with my blanket. It wasn't my illegitimate birth that was torturing me. Yes, it was this man [appeared in my dreams] who was torturing me. The fact that I had been left alone tortured me. I was dreaming of building a new nest. But in all probability I was that kind of a person myself. I was myself a Versilov. My dreams: <to become a> farmer. I am shining shoes.

Then, a wealthy friend. But I wanted something immeasurably larger—pride.

First place—but mysteriously. A professor. Ungern-Shternberg.[36] Finally, Rothschild. Save—not acquire it unnaturally! Finally, the triumph of lack of talent and mediocrity. That's what I arrived with. Don't tell that. Don't tell that under any circumstances.

I entered my mother's room. Sunset. Description of the evening. [I had come in with the notion that I was going to break <with them> that day, or the next. Guilty all the same... Versilov not in.]

["What has this day given me? Vasin—I'm not going to join him." I was on my way <to Petersburg>: that document of the Princess's was with me. He entered; mother's gentle eyes. Versilov entered.]

[There they have banks, business offices, playing the stock market; I knew nothing of that. Of course, one does run into people; eventually I would have worked out something.]

I was imagining that proud creature of high society, the Akhmakov woman, and there, myself, taking the side of Versilov. I am the possessor of the document. Not just a help to Versilov: her tears, high society. Now everything appeared so childish.

I remembered how I had shuddered during our recent meeting.

[About how I clashed at Dergachev's. For me, it was important. I was timid, I feared for my idea: "They are thinking that I am a misanthrope. I know their ideas concerning private property."]

[The idea was calling me.]

Versilov's first talk.

"My friend, it seems that your birth is bothering you. I am very sorry that you love me so much, considering that I haven't been able to do anything for you."

"You are so sure that I love you."

"Didn't you say yourself that you were fascinated by me, and that ever since that time, your dreams were wandering around me?"

I remained silent, clenching my teeth. (How could he have guessed?) "Tell me, what kind of a person is my father?" (About Makar). "Tell me, what kind of a person is my father! What kind of a person is Makar Ivanovich?" Versilov's story. (Chases him out.)

"You must have suffered a lot from the Princess. I saw her today."

He: "I have noticed that you are taking an interest in many things and that you are worrying too much."

---

[36] See note 3 of Part II.

I was looking at his face. "Tell me, what kind of a person was my father? Leave me alone."

Having left Kraft <. . .> I didn't want to go to Vasin. The terrible document was in my hands. Sewn into my clothes. "Nobody can love me."

And suddenly, as I entered the house—the gentle eyes of my mother.

At my mother's, after Versilov has come: "If I dream a lot, if I'm a dreamer, who has made me one? It is he who has made me become what I am."

I, at Touchard's, but Touchard is an honest man.

N.B. And generally, make that scene at mother's shorter, straight on to Touchard, which would correspond to that mood of desperation and "break with them," in which he returned from Kraft's.

ORDER. Very important. When meeting the Princess for the second time, at Tatiana's <. . .> I was seeing her for the second time; circumstances and the events of the preceding day had erased her image in my mind. (A strong impression this second time.)

And later, he is *too insistently questioning Versilov* to find out: does He, or doesn't He love the Princess, in order to learn whether he can love her. Avenge his father.

MY OWN IDEA, the way I understood it at the time.

Let there be envy, let me be worst of all <morally>, but to make up for it, I'll be superior to everybody. The moment somebody in Moscow got to be superior to me, I immediately quit speaking to him. Just the other day with Vasin, and there I am, already I'm beginning to love him less. Good or bad—that wasn't my worry. There was nothing but a feeling there. I needed power, with arguments of "right" and "wrong." I wasn't even embarrassed; on the contrary, I saw an indescribable beauty about it, and I still feel, even today, that nobody could have defeated my arguments. I am not crude, I knew what the ideals of good and of light were. Yet my own ideal seemed best of all to me. Was it simply that of a saver and moneymaker? I saw here only the brilliance of power and a guarantee of my own will, and that I'd be better than everybody else. How I would direct my will and my personality, whether I would take my vengeance on people or become their benefactor—all this would be within my powers. Though I was afraid of books, I knew the social arguments against my idea—about private property, and about capital, and that private property was nothing but organized fraud. Yet <their> paradoxical nature was obvious to me, and altogether I hated these new teachings, had a deep contempt for them on account of their erroneous premises concerning basic and primary ideas, their faulty interpretation of the same, their theoreticalism, and the impurity of their ideal. "However, the devil take this all," I was thinking. "What matters isn't theory, but beauty; what really matters is power, power is the whole thing. The most important thing is *I*."

Still, at Dergachev's I didn't have a chance to express myself. But could their views, their laughter, ever make me join them?—never! Insofar as I would always be inferior to somebody as far as talent is concerned, I'm not even going to make a try in that direction. I'll have the money. Even better, to get even with them, let me be a nonentity. I am not regretting <to have thought so> even today.

I am putting this down not to beg anyone's forgiveness; it may well be that I haven't changed at all. Just that my idea has grown up.

If I am going to fail, I am not going to join their association so that I can lean on all of mankind. I'll simply shoot myself, and let that be the end of it. I won't even be a beggar. But it would be in vain if I tried to explain all this graphically, in words. This is the weak side of my *idea*. What could I express in words? What I've got here is a feeling.

I am convinced that I couldn't tell anyone about it: nobody would ~~understand~~ understand. I am convinced that even now, as I have written it down, no one will understand me. Words are nothing but nonsense. The real thing is left in those unsaid words, because they couldn't be expressed. Words are nothing but nonsense, the real thing is in what remained unsaid; that's the way it is, always, always!

[*My own idea,* the way I understood it then.]

I've got an assurance here, yet subject to all the chances of the card table, and still an assurance.

Live some. To spend it is something of no consequence. Not money, but pleasure. Earthly blessings, a hotel, a wife, ~~aristocracy~~ an elegant circle of friends, all this ~~isn't exactly~~ is actually base, that is, it isn't exactly base, but rather something petty, small. Some sort of exceeding narrowness of life. That is not the thing, it's better to sew it up in your clothes.

No matter how educated I might be, there will always be people in the world who are more educated.

"Vanity?" you're going to say. "Oh, my God, I am not seeking to justify myself, I'm begging no one's, but no one's forgiveness."

What if eventually I were suddenly to give everything to orphanages, to education, to schools, to almshouses, to foundling hospitals?

The case of the abandoned infant.

I could not stand those gentle eyes.

Why was I running after this man who wanted no part of me?

A gorgeous lady. I was stung by my recent impression, that document <. . .> Sewn into <my clothes>. I only smiled. Why should I go there? Why, she is going to extend her hand to me, if I return it to her first. But if I give it to Versilov, he is going to embrace me, and tie me <to himself>, but will it be for long? Everybody thinks that I am just a youth. I'll forget about all of them, and I'll forget about the document, too—having left it on my person, sewn up in my clothes.

I am not going to Vasin's. I am quitting loving him. Why should I be reproaching myself for it? For my own vanity? No, it is much better not to beg anyone's forgiveness. If there is something wrong with this, let it stay right here, with me. I'll go after my freedom, my will, into my shell, into my idea.

Here, too, I kept seeing the eyes of my mother before me. Since my childhood. I once met her. Yes, that impenetrable environment. But I was feeling sorry. Sometimes I would come and be nasty and rude. Even this time they stopped their conversation as I entered (Tatiana Pavlovna). I sat down more cheerily. I had given my word that I wasn't going to be rude. <She'd like> to stroke my head, but she won't dare. She would address me as she would her squire's son. My own kind words. Tatiana Pavlovna turned her back to me; she quickly kissed my head, as if she felt guilty. Then, Versilov came in.

My own idea, the way I understood it then.

Most important: STUBBORNNESS and moderation, but this you can't explain to anyone, ~~it's not money that matters here~~ it is a feeling.

Having attained power, all these Kokorevs,[37] etc. I'll be reselling—what exactly, I don't know, but I'll swindle them.

In trying to make a profit, people are after a maximum profit, [while you] are shooting for the minimum. I've bought some shares, bought my way into a company. The shares may go bust, or they may yield 50, 60 on a hundred. But there's a big capitalist who regrets

---

[37] Vasily Aleksandrovich Kokorev was a financial power in the middle of the nineteenth century. He started from nothing and amassed a great fortune. He is in some sense the prototype of the Youth's Rothschildian motives. In the fifties and sixties he published articles on financial subjects and it is possible that Dostoevsky was acquainted with him. There is a reference to him as a type in the final version, Part I, Chapter 5:2.

that he isn't a shareholder, and the business has just started to move. He'd give 10 percent. I paid 100 thousand, and I sell him my shares for 110. People tear into me, shouting that I could have taken so-and-so-much. "All right, gentlemen, my 10 percent is already in my pocket, while your 60 percent is still a question mark." This is how I imagined it. And if not exactly like that, then certainly something of that kind.

Order. Farmer. General. Scholar. Ungern.[38]

They'll say: So he has saved a lot. Why not live like everybody else? A hotel, a family, social connections, etc. But here you have people who are stronger than I, more clever than I, and I am a second-rate figure; no—better *untouched* power, even a beggar with his money sewn up <in his clothes>—that is somehow more chaste.

[Here] *Socialism*. Don't worry, though I haven't read any books, I used to know a thing or two, and besides, I had sometimes talked ~~to N.~~ to Nikolai Semenovich, and it is hard to be better educated than he is.

Why did Maria Ivanovna hand it over to me? It is her free will, her opinion.

And so Jove is surely pretty tired of his thunderbolts, and he hardly thunders with them, except perhaps around St. Elias's day, but if some wretched little clerk were put up there, or some newspaper correspondent, or some shyster lawyer, or some stupid peasant woman—we'd sure have [it will turn out] a lot of thunder, a lot of thunder.

I can see that this whole thing—<being> a farmer, etc.—is turning out so embarrassing in writing that... ~~a man may invent all kinds of stories and it would come out both beautiful and interesting~~ [It is easy to invent <a story> so that it will be beautiful and interesting: all you have to do is sit down and start lying; no, better write down the truth!] [Why, I can't even write, I am writing these notes with disgust, for I know that I have now entered the circle of *littérateurs,* and there, everybody writes better than I, for they're writing to show off their elegant style, and not to tell you the truth.]

Start off with "Woe from Wit" and the story of <my> defeat. If I'm going to describe what happened at Touchard's, then immediately after Touchard a curse to all writers who describe the years of child-

---

[38] See note 3 of Part II.

hood in their works. (Copperfield.) And then about how ~~to flog~~ I'd flog them, those orphans.

I bought a rose for that little girl, Arinochka, when she was lying in her coffin, and put it into her little hands.

She didn't cost me even as much as 25 rubles. I returned this money from the money I got from Versilov; he had sent me 30 rubles [at the time] for my trip from Moscow.

It was my idea to become a Rothschild. I am asking the reader to remain serious.

The Youth is stunned by Kraft's death, when he is eavesdropping at Tatiana Ivanovna's. He let "the spy" go, but when Kraft was mentioned, he came out: "Is it true that Kraft has shot himself?" She is puzzled. "I am going to return the document to you." Runs off. Later, having learned that the letter concerning the inheritance had been produced by the Youth, the Princess falls to thinking: "Could it be that he has got the document also?" (Maria Ivanovna.)

[*My own idea.*] What I needed wasn't money; what I needed was property.

I <had to be> in the forefront everywhere, first everywhere.

In the 1st chapter of the first half of part two.

Do not forget that, having arrived from Moscow and entering the house, he meets his mother rather coolly. That "I cried, and cried" of his childhood years has become effaced.

In my dreams everything goes marvellously and under great power, so long as I remain alone. But the moment I get rich, and get married, or return to my father, i.e., the moment I am back among people, I somehow become weak and confused, because there, quite naturally, I lost my superiority. I found myself in the general rut and, consequently, immediately met people who were superior to me in beauty, wit, talent, wealth, and physical strength, whereas I couldn't imagine myself being anything but first.

My own idea.

I started trying to have just a piece of bread for my meals, to wear my clothes for three years, shoes—difficult, bad as our pavements are, a brush! How happy I was in those days of privation and a hermit-like existence! Though my idea hadn't as yet started <to be transformed into action>, and wasn't going to start for a long time yet, I still wanted to try it out, I was dying to try it out.

This was my poem on independence. Why then, that Akhmakov woman, why the document, why did I want to save Versilov from his enemies—by doing all this, I was only betraying my idea.

... [Besides,] there wasn't a chance to learn the banking business [before finishing] <illegible> Besides, it isn't necessary, I'll start by <working> right in ~~the street~~ the street, ~~and~~ and one can learn how to work the streets only from experience. Having a corner to sleep in, a few kopeks for food, and 100 rubles operating capital—no, that way I couldn't fail. And as for high finance, there would be time to learn it in between.

There is nothing immoral about it, I am no crook and no ~~thief~~ thief. And besides, everything is in my own hands, etc.

I do realize that, having become a Rothschild, I have excluded myself from society, no matter how much I might be giving to hospitals and institutions.

People are not nearly so fine as to justify doing something for them. Why don't they, on their own part, approach me directly and openly? I am a grateful creature—I would become sincere myself right away, and would begin to love them; yet each time this happened to me, I immediately found that I had been mistaken. But they went on to cheat me right away, and <thus> immediately shut me up again. Only Lambert, who beat me more than anyone else, was always sincere with me ~~though for~~.

Introduction. The 19th day. Various people and I. At Kraft's. "My own idea."

Most important. When he is spending the night at Vasin's he explains a part of the essence of his idea to him (Sancho Panza).[39] Vasin responds from the socialist point of view. He counters with bitterness. Suddenly he gets up:

"Vasin, I can't stay here, I've come here by mistake, we are two different bodies (our differences are not limited to ideas)."

Vasin makes his bed for him.

"Are you really going along with these muddle-headed people?" (Dergachev).

Vasin replies by <expounding his theory of> *The Machine.* At this point, about Liza and the Prince. A hint. And suddenly, the poisoning.

[Here] On the second day thereafter, when the Youth breaks with Versilov in connection with the-girl-and-the-letter, he hands him the letter telling him that Kraft, who had shot himself the day before,

---

[39] Sancho Panza's dream that he would become the ruler of a Baltic island bears some resemblance to the Youth's fervent belief that he will become wealthy.

had given him that letter three hours before he shot himself. The thought immediately occurs to Versilov: couldn't he have also handed him that most important document, the one which concerns the Princess? *Versilov's visit to him on the following day* is later ascribed by the Youth to that very circumstance, namely that Kraft might have handed him that document.

At the tavern, Touchard simply <. . .>

To keep me separate from the Counts and Princes Touchard actually considered to be his sacred duty.

I cannot understand how a person could not be moved by a boy who was eager to kiss his hands, and I was eager to kiss his hands.

I had a feeling of surprise and cheerful forgiveness. I was not as yet familiar with shame. I would have liked to say: "Of course this is so, and we shall be playing together happily again, just as we did then."

It was Lambert who explained to me what a "son-of-a-whore" was.

Still during my period of innocence—run away.

After my mother had left he pinched my cheek.

I was dreaming all the time that one day, suddenly, somebody would come and take me away.

I don't want <to make any "David> Copperfield<" out of this>.

"I'd be flogging <them>."

But I only want to tell about my idea.

Now that I am advancing deeper into my novel, I want to tell about my idea.

The finale. Leave it. Mother's eyes, holding the door handle.

[Here] My own idea—the way I saw it at the time.

This man is, [maybe,] himself, a Moscow gossip, just in a little bit different form.

He is an unworthy person, break outright. What good is it, to that Akhmakov woman, the devil take him, <I'm withdrawing> [into my own idea.]

He: "I'm beginning to think that everything that bears the imprint of common sense in this country is designated by the general term of 'Slavophilism.' "

BECAUSE WOMAN IS A GREAT POWER.

THE YOUTH IS FASCINATED BY THE LEGEND OF "ALEXIS, MAN OF GOD," WHICH HE HAS NEVER HEARD BEFORE.

[February] "I'm not too venerable as yet," says the old Prince.

He: "One must learn how to love people. In Russia, no one has ever made a strong effort to cultivate himself. Without a conscious effort there won't be any love, if there hasn't been any in the first place. Nobody is born a ready-made person. It is only natural that you have no respect for people. It is very difficult to love them."

It is He who talks about socialism.

People must be treated without respect.

Vasin, about his group: "Yes, they are moved by a live force. They are needed to give uninterrupted proof of the fact that there is real life (force) away from the center. Let them be weak, and insignificant; yet they are needed (necessary) for the continuity of their example. They never stop and they never run dry. ~~And later~~ Don't be disturbed by their insignificance: later, when we get to the real thing, both wisdom and knowledge will make their appearance. These are only the vanguard of the crusaders, all of whom perished, too, and before they ever got as far as Asia, and it is said that they perished disgracefully, wretchedly. [The law of the demand of live force is apparently the same everywhere."]

"Look how successful the Shtundists are,[40] yet doesn't it appear to you that they stand for something that is quite contrary to the Russian national spirit?"

November 25.

The rude and insolent tone which the Youth displays in the early part of his notes must ~~be~~ change in the last few parts. "It wasn't in vain that I sat down to write this; I have seen my spirit brighten, and presently I feel things more vividly and more truthfully..." Warmth, and an admission to his father. An admission that he loves the Princess: "If I should ever manage that she might hear of me." By what means and how could this be done?

These are the concluding words of the novel. "Forgive them (such simple-heartedness). Fooled me. Forgive me that I am talking about myself all the time. I'm not going to plant a tree. Oh yes, I forgot."

We haven't got any men of action. There's no one around who can get things done.

"~~I~~ Best of all, leave everything as it is, and withdraw to your own place."*

"Where to? To America?"

---

* *Uiti k sebe* is ambiguous, meaning, literally, "to go away to oneself," but normally simply "to go home, to go to one's own place."

40 A sect that had its origin in the south of Russia in the 1870's. The Shtundists denied the dogmas of the Orthodox Church and believed in the efficacy of individual prayer.

"That would mean to go see someone else, wouldn't it? To my own place, simply to my own place!"

"Have you got such a place?"

"Oh yes."

About the document.

I replied nothing to Kraft's words. This was a complete secret.

The Youth did not believe Kraft's story.

"But if this document does exist?"

"It exists, right here in this room."

"~~But how could that be?~~ Really? Then what should I do?"

"Do as you please; I'll be glad."

"Have you seen the document?"

I submitted, for the time being.

Oh, for a tree again, and like everyone else.

As I have already mentioned— eleven years; and this was the stimulus.

I would like to present a few traits from my biography, just a few traits.

[Here, November 26] I hate the biography of <David> Copperfield, but I want to put down in writing, at long last, my idea, which could not be understood without the circumstances under which it was conceived. I wouldn't understand it myself, though everything about it is so simple. I think, when Columbus—I'm not in the least comparing myself to Columbus, really, it would be embarrassing to me if people thought so. <I was drawing> this comparison because there isn't any. I was merely talking about simple ideas. Nothing is more difficult than to understand a simple idea. The simplest one; the simpler, the more difficult.

Until he was transferred, as far as I am informed, by one of the newly appointed Ministers <. . .>

My heart, too, was breaking, to say good-bye to Versilov. But my mother's tear <. . .>

I was thinking very hard.

I was waiting constantly for somebody to come and take me away. And there, a certain event took place the meaning of which I later made clear to myself.

Eh, do they really think that I <am telling this> to stir their pity? No, much rather I shall, as I am advancing deeper into my novel, give an account of my idea.

It was night already, past seven o'clock. As I approached the house, I remembered that ~~still the other day~~ the Princess had arrived from

Moscow. I decided not to go to Vasin's. Part now. Why go and make inquiries with that Akhmakov woman, I had thought when still in Moscow. The letter is sewn into <my jacket>, but... I'll quit everything. I'm not going to Vasin's. When I touched the door handle I strongly wished that Versilov might not be in. Well, and what could I expect from Kraft, what new information could there be? Now, as I am about to embark upon my Petersburg adventure, I'd better tell you about my idea. Besides, it will be easier to tell the story.

An official record.

Touchard. Frighten the child; I have many perverted fancies.

Who was sending him money to pay for me? I didn't dare to ask any such question.

I became a lackey.

There was a bookcase full of books.

However, I am not describing my childhood here. That time, as I had left Kraft, I was carried away by my memories.

I entered a tavern. I sat down and fell to thinking. Eh. I'll tell you about my idea!

"Even without it, we're being fed well here."

Hadn't seen <her?> in 5 years. *Alone.*

"Are you angry?"—making a timid advance.

She became embarrassed and stole a glance.

"Are you really ashamed of me?"

I remained silent.

My Lord! She kissed my head.

She began crossing herself, facing the church.

"Stop it, they may see it," I said.

"Are you really ashamed of me?"

I said nothing.

I can see him as if he were here now, in the flower of his prime, handsome. *"Il faut le rosser."*[41]

And this is all. This is the only appearance of this man in the course of my entire childhood; this is how often I saw him. But then, a certain event took place.

If he'd shown up now, I'd have stood in a corner and tried not to take any notice of him until he'd stepped up to me himself. Then, then too, I'd not have started to cry and to complain, but instead, I'd have started to laugh most ingenuously, as if we had parted only the day before. To be sure, I would have been cool, or so it would have

---

[41] French: "You have to beat him."

appeared—cheerful, but cool. I'd be talking wittily, of course, but about trifles only, and I'd not be bringing up any subject myself, but would merely be answering his questions. And only later he would have gotten the idea: "Ah, for goodness' sake, what have I done!" All this I was dreaming up, dreaming up, dreaming up.

He was short of stature, an insufferable boaster and braggart.

When Touchard died of a stroke, Tatiana Pavlovna suddenly appeared out of nowhere and relocated me with Nikolai Semenovich, under whose tutelage I began to attend high school—where, in the beginning, I used to beat the smaller boys myself. There, things went differently.

"All right, so I am a lackey, ~~all right~~." That is to say, I wasn't agreeing with it at all, but was doing it out of spite only: "There you are, I can be a lackey, too." Incidentally, it is unlikely that I could really understand what I was trying to say. This was just a feeling, but it was growing all the time, growing and accumulating.

It was a fateful moment. I had to make up my mind, finally. "All right, can you make up your mind, or can't you? What is it, what is it that you feel sorry for? Or are you afraid to go out into this dark night?"

He had been slandered and disgraced; all these wretched people weren't worth the sole of his foot.

The thought that I'd be at his side, that we'd be walking along hand in hand, and, most recently, the thought that I'd be coming there to defend him.

And so this is the man for whom my heart had so long been beating.

Ate at a tavern.

It is a long way from the Petersburg side to Semenovsky Barracks. I just kept walking, lost in thought, without paying any attention to the way. I had also forgotten that I hadn't eaten. I entered a tavern and sat down by the window.

He flashed by me 10 years ago.

By the way, here is his official record.

Having finished with Touchard (would flog orphans).

I made my way to <his> study and saw <him> in front of a mirror.

I can't stand talking about <my> childhood—I'd better tell you about my idea, ~~embarking about my novel~~ as I'm embarking upon my Petersburg adventure.*

---

* *Peterburgsky roman.* Could also be "my Petersburg novel."

Eh, here I'd better tell you about my idea.

I was not bothered by the fact that I had not finished. (See.)

I liked none <of> those who were ahead of me in school, I didn't even like Vasin, and I even disliked Kraft a bit, for his having steered me to the door the other day. ~~Strange, though I did know that he~~

An idea.

A small child.

In brief, what ~~about him~~ do I care about him, the document ~~is on my person~~ is sewn into my pocket.

To be sure, I did want to find out about my father from her, that's right, just go there and find out, but there was something about that document, something that reminded me of an island in the Baltic Sea—Ungern[42]—something that filled me with an irresistible longing. I smiled sadly at this stupidity of mine. I couldn't remain a daydreaming ass forever!

No, not 20 nor 5, but rather, he wants—and why shouldn't he want —to be a man of property, and if this is indeed so he is unlikely to be capable of stubborn saving.

Not so very eager to become a beggar, if that were absolutely necessary, and certainly he would not resist the temptation to eat a piece of bread, or to give a piece of bread to someone else.

I got the idea to run away. Oh, how my heart was beating when the sun set!

Run away, but not to him.

This simple line of thought dawned upon me when I was still 17; there, perhaps, rests my whole tale.

As briefly as possible. Show your conciseness in the Touchard episode.

Directly and simply: He flashed by and fascinated <me> by his theatrical *"il faut le rosser."*[43] But aloud, a different reminiscence, ~~a long way to the tavern, sunset.~~ Unfolding the roll <of memories>, all about Touchard and my "lackeyism."*

I wasn't beaten.

I'd be beating them.

Copperfield.

I entered a tavern, sunset, ~~mother and dinners~~ and sat down to

---

* *Lakeizm,* as much of a neologism in Russian as "lackeyism" is in English.

[42] See note 3 of Part II.

[43] French: "You have to beat him."

think. I was perturbed... ~~No~~ crushed and blown to bits, like that canary, into a hundred little feathers.

I don't want to develop my thought (my idea).

Illegitimate.

Used to stand aside.

I don't like either Vasin or Kraft.

He took <over> all of my thoughts, but my dreams were somehow revengeful. Dreams about <becoming> a farmer, etc. <Then,> came my own idea.

As I embark upon my novel, in the course of which I actually did get to know this man, and perhaps myself as well, I want to tell you about my idea.

November 26.

In the latter part of part one introduce the sister, and an encounter with the young Prince.

(If necessary, even Lambert.)

In the 1st chapter of part one, the Youth gets angry at his mother for having told <him> about the money. The chapter is based entirely on this <circumstance>.

Upstairs, he does not become reconciled to him; they part enemies.

2d chapter. However, I did not deliver Kraft's letter.

At Vasin's, new and final variant.

At first, the Youth *is seeking to elicit* from him, whom he knows to be a socialist, some information concerning the weak points of <his> idea; but later, since their opinions differ so much, he would like to leave. He stays and tells him about the things he loves, as well as about his daydreams (one can "live by romances, like that timid farmer," Ungern).[44]*

But after the turmoil in connection with the girl who had hanged herself, he begs his forgiveness.

The night before, at Versilov's, he tells his mother about Touchard and everything. ("I disgraced you.") And announces that he is leaving. He comes upstairs. Conversation about <his> father.

"I don't love you. Go away. I've always been dreaming of how you would come. Of how I would run away." He: "This is terribly serious." "No, this is nonsense—but then, that story about how I became a lackey is more serious. A lackey." Then about my mother, then

---

* Ungrammatical in the original.

[44] See note 3 of Part II.

upstairs, to Versilov, in vain, illegitimacy. "Go away, I do not love you," etc.

"In the main, this is the cheapest trash that could possibly exist," he says about Dergachev's group, but only *toward the end.*

"Oh, we have here a lot of people," says Vasin, "who are quite crude and who have no convictions whatsoever, and who are merely exploiting our ardent and pure youth for financial profit—in literature for example; yet all this is useful and therefore to the good."

Occasionally, the young Prince would exclaim: "Oh, how uneducated I am!"

He is frankly convinced that the independence of Russia as a nation, and of each Russian as an individual, is quite impossible, and that this is a proved fact.

Vasin's weakness is to think of himself as a statesman and administrator; he has become a captive of glory, which he ostensibly detests.

He is the personification of a broken-down feeling of absolute humility, based upon constant intoxication with his own superiority.

Once, at sunset, Liza and the Youth, in an inspired state of mind: "Let us swear that we shall always be kind and good." Locked in an embrace. "Well, good-bye, good-bye. Did you want to say something else? All right, leave it to yourself, and Christ be with you."

A Trait. Never present him other than in words which carry a deep irony.

"You can't live without accepting any ~~responsibility~~ responsibility," says the Prince.

He. He gives his opinion on contemporary literature—that the types created by it are rather crude; Chatsky, Pechorin, Oblomov,[45] etc. Many fine nuances have passed unnoticed. There was too little understanding.

When the Youth has been accused of theft, He straightens out the matter, i.e., really brings back the news that the real thief has been apprehended, but the Youth embraces him impetuously and fervently thanks him, as if he were his savior.

A shabby little fellow had stolen the money, then had quarreled with his partner, who then turned him in on the following day.

But when the young Prince apologizes (with reserve) to the Youth

---

[45] Chatsky is one of the protagonists of Griboedov's *Woe from Wit* (1822–25); Pechorin is the hero of Lermontov's *The Hero of Our Time* (1840); and Oblomov is the hero of Goncharov's novel of the same name (1859).

for having, himself, suspected him, the Youth replies: "No, I won't forgive you," And says that, actually, he *is not* glad the thief has been found, and that he wouldn't have cared if they had kept him in suspicion.

SHOULDN'T WE LET THE YOUTH'S LANDLORD HAVE A LITTLE BOY? THE LITTLE BOY AND VERSILOV.

In his last showdown with the Youth, at the end of part one, Versilov discusses that slap in the face in connection with the subject of *mice*. "I have become ashamed of my challenge of yesterday," he said ~~us~~.

During their last showdown, the Youth to Versilov: "Would you believe that I have had to regret a thousand times that I am not vindictive?—sometimes it is so annoying to be kind." (Just as it is to keep running after somebody.)

The Youth at Tatiana Pavlovna's, eavesdropping.

"Why have you been eavesdropping?"

"I'll show you, 'eavesdropping!' "

Tatiana Pavlovna, to him: "What document? what letter?"

He, to the Princess: "You shameless woman, you!"

"You are all without shame, men and women alike!"

Vasin to the Youth about Versilov, after the latter has refused to accept the money: "Such things aren't done to show off, but rather they conform to something basic, something inward."

"No, Vasin, you are wrong."

The Youth at Vasin's about Kolosov,[46] a characterization, "if they're crooks," etc. Asked about Dergachev.

December 7.

He. He has a high ideal of beauty; the chains <worn by ascetics as an act of penance> needed in his feat are easy to come by, for <His> ideal is humility, and all humility is based on pride. In agreement with the Youth's "idea." For example, the most shameful and the most terrible memories mean *nothing* to Him, nor do they cause Him any feeling of remorse, because He has got "His own idea," i.e., an ideal. It is an impure ideal. Self-deification. People are, for Him, no more than mice. (The character of the Princess is of the essence):

---

[46] The real-life prototype of Stebelkov. He was convicted, along with others, of counterfeiting shares for the Tambovsko-Kozlovsky railway. Dostoevsky followed his trial in 1874 very closely, and many of the real-life characteristics of Kolosov are preserved in the portrait of Stebelkov.

<He> undertakes terrible feats, of a kind that frequently goes beyond the common sense of practical life. On one occasion He makes a full confession before the Youth. And all in all, He casts his spell upon the Youth who, lonely as He is, ~~and all~~ keeps breaking with Him, only to make up and become friends again (i.e., according to how much he is disenchanted or fascinated by Him). No disgraceful fall would ever stop Him: time and again He would get new comfort and new hope from the idea that, in spite of everything, people were still as good as mice, so that tomorrow He would again stand above everybody. This last fall shocks Him deeply. This woman is killing Him. If He had not gone out of his mind, He would have shot himself. [A born gossip.]

The Landlord with his theory that woman is a *carnal* creature.*

A dreamer.

The wife who is going to be fried.

And the high school student who makes three attempts to shoot himself.

And the young Prince.—All still in part one, find a place for him.

A visit by the old Prince

At Vitia's regarding a challenge to the young Prince.

Something about his sister.

Give an outline of the characters of the young Prince and of Vasin.

The young Prince is a fop, disorganized, the last of his family and a degenerate; a spendthrift and a gambler; secretly, a coward. At times sincere, at other moments he turns up his nose in the vilest fashion. "I can't behave when I lose." Shoot himself. Exalted and sincere dreams. About the essence of being a nobleman, and a nobleman's calling, also about how he is going to marry Liza. Scenes with Liza during one of which the Youth is present, allowing this to happen. In the beginning he gives the Youth some money, but when the latter loses it gambling and asks for more, he quarrels with him. When some money has disappeared from the gaming table, he shamefully *deserts* the Youth. Back home he tells him to his face that he has been *selling* his sister to him. Dreams about starting his own roulette; in a word, all kinds of contradictions simultaneously. Fragments of thoughts and emotions, a quickness of wit and of understanding, as well as a lack of character. He does, however, spare Liza. The old Prince at

---

* *Sushchestvo miasistoe,* literally, "a fleshy creature."

one time had the idea of getting him married to Anna Versilov, but things took a different turn (N.B. Anna comes to find out from Versilov if he is in love with the Akhmakov woman). The young Prince alternately brags that the Akhmakov woman is in love with him and is afraid of her. He had been expelled from his regiment and was living in Luga, under terrible conditions. Vasin knows him. The Akhmakov woman patronizes him and would like to save him, unfortunate man that he is, but she does not love him. Interested in Liza. ("Bear it!") The Prince perishes together with Lambert. (Everything more concisely.)

Vasin and the Princess are both needed. The Princess *loves* Versilov. Vasin, who has such a strong mind, is stupidly caught as the author of a proclamation.

A detailed plan.

But in the first part there can't be any particular delay.

December 12/13.

[February] New program of characters, December 13/14.

The young Prince is a somber creature, almost narrow-minded (?), always sincere, proud, short-tempered, in whom high society has awakened a sense of indignation and ambition (he and the Youth are of a kind, which is why they become friends), unbearably proud, pure in his intentions and in his ideals.

He loses <at cards> on account of his pride, quits in anger, and sends the Youth to hell (though he later receives proof of the latter's innocence). He has a terrible temper, picks fights ("an outrage"), but in his narrow-minded way is pure and firm. For example, he admits that he is uneducated, yet at the same time he is immeasurably proud of his noble birth.

[Liza alone can mollify him.]

He had fallen in love with Liza by accident, in Luga, where he was then living after having been injustly cashiered from his regiment. She is the sunshine of his life, and only in her presence does he have a feeling of light and of peace. Having met her in Petersburg by accident, he takes possession of her. Initially he had no intention of marrying her, but after those gambling losses, and seeing that he was going down the drain,* he decided to do the honorable thing. Liza awakens even more feelings in him. The General's widow is in love

* *Ogovnialsia,* literally, "turning to shit."

with him, and they are practically engaged. He turns down the General's widow. Finally, he decides that he can't be without Liza, marries her, transfers to the Army* and goes to Tashkent.

He ~~tells~~ prophesies to Liza that her husband is going to be her ruin.

A scene at her parents', her mother and Makar Ivanov, when the Prince comes to ask for their daughter's hand. [At first, Liza refuses, and ~~he~~ the Prince says farewell to her. ("Bear it!") But suddenly the Prince comes back and takes her with him.]

N.B. At first, *He,* who has cast quite a spell on the Prince, makes the latter jealous of the Youth, who, in turn, is the object of the Princess's advances, and the Youth knows why, but the Prince chases them all away. ~~The Princess, in her turn, is enamored, to the last degree, of the young Prince. She feels insulted when he abandons her.~~

~~She is compassionate (a comic trait of her character). She married the General out of compassion, out of compassion <she loves> Him, and, finally, out of compassion, the Prince.~~

N.B. When the Prince arrives in Petersburg, he has already been "moved" by an urge for regeneration; the ferment is present in him. A new attempt to restore his name—it becomes repugnant to him. The WRONG way! And he takes Liza, *not to atone for his guilt,* but because "she is my sunshine." ~~CHRIST~~

A somber and hypochondriac person, at one time he wanted to become a monk. ?(*C'est le mal qui anoblit*)?[47]

A perennial, hidden anger at the outrages and established ways of the world, as well as at his own. He starts changing this by <beginning to change> himself. "Then I shall be a true Prince."

IN OUR society there exists a thirst for regeneration, for new and righteous ways, and for resurrection, something that K——v has failed to observe. "This is enthusiasm," says He; "They even reject God religiously."

He says this to the young Prince and to the Youth, while placing himself (inside) magnificently above all this. But in a direct sense, a thirst for regeneration.

This is the idea of the novel.

"Cher," He *finally* says to the Youth, "this whole idea of yours is: 'I am retiring to the desert.' "

---

* *Armiia,* "Army," here in juxtaposition to *gvardiia,* "the Guards."

[47] French: "It is misfortune that ennobles one."

"I would like to change many things in the early portion of my manuscript," writes the Youth.

A spirit of regeneration, of searching for the right way...

[An idea.] The Princess is cheerful in a graceful way, and outwardly frivolous. She likes a good joke. She can be passionately bewitching. The Prince finds that she lacks seriousness; but she is uncommonly clever and can see right through Him.

~~The Youth~~ is passionately enthralled by her graceful image. He is in love with her, but makes himself believe that he hates her.

The Youth He The novel ends, and the reader can see that he is in love and wounded, and that he escapes into ~~daydreaming~~ his idea out of spite.

The Youth's finale.

The dream to distinguish himself somehow, so she would hear about it ~~and~~, and, angry at himself for this dream, he escapes into his "idea," about which he is having awful doubts. For the time being, however, he takes a job so that he may support his father.

It is necessary that the Princess make fun of him throughout the entire novel, most gracefully so, but it makes him angry. But later she begins to despise him. This makes him even more bitter.

"This was such a dark moment in my life," says the Princess to Tatiana Pavlovna, "I am not afraid to lose the money, but I'm afraid to lose his respect", i.e., her father's, the old Prince's.

December 14.

THE NEWEST.

An idea.

The Princess has an important suitor, so that the young Prince, whom He has made believe that he might have a chance, is making a fool of himself.

The young Prince, who has been carrying on disgracefully, definitely marries Liza.

The Princess has had a rendezvous with the Youth.

He suspects that the Youth may have the document. He is jealous of him, and also makes him jealous of the young Prince (or just so he detests him).

The Youth is disgraced, since he is suspected of theft: ~~this idea~~ The suspicion must be growing stronger (for a month or so).

The Princess and everybody else all sever all relations with him, as the Youth withdraws into his corner (his flat—details).

Meanwhile the young Prince was greatly impressed by Makar Ivanov. (He met Liza at Vasin's.)

He proposes marriage to the Princess (a scandal).

The important suitor summons Him and threatens him, telling him not to make any more slanderous statements affecting the Princess.

Vasin is arrested, and He is also arrested.

The Youth gets quite mad at Him.

Catching the Princess, together with Lambert.

Meanwhile the old Prince is practically in open rebellion. He is at the Youth's flat, being afraid that his family will put him in ward.

He is released from custody.

The arson scene.

The old Prince dies and leaves everything to her.

He <lives on> as an idiot.

The Prince takes Liza with him.

The Princess marries the important personage. She keeps seeing the Youth, etc.

And all in all, He is corrupting the Youth. When the latter is in the Princess's good graces, He suspects that the Princess, by being kind to the Youth, is actually trying to establish a liaison with him; yet He is also jealous.

Later, when the Youth has fallen into disgrace, He is actually in contact with Lambert, after having found out the whereabouts of the document.

~~See in the old book~~ The young Prince is under Versilov's spell, but his pure heart allows him *to see through* Versilov's unhealthiness and impurity. He does not believe that the Princess is engaged in debauchery with the Youth, but he despises the Youth for his *foppishness.* [(In <the latter's> reports about the Princess),] he does not like him. The Prince *would rarely forgive anything at all.* He is a hypochondriac who feels oppressed by the world. At one time he wanted to become a monk. He fell in love with Liza because she brought light into his life. The idea of marrying her seems terrible to him. He seeks the Princess's advice (with whom he has a relationship resembling my own with E. P. while her husband was still alive).[48] But he, with

---

[48] The initials stand for Elena Pavlovna Ivanova, Dostoevsky's sister-in-law (the sister of the husband of Dostoevsky's sister Vera Mikhaylovna). Dostoevsky's relations with her were friendly, and it was thought at the time her ailing husband died that Dostoevsky would marry her. She bears some characteristics of Anna Akhmakova and may be considered a life prototype of her.

comical seriousness, assumed that this was true; and suddenly the Princess tells him that she is going to marry Lanskoi. He is glad; a little hurt. He is sad that the Princess is so frivolous on the surface, but he knows that she is clever and admires her very much. He discusses Him with her quite openly, and receives some strange comments. He is completely overwhelmed by Makar Ivanov. A need for regeneration and renewal. He takes Liza and leaves with her.

In the beginning there is something like a liaison between the Youth and the Princess, that is, when he used to be with the old Prince every day. Their conversations. The Youth would threaten her with the document, *letting her know*. She would allow herself to be amused by him, just for fun. Princess Kitty's gracefulness. Later she contemptuously abandons the Youth.

[This is necessary] Her scenes with Him. She is the only person who completely understands Him.

He is a gossip. He corrupts the Youth and incites him against her.

Vasin—a desire to become a Field Marshal. At the time of his arrest the Youth is with Lambert. He learns from Lambert that He had the idea to rape the Princess, together with Lambert, and that he had praised <. . .>

The Youth, who had had the very same idea, is indignant at Him: "How did He dare to want the same thing?"

In the meantime, the Prince refuses to take Liza's innocence, though she offers herself to him. A scene of struggle.

Do not leave the Youth out of sight for a single moment. The Youth is *the hero*. Make his personality more attractive.

It is absolutely necessary that the Youth, while seeing the Princess almost daily for a whole *month*, fall deeply in love with her, and that he tell her everything, including the story of his past... Later, the Princess hurts him deeply by making fun of him.

Expressions.

The novel: *Disorganized forces*.

[February] "Resting, so-to-speak, with my own capital."

"Exceptions, if repeated time and again, eventually become the general rule."

"I want to learn all about this high society" (so he hires a dancing instructor.)

The young man on the train (an animal) takes out his money and counts it, while the Fool is looking on: "Money?" [About.] The other man answers: "Money."

This stinking soul.

"A youth grown old, a toothless youth."

"So what, I have enemies! That's why I'm talking (that's why I've started talking), so I would make some enemies."

"To shut oneself in, to snort, and to take out one's own insignificance on others (that's it, that's it, clever, very clever)."

At Vasin's.

"There is a good deal of ~~proud~~ some sort of a proud challenge in your present fit of sincerity" (about Ungern).[49]

"And you are a Field Marshal. I am sincere because I am breaking with everybody as of tomorrow."

[At Vasin's, the Youth discusses the scene at Dergachev's place: "The more so, since I was absolutely right."]

Belle idée! N.B. Versilov had come to see him solely because he thought that the Youth might have the document. His lie had been a sly maneuver—would the facial expression of the Youth change, or would his behavior?

The young Prince says: "The plain people are given to frightful depravity, they care for nothing but themselves and debauchery—bestial, terrible debauchery; they are given to it without regrets, given to it consciously. Given to it irretrievably. Ours are terrible times." (This he tells Liza.)

But to emerge from a woman's bedchamber appeared as something so monstrous to me (in Tatiana Pavlovna's bedroom, while the Princess was there) <. . .>

Liza: "Mother said: Think about the thing I wouldn't dare to beg of you."

Versilov about Vasin: "Yes... he is a decent fellow."

"Is that really all?" (I would have died if somebody had said that of me.)

"No, that's all."

Vasin: "Have you ever had command of a Russian army?"

"Been down on <my> knees in the Senate."

"Or, when like a shyster lawyer he ~~is going to~~ is going to get rude with me."

He went to see Vitia, on account of the duel.

"Why, you're too little for that."

"Of course I am."

---

49 See note 3 of Part II.

["You're growing." "No, you'll grow some yet." "You are tall and such a puffy one."

"No, I won't go, I'm afraid they'll kick me out."

"So you're afraid."

"I sure am."

"He'll tell his lackey to kick me out. What am I going to do then?"

"How dare he kick out a second?"

"Come on, I'm still a boy, how could I be his equal?"]

And here a scene took place which had so much real-life truth in it that it was positively repugnant.

"I am already nineteen, I have my rights as a citizen."

"Still you are too little."

"It's a full year since I am allowed to get married."

"Go ahead and get married, you'll still be a green kid."*

Sullen and serious, like a caged bird that has ruffled up its feathers, and to top it– a mocking expression. People who haven't the right to display a mocking expression and who don't know it are revolting.

Belinsky was a precocious man, and nothing more.

During the final showdown: "My friend, I've come to get reconciled to you. I knew that you wanted to come and see me yourself, wanted to do it all day, but I also knew that your pride overcame your generosity, and so I have come myself."

When Versilov has returned the fortune, the Youth is gravely affected by the circumstance that Versilov had, for a whole month, heartlessly displayed before him nothing but his bad, foppish traits, never thinking of deigning to show his deeper features as well. "A careless and indifferent attitude toward my opinion. Can it be true that I was such a stranger, and so unimportant, to him?" N.B. The Youth states this in his conversation with Versilov.

Finale of part one. He was doing it because, in his scheming and far-seeing mind, he was suspecting that I might possibly have that other document as well. For my part, I suspected nothing of the kind for the time being (it became clear to me later).

In the morning, after <the episode of> Versilov and the girl who hanged herself, Vasin asks, having explained the matter involving the return of the money to the Prince, as well as the Prince himself (a hussar, etc.): "Are you very close to your sister?" That same morning,

---

* *Shibzdik,* a word which I don't find in the dictionaries, but the meaning is obvious from the context.

the Youth meets Liza, talks ("a ray of sunshine") about Luga, and suddenly about Vasin: "Why did Vasin get to talking about you immediately after he'd been discussing the Prince?" (The Prince had been in Luga also.) And it is at this point that Liza says: "Let us always be wonderful people, let us always be honest, let us always remember this morning." Etc.

Finale. "People are ~~mice~~ mice..."

"Perhaps now you're going to change your opinion, but now we're together, together; you never had a friend before."

Vasin's action irked me.

Having learned that Versilov was innocent, the Youth is delighted, rents a flat and fixes up his room. (Not telling the reader that Versilov is going to visit him.)

Finale. *Versilov:* "I've come to make up with you," etc.

The Youth: "I've been waiting for you."

Versilov: "Thank you for having waited."

HIS CHARACTER (in the final version).

In order to gain possession of the document and to take advantage of the Youth, he unmercifully lures him into debauchery and moral degradation. He takes advantage of his love for the Princess; he takes advantage of his thirst for a conflagration, his vanity—which he kindles into a terrible flame—his vices, and his pride. Having sensed a superior nature in him, he would, occasionally but casually, throw him a crumb of some superior thought (socialism, Christianity). However, this deceit, this coaxing the document out of him, all this does not proceed in any Jesuitical or systematic manner, for His very intentions are undefined.

First, He does not know himself what he wants to do with the Princess, and therefore, much to the Youth's surprise, he would suddenly become very casual with him, antagonize <him with his?> cynicism, as if he had lost sight of <the> goal, and all in all, begin to pursue *his own goal* in the novel, and <then again?> cast it <off?> *convulsively* many a time.* At times he would say flattering things about the Youth's "idea" of <becoming a> Rothschild and proud solitude, then again he would suddenly speak of it with casual skepticism, and <treat> the Youth's soul with cynicism. In spite of his self-adulation, he is restless, for he is often dissatisfied with himself. He wants the feats of a superior man, he wants chains and sacrifices, but his *attitude*

* Ungrammatical and very unclear in the original.

*of considering people as being no better than mice** as well as his pride justify Him to His own conscience every time. It is impossible to love people. The idea that he may be in love with the Princess is humiliating to Him, [and eventually leads to his ruin.] His restlessness makes him a gossip. He has failed to gain a real insight into Vasin's soul, for he sees in him nothing but a narrow-minded Field-Marshal. Furthermore, he cannot exist without a circle of admirers, starting with poor Sofia. He likes to be adored even in the most petty ways and would be unhappy in a trivial way even if a Tatiana Pavlovna turned away from Him; yet it would never make him lose heart. A passion for the Princess. This is what he has to say about Vasin's stepfather: "A scoundrel, a liberal of the 1850's (Kolosov),[50] then there's Lambert, still less complicated, finally, the Youth—and there you have all the types of this generation." But his love for the hunchbacked child of the Youth's landlord and his relationship with ~~the young girl, when the young girl~~ Kolosov's wife, [or with the girl whom Kolosov wants to marry] whom the latter had sold to be the kept woman of the Aide-de-Camp's father, are strange phenomena about His character. He watches the Prince and Liza skeptically.

[Vasin is a little Field-Marshal. Lambert and Kolosov had been forging stock certificates together, and Lambert had demanded his share, whereupon Kolosov denounced Dergachev to the police.]

Makar Ivanov is an Orthodox Christian, the highest contrast to Him.

N.B. Kolosov's wife, who loves Kolosov, but has been sold to the Aide-de-Camp's father and is seeking Vasin's protection.

(Couldn't it be Andrieux?)

Sketches of December 15.

The Princess is a depraved woman-of-the-world. *He* didn't "have" her even once; rather, she chased Him away. (Wanted to save <her>.) He also wanted to save that young girl. She sent the young Prince on his way having made sure that he had been unfaithful to her. Versilov strongly supported her in taking this step. Meanwhile the Prince became infatuated with the Princess. He left for Paris, not knowing that she was pregnant. Versilov offered to marry the young girl. The Princess was against that. Meanwhile no one was aware of the fact that she was pregnant. Suddenly the young girl dies in childbed (phos-

---

* In the original, simply *myshinyi vzgliad,* "murine attitude."

50 See note 46 of this section.

phoric matches). Versilov is being accused of having made her pregnant. Versilov *says nothing,* but he has a document and the child (i.e., the girl's letter).* The Prince can't have any doubts on that score. The Prince remains in bondage as the Princess's lover. He breaks with her, wanting to be honest. Versilov attacks him vehemently. Having learned the secret of the child from Versilov, and also how the Princess has deceived him, making him believe that Versilov was the young girl's lover—the Prince is quite beside himself, and in spite of the fact that he loves Liza he insults the Princess. The Aide-de-Camp. (The Aide-de-Camp is under <her> spell, but figures on her dowry.) The Aide-de-Camp knows about that compromising letter and wants to threaten Versilov so that He will hand it over.

Or. The Princess isn't guilty of anything at all. It is Versilov who has (out of sincere conviction, though the Princess thinks that it was with an ulterior motive) *made* the young girl *believe* that the Prince has been unfaithful to her with the Princess. The Princess had actually been opposed to Versilov's marrying the young girl, hoping that the Prince would marry her. But the Prince was chased away by the young girl, nor did he know that she was pregnant. He can never forgive Versilov that. Versilov, on the other hand, being fully convinced that the Prince has been and still is the Princess's lover, unveils the story of the child before him and tries to incite him against the Aide-de-Camp. The Prince can see Versilov's spiteful jealousy and despises him for it. But as if to make up for it, he fully succeeds in making the Youth believe every detail of this story, including that the Prince has always been her lover, and that he, Versilov, has always found her repulsive, for didn't He sever his friendship with her when he noticed that she was beginning to run after him? Then, the letter and the Aide-de-Camp just as before. He motivates <his actions with regard to> the young girl by his desire to save her.

However, after this story with Lidiia, the Prince's conscience kept bothering him, and even though he was courting ~~the daughter~~ the wife of Kolosov (~~having been~~ he was in Luga), etc., he finally took up the search for the child. Troubles in the service. Finally, having received the inheritance, he made an attempt to stifle his conscience by debauchery. It is at this point that Versilov shocks him (showing him the letter and the child) and turns him into the Princess's enemy.

* *Dokument i rebenok,* "a document and the child," may be a hendiadys meaning "a document proving who the father of the child is."

? In the end, the Prince begins to realize that Versilov is jealous of him, thinking that he has had a liaison with the Princess. But Liza. He quits everything and leaves for Tashkent. He had completely submitted to Versilov's will.

[Think it over here] Kolosov knows about the child ~~and is convinced that it is Versilov's~~ that it is the Prince's, and that Versilov might get a large sum of money if he wanted. [But that he had a different scheme, that is, <to marry?> the Princess. That even if he got nowhere with the Princess himself, He could at least spoil things between her and the Prince, by letting <her> know about the child.]

But absolutely the time in the first scene.*

?Kolosov is one of the Princess's temporary advisors, during her stay in Germany, in the matter concerning putting <her> old man in ward. It was also he who delivered the letter to Andronikov.

Versilov had already proposed marriage to the Youth's mother when he suddenly, and on the eve of the wedding, asked for the Princess's hand.

N.B. The Prince would like to break with Versilov, but he won't dare, because he loves Liza, although to make up for it he kicks out the Youth.

The Youth, having been kicked out, gets together with Lambert to set a fire. After the fire, the Youth gets in touch with the Princess. She explains the truth to him, as does the Prince. It turns out that Versilov is out to save <her>. But it is quite clear to the Youth that he is in love. Then, on the eve of his wedding with his wife,** he proposes marriage to her, fully convinced that she is in love with Him. N.B. N.B. (Here, the dénouement requires something stronger than a fire.) (The old Prince goes out of his mind.)

Or thus:

The fire comes in the end. ~~But~~ And it is only the Youth who, in the course of the entire novel, has full faith in him and who has the <same> attitude regarding the depravity of this whole society, the Princess, the Prince, etc. Versilov *does not reject* him after he has disgraced himself but, on the contrary, takes him under his wing. *He* teaches him selflessness, contempt for people, and how to save others. The youth has the idea to disgrace the Princess. (They take the old Prince over to their place.) [?] The Youth becomes involved in all of

---

* Incomplete and unclear in the original.

** Really Makar Ivanovich's widow.

his schemes. It is the Youth, and not He, who lets the Prince know that they want to put him in a lunatic asylum. Versilov also entrusts the child to the Youth, after it had been with the blind woman, Tatiana Pavlovna, who keeps repeating: "What a saintly man he is, Andrei Petrovich." The Youth finally decides that he is a saint. <Somebody> insults Versilov. The Aide-de-Camp. He is arrested for three days. All of which incites the Youth to take final action. WHAT IS MOST IMPORTANT, he is incensed by the fact that he had been feeling guilty of a crime against his father, having been at one time in love with the Princess, as a result of which she becomes doubly odious to him. Finally, Versilov comes back to marry <the Youth's> mother but at the decisive moment he chops up those icons and disappears. Then, he makes his last proposal to the Princess. THIS gives the Youth the idea that perhaps He loves the Princess. The Youth then decides to let Him have the document, and it is then that the catastrophe of the conflagration takes place.

"Forgive her!"

After the fire the Princess explains everything to the Youth.

He gets the Aide-de-Camp confused by letting him know about the Princess's liaison with the young Prince, and also that while she is running after him He, Versilov, has rejected her. The proposal to the Princess is made in scandalous fashion, which is why the Aide-de-Camp intercedes. <Her> father. He tells her father that she wants to put him in an insane asylum. The old Prince flees. The Aide-de-Camp, embarrassed by the scandal and by public opinion, demands an explanation from Him. Versilov says, in his explanation, that she has always been in love with Him, and that, by proposing to her, he merely wanted to rescue her from herself. (He also points out her immoral liaison with the young Prince.) Everything turns out to have been a lot of nonsense. The Aide-de-Camp could be reconciled to the Princess, except for the document. At the crucial moment, when the old Prince is in <their> hands and the document could accomplish everything (N.B. The Aide-de-Camp and the Princess return the old Prince from the Youth and Lambert's to his own home, thanks to Tatiana Pavlovna). It isn't the money the Aide-de-Camp needs; yet he understands, in particular, the fact that it might be dangerous to show the Prince the document in his present condition. It is at this juncture that the Youth shows Him the document. "Forgive her."

An idea: The Youth is constantly under His influence and is fanatically devoted to Him. Versilov, in the full meaning of that word, controls his ideal and gives it any direction he may choose; <at times> he would show him the edge of a new horizon.

Memento: The ideal. Field-Marshal General. Scandal-mongering at the flat of the Youth's landlord.

A romance—invent a romance between the Youth and the Princess, and how He saves her, everything invisibly and inaudibly.

December 24.

Vasin's ~~father~~ stepfather, someone like Kolosov, has launched some forged stock certificates (Lambert), a liberal of the 1850's, conceited and very sure of himself. A blockhead, respected by Vasin, even though the latter has been working as a clerk at his savings and loan association. A businessman, uncomplicated; to protect himself, he reports Lambert and his other associates to the police, for the forgery, as well as Dergachev <for political conspiracy>. He wants to marry the Aide-de-Camp's mistress for some money. With a capital of 50,000. He was once mixed up in some affair, had "suffered" (a month in prison), and drawn all possible advantages from it. On account of this, he has access to good society. He is making up to the Youth in order to use him for his own ends, etc.

December 25.

Kolosov, the editorial office. Vasin's stepfather, something like Zhemchuzhnikov, has the reputation of a capitalist, knows the old Prince through his business. At one time he toys with the idea of paying court to Anna Andreevna (meanwhile he is just an ephemeral fraud, and forges stock-certificates). However, Anna Andreevna sees through him and sends him on his way (he was expecting a dowry from the old Prince and was giving advice to Anna Andreevna) and, herself, makes the Prince marry <her?>.

But the old Prince, having heard of the document and about the threat of being taken to an insane asylum, flees to the Youth. At this point, Kolosov and Lambert demand that Anna Andreevna give them 50,000, for which they promise to arrange her wedding. Meanwhile, Kolosov is suddenly arrested (he had himself informed the police), and so forth (Vasin warns the Princess). (The young Prince *severs* all ties.)

Plot, January 13.

Lidiia is a madwoman. The Prince has made her pregnant, then regrets it, and, in very mean fashion, rejoices when Lidiia herself chases him away. Meanwhile he has started to run after the Akhmakov woman and, since she is off to Paris, he's off to Paris also. N.B. He is passionate, disorganized; yet, by that time, he has already experienced fits of an urge to become honest. In Paris, the Princess flirted some with him, but there was no liaison. Meanwhile, his conscience is starting to bother him. He makes a clean breast of it to the Princess.

She initially demands that he marry the girl, but then, how could he marry a madwoman? The Princess quickly returns to Ems, where everybody has gathered coming from ~~Italy~~ Switzerland. She finds the young girl still in love with Versilov. The Princess is opposed to a marriage to Versilov, writes a letter to the Prince, the latter having, however, suddenly become infatuated with Kolosov's wife. No answer. Finally, a date is set for the wedding, but Lidiia suddenly bears her baby two months prematurely and suddenly dies. The wedding with Versilov didn't come off because everything turned out differently than expected. The Prince returned; Versilov called him "a heel." The Prince challenged him. Versilov didn't want to fight a duel. The Prince slapped his face in public (disorder). Thereafter, the Prince was in Luga, with a female relative of his, at first, looking for <his> daughter, found Liza. Having returned his inheritance to him, Versilov challenged him to a duel, but then withdrew his challenge. Versilov became firmly convinced that the young Prince had been the Princess's lover (the young Prince was not aware of the pregnancy). He found out about it from the young girl's letter, shown him by Versilov, ~~Meanwhile the Princess is convinced that it was Versilov who made crazy Lidiia pregnant~~ only toward the end of the novel.

The romantic intrigue lies in the fact that the young girl had chased the Prince because Versilov had made her believe that the Prince had a liaison with the Princess.

But when the Princess, upon her return from Paris, insists on Lidiia's marrying the Prince (she also had been writing him to Paris), Versilov tells her, while Lidiia, the old Prince, and <her?> husband are present, that she has had a liaison with the Prince all along, which is also why she is carrying on this intrigue (the letters to Paris notwithstanding) to prevent the Prince from marrying Lidiia. Thereupon Lidiia dies unexpectedly, at a time when nobody had been able to reach any decision.

THE VERY LAST VARIANT. January 13/14.

The young Prince (disorder) has made Lidiia pregnant. But she is mad. He conceals it, which is possible, since Lidiia is fantastically deranged. He had her by accident, without love. However, he does not know that she is pregnant. But he does conceal the fact that he has had her. This is also what he tells the Youth, in all sincerity, in a few pages. And suddenly, for the first time in his life, he meets the Princess; they are all in Switzerland at the time, whereas the Princess just passed by en route to Paris. He immediately falls passionately in love. The Princess was accompanied by her father. He follows the Princess and the old Prince to Paris. (N.B. Since that time, the old Prince takes a liking to him, and begins to need him.) Also there, the Princess, sensing her husband's imminent death, does some flirting with him. Finally, she falls in love. She understands that the old Prince will give her another dowry. (N.B. While still in Switzerland, she had been imprudent enough to write, together with Kolosov, that letter to Andronikov.) In her flirting with him, she drives him to a frenzy, but *does not submit to him.* In the meantime, Kolosov has returned from Russia. He <is?> a doctor, ~~Versilov~~ an obstetrician. Versilov was seeking his advice (it is also from him that he learned about the letter to Andronikov which, incidentally, was actually sent, in part, upon his own instigation). Versilov, ~~with K~~ through Kolosov, lets the Princess, who is now in Paris, know what kind of a person the young Prince is, and what he has done (all this, out of jealousy). In the meantime, in Paris, the young Prince, though he is very much in love, is also thinking of the young girl. He is thinking various somber thoughts, and is full of remorse. Suddenly, Kolosov arrives. The Princess learns everything, questions the young Prince, demands that he marry the girl, travels to Ems. From Ems, <she?> writes to Paris, for <she?> does not want Versilov to marry. The young Prince is procrastinating, he is in ill health (he has lost some money gambling, a bad incident in his regiment), fails to reply <to her letters>. She dies. The Prince shows up. Finds out from the Princess that Versilov has been carrying on an intrigue against him, with Lidiia; but he also learns from Kolosov that it was Versilov, too, who had dispatched that same Kolosov to break up his liaison with the Princess, having revealed his true nature to him. *What is most important:* though the young Prince, during his stay in Paris, had fallen to thinking a lot (gloomily, fits of honesty), he still wanted to conceal his liaison with Lidiia from the Princess, and at any cost. When he arrives in Ems, the Princess receives him most ungraciously. This is where he attacks Versilov. Versilov sees that the Prince is so passionately and so blindly in love that he actually shows no human feeling for the deceased Lidiia or his daughter. He does not deliver the letter, and keeps the child with himself. For this, he has his face slapped. Later, the more time goes by the more he starts grieving for Lidiia. Luga and Liza are having an effect on him. Then, the lawsuit and a trip abroad, back in the service. An important mission to Berlin. Having returned to Petersburg <to attend> to the lawsuit, he suddenly gets the inheritance and a challenge from Versilov. But he has already changed his opinion of Versilov, and also knows himself that the Princess is

<now going> with the Aide-de-Camp. He makes friends with the Youth, meets Liza. Versilov hands him the letter and his daughter. Everything would be fine, but suddenly he runs into the Princess again. He takes to carousing, out of vanity and jealousy, so that he might encounter [and meet] the Aide-de-Camp, to whom he has previously lost some money gambling. The Princess has completely overwhelmed him. At this point Versilov suddenly gets complete control of him, assuring him that he has never been in love with the Princess, but that, quite to the contrary, she with him; right there in Paris, the Princess had been mentioning Versilov very frequently and had tortured the Prince by making him jealous of Versilov. Versilov incites him against the Princess and the Aide-de-Camp. She treats the young Prince with contempt, insults Liza. N.B.? Perhaps still while Lidiia was alive, the Princess either told or wrote the Prince that Lidiia was, perhaps, bearing Versilov's child. And he did not know for sure: whose child? etc. (to Andronikov). As for Kolosov, he knows about the letter both because the Princess was later looking for it with him, and because Versilov was questioning him about it. N.B. *Most important.* Kolosov could know (as an obstetrician) only about Liza's pregnancy; but from whom?—This he did not know. Versilov, on the other hand, when he wrote to Paris, ~~said~~ wrote nothing but this: "Make inquiries about Kolosov, only about the facts."

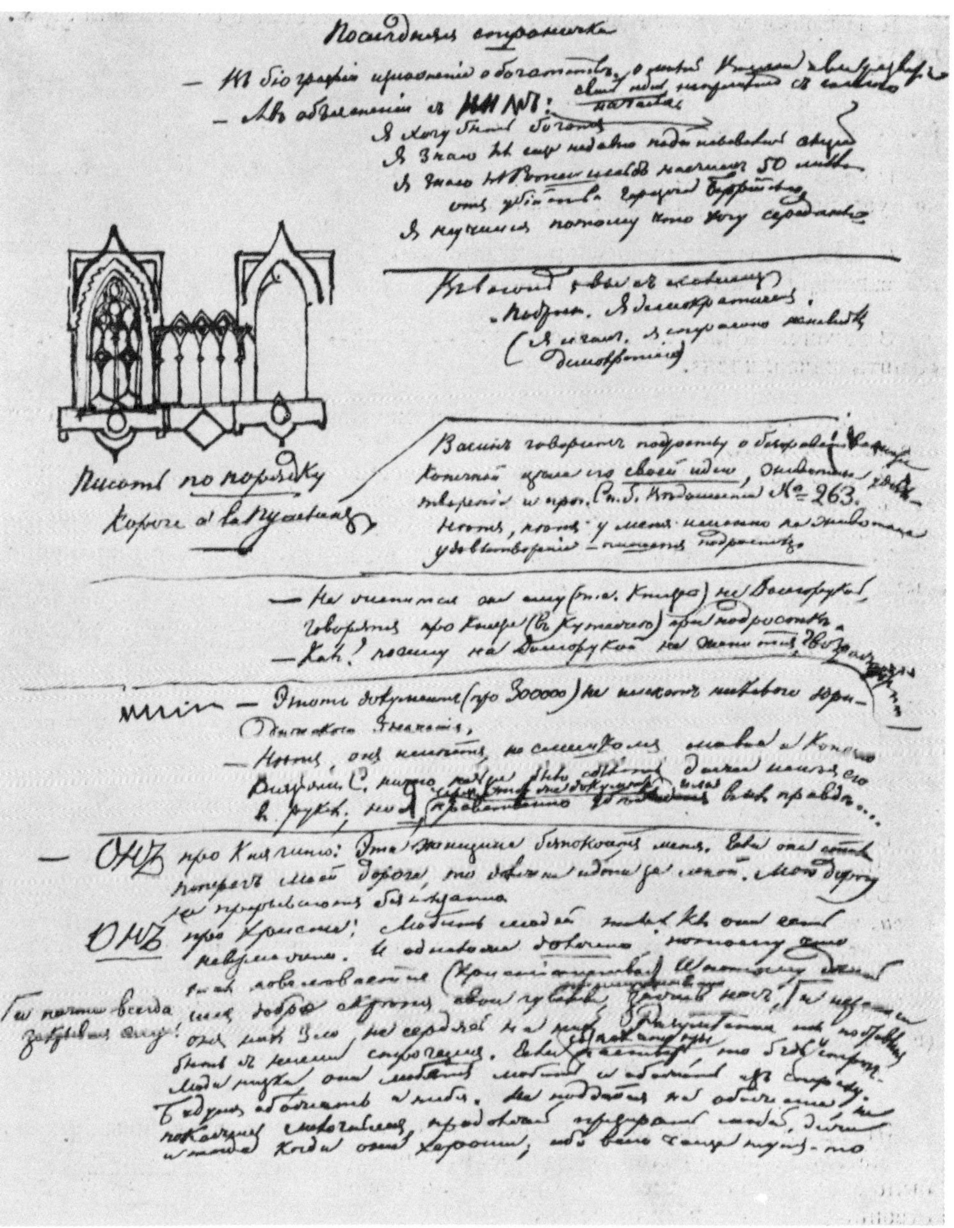

This facsimile contains typical features of Dostoevsky's notebook pages. The handwriting is neat and evenly lined; different comments are separated by lines; large letters are used for emphasis, as, for example, the large He *in the lower left-hand corner; and a typical drawing of gothic windows appears prominently in the margin.*

V

Notes to the Second Part of the Novel

The notes for the second part of the novel refer at some length to the following events and situations: Arkady's meeting with Katerina Nikolaevna (the Princess), Versilov's character and his conversations with the Youth, the ambivalence of the Youth toward Katerina Nikolaevna and toward his father, the Youth's gambling sprees, an account of Katerina Nikolaevna's and Versilov's early relations and an account of Versilov's motives toward her, and, at considerable length, Prince Sokolsky's relationships with Katerina Nikolaevna, the Youth, Liza, Anna Andreevna, and Stebelkov. Near the end of this section of notes Dostoevsky defends himself and his place in Russian literature and insists on the universal importance of his discovery of the "underground" type.

These situations correspond roughly to those in the novel itself, but there are substantial differences in treatment and emphasis. By and large we find less mystery and obscurity in the notes that we do in the novel. Some of the ambivalence and obscurity of Versilov's motives and reactions toward Katerina Nikolaevna are eliminated by an account Dostoevsky gives us of the hostility which arises in their first meetings. Dostoevsky tells us the following of their early friendship: "Two years earlier, he had fallen in love with the Akhmakov woman —and, terribly naïvely, told her about his strivings. N.B. Price: 'Since she has learned about my thoughts and I have revealed my soul to her, she should have appreciated that. But she...' She was stunned, but only laughed at his sinfulness." He leaves the Akhmakov woman—filled with shame and anger—for Lidiia, who, however, dies—perhaps from remorse—when she learns about the other woman. His hostility, as well as his attraction, seems to have been motivated by her lack of appreciation of him, so that "He is dreaming of saving her, and of punishing her, and of forgiving her, etc." Versilov burns on the hate of spurned love and on the humiliation of ridiculed confession. Like so many of Dostoevsky's characters, Versilov is motivated by spite and revenge, but the Predatory Type of the early notes has been progressively transformed into a charming type with "moral predatoriness," which has been systematically obscured and made ambiguous. This process is clear if one contrasts the account we receive here of his early relations with Katerina Nikolaevna and the account that we receive in the final version of the novel.

Versilov's character receives fuller treatment in this sections of notes than it has up to this point, and what we learn about Versilov lends light to crevices of his personality that are never illuminated in the published version. Much of the obscurity of his motives, for example, is dispelled by the following quotation:

> 1) Versilov is convinced of the loss and of the stupidity of every ideal, as well as of the curse of stagnation that has hit the whole moral world.
>
> 2) For a while he forced himself to believe in Christ.
>
> 3) But his whole faith went to pieces. There remained only a moral feeling of duty ~~as such~~ telling him to strive for self-perfection and good <deeds> *under any circumstances* (i.e., regardless of any loss of faith, or any kind of moral despair), owing to his own conscious will, a certain uncompromising desire. "Though my ideal may be lost and I may not know good from evil, still, I shall follow my conscience and, gropingly, seek to perfect myself—and I shall somewhere." Having lost his faith he decides, instead of succumbing to despair, to start straight from himself, and he believes that he will get somewhere, and that something will be revealed to him along the way (the chains).

Up to this point in the notes, Dostoevsky, and the Youth, had been unable to determine whether Versilov's faith was sincere or not. We must remind ourselves that Versilov's preaching of Christianity and his wearing of chains (apparently as acts of penance) are repeated refrains in the notes. The same ambivalence is present in the novel, and more than one critic has taken Versilov's Christianity as true coin. This passage makes it clear that Versilov is neither a hypocrite nor a believer. The situation is more subtle, for Versilov is both sincere and an unbeliever. He wants to believe but he cannot. He thinks like a believer, acts like one, but does not *feel* like one. His is a forced faith, and as such not faith at all. It is from this delicate situation that the frustration, rage, and inconsequent actions of Versilov arise.

Versilov's motives in the quotation above are "explained" in the way that they are not in the novel. In the notes Dostoevsky analyzes Versilov's character directly and permits him to analyze himself. In the novel he gives the point of view to the Youth, and with the point of view come all the ignorance, confused emotions, and willing blindness of the son toward the father. The Versilov the Youth sees and Dostoevsky conveys to us in the novel is enigmatic, contradictory, and ambivalent. Dostoevsky apparently wanted him that way, but we have, at least in part, in these notes an unenigmatic and unmysterious Versilov. Between the notes and the novel intervene all the "techniques" by which Dostoevsky accommodates himself to his audience and to the demands of the novelistic art of stirring interest and holding attention. But more than rhetorical effects engage the reader's attention and more than interest is gained by the mystery and ambiguity. To some extent the technique mirrors the actual ambiguity present in a faith that is striven for and desired but is incapable of realization because it is "forced" faith.

Despite the fact that Versilov comes to occupy the center of the stage, both in these notes and in the novel, Dostoevsky continues to assert that the Youth is the hero of the novel and that all other characters have reference to him. Dostoevsky says:

> N.B. And so, the whole *project* consists of three main and major sections (aside from the minor ones, *all* of which must be remembered).
>
> N.B. 1) regarding the relationship between the Youth and Him,
> 2) between the Youth and the Prince (Liza),
> 3) between the Youth and the Akhmakov woman.

The Youth vacillates greatly from paragraph to paragraph in his intentions concerning Katerina Nikolaevna. He loves and he hates her, and wants to save and to ruin her. His feelings toward her are not unlike those of Versilov, although more open and direct. The question of sexual rivalry, which was put forth boldly and even coarsely in the very early notes, continues to present itself to the Youth's attention and consternation. There are repeated displacements and sublimations of the Youth's sexual feelings for the Princess in the notes and in the novel, but one of the most curious, if not the most revealing, is to be found in the following statement by the Youth to the Princess: "You are now like a mother to me." The Youth is tempted repeatedly to make coarse use of the document to gain power over the Princess, and Versilov has the same temptation. There is even a structural parallel to support the analogy of father and son in their relations toward the same woman. The climactic scene of Part II may be said to be the rendezvous between Katerina Nikolaevna and the Youth, and the climactic scene of Part III may be said to be the meeting between Versilov and Katerina Nikolaevna. The disorder that Versilov embodies on a moral level is the disorder that is acted on by the Youth in his reckless gambling and his high living. Dostoevsky seems to have contemplated a similar analogy between Prince Sokolsky and Versilov. This is not surprising since the notes, and the novel, make clear that Versilov was supposed to embody in some form all the disorder of society. Dostoevsky explicitly reinforces the analogy between Versilov and the Prince in the following note: "Versilov and the Prince have some points of contact: refusal to accept the estate, Lidiia, the child; both hate the Akhmakov woman, and <their> nobility." The inner disorder of Versilov is compared to the "outer" disorder of the Prince. Versilov represents on the level of consciousness a moral disorder that the Prince represents on the level of action. It is perhaps significant that the Youth falls into disorder because he loses faith in his father and lives with the Prince when he gambles and carouses. Dostoevsky says: "N.B. Versilov's cynicism was in part the cause of <the Youth's> passion for gambling."

The tie between the young Prince and the Youth as double reflections of Versilov's inner disorder is found confirmed in the attitude of each to Liza. The Prince "dishonors" Liza in act, and in the notes the Youth "dishonors" her in attitude. In the novel the Youth does not suspect that his sister has had an affair with the young Prince, but in the notes he hypocritically blinks at the affair and in one marginal note he cynically approves of it:

> For instance, he already suspects that Liza may have something with the Prince, but in his depravity he remains silent, lets it go, closes his eyes to it—only once does he make Liza an angry, unfair scene (that happens right before her *disgrace;*) and on the very last day <before> her disgrace he catches her, and is almost a witness of a scene between the Prince and Liza. [Or, he even pretends that he has become shamefully "civilized," and suggests, by various jocular and cynically vile hints, that there might be some *very light sort of* relationship between her and the Prince.]

The object of the Youth's and Versilov's passion, the Princess (Katerina Nikolaevna) figures importantly in these notes, but little light is thrown on those qualities of her character that so violently provoke father and son. Neither here nor in the novel does Katerina Nikolaevna fit the role Dostoevsky gives her. Versilov's entire program of moral improvement without faith comes to shoal on the mysterious attraction that she exercises on him. And the Youth's idealism is wrecked in part by the emotions she generates in him. Yet the reader will search in vain, both in the notes and in the novel, for qualities that seem of sufficient importance to provoke such effects. She is mystery without substance, and some of Versilov's condemnations of her as a shallow and worthless woman seem justified. The Youth in these notes during his rendezvous with her calls her a saint, but we are not told what her saintliness consists of. At best she is a woman who had once callously suggested sending her father to an insane asylum, and who during the course of the novel is intent upon retrieving those rash words in order to safeguard her position and legacy. Her ambition seems to be to assure herself the calm and the dignity of social eminence that marriage to Baron Bioring will bring her, and the financial security that retrieving the letter will bring her. She is most decidedly not a sufficient "objective correlative" for the emotions and conflicts she arouses in the Youth and in Versilov.

Her portrait in these notes is closer to that of the final version than that of the early notes. Like Versilov she has lost something of her predatoriness, although there is a passage in the notes in which she contemplates seducing the Youth. Parenthetically, however, she explains that she does not know how to seduce a man. Versilov's early coarseness is softened to subtleties and ambiguities, but her early coarseness evaporates and only a kind of vague innocuousness remains.

Finally one must draw attention to several pages of biographical reflections by Dostoevsky on the nature of his art, near the end of this section of notes. Dostoevsky defends his portrayal of the "underground type" against his critics as the true representative of Russian society. He has in mind, in contrast, the "normal" lives of Russians as portrayed by Tolstoy and Goncharov: "Tolstoy and Goncharov thought that they were describing the life of the majority; in my opinion, what they were describing were the lives of some exceptions. Quite to the contrary, their life is the life of exceptions, while mine is the life of the general rule. Future generations will find that out, because they will be more objective, and the truth will be on my side. In this I believe." To this he adds his comprehension of what the "underground type" consists of: "I am proud to have presented, for the first time, the real image of the *Russian majority,* and to have exposed, for the first time, its misshapen and tragic aspects. The tragic lies in one's awareness of being misshapen." A few lines later in the notes he continues: "I have been the only one to bring out the tragedy of the underground, which consists of suffering, self-laceration, an awareness of a better <life> coupled with the impossibility of attaining it, and, most important of all, a strong conviction on the part of these unfortunate people that everybody else is like them and that it is, therefore, not worthwhile to improve oneself: ~~What~~ What can sustain those who do try to improve themselves? A reward, faith? Nobody is offering any reward, and in whom could one have faith? Another step from this position, and you have extreme depravity, crime (murder). A mystery."

Dostoevsky, in his self-justification, has Tolstoy in mind, and he feels aggrieved that Tolstoy's reputation is greater than his, since he has seen more fully into the depths of reality. He adds, and not without some credibility, that "Bolkonsky reforms as he sees Anatole's leg being cut off, and we've all been shedding tears over it, but a genuine underground man wouldn't have reformed."

January 20

The Prince had been seeking Lidiia's hand, but was diverted by the General's widow, and Lidiia chased him away. In the meantime, Lidiia gave birth to his child.

(N.B. The General's widow did not know, as she was enticing him, that he had a liaison going with Lidiia, but <thought> that he was merely wooing her.) On his return, the Prince finds Lidiia dead and learns that there had been a child (this, a long time after). He is stunned by all these developments, and already in the beginning of the novel, he has broken both with the Princess and with Liza. But then Versilov either brings them together again, so as to tear them apart later, or directly incites the Prince against her. Or brings them together again. As for himself, he proposes marriage to his "wife," after Makar Ivanov's death, and chops up those icons. She turns him down. At this point the Youth turns up with the document. (Liza, "Bear it!")

January 20. Second variant.

The Prince is pursuing the General's widow. He is in love with her to the point of *idea fixa.* Now, he has come to town in connection with the inheritance and has sworn that he won't let her (the General's widow) marry the Aide-de-Camp. Having received the money, he flings himself into all the social gatherings at which the Aide-de-Camp is present. Versilov makes friends with him and encourages him. Then she surrenders herself to the protection and guidance of Versilov, hoping that he might save her from the Prince. [Or else, he saves her of his own accord, without her having asked him.] Versilov takes up the matter, gets everything arranged, then, at the crucial moment, smashes everything to bits.

Liza?

Vasin's wife. She does know what to do with him, constant arguments. Vasin's smugness. Stebelkov, scurrying around near Vasin, for he ~~has gotten wind~~ has gotten wind of his marriage. (But Vasin won't tell him anything about it.) Stebelkov is compromised in connection with the <forged> shares, but he isn't at all scared, but actually expects to celebrate a triumph; Vasin, though, is hardly compromised at all. She is complaining to the Youth about Vasin, and makes fun of him. And only in the end it becomes apparent that she is Vasin's wife. Vasin goes out of his mind, and then the scene of the conflagration.

N.B. He won't live up to his duties as a husband. About a divorce.

January 24.

The Prince has gotten mixed up with Kolosov. His character is such that he is perfectly capable of making Lidiia pregnant. He was drummed out of his regiment by the other officers. Now he wants to try his hand at everything. Hatred for the General's <widow>, love for Liza. Kolosov is his ruin. Versilov puts him back on his feet again. The General's widow seeks Versilov's protection. But the ~~Princess~~ General's widow loves Vasin; the latter is *impossible*. The Youth is convinced, through the entire novel, that there is no love between Him and her. He finally learns about her love for Vasin. And, toward the very end, about His love for her (after He has unexpectedly proposed to her). Besides, he had made the proposal virtually on the eve of her wedding to the Adjutant-General. Then the Youth gives the letter to Versilov. N.B. The letter, in the meantime, is becoming more and more important as her wedding to the Adjutant-General is approaching. (If Vasin is to be made into a madman, oughtn't Versilov, in that case, have guessed long ago that this was so?)

[Here] Vasin's idea. You can live happily only if the people who were there before you are good. But people are good only when they are happy. And therefore, everybody ought to be applying all his efforts to the end that everybody be happy. Consequently, <society> should be organized as a company of shareholders. A shareholder will be a lover of mankind whether he wants it or not, for if he won't, people will treat him badly, and he will be unhappy.

Vasin: "I need nothing, not a single ruble more. What's the difference between Vasin in a suit of gold and Vasin as he is?"

"Tasty morsels do not tempt me, neither do honors. What is the pleasure received from a tasty morsel in comparison with mine? Can any honor be compared to the position which I am now deserving of?"

[February] "I am never bored. There are certain thoughts which will never allow you to get bored."

"I know of nothing in the world that I wouldn't be familiar with. [Are there any ideas with which I am not acquainted?] I do not know of any. Of course I don't mean, in any special field: I couldn't be familiar with such-and-such invention in the field of railroading, but this isn't higher knowledge, of course."

The governess has hanged herself. Vasin says: "This will go on forever."

He has words of praise for Versilov, but just a tiny bit, just barely. "Yes, but everything ought to be in one piece. And this thing is too particular, and it is quite likely that he is motivated by considerations of personal advantage."

The Youth is surprised that Vasin is so kind to him and talks to him as if he were his equal.

"This isn't so, nor is it because of this," says Vasin. "It is because I see absolutely no difference between you and everyone else. I certainly don't consider you to be more stupid than the clever ones, more wicked than the good ones, or even younger than the old ones."

"How could that be? Don't you really see any difference?"

"Oh yes, of course, everybody differs from everybody else in something, but those differences do not exist for me. In my eyes everything becomes level with everything else."

"But what about yourself?"

"So far I have not entirely determined ~~my own~~ my position in this changing world.* I don't know. I am always satisfied with myself."

"And you are never bored?"

"No, because there is a lot left to desire. There are many things to be achieved yet."

"People like Christ, Mahomet, Moses..."

Expressions.

Surnames: Miss Comforting, a young girl;** Mrs. Perchatkin,*** a widow; Assafetidov,**** a divinity student.

The chatterbox: About how the English were going to give Zavialov five million for his firm.

About Chernyshev,[1] the Minister, and about Victor Hugo and Dumas on the marriage contract.

"She isn't what you'd call 'well scrubbed,' she is 'well laundered.' "

"He has as many virtues as he's got shortcomings."

"Ah, you are flattering him too much."

A delicate handwriting.

---

* *V mirovorote,* literally, "in the whirl of the world."

** *Uteshaiushchaia,* participle of *uteshat',* "to comfort." The verb is used with an obscene connotation.

*** Literally, "Mrs. Glove," but apparently not suggestive of anything.

**** From *as(s)afetida,* "asafetida," an evil-smelling resin.

[1] See note 17 of Part IV.

"And he is sitting at the most important spot in the world of learning?" (i.e., in the Academy, speaking of Str<akhov>).

Nothing dies. On the contrary, everything continues to live organically; it just is reincarnated in different forms.

"Everything is falling apart in this country. What we need is for educated people again to be at the head of our society."

Rossen: "Isn't it true that educated men are even now at the head of our society?"

Versilov: "Yes, if you see it that way, perhaps..."

"It is necessary that mankind be given justice; then it will remain at peace."

"But what about freedom, equality, brotherhood...?"

"These are all no more than very fine wishes, nothing that has been realized. They lack authority."

"What about science?"

"Contemporary science hasn't even started to make any moral conclusions to make, and if you want to know the whole secret, it is none of its business either. Science knows this very well itself, and this is why so far it has played merely a negative role relatively as regards the past; it has created nothing, only destroyed. Science does not create, it destroys. What it can create and build are railroads, and nothing more."

"Isn't that a great deal?"

"The point is not that it is too little; the point is that it isn't enough. The point is that it is really not nearly enough, which I can prove to you right now. Would you be satisfied with having railroads and nothing else, or would you like to have something else, too?"

"Surely I shall want something else, absolutely."

"And this is precisely what science will never be able to give you."

"Do you really think so, do you really?"

"I'm not trying to find fault with science at all: it won't give you <"that something else"> because that isn't any of its concern—that's all there is to it."

"This is really the heart of the matter, as I see it."

A good-natured person, but not a good man, as are most shallow people.

Tatiana Pavlovna to the Youth: "I am convinced that you are thinking that he is doing all this just for your sake—I mean, decline the inheritance, and challenge the other man to a duel—all this solely to become worthy of Arkady Makarovich."

—She was beating me terribly, but I was kissing her.

They served a mass for Olia.

On February 22, after his arrival in Petersburg, the Youth says: "I cannot understand how I could then, in my mother's presence, tell about Touchard! I never even thought that I ought to be ashamed of her!"

"In a word, he has as many virtues as he has shortcomings."

"My God, how you are flattering him! How could anyone have so many virtues?"

The Youth to Versilov: "I always knew that we should never part. That time, when I was telling about Touchard, I was merely having a good time of it, even though I was feeling that I had broken with something: [absolutely.] Broken, yes, but not with you, I knew that we two would get together again. That time when I insulted you by chasing you from my room, my heart really sank <after I'd done it>. To be sure, I was terribly mad at you that time."

"Acquire then, a feeling of shame, and at least a little bit of restraint in your anger."

The Liar, a General on the railroad, they'll wait, and <in the meantime> the train would be gone. (Vasin's father, who sold his wife.)

(*Memento.* Turgenev, in his opinion of <this> murder, called <him> "a Marquis"—while, in this case, the murderer displays nothing but his dullness of imagination as well as of reasoning.)

February 25.

After Petersburg.

1) Versilov is convinced of the loss and of the stupidity of every ideal, as well as of the curse of stagnation that has hit the whole moral world.

2) For a while he forced himself to believe in Christ.

3) But his whole faith went to pieces. There remained only a moral feeling of duty ~~as such~~ telling him to strive for self-perfection and good <deeds> *under any circumstances* (i.e., regardless of any loss of faith, or any kind of moral despair), owing to his own conscious will, a certain uncompromising desire. "Though my ideal may be lost and I may not know good from evil, still, I shall follow my conscience and, gropingly, seek to perfect myself—and I shall get somewhere." Having lost his faith he decides, instead of succumbing to despair, to start straight from himself, and he believes that he will get somewhere, and that something will be revealed to him along the way (the chains).

4) Two years earlier, he had fallen in love with the Akhmakov woman—and, terribly naïvely, told her about his strivings. N.B.

Pride: "Since she has learned about my thoughts and I have revealed my soul to her, she should have appreciated that. But she..." She was stunned, but only laughed at his sinfulness. For there are two types combined in him—the idealist and, time and again, his former self, a most sinful and petty person. Yet Versilov was more right <than she was>: realizing his own sinfulness and his <many> falls, he did not become confused, but admitted these to himself and, thus, lifted himself up.

5) Then he left <the Akhmakov woman> for Lidiia, while jealously accusing the Akhmakov woman of sensuality and narrow-mindedness. Besides, he was terribly ashamed that he had bared himself so completely before the Akhmakov woman (about self-perfection, "You've taken off your chains, haven't you?"). [Lidiia, on the other hand, accepted him in an entirely different way, fool in Christ that she was, and followed him rapturously, and bowed before Him, as before a prophet.]

6) But Lidiia died. ["She died because she realized that I still loved that other woman."] Full of shame, and continuing his <program of> self-perfection, he lived another year and a half (he refused to challenge <the Prince> to a duel, for instance, after having had his face slapped, and did so to show his willpower, did it as a moral feat).

7) At this point, the Akhmakov woman makes another appearance and the romance takes its course. (He is dreaming of saving her, and of punishing her, and of forgiving her, etc.) He has made himself believe that he does not love her, but that he, rather, has a tremendous amount of compassion for her, etc. In his pursuit of her, and in his love for *her* He sees his own weakness and his own fall; but in self-control, and in suffering her insults, he sees—salvation. He has expressed his task in these two points, altogether too naïvely, almost childishly—and therein lies the beauty and truth of it.

And so, *Nota bene:*

In the 2d part he does nothing but bare himself quite unexpectedly and in a most disorganized way, [but most of all, quite unexpectedly,] thus surprising the Youth by his unsuspected and ideal aspects.

[His action with regard to the Akhmakov woman comes entirely unexpectedly. A letter to her, or an insult to the Aide-de-Camp.] In the third <chapter?> when the Youth has fallen (that same night), he bares himself completely before him; [their friendship, and] here, suddenly, his terrible fall; his exceedingly mean action (denunciation) against the Akhmakov woman. ~~A letter to her and something with~~

~~the Aide de Camp.~~ The Youth leaves him, and he abandons him (perhaps, marriage to <the Youth's> mother?). He chops up those icons and leaves. A marriage proposal to the Akhmakov woman and, finally, in the 4th <chapter>, the Youth and Lambert, and all the dénouements, arrests, Stebelkov, the Prince, Liza, etc. [Here, too, the Prince's marriage.] The old Prince's wedding, and his death, and the affair with the Akhmakov woman, and the document.

[Meanwhile, the Youth with the Princess, the Prince, Makar, and gambling. Makar in the third <chapter>?]

In the 3d part, when He has undertaken to save the Youth and wholly bares himself before him—and besides, there is also Makar Ivanov—the Youth, *though he is saved, still retains a certain amount of hidden, revengeful anger and spite,* and though he has sincerely *surrendered himself* to the ideals of Makar and Versilov, Versilov's fall (proposing marriage to the Akhmakov woman, and the icons) distresses him greatly and awakens in him a boundless bitterness, and at this point—Lambert. But it isn't just the fall that has such an impact on him; it is precisely while overcome by the tenderest of emotions, after having heard his offer to set out on their pilgrimage into the desert, that he suddenly joins Lambert. (He also meets Alphonsine, and is glad he does.)

He merely answers all of the Youth's questions most genially, while saying nothing on his own part (Speshnev).[2] Yet he visits him frequently and is affectionate and *responsive,* which moves and delights the Youth.

N.B. In a very rapid narrative à la Pushkin.

Notabene's. Versilov is firmly convinced that the young Prince used to be the Princess's lover.

February 25. Create <the image of> *the Princess!*

February 26. *The role of the young Prince.* (Beside everything else, beside his sufferings which are due to his sense of duty and his insignificance.) He is terribly inclined to yield to his evil instincts. (The money which is his as a result of the successful lawsuit.) And, again, he is jealous of the Princess, on account of the Aide-de-Camp. The slander he has spread (under Versilov's hidden influence) about the Princess. The Youth, in his meetings with the Princess, wants to set all of this straight *for her,* and be of some service, and so he develops, if not an outright hostility, at least an antagonism toward the

---

[2] See note 23 of Part II.

young Prince. But somebody talks some sense into the Prince. He admits that he was lying (this is already in the third part) ~~Here, with Liza and~~, when caught together with Stebelkov. This is where Liza enters the picture. Tashkent. And so on.

In the end of the 2d part, only a quarrel, involving *the despotism of love,* between the Youth and Versilov. (Besides, Versilov suddenly writes a letter to the Princess, asking her not to corrupt that adolescent.) A terminal quarrel, *that is, a quarrel which the Youth thinks is terminal.* But when, in part three, He comes to the Youth's rescue, soothes and revives him, new ties are established, which are now complete as well as sincere. Versilov bares himself *down to his chains;* and yet the whole thing ends in his proposing marriage to the Princess, and exactly after Versilov has been insulted by the Aide-de-Camp.

And so.

In the 2d part, Versilov has merely become *inexplicably* attached to the Youth, but does not bare himself completely. A good deal of mystery is still left. The Youth would like very much to find out more about the Princess, but he does not get the whole information from Him, but rather gets it from the young Prince, from the Princess, and from Anna Versilov.

In the end of part two, Versilov suddenly comes up with a *mean* trick, stunning the Youth. Besides, Versilov leaves his *wife,* nor *does he pay any attention* to the way the Youth is living and gambling. The latter fact greatly affects the Youth, so that he quarrels with him out of "a despotism of love." (In fact, Versilov disappears for a time.)

The story with the card game, night (absolutely, the encounter with Lambert).

2d part.

Versilov's letter to the Akhmakov woman, asking her not to corrupt the Youth. A threat to tell the Aide-de-Camp. *She* complains to the Aide-de-Camp herself. The latter clashes with Versilov. Versilov is disgraced and disappears from the house. The Youth feels indignant. Cynicism gains a hold on his soul, debauchery, cards.

Then, in PART three. In part three, the Prince's remorse and despair, and in the end he gets involved in that affair with Kolosov and Lambert. Versilov saves him, and here, now, everything becomes clear, and they join forces against the Princess, etc. Also, Makar Ivanych, and all those stories with the old Prince (Lambert and Kolosov), and the young one. But then, the chopping of the icons and part four.

The Youth is embittered, and all of the dénouements, he joins Versilov only at the very end. Conflagration.

N.B. Lambert, in vile fashion, entices the old Prince to come to <Mme> Andrieux's place (he wants to make him marry her). The old Prince escapes, rescued by the Youth and Anna Versilov, and—already in *part four*—the Prince flees to the Youth's place (here, again, Lambert, and Kolosov, and the Youth, and Anna. But the Aide-de-Camp and the Akhmakov woman take the Prince away. But he still wants to get married, and dies suddenly).

[In part four.] On one occasion Lambert says to him: "Why won't you fuck <Mme> Andrieux?" He agrees and stays with Andrieux; however, they both start crying, nothing comes of it. That is already in part four.

About how to set the city on fire, become a thief (a hellish night).

Composition of the whole novel, already a definitive one, general *summarium, assigning their respective places* to all the personages and stories in the novel, *according to parts* of the novel. (In general, but not in detail.)

An embryo.

1st chapter of part two. The flat (a month later). Versilov's visit.

The story of how he came to see him for the first time. Characteristic discussions, arguments, and lectures. "I made a point of not mentioning the Princess or the Prince, nor did He say a word <about> what we'd be living on. Nothing about me and my affairs: I found it both reassuring and irritating (it worried me). Out of pride, I said nothing." The story with "that passive creature." Found that child. Versilov and his family. A small quarrel on account of "that passive creature" and the family. The Youth suddenly realizes that he is still very remote from Versilov.

2d chapter (or 3d). Meanwhile, a liaison <has developed> between the young Prince and the Youth's sister. "I found out that there was something new going on between Versilov and the ~~young~~ Prince. Connections. The Prince is delighted. Getting to be close with the Prince. A night—suddenly the Youth wins <a lot of money>. The devil take it all!

3d chapter (or 4th). Meanwhile, about the Princess, ~~relations~~ an anecdote about how he established contact with the Princess. It was a secret—both on Versilov's part, and the Prince's. The Princess suddenly takes him into her confidence, seduction. "You are seducing me." Quarrels, young love. (Introduce Vasin, Stebelkov, the child, and the rest.) [About Liza.]

5th chapter. Playing cards with the Prince—life is really in full swing. A big quarrel with the Princess. The Aide-de-Camp. Some sally on the part of Versilov, in connection with a document, or something. The Youth treats him condescendingly. Anna Andreevna, the Prince—"I'm getting married." (Stebelkov.) ~~(Perhaps, an encounter with Lambert.)~~

6th chapter. Reconciliation with the Princess, and her betrayal <of his confidence>. ~~Versilov~~ Full of hatred, he gives Versilov a strong hint about the document. Here, suddenly, he meets Lambert. The money. Meanwhile the Youth has lost a lot of money gambling, and the Prince is beginning to sniff. A quarrel with the Prince, the last word about Liza, prior to that terrible night. Lambert has got money. The scene involving his loss. The terrible night. ~~Meet~~ Lambert. Meeting with Versilov—i.e., the plot stays the same all the way.

Part three. Solitude. "My idea." Versilov, friends again, but in a higher sense. Makar Ivanov, his death. Everybody is arrested (including the Prince). Liza. Marriage. Versilov. Proposal to the Princess. Versilov and the Aide-de-Camp. Versilov's sudden fall, after <a period of> ideal magnanimity.

Part four. Goes directly to Lambert. ["No, evil is better!" Cynicism.] Meanwhile he has got everything worked out with the Prince. (The old Prince is, in effect, frightened by Versilov's revelation concerning the document.) [More about the old Prince in part three, save him.] Lambert *et al.* drive the Prince into a panic. He flees to the Youth's place. The Aide-de-Camp and the Princess save him. (Meanwhile, the story of the young Prince and Liza is coming to its end. Tashkent.) (N.B. The young Prince (out of stupidity) says disgraceful things about the Princess.) Suddenly the Youth, after all that has happened, decides upon the conflagration. He breaks with Lambert, arranging everything by himself. At the last moment he goes to Versilov. Both of them together. The conflagration. Explanation, and general dénouement.

February 27.

Detailed composition of part two. (A big job.)

(At first a general, but detailed, idea of part two, and later according to chapters. Then, the composition of the separate chapters, and most of all, *the first*. Separate and detailed reading of *the material,* with distinct marking of the selected passages.)

N.B. N.B. ~~M. St.~~ The contacts between the Youth and the Princess in part two are kept secret *from everybody*. Think up a story about how the Youth was able to take up these contacts, and the first rendezvous. Just as with Anna Versilov.

[Find out about Rudin] N.B. And so, the whole *project* consists of three main and major sections (aside from the minor ones, *all* of which must be remembered).

N.B. 1) regarding the relationship between the Youth and Him,

2) between the Youth and the Prince (Liza),

3) between the Youth and the Akhmakov woman.

For instance, he already suspects that Liza may have something with the Prince, but in his depravity he remains silent, lets it go, closes his eyes to it—only once does he make Liza an angry, unfair scene (that happens right before her *disgrace*); and on the very last day <before> her disgrace he catches her, and is almost a witness of a scene between the Prince and Liza. [Or, he even pretends that he has become shamefully "civilized," and suggests, by various jocular and cynically vile hints, that there might be some *very light sort of* relationship between her and the Prince.]

(N.B. By the way, he is mad at the Prince because the latter is telling him things about the Akhmakov woman, because he is after the Akhmakov woman, and because he wants to spoil her relationship with the Aide-de-Camp.) The Akhmakov woman suddenly shows him the door and disgraces him (after Versilov's <outrageous> sally, when he writes her a letter asking her not to corrupt the Youth). It is after this incident that the Youth, quite beside himself, goes gambling (the disgrace). (N.B. The Prince, also, disgraces himself with the Aide-de-Camp. The Prince is angry (on the last day <before> the disgrace), and breaks both with the Youth and with Versilov.) At this point, a brief, but mean, conversation about Liza.

(N.B. In the last scene, *at night,* Lambert *lets him know* that he has been with the young Prince for a long time already.)

The role of Olia's mother. (And that of Vasin, the Dergachevs, etc.) (N.B. Start with this in part two, but the main dénouement is in part three, i.e., as far as Vasin and the Dergachev group are concerned.)

Stebelkov is at Anna Andreevna's and is involved with the Prince as <his> money-lender.

In part three: A full, childlike confession and Christianity on the part of Versilov, until the chopping <of the icons>. Yet, already in part two, some hints. For, though he is playful and cynical, or very deeply melancholy, as far as the Youth can see, his urge for those childlike, tender revelations, which come up in part three, comes through here and there in part two.

N.B. Absolutely essential:

It is absolutely necessary to compose only *one* learned discussion between Versilov, the Prince, and the Youth, and besides, thousands of questions and answers between the Youth and Versilov: *most difficult.*

N.B. *Very important.* Throughout part two.

A whole series of contacts with <his> mother, with Liza, and with Tatiana Pavlovna, all of them quite abstract. Just as with Versilov, not a word ~~about~~ reality, but merely about various memories, jokes —in a word, about all perfectly *happy* relations, which must be also *explained to the reader* (i.e., that strange alienation from reality, and flight into the abstract). And so, continue in this fashion right up to the last scene with Liza (which is real, acrid, terrible).

But finally, Liza, his mother, and Tatiana Pavlovna get worried about his carousing and gambling, and this in spite of the fact that things have gotten right up to Spinoza;[3] and so, when it happens, already toward the end of part two (~~when~~ at a trying moment, when his heart is overflowing with pity), that Liza—replying to his reproachful question, ~~why~~ uttered while they are alone, why she was disturbing their mother by telling her about his carousing— suddenly starts talking to him quite seriously about his conduct, he responds, with a cynical and bitter laugh, that he isn't interfering with her freedom <in carrying on> with the Prince either, leaving her much embarrassed. And in an even more <climactic?> scene that follows,* on the last day, he suddenly attacks her, bringing up the subject of her shamelessness and depravity; he acts as if he feels hurt and leaves, but later makes up with her, so that Liza still talks to him, though in a casual way only.**

N.B. Important task. It is absolutely necessary to specify the participants in the drinking spree, and the officers.

Another task: About the flat, description of the flat and its occupants. He makes <the Youth's> sister and mother laugh at his stories.

N.B. (Tuck Olia's mother away somewhere.)

---

* *A v eshche bolee posleduiushchei stsene, literally,* "in a still more following scene," where obviously one or two words have been left out.

** The whole sentence is very awkward in the original, just barely grammatical.

3 Dostoevsky became acquainted with Spinoza most likely from an article published in Dostoevsky's magazine *Vremia,* by N. N. Strakhov, "Spinoza's Teaching About God," in the September issue of 1861. During the writing of *A Raw Youth* four volumes of Strakhov's translation of Spinoza appeared and Dostoevsky may have had firsthand knowledge of Spinoza. There is something of a parody of Spinoza to be found in the words of the old Prince in Part I, Chapter 2:3. The old Prince says: "If there is a higher being," I said to him, "and he exists as a person and not as some kind of diffused creative spirit, as some kind of fluid (because that is even more difficult to understand), then where does he live?"

N.B. *Important.* The young Prince abandons him and rides over to Vasin's place to get some advice, or, in his presence, honors Vasin outrageously, thus terribly hurting the Youth.

N.B. The Akhmakov woman also has something to do with Vasin—jealousy.

N.B. *February 28.*

In part two, when the Youth discusses his relationship with the Akhmakov woman, he says: "And now I am getting to the most secret and confidential part of my story, which is in fact still confidential: *that morning I had an appointment with...*" and so on.

N.B. *The most important and the main thing, absolutely.*

In part two, Versilov says this to the Youth:

[On one occasion he said this to me, and I've completely forgotten in what connection:]

"My friend, you do remember, don't you, how you were asking questions of me, in that *coffin* <of yours>, concerning your mother and Makar Ivanych—remember, then, how free and easy you were on that occasion? Was it proper for a son to speak of his mother in such terms, to show such curiosity regarding his mother? Nor were you blushing: I was looking at you, watching you on purpose, and I saw no color in your face... Why, now you are blushing..."

[For part three, for <his> generation.] "But what about you, yourself—weren't you rather casual in your story about Makar Ivanovich, too [that time?"]

"I ~~purposely wanted~~ was out to embarrass you, [You ought to be chasing me out right now] I was feeling you out, I was expecting you to blush..."

"And so you merely deceived me, making the pure spring of my soul even more turbid than before. Yes, I am a wretched youth who does not know, from moment to moment, what is evil, and what is good. Had you then done even the least bit to show me the right direction, I would have taken your hint and jumped on the right path right away. But you merely got me confused and angry. ~~But~~ I swear to you, all the time you were telling me this, I was suffering and blushing deep inside; particularly since I had my cue: you were speaking with affectation, you were being witty in an unnatural way. I saw this and instead of blushing ended up by getting rather angry at you, and terribly angry at myself. But this was precisely ~~instead of~~ what substituted for my blushing. This was precisely <what you just called> *the color in my face*. Now, of course, it is something else again, now it is all different again!" (for part three).

"I saw all this perfectly well, I had noticed it, and fully understood you, and it is for this sole reason that I even then, immediately, [and with all my heart] forgave you the terrible thing you did to me on that occasion: for you literally showed me the door then, didn't you? But I was perfectly aware of the fact that you weren't angry with me, but with yourself, and precisely *instead of blushing*. ~~This is why~~ I was actually glad for you, and ~~on the next~~ regained my composure... I knew that, somehow or other, we would get together again..."*

"We got a lot of things straightened out," (the Youth remarks,) "in those days we were incessantly and eagerly trying to communicate with each other."

February 28.

Final task: Distribute the whole content of part two among 10 chapters.

About Spinoza, he to Versilov, in desperation [and despotically:]

"Why then were you just sitting there and not telling me that I was a fool?"

"If I had done that, you would have cursed me forever. As it happened, you were able to speak your mind, to cuss me, but good, and to return <to me> right away. And it all came out marvelously, and with grace. As for your coming back to me, I never doubted that for a moment... You are acting like a despot with me."

March 1/2.

Solution of a problem.

Start part two with a single event, rather than splitting it up into four acts. Express everything that is of importance through artistic action, <that is> the words and actions of the characters. As for the historical part of the whole thing (i.e., how things happened to take this course), insert it, too, wherever necessary, in sections and fragments. There must be a unifying plot (the search for the child, for instance, as far as the Akhmakov woman is concerned) ~~or~~ (the Akhmakov woman is trying to find out from him what Anna Versilov wants of the child, and he is both trying to dodge her prying, and yielding to it). As the action begins to unfold in part two, it should be apparent that he is already, in spite of all his successes and joys, beginning to have his doubts and to feel very depressed at times (he is in debt, the Prince is being rude and equivocal with him, Versilov). *Later,*

* There is some indication that this paragraph was meant to be crossed out. Ambiguous in the text.

<show> through scenes as well as the narrative, how such a scene could come about. A major quarrel, with the Aide-de-Camp involved in it, on account of Versilov's letter in which he warns against corrupting the Youth. The Aide-de-Camp had been threatening the Prince even before. The Prince tried to communicate this to the Youth, but then quarreled with no one but the Youth himself. In passing, a scene between the Prince and Liza, witnessed by the Youth —and he remains silent on account of the money (screams of remorse directed at the reader). After Versilov's letter, the young Prince, having discovered that ~~the latter~~ the Youth has been in contact with the Akhmakov woman, almost attacks him—sneers and anger and contempt for him—after he has been a witness of that business with Liza. (N.B. The young Prince had been laughing most heartily even the other night, when the Youth had been thrown off a sleigh.) Lambert, etc. "His own idea" emerges toward the end of part two.

Suddenly, one night, in the street, to Versilov: "Dad, father. Why, you are my father, and I haven't ever called you father yet!" (this, right after Spinoza.)[4]

N.B. (Important.) This man Versilov does everything in spurts: at one time the Prince's family wouldn't have a chance, then again he relinquishes the inheritance of his own accord; he would challenge his man to a duel, then withdraw his challenge. He would be silent for a while; then suddenly, that insolent, insulting letter to the Akhmakov woman, which violates all the rules of decency and is altogether immoderate (Heeckeren). "I cannot understand how such capers could occur to such a composed, even-tempered, calm, and firm gentleman as Versilov" (remarks the Youth).

"His own idea" comes altogether to the fore *in its entirety* during that hellish night,* while it had hardly been mentioned in the 2d part. (Only, perhaps, a thing or two while he is gambling, but otherwise he *simply had no time for it.*)—<Start part two?> *with a single event* in order to have the time to prepare the dénouement involving the gambling incident, and that whole episode.

Regarding *Lidiia* Akhmakov, let something *flash by* in part two, through the young Prince and, perhaps, through Versilov, *where it is understood* that it is precisely Versilov's account of Lidiia's story ~~the~~

---

* "In its entirety" is underlined twice.

[4] See note 3 of Part II.

~~Prince~~ that shocks the Prince so much, and *immediately* wins him over. That this is how it actually happened, the Youth learns from the deeply shaken Prince, but he does not as yet, in the 2d part, that is, know the very *plot* of Lidiia Akhmakov's story (he merely lets the reader know that there probably must have happened something terribly shocking, but that he learned about it only later (in part three) and would communicate it to his reader at the proper juncture). And so he learns the whole graceful and fantastic story of Lidiia only in part three, already from Versilov (who is in an exalted frame of mind at the time), and Versilov's raptures leave the heart of the Youth deeply shaken. Right here, in part three, we also have Versilov's confession, to the Youth, about the Akhmakov woman, though it is not a true confession but rather presents things the way Versilov himself wanted to understand them, including remorse, etc. On this occasion the Youth concludes *definitively* that He does not love the Akhmakov woman (and suddenly, in part three, He proposes marriage to the Akhmakov woman), and so on.

At dawn, after that hellish night, the Youth has a mass served for Olia (his last ruble). Without explaining to the reader to what end, or why. After mass, he runs into Versilov: "He took me up to his place" (last line of part two).

The Stolbeev woman has left for her country estate: so the Prince is alone at the apartment.

At first, the Youth won some money at faro. At one time they were considering pooling their accounts, the Prince and he, that is.

There is one scene where the Youth and the Prince get to be quite close—that's <during their discussion> *about the spirit* of the nobility. It was the Youth who was doing the talking. All of a sudden the Prince began to treat him with extraordinary respect (and then, later, accounts).

Anna Andreevna asks Versilov if he is in love with the Akhmakov woman, even in part two. [Especially toward the end, after the row with the Aide-de-Camp in the Youth's presence].

In part two, the old Prince has fallen ill. Anna Versilov is in attendance, while the Youth chooses to neglect him. He had been thinking of borrowing some money from him, but was ashamed to ask him. Prior to that, he had consulted with Anna Andreevna, who apparently approved of it. Something like friendship between the Youth and Anna Andreevna (Varia).

In part two, Versilov sometimes actually doesn't seem to notice the *insults* and the *tyranny* which he suffers at the hands of the Youth, and comes to see him meekly, in childlike fashion, which surprises and delights the Youth.

??? A vital task: the Youth's flat.

! A PRECIOUS scene. Practically on the last day (of part two), his mother suddenly pays a visit to the Youth at his flat, something she had never done before.

! In the course of part two the Youth tells his mother about how he had met her at Touchard's.

In the final scene, Liza makes a confession to him, but only casually so.

In part two, Liza is jealous of the Prince on account of the Akhmakov woman. Humiliations, but also tenderness, on his part.

March 1/2. Compose chapter one in detail, the rest, what with the material already on hand, *will come by itself.*

The point, the pivot from which to start, the point of departure, the essence of the plot!

!Reading the material!

March 2—reading the material,

March 3—composing the pivot,

and March 4—start <writing>!

N.B. He has been thrown from a sleigh, snow... If this is all to be developed, the Youth's drinking spree must start *at the very beginning of part two.*

Part two in 4 stories.

1) The story of the Youth and Versilov (the flat, Liza, mother).

2) About the Youth and the Prince (the Prince's relationship with the Akhmakov woman, the beginning of the drinking spree, the Aide-de-Camp), etc.

3) About the Youth and the Akhmakov woman.

4) About the drinking spree and his quarrel with his father.

?? Here, this question: How much should be given in the form of a narrative, and how much as outright action? Should one start with outright action immediately (introducing the preceding in the form of narrative passages within the action), or would it be better to have <a series of> narratives?

In part two, the Youth suddenly says: "I am now writing the book of my disgrace."

N.B. Perhaps one shouldn't bring out Versilov's opinions and theories *too much* in this second part.

March 1/2.

[So] ~~He~~ or the Youth arranges for some intimacy between the Prince and Versilov, or of their own accord, they—that is, the Prince and Versilov—get together even before the Youth <is around>, through the child (the infant child). An encounter with Anna Andreevna and the beginning of her schemes <connected> with the infant child. On the occasion of that encounter, Anna Andreevna suddenly invites the Youth to her place. Olimpiada is at her place. A conversation concerning the possibility of Olimpiada <. . .> The Youth strikes a tone. Tableaux vivants.* Junior Chamberlain Versilov.

(N.B. Junior Chamberlain Versilov is a silent and disdainful witness of the Youth's *disgrace*.) Prior to this, the Youth complains to Versilov about his brother.

N.B. Perhaps a scene such as the following should be inserted. Once the young Prince has become fascinated by Versilov and is giving out shrieks of remorse, saying that he, the Prince, is an ignoramus and the unworthy scion of a great family, the Youth begins to preach to the Prince, and they become awfully close friends. Then, very quickly, comes the scene about the accounts and <mutual> loathing. Also, about the Princess...

As for "about the Princess," that's because I...—and this is where the story of his romance with the Princess begins.

N.B. His conversations with the Princess frequently approach the topic of the *document,* but the Youth keeps dodging her questions, nor does he explain this thing to his reader, not in part two. The same holds true for Versilov as well, as the latter, too, is out to get the document, without any explanation on the part of the Youth (except for these sudden words to the reader: "Inasmuch as I was seeing that he was after the document"). He is also confused by the fact that Versilov is apparently encouraging the Prince to pay court to the Akhmakov woman.

N.B. Once, during a drinking bout, somebody says to the Youth: "Listen, Prince," but it is said naïvely and in a friendly way, and he does not take it up.

?A fantasy: He has been teaching Liza and his mother philosophy (also, Tatiana Pavlovna), and then quarrels with them about philos-

---

* *Zhivye stseny,* literally, "living scenes," "lively scenes," but here apparently in the meaning of *zhivye kartiny*. However, "some lively scenes," is a likely alternative.

ophy (the absolute, Spinoza). He screams at Liza: "You are no longer my sister!" ~~and later~~ And to his mother: "I curse the day I was born." Later he admits that he knows nothing, even though he wanted to enlighten them (N.B. This might come out quite graceful.)

And later, to the reader: "I am putting in this lowly, humiliating scene, etc. It is very precious to me, but if the reader does not want to, he must not read it, let him throw it out, and enough of it."

N.B. *Important.* Characterizes the Youth.

For some reason, the Youth avoids, throughout part two, approaching or questioning Versilov regarding those real essentials (or secrets), i.e., the Akhmakov woman, the infant child—even his intentions so far as his mother is concerned—but rather tries to make his own guesses, or to find out about these things by roundabout ways (the child, for instance). "Was this because I was ashamed? Or out of my adolescent stupidity... I believe that the latter was the case, for any shame was sheer stupidity <under the circumstances>. It would have been quite possible to skip over <to any of these topics>." Yet he discusses nothing but abstract themes with Versilov... All this he then admits to his reader, adding a detailed explanation of this foolishness, and of its consequences. (For instance, that it depressed and angered Versilov. In connection with this, mention Versilov's humility.) [So. March 1–2]

?N.B. He sees Stebelkov at Anna Andreevna's and learns that Stebelkov has been in contact with the young Prince. He assumes that as a moneylender. On one occasion he goes to see Stebelkov himself, to borrow some money. [*Arseniev.*][5] Stebelkov, by way of repeated hints, suggests to him a project to sell Dergachev <to the police>, but seeing that the Youth is growing furious, adroitly changes the subject (dissuading the Youth by putting on an innocent expression, and also by *pretending* not to understand why the Youth is getting so angry) and lets him know that one might take advantage of the old Prince (something like <Mme> Andrieux).

Lambert, then, as he runs into the Youth in the final scene, after the latter's disgrace, makes some strong hints regarding la Andrieux, the old Prince, the young Prince, etc. But he explains nothing, just strikes terror into the Youth's heart. 2,000, took them and lost them.

---

[5] A possible prototype of Stebelkov. Il'ia Aleksandrovich Arseniev was a journalist, owner of several newspapers, agent for the third section, and a thoroughly disreputable person.

N.B. The Prince has just rudely refused to give the Youth any <more> money, and has rudely spat at him with 100 rubles, (the latter accepting them) as Lambert shows up, 2,000. He ~~loses~~ rides *to the gambling house,* returns the Prince his 100 rubles, loses 2,000, and—night, flee to America. "HIS OWN IDEA." (Or, the other way around, Lambert after his disgrace, that night, 2,000, but the Youth refuses the money and runs away.) Mass, Versilov. (N.B. But the earlier program is better. He loses 2,000, and Versilov somehow rescues him.) [Here.]

Anna Andreevna's plan involving the old Prince, i.e., making <him> marry <her>, in part three, but in part two only some mysterious preparations and one scene with Versilov.

N.B. IMPORTANT. In part three, Anna Andreevna takes her step *fully*. Though the Youth is *isolated* at Versilov's (Makar's death also plays a role), he is, in a remote way, held in servitude by Lambert and in the beginning willy-nilly participates in the project (negatively, freeing the Prince); but later, Lambert, having learned about the project involving Anna Andreevna from Stebelkov (which Stebelkov has been keeping to himself), cooks up the whole crazy scheme according to which the old Prince is to flee to the Youth's, greatly frightening the old Prince (to which Versilov contributed [by his denunciation] of the Akhmakov woman), which, incidentally, is also embarrassing to Anna Andreevna—and demands that the Youth help him.* But the Aide-de-Camp and the Princess rescue the Prince. On this occasion there is a scene between the Aide-de-Camp, on the one side, and Versilov and the Youth, on the other, the latter being, on the contrary, innocent, and after all this, Versilov's *proposal* to the Akhmakov woman and the chopping up of those icons. But the chopping up of those icons makes the Youth waver. The Youth now surrenders himself to Lambert, and at this point Lambert explains everything to him.

The most characteristic feature of part three is that Versilov has the Youth definitely convinced that he never did love the Akhmakov woman, but merely wanted to save her.

Part four, all the dénouements, the plot involving the fire, the final scene, the young Prince with Liza and on trial, the old Prince dies, etc.

March 2/3.

---

* The sentence is ungrammatical in the original.

I, all dressed up. 1½ months later. Let the reader try to imagine. I was overjoyed, but never again was there to be such shame. What's right is right.

"He has rejected that conscientious and talented Frenchman, Charmeur, <he has> thousands, what thousands? Even Versilov hasn't told me a thing."

Why so silent, why didn't he say anything—why didn't he guide <me>, abstract topics?

I was staying at that flat—a small one—I was hardly ever there. [Here] Versilov used to sit around there.

This happened one evening. He came in. ~~I [expected] you~~

[Take it from the material] "I expected you." He remained standing in the middle of the room.

"So you expected me? Really? Well, thank you, thank you very much for that."

A conversation about everything (just as with Shatov), about God... Changed to the landlord. The landlord.

I went out to see him off. Went out to finish that conversation. Was ashamed to ask, about this and that.

(In the same chapter.) "But I have stopped at what happened 1½ months later. I was on my way to the Prince's"—etc. (will be continued later).

At the Prince's, I ran into Versilov, about how they got together through the child. (A pathetic scene. Versilov is the winner), about the nobility. The Youth has a discussion with the Prince; they are both delighted. Immediately thereafter, settling accounts on gambling. As if somebody had thrown cold water <on me>.

N.B. Important: In part two, the Youth casts an inquisitorial glance: Is there, or isn't there anything going on between Versilov and the Akhmakov woman? Getting carried away himself.* Lets Versilov know. Conveys to the reader that it was then that he finally became convinced that there had been nothing... and suddenly—Versilov's crazy sally!

An account of how it all happened (gambling) and what was going on in his soul—any breadth, or none, etc. A hint about Liza. Used to pay visits to Tatiana Pavlovna. Two meetings, at the child's, with Anna Versilov.

---

* Or: "Becoming infatuated himself."

At first, a scene with the Akhmakov woman, and then a description of how they got together. (The old Prince, etc., sick.)

And one mysterious thing about the Akhmakov woman.

At night, at his mother's. ~~A quarrel with her.~~ Spinoza.[6] Kissed her hand. Versilov, "dad." An accidental win, etc.

N.B. His relations with the Akhmakov woman are of a mysterious nature, but the Youth finds it *necessary* to let Versilov know about them. *And so from the very beginning of part two.* Versilov had had a presentiment about it, and had foreseen it. Their mutual relations and their *opinions of each other* after this revelation.

N.B. *And altogether,* in part two, the Youth is *bossing everybody around.** (Everything works well for him, and there is no holding him.) He even *exuberantly cracks jokes* in society <and> at cards, tells anecdotes, comes up with witticisms, disgracing himself (in bad taste)—about Chernyshev[7] and other things. [He even tells lies, and is caught.] He also bosses the Akhmakov woman around, as if she were accountable to him. She asks him a number of questions about the young Prince, while he tells her about Versilov. He is pouting about her becoming involved with the Aide-de-Camp. Won't keep an appointment. Does some eavesdropping. Follows her to a masked ball.

[On one occasion,] Versilov can't stand it anymore and gives him a lecture about Chernyshev, the rock, etc. Very sharp and caustic.

"Why didn't you tell me before?" the Youth asks. "You kept saying nothing (failed to give me any guidance)." "This was a stretch of time when I got carried away by the game and got entangled in my own lies," says the Youth, "and altogether, it was a period of disgrace."

(N.B. But these trifles concerning Chernyshev, etc., He definitely considers on a par with the most serious and the most tragic events.)

I discovered that some tales about the cossacks of 1812 were still alive at the time, *The Goat,* etc.

This all originates from the milieu of petty government clerks, yet such tales are the height of dishonorableness.

The young Prince had spread some kind of slander about the Akhmakov woman. The slander made its rounds. (The Aide-de-Camp.) On account of this, the Youth quarreled with the Prince and called him a slanderer. The Youth feels sad as he sees that Versi-

---

* *Despotiruet,* "is acting the despot," a neologism as far as I can see.

[6] See note 3 of Part II.

[7] See note 17 of Part IV.

lov is apparently inciting the Prince to make these slanderous statements... This happens in the very beginning of part two. This, precisely, is the plot.

~~Versilov~~ The Youth would like to brag some about knowing such a charming lady (the Akhmakov woman). Even if it be just to Tatiana Pavlovna. To Liza.

Versilov and the Prince have some points of contact: refusal to accept the estate, Lidiia, the child, hate for the Akhmakov woman, and <their> nobility.

[This is the last page of the first half of part two.] At one time the Youth made an attempt to discuss Liza with Versilov, but he saw that the latter did not want to listen to him.

This is Versilov's second disappointment, and the beginning of his doubts, in the Youth:*

1st. His taciturnity.

2d. There is a suspicion of <his> hatred for the Akhmakov woman (though not of love). The Youth is convinced that he loved Lidiia, and has heard about it from the Prince. "It is impossible to speak of Lidiia with such warmth of feeling without having loved her," thinks the Youth.

3d. That Versilov is inciting the Prince to a frantic sally against the Akhmakov woman (secretly, Versilov is jealous of the Prince).

4th. That when the Youth has admitted to Versilov that he is in contact with the Akhmakov woman, something quite inexplicable begins, as if he had stroked him the wrong way.

5th. That Versilov does not want to hear anything about Liza.

6th. That he *definitely* is trying to approach the subject of the document.

In spite of all this, the Youth stands up for him every time and breaks lances for him as if he were his most devoted servant. And so it goes, right until Versilov's crazy sally, his letter to the Akhmakov woman in which he asks her not to corrupt <the Youth>.

The Akhmakov woman finds out everything from the Youth (about Anna Versilov, for instance). The Youth, though he is giving in to her and telling her things, owing to his weakness <of character>, is also taking note of everything, and is merely angry at his own weakness: *Why is he yielding?*

Versilov has been telling the Prince a lot about the nobility, but

---

* Apparently a *lapsus calami:* It ought to be the other way around.

the Youth clearly realizes, on that very same day, when he meets Versilov alone, that the latter does not believe in what he is saying, and proceeds to let the Prince know about it in a half-facetious way just to tease him a little.

Stebelkov is paying court to Anna Andreevna; he is having hopes, is expecting a dowry from the old Prince, and is instructing Anna Andreevna how to wheedle it out of him. But Anna Andreevna has kept him around just to find out everything about the Akhmakov woman and about Versilov, has given the appearance of being his willing pupil (and then some), and then she suddenly makes a fool of Stebelkov and all his hopes by picking the old Prince for her fiancé. Versilov is worried during the entire time of Anna Andreevna's intimacy with Stebelkov. This is in part two.

N.B. Even a long time before that, the old Prince would on occasion say words of praise about Anna Andreevna.

The Prince is toying with the idea of setting up his own roulette.

The old Prince is aware of the fact that Stebelkov is wooing Anna Andreevna. He is quite interested in this circumstance, but won't stand for it, figuring, rather, on Prince Serezha as <her> suitor. Conversation between the old Prince and the Youth about Stebelkov.

Absolutely, about "that passive creature."

?! Important N.B. A remark to the effect that the Prince is not accepted in the highest society. "At the Sportsmen's Club, what a game you can have there!" His application was turned down. The Prince is having some visitors. A retired officer, a member of fashionable society, is running a roulette. The Prince is outrageously flattering and fawning on persons belonging to fashionable society. This bothers the Youth a great deal.

The old Prince: "I see a new type of people in the streets, all bearded; it would be interesting to walk down the street just with the idea of reading from people's faces whether they have read *The Pickwick Papers*,[8] or not."

"I am not too... venerable as yet," says the old Prince.

Sometimes the young Prince would exclaim: "Oh, how uneducated I am!"

Tatiana Pavlovna says: "I am convinced that you think He did it all for you, and no one else—challenged <the Prince> to a duel, and

---

[8] See note 33 of Part IV.

turned down that inheritance—solely to become worthy of Arkady Makarovich."

"A brilliant idea!" exclaims the Youth, "but... so help me God, I wasn't thinking that! And yet, absurd as it may sound, by God, it may be true!"

The Youth to Versilov, about the Prince: "In a word, there are as many virtues in him, as there are shortcomings."

Versilov: "But my dear friend, you are flattering him immeasurably; if he really has so many virtues ~~as he has shortcomings~~, he is the most righteous man or else the Apollo of Belvedere."

"Or a general on the railroad: they'll wait, and meanwhile the train is gone."

The young Prince was originally thinking <of wooing> the Princess, but then he met the Aide-de-Camp and, through Stebelkov, Anna Andreevna (hoping to get a salaried position) (this, in the Youth's narrative); thus, he betrays Liza.

See February, December 13/14, character sketch of the Prince.

The Youth was always wondering why Stebelkov was moving in good society, why he was received by decent people. What had happened was that he had "suffered" at one time, spent a month in prison; that's why some decent people would receive him, and he knew how to turn it to his advantage.

The young Prince is *honest,* but his judgment is most irregular, as are his impressions. His relationship with the Princess resembles my own with E<lena P<avlovna>.[9]

About the young Prince, see *February,* toward the end of the book!

Various cute expressions in the beginning of the book. See February.

"I've come to make up."

"I've been expecting you."

"Well, I thank you for that."

Initially, the young Prince was counting on the Akhmakov woman (El<ena> Pav<lovna>). Then, on Anna Andreevna, which makes the Youth suspect that he apologized for the slap he gave <Versilov>, because he saw an advantage in it, but this is not true. The Prince begins to hate the Aide-de-Camp. Whereas the news that the Youth is also in the picture makes the young Prince very angry, as he is dreaming of Anna Andreevna. And what about Liza?

---

[9] See note 48 of Part IV.

VERY IMPORTANT. Not so firmly and radically about gambling in the 1st half of part two. There haven't been any scenes yet, nor have there been any scenes involving gamblers (or gambling), or any details. Everything concerning gambling enters its mold only in the 2d half of part two. [About gambling]

The young Prince. He suddenly starts reading Belinsky.

Lambert relates how he was living in the provinces and how he "had" Viktoriia (a Kirghiz).*

March 3/4.

*Versilov in part two. (Words and cute expressions.)***

Versilov is worried about Anna Andreevna. Having heard about her from the Youth, he asks him many further questions. He is worried about Anna Andreevna being on such intimate terms with Stebelkov. The old Prince also praises Anna Andreevna to him.

He tells the Prince about the nobility. Deprived of everything, the nobility has even less than the other estates. And it would appear *incomprehensible* why it should still be an estate. But all of a sudden it is addressed <by destiny> and handed the guardianship of the spirit of the Russian nation, put at the head of <its> education.[10] And so, the banner which it is bearing remains a spiritual one. Now, after the abolition of serfage, this has become even more evident. I am in favor of the abolition of serfdom, a condition which the nation*** could have blamed on the nobility. What remains now is the pure banner of <our> spirit. The nobility has been entrusted with Russian honor, a sense of responsibility. The banner is now more readily visible. Let it be an ideal, let just one in a million <hold it up>, but that is enough for it not to die. In order for the nobility to be regenerated, the gates to it are wide open. The nobility is the intelligentsia. The only ones who are laughing at the idea are those who are glad to have acquired the right to be dishonorable. The merchant and the scribe.

The Prince remarks that this is all ideal and won't last without having any material roots. Versilov replies that it might be precisely the peculiar quality of the Russian race to be able to sustain an ideal without any material roots.

---

* "A Kirghiz" is in the masculine gender.

** *Slova i slovechki,* where the latter means literally "little words."

*** *Narod* is ambiguous here; it could also mean "the people."

10 See note 26 of Part I.

"You are descended from Riurik. Set up yourself as an example. Self-perfection. Even a limited field of activity will do. These small efforts will not remain without recognition. The banner, etc., are important. This may be just the breadth of our Russian nature," Versilov says jokingly. "At the present time, though, this breadth (i.e., ardent faith and, at the same time, cynicism) is getting somehow more narrow: the Krafts are shooting themselves on account of the idea that Russia is second-rate. Whereas we only used to *grow more handsome* from such ideas," Versilov adds. After Versilov, the Youth, friendship, accounts.

That night, Versilov says the same things to the Youth, this time with open cynicism. The Youth is surprised and angry.

"One must have no respect for people. And I'm starting it with myself."

Conversations about how he expected the Youth to blush while Makar was telling his story.*

N.B. Versilov's cynicism was in part the cause of <the Youth's> passion for gambling ("had he taken me firmly into his hands that time," etc.). But on the other hand, Versilov's tender treatment of the Youth, his visits, etc.

Discussion during the first showdown.

Discussion about Chernyshev.[11]

Versilov definitely approaches the subject of the document. An unpleasant impression on the Youth.

"A man of indubitable mental faculties, yet... still not a very clever person."

"A witty, but not a clever man."

Versilov: "One must learn how to love people."

"No one among us has ever tried to cultivate himself by force."

"No one is born a ready person."

"In our country, what they like is precisely to have things ready for them."

"Lots of things in Russian life, and among them some of the most important, are sustained precisely and only by this quality of the Russian people."

---

* Though this is what seems to be the only possible translation, the real meaning ought to be: "While listening to <Versilov's> story of Makar <and his family>."

[11] See note 17 of Part IV.

"It is natural for one not to respect people. It is very difficult to love them."

Regarding contemporary literature, Versilov says that the types presented by it (Chatsky, Pechorin, Oblomov)[12] are rather crude, and that many fine nuances and much that was undoubtedly real has slipped away from it; immeasurably more has slipped away than was actually captured by literature. For we have failed to understand ourselves all along, and the moment some light was cast on one tiny bit <of our life>, it suddenly turned out that there was even more darkness than before (during the past twenty years).

MICE.

"As many virtues as shortcomings" (see).

Versilov says: "We have, in our society, on the one hand despair and purulent decay, and on the other, a thirst of regeneration, and enthusiasm. They are even rejecting God religiously."

[Here.] For other statements by Versilov, see *February,* toward the end of the book.

"Fight with words. [Ideas] Children fight precisely when [because] they haven't learned to express their thoughts yet."

Or, they will insist on telling you in a whisper how an extremely important personage was, at one time, kneeling in the Senate before the Senators...

The trial of Christ in England.

"I have come to make up with you."

"I've been expecting you."

"Well, thank you for that."

~~The young Prince~~ "I have in me all the depths of degradation. But, to make up for it, I also possess all the sensations of 'exalted thought.' "

The Youth is <at> the old Prince's, a learned conversation about how rocks will be flying <through space>.

The old Prince: "Oh, my dear friend, why should you be worried about that, let them fly."

~~the young Prince began to read~~

He, to the Youth: "My friend, I am generally afraid of formulating. You see: suddenly, I believe in nothing and yet, at the same time, know firmly and at all times that 'I believe in a great idea.' My position is of course untenable, for the whole trouble lies precisely in the

---

[12] See note 45 of Part IV.

question: 'What then, does your great idea consist of?' What's both funny and absurd is that it never has been formulated: the moment I would formulate it, I would be the first to ridicule it myself. And that's the way it always happens."

The Youth: "It seems to me that there's nothing to worry about here: a great feeling will appear as an impression—well, and that's enough. You go along, meet a certain fact, and say—'this is good!'..."

He: "That's precisely what is wrong with it."

The Youth: "You mean, it is too little, it's not enough to have just the impression... Listen" (at this point, about something else, about the Prince, for instance).

He: "There's an excess of happiness boiling inside you, and I'd certainly hate to cool you off. That's why I am not even touching you."

He, to the Youth: "My friend, I've been frequently telling my wife, your mother ~~here, I will~~, at the beginning of our union, incidentally, in the beginning as well as in the middle, and in the end: 'My dear, I'm torturing you, and I shall torture you to death, nor am I feeling sorry for you, not as long as I have you before me. But if you should die, I do know for sure that I would [torture myself] to death, for having caused your death.' "

He: "If at least I were a weak-willed nonentity, and could suffer from my awareness of that! But no, for I know that I am infinitely strong, and through what, would you think? Well, precisely through that immediate power of vitality and adaptability, so characteristic of all clever Russian people of our past generation. Nothing can destroy me, nothing can kill me, nothing can do me in. I have the vitality of a watchdog. I can most conveniently experience two contrary feelings simultaneously—nor would it happen of my own volition, I can assure you. It is dishonorable—and precisely because it suggests that, in certain instances, the kinds of me can be exceedingly prudent. But just imagine, I have lived to the age of 50, and [to this day] I don't know myself if I have lived well, or badly. Of course I love life, which really follows from the rest of it. Yet, it is base for a man such as I to love life. Lately, there has been a new trend, and the Krafts <no longer> adapt themselves to things, but shoot themselves. But [it is obvious that] the Krafts are foolish, ~~well~~ whereas we are clever, [on the other hand] and consequently, it is once more impossible to say ~~whether it is good or bad~~ anything. ~~But if~~ Could it be really true that the world exists only for ~~clever~~ people such as myself? Most likely so, but this is really much too dismal a notion, for, if the Krafts are stupid, then, [on the other hand,] we, the clever ones, are dishonorable to the marrow of our bones, and what is even viler, we are glad that this is so." ~~We are shameless, depraved people, and nothing else.~~

Versilov, on education: "I was almost glad that, during the past 15 years or so, our whole intelligentsia, stimulated by Russia's needs, began to specialize in a variety of branches, and, so help me God, I was honestly glad about it, and I am, in this respect, really an enemy of any other kind of 'educational reform' as well as of any kind of external 'raising of the level'...: for, in our dear fatherland, to raise the level of education invariably means to also raise the level of suffering...—at least this is how it has been up to now... ~~but~~"

"Listen," I interrupted him, "I've always suspected that you are saying these things merely out of spite, or suffering, and that secretly, in your own mind, you are perhaps the fanatical devotee of some higher idea, which you are simply concealing, for some reason, or are ashamed to admit..."

"Do you think so?"

On that occasion I went on to bombard him with a variety of questions [too much so], and I remember he answered all of them readily and straightforwardly, though somehow much too briefly and abstractly, [and the world] veering off into the most commonplace aphorisms toward the end of each statement. I don't know whether or not he was just chatting with me, for he really didn't have anyone else to chat with. But it seemed to me that this was not the case. And yet ~~really~~ all of these questions had been bothering me all my life and, let me admit this much, while still in Moscow I had been postponing their solution precisely until we would meet in Petersburg. I told him so directly, and he didn't laugh at me at all, but on the contrary, I remember, actually shook hands with me. Regarding general politics and social ideas, I was able to ~~extract~~ elicit next to nothing from him, and yet precisely those questions were, in view of my "idea," bothering me almost more than anything else. Regarding the likes of Dergachev I once wrested a "they're below criticism" from him; yet right there he added that he would "retain the right to consider his opinion utterly devoid of significance." [~~well~~, and we are so clever] Then, concerning the eventual end of the state and the world as we know it, and the future regeneration of ~~Europe~~ the world, he dodged my questions for a long time, until I finally wrung a few words from him. "I think that all this will happen most simply and ordinarily," he once said, "very simply, all these different states will one day, in spite of all these balances and budgets, in spite of the absence of any deficit and the presence of perfect controls, get all tangled up in their finances *un beau matin,*[13] i.e., every single one of them, and I mean every single one, will decide that he is no longer willing to pay his debts, so that a general regeneration by way of general [and solidary] bankruptcy will be in order and so... a new and regenerate life may start—[i.e.,] with new loans, new budgets, and a new bankruptcy. Meanwhile the conservative element in the whole world will be opposed to this, for it is they who'll be the shareholders and the creditors who won't like to allow this bankruptcy to happen—even if it promises to regenerate the whole world. Then, naturally, there will start what you may call a general oxidation; there is going to be some forced oxidation, accompanied by a perfect awareness of one's own turning sour, whereupon all those who never have possessed any shares, who in fact have possessed nothing at all, i.e., the paupers, naturally will refuse to participate in such oxidation, for they won't have anything to lose. A struggle will start, and after thirty or 70 defeats the paupers will destroy the shareholders, will take their places, and... maybe they're going to say something new, and maybe they won't... More likely than not, they, too, will go bankrupt. Further than that, [For the time being] my dear friend, I find it impossible to foresee anything at all in the fortunes ~~of Europe and the world~~, which the face of this Earth has yet to see. [Incidentally,] you may look it up in the Apocalypse."

"Is all this really so material, is the world as we know it really going to come to an end because of its finances?"

"Of course not, I was merely taking one hundredth of the total picture, just one section of the whole business. But that small section, too, is connected with all the rest of it and, one might say, connected by indissoluble ties."

"What then, is there to be done?"

"What are you to do, my dear? Be honest, never say a falsehood, do not covet your neighbor's house; in a word, read the ten commandments; that's where it has been written down forever. ~~And if life turns out to be just too boring, then over and above that try to love somebody or something.~~

"Eh, come on, this is all so old, and besides, these are only words."

"Well, if things turn out to be too boring, then over and above that try to love somebody or something..."

---

[13] French: "One beautiful morning."

"Eh, of course, you're right, but that isn't the real thing either! What is of the essence is something to do, something to be done, and what is there to be done?"

Versilov: "Ah, my friend, it is better not to do anything; at least you'll have a clear conscience knowing that you are not a party to anything."

"And besides, what am I alone going to do with your ten commandments? That's nothing but a joke."

"Well, you just go ahead and fulfill them, in spite of all your questions and doubts, and you shall be a great man."

"Unknown to the world."

"There is nothing <so> secret that it will not be made manifest."

"Why, you are making fun of me!"

"Well, if you are taking things so much to heart, it might be best if you'd try to find a specialty as fast as possible. Become a building contractor, or a lawyer, [or start making money]...and then, being busy with ~~a serious~~ a real and a serious activity, you will naturally calm down and forget ~~all this nonsense, and quit~~ <about> asking abstract questions."

I remained silent. Really, it appeared to me at the time that he was sometimes laughing <at me>, [which] made me sad. And yet, perhaps he wasn't after all, because after each such discussion I would fall to thinking and would get very excited. I saw that he was still guarding some kind of a secret: and it was that secret that was attracting me to him. I was becoming more and more attached to him. And this even in spite of the fact that I was beginning to have my serious doubts about him. About that, later, and separately. I was postponing my telling him about "my idea"; it wasn't the proper time for it, I could see that, and besides, I was hardly capable of making up my mind to go through with it: to reveal it to him meant to deprive myself of everything, no matter what the outcome. But what was most important, it wasn't the proper time. God knows what kind of time it was, a time of enthusiasm and of disgrace all at once.

"I swear to you that I felt no anger after he had slapped my face. I can remember how I told myself: 'Surely, I am feeling no anger because I actually deserved to have my face slapped.' But this was merely a pun: actually that slap in the face was undeserved; I really wasn't guilty."

Once, in anger, the young Prince says ~~about Versilov~~ to the Youth: ~~He~~ "You simply haven't done anything to deserve anyone's attention, and this is why you are envious of everybody, that's all there is to it."

The Youth asks: "Once you mentioned certain 'Genevan ideas,' and I failed to get it."

" 'Genevan ideas,' that's virtue without Christ, the French ideas of today or, rather, of today's entire civilization...In a word, this is one of those long stories which it is so boring to start <explaining>, my friend, ~~nor is it really worth~~ so let's rather talk of something else."

Versilov: "My friend, being the youth you are, you are dreaming of a resounding life, you desire to pick too conspicuous a lot—that of Napoleon the First, for example. But, you know these dreams are really something very primitive; and besides, that lot as such is ~~a fussy one~~ none too tempting, really: you are too much in the public eye, you must grimace and act, and pretend too much. Well, there are different tastes; simple freedom is certainly to be considered also."

"And mystery."

"What?"

"Mystery. Besides freedom, I also love mystery."

"Ahem. It may be that you've just said something very profound... Though on second thought, I may be wrong. By the way, you really do have some sort of an 'idea,' don't you?"

"Oh yes, but we'll discuss that later."

"That's right, later, let's do it later," [he agreed, apparently] very glad <to stop it right there>, "and you know what, I do happen to be in a great hurry, good-bye then."

The Youth asks: "What are you going to live on, having given away the inheritance?"

He didn't even ask that either.

Versilov: "I am one of the old, and I don't see any new men; and what I do see isn't serious."

About Dergachev: "These are the fruits of the bankruptcy of the old generation. We haven't passed on a single edifying thought, not even a single solid thought, to the new generation. Yet, all our lives, we were suffering from a thirst for great ideas. Well, what could I, for instance, pass on? I have nothing at all to pass on to you. I am a beggar myself. All my life I believed that I was rich, that I would never come to grief, and there, on the threshold of old age—I must beg my bread ~~beg my bread, beg my bread~~."

"The fools are many, but the wise men are few. The wise [always] go away, while the fools [always] stay behind."

Versilov: "It isn't that he is immoral, he's just an all-around scoundrel, though that is really a good thing."

"Why is it a good thing?"

"It fits him better... ~~It won't disturb~~ For harmony."

"Ah, my friend, we haven't got a nobility, and perhaps we never did have one."

"Yes, he is acting the role of a very solid citizen."

"In our society this is far from clear."

"I know only that I suddenly looked around, and found nothing."

"Did you look around only when you got to be forty?"

"Le temps n'y fait rien.[14] But, never mind, 40 years of age."

And besides, an insatiable appetite for life, for everything in life.

"He even talks in a taciturn manner."

"How's that—'talks in a taciturn manner'?"

"Well, there are some people whose talking is as good as silence."

"Yes, it is a felicitous expression."

"Really, to talk the way we've been talking is just as good as remaining silent."

"Ever since the moment when I realized that I would never become a serious person, I have been determined..." etc.

"All this nervousness... Better let's be silent about something."

"My friend, remember that it is incomparably more advantageous to be silent, than to talk. And this is true in every single instance, without an exception. To be silent is good, safe, and beautiful—what more do you want?"

"Beautiful?"

"Of course. Silence is always beautiful, and a taciturn person is always beautiful; but more than anything else, it is to one's advantage."

"[Well,] that 'these stones be made bread'* ~~this~~ is a great idea."

"No, my friend, there's more to this idea than you might think.** It is a great idea, I won't argue that, but it is a secondary idea, and great only at a given moment. ["No, my friend, there's more to this idea than you might think. It is a great idea, I won't argue that."] ["But of course, all this is quite abstract."] A man will eat his fill and not think of it anymore; ~~what is~~ on the contrary, he will immediately say: "All right I have eaten my fill, and now, well, what

---

* Matt. 4: 3.

** Literally, "this idea has got a hook."

14 French: "Time doesn't have anything to do with it."

am I going to do now?' And so you are facing the same problem again: what should a man do?"

"Mankind always does it that way. It is incessantly thirsting for a great idea. But the moment it is born ~~it laughs at it and, with all its force, tries to present~~ it considers it to be its duty to go right ahead and spit on it, and to put it down, below itself."

The Youth: "What, in general, are you calling a great idea?"

Versilov: "I don't know what, my friend. I only know that it has always been that thing from which real life flows, that is, ~~immediate~~ life that isn't of the intellect ~~but immediate not manufactured~~, that isn't made up ~~in other words~~, and ~~not~~, but beautiful, cheerful, and never boring; so that a great idea ~~is great because~~, from which all of this ~~this~~ emanates—[a great idea is absolutely essential for every society,] to everybody's chagrin, of course."

"Why chagrin?"

"Because it is boring to be living with ideas, whereas without ideas ~~well always~~ it is more cheerful ~~and incomparably more comfortable~~."

[The Prince swallowed his pill.]

"And what, in your opinion, is real life" (he was apparently getting angry).

Versilov: ~~Versilov: Real life~~ "I don't know that either, [my ~~friend~~ dear Prince,] I only know that it ought to be something awfully simple [and even] trivial, something that would catch your eye every day and every minute and so simple we couldn't possibly believe that the whole thing was so ~~easy~~ simple, and so, quite naturally, we keep walking by it, already for many thousands of years, ~~even~~ without noticing it ~~let alone~~ or recognizing it."

He had some amazing ideas about nihilism, for instance ~~says the Youth~~. Once, I remember, I told him:

"The sequel of nihilism is going to be idealism."

Versilov: "On the contrary, my friend, on the contrary, the sequel of our nihilism is going to be the most salutary and the most sobering positivism, for nihilism itself [is] nothing but idealism, but only in the very highest, and so far unheard of, degree. Nihilism is the ultimate stage of idealism."

"My friend, I am not drawing any definitive conclusions because I do not want to pass judgment on anyone."

"Why don't you?"

"I don't know why, but I have an aversion against it. A certain wise woman has told me that I haven't the right to pass judgment, because I don't know how to suffer, and, in order to be a judge <of other

people>, 'one must acquire the right to be a judge by one's own suffering.' It sounds a little pompous, but, if applied to me, it may be true."

"It's awful how you always speak in such abstract terms."

"So don't bother me with your questions."

Versilov: "There isn't one honest man among a hundred thousand."

"I know one."

"Who would it be?"

"He is sitting right here and talking to me."

Versilov (whispering in his ear): "He is lying." (He gets up and leaves.)

Having only a single idea. People who have a single idea.

"Our nihilists? Don't tell me this is a pure type, something equable and stable! It certainly is not! I had a premonition of what they'd be like even before they actually appeared, and, I must admit, they are exceeding my expectations. A real nihilist cannot, must not, dare not get reconciled to anything at all that is now in existence. He dare not make any deals, under any circumstances, and he knows full well that no deal is in effect possible. Well, and now ours: where's the negation in our nihilists? With them, even the negation of religion is turned into religion. Their whole nihilism is nothing but a passionate faith; ~~something medieval~~. These people are perpetually praying, they are monks and hermits. There is something medieval about them, with the same kind of blind and passionate authority. Naturally, I'm speaking of nihilists only, and not of scoundrels, or of people who are doing business with this idea. There is an awful lot of businessmen among this group, though even more are mere fools, granted that the latter don't count, for they are of no consequence."

["One must believe <in> God. Eh, the devil. And if I don't believe in God? A very fine sign of that idea. How come, very fine?"]

"[That atheist] The Russian atheist, if only he is a genuine atheist, and a little bit intelligent, is always inclined to show a real affection for God, for he is invariably [also] a kind person, being kind for the reason that he is immeasurably satisfied with his being an atheist. To our atheist, atheism is a source of honor and enjoyment, and certainly not of suffering. They are really fine people, honorable and loyal in the highest degree, the pillars of the fatherland, so-to-speak."

"Pillars of the fatherland? Come on, you're letting your tongue run away with you!"

"You are all wrong! Why, that liberal of ours is really a most conservative person—and it has always been that way, which happens to be a fact well known for a long time to those...who take a [special] interest in these things."

"We have survived the Tartar invasion, then two centuries of ~~invasion~~ slavery, solely because ~~this~~ one as well as the other really happened to be to our liking. Now we must survive freedom. But are we going to make it? Will it be to our liking, I mean freedom?"

"In your opinion, what is philosophy?"

"Philosophy, my friend, that's something about the laws of the essence of things, where 'essence' must be absolutely and ~~Eh, we know that~~ under any circumstances above human reason, and this for the sole reason that man may seek to define it all his life, without succeeding in so doing. ~~This is, so to speak, an advanced version of blindman's buff.~~ Moreover, it is absolutely necessary that man should never discover anything about the essence <of things>: it is more seemly that way, and that's what this thing is all about. This is, in a manner of speaking, an advanced version of blindman's buff—that's all there is to it."

"What do you think of progress?"

"That whole progressive movement of ours during the past 15 to 20 years has shown, more than anything else, that we are terribly uneducated."

"If there weren't any misfortunes, life wouldn't be worth living."

"You know what, sometimes you are a terrible reactionary," says the Youth.

"My friend, I couldn't care less."

"Why then, didn't you come yesterday?"

"Well, I was afraid that you might give me a tongue-lashing."

N.B. The Youth tells him about his virginity. (He is telling him about the dangers of fornication: "Abstain!" This makes the Youth angry.)

N.B. The Youth remembers that, at their first meeting, He very nearly began to cry.

Versilov: "But, my friend, this very dullness may sometimes make a woman attractive. 'A foolish woman is good also,' says Iaichnitsa.* This isn't really the same thing, but the most depraved creature may sometimes be more attractive than an angel. But if she is dull, and unfair <to you>, so much more so, once she has had an impact on your feeling."

---

* In Gogol's comedy *The Marriage*.

"You are corrupt to the marrow of your bones, that's what."

"May be this is so; like all Russians, by the way."

Versilov, to the Youth: "My friend, I am not trying to tempt you with some kind of bourgeois virtue, offering it as a substitute for your ideals, nor am I trying to tell you that happiness is superior to heroism. On the contrary, my dear, heroism is superior to any sort of happiness, and the very ability to be a hero is a token of happiness. It is precisely for this that I respect you, as well as for the fact that you've got some kind of an 'idea of your own.' (Don't worry, I remember it only too well.) Yet in spite of all this, one must not forget to retain a sense of measure, for right now you wish to set fire to something, to smash something to pieces, to elevate yourself above all Russia, to sweep past like a storm cloud, leaving everybody behind in fear and in wonder, and then withdraw into the desert, or to the United States of America. I'm sure that something of this kind is going through your mind, which is why I'm considering it necessary to warn you, for I've grown sincerely fond of you, my dear."

"Have you told this to your children?"

"No, I do not intend to ask for their permission."

"And what is most important, don't fall too much in love with yourself."

N.B. "But what if she hates you?"

"No, she adores me, and it is I who doesn't like her."

"But she won't admit it."

"Give her time; maybe she'll get wise enough to admit it to herself."

N.B. She is bashful.

"If she is bashful, what kind of a Messalina can she be?"

"You wouldn't understand it."

The Youth: "How come you, *being a Christian,* praise me for my hatred, and encourage me to persist in my hatred?"

Versilov: "My friend, what I am praising is merely the fact that, in this jellylike age of ours, you were able to experience a profound feeling, to nurture it within yourself, and not abandon it. You say that I am encouraging you to persist in your hatred, don't you? But perhaps you don't as yet know yourself that, hidden below your hatred, there is even more love (just as, vice versa, many a love is really hidden hatred). You are still going through a certain phase in your development; wait a bit, you'll enter the next phase, and see things more clearly. I don't want to stop you from doing anything, since I believe in the principle [sticking to the principle] 'live and work yourself.' At any rate, I am not your nursemaid; live as best you can, and do what you think is best for you."

The Youth about the Princess: "That woman was worrying me. Once she crossed my path, she would have to follow me; no one stops me on my way with impunity."

Versilov: "It is impossible to love people the way they are. And yet, one must love them. And therefore, do good unto them, checking your emotions, holding your nose, and closing your eyes (the latter being almost inevitable). Suffer the evil they will do to you without getting angry with them, remembering if ever you can [keeping in mind] that you are, after all, a man, too. Naturally, it is your duty to be stern with them. People are base, they like to love ~~and to adore~~ from fear; so they will adore you, too. Do not succumb to their adulation, do not prove to be petty, and continue to despise them. Keep despising them even when they are good, for this is precisely where, more often than not, they are at their worst. Without any doubt, Christ couldn't have loved them: he put up with them, he forgave them, but, quite naturally, he ~~also~~ despised them. Personally, at least, I cannot understand his personality otherwise. Love of mankind must be held in suspicion, ~~in the ideal~~ toward a perfected <mankind>, one which exists ~~only~~ ideally, that is, in your soul, one that perhaps [probably] [most likely] will never come into existence—though, let this be said, this circumstance should in no way interfere with any of this."

"It will never ~~?~~ happen."

"My friend, I agree that this [apparently] is rather stupid, but this is not my fault; my opinion was not heard at the creation of this world, which is why I reserve the right to have my own opinion."

"After all this, how is it possible that people are calling you a Christian, a monk who wears chains, and a preacher?—I can't understand it."

"And who is it that has said these things of me?"

I told him, and he listened most attentively. But our conversation had come to an end.

"You know what, it is precisely you [however] who is a fanatic."

It was in a strange way that he spoke about <his> contempt for people. Even his eyes were flashing, and yet at the same time I did not believe him, for it couldn't be that he would talk to me so seriously about such things."

"Why do you love me so?" He suddenly says to the Youth.

Here: "If you want to, quit your job with the old Prince."

Versilov, at the end of part four, after the Youth has been telling him about the Akhmakov woman: "Let me kiss you just once—come to think of it, I haven't ever kissed you yet!"

"A lawyer is a hired conscience."

"Everything has a limit, even our all-Russian stupidity, which is nevertheless boundless."

He: "What we are having everywhere is *lazy atheism.*"

He: "Meaning: *Chacun chez soi* and *chacun pour soi;*[15] and ~~that~~ what will come of it, will come."

The Youth: "I rushed over and started kissing the spot on which she had been sitting. I wouldn't have admitted that at confession."

The Youth: "I was engulfed by disorder ever more and more."

The Youth: "I felt that He, too, had his 'own idea.' "

He: "I am one who denies everything, and I am desperate about not having anything to grasp at, yet at the same time I am attached to everything. Any nihilist, as long as he is not stupid, must think that way and feel that he is attached to everything. And as for the fact that people kill themselves with ease, ~~it decidedly~~ it really happens because it is the easiest thing to do and, [what is most important,] does not ask for too much thinking power."

He: "My friend, I dislike having to expound anything at great length; what I like is to believe quietly in my own idea and to be silent about it. <In this respect> I am a lot like you. And here is another strange thing: whenever it happens that I begin to expound an idea of mine, an idea in which I believe, I swear it to you, it almost invariably happens that by the time I am through with my explanation, I have quit believing in whatever I had been explaining, even though I'd been believing in it for three years. Later, if I continued to support that particular idea, it would be, so to speak, out of a sense of responsibility only. [Well, this is why I much prefer to feel, rather than to formulate."]

The Youth: "My God, how many things you're telling me there, all of which require some thought, and which I had suspected even before."

"Not a grain of truth."

"What kind of a nobility is this? This isn't any nobility anymore, but rather some sort of a masonic lodge, the kind about which you were sermonizing this oaf the other day."

---

15 French: "Everyone at home. Everyone for himself."

"That is, ~~the whole~~ all of freemasonry, [the whole idea,] and not [just one] lodge, i.e., [the whole idea,] and not to any oaf, but to a person well capable of honorable feelings."

"I am sorry, not to any oaf, for I am no better than he is; but then, in that case, ~~this is merely~~ we really haven't got any kind of nobility, nor have we probably ever had one, if it must be thusly reformulated, isn't that so? And besides, can it really exist in this form? Hardly, except with constant and innumerable exceptions, wouldn't you say so?"

~~"It did exist before Peter <the Great>, and precisely in the sense I was sermonizing about today."~~

~~"Hardly, except with innumerable exceptions. Fie! What impossible things you are bringing up!"~~

"What exceptions? Exceptions pass on and come to an end, and they mean nothing, as long as there is a pivot, as long as there is but the tiniest light, shining in the deepest darkness. The tiniest fire can give birth to a universal conflagration. You have exactly the same thing ~~here~~ with an idea—one fiery spot in the deepest darkness, [provided it is not extinguished.] However, you are making me tired... Let us leave all these things, I beg you, and you know what, let's leave them for good."

~~In the West, kings and emperors always were no more than the leaders of victorious parties, at first the knights against the plain people, later the cities against the knights, and so on. Our Czar has been something entirely different.~~

" 'And the light shineth in darkness; and the darkness comprehended it not.'* And so it has been at all times, and with all great ideas. However, my friend, you are making me tired..." etc. (N.B. Right here, also: *About, "what I explain to somebody, I quit believing."*) I.e.: "You ought to have compassion with me, an old man, and spare my feelings..."

And so he was always getting off the hook, as a result of which it was difficult to determine if he had said these things in all seriousness, the other day when he was talking to the Prince, or just to be diplomatic. I was inclined to believe that he had been pursuing some political end.

The one of them, all fancy and enthusiasm, and all but saying: "Why won't you let me make this up, and you'll see how fine it will come out, and what a pleasure it's going to be <for you to listen>."

---

* From John 1: 5.

And the other, all prose, all spleen and bad manners: "No, I won't let you make up anything!"—"But for goodness' sake, my friend"—he got to talking about that rock—"why, that rock is still there; I guess it's on Malaia Millionnaia Street, and was never dropped into any hole." But I didn't take him up on it, I said nothing, out of tact, out of gentlemanliness, out of embarrassment, ~~for the reason that I wouldn't be~~ for aesthetic <considerations>, so-to-speak, for if I had acted otherwise, what sort of a gentleman would I have been after that?"

"Oh, my God, that's what I mean, it is standing right there even now."

"Well, yes, it's standing there all right, for this is really a delightful anecdote: 'and so things got before the Emperor.' "

"Why, his soul must have been overflowing with joy during that moment when he was presenting ~~his ideal~~ his hero to the Emperor."

"Always let the other man tell a small lie, it is quite innocent. Even let him tell a big lie. First of all, this will only show your tact, and secondly, they'll let you tell your own lies in return—two tremendous advantages at the same time. *Que diable,*[16] one must love one's neighbor."

"In exactly the same way you may repeat the witticisms of Prince Menshikov and the one about *voilà Monsieur, qui se leva* (Kiselev, that is). However, this one is a bit more genteel. All this survived to my own time. In fact, it exists even to this very day."

"Or the one about Zavialov, whom the British offered a million for not putting his label on his goods."

"My friend, there will always be an individuality, and the socialists have overlooked that."

"Make sure you won't dare tell any of these anecdotes—it is a most dishonorable thing to do—and once you've taken the first step in this direction you'll be drowned in that cesspool on your second step."

Also in part two, the Prince is having certain connections with Stebelkov, definitely something *suggestive* of what is going to come later, something that worries the Prince and makes him irritable; it is precisely at one of these moments that the Youth runs into him. In a word, make it so the reader will have a foreboding of the further developments (i.e., those Tambov shares). Also in the 2d half of part two, the Youth goes to see him for some money he'd like to borrow

---

[16] French: "What the hell."

from him, and—N.B: also without letting the reader know beforehand that he has been in contact with Stebelkov.

Versilov is discussing communism: "It will start right here, in Moscow. There won't be any firewood left to heat homes, so there will be communal dwellings, and people will quit leading a family life. As a result of which, new customs are going to develop—etc.," in a mocking, lampooning mode.

The Youth starts that hellish night thinking of Lacenaire.[17]

Drop a few ~~things~~ words in those conversations with Versilov to suggest that the ideals of Lacenaire, etc., are present in the Youth's mind.

Ungern-Shternberg,[18] *maybe,* in part three.

In the second half of part two, the Youth's eyes are suddenly opened to Liza: he intercedes and is rebuffed by the Prince.

A series of forceful witticisms on the occasion of his winning at roulette.

[At Anna Andreevna's. About El <ena> P <avlov> na.]

The Prince is an idealist. He is still fascinated by Versilov, but is no longer under His influence. He is a single-minded person: either the full truth, or you're a scoundrel. He is sullen, sarcastic, and a fiery seeker of truth and beauty. "I am my own judge." He dislikes the Youth because he is taking money from him (selling Liza). "Versilov —why isn't He himself a man who lives what He preaches?" Versilov's idea about the nobility does not strike him as something impossible: he believes in it as if it were a trivial everyday thing; but "why isn't He like this himself?" he says to the Youth. It is precisely this idea that the Youth registers even as early as the 1st half of part two. The Youth is asking himself this question: "What is it that makes Versilov fall short?" and he *conveys this question* to Versilov (in his confession). The Prince won't say: *"What is it that makes him fall short?"* But in the second half of part two he says to the Youth: "He was making me run after the Akhmakov woman, and I could see that he was doing it with a purpose." About the Akhmakov woman, he says: "I wouldn't have her for nothing now ~~but~~, after I've found out what a treacherous

---

[17] Dostoevsky, as co-editor with his brother of the journal *Vremia,* published in 1861 an article on the trial of Pierre François Lacenaire, a thief and murderer. It is clear that what fascinated Dostoevsky was Lacenaire's emotional indifference to the suffering of others and the worth of life. When Lacenaire left the courtroom, he said, "My life to me is worth as much as a five sous piece."

[18] See note 3 of Part II.

person she is, but why did she betray me?" *The betrayal lies in the same as with El<ena> Pav<lov>na.**[19] The fact that he has become involved in that business with the shares worries and irritates him, but he doesn't even suspect that Stebelkov, whom he hates, will dare to implicate him as his accomplice. However, Stebelkov tells him so in the second half of part two. The Prince shows him the door, but is frantic himself and would even like to shoot himself. He has a liaison with Liza, but he wouldn't even think of marrying her ("I'm a Prince, after all!"). But Liza, in the 2d half of part two, lets him know that she is pregnant. ~~Later~~ He, in turn, lets the Youth know about it, and there is a scene between Liza, him, and the Youth in the 2d half of part two. Then he declares this to the Youth: "You've been selling your sister to me, you've been taking my money," and kicks him out. "I'm my own judge, no one else will be." The Youth bitterly and insultingly reproaches Liza. What amazes him more than anything else is the fact that Liza takes it to be *quite unthinkable* that she could become the Prince's wife. It is at this point that he runs to see Stebelkov about some money. The latter refuses to loan him any money, but gives him 300, suggesting that he exploit the old Prince. The Youth is reduced to such straits that he apparently agrees (this is the idea involving Anna Andreevna) ~~right here, too~~ (to let her marry the young Prince). What happens is that Stebelkov is offering Anna Andreevna to the Prince, which would mean a healthy commission for him, and a dowry from the Prince. Stebelkov is very friendly to the Youth, in part two, but when the latter comes to him for some money he offers him 100 at first, then 300, and finally even 1,000, but the Youth yells: *"with no conditions attached!"* <This,> in order to quiet his conscience, though he is in effect accepting the other's terms. (But the Prince rejects Anna Andreevna?) But when Anna Andreevna comes up with her *tour de force,* Stebelkov is beginning to threaten <the Prince>. Whereupon the Prince himself reports everything to the police: "I am demanding to be punished, to be punished!" But he is acquitted. He would have liked to shoot himself, but he feels sorry for Liza. It is she who saves him. "I'll be tilling the soil." Etc.

The Prince discusses noble and ignoble vices with the Youth.

The Prince to Liza: "If you're going to drown yourself, I'll shoot myself."

---

* The Russian sentence is ungrammatical.

[19] See note 48 of Part IV.

And later, after the trial: "How are you going to marry me, a vile convict?"

"But you've been acquitted!"

"It doesn't matter, I'm still a convict. You can't marry me."

But Liza saves him. The Aide-de-Camp, the old Prince, and everybody else show their concern. He says that he won't need any money, "<give me> a few acres of land, I'll be tilling the soil," and then, having made this decision, he suddenly shoots himself.

"The world is in disorder," the Prince keeps repeating all the time.

After he has shot himself, the mother says to Liza: *"Bear it!"*

[Versilov, cute expressions.]

"The ideal is as real as everything real," says Versilov.

"The most ~~intimidated~~ intimidated crowd, even it..." etc.

March 5.

[1st half of part two.]

A series of points.

General information concerning clothes, the Prince, Versilov, the flat, and the reconciliation. Accounts. Nobility. ~~The Akhmakov woman.~~ Conversations. Puzzlement and Liza. ~~Card games.~~ The Akhmakov woman. At night, with his mother. Spinoza.[20] With Versilov, told him about the Akhmakov woman. Pushed off a sleigh. Playing cards. General information in narrative form. The rest in scenes.

[First half of part two.]

[Slander against the Akhmakov woman.] November 15. First I shall tell in brief how this all happened. Then, the scenes of November 15. On the nobility, etc. (and, along with the scenes, explanations). Prior to the rendezvous, as He is waiting <for her>, this story, too <?> (i.e., how it all started with the Akhmakov woman), in narrative form, then, on to the end, up to where he wins all the money. [Not a word about the Akhmakov woman, right up to the very rendezvous.] A conversation about the Aide-de-Camp (in this scene). First meeting with the Akhmakov woman at the old Prince's. Prior to that scene, a whole chapter. The first chapter is about how it all came about. The 2d chapter—the nobility. The Prince. Visitors. Liza. Accounts, puzzlement. The Akhmakov woman slandered. Versilov does not, in his presence, discuss the Akhmakov woman with the Prince. The 3d chapter is about how it all happened with the Akhmakov woman, and a scene with her (about the Aide-de-Camp), kiss. 4th. At night,

---

[20] See note 3 of this section.

at his mother's. Spinoza. With Versilov, an admission concerning the Akhmakov woman. ~~Shoved off~~ 5th. Playing cards. How it happened, and what *came of it*. They give him some gold, quarrel with the Prince. About the idea, dreams, as he falls asleep.

N.B. After each of the first two conversations, the Akhmakov woman had forgotten about him. It was he himself who was trying to catch her attention, obtaining information, etc.

About how I developed a crush on the Akhmakov woman, and at this point, a story. How he got together with the Akhmakov woman, [with Anna Andreevna] ("I shall be at Tatiana Pavlovna's tomorrow"). But keep in mind that the reader shouldn't hear a word about the rendezvous, <for> the reader hears of the rendezvous quite suddenly, toward the end of this, the 3d chapter, and <without> any preliminary information. 4th chapter, the rendezvous, and his mother (Spinoza), with Versilov, an admission concerning the Akhmakov woman, etc. And chapter 5. "I am late": and straight on to the drinking spree, in scenes, without *forewarning* the reader, and only after he has won all that money, only a few words about how he got sidetracked. Here: at home, a quarrel with the Prince, he returns the money, enthusiasm, daydreams and the oppressive idea that he has been sidetracked. Don't forget about Anna Andreevna's flat.

And so: about <his> clothes, and about the 1,000—however, *without any explanation*—then, after his quarrel with the Prince on account of <his> slander of the Akhmakov woman—the story how he and the Akhmakov woman got together, but *without any mention* of the rendezvous. Later, dinner at his mother's, but prior to that, *not a word* about <his> relationship with the family, and, finally, he is late to the card game, and the card game without any *comments*.

In the 1st part <of> chapter two, about the Prince in detail, and after Versilov, there is a touching scene between them, as they get things straightened out between each other, and are reconciled. Later, a hint regarding the Akhmakov woman. The Prince falls to thinking (about the Akhmakov woman).

It is already after he has won all that money that there is a real quarrel between him and the Prince on account of the Akhmakov woman. He returns home for the night, recalls certain equivocal statements at the gambling house (a few insulting words, and persons), about the Akhmakov woman and the Prince, about "his own idea"—about the document. He is drunk, his head is going round.

About the fact that Versilov hardly ever mentioned the Akhmakov woman at all.

By November 15 all of my suspicions had become stronger.

In the narrative part, how he got together with the Akhmakov woman; he relates some details, what he's been telling her about Versilov and, in chapter four, some information about Versilov also, an announcement, and precisely on the current state of affairs (about the document, a quarrel on account of the document, as well as the Aide-de-Camp and the Prince). (N.B. Make it so the Akhmakov woman won't appear to be too clearly inquisitive <about the document>.)

At his mother's. With Versilov, and then the gambling episode. At the gambling house, the Prince's betrayal <of the Youth> *as an actual fact.* They quarrelled about the Akhmakov woman.

So then, the plot of part two is this: the descriptive part aside, how the Youth got involved in a card game, and how he fell in love with the Akhmakov woman.

N.B. Develop some kind of a scene in which Olia's mother comes to see him: "I have no one to turn to," and suddenly she begins to cry and presses herself against him.

He meets Liza somewhere in the street (the Stolbeev woman has left).

"Why are you taking money from him?"

Back home, Olia's mother drops in on him, begins to cry.

He walks over to the roulette game.

Everything ~~in narrative~~ in scenes, November 15.

Only in the beginning, for half a chapter, Versilov.

The scene with the Akhmakov woman *without any preliminary comments.* At Tatiana Pavlovna's flat.

She—I am waiting for her. "I, for a whole month <. . .> I am giving you information. Who do you think I am, a *petit espion*?[21] ~~You know that there is no letter.~~ Who am I to you?"—"A dear boy"—about the Aide-de-Camp. She captivates him. He kisses the floor.

N.B. In one scene, without preliminary comments. He leaves intoxicated.

THE VERY LAST PAGE. Final <and> correct composition. March 7/8, in scenes.

November 15. The flat. Versilov. By way of narrative. Brought him together with the Prince. A point of contact ~~with~~ <is found in> the child and Lidiia—[and so on.] ~~This story later. I knew what he was~~

---

[21] French: "Little spy."

~~like *during that period* only from the Prince's accounts. I was convinced of only one thing, namely that it was precisely this thing that was weighing upon Versilov's soul, and was serving as a point of contact with the Akhmakov woman.~~ How then, did all this happen? The story of my disgrace. In scenes, at the Prince's. Versilov, nobility. Versilov is gone. "I am an ignoramus, I know nothing." Our tirade, and comments. Warm. 500 rubles. Better not take them, let it go at that. Stebelkov and after him, Baron Ditrin. [The Prince is afraid of Stebelkov.] Talks about a bank, "why not start a roulette?" News of the Aide-de-Camp. The Prince, a sharp word about the Akhmakov woman. He leaves. Stebelkov also leaves. Conversation about the Akhmakov woman. The Youth becomes persistent, an insulting word of His, directed at the Youth. Wants to return the money. "Take it." (They leave, having kissed each other.)

~~He runs across Liza.~~ Liza, at Anna Andreevna's: "Why are you taking money from him?"

"Here, give it back to him." "Lizochka, I have hurt you." (And here, a few words on his own behalf: "Yes! I had been neglecting <her>.) Perhaps much of this will be forgiven me; I wasn't quite myself: the Akhmakov woman!"

["Why should I be at Tatiana Pavlovna's tomorrow, why not at my own place?"]

Rendezvous scene with the Akhmakov woman. A full explanation. (The whole art.) The Youth would like to make an admission, but hasn't the courage to go through with it. About the Prince, about Lidiia. A firm conviction that the only thing on Versilov's conscience is Lidiia. The Aide-de-Camp. (Enter Tatiana Pavlovna.) She leaves. He kisses her tracks. Tatiana Pavlovna.

Home in an enthusiastic mood. (Have dinner at mother's.) Tatiana Pavlovna is there. Spinoza. With Versilov, told him about the Aide-de-Camp. Confessed about the Akhmakov woman. Versilov, a few words about the Akhmakov woman (but certainly none of the kind that would presage his crazy sally). At home. Olia's mother comes to see him. ~~She began to cry at the Akhmakov woman's.~~ She had had a good cry at the Akhmakov woman's. The drinking spree, roulette, winning. Settled accounts with the Prince. Quarrelled <with him>. At home—a palpitating heart. Intoxicated. A message for Anna Andreevna. "Why are you gambling?"

Visited Anna Andreevna, to find out about the Prince, since <he> hadn't been in that day. A whole scene. N.B. Give this some more thought.

And then, home. Olia's mother.

"Why do you love me?" He pressed <me> to his heart.

"No, I won't be seeing you." And this, at such a moment.

"I won't ever forget it."

Last page.

N.B. "I shall be at Tatiana Pavlovna's tomorrow."

"At what time?"

"At three."

All the time, while they were talking, he was waiting for her to mention the letter. (She didn't!) Why here, and not at his own place?

"Just for charm," (Versilov says to him).

In the evening, after he had made his admission to Versilov, the latter started questioning him: "How did it work out?" By way of narrative. "No, I'm not going to speak ill of her." And at this point, a detailed narrative account of how he got together with the Akhmakov woman. [Being fully convinced that Versilov does not love her.] Then, to himself: "What have I been doing! What have I done!" (i.e., having told Him).

Furthermore, he goes to see Anna Andreevna before <seeing> the Akhmakov woman, at half past one, and meets Liza at her place. (N.B. At Anna Andreevna's, regarding a possible match with the Prince. A description of his character.) ~~Another word~~ At Anna Andreevna's, he talks freely, but is rather depressed. "Ever since I got to know you," etc. [N.B. About Anna Andreevna, in more detail.] Why is Liza here? But still another rendezvous. And here, a scene with the Akhmakov woman. At night, when he makes that admission to Versilov, he is presenting it *as if he were in a hurry,* but it turns out quite detailed.

Most important. N.B. Liza is at Anna Andreevna's in order to find out (spy out) everything about Versilov, i.e., *first of all,* whether or not he might be capable of proposing marriage to the Akhmakov woman. Anna Andreevna confirms the news about the Aide-de-Camp to the Youth. The Youth tells her outright that Versilov wouldn't even think of being in love with the Akhmakov woman.

"But what about her?" asks the Youth.

"Her?" answers Anna Andreevna, "I don't know."

"Can there really be any doubt here?" the Youth shouts.

[Why is Liza at her place? "I swear, I knew from the very beginning that she is *keeping* us here just to get something out of us."]

[As for Olia's mother, she has come to talk about the infant child.]

And then, the rendezvous scene.

The very last page.

Versilov, after the confession: *"Why is it you love me so?"* Later: Didn't he go over to the infant child's himself, and find Olia's mother there, *a scene?* And from there, on to the roulette.

And so there is hope: if told in a brief narrative, sticking to the most essential, it ought to turn out well enough.

The Youth ~~to the Akhmakov woman~~ to Anna Andreevna, about Lidiia: "If you only knew, if you only knew what Lidiia means!" *His* heart is bleeding.

*The Akhmakov woman:** "Who told you?"

The Youth: "Tatiana Pavlovna."

Anna Andreevna confuses the Youth by telling him that Versilov is in love with the Akhmakov woman. He has a showdown with the Akhmakov woman and is told about the Aide-de-Camp in no uncertain terms.

Versilov, to him, about his blushing. (This is in the beginning.)

The Youth says: "We only had a couple of showdowns: the one about my blushing, and then that other one about..." See.

[Most important] The Youth, as he makes his confession about the Akhmakov woman to Versilov: "I was sitting there, not knowing how I was hurting his feelings." "Why is it you love me?" I shall never forget it. *A tirade.*

Or: He was terribly calm. I can remember all the details.

~~In the 2d half of part two, the Youth's eyes are suddenly opened to Liza.~~

[Not necessary. Quite the contrary] The Youth admits: "Well, I did have a vague and remote notion that He loved her. For a moment there, I wanted to shout to Him (more gracefully): 'All right, so love her, I shall go away and...' "

Versilov** asks: "Why the rendezvous at Tatiana Pavlovna's?"

Versilov says: "You know what, my friend, she was there! I entered through the rear door, and there she was, in the kitchen."

The Youth to the Akhmakov woman, about the Prince: "This is a man who has only one idea." Actually, the Akhmakov woman is afraid of a scandal on his part, because she is greatly concerned about not losing the Aide-de-Camp, who is a truly brilliant match.

The Youth's meeting with the Akhmakov woman takes place, *maybe,* at the old Prince's.

---

* Apparently a mistake; should be: "Anna Andreevna."

** Apparently an error; should be: "The Youth."

[*Or better*]—at Tatiana Pavlovna's, mostly because the Aide-de-Camp arrives and the Youth quarrels with him, announcing that he won't be coming back.

~~Besides~~ The Akhmakov woman is herself afraid that somebody might disturb them. But most of all, in order to flatter the Youth with the notion of a rendezvous. The Youth understood that she had talked things over with Tatiana Pavlovna beforehand. (The latter was sitting in the kitchen!) And subsequently, the Youth learns that Tatiana Pavlovna had actually been present.

Both are convinced, after this meeting, that the Youth hasn't got the document. The Youth lets the reader know about this detail beforehand.

~~The Youth~~ The Prince says to the Youth: "Seeking to support my princehood, I did some gambling and got stuck."

The Youth: "To support one's princehood isn't such a base thing; rather, it is a thousand-year-old debt."

"This seems to you that way," says the Prince, "because you... (i.e., aren't of princely blood). Admit that you would like to be a Prince."

N.B. This, either toward the end of the 1st half of part two, or toward the end of part two.

"There is disorder in society," the Prince keeps repeating. "You yourself are the product of nothing but disorder," he tells the Youth.

"You haven't even managed to formulate this."

"What you've got isn't logic, what you've got is some sort of an emotion," says the Youth to the Prince. "You aren't able to refute Versilov's idea, and so you're merely saying: 'Why isn't He like that himself?' This is your logic, but this is rubbish, not logic. He could actually be evil himself, but at the same time He could be telling us the loftiest truth."

"No, this isn't so at all," replies the Prince, "if you are telling a lofty truth, be a righteous man yourself."

"Let's not talk about this. You seem somehow unhappy. Tell me, what is it you're accusing Versilov of?"

The Prince won't answer, but says: "I slapped his face, which only ties me down. But I don't know if I still have a right to suffer this tie (string) to exist."

"So this is it. Why didn't you say that? I would have let him know about it."

"Well, I'm suffering you to be around, am I not?" says the Prince.

The Prince says: "I've received a letter—my younger brother has died in Moscow, my father is decrepit and can no longer have any children, and I've got only two sisters left. This means that in my person, the family of the Princes Sokolsky, a family that traces its lineage from Riurik, is coming to an end."

Old Prince Sokolsky, though from a more recent branch of the family, does not have any children.

[*Most important.*] Stebelkov says: "His younger brother died. The old Prince has no children. Prince Sergei is the only representative <of the family>. If he were to marry ~~the Akhmakov woman~~ Anna Andreevna, the old Prince <might give> him his entire fortune to preserve the family—that's an idea!"

The Youth, definitely and even several times, repeats to himself: "I've behaved very badly, I've been making some bad jokes, a lack of discipline. I've been coming to the Prince's, *as if I were living there.* I've been talking to his friends, as if they were my own acquaintances."

In this first half, too, the Youth says a few words to Stebelkov, even though these are arrogant words.

When Ditrin is about to leave, Stebelkov tells him that they haven't received that forged promissory note.

Stebelkov takes the Prince *à part* and says something to him (he is trying to scare him).

Anna Andreevna has summoned the Youth decidedly in order to question him about the Prince.

The Youth has an appointment with Stebelkov. "I can always give you some. Money. You get one half. To provide for your sister." The Youth listens to what he has to say, but arrogantly so.

["Why won't you borrow it from me?"]

Stebelkov about the Prince: "He can also provide for *many others* (i.e., Liza)." When he said that thing about Liza, the Youth jumped to his feet and said, with indignation: "You are a scoundrel." "Well, forgive me, forgive me, I know nothing at all."

The rendezvous with Anna Andreevna. She actually had invited him herself, but as he was sitting there, she *was pretending* all along that he had dropped in accidentally, and persisted in this attitude to the very end. And finally, there was Liza.

With Liza, a mild scene before dinner.

"A hypochondriac!"

Or thus: "I had been asking Liza before. This is how it was. There is a little story to be told here." Liza said to him: "I am going to tell you all about myself, when the time comes for it. When the time comes for it—that's when I am going to tell you."

Stebelkov, as he is sitting at the Prince's, pretends that he absolutely didn't invite the Youth over.

The Youth is at Anna Andreevna's, and suddenly, right in the middle of the scene, he addresses the reader and says: "I am going to tell you right here, she was trying to find out from me... However, there was something indescribably charming about her."

In this particular scene with Anna Andreevna, express, in artistic fashion, the dissipated swagger of the Youth during that period of his success and good fortune.

N.B. Anna Andreevna and I met at the Prince's. [N.B.] Versilov showed a good deal of interest in what Anna Andreevna might have been doing at the Prince's.

Olia's mother had been wandering about in the streets for three hours: "I think I might go and see him, he is so kind. You will forgive me, won't you?" N.B. She had been seeing <me> even before, but very, very rarely.

Toward the end of the 1st half of part two, the Prince says to the Youth: "Come on, don't be angry, do not be ang-ry!"

~~Toward the end of the 2d half~~ The principal feature of part two is that the Youth keeps placing *himself in the foreground* all the time. He is by no means describing the adventures of ~~strange~~ the other characters, but precisely *his own adventures, nothing but his own,* and those of other people only insofar as they pertain to his own adventures.

In the 2d chapter of part one, the Youth, upon beginning to relate his meeting with the Prince, reveals that, even then, he was not trusting Versilov, and suddenly exclaims *abruptly:* "I can't understand how I could be visiting him then, at a time when I already knew so much, and, alas, at a time when I was already beginning to suspect a good many things. No, I shall never seek for any excuses!" And here: "My lack of discipline, I used to come to his place, as if I were living there," etc.

Very important. What was also tying the Prince to Versilov were the accounts <they had yet to settle>. This was greatly worrying him. He made a strong effort to induce Versilov to accept one half: "My father is mentally incapacitated and for 10 years has not been legally competent, my younger brother is dead, and I am alone now, but, imagine, I am not as yet capable of assuming possession. But one half I could not, for—after all, my mother wouldn't agree."* Versilov

* The last two sentences are unclear and ungrammatical in the original.

was taciturn when he met him, and he didn't mention it with a single word, so that the Prince could not but acknowledge his disinterestedness. (Meanwhile the Youth had already been taking advantage <of the situation> and had, little by little, received as much as three thousand <from the Prince.> The Prince says to the Youth: "Let Him have at least 20,000. I was going to get at least 10,000, and was calling for that rascal (Stebelkov), but he is trying to weasel out of it."

When the Youth comes to have dinner with his mother, he says, for the first time, that the *doors** of society have been opened to Versilov. Though he did show up at one or two places (I know this much), he continued to live at home.

March 8.

Stebelkov: "Look, this is the most important person around. Everywhere in the world, you have your number two man. There is number one, and there is number two, and it is number two who is the head man. Number one will be doing things, while number two will be taking things. Which means that number two is really number one, and that number one is really number two—you just watch it. [Is it, or isn't it so?"

The Prince was looking for something in a book.]

There was a revolution, and everybody was being executed. Then came Napoleon and took everything. The Revolution is the number one man, while Napoleon is the number two man. But then Napoleon became the number one man, while the Revolution became number two, isn't that so?

"Let's go," said the Prince. ~~having gotten up, the book.~~

My position.

[Return the 300 here] Already toward the end of part two, and during his ~~meeting~~ second meeting with the Youth, Stebelkov speaks of the impossibility of arranging a match between Anna Andreevna <and the Prince>, because of Liza's pregnancy—two sisters. This, the second time, he is already more firm and more frank. He has, however, gotten the idea that there might be the chance of a marriage between the old Prince and Anna Andreevna. (Whereas the latter has just been asking Versilov if he were in love with the Akhmakov woman.) And so on.

---

* Literally, "the houses."

~~Olia's mother: to come~~ "You could see that *I wasn't giving* you any signs."*

N.B. When Stebelkov is starting to tell the Youth (at their first meeting) about a possible match between the Prince and Anna Andreevna, the Youth cuts him short: *"I know about this idea."*

N.B. In this fashion, everything will come out in scenes, rather than in words. And then, when he goes to see Anna Andreevna, the Youth tells her about this idea of the old Prince's, about the old Prince and Anna Andreevna, how she met him at the Prince's. By chatting about the Prince while with her and maligning him, the Youth was unwittingly causing Liza great suffering.

N.B. Stebelkov has the idea that it might be possible to transfer the entire fortune of the old Prince to the young Prince, through the latter's marriage to Anna Andreevna, <thus> bypassing the Akhmakov woman.

Stebelkov suggests that the Youth help him to arrange this match for Anna Andreevna. An honorarium: if he could only exert some influence on the old Prince. Ruin the Akhmakov woman.

The idea of breadth.

The Youth to Stebelkov: "And you have the gall to believe that I'm going to work for the Prince for money!"

"Aren't you taking his money now?"

"How do you know that it isn't that <other> money, the money he owes to Versilov?"

"But... you aren't a Versilov, are you? Aren't you a Dolgoruky?"

Got angry: "What's the difference!"

March 10.

The most important about Liza.

The Youth knows nothing, and suspects nothing, about the Prince's relationship with Liza. Stebelkov did tell him something, but he failed to get it. "I was acting like a fool!" I kept exclaiming. He meets Liza at Anna Andreevna's, and insults her. At home ~~he talks,~~ before dinner, he talks to her upstairs, quite beside himself with delight, and make it so that Liza does already realize that he has insulted her, while he does not. And only later, after he has won all that money gambling, a hint by the Prince—still vague. Doubts; but his ecstasies over his winnings, and other ideas, are clouding <his judgment> altogether.

---

* The gender of the verb suggests a male speaker.

N.B. However, *the narrator* should mention, and make some hints (without going into the *circumstances*), that Liza has been there, and that she was *already then having an affair* with the Prince.

The most important about Versilov.

In the 1st chapter, His visit to the Youth's comes about somehow without any explanations. He did, for a moment, make a move to accompany him, but nothing was said. And this is why it so developed, from the very first step, that he got to be ashamed of asking any questions; though, on the other hand, he was having a despotic sway over him. And only toward the very end, after his confession about <that?> *woman:* "Why is it you love me so?" "Why, I was waiting for you for three full days then, knowing that you would come." He answers: "Well, thank you, thank you," etc. *in a more touching manner.* But after he has won all that money, he accuses Versilov of "having been keeping away from him and from Liza, and of not having been like a father at all," and all this because, the Youth adds, "I could see something wrong and something awkward (jealousy) about Versilov's reaction to my account of my contacts with the Akhmakov woman. I was only feeling it, though I wouldn't have ever admitted consciously, not at any cost, that all this was indeed the case!"*

Last and most important: during his confession, the Youth inadvertently almost lets out the secret of the document and, after having won all that money (in the 2d half of part two), he is terribly afraid that he may have actually let it out. Also in the 2d half, *there is a phrase,* a trait of Versilov's insulting tone toward the Akhmakov woman which, obscure as it might remain to the outsider, proves that Versilov has already guessed that the document is in the Youth's hands (He has found out about it from Tatiana Pavlovna).

N.B. When the Youth has been kicked out from the roulette place, he screams: "I'm telling you, I'll report ~~you~~ to the police, I'll get the police and tell them that you've got a roulette here!"

Versilov has not been seeing the old Prince.

The Youth, after he has won all that money, says to the Prince, when the latter, irritated and angry, gives him a *very slight* hint regarding Liza, which the Youth *fails to understand:* "What is it you are insinuating? What could my sister have to do with this?" The

* This sentence is not quite grammatical in the original.

Prince, with a malicious guffaw: "Nothing, of course, I just mentioned it, *on ne parle pas d'une corde...*"[22]

Stebelkov: "All right, all right. He could provide for many others."

"I don't want to."

"All right, so don't take it, very well, very well, [so don't take it] (even though you are taking money, too), but you aren't alone: he may provide for some *otherrrs,* too."

~~Versilov~~ "Why, you must be out of your mind!" He'll become a Versilov.*

Stebelkov is looking in his face, straight and for a long time: "You don't understand. [The other day I was mentioning that On<isim>-ovna lady, wasn't I?] Well, all right, all right. It's all right if you don't understand. If you actually don't understand, [that's really very good, I am very glad that I've found that out."]

["You don't say!] Well, you better leave me alone; really, to be bothering me with such trifles!"

"These aren't trifles. You are leaving? You know what, you're going to be back."

"No."

"You'll come... and then... Then, we'll have a different kind of discussion. We've had one discussion, but there will be another one, the main one."

Stebelkov. Also, Stebelkov definitely confirms, *by a hint* on his own part, that there exist unbreakable ties between him and the Prince, and even that he's got the Prince in his hands. Also, a hint about Dergachev.

March 12.

Actually, Stebelkov calls in the Youth in order to talk him into supporting the Prince's marriage to Anna Andreevna (the old Prince is to marry Anna Andreevna). Believing, mostly, that the Youth would be opposed to it on account of Liza, having, at the same time, [a certain] influence on all of the Princes. The Prince tells him that night: "Stebelkov promised that he was going to make you do it by giving you some money; did you take his money?"

N.B. In this 1st half of part two, Stebelkov isn't as yet too well acquainted with Anna Andreevna.

---

* Unclear in the original. The translations is questionable.

22 French: "One doesn't speak of a cord."

March 13.*

[Here] With insolent naïveté, Stebelkov makes the Youth feel that he is really *ashamed* of spending the Prince's money, for isn't the money really Versilov's?

"But I am a Versilov also."

"No, you are a Dolgoruky, and besides, since when do children dispose of sums belonging to their father?"

"Enough, enough!" (Arrogantly.)

Such a lesson, and from whom? From Stebelkov! I also knew that it was a vile thing to do, but I had to win, just win!

The Prince: "[Last night] Stebelkov promised that he was going to make you do it by giving you some money; [did you take his money?]"

At the end of the novel, the Prince says: "A few acres of land, not more, and I'll work <them> myself." And having made this decision, he shoots himself. He says, in his suicide note: "The Court has acquitted me, but I don't want their charity. I am putting an end to my life because it has become repulsive to me. After some initial pain, Liza's wound will heal, and she ~~is going to remember me~~ will remember me with a good feeling. But if I remained alive, I would ~~exhaust~~ torture and weary her heart, and she surely would have quit loving me, and instead, would have begun to loathe me. I know that she couldn't stand my character. Really, all of that time, I couldn't understand what it was that made her love me. The last moment. Liza's image is with me. Liza, farewell, and forgive me. Remember Lermontov's line: 'But in a better world, they failed to recognize each other.' "

Toward the end of the 2d half of part two, the Prince learns about Versilov's compromising letter ~~and~~ to the Akhmakov woman and, being awfully angry with the Youth, tells him that he has been selling his sister to him.

The Youth: "Was it you who called him an old wives' prophet?"

The Prince: "No, it wasn't I. I can recall this sobriquet, but it wasn't I <who invented it>. [I am not so good at putting labels on people.]"

The Youth: "Stebelkov tells me that it was you."

The Prince: "He is lying. It was he himself who gave Him that

---

* The original has "May 13," but this is wrong. It should be March rather than May, since this conversation with Stebelkov was printed in the April issue of the Journal.

name, I can remember. He was afraid to tell you that it was he."

The Prince was *worried*. Oh, at the time I could not as yet understand all that was causing his restlessness, not being aware of the facts, and therefore I was, quite naturally, getting on his nerves—either by my casual, easy tone, or by the insolence with which I was asking him certain questions.

It is necessary to insert some strong *hint*, suggesting that *something* is tying the Prince inseparably to Stebelkov. The Youth may simply say: "It appeared to me then, that the Prince was tied to him by something, inseparably and painfully, and that it was quite implausible how the Prince, who sometimes would be sick after having been with Stebelkov, would still tolerate his presence and steadfastly continue to receive him. However, I attributed all this to their financial dealings, since I knew only too well that Stebelkov was giving him money. The remaining instances of his perplexed and nervous behavior I attributed to the Prince's bad temper."

A certain change. March 12. About the Prince.

Stebelkov is instructing the Prince to marry Anna Andreevna; if otherwise, he is threatening <. . .> But the Prince is moved, (1) by his outraged pride, (2) in spite of everything, by his honest realization of Liza's condition, since, by now, she is pregnant, and (3) partly by a remote but mad hope to win the Akhmakov woman. Having learned from an important visitor that a marriage between the Aide-de-Camp and the Akhmakov woman is a possibility, The Prince flies into a rage. The Youth can see through all this and is infuriated by a few things the Prince says about the Akhmakov woman.

N.B. The Youth, for some reason, is in favor of ~~his~~ the Prince's marriage to Anna Andreevna. In the morning, the scene between them comes to a fortunate, though ambiguous, conclusion. "Why are you defending this lady?" asks the Prince. But that same night, the Prince gets mad and (after the Youth has won all that money) tells him of Liza's pregnancy, and that he <the Youth> has been accepting money for it. The Youth is crushed. The Prince's sarcasms ~~most important~~. Maybe, the Prince has been seeing Anna Andreevna and has proposed marriage to her, but has been rejected. That's why he is so furious. This is why, that night, he tells the Youth that he had been obliged to do this, otherwise he'd be lost, and so, for his scoundrelly action, he got this refusal. "But why 'scoundrelly action'?" exclaims the Youth. "Because Liza is pregnant," answers the Prince. Then the Prince, in the 2d installment of part two, wants to vie with the Aide-de-Camp. [In the 2d half of part two the Prince is seeking

Vasin's advice.] Besides, the Prince had been supremely confident that Anna Andreevna would immediately give her consent!

Or rather better, make it so the Prince *has not proposed* to Anna Andreevna and *Liza* is *delighted.* As for the Akhmakov woman, he is merely angry with her. And as for the Youth, he reproaches him for being in Stebelkov's pay. The Youth is furious, and the Prince holds up Liza's pregnancy to him. But in the 2d half of part two the Prince definitely wants to marry Liza. He is, however, secretly infuriated by Stebelkov's threats, and is himself threatening the latter to report the matter of the <forged> shares to the police. And he is the first to make a report (in part three). As for Stebelkov, it is he who, in part three, informs on the conspirators.

In the 2d half of part two, the Prince responds to the Youth's demands with haughty condescension. But in that scene with Liza, he does want to marry her, "but for this business, this business!" The Youth thinks that he is referring to his gambling losses, while the Prince is worried by the nagging thought that Stebelkov is threatening him. Meanwhile *there is some talk* ~~about~~ in society about the discovery of some forged <shares>, and in part three the Prince turns himself in.

[The Youth, to her about the Prince: "I love him, I love him. He had me enthralled later."]

Anna Andreevna had called him, mostly in order to ~~Liza~~ find out: Does He, or doesn't He love the Akhmakov woman? And there, the Youth says to himself: "Now I know that she, of course, called me in order to find out whatever she needs to find out. Without having dropped a single inadvertent word herself, she has gotten a lot of information out of me. *Oh, in those days many people were getting a lot of information out of me.* [With Versilov alone an exception.] I was serving as an *espion*[23] and kept letting out secrets all the time (out of the goodness of my heart). [But let me add one thing: I had nothing but the greatest contempt for her suspicion that Versilov might be in love with the Akhmakov woman;] it seemed both ridiculous and absurd to me, and—I swear it—I am saying this in all sincerity."

Anna Andreevna. When I had hotly disputed the notion that Versilov might be in love with the Akhmakov woman (and also <that rumor> about Lidiia), Anna Andreevna had been listening with

---

[23] French: "spy."

obvious satisfaction. (She was a marvelous listener.) She lowered her eyes when I was telling her Lidiia's story.

"It seems that you are on friendly terms with Mrs. Akhmakov."

"Oh, I've been seeing her."

"I know that you've been seeing her. Don't fall in love with her."

I blushed.

["You used to mention her with so much indignation, it's quite different now."

"A young and beautiful woman invariably elicits a feeling of indignation in a young man of your age."

"Why so?" etc.

"How clever you are, and how... experienced." (She blushed.) "Forgive me" (ardently). "But you are wrong. I felt indignant with this woman only because I was considering her to be an enemy of Versilov's. Versilov. He was spreading the rumor that she was in love with him."*—"Do you know this for sure? That is, that Versilov is not in love with Mrs. Akhmakov?"

"For goodness' sake, what an absurd idea!"

"This... That man. But if you knew the story of Lidiia." (She blushes.)]

The Youth explains the story of E<lena> P<avlov>na[24] to Anna Andreevna.

"This was a prank, I have firsthand information."

Anna Andreevna only smiled. (She blushed slightly. A delicate glow.)

N.B. She was somewhat ashamed of Versilov. A strange relationship. A few words about this relationship.

The Youth to Anna Andreevna: "Versilov on the nobility. He started out as a retrograde, but later he showed some improvement. [Perhaps,] He was preaching a Utopia, He has a tendency to do this kind of thing, but who is the Prince to pass judgment on him?"

The Youth: "I liked her austere, almost ascetic character... Fascinated by her after a visit with her, I would sometimes feel sweetly consoled, thinking that, perhaps, I wasn't quite so bad after all, as I sometimes think I am, for couldn't I, too, experience thoughts that were noble and beautiful, etc.?"

Anna Andreevna was managing to get along even with the Fanario-

---

* Here, it is not quite clear to whom these words belong.

[24] See note 48 of Part IV.

tov woman, who already belonged to the very <élite,> court society, and not at all after the fashion of the ward in Pushkin's "Queen of Spades."

She was very well educated, much more so than I; she knew mathematics.

["You haven't distinguished yourself by anything, and that's why you are mad."]

"You would like to be a Prince."

The Prince. Already in the morning he got excited: "I am not responsible to you, I am my own judge. I am not obligated by any, not even the slightest, obligation."

The Youth: "If you are speaking of the money which you owe my father, he isn't bothering you at all, or is he?"

[For the 2d half, finale.] "I am not obligated to pay that money. It was of my own free will, my own desire, though I wasn't speaking of that money, for I wasn't speaking of your father, but of you, solely of you..."

"But am I not taking some of that very same money from you—so, really, isn't it all the same if you are speaking of me, or of my father?"

"Not your father, but you, you alone, and [if you] <. . .> insist on speaking of that money, why, I couldn't be giving you somebody else's money, your father's without having that person's permission. I've been giving you my own money, [and I've been giving it, naturally, without expecting to get it back.]"

"How do you mean, your own? But in that case, for what?"

"Surely for friendship?" the Prince grinned, *"pour vos beaux yeux."*[25]

"To hell with your friendship—take it all. I'm not going to take your money, like a beggar!"

"As if you didn't know that you were getting it for... for your sister," etc.

The Prince: "Oh, in the beginning I took you for an honorable person."

Very definitely, the Youth is angered by a few words said about the Akhmakov woman. ~~He said it so Ditrin~~ Ditrin said frivolously: "Well, it would seem that she was a little lady of easy virtue. ~~Perhaps~~ I've

---

25 French: "For your beautiful eyes."

heard that you, too, Prince, might have something to say here." ~~Here~~ A sharp word by the Youth. Here, about Liza, etc.

But when the Youth and the Prince were left alone, the Youth began to talk of the Akhmakov woman, and the Prince jumped to his feet: "Nobody has the right" (hints about Liza).

"Don't take the knife."

The Youth says: "You always had something against the Akhmakov woman, because you were counting on her." (N.B. This, perhaps, at Stebelkov's, or at Anna Andreevna's.)

"How could I, then, go back and take another 300 rubles! But, let me repeat it, I was then dwelling in higher regions."*

Letter by Prince Serezha to the Youth, from prison: "Forgive me, I have done you a grave injustice... My dear friend..."

"As if you didn't know that your sister is seeing me."

Begins to cry.

"Not about myself, about her."

That very morning Liza says to her brother, in the *2d half of part two: "Do not tell them"* (i.e., Versilov and her mother).

~~In the 2d half of part two, the Youth is seeking to establish Liza's happiness. The Prince wants to marry <her?>. One must get some money. They agree to try their luck at gambling. And the hellish night.~~

~~N.B. The Prince had hoped, for a moment, to buy his freedom from Stebelkov. All that was needed was that Stebelkov return those fateful documents, the Prince's letters. It goes without saying that he is convinced that Stebelkov would never turn himself in. However, there is already some talk about those shares, that they have been forged, and discovered to be false. But Stebelkov refuses to give him those documents. The Prince realizes that the whole affair will *certainly* be exposed, and so he turns himself in. (But this is already in part three.) *Liza alone was aware of all these things.* All this is exposed in the end of part two, when Versilov looks up the Youth. But in the end of part two none of this has been exposed as yet.~~

?N.B. But Liza's position in part three? (Must be defined.): AND THEREFORE, HAVE IT THE OLD WAY, LETTING THE PRINCE REPROACH THE YOUTH, IN THE 1ST HALF OF PART TWO, WITH LIZA'S PREGNANCY. THIS HAPPENS ONLY TOWARD THE END OF PART TWO. (THOUGH IT IS VERY HARD TO SAY.) IT SEEMS THAT IT MUST BE THAT WAY.

---

* *Pelo v dushe,* literally, "my heart was full of song."

[Here] Most important. March 13 ~~He~~ The Prince may reproach him, he also may get excited. However, he goes to the authorities and turns himself in only at the end of part three, when Stebelkov has worn him out, and there already have happened the whole business with the old Prince at the Youth's flat, Versilov's proposal, and the chopping of the icons; and that's when the Prince is arrested. Meanwhile, in part three, Liza is simply at home, being the only one who is aware of the Prince's secret. At the same time, the Prince is very excited and *extremely busy*. Though perhaps in part three the Youth also knows the Prince's secret.

March 13.

Liza.

Couldn't it be arranged so that Vasin proposes marriage to Liza, who unexpectedly hurts him by her refusal?

N.B. Couldn't it be arranged so that Vasin entrusts Stebelkov with the documents of *the cause,* and so that the latter denounces <the secret society> to the police on the basis of these documents?

Most important. So that in part three, Liza is awaiting a decision of the Prince's fate. Makar Ivanov is also there.

[N.B. Stebelkov's role is as such a minor one; however, he is clearly indispensable for the Prince's *fate,* and later, for Vasin's. N.B. Stebelkov without Lambert. They do not know each other.]

N.B. Inquire: The Prince, while he is under arrest, can he be seeing all of them?

In the 2d half of part two.

"The awakening was terrible"... Liza came. ~~Liza, what~~ Savage reproaches.

["What could you find in him? Oh, I am cruel, cruel!)"

The Youth: "If our mother has been living that way, why must we all live in disgrace?"]

Liza left. I ran after her and asked her to forgive me.

"Liza! Does mother know?"

"I told her."

"What does she say?"

"She said: 'Bear it.' "

"Oh, do bear it, do bear it, Liza!" (i.e., "don't drown yourself!")

"I came to ask you not to tell father about it."

Liza is telling her brother about the scene with the pocket knife.

"How do you know that?"

"Mother is begging you to think of what she won't dare beg of you."

"Not to do any gambling, that is!"

LAST DECISION. *March 13.*

Both the arrest [of the Prince] and *everything,* perhaps, at the end of part two. Then, in part three, Vasin could propose marriage to Liza, who has been left alone. He admits that Stebelkov has got the papers, and Stebelkov denounces <the rest of them> so as to get a lighter sentence. The old Prince does not flee to the Youth's *of his own accord,* without Stebelkov. [Versilov and Lambert may be there.] But Lambert exerts an influence throughout part three. And when the Youth's depressed condition has assumed frightful proportions, especially under the influence of Lambert and his sneers, he conceives the idea of quitting everything, breaking with everybody, and going off to America. At this point, the conflagration. Thereafter, the Prince's acquittal.

Vasin. March 13.

Should it be arranged so that Vasin, who keeps giving advice to the Youth, gets caught himself, like a fool, with those documents and Stebelkov? He also offers his hand to Liza. Doesn't he, in the 2d half of part two, warn the Youth about doing any business with the Prince, as well as about the latter's dealings with Stebelkov? And later, also about the fact that ~~he~~ some important documents of Vasin's were in Stebelkov's hands.

After the Prince's death, Vasin, who has been acquitted, proposes to Liza, etc.

Lambert. ~~Lambert's appearance may take place toward the very end of part three, after the chopping of the icons.~~ Perhaps one could altogether dispense with Lambert, and make it so that toward the end of part two so much spite has accumulated in the Youth's heart, so much spite and envy, that he decides to launch the document of his own accord. The document is tormenting him. Power.

Or, perhaps, Lambert might be left in.

Lambert used to be perfectly ingenuous and frank with me and, what's most important, I was struck by the fact that he never for a moment doubted that I was his friend. But not altogether a Russian. Not a Russian character—a villain, but not a Russian. No sullen dullard. (The sacramental act of a crime committed, with an incessant view of taking vengeance on society, vicious because stupid and backward, and deifying his own spite, callousness, and negativism.)

Olia's mother.

"I'm wandering around, wandering around, pushing through crowds of people, sick of it. My sorrow."

The Prince.

Mention, in the beginning of the 2d chapter, that ~~the Fanariotov woman~~ the Stolbeev woman is out of town, so that the whole flat is at the Prince's disposal.

The Youth had been thinking that Liza was seeing <her?> old nurse.

"Come on now, could you have ever believed such nonsense as her going there for Varvara Ivanovna's sake only?"

(The Youth, to himself: "I swear that this is what I was believing; no other thought ever entered my mind.")

Ditrin asks: "Who was that sweet girl I met there?"

Stebelkov: "Lizaveta Makarovna."

"Ah, what if this is an indiscretion."

The Prince: "She is seeing <her?> nurse. [Olia's mother.]"

All of which was quite awkward.

At the end of the 1st half.

"Your sister is pregnant. Here is your money!" I wanted to lunge at him—*and suddenly I began to cry!*

Most important. March 14.

The Youth's admission, in chapter two, that he used to enter the Prince's flat as if it were his own, make it ~~after~~ on the occasion of a visit by some important guest, or something of that kind.

The Prince: "Don't take that knife. You dare not take that knife." He stamped his foot. I threw those 300 roubles. Apologized. Mutual explanations. 300 roubles. "Take them, take them."

But I had something entirely different on my mind, my heart was full of something else.*

"You know what, I want to gamble, I want to win, gambling is abominable, but..." (and I had forgotten everything, as I was walking up and down the room in a state of exaltation. I repeat, something entirely different was filling all my soul).**

Organize a roulette. Wouldn't go if you're in the service. I looked back and saw that grin on his face. This was one thing I hadn't expected.

"Naturally, I shan't carry it to ~~a certain~~ any excessive amount. Versilov is going to pay you" (How could I be saying things like that!).

"I've never urged you to return any of the money," said the Prince.

* Literally, "something was singing in my heart."

** Literally, "something else was singing in my heart."

He hadn't been talking this way before. Before, he used to get up, shake hands with me, and wouldn't even let me finish. To be sure, even then, there were times when he would smile strangely... However, I had attributed this simply to the mechanics of his smile, i.e., that his smile was always like that, and that by its very nature it hadn't much of good nature in it.

Stebelkov.

Stebelkov to the Youth, still at the Prince's, nodding at <his> clothes, tailored on Bolshaia Millionnaia <Street> (i.e., clothes) <. . .>

The Youth comes to see Stebelkov (he had been looking for Vasin): "Why didn't you tell me over there (at the Prince's) what you needed?"

"And you, why did you, too, remain silent there, and now you are coming [to me.]"

St<ebelkov>: "You wrote me that you needed some money, I've got money."

"Don't bother, I got some from the Prince."

"Stop, it wasn't yours."

"And he always smiles so when he is giving you money."

"How do you mean, 'smiles'? He does not smile at all."

"Today, for instance."

"I'm attributing it simply to the mechanism of his smile. This is how God made him."

"It isn't just the mechanism," Stebelkov said, with a wink.

"What then? What is it you want?" I shouted.

Stebelkov about Ditrin: "So they cosigned the note, and the moneylender grabbed the promissory note allright, but didn't give them any money, while keeping the note—so that's where the fun started."

"Aren't you the moneylender?" I asked.

"I own a bank, I have a *Mont de piété*. Have you heard what a *Mont de piété* is in Paris?"

The money was Versilov's, no matter how you looked at it: how could I, then, reason in that fashion? However, it seemed to me that it really had to be that way, and not otherwise. At least it seemed that way two-thirds of the way, the remaining third [to be scored] to a guilty conscience.

"Today I delivered a nice round sum to him" (speaking of the Prince). "At first he used to <see a lot of> the Akhmakov woman, but now it's gotten to be Anna Andreevna. Might get away easily."

The Youth: "I never spoke a word with him about Anna Andreevna."

"I understand, I understand that you really couldn't be talking about Anna Andreevna" (Liza).

Stebelkov about the Prince: "He is putting on a big show... but..."

Stebelkov about the Prince: "He is furious" (about the Akhmakov woman).

"Nonsense, he can't have any hopes."

"He hasn't got any hope, but he's still furious."

"I'll give <it?> to that *littérateur*. He's sold his wife to a General. I'll give <it?> to him."*

"What filth!"

"No, he is *good and clean,* very good and clean, all scented. He gets very mad whenever things aren't clean enough for him. Even if he feels like spitting, he'll always be looking for the very cleanest spot, before he'll spit there."

The Akhmakov woman (the rendezvous).

She: "So you really think that I've come here because of you."

The Youth: (My heart sank. That's precisely what I'd been thinking.) "Yes, I've been thinking that you were coming precisely because of me," [I suddenly blurted out, flinging myself into the abyss, with chills going down my spine, but with my eyes flashing.]

She: "No, I've let you go too far."

I: ("Stay here, stay here")—"in order to... steal the document from Versilov."

The Youth is most curious and excited by the fact that the Akhmakov woman has decided to take this step, making this appointment with him: so he is anxious to find out what precisely made ~~him~~ her do it. He almost knows it himself: that is, <she is trying> to find out for sure whether or not Versilov has the document. He thinks that perhaps she wants to make him steal the document. This thought causes him intense suffering: it would mean that she sees in him a spy, and not... a friend. He even makes up his mind to let her have the document, if *she is going to conduct herself loyally.* [Yet the news of] ~~But~~ the Aide-de-Camp leaves him bewildered. He is jealous. N.B.? However, she conducts herself with dignity and charm. He hints that

---

* The context does not tell us what the object of "give" might be: "he," "she," or "it."

he might get the document for her. She suddenly gives him high hopes, leaving him enraptured.

The Youth to her: "Fear nothing, I am your protector, I feel that you are the summit of perfection, though I used to think you were the summit of pride and... of passions.*

The Akhmakov woman: "Where did you find out all these things (about the document)?"

"From the late Kraft. Here's how the first lines <of the letter> go" (he says them).

"So what? I am so confident of my father. And you've been thinking that I wanted you for a spy. Oh, how depraved you are (forgive me)."

I was thinking of taking it out and giving it to her. "But what if she is lying? Look at her eyes (is she, or isn't she lying?). If I'm going to hand it to her, I'll be ashamed. (I'm not going to give it to her.)"

"I am giving you my word of honor that this document does not exist and that Kraft tore it up in my presence."

"Did you see it?"

"I did."

"Yourself?"

"That's right."

"Kraft tore it up. Thank God, it was a bad thing to do, but I..."

She, about Versilov: "(Perhaps I was not worthy of him.)"

"No, you have given me great pleasure."

"I can always be your friend."

The Akhmakov woman: "You are still little, but you are already so depraved."

The Youth (quite beside himself): "If you will prove to me right away that you aren't [depraved yourself, and that you are not] lying now, but are telling the truth, you don't know what I am going to do for you!"

The Akhmakov woman: "Now this certainly oversteps the limits."

The Youth: "No, please, sit around for a while, and prove to me that you are a superior woman."

The Akhmakov woman: "What if I am going to prove it to you?"

The Youth: "First: did you seek an appointment with me here, or didn't you?"

---

* The Russian sentence is as awkward as the translation.

The Akhmakov woman: "Yes, I made an appointment with you" (blushing, and with a pleading smile).

The Youth: "It is about that letter, isn't it?"

The Akhmakov woman: "Yes, I was fearing that letter, but I swear, not as much, not as much as you think. That time, at Tatiana P<avlovn>a's..."

The Youth: "So then, I was merely a spy."

The Akhmakov woman: "No, so help me God, I was also in love."

The Youth: "I'll tell you about this letter. But let me tell you that I esteem you immeasurably higher than myself, because right now I'm telling you lies, while you aren't telling any to me, so it seems. However... however, I am your friend forever. I am going to tell you soon, very, very much I'm going to tell you."*

The Akhmakov woman: "Set my mind at rest on one thing. Is it with Versilov?"

The Youth: "N-no! He hasn't got it."

The Akhmakov woman: "Who then?"

The Youth "Kraft... he destroyed it... with my own eyes..."

The Akhmakov woman: "Thank God."

The Youth (alone): "... I lied to her! Oh, how immeasurably below her I stood then, and how I despise myself at this moment! But perhaps I was thinking at that moment: 'It is still in my powers to give everything back to you, and I shall reward you!' Was there any suspicion? Yes, there was. There was also a desire to hang on to the document. Oh, what a vile, oh, what a dismal character! I rushed to kiss the tracks of her feet. But I was happy and cheerful. I was singing and thinking: 'If things are vile in this world, it is only I who is vile, but there is also beauty in this world.' "

Was it frivolity? Or was it extreme vanity?

And later, in the scene with Versilov, he also speaks about the document with him, and also tells lies.

After having discovered this thing about Liza, he is thinking of the Akhmakov woman.

The Akhmakov woman: "You have been at my place several times, <and> several times I've been meaning to find out for sure... Only I don't know how to go about it."

The Youth: "That time, Tatiana Pa<vlovna> said: 'Seduce him.' "

---

* Equally awkward in the original.

The Akhmakov woman: "I don't know how to seduce <a man>... What good is it if nothing comes of it?"

To pucker her little lips in laughter—this is her <typical> gesture. Toward the end, she pursed her little lips <speaking> of the Aide-de-Camp: "Only, this would be just too funny," she said, as if begging forgiveness, and then suddenly burst out laughing.

The Youth: "I am not jealous, I am not jealous. Let it be that way."

The Youth: "I deceived her, and Versilov, (about the letter), yet I was full of good cheer. But I was strong... 'But if this woman ~~has~~ is deceiving me, I shall know how to protect myself.' " (See, somewhere, an earlier N.B.)

The Youth is telling her how he likes honesty about a woman, and adds a description of Anna Andreevna.

Later, the Youth says, *after the rendezvous,* that he managed to remain sober, i.e., to believe that she was perhaps deceiving him, even though completely overwhelmed and carried away by his feelings, which is also why he himself deceived her. "I acted in precisely the same fashion that night, with Versilov," he says. "Well, was it courage? Strong nerves, or that *double monster,* which is sitting inside me, and which Versilov esteems so highly, higher than singlemindedness," etc.

N.B. The Akhmakov woman still did not belong to the [very] highest society, but Baron Bioring's proposal was about to elevate her to the very highest circles.

"Yes, I was at fault."

"How could you humble yourself so... No, no, humble yourself in such a noble way. How could you confess to a person such as myself—and just to find out about that thing!"

"No, I was very much interested in you."

"I have asked you to never mention Versilov in my presence."

The Youth: "You are merely repeating yourself. And in the meantime, I've told you everything."

"The letter has been destroyed. Kraft told me." (~~Even her I~~ I was deceiving her, too. I was only ashamed to admit that I had been putting on a show. All these superior women were having a purifying effect on me. That very moment I made the decision to tear up that letter that same evening and to put an end to this "base and ridiculous intrigue.") When she heard about Kraft, she said to me: "Thank God." I was not lying to her. [I was pure. These women were having a purifying effect on me.]

And, as I was leaving:

"Listen, are you marrying Bioring, the Aide-de-Camp?"

"Oh, I, never mind me, never mind me" (her little lips were trembling with laughter).

N.B. A tirade: "What you meant to me!"

She has a feeling <for him>.

"My dear boy, don't be angry with me."

"This is all I want. I ~~only~~ shall never know another woman."

She turned away, her little lips pursed: "Let me laugh a little." Then she turned back to me: a single tear. "I am a bad, I am a vile woman. If you should ever remember me: think something good of me."

In his confession before Versilov, the Youth says to Versilov: "She was worried about the document."

Versilov: "But you haven't got that document, or have you?"

[I was expecting Him to ask me <outright>.] And what I really needed was this question. All this time, all of these two months, I had been asking myself: Why doesn't He ask that question, why is He remaining silent? For don't I know that He has his suspicions? However, He remained silent even this time. I was very much ashamed deep inside.

N.B. In part three, not a word about the document either (though this was not the prime concern of that period, nor did it fit in with our mutual emotional attitudes, or with the words which were then exchanged. And then, all of a sudden, I find out *for a fact* that He ~~is looking~~ has been looking for the document [in a certain place]).

?N.B. *Maybe.*

Among other things, Versilov lets the Youth know that the Prince has formally proposed to Anna Andreevna, but ~~she~~ that she has rejected him. "And she also asked me a very strange question: 'do you love the Akhmakov woman?'."

"Womanly curiosity."

"Oh no, a categorical question. Don't you know something?"

Confession. [Precious.] Suddenly, after all these stories about the Akhmakov woman, the Youth asks: "Listen, tell me what is philosophy?" And a little later: "Why won't you give me a kiss?"

Versilov, at the confession: "Kraft tore it up, didn't he? You aren't lying to me, are you?"

And suddenly, that night, after I had returned from the Prince's, I suddenly recalled my recent conversation with Stebelkov. Stebelkov was bribing me so I wouldn't interfere with his matchmaking for

Anna Andreevna, or intercede in Liza's favor, and what's worse, he was saying: "My money is better <than the Prince's>!"*

Falling asleep: "Really, there had been so many hints (about my sister). Really, after all this, I must have simply been stupid not to have realized what was going on. No, that can't be it: ~~This~~ it must have been egoism, not stupidity, an egoism of the heart and—and, perhaps, a belief in the saintliness of other people, a belief that everyone else was above me morally. Oh, of this I had always been convinced. But what was perhaps the most important fact was that all these different hints ~~as if on purpose~~ had come into a focus only on that day, so that I hadn't had the time to realize what was going on, and besides, as if on purpose, I happened to be preoccupied with entirely different things, being distracted by the Akhmakov woman. As a matter of fact, Stebelkov had, [on that same day]... Do they force people to marry in such cases?... pistol in hand... I don't know. I shall act as an honest man should. Versilov—I wonder what Versilov's position might be, did he or didn't he know?"

Liza entered.

About E<lena> P<avlov>na.[26]

"Sure, you know all about youths such as myself."

"This," said Liza, "is all because you are still *little*. You'll meet a beautiful woman, you'll fall in love, your heart will stand still... and later you'll begin to hate her."

"Well, and what if she prefers me to a grown-up man?"

"That's when you will perish at her feet."

"No, I'm not going to perish... No, I won't perish. Rather, if a woman should ~~in my way~~ get in my way, she must follow me. Nobody crosses my path with impunity."

She began to laugh.

"How I like it when you're laughing at me! How I like to be with you!"

I leave purified.

He is leaving. Liza catches up with him, "Don't gamble," 300 rubles.

"How do you know?"

"Onisimovna told me."

About the Aide-de-Camp.

---

* The original says: "so I wouldn't interfere with his seeking Anna Andreevna's hand." However, this is hardly what Dostoevsky wants to say.

[26] See note 48 of Part IV.

The Prince somehow unhappy. He is a generous, kindly man.

I'll admit that I had been invited, whereas she absolutely pretended that I had dropped in by accident.

Is this breadth?

"What I've got is undisciplined dashing. I am gambling" (as I am leaving).

"Come back more often."

Versilov, it seems, was interested in knowing what Anna Andreevna had been doing at the Prince's. "He keeps asking me questions about you," he says to Anna Andreevna.

"How pleasant it is to say something pleasant to a person." [Olimpiada]

"Ever since I got to know you."

"He does not love <her>,
But does She love Him?"

"And when he (the Prince) and I quarrel—it hurts me."

Having left Anna Andreeva, <I> rushed along. I was late.

"Is it true, is it really true that she has made an appointment with him?"

To Liza (as he is leaving): "You were at Daria Onisimovna's the other day, weren't you?"

"I am looking at Russia."

"Listen: we have withstood the Tartar invasion, then two centuries of slavery, ~~solely~~ i.e., both the peasants and their squires, solely for the reason that they found both things to their liking. Now, we have to withstand freedom: are we going to do it, is freedom going to be to our taste?"

Anna Andreevna got up and left.

Liza: "Exactly like your father. Why, you must have taken this from him."

"So you're denying that I have a mind of my own?"

"Come on, don't talk that way."

Kissed Liza's hand.

Liza: "You are kind and very nice."

"With that whole progressive movement of ours during those past 15–20 years, we have proved first of all that we are terribly uneducated."

Liza: "It's terrible how abstractly you talk these days."

The Youth: "Why are you picking on me, Liza?"

The Youth: "I carry in me all the depths of abjection!"

"Here you go again. You are finding that Versilov, such an extremely honorable man, is dishonorable. <Yet,> you couldn't even express it."

The Youth: "One should not respect people, and so I make a start with myself."

About the forged stock certificates.

The Prince.

"You know what, I want to gamble, I want to win some money, gambling is an abomination, but this is all temporary only, just so I could win a certain sum... and... then..."

I looked at him and saw a grin on his face. "Of course, I am not going to take it past a certain figure."

"You want both to retain your innocence and to acquire a capital. ~~I want~~ I want you to take it! You don't know what I've got!"

"If you and I will kiss..."

"If you will kiss! What tenderness all of a sudden."

He kissed me with aversion.

"We used to be friends."

"All right, all right... that'll do..."

"I really don't know, those 300."

"Take them, take them." And I took them.

If you only knew what was in my soul. Oh, had he only known what was in my soul!

And I took the money. I could have gotten it <elsewhere>. I could have gotten it from Stebelkov, and I had gone to see him for everything but money. Yesterday I had received a note.

In Stebelkov's presence: "You've got another Bioring there. You are educating yourself, my Prince." "I beg you to put this book down."*

About Stebelkov (Well, at least he's brought the money).

"Makes no difference."

"Come on, I've brought it for you."

"Brought it, brought it."

A visitor arrived. An individual such as Stebelkov, naturally, had to catch his attention. It goes without saying that on occasion I did know how to behave, and the Prince apparently ~~that means~~ was ashamed of me also. This notion made me furious.

In Ditrin's presence, "The way out is to shoot oneself."

"I have the pleasure of knowing Katerina Nikolaevna personally."

After the rendezvous.

---

* The whole paragraph is quite unclear in the original. One might also translate: "In Stebelkov's presence, you've go..."

Something very intimate from the Youth's recollections.

There was something wrong there, something apt to humiliate Liza.

St<ebelkov> about Ditrin. "This isn't done" (the promissory note).

"What do you want? Why did you keep sitting around?"

"But... about that, that... How do you mean, my Prince?"

"No, no, and no."

<He went> to the door. "I'm not afraid of you," then suddenly ran after him and started talking <to him> very rapidly. Stebelkov was listening with his eyes screwed up, then shook his head: "Come on, we know that," and left. The Prince returned, all trembling. He made a move to sit down, but took a look at me and remaind standing.

It was as if his eyes were saying: "Why have you been sitting around here?"

"I, my Prince," I started.

~~"Eh, what's the use"~~

"Honest, I haven't got time, I must be leaving right away."

"All right, so take your 300 rubles first."

When I was telling of <my> meeting with the Prince

I admit, I was abasing myself, but invincibly <. . .> So as not to prevent from transporting <. . .>

About the nobility, about faith—at the Prince's.

"Now this is already something ideal, some sort of masonic lodge" (the Prince was terribly uneducated). Versilov realized that he was trying to put up an argument for spite only.

"This is tantamount to annihilation of the nobility."

"If you want to put it that way, it may well be that it has never existed," etc.

"Only in the beginning did his words seem reactionary to me. Later I liked the idea" (repeat three times!).

"Our society is in disorder. You yourself are nothing but a product of disorder."

From among courtiers and slave owners.

"My God, how you are flattering him."

"He's got as many virtues as he's got shortcomings."

"My God, how you are flattering him."

"Flattering, how come? <I said> not understanding him right away.

"You were trying to say something, but didn't succeed in expressing it. There is Bioring for you."

"Please, leave me alone with your laws."

"Well, what you've got there isn't logic; what you've got is some kind of a feeling." Oh, how unsophisticated I was. To be sure, I had something completely different ~~in mind then~~ filling all my heart.*

"Why, his relics will perform miracles, if he has this many virtues."

In this sense, the Prince was more clever than I: he immediately noticed that the other man was using a joke to get off that subject. Something like baring his teeth.

"You say about Versilov, 'Why isn't he like this himself?'—this is your logic. But it's rubbish and not logic, for even if he weren't like this at all, he could still be preaching the truth. And secondly: What is so wrong about him?"

"Oh no, once you've begun to preach your higher truth, you've got to be righteous yourself."

"Was it you who called him an 'old wives' prophet'?"

It says in the Koran that one should look upon such people as if they were mice, and stick to one's business.

1. A notion just as monstrous as that other slander about her, namely that she had promised to marry Prince Sergei Petrovich, even while her husband was still living.

2. "This was just plain stupidity, I know, for I have firsthand knowledge," I explained.

This was a gay, light, facetious conversation at a bright, cheerful moment, when the Prince, in view of her impending widowhood, had insinuated something to her, and she had answered, with a smile: "Maybe." This was frightfully frivolous, I agree, but what could her "maybe" possibly mean? I know only too well that the Prince could not possibly attach any importance to this kind of a promise. "And having no intention, besides," I added, realizing that I had said a little too much about the Prince, and seeking to correct my mistake... "I love him very, very much," I suddenly started again, "in spite of all his shortcomings, he is a very nice person. There is a certain single-mindedness, a certain abruptness in his thinking, to be sure, but all this has a most honorable foundation: 'That's right, if ~~you yourself~~ you are talking of honor, you'll have to be an honorable man yourself; if not so, I'll attach no value to your words.' This is illogical, for a man who isn't honorable himself may very well express a truth. However, such thinking does reveal the Prince's noble aspirations and desires ~~notwithstanding the fact that he has been reduced... However~~

* Literally, "singing in my heart."

~~... Show me... I~~. Oh, my God, is it already three o'clock?" I suddenly exclaimed, looking at the clock.

"Ten to," said Anna Andreevna.

I began to take my leave, *dithyrambs.*

"Really, one might suspect that you are under the influence of some woman."

3. "Mother is begging for something she's afraid <to ask of you>."

"Sometimes, I am most wicked. Well, I shall leave you to your little secrets. Especially since I'm in a hurry."

"Liza, why were you not quite so kind to her? Why were you tugging <at my sleeve>? Isn't she a wonderful girl, isn't she?"

"I, I'm sometimes most wicked."

"She is no good."

"All right, Liza."

"Well, in that case, I'm no good."

After the meeting with Anna Andreevna, Liza went into the other room with him. "Don't gamble. You've been taking money from the Prince." And suddenly she pulled him over with all her strength: "Let's stand over here. Behind the door-curtain." The Prince walked past. Spurs.

"This is the Prince. What are you afraid of?"

"Oh, nothing. I just don't want him to see me."

"It sure gave you a scare. Could it be that he is running after you?"

"Enough of that."

"I'd really let him have it..."

"You are against him, you dislike him a great deal."

"No, Liza, I like him. Why did he insult me?" About those 300 rubles.

"How do you know? The Prince."

"He wouldn't get too far, would he? My little Liza couldn't possibly fall in love with the likes of him. But you know, really, I am ready to forgive him. He did insult me, but I am ready to forgive him. When one is happy, one tends to be kind."

"And you are happy?"

"Terribly, terribly happy—~~altogether~~ I'll tell you everything later, Liza."

"Well, of course it is all nonsense. Forgive me. ~~I shall win back the money I lost, and return it to him.~~ You know what I'm going to tell you..."

"No, let's go out. I don't want him to know that I come to this place at all."

"Aren't you on your way there?"

"No, I'll go with you."

"Did you say good-bye?"

"I did."

We left.

"What I was going to tell you is that he came here to propose marriage to her."

"This couldn't be true."

"Why not?"

"You know what, you go ahead and take your cab, while I ~~I'll immediately~~ will walk."

"Are you going to have dinner with us? I'll be there."

"Mother has asked me to tell you something she does not dare tell you."

"Liza! I know that this is all but petty faint-heartedness, but... these are only trifles. But you see, I've run into debt, and I want to win some money so I can pay my debts. It's quite possible to win. It's easy, as long as one isn't carried away. I am going to count every ruble, but I shall pay my debt and call it quits, and then I'll be all yours, inseparably yours, and do tell Mother that I'm never going to leave you. But today..."

~~Yes~~ "Are you going to have dinner with us tonight?"

"Oh, sure. I'll be home for dinner, as I promised. Half-past four."

"Are you very happy? You just said that you were happy."

"Give me your hand, for good luck."

"For good luck, my hand—never!" she said.

"I'm leaving. Lizochka, my dear ~~What have I done to you, how I did torture you~~." I can remember her glance when she said to me: "And are you happy?" There must have been something there, in your heart. Wretched, wretched mole that you were: I could see nothing, understand nothing.

[And perhaps it was precisely that happiness of mine that was the main reason why I couldn't understand anything of what was going on.]

"Not only have I not been in your room..."

"Why, he has come to propose marriage to her."

"N-no," she said, smiling a kind of pale smile.

I was riding along, just as sunny. "Three o'clock, three o'clock," I was thinking. My heart was palpitating something terrible. At three o'clock *she* was to be at Tatiana Pavlovna's. "Is she really going to be there?"

"What shall I need, boldness or timidity? Eh, I won't fail!"

I entered. Nobody home. I'll wait. I entered: *she* was sitting there, *waiting* for Tatiana Pavlovna.

"Yes, I haven't met her." "You probably forgot to tell her."

"I... I haven't even seen her."

"But didn't I ask you to tell her, last night, that I would be at her place at three o'clock?"

"Either I didn't hear you right, or you forgot to tell me."

"It is hard to imagine that I would have forgotten it."

So this is how it was! And I, I had been thinking that she was giving me a rendezvous!"

"Oh, my God, why are you here? Oh, my God! Why have you come here?"

I was getting ruffled. She began to laugh.

"Yes, you cannot help laughing!" ~~You~~ (Angrily:) "You aren't like Anna Andreevna."

"Have you been at Anna Andreevna's?"

"Yes, I've been there, and I heard that you are getting married."

"To whom?"

"To Baron Bioring."

"Did you hear that from her?"

"No, not from her. At the Prince's" (good-naturedly).

"I like your good nature."

"Everybody praises me for my good nature, while I am really wicked. Incidentally, Nikolai Alekseevich made that wisecrack about my being acquainted with you, that young men... from a corner..."

"They told me, and I said that if anybody should be standing in my way... They laughed. I am humiliating myself so terribly with you."

"I do not want that... because I have you <illegible>." N.B. Or so, with the Youth still speaking: "Do you want me to tell you what kind of a person you are?" And he goes on to develop it.

"I'll tell you everything. The document. Is it true?"

"Tell me, really, and I shall forgive you."

"I am glad that you have started to talk <of your own accord>."

"But why didn't you start to talk yourself?"

"Well, I don't know how."

"You know, I've been afraid of you all the time, and I'm still afraid of you."

"Afraid of what?"

"Well, that you might jump up and do something violent, like breaking this wall."

"I'm not going to break any walls."

"Really? without making fun of you, and without any second thoughts." (Simply because you don't believe that I'm not going to break anything.)

I: "Where do you get these cute expressions from?"

"Why, the very idea that somebody might believe I might break a wall."

"What am I to do with you? Why must I always laugh when I look at you? You are a joy" (a dithyramb).

"Forgive me, but would you mind shedding your pride for just one moment?"

And then, in the end, he suddenly, just before leaving, produces another dithyramb.

"I was thinking of a poor boy, a neglected, unhappy boy. I came to love you because you were unhappy. 'My dear boy,' as my father calls you."

"I like to have a confidant such as you. Yours is a pure soul."

"Like cat and mouse..."

"What kind of a cat am I?"

"Let's each suggest some good idea to the other."

"And you aren't jealous about my getting married?"

"No, may God give you happiness. Love him. This is higher than thoughts could be, isn't it so?"

And yet I deceived her. I was capable of deceiving her (about the document). Is that "breadth"? No, I wasn't deceiving her. I was going to tear up the document that very night.

But there is still another trait, typical of those days, which would let you commit your villainy while you'd be saying: "Later."

"Listen, when I was taken out for the first time <. . .>

Not one single bad experience.

Because nobody can see it.

Ambiguously about Versilov: "What is He doing, how is He doing?"

I. "It may be that I am very guilty before him."

"How?"

II. "I do not know. By showing myself to him, frankly and openly, as I am doing it before you right now, <by baring> my whole soul, with my evil vices."

III. "Which would be?"

"Frankness. A desire to conquer, to attract, to make happy immediately."

N.B. IV. "How can that be? A woman shouldn't be frank the way

I am. She shouldn't attract without love. While I—I really love no one... I love everybody. I am destined to love *everybody,* and so no one."

V. "Why did I let this happen? Only because no one is going to find out about it. Well, and even if they did find out."

"But you are a chivalrous man. You are going to say: She was mad. But you'll smile and—forgive me."

Some kind of trifle, as a result of Liza's *action.*

[Here.] First chapter. After the rendezvous, going home: "The fact that Liza had been so ungrateful, even before Anna Andreevna the other day, worried me particularly. And why are they so easily angered, so irritable? They don't know life. Life is quite different from what they think it is; everything is so good and so clear."

For the monologue.

"Your passions..." She shuddered. "You are full of fear, and yet even in your fear, you smiled." (She smiled.)

"I have become so attached to you precisely because you have such simplicity."

"I wouldn't have started talking unless I hadn't actually reached a decision."

"If you want it, happy as well."*

"I, afraid to leave you?"

"Is this to say that you weren't thinking of how you could wheedle the document out of me all the time?"

"Oh no, I was forgetting it altogether quite often."

Jesuitism, cunning, a spying serpent... and what I discovered was honor, glory, a student.

"Tell, what has made you laugh just now?"

~~What's so~~ "You've got such words... what is a 'spying serpent'?"

"No, I am thankful to you for having broken the ice. You've done it in a terribly ~~thankful~~ original fashion.

"About the blessings, he knows."

"Versilov has been telling me that Othello didn't kill, and then killed himself, because he was jealous, but rather because he had lost his ideal."

"I can understand that."

"This was really well said by him."

She was getting ready to leave.

---

* Unclear in the original.

I got up, not knowing what to say. There was, at first, a certain moment after which I had suddenly made a tremendous decision and knew that I was going to fulfill it. Having once accepted this decision, I immediately went mad and began to talk—as I had never talked before.

In the sleigh, a marvelous idea occurred to me. "This then, is real life," I thought, "the real life Versilov has been talking about. He has failed to understand that she is so very simple and has accused her of all kinds of vices. But he has never had any real love for her, but merely wanted 'to save her'—there's the solution of the riddle—also, about Liza's thanklessness. That's what she has always been like, all the way."*

"This is precisely what people fail to understand (about real life) and what Versilov has failed to understand."

There was one most precious word here: how could she say that "I counted on your ardor"... All right, she was a saint, even according to her own admission, but this still would have to be what amounted to a truly monstrous frankness, for a woman of the world (but not in these words; as a woman of the world, she could have avoided it to preserve her own dignity), yet also saintly, for by saying this she was, in her purity of spirit and out of deference to me, to my condition as a youth and unprotected adolescent, actually blaming herself.**

I recalled <her> cute little sayings, following the example of earlier meetings.

And so by baring her own guilt before me, she was, by virtue of doing just that, and quite perceptibly to me, already now and forever stopping that game—that game of enticing a boy—and was now not only educating him but also elevating herself to a higher point.

Though *this* means nothing, for she is a saint all over.

N.B. Leaping across all my many falls, I shall say: That's what she really was like—saintly and righteous!

"Now it is no longer possible, now it would be even sinful! Oh, how much frivolity there was on my own part!"

"I liked to listen to my husband. I used to love Prince Sokolsky's quest for honor."

Versilov.

"I was then sitting behind the door-curtain. You were talking about

---

* The end of this paragraph is somewhat incoherent in the original.

** The sentence is awkward and curiously involved in the original.

the letter. I jumped out from behind <the curtain> and let out my secret. You were bound to realize that I knew something. Wait, don't answer me yet. Your suspicions were well founded. Kraft. Kraft had it, he shot <himself>."

She: "Is that really so? Did you see it yourself? Thank God!"

(N.B. I wasn't lying to her, I was pure.)

"Tell me then, why were you attracting me to yourself, why were you being kind to me, why were you receiving me? Don't hurry your reply. I'm not going to be angry—there's nothing to worry about—if it is the document that has been worrying you."

"Tell me, was it because of this?"

"It was."

"I'm guilty."

"Wait a moment, you've got me stunned, and I can't understand a thing. If it's true that it was because of this, why don't you get up and leave? Instead, you're saying: 'I'm guilty.' How could you humble yourself so much? Listen, nine-tenths of all ladies would have left..."

"Why then?"

"Because you are not afraid of me, because you believe that I shall open the door myself."

"I can see that I was really most guilty."

"Tell me, why didn't you say anything before?"

"I didn't know how. I was ashamed. Later, I got attracted to you, I thought that you might notice it, and I felt ashamed. I was forgetting."

"And why did you make this appointment here?"

"Now the time has come. I was thinking that things might *go more smoothly* at this place, that I might succeed in making you talk while we were here." (She smiled, as if asking for my indulgence.) "Oh, I've been very imprudent about this thing! Just as in everything that pertains to this story with that letter. This document is one of the saddest and most imprudent things (actions). ~~Later~~ I actually did think that you had it. But then you started to come to our place <regularly>, and I became attached to you."

"How could I, a poor youth, how could I..."

"I rather dislike society, my husband, like students—you've got such words... Versilov—all the vices."

"~~Enough, you have planted paradise~~ What vices? You haven't got any."

"Oh yes, I do."

"What specifically? Tell me! To be sure, don't tell me if you can't, but better tell me."

"I wanted to be liked by everybody."

"Could it be true that this includes me?"

She looked up and smiled.

"Enough, you have planted paradise <in my heart>. I am grateful to the 'spying serpent'..."

"What words!" She smiled.

"But now, now don't come to see me."

"It won't go, it's my fault. Sinful. A poor, dreamy boy."

"Not so often."

~~He~~ Othello, jealousy.

"Is it true about Bioring?"

"I don't know. He is a very clever man. A clever and firm man. Kind and generous."

"Yet he didn't believe <what I said?> and became my enemy, enough of him. I beg you to never mention him again."

"God bless you."

"No, I shall only retain the ideal in my heart, which is good enough for me."

She: "Shall we never talk that way to each other again?"

"Never, never."

"No, you must leave *before.*"

"Yes, I didn't know how. Actually I do know how, but I don't like it, and that's why <we shall be> like students."

"But this means nothing, for you actually needed something <from me>."

"No, I didn't need it so much, you are putting me to shame. I did make a mistake: ~~I'm very much~~ for I actually was counting on your ardor. But why did Kraft tear it up? And do you know for sure that he did?"

[Here] "Yes! Yes!" ("I'm going to burn it right today," I was thinking.)

"You are now like a mother to me."

March 22.

For the preface.

Facts. They are passing by. They don't notice. There are no *citizens,* and nobody wants to make an effort and force himself to think and to notice things. I haven't been able to tear myself away, and all the shouts of our critics, ~~haven't dissuaded~~ who say that I am not depicting real life, haven't dissuaded me. Our society has no *founda-*

tions, it hasn't worked out any rules <of life>, because there really hasn't been any life either. A colossal shock—and everything comes to a halt, falls down, and is negated as if it hadn't ever existed. And not just externally, as in the West, but internally, morally. Our most talented writers, who have been describing, in highly artistic form, the life of our upper middle class (from the vantage point of the family)—Tolstoi, Goncharov—thought that they were describing the life of the majority; in my opinion, what they were describing were the lives of some exceptions. [Quite to the contrary, their life is the life of exceptions, while mine is the life of the general rule. Future generations will find that out, as they will be more objective, and the truth will be on my side. In this I believe.]

It has been said that I was describing real thunder, real rain, just as on stage. Where then? Could it be true that Raskolnikov, Stepan Trofimovich (the principal heroes of my novels) may give grounds for such an assertion? [Or Akulka's husband in *Notes from the House of the Dead,* for example? It was precisely this (civic) feeling that made me, for a moment, consider joining the Slavophiles, with the idea of resurrecting the dreams of my childhood (I had read Karamzin, <and was familiar with> the figures of Sergius, Tikhon).] And what about the underground and *Notes from the Underground?* I am proud to have presented, for the first time, the real image of the *Russian majority,* and to have exposed, for the first time, its misshapen and tragic aspects. The tragic lies in one's awareness of being misshapen. As heroes, those beginning with Silvio and the Hero of our times down to Prince Bolkonsky and Levin stand for nothing but petty self-love, which is "not good," they were "brought up the wrong way," they have a chance to improve themselves, for excellent examples are available (Saks in *Polin'ka Saks,* also the German in *Oblomov,* Pierre Bezukhov, the tax farmer in *Dead Souls* ~~and many others~~). But this is so because they are representative of nothing more than ~~poets~~ heroes of petty self-love. I have been the only one to bring out the tragedy of the underground, which consists of suffering, self-laceration, an awareness of a better <life> coupled with the impossibility of attaining it, and, most important of all, a strong conviction on the part of these unfortunate people that everybody else is like them and that it is, therefore, not worthwhile to improve oneself! ~~What~~ What can sustain those who do try to improve themselves? A reward, faith? Nobody is offering any reward, and in whom could one have faith? Another step from this position, and you have extreme depravity, crime (murder). A mystery.

They are saying that Olia has made it insufficiently clear why she is hanging herself. However, I am not writing for fools.

Bolkonsky reforms as he sees Anatole's leg being cut off, and we've all been shedding tears over it, but a genuine underground man wouldn't have reformed.

"Underground, underground, *poet of the underground,*" our feuilletonists have been repeating over and over again, as if this were something derogatory to me. Silly fools, it is my glory, for that's where the truth lies. It is that very underground which made Gogol, in his solemn testament, speak of his [last] narrative which had risen from the bottom of his soul, *like a song,** and which actually ~~would~~ didn't even exist. Why, it is quite possible that, when he began to write his testament, he didn't even know that he would write this thing about his last narrative. Now, what is this power that makes even an honest and serious person lie and clown in this manner, and what's more, in his own testament? (This power is peculiarly Russian, in Europe people have more integrity, while our people are dreamers and scoundrels.)

The reason for the underground is the destruction of our belief in certain general rules. *"Nothing is sacred."*

Unfinished people (as a consequence of the Petrine reforms *in general*), like the *engineer*[27] in *The Possessed.*

Continuation and conclusion of part two. April 4/5.

[MORE BRIEFLY] Dinner at mother's. Versilov is grumbling. Tatiana Pavlovna approaches <him?>, very mean with him. The Youth is both full of joy, and awkward. Upstairs, he surprises his mother and Liza in an embrace. He says something stupid to Liza, but accidentally it is an obvious hint. Leaves with Versilov. Conversation. More briefly. At home. Olia's mother. Gambling. The scene with the Prince. Learns everything. Tomorrow, Liza. The Prince to the Youth, in Liza's presence. Definitely, a scene between them. Goes to see Stebelkov. The latter (Arseniev).[28] He <goes> to see Vasin. Vasin warns him. [At the landlord's,] [(scene between the Prince and Liza).] His relationship with the Prince. The Youth's sufferings and cynicism. Versilov is cool toward him. Suddenly, Tatiana Pavlovna asks the Youth: "What has he been doing? Versilov has written a letter on

---

* *vypelas' iz dushi ego,* which I found untranslatable.

27 Reference to Kirilov of *The Possessed.*

28 See note 5 of this section.

account of it." A whole story, and scenes, in connection with the letter. [Tatiana Pavlovna says that she had been behind the door that one time.] The old Prince. Anna Andreevna. The Youth is really mad at Versilov. The old Prince, [through Anna Andreevna, shows the Youth the door.] The latter is desperate. [To the Akhmakov woman, encounter with Bioring.] [Insulted by Bioring.] Fireworks of ideas: to America. (There's a funeral at his landlord's.) A quarrel with the young Prince on account of Liza, and another quarrel, this one with Liza. He gets some money. Win back the money he had lost and quit everything! Losing, and the scene at the roulette. "I'll inform the police." A terrible night, encounter with Lambert. Andrieux. Fantastically.

N.B. Pay more attention to Liza, *more warmth*. After the letter, Versilov doesn't show up at home. (A visit to the child, and a mass for Olia.)

MORE RAPIDLY.

She's cold. A little girl. A little girl (cold). He needs her throughout the novel as a refuge from Versilov, Lambert, Liza's distrust, his mother's *apathy*. He secludes himself with her. The little girl dies right before <the execution of his> scheme—the decision to <assault> the Akhmakov woman, downtrodden. Her death makes the Youth desperate.

However, the scheme against the Akhmakov woman had come into existence while Makar was still alive. Here, one might introduce, still during Makar's life, a sudden sally of his against Bioring, the Aide-de-Camp. The Youth is insulted.

Arrival of Maria Ivanovna.

The landlord's wife does not die. He merely reconciles the landlord to the landlady. However, the landlord will come in handy when the old Prince flees to the Youth's flat.

He wanted to set fire and <. . .> She is so cold. They've given her a beating at home ~~drown oneself~~. Drown oneself. Lambert.

The 2d part MORE RAPIDLY.

Current matter. April 4/5.

The Youth admits to Versilov (after dinner) (at the entrance to the tavern) that he has met the Akhmakov woman, but referring to her in a haughty manner, without admitting that he is in love with her and saying merely that she has been asking him about the document. He does everything just to say it, treating the Akhmakov woman with haughty condescension at first, then suddenly giving himself away and admitting that he loves her. Versilov asks him all kinds of questions.

<He tells him?> everything, in his enthusiasm. Here, also about happiness for mankind and about philosophy. A kiss. ~~"I'll give you one."~~ Versilov at the tavern. More lively. ~~At home, Olia's mother. Gambling.~~ At home, Olia's mother. (He is still in that enthusiastic frame of mind.) Gambling, and the Prince. The awakening. Liza at his place. Enter the Prince, too.

Toward the end of part two, already after the betrayal, <he goes> to <see> the Akhmakov woman, to tell <her> that it is now almost impossible for him to quit the game. "The idea." "Some day she will learn about my idea, but should I really turn myself into a mouse now? I must meet Bioring in society... I ~~prove~~ am obliged to meet with Bioring now."

Before the General's widow's betrayal: "There are moments when the truth of reality descends upon ~~his~~ my heart: so what, let my sister be somebody's mistress, and a kept woman—isn't everybody? Why, Versilov is not ~~terribly~~ embarrassed, or is he? Eh, Versilov! Versilov—a phrase..."

"I was ready to kiss." I was kissing. I threw myself on the floor a couple of times, kissing the rug on which she had been standing.

At dinner, Versilov acts bored. Show more clearly that it is *for that very reason* (Bioring).

Versilov, with much ardor, tells him about *légion d'honneur*. This could ~~preserve~~ happen in two different ways, either through the government, or privately.

Versilov again tears him away from the family and from Liza. The Youth has made an appointment with Liza to get reconciled, etc.

From Versilov's letter to the Akhmakov woman: "...This document exists: I could see it from the eyes of that little fool, who wanted to make me believe that it had been burned. But it hasn't been burned, and therefore, beware."

THE PRINCE. *The Prince:* "Maybe I shall marry your sister."

"Eh, this has been all nothing but thoughts, now some action."

"Your sister has also told me that you knew nothing, though I still couldn't make myself believe it."

Versilov's words: "As for Petersburg, these are all paper people, really almost people made of paper."

Versilov, speaking of the Prince's liaison with Liza: "How can I help it, the human heart is free."

When Liza's pregnancy has become known to him, the Youth asks Versilov: "How could you, suspecting that I am aware of Liza's liaison with the Prince, and seeing that I am, at the same time, taking money from the Prince—how could you keep talking to me, shake hands with me, fail to despise me worse than a dog?"

Versilov: "My friend, it's all a matter of one's conscience. I have been meddling in other peoples' consciences more than enough, earning nothing but rebuffs and sneers for it; I don't give a damn about the rebuffs, but what really matters is that this kind of maneuver will take you no place: nobody is going to listen to you." And at this point, about <the Youth's> blushing.

"How could you, suspecting that I knew of Liza's liaison, stretch out your hand to me?"

Versilov: "How could I?... Perhaps I, too, was afraid to lose my ideal and to face a scoundrel, instead of my ardent and honest boy. Why couldn't you suppose there was something other than perfidy in me, something closer to naïveté?"

["So you were not sure, not sure."

"I am an old man. I don't know young people."]

In part three.

"I do believe, my friend, I do believe in stinking Lizaveta, I believe in her with all my strength."

(Stinking Lizaveta, according to legend, screams to Christ: "All right now, Christ, you won't dare refuse me thy Kingdom... And if you refuse, I'll still shout 'Holy!' to you. You may elevate others, and I'll shout 'Holy!'—cast me in Hell, and it's still 'Holy!' Let me be in the hellish fire, with the devils, and I'll still be yelling 'Holy, Holy, Holy!' " (N.B. Mad frenzy, fakirism.)

... And always smut on <her> nose.

[The Youth's mother.]

THE VERY LAST DECISION. APRIL 4/5.

In part two, introduce only Stebelkov's offer to sell *those people* to him. The Youth is outraged and goes to see Vasin, whereupon Vasin warns him of the Prince (the stock certificates). Then, in part three, Vasin, even though he is compromised by Stebelkov, entrusts <his?> manuscript to the Youth. *The latter,* even though he is under Versilov's and Makar Ivanov's influence, wants to join the conspirators himself, being under the impression that the manuscript has been entrusted to him. When [Lambert] informs the police of the manuscript, Vasin is arrested. The Youth meanwhile had spent a night at his place. Vasin suspects that it was he who informed the police, and since the Youth is suspected of having informed the police about the roulette, he is quite crushed by this suspicion and wants *to set everything on fire.*

April 7.

THE LITTLE GIRL. Liza has rejected the Youth, so it appears to him. It seems to him that everybody is wronging him, so the little girl is the only one he's got <in the world>.

April 15.

The girl is quite frozen. As she dies, she says: *"It's all right!"* (Bismarck's ring.) Instead of being affectionate, she says to the Youth: *"Here!"* and gives him some treasure of hers, a toy or something.

(To Liza, as she is leaving:) "Liza, I think that you are a strong individual; I've been talking all the time, while you have told me nothing, and are leaving as the winner. Yes, I believe that you're going to subdue him, and that you're going to subdue me also."

"I take a dim view of everything. I'll earn my spurs before her. Don't tell her. Listen, I told you about (the marriage proposal to Anna Andreevna), because it has been bothering me too much."

"It isn't I who refuses <to marry her>, it is she who has turned me down. I am gravely afflicted by it."

"You have proposed to her?"

"Yes, I was there to propose marriage to her."

"And later, I didn't go through with it; I said nothing, but only because I didn't get around to it. She forestalled me and said that this was an idea <only>."

"Which means that it was just as if nothing had happened, and your pride must be..."

"Still, before Liza I'm a scoundrel—don't tell her."

Earlier, we had been talking of roulette.

At night, I found a note from Stebelkov. Saw Versilov in a tavern. Anna Andreevna. After the Prince, in the morning, Tatiana Pavlovna. At Stebelkov's (about Anna Andreevna). At Vasin's (a second). To the old Prince—about Anna Andreevna, and the letter. At the entrance, a kick in the arse by Bioring. Came running to Tatiana, weeping: Versilov's letter. To Versilov: Baron Roden (mother and sister upstairs): "You are a maniac. You will be summoned before a higher agency. In that case he is going to protect himself, and you will be summoned to appear at an altogether different place. Bioring, so far, is not involved at all. Let the young man be here." When Roden has left, Versilov laughs: "You know, I made them sit upstairs in the meantime. Eh, leave me in peace, let's go." At this point, a letter from the Prince.

"Isn't it wonderful to be dealing with a person who can express himself so clearly and so concisely?"

"Oh, you are witty—I have heard about that—but wit is not always wisdom."

"A most profound observation, Mr. Baron Rossen."

"Oh, I have heard that you are a witty man, but you know that wit is not always wisdom."

"The devil take it, you are really tempting me."

"A retraction of one's words such as you are giving me is almost tantamount to reaffirming them."

"Is that really so?" Versilov said with a smirk.

On the next day the Prince gave himself up. His letter to me. Mother, Liza. *(She* keeps her wits.) To America, win some money. The scene at the roulette table.

Vasin: "There's nothing to it, believe me; in reality there is nothing to it at all. Nothing but talk. I am telling you this confidentially, and as to a person whom I trust. However, I am still grateful to you... He knows only too well that I'm not a party to it."

Versilov: "This marriage (of Anna Andreevna's) is quite typical of society."

"That she would like to have some money, and a position in society? Why, isn't this worth it?"

Bioring won't like the taste of this a bit.

"And it has been made public?"

"No, nothing has been. I have it from his son, Andrei Andreich. I don't know how it was done; nor whether it is still a big secret or not; but all I have told you is true."

"What about the old Prince?"

"That's precisely the point, he is delighted. And of course there is a lot of commotion over there. You can understand this. So they laughed at you over there! Ah, poor boy!" (And he laughed right to my face.)

Everything is in confusion, the roulette.

The Prince in his letter: "I told her that I had proposed marriage to Anna Andreevna. She forgave me everything. And there is one more thing: I must tell you that I am actually more guilty in that business (the stock certificates) than I let you know yesterday."

"I find it awfully base to love generosity in the ideal, yet allow oneself to go from degradation to degradation."

The Prince, before they go to play roulette: "Don't you find this sordid? (We've been doing it a thousand times.)"

The Youth: "Money is always sordid."

"A kopek earned by hard work isn't."

"Let's do it one last time, and then repent."

"This is what I've been telling myself a thousand times. This has been my ruin."

"You are so right, but what if there's no other way?"

"No, there is a way out, the *princely* one."

"And that would be?"

"Later. Let's go."

Let's try it once.

My jaw was trembling from nervousness all night. "Is he really so noble (Bioring), selling himself; and Anna Andreevna, too, is selling herself, selling everything. And Versilov is a maniac." I laughed spitefully. "Yes, a maniac, a maniac" (jealous of Katerina Nikolaevna). "You <withdraw> into carnality, and I, and I, into my idea. But that woman, that woman. Oh, this is lower than the lowest."

PS also in the letter: "I have told you that there is a way out: the princely way. *I* have taken it. However, even with this, I was late. I shouldn't have gone gambling."

Versilov: "What's worst of all is that you've been rubbing elbows with these people, gambling; however, I am not judging you."

After Versilov's showdown with Bioring: "Let's give it one try (roulette)." The Prince smiled: "I'll think it over. Right now I'm sick."

To the Prince, at the roulette table: "You have renounced me!"

"What else could I have done? Even without it, I am quite crushed by the very fact that I decided to follow your advice and that I've come to this place."

"You are a vile little aristocrat."

"I'll prove to you that I am not."

At the roulette table: "Yes, I can testify that Mr. Dolgoruky cannot have stolen <that money>, at least so far as I know him." (Before he is searched.)

"Is this to say that you do not know him well enough?"

"I'd rather like not to answer certain questions."

In his letter: "I did not renounce you; I could, however, have acted in your behalf more resolutely."

At the Prince's, that night. Story of the Ensign. "I wanted to write to the Officers' Club and to the Ensign while I was in Luga. I was wavering and suffering. It was then that I made a clean breast of it before Lizaveta Makarovna."

"What did Liza say?"

"Not to write."

"Set that straight." <?>—"She told me, of course not directly, but in all too transparent terms, clearly and tactfully, that this was an impossible idea."

"She decided the matter as a woman would."

"She said that I would <in that case> love myself just as much.* Is that so? Is that so?"

"Yes, I think that they don't have full proof. But what about having to lie to them?"

"Does Liza know about it?"

"No, she does not know everything. Because I myself have found out all about this affair only now, from Stebelkov and from Zhirondsky. I had already forgotten about it."

"But listen, if they tell the police about it, they are really turning themselves in, aren't they?"

"But to be in partnership with these crooks! To be their associate for ever and ever! What are they talking about now, what are they threatening to do, what do they want money for? They are saying: ~~you know, her~~ 'Of course we shall not give <you> away, but in case...' It is Zhirondsky who is uttering these threats, and Stebelkov is passing it on to me. This Zhirondsky, it seems, is planning to steal something, some money entrusted to him, and to go to America. Stebelkov has explained something along these lines to me. Well, that's what it is, he needs some money to go to America."

After the scene with Bioring's second I came running to the Prince's, and he said to me: "I almost decided to go and play some roulette! Will you despise me..."

"No, I also, I also..."

"Don't you find this sordid?"

"Money is sordid, but... I've run out of money completely, and I have to go out no matter what happens."

"What hatred!" I exclaimed.

"Hatred!" Tatiana hissed, laughing venomously to my face.

"I have come to the conclusion: no, there can't be a duel."

"Perhaps so much the better for Baron Bioring."

"Oh, I know that you are a witty man, but wit is not wisdom, and moreover, I admit that I am most grateful to you for saving me all this trouble. I so dislike all this nonsense."

---

* Not quite clear in the original.

"Yet you are allowing yourself..."

"We are not living in the woods, but in a well-organized state."

"Is that what you think, my good Baron Rossen?"

"I'll admit that you are greatly tempting me to show you that I'm not so very much 'your good Baron Rossen.' "*

Only *one* strange sensation stuck in my mind, namely that I had told Lambert that I'd got a document by which I could destroy everybody and everything.

When I woke up—I felt so glad that Lambert did not have my address, but how great was my surprise when I realized, after a moment's thinking, that I did not have his address either. I had completely forgotten where I had been. I could remember the room, Adolphine, but where it had been, in what street, I had forgotten.

Suzdal' boyars.

"First of all, the question regarding Katerina Nikolaevna Akhmakov *must be* completely eliminated."

"There might have been other ways to bring you to reason, but certain allowances were made. You are proving to be unworthy of such indulgence."

Jealous of Versilov on account of Katerina Nikolaevna. Was this a monstrous idea? Everything was possible, I was a medley of sensations which were staggering me, and of which I was not consciously aware. There ~~was~~ remained a single point of rest: *my idea,* and that's what I was clinging to.

It appeared, that she had some close connections with *la maison Andrieux,* and that she actually came from *la maison de monsieur Andrieux,* but was then torn away from *la maison Andrieux*. It was hard to imagine that she was his mistress, but even that could be."

"Où allez-vous, monsieur?" she screamed in a torn, broken voice.

This stern face, this stern and beautiful face, is the face of the best, of the most marvelous English etching.

David—Salomon, everything is going round in my mind.

Anna Andreevna told me this herself. This was perfectly chaste, pure, and wonderful, something like a poem... I kissed her hand and began to cry in delight...

(And he began to cry.) "Let it be only a dream... But don't let them take this dream from me. Let me die with my dream. Even Katerina

---

* A pun, difficult to translate: *dobryi baron Rossen* could also mean "kind Baron Rossen." The Baron is implying that he could be quite nasty, too.

Nikolaevna has promised me this. We have started this romance, so allow us to finish it. Let it be a dream... But don't let them take this dream from me. Let me die with this dream."

"Life with friends, with my family, with my dear ones. This is heaven. I would forgive them all. I want to forgive everybody; I haven't been angry with anybody in a long time. Katerina Nikolaevna is smiling to my face: but, *ma chérie,* I am not saying at all that I am altogether King David. Never mind, it is just a simile, *la poésie dans la vie.* I say, what is it that makes you smile? *Chère, chère,* I want to do harm to no one. But I am strong, I have support. *Quelle charmante personne,* ah?"

"But how long it is since you were here, my friend, and how very-very-very much has happened since."

"I don't know why life should be so short; I suppose so we won't get bored, of course, for life is the Maker's work of art, something like a poem by Pushkin. At least one should let those who are not bored live longer. I, for instance, am not bored. *Les chants de Salomon, mais non, c'est David, qui mettait les jeunes belles dans son lit pour se chauffer dans sa viellesse.*[29] My dear friend."

The old Prince: "History remains silent on this point, but otherwise, what's the difference? So this is what we have decided. This should stay in the family, strictly in the family. I told Katerina Nikolaevna about it only because I feel guilty before her. Every matter can be both majestic and ridiculous. In <a novel by> Paul de Kock this would have become une *une scène de bassinoire*[30]."

"Paul de Kock lacks elegance; otherwise he would be magnificent. They've got no taste, I swear, *le goût est chez nous,*[31] in Russia, in our ancient mansions... those which are still standing. In this respect, I am a patriot."

---

29 French: "The songs of Solomon, but no, it's David who placed the young beauties in his bed to keep himself warm in his old age."

30 French: "a scene with a hot water bottle."

31 French: "we have the taste."

This notebook page is a good example of Dostoevsky's "contained chaos." The page gives the impression of messiness because of the drawing, interlineations, marginal additions, and crossings-out. On closer examination, however, the effect is one of control and order.

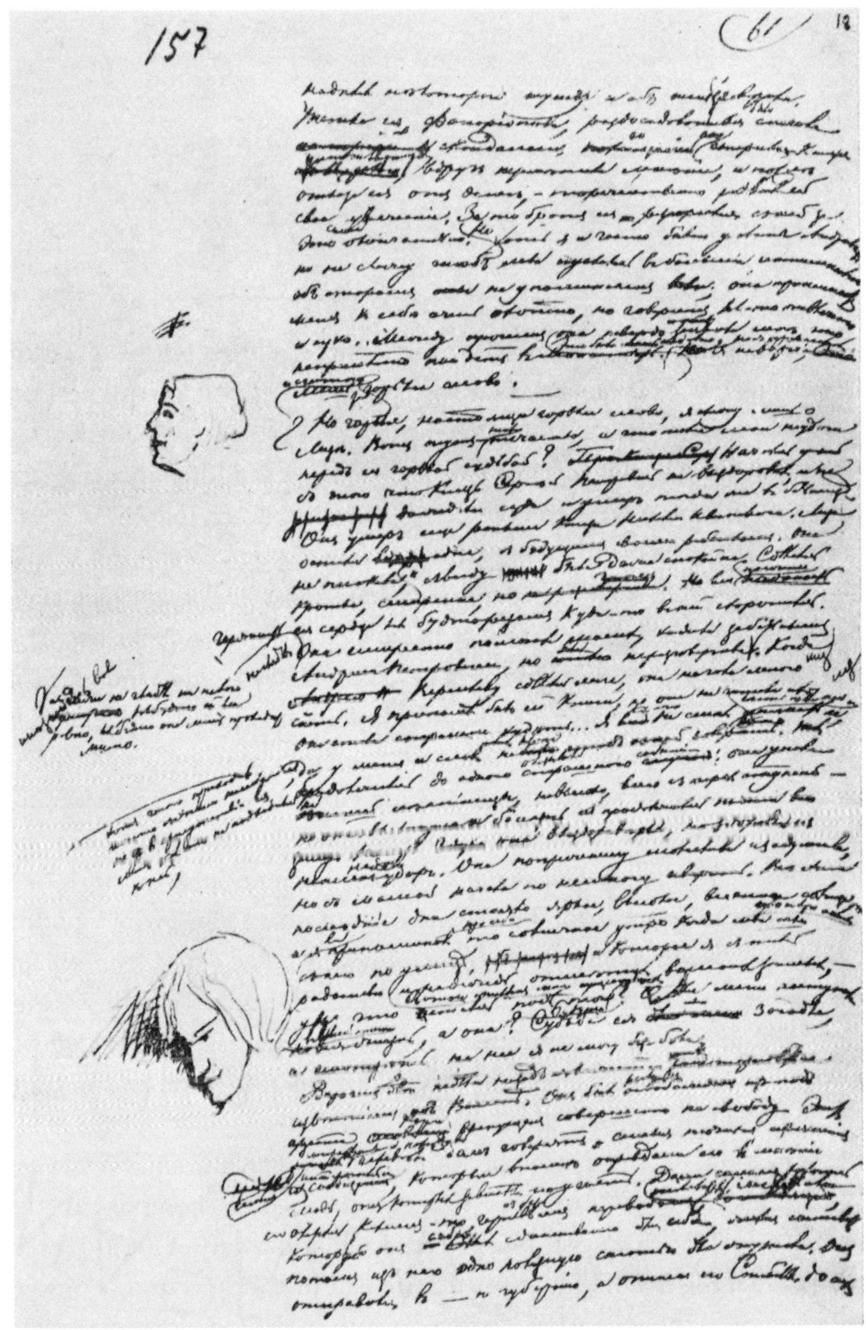

The heads of men on this page are typical of drawings in the notebooks. Note the meticulous evenness of the left-hand margin. The features of the drawings are precise and clear, and even the shadow of one head is composed of straight lines. Although there are many crossings-out and substitutions, there is no smudging and the interlineal substitutions are neatly entered.

VI

Notes to the Third Part of the Novel

The confession of Versilov to Arkady and the meeting of Versilov with Katerina Nikolaevna hold the center of interest in this section of notes. In both notes and novel Katerina Nikolaevna is intimately tied with his fate and in some way she represents and confirms Versilov's fall. In the novel the connection between Katerina Nikolaevna and Versilov's failure is dramatically implied, but in the notes it is explicitly insisted on: "Here, *Finis.* [What's most important.] Versilov says: 'I hate this woman, for she has stolen my peace from me. If I were to fall in love with her, I would ~~myself~~ kill either myself, [or her]." Neither she nor Versilov, nor indeed the Youth understands why Katerina Nikolaevna should exercise such power over him, but by his contradictory statements and his violent actions Versilov confirms the power. Katerina Nikolaevna cannot understand why he loves her: "You see how nasty I am, really, why should you love me? What else can you want?" The Youth cannot understand why Versilov loves her, and he feels ashamed for him and ashamed of himself for loving her in competition with his father. His suggestion that Katerina Nikolaevna be humiliated by Lambert is a desperate effort, born of bruised love, to restore to Versilov his lost pride and to himself the ideal that he has of his father.

Some light on the power of Katerina Nikolaevna maintains over Versilov is cast by the meeting between the two in the notes. In the novel she assures him that he is a respected and a valued friend, even while rejecting him. The implied criticism in the rejection is powerful enough to the sensitive Versilov for him to explode into expletives at junctures in the meeting. But in the notes the criticism of Versilov is direct, explicit, and even scathing. Katerina Nikolaevna does not speak to him in the novel as in the following passages taken from these notes:

> She to Him: When falling in love with me, you were falling in love with no one but yourself, and, besides, you certainly couldn't have forgiven me that confession which you made before me, for you saw it as a humiliation. You vain man, you couldn't even stand *that*. How then was I going to help laughing at you.

A little later in the meeting, she adds:

> *She:* ("Lack of all form") I have seen your pride, which consists of the idea that, inasmuch as I have learned about your thoughts and you have exposed your soul before me (you have deigned to open it to me), I should therefore value this very highly. I have seen this in every movement of yours, and I've made a point of ceasing to value it; quite on the contrary, I've often been laughing at it. This alone is utterly disgraceful.

At one point she states quite openly that she considers him to be false:

> Versilov *to her*. "I'm one of those people who cannot remain indifferent when they have nothing to believe in."
>
> "You are exaggerating, as always," *she* says.
>
> "No, with a single glance, with a single smile, you have been destroying the whole path to my salvation."
>
> "Because I saw through <its> falseness.
>
> "There was no falseness."
>
> "I am not talking of any kind of fraud. What I saw was simply the falsity of the idealist, the stiltedness, the affectation." [NB. *Lidiia.*]

Also: ["I have seen your moral disorder..."]

But Katerina Nikolaevna recognizes only the symptoms, not the causes. She sees the stiltedness, affectation, posing, and pride, but she does not see what has brought Versilov to this state. At one point in the notes she asks Versilov about his "idea," and he delivers a long analysis of it. The explanation is not given in the meeting between the two in the final version, and yet it is the key to Versilov's character and to the connection he sees between his efforts and his failure. Versilov says:

> I conceived, at that time, my original idea: seek to perfect yourself, try to break your own resistance as your conscience and your faith will tell you, to the best of your ability, and, once having conquered yourself, you may perhaps also find that ultimate idea, your own solution to "what to do?" and "what to preach?" I passionately clung to this idea. You were all laughing at my chains. Why? I was actually wearing them, but you didn't know what was going on in my *soul.* Yes, it may be that, finally, I did persuade myself that mine was the right way, but then you appeared before me, and I suddenly realized that without you I am nothing, and that my idea is unrealizable.

The intent seems to be admirable. Versilov had lost his faith in but not his yearning for something to believe in, and he formed a program to discover by discipline and self-perfection what to believe in. Culture, wisdom, firm will, sacrifice, and devotion to his program would restore what history had robbed him of. But, as Versilov tells Katerina Nikolaevna in the notes, "With a single glance, with a single smile, you have been destroying the whole path to my salvation."

Why should this be so? Why should a trivial woman destroy what refinement, will, and culture have achieved? The notes tell us why. Versilov's vanity had been touched by her rejection of him in the beginning, so that he turned to a sick half-wit for the adoration Katerina Nikolaevna would not give him, and his vanity is touched again later when the hope of reconquering Katerina Nikolaevna is threatened by her intention to marry Baron Bioring. According to his plan Versilov was supposed to be the master of his fate: he would believe in what he had created, rest in superior isolation in a world he had constructed and in beliefs that he had erected. But his love-hate of Katerina Nikolaevna irrationally breaks down his solipsistic world, and hence his fury and rage. What threatens him, he attempts to destroy. One way or the other she too must be brought under his command: either by loving him and acknowledging his perfections, or by being unworthy of his love. She must be the best of women—if she loves him—or the worst of women, if she does not. Thus the agonizing and violent contradictions of word and feeling. Even Versilov has a moment of sane penetration to his motives when he says to the Youth: "I am afraid of one thing," he said suddenly, "namely, that we are both vile, which is also why we wish that she were vile, and not at all because she really is vile."

At bottom what Dostoevsky is telling us about Versilov is what Katerina Nikolaevna herself partially perceives when she says to him: "When falling in love with me, you were falling in love with no one but yourself..." Dostoevsky had told us many times before and he was to tell us again in *The Brothers Karamazov* that when one loses one's belief in God, one has only oneself to believe in. Beneath the culture, refinement, and intelligence, and despite the efforts to believe and to be virtuous, there was in Versilov only the vanity and impotence of the self. Dostoevsky is thinking of Versilov as a representative of contemporary man, when he says of the contemporary man:

> The ideal, its presence in one's soul, a thirst, a need to believe in [something... to worship something] and the absence of any kind of faith. This gives birth to two feelings in <the soul of> a high type of contemporary man: boundless pride and boundless self-contempt. Observe his hellish sufferings, watch him trying to convince himself that he is actually a believer... And then, his clashes with reality, where he invariably shows up so ridiculous, so ridiculous and so petty... and so insignificant. *He* suspects that what one must do is work on oneself, restrain oneself, and that this would cost an endless effort. And so he does tax himself with the duty of self-perfection, does it gladly, enthusiastically... [choosing for himself nothing but chains all along.] Occasionally, he would be bothered by a feeling of tormenting unbelief and skepticism, but He stands firm and, finally, it appears that he has come close to his goal... And there, as he clashes head-on with reality, he takes a terrible fall, showing himself feeble and nerveless. Why? <Because> He is uprooted from the soil, a child of his age...

We find neither an explicit analysis of Versilov's idea, nor the explicit and scathing exposure of its falseness by Katerina Nikolaevna in the novel itself. There is a brief allusion to the idea of mortifying one's will by monastic discipline in the novel by the Youth as he re-creates what Versilov said during his confession. But the decision to discipline the will is put forth as a consequence of his break with Katerina Nikolaevna, as some kind of punishment of himself for having been attracted to her. In the notes the "idea" to discipline his will, which is analyzed much more fully, predates his relationship and break with Katerina Nikolaevna. One is at a loss to see what—except for mystery and vagueness—Dostoevsky gained by these changes. The notes tell us quite fully what Versilov's "idea" was, why he is so violently attached to Katerina Nikolaevna, and as a consequence what moves him in his irrational acts. We do not know these things from reading the novel alone.

The grand theme of the novel is order and disorder. Versilov is disorder and Makar is order, and the Youth stands between both. And as Lebedev in *The Idiot* exposes by caricature the disorder of the society about him, so Lambert in caricature makes evident the disorder that Versilov conceals and the Youth attempts to avoid. Makar is supposed to be the antipoise to Versilov in both the novel and the notes, but in neither do his anecdotes, biblical sayings, or his aphorisms convince the Youth or the reader. Several times in these notes Dostoevsky tells us that Makar's influence on the Youth is immense, but nothing in the Youth's actions or thoughts or feelings confirm what Dostoevsky desired.

One must point finally to a number of passages, some of which reappear in Versilov's confession to the Youth, where Versilov expresses ideas that were sacred to Dostoevsky. Dostoevsky himself could have said what Versilov says in the following passage:

> Society must be built upon moral foundations; nothing can be founded upon the flesh, upon an economic idea, upon making stones into bread, and so far our politicians are fooling only the gullible. The moral ideas of a nation are derived from religion, or are formulated by popular religion. Anyone who wants to reject and *break up* the old foundations, such as private property, family, etc., must break up the old faith... For a Russian nobleman is the universal reconciliation of ideas. For, in our time, educated Russian thought is the universal reconciliation of ideas. The educated Russian type is a uni-

> versal human type, and up to now it has been only the Russian nobleman. A Frenchman is only a Frenchman, but a Russian... a Russian is a progressive; his thinking is very much ahead of everyone else's. The bearer of a universal ideal.

But these are only ideas, and not beliefs, and the difference is insurmountable for Dostoevsky.

May 9.

Makar has a shattering impact on Liza, awakening in her a passionate religious feeling. She says: "I knew nothing about this." Then, suddenly, she is angry with Makar, pouts. Later, she is listening to Versilov (his ideals) also, and accepts a good deal of it. She is, however, a practical person. Marriage to the Prince. The Prince has been acquitted, is full of enthusiasm, and—shoots himself. (N.B. He must elicit extreme sympathy.)

After <his> illness, the Youth, in spite of Makar and Versilov, develops a very somber emotional attitude. Feelings of vengefulness and jealousy make their appearance. A yearning for the ideal.

(1) The idea of self-perfection, and (2) to become famous as quickly as possible, [in order to take his vengeance]—a struggle between these two ideas.

Meanwhile, the "idea"—this he realizes only now—was nothing but an outgrowth of <his idea of> revenge for everything, for everything, even if it took him 50 years.

N.B. Versilov's terrible ingenuousness makes a tremendous impression on him.

See in the yellow book, February 25.

"Shut up and say nothing to anybody! This is my new rule."

Versilov is an enthusiast, which is why he was discussing socialism. *(Ingenuousness.)*

After his recovery, Versilov and the Youth—they're related <spirits>, fervent compassion for Versilov, <though> mute.

They abduct the old Prince.

After <his> recovery, the Youth <is obsessed> by the idea of *her,* a yearning for the ideal. And through the remaining two parts, he either has spells of a passionate renascence of his faith in her purity [("a forced faith," says Versilov),] or experiences an even deeper fall. Finally he becomes convinced of her guilt (through Versilov). Then, disenchantment, cynicism, and Lambert. The somber idea to catch her using the document as bait (the conflagration). But right before the execution <of this scheme>, a more noble thought: hand over the document to her, i.e., *fulfill the duty of honor, and pass on,* into "his idea." (?N.B. *Perhaps:* Alphonsine hides him. Lambert and Versilov attack her, the Youth saves her.) They steal the document, and resew the pocket, with Alphonsine doing the sewing.

After <his> recovery: a yearning for the ideal, the idea of revenge and jealousy, and *the struggle with the ideas* of Makar and Versilov. Versilov finally explains to him his own relationship to the Akhmakov woman. At this point, a quick meeting between the Youth and the Akhmakov woman, and another insult from Bioring (in connection with the old Prince's flight to his place). He once more becomes disenchanted with the Akhmakov woman.

Liza: All of a sudden, she develops a religious feeling. And while the Youth and Versilov (after Makar) are still making their preparations, she decides, after the Prince's death, to enter a monastery. But the child.

[2d chapter] Besides her religiosity, there is also haughtiness in her. It is well possible that she fell in love with the Prince partly because his character was inferior to hers (weaker), and he needed her help. (Her character resembles that of Versilov. What is needed is a scene featuring her and Versilov. Also, her and Makar.)

[Regarding the monastery, she contradicts and argues.]

[*Here.* NB!! That is the beginning of the 2d chapter.]

Versilov's mad and morbid letter to the Akhmakov woman has been dispatched, not just in a delirium or with the sole desire to insult her, whatever the cost, but also with considerable forethought: inasmuch as *she* was about to marry Bioring, and knowing ~~how they~~ people like Bioring, he was figuring on stopping him by his fear of a possible scandal, thus destroying (severing) their budding marital union. And to be sure, he ~~was~~ very pleased with the fact that Bioring, in sending Rosen to him, was was particularly insisting that everything pertaining to *that lady* should be removed from their declarations.

July 30. [N.B. Going to bed: "Why is she alone pulsating in my head? Even Lambert doesn't have this strong an effect. The thing is that I love her."]

Versilov: "It is Christ who is going to save Russia, for that is the only thing she's still got that is national; really, Christ is the only national element [Russia] ever had. If their faith in Christ comes to an end, this will also be the end of the Russian people."

Practically—preach, feats.

"Let us perform some feats" (naïve agreement).

["Yes, my friend, go right ahead." (And here, He makes his confession about *her*.)]

"Marry my mother."

"Yes, my friend, if you please, my friend."

(Makar had willed the same thing.) (He chops up those icons.)

"Let us perform some feats." (And at this point, this confession about the Akhmakov woman.)

"What does an ancestor, or the memory of an ancestor, mean?" (Makar).

"Thank <God> for your soul."

"Every blade of grass is singing a song."

"A new nation is arriving" (a patriot).

"Silly little deniers of God, nihilist and nihilist woman."

The Youth: ["I have been thinking of you, but your hermit doesn't even know the laws law of gravitation."

"Why do you think so? There are different kinds of knowledge."

"What kind of people go there?"]

Forests—meadows, nature.

"At first, while amidst nature, I was feeling *sorry* about being *alone*, but later I found out that I was *with everybody*. And so a hermit, forty years in the desert, yet he is *with everybody*."

"But where's the profit?"—"God won't let anything pass without a profit, he'll make it manifest, too, Mary of Egypt."

Makar and the children. "What is a child?"

About how Christ will come.

About how the third part of all grass will be burnt up (power).*

"But Christ... Ah my dear ones, have you forgotten, look at this grass... this birdie."

"Remember your forefathers, but even if you will not remember them—that's all right, *for I am with you*."

A village cemetery.[1]

"I am too kind," says the Youth, "I ought to be meaner, this way I won't get through life."

---

* Quoted inaccurately from Rev. 8: 7.

[1] Reference to Zhukovsky's translation of Gray's "Elegy Written in a Country Church-Yard."

[For chapter two (2d part)] My whole "idea" is nothing but a lot of kindness, it is funny and comical, and therefore base. (As he is sitting down to start listening to Makar.) [(Lambert isn't the one who makes him confused, but he's got his own idea, i.e., a kind of conflagration, a ~~great~~ revenge of magnanimity.)]

The idea to become a pilgrim, to suffer from everybody, while loving everybody, or else the darkness of <his> idea.

"Suffer, suffer," (says Makar,) "and then you'll even quit suffering (for your heart will be filled with love). You won't even feel your suffering."

See St. after Petersburg. February 25.

[(N.B. The age and contemporary man.)]

It isn't the fact that Versilov has experienced another fall that confuses him; rather, even while he is still deeply moved and right after he has offered to join Versilov on a pilgrimage, he suddenly meets Alphonsine, and is glad about it, and goes to see Lambert, and talks to him. ("This man is more akin to me, a little sordid.")

On the contrary, Versilov's fall (the icons) elicits his compassion. Whereas the fact that he is glad to have met Lambert is <to be explained by> his hidden anger at those who had insulted him, and at her.

And there she suddenly offers him a rendezvous.

Finish part three with this, i.e., with the Prince's flight, the chopping of the icons.

Makar: "Let us weep until we get justice from the Lord. [Sometimes, in the springtime, a whole crowd of poor people will be seen weeping.] You raise your head, they're asleep, it's cool, a child, you give a sigh and fall asleep again. [Every little leaf, the birdies, and there's a tree standing there, and the tree is growing, and a little leaf. Isn't this a mystery? We rejoice at it."]

"God's little birdie is a mystery, and isn't it marvelous (that it is a mystery)?"

"What is there to be found out?! Even if you did find out, you would still have even less understanding, for it is not for your mind to deal with these things. What is this? God's green grass, let it grow (in peace), God's green grass. You look around, and you see beauty (everywhere). God's mystery." [For chapter two]

"Are you a pilgrim?"

"A pilgrim, my dear. And sinful and vain while I was still of this world."

"What is it that makes you rejoice so much?"

"One rejoices at the Lord."

"That is, that He is merciful?"

"Both for the innumerable times He has shown mercy to us, and just simply so, just rejoicing that He is there," he answered, quite unaware of the insidiousness of my question about God's mercy.

Liza, having learned of the Prince's decision, and of his arrest, says: "That's the thing I have been afraid of. I knew that he is too wonderful and is capable of anything great."

And so she makes home a hell for everybody: she is suspicious of everyone, fearing that they might attack and slander the Prince, but when somebody is speaking well of the Prince, she refuses to believe in that person's sincerity, thinking that whatever was said was only meant to console her. This goes even for her mother. But when somebody is giving sincere praise to the Prince, she gets angry, claiming that he isn't getting enough recognition, [that he has suffered] that he stands higher than anyone else, and is so much nobler, so much so that even those who praise him couldn't possibly grasp it. The whole reason for this is that she can herself very clearly see how worthless a person the Prince is. But then there is love. She receives Makar's sermon with hostility. Finally, she becomes openly *defiant,* and admits before Makar that she is pregnant. The latter, something like the woman who was granted forgiveness in the temple,* gentle and timid. Suddenly, Liza is defeated. She actually admits right there (abruptly, inadvertently) that the Prince is a worthless person. ("But he is dear to me.") The Prince's jealousy throws her into a frenzy. She keeps running to visit him, to see his lawyer, she is rushing to <plead for him with> the authorities, to the courts; marriage...

In this fashion, Liza's role is *established.*

Even amidst such inconsolable grief, occasionally laughter and jokes. (Rays of sunshine continue!)

[2d chapter] And only after the Prince's death, Liza, terribly shaken, forever <her> mother.**

"So you rejoice because there is mystery."

"Your repose is mystery, and your sigh is mystery."

"So it is just wonderful that there is mystery? I shall remember this. However, in the light of reason... this isn't how I myself under-

* John 8: 1.

** The phrase is unclear in the original.

stand it, I have been grumbling myself. It seems to me that people know very little, and that they are much too proud."

"You've got such a mind..."

"A microscope is even more of a mystery."

"You may, perhaps, not know it yourself, but what you've said there is true."

"Know, oh elder: the more a man has learned, the nearer he is to God."

"Well, it is not always that way."

"Not always, my friend. I have seen many learned men."

"The deeper the mystery becomes, the nearer it takes you to God. But whosoever will say, in his pride: 'There is no more mystery, I have learned everything,' forsakes God and the true light and falls into darkness, and is having a bad time of it in the darkness. Yes, my friend, and in the meantime the mystery continues inviolate."

And I remembered these words.

Memento. (Supporting details.) In the yellow book: beginning February 25. In the same book: page X^0. (Versilov's words and cute sayings at the end of the book, see February, and also at the beginning.) Then, according to names: Vasin, the Prince, the Akhmakov woman, etc. Then, p. *YZ*—Versilov's words. *ZZZ* at the very end (November 26). In the beginning, about Vasin, 570.

Ems.

[2d chapter] N.B. I was pretending that I wanted no part of that business; yet I was stunned by this remote news about Katerina Nikolaevna.

Here, Anna Andreevna is asking N<astasia> Egor<ovna> to pay her a visit.

Nota bene, important. Rumors the effect that Katerina Nikolaevna, who had previously shunned high society, had made a new appearance there and was having extraordinary success. Simultaneously, the news that the episode with Bioring had ended in a separation, which isn't quite correct; rather, a certain coolness developed between them as a result of the fact that Bioring, after *Versilov's letter,* took fright and wavered for a moment, showing a desire to withdraw. But not entirely so. The caution with which Bioring had separated *his* from *hers* in Versilov's letter had offended Katerina Nikolaevna. Her success in society had again turned Bioring's head.

The Youth is jolted by the news of Katerina Nikolaevna's success in society, which fills him with *hatred* caused by jealousy. (The image of a youth, standing in a corner during a ball, while *his* beauty is surrounded by a throng of dandies.) Jealousy and hatred, and when she grants him a rendezvous in passing, as if throwing it to him like *charity* (while he is actually delighted), he really does begin to hate her, whereupon he immediately joins Lambert...

? (N.B. Versilov has proved to Bioring that the Prince is going to disinherit her; or, he has succeeded in getting Bioring involved with him, etc.). [Such is the Youth's suspicion.]

Liza is now in close contact with Vasin and is using his advice (without the Youth's knowledge), and at home she is short-tempered with everybody. The Youth thinks that this is "because she feels that I have little love or esteem for the Prince." Whereupon his mother says to him: "Leave her alone, she is doing it out of pride; she is finding it hard to face our pity for her, and for him" (i.e., for the Prince).

"I am the happiest woman in the world," says Liza, "he is great, he has done something you would never have done."

Meanwhile, Vasin suddenly proposes to her, and is angered when she turns him down. Liza is terribly offended and irritated by the proposal.

[2d chapter] The Youth discovers that Liza has been secretly in touch with Versilov. Like a pupil with her teacher, and he has had a strong influence on her.

The Youth to Makar, speaking of <his> scalded hand: "Don't tell me about it, don't embarrass me."

Meekness is strength. Meekness will conquer everything.

Versilov: "Meanwhile I have returned to my former filthy condition."

~~News~~ "Don't you think that your mother's soul is gravely afflicted by her sin?"

"And I thought that you were in favor of all those new ideas?"

"There are no new ideas: the ideas are still the same, beginning with Job. Proudhon and Job—the temptation of Christ."[2]

---

[2] Dostoevsky wrote to his wife about the "Book of Job" on June 10, 1875: "I am reading the book of Job, and it brings me to painful ecstasy. I leave off reading and I walk about my room for an hour, almost crying. This book, Anna, strange, it was one of the first that made an impression on my life; I was still then almost a child!" The influence of the book of Job is pervasive in *The Brothers Karamazov,* especially in the words of Father Zossima. Proudhon's *La Célébration du dimanche* was one of two forbidden books found in Dostoevsky's apartment when it was searched at the time of his arrest in 1849. Two books on Proudhon appeared also in Russia at this time: *Zhizn' i perepiska Prudona* (The Life and Correspondence of Proudhon) by A. N. Pleshcheev in 1873, and *P. Zh. Prudon v*

[Here, chapters 3, 4] About Makar: "Two views. Self-possession or independence of anything in the world. This has also been the same since the beginning of time." (Freedom of will.)

"I shall not relate what we discussed on that occasion. Oh, those days, I consider them sacred to this very day."

His naïveté and ingenuousness, his *childlike nature.* Those who are difficult to reach, who seem to be mocking everything and, most often of all, children when they are truly beautiful, are exactly like that.

Lambert: "Remember our gang of robbers?" And some day you are yet going to gain the kingdom of God.

Lambert is actually a good man. Lambert believes in God. It's because he is healthy, that is why he is a villain. Let him grow old, or fall ill—and he'll start buying candles for the Church. Every *average man* is like that.

Makar Ivanov. About the landowner, who rebuilt a village that had burned down. About how the children were begging the merchant, yet he didn't forgive. About how the little boy drowned himself, the siskin. About how he used to rake out oats from a horse's <crib>. Stinking Elizaveta. About how some holy monks killed another monk. And so on.

Mother's name day. Versilov brings a bouquet and ends up chopping up the icons.

Makar: "The siskin. I wonder what that little soul (the boy's) said to God?"

[Chapters 3, 4] "Why, you are telling things which are right against you<r ideas>!" shouts the Youth.

"Don't you get upset about it. (The world is always like this, what's important is only that truth never die in it.)"

Versilov: On God's ways, Philidor and Lagrange.

[2d chapter] The Youth (to himself): "I haven't told Him a word about his turn of speech in that letter to *her,* that the document is intact (as if nothing had happened)." But later He says to Lambert: "The document is intact, and he's got it."

Lambert: "How can you know that for sure?"

Versilov: "Because he has not told me a thing about those words in

---

pis'makh (*P. J. Proudhon in His Letters* by P. D. Boborykin. Dostoevsky may also have been acquainted with Sainte Beuve's *P. J. Proudhon—sa vie et sa correspondance, 1838–1848* (1872). In linking the two, Dostoevsky may have had a contrast in mind. There is a reference to Job in the final version of *A Raw Youth* in the words of Makar Dolgoruky, Part III, Chapter 4:2.

that note of mine, even though he knew them, [having read the note."]

Here, *Finis.* [*What's most important.*] Versilov says: "I hate this woman, for she has stolen my peace from me. If I were to fall in love with her, I would ~~myself~~ kill either myself, [or her.] On the contrary, I hate her and I'm glad that I do."

And he actually *does hate* her.

In his letter to her: "Take me, I shall be nothing before you."

(N.B. Let Lambert, or somebody, give the Youth a chance to be the secret witness of a meeting between her and Versilov.)

She says to Versilov: "If you'd love me less, I would have married you."

"Go into the desert, serve ~~in chains~~ God in chains, those chains which you have displayed before me, and you will thus subdue your pride."

"I hate you, I don't love you," says *he.*

She to Him: "I am afraid of such passion, I am an ordinary woman."

She to Him: "Why are you being unfair to that wonderful woman, the mother of your children, I know all about her; I have been watching her."

She: "You are a *hero,* and not an ordinary person, which says everything."

"Haven't you been making fun of me, you frivolous woman, you, which is why I have cast you off, like a rag, before whom?"

He suddenly begins to reproach her for her vile actions, for her animal voluptuousness, <saying these things> to her face (while she is pure, and he knows very well himself that she is pure).

~~She~~ to ~~Him: "I~~

He to her, upon her mocking remarks about his chains: "If I had only known that this might seduce you, I would have spent 30 years as a stelite, standing on one foot."

She to Him: "On one foot, that is too much. No, I am an *ordinary character,* and this won't seduce me."

"Don't talk this way, don't. I am thinking of you at night. Something frenzied, nightmarish."

She to Him: "Listen, I feel sorry for you; I swear, I would love you if I could, but I can't. I love you even now; I loved you even before, precisely because you are suffering, and tormenting yourself so much."

"What kind of suffering this may be, and what it may consist of, is not for me to judge, but you were suffering, and I came to love you. But remember, this is only compassion, and not love. I don't know why I can't love you. It may be because you do not command my respect. Though your sufferings are sincere, there is something very false about you."

"Forgive me, sometimes I felt like laughing at you. ~~Look what kind of a person I am.~~ Perhaps it is all my own fault, that I do not understand. You see how nasty I am; really, why should you love me? What else can you want? Love from pity—could that be it? Would you really want that? Oh, do forgive me this, my feeling sorry for you."

He: "I haven't any pride, not even that. A beggar cannot help despising himself. *Before you,* I am a beggar. ~~Please, love me even if it be for pity alone~~ I've been already begging for charity. I'll accept it."

She to Him: "Perhaps I might get to love you. Right now, I feel in my heart that I could get to love you, but you will later take bitter revenge on me for having been a beggar before me. I am scared. I can't."

[At this point, about *mother.*

"Don't you dare talk about her. Nor shall I forgive you that I've been ridiculous.]"

["I know you're a Catholic monk, I know you are a ~~Jesuit and~~ pilgrim, a hermit. I know that you've spent a year there and that you've come out only to make propaganda, and that's where you met me."]

N.B. *What's most important.* Up to this time, He has been suggesting to the Youth that she is the most depraved woman in the world. *After having witnessed this meeting,* the Youth, who had practically agreed to join Lambert in "setting the fire," (or even without Lambert's knowledge), abandons these plans and goes to see Tatiana. And this is where the document is stolen from him. And this is then where the final scene of the conflagration follows, with the Youth saving her.

Tatiana had a lawsuit with her cook pending at the Justice of the Peace.

All the vices.

Versilov: "She is supposed to be perfect in everything, meanwhile she is vain, jealous, cowardly, a tease, stupid—exactly like all ordinary women!"

The Youth: "Why is she supposed to be perfect in everything?"

Versilov: "Because she is beautiful, because she is kind, clever, generous..."

The Youth: "But you are contradicting yourself, aren't you? You were just saying that she was stupid and jealous."

Versilov: "No, I am not contradicting myself; she is depraved like no one else, depraved as all women are. She is vile, the embodiment of vileness. She is supposed to be perfect in everything. Nor can she be like all other women, she alone in the whole world. Nothing but compassion led me to her. I wanted to save her from herself. I wanted to restore the ideal... I did not love her, or loved her as my future creation: my proof—I don't care whom she marries. You know what, Bioring has left her."

The Youth: "Listen, I am convinced that you didn't write that letter simply to insult her, but also to scare away that German, Bioring, so he'd leave her alone and run away from her."

"Why, it's you who did it."

And later he comes to see the Youth: "I cannot stay here. I am going to marry your mother and leave town."

"Where to?"

"I do not know." [(By the way, he thinks up some scheme.)]

Versilov, suddenly *ex abrupto* to the Youth: "Do you think that I was envious of him (Makar)?"

"I have never thought that."

[2d chapter] See the *finale* of chapter one, Versilov's opinion of Makar.

The Youth (to himself): "I had the desire to hurt somebody, so that I could then immediately say to myself: Look how kind I am, look how generous I am."

[2d chapter] The Youth suddenly develops a desire to get close with Liza: "We are both disgraced."

Versilov: "Oh, I have never loved her; oh, if I could but love her, I could bear anything."

She to Him: "When falling in love with me, you were falling in love with no one but yourself, and besides, you certainly couldn't have forgiven me that confession which you made before me, for you saw it as a humiliation. You vain man, you couldn't even stand *that.* How then was I going to help laughing at you?"

He to her: "Why laugh? Why laugh? That's what is most important."

"So you really wanted me to cry?"

"No, just not to laugh, even that would have meant a helping hand to me. That alone. I would have valued it greatly."

"But what business was this of mine?"

"What do you mean? You were in my debt, you were obligated to me!"

Final plan. June 16/28.

A few introductory words. A ray. First meeting with Makar. Went to his own place; about the family and the doctor. Versilov and the family. Mother's role. When I went down to see Makar on the next day I found everyone present there. News that Tatiana Pavlovna's trial is up; Versilov's story. Tatiana comes in. Liza comes in. Her relationship with Makar. Something like a quarrel. Makar's story; wanderings and anecdotes. "Wise guy! Wise guy!" With Versilov, on family affairs (not a word about "that"). I adjusted my clothes and left. Nastasia Egorovna—Anna Andreevna. News about *her,* very much excited. Went to see the Prince, Vasin, very much excited, found out from Versilov. A feeling of disorder. Came back home—again to Makar. About Elias and Enoch. A hot discussion with Versilov about communism, and Christ, and Makar.

But the Youth restrains himself; he is hurt. Yet to himself he is saying that he has never been more devoted to Versilov than he is now. A feeling of hatred for her.

Liza's episode with Vasin. Liza is hurt. The Prince is jealous. Vasin is suddenly arrested. [At this point, first encounter with Lambert. Again the document.] Charity. [He goes to see Versilov.] ~~Encounter with Lambert.~~ The Youth goes to see Him at the flat, and tells Him about his meeting with *her*. An unexpected meeting with Lambert. The latters tells the Youth that he already knows Versilov. The Youth even drops a hint about the document. Again, some disgraceful happenings. ~~The idea of "the disgraceful."* A depressed feeling.~~ Makar's sudden death. [½ of part three]

On the day of Makar's death, He comes to see him. At this point, feats, the confession; they become friends. About the "idea," and even about Lambert. The Youth reports, with almost too much conviction, what an impact Makar has had on him. [The Youth tells about his meeting with *her*. (*He:* "I used to hate her, but this must now end." The Youth is glad: "Versilov has risen from the dead!" Har-

---

* *Bezobrazie* is hard to translate; literally, "absence of all form," "deformity," "disorder," "disharmony."

mony.* At this point, once again news of Bioring and <her> wedding. A letter containing a marriage proposal.)] ~~Anna Andreevna, in~~ About the Prince, about Liza's wedding, etc., about those under indictment. Suddenly Anna Andreevna conveys His marriage proposal to *her*. Mother's birthday, a bouquet, chopping up the icons, Versilov disappears. He is looking for Versilov. Versilov's rendezvous with *her*. He goes to see Lambert. Very nearly a plan. But as he is leaving, he decides to go it alone. [He hates her, i.e., he is jealous.] The insult. The police station. Flight of the old Prince. [End of part three] The Youth suggests that Versilov take some action with the aid of the document. ~~Highsounding words.~~ N.B. How does Versilov show up? ~~His liaison with L<idiia>.~~ The Youth goes to see Lambert (but decides to go it alone). They cut open his pocket, put a blank piece of paper there. A night of doubts. The Youth to Tatiana. And here, the whole story. Then, the dénouement: the young Prince shoots himself, the old Prince dies. Versilov an idiot, and *she*, her image. The "idea." But most important of all: *the memory of Makar*, a colossal role.

An important *remarque*. When they had cut open his pocket and he woke up, he found himself alone with Alphonsine. He gives her an explanation, overcome by a strong emotion. He wants to return the document. He wants to ask Alphonsine to come with him when he goes to see *her*. No, Tatiana. *Chez qui, chez qui*, and [Versilov gets an idea, the cook.]

Versilov says: "Having lost my faith, I have fixed my attention on the idea of self-perfection."

"What a wonderful idea!" *she* exclaims.

"Take your time dying of despair," I was thinking to myself, "seek to perfect yourself and later you will perhaps tell yourself something entirely different, and you may even find something to believe in. What was so funny about this? Where is my idea wrong?"

"I met you, and everything about you was telling me that there was something wrong with me."

"I was myself glad to have encountered your idea, quite the other way... Yes, you are going to need your chains for a long time yet, if you want to contain yourself; you haven't got any self-restraint," *she* says.

---

* *Blagoobrazie* in contrast to *bezobrazie*. See preceding note.

She: ("Lack of all form."* "I have seen your pride, which consists of the idea that, inasmuch as I have learned about your thoughts and you have exposed your soul before me (having deigned to open it to me), I should therefore value this very highly. I have seen this in every movement of yours, and I've made a point of ceasing to value it. Quite on the contrary, I've often been laughing at it. This alone is utterly disgraceful."**

"Why were you laughing? You should have helped me."

"I am no charity worker."***

"You were obliged to."

"In a word, I was not aware of your complete sincerity at the time, nor did I understand it, which is also why I was not obligated to be compassionate, or to help you with acts of charity."

"But now you see my sincerity."

"I see it and I am surprised... but I still do not value it."

"It's not worth it?"

"It is not. Side-by-side with a positive feat, you'll be ready to commit a crime. You haven't got any self-restraint. I repeat, there is disorder inside you. No, you'll have to wear your chains for a long time yet."

"Incidentally, do you remember Lidiia? Angry because I had rejected your love, you made yourself believe that you loved her... and ruined her. Oh, I am not accusing you of anything, you were sincere then, but I did value the heart of that unfortunate imbecile-in-Christ, and you took it away from me."

["I say: imbecile-in-Christ."]

"And this dissolute Prince was capable of taking advantage of such a high-minded girl. There's another type of moral deformity for you!**** You have it in all of contemporary <Russian> society. Where is one to find anything better?"

[There is something ridiculous about you.] ~~Or among such Makar Ivanov~~

"Rather among such fools as Makar Ivanov, or in a revolver."

She: "I am marrying Bioring most of all because I shall have peace with him: I will retain possession of my soul."

---

* See n. (*), p. 454, above.
** See n. (*), p. 454, above.
*** *Sestra miloserdiia,* literally, "sister of mercy," normally "nurse."
**** *Nravstvennogo bezbraziia.* See n. (*), p. 454, above.

"I'll admit, I like this captivity, and even our high society. In it, everything is a lie, a falsehood, deceit, and complete disorder. Not a single one of all these people will pass the test: complete immorality, perfect cynicism in each and every one of them. They are all robbers and petty crooks, all and sundry. Do you think that I don't know this?"

"Why then are you joining them?"

"But then there is that exterior, an external appearance of something stern, moral, stable, something that holds together these scoundrels. They submit to it, and there are even some who (as a result of this) believe in justice, while still remaining robbers. What is there to be done? There is no better place to go—you really ought to feel sorry for me. I would myself join a conspiracy and start wrecking it all, if only this would lead to any end."

"Why won't you try a <spiritual> feat?"

"Feats can be performed anywhere, they won't run away from me, if I decide to do them, but you show me a righteous man, and I shall follow him. But you are not a righteous man, which is why I don't believe in you; all you could be is a sufferer."

"That's enough from you."

"What a strange thought: to sacrifice everything for the sake of such a sufferer, merely out of compassion." (And here, about compassion.)

For the first time, a feeling of moral deformity.* I decided to leave everybody alone, and went to visit them all, in order to *have done with them.* A feeling of being humiliated. Admits that he wanted to take some action with the aid of the document. He had this idea while in bed. For the first time, perhaps, he dares to *criticize* Versilov. He takes a cynical look. He looks and sees how he and Versilov have both been lying to themselves, and about what.

An important change in the plan.

After *Versilov's* rendezvous *with her,* when *He* has disappeared, the Youth goes to see Lambert (this is earlier), *almost the plan.* Then to Versilov; he suggests that they act with the aid of the document. Then, the flight of the <old> Prince. A turmoil, police station. Leaving the police station, dark night in his soul. At Lambert's, drunk, they cut open <his pocket>. And here, remorse and *the whole conflagration.* [*That is,*] the flight of the <old> Prince and the police

---

* *Bezobrazie.* See n. (*), p. 454, above.

station have had an influence not in the direction of vengeance, but in that of a more sober attitude.

Versilov learns about Lambert's trick and says: "That's the boy!" He also laughs about the police station.

On the day of Makar's death, *He* comes to see him. *He* has some tender recollections of Makar, of <the Youth's> mother, says that Makar had the right idea.

Versilov has disappeared. The old Prince flees *even without Versilov.* [Here] At this point, Lambert.

Lambert has brought him a photograph and some prints. (From the Youth. The latter had not given him a letter of recommendation.)

After this meeting the Youth conceives the notion that *she* is not a saint, and that Versilov is needlessly suffering on her account: *she* is not worth it.

Versilov says or thinks: "My friend, in that case I shall begin to love her 10 times more than I do now."

She says: "It goes without saying that *one does not speak* about such ideas (as self-perfection); whereas you, having introduced me to that idea, immediately *demand that I respect you,* etc."

"Don't marry Bioring, don't marry him! If you do not want me, do not marry him... or... or I shall do something."

She: "Be my friend, stop this, and I'll appreciate it."

"Help me, give me a helping hand..."

"I can't."

The Youth decides not to leave Him, but to save him.

Psychological development of Versilov's character.

During his confession and so every other time (right up to his meeting with *her,* secretly witnessed by Versilov)* He tells the Youth that *she* is the epitome of corruption, vice, a moral monster, in spite of her apparent beauty and harmony. "I hate her," He says, and the Youth correctly observes that He isn't lying, but is telling the truth.

But during their meeting, His passionate love for *her* is plainly visible: "Why is it that you have the gift of harmony for naught?" He says to her. "Because you are perfection itself."

"I have suffered, I have arrived at the idea of self-perfection, and I would never have thrown off my chains, you can rest assured of that; rather, it is you who have taken these chains off me. You have done it by returning me to my former condition of faint-heartedness. That

---

* Obviously an error; should be: "the Youth."

which others achieve through suffering and feats, you have received for nothing," He says.

Versilov *to her:* "I am one of those people who cannot remain indifferent when they have nothing to believe in."

"You are exaggerating, as always," *she* says.

"No, with a single glance, with a single smile, you have been destroying the whole path to my salvation."

"Because I saw through <its> falseness."

"There was no falseness."

"I am not talking of any kind of fraud. What I saw was simply the falsity of the idealist, the stiltednes, the affectation." [N.B. *Lidiia.*]

"There was no stiltedness. If you are beautiful, you have an obligation before the world. Why didn't you want to follow me?"

"Where to? That is, promise you that I would marry you, [when you were running after me?"]

"That's not it, but ~~perhaps~~ suppose it is?"

"I could not love you."

"But you are obligated for the sake of the idea, for the sake of the whole."

"As if you were such an idealist yourself."

"To be an 'idealist' means to be false, a fraud. As far as I am concerned, go ahead and marry Bioring. But what have you found in Bioring? Do you want me to tell you? You are seeking a *position in society,* like the coarsest of women."

"I never vowed to perform any feats."

"But you were obligated."

["I have seen your moral disorder..."]*

And finally *she* says to Him: "Be my friend and leave me alone. Make this your feat."

"I threw off my chains and spat on my feats because of you, but so far I have not become a villain. However, you are going to turn me into a villain. Yes, I am going to be a good husband..."

Then, the Youth goes to see Lambert and almost states his plans to him. However, he decides right then and there to go it alone (i.e., to expose *her*). The Youth develops a hatred [simply jealousy] for her in connection with the fact that *she* is not nearly perfect, but falls at the first opportunity.** Then, the flight of the <old> Prince ~~through~~

* *Bezobrazie.* See n. (*), p. 454, above.
** The original is equally awkward.

~~Versilov~~. The Youth is insulted. However, the affair is settled honorably after all. Nevertheless, having settled that affair with honor, he goes to Versilov and conveys to him his devilish plan of violating <her> (his own plan). "She is not to stand up under pressure; she will fall, and you will see that she is not nearly so perfect. You will be cured..." Versilov is in full agreement with him. Versilov guffawing in a state of frenzy. When the Youth leaves him, the darkest night has gained possession of his soul. He gets drunk, they cut open <his pocket>. Then, the whole next day he is in a daze: he could never forgive Versilov for his agreeing <to his scheme>. He makes up his mind to go on a pilgrimage all by himself. Makar. "Get rid of everybody." However, he goes to see Tatiana instead; he tells her everything with tears in his eyes, his only wish being to hand over <the letter>. "She is an ordinary woman, but I am just as ordinary myself. I shall return the letter, and we shall forgive one another." In the meantime, a hellish intrigue.

Definitive plan.

June 18/30

A few words of introduction. Offended, spite<ful>. He is so mad he begins to cry. "Keep quiet. I have been watching them." They haven't been asking any questions, which is both a good thing, and insulting. Liza and Versilov—insulting. Lambert. A new idea, but—keep quiet. (*A ray?*) "God beware. Who is it? I've been wanting to ask for a long time, but I haven't, out of spite." Got up and left. "And I must admit that I find it most annoying to have to tell all this in my own name. Of course, I am a different person now." (See the large sheet.) First meeting with Makar, about life and the elder. Comes back. At this point, for the first time, a ray <of light>. (A surge of energy. Edgar.) He says to Makar: "I like the way you are so decorous.* He has to make an effort not to start crying (a ray) (joy). Great curiosity.

About the family and the doctor. Versilov and the family. With Versilov, not one word about the main thing. Mother's role.

"When I went downstairs to join Makar the next day, everybody happened to be present. After me. I thought that they weren't there. I was annoyed but refused to show it. Versilov's story about the trial of Tatiana Pavlovna. Tatiana shows up. Makar is drawn into the con-

---

* *Blagoobrazny*. See n. (*), p. 455, above.

versation. Episode with Liza, something like a quarrel. Makar's story, <his> wanderings and anecdotes: "You are contradicting yourself." "Wise guy, wise guy!' '

With Versilov, about all kinds of domestic matters, but not a word about *that.* He goes on to tell him some things about Makar. I adjusted my clothes and left. Nastasia Egorovna, Anna Andreevna (excited by the news about her).

I decided to leave them all and visited each of them to have done with them, Vasin, the Prince. (Vasin and Liza.) "I've got an idea. *I am free."* I sadly admit that I did have the intention of acting through the document. Return the document. Decides to criticize Versilov (to make someone else responsible), takes a cynical look. He takes that look and sees how and why both he and Versilov have been lying to themselves.

A sudden meeting with Tatiana. Tatiana, having learned that he is intending to leave, whispers to him, mysteriously: "Be at my place." His heart sank. "Charity." A conversation with Tatiana about Versilov and about everything (more briefly, just a few words).

Returned home with a joyous feeling. Elias and Enoch. Versilov about communism and socialism. "It's <like> a thicket inside him."* The Youth is restraining himself, but he is deeply moved. He is devoted to Versilov; toward *her,* a feeling of hatred (later, make it clear that it was really jealousy).

N.B. Here. The episode between Liza and Vasin. Liza is offended. *Liza and Makar.* [The main thing.] *The Prince* is jealous. Vasin is suddenly arrested. (A denunciation, N.B.) News about Bioring, excitement. An unexpected meeting with Lambert. He is glad. It is here that he tells the Youth that he already knows Versilov. First hint about the document. (A feeling of moral disorder, again to Makar.)

Makar's sudden death.

On the day of Makar's death, He comes to see him. Right here, feats, confession, they become friends. "About the idea," and even about Lambert. The Youth expresses, with all too great conviction, what an impact Makar has had upon him. About her. He: "I used to hate her, but this must take an end." "Versilov has risen from the dead!" Harmony. He talks about charity. Makar's got the right idea.

---

* *V em gushchina.* A crassly dialectal phrase, definitely "sub-standard."

Tender recollections. A lot about mother. "How wonderful you are!" naïvely and ingenuously.

About the Prince, about Liza's wedding, and about the other defendants. Something with Bioring. (An escapade is needed: Versilov and Bioring.) The Youth won't believe the rumors. Mad at *her*. Mother is crying. Tatiana is out of countenance and has her hands full.

Anna Andreevna calls him in. A letter containing <his> marriage proposal (through Anna Andreevna). This is why Tatiana and Mother were out of countenance *the other day*.

[3d chapter] I. Evenings. Conversations at home. Versilov used to be most affable. About the Chinese. ("Makar Ivanovich likes politics," He remarked to me.) (Suddenly, a retort by Mother regarding the Chinese.)

Conversations in the evenings. About a doctor. "I want no part of the present generation, I belong to a new, a future generation, and if it isn't going to be like me, I shall be the only one of my kind..."

Here, N.B. Having awakened from his feverish ravings, *He* kept daydreaming about her, and the longer the more so. He was making inquiries regarding Bioring, Anna Andreevna—and suddenly, *charity*. That bit of charity gave him a real shock: he was now hopelessly in love, but at the same time had begun *to hate her terribly* for her charity (as if he were a small boy). And here then, for the first time, Lambert. "No, this Lambert ought to be kept in store," he says as he is leaving his place. But immediately thereafter he is sad about his own degradation. There is something vile weighing upon his soul, and suddenly, Makar's death. Spiritual purification, a pact with Versilov. The Youth gives Him his own spontaneous opinion of *her*. (And here the Youth consciously expresses his *hatred* for her, defaming her before Versilov.) Her meeting with Versilov merely strengthens these thoughts of his. Launch the document. He would like to kiss her, at night he sees her in his dreams. Frightening audacity while wide awake. Red-eyed and quite beside himself, he offers to dishonor her. But he definitely makes up his mind to join Lambert, and not Versilov. At this point, the flight of the old Prince, and the insult from Bioring, the police station. And only now, *immediately after the police station,* or during the very night <he spends at> the police station, he conceives the thought of Versilov's fall. "No, I am going to show her my generosity. I am her knight, I love her, but to meet her, to meet her, for the last time, and then off into the desert, into <my> idea!" ~~Tatiana~~ *Makar*. Tatiana agrees, and here then, the plot and the conflagration. Keep in mind: the Youth's irrepressible love.

"Please do forgive me!" Her final words in the epilogue.

July 23.

Here, for the first time, he accidentally mentions the document to Lambert quite unmistakably, and that same night (when he is drunk) his pocket is cut open. In the morning he returns to his home. He finds the old Prince at his flat. A funny day. He communicates his plan to Versilov, and in the evening he is insulted by Bioring and <taken to> the police station. At the police station. He leaves the police station a new man. [An encounter with Lambert, and a quarrel.] To Tatiana. The scheme and the conflagration.

VERSILOV'S SON.

Mother's birthday, a bouquet, chopping up the icons [("At least say good-bye, Andrei Petrovich!")] (I had seen it coming: that moral disorder again.) Looking for Versilov. At Lambert's. About the old Prince. *Almost a plan.* He lets out the secret, like the youth he is. A depressed feeling. But it is impossible to break it off. [Makar] Versilov is dear to him. *His meeting with her.* The Youth witnesses it. The Youth is indignant. A night of doubts, his whole jealousy breaks loose. Dreams of a conflagration.

1) Meeting with Versilov, he tells him of his plan to cause a conflagration. He leaves ~~to Lambert, etc.~~.

2) Back home, suddenly, the flight of the old Prince. [Lambert has arranged it all by himself.] (*Le carême.*)[3] The insult. A night at the police station. He leaves the police station realizing to his horror that Versilov had raised no objections. And then on to Lambert. (See 3) Makar.

3) He goes to see Lambert. Drunk (they cut out the paper). Lambert: "You don't know how to do it."

"Lambert, I'm going to pay you back for everything, for everything, for my childhood."

Drunk. In the morning, Alphonsine. The Youth explains to her, overwhelmed by a powerful emotion, that he is about to return the document. At first he wants to send Alphonsine to *her,* but then he changes his mind: to Tatiana. *Chez qui, Chez qui?*[4] Makar. The whole *plot.* The conflagration.

---

[3] French: "Lent."

[4] French: "At whose place, whose place?"

Dénouement: the young Prince shoots himself, the old Prince dies. Versilov, an "idiot." She and her image. "The idea." And above it all, Makar. His concluding tirade. 3d chapter.

[2d chapter] A sudden explanation regarding himself, addressed to the reader (for the sake of CLARITY à la Leo Tolstoi).[5] After "hatred."

I suppose that I was simply in love with her, madly in love, yet at the same time also hated her, I don't know why, or as a matter of fact, I do know why... (like somebody standing in a corner at a ball). I WAS JEALOUS. But at the time, this idea would have made me furious. *The document.* "I'll let <her?> know, but I'll fail to mention," <. . .> everything is up <. . .>

[2d chapter] At the end: join Dergachev's group, becoming an ardent supporter of their role. Or study (Tatiana). "I don't know. But I've still got that idea, I'll never let go of it."

"Dergachev... is this really ignoble? They were in error, they understood things too shallowly, but they did sacrifice themselves to a great common cause, even though they had no understanding whatsoever of it, of course. But I could introduce a new idea. It would just be necessary to study all these things. My knowledge of socialism leaves much to be desired, though I do know enough."

"Too bad that Versilov" <. . .>

(And still, Makar comes to the fore.)

I have noticed that Russian youths have an urge to sacrifice themselves. Yet I have done so very little.

But as for the fact that among those youths <there are also some> who became shyster lawyers or railway engineers (Aleksandr Aleksandrovich)"[6] <. . .>

Versilov on the inevitability of communism. People's life consists of two parts: the historical, and the one the way it ought to be (the one that finds its justification in Christ incarnate). Both parts have their own unchanging laws. According to these laws, communism will triumph (regardless of whether the communists are right or wrong). But their triumph will be the farthest point of withdrawal from the kingdom of Heaven. Yet this triumph is something we have to expect. Nevertheless, *none* of the rulers of this world is *expecting* it.

---

[5] Dostoevsky may have had in mind Tolstoy's *Childhood* and *Boyhood,* which served as models for the Youth's confession.

[6] This is a reference to Dostoevsky's nephew (the son of his sister Vera Mikhaylovna). He was a railway engineer by profession.

Still, what a great thing it would be if *Russia* could understand European communism, understanding, by the same token, how far removed from it she is.

Versilov sent Lambert out in front, while hiding himself, because he decided in his own mind: "In my presence she won't dare; she is proud and would rather lose her fortune than humiliate herself before me. Whereas Lambert is incognito, somebody who just came and went. What I'll do is come out when everything is over between her and Lambert, thus ~~catching her in the act~~ catching her in the act."

[Finale] When the Youth has told Versilov about his plan of causing a conflagration, and Versilov has accepted it, the Youth says to himself: "Oh, I shall never forget this, nor shall I ever forgive him this; He has filled my heart with sadness. Better if it had been I, rather than he." He is struggling <with himself> during the night—the result: "Let everything go to the devil with a big bang, *all this disorder deserves it;* and then, my own idea."

The result: Give Versilov some more attractive, *childlike,* ingenuous traits.

His project together with Lambert: "This was a complicated and clever thing, also risky," says the Youth.

His meeting with Katerina Nikolaevna: when *she* displays so much kindness, Versilov exclaims: "How kind you are, how kind you are! You are overwhelming me."

And later, He to the Youth: "SHE? Why, for the sake of her own *order* and peace, *she* is willing to do *this thing,* that is, any kind of baseness. The Youth believes him and tells him about his plan. Versilov approves of it with reckless abandon. The moment he is gone, the Youth immediately gets very sad on account of him. A night of <internal> struggle, etc., he almost hates *her* because of this, etc., and in the morning, Alphonsine.

[Finale] Liza keeps contradicting Makar as long as he is alive, but when he dies she is terribly sad.

Versilov to the Youth, during the confession: "I am afraid of one thing," he said suddenly, "namely, that we are both vile, which is also why we wish that she were vile, and not at all because she really is vile" (naïveté).

An important page.

Elias and Enoch.

In the *charity* <scene>, *She* tells the Youth about Him, describing his character (the beauty of all-forgiveness, of forgetting an injury).

[More briefly] "He used to get hurt by all kinds of trifles," *she* says and recalls some *examples* (however, she does not conceal the fact that *He* was most charming in his ingenuousness; and altogether, the Youth can see that *she* willy-nilly respects Him, that she actually would like to become His friend).

This "charity," and the whole meeting––though they captivate the Youth and have a great impact on him, still, he immediately feels that he is *angry:* after so much suffering, He still has not achieved that harmony which she has received for nothing: *she* was born that way! And in connection with this, in the recesses of his soul there develop an increased and nurtured suspicion and hatred for her. He hates her, exactly in the same way *He* does, namely for her being perfect. He would be glad to be a witness of her degradation, of her vice. He is taking His side.

Even at the time of <her> "charity" he is arguing with her, telling her that He never loved her, assuring *her,* presenting proof to her, retelling conversations with *Him.*

N.B. She explains His noble actions to him, his refusal to accept the inheritance; yet she is calling him a child of his age. The Youth is deeply hurt by her comparing him to a child.

"If this is beyond your comprehension, and if you have received this gift for nothing, you must still respect the sufferings of others."

Later, after *she* has left, a conversation with Tatiana about Him. An old spinster; cries; tells him a part of <Versilov's> past; tells him about his mother.

The Youth tells Him about the meeting <with her> in detail (i.e., even that she loves Him and that she wants to be His friend); he inflames Him by telling him these things. But they both decide that *she* is merely a society lady, who wouldn't stand the test. Still, the Youth does not dare to tell him about the document, whereas He drops a few hints concerning the document.

The Youth leaves, with the seed of an idea *of taking revenge* on her and *exposing** her. The encounter with Lambert. (He learns, among other things, that He is already acquainted with Lambert.)

[MORE CLEARLY] At this point, Makar's death. A rumor about a marriage proposal on His part. Mother's birthday, a bouquet, the icons. The Youth leaves, with the idea of "disorder" in his mind. His rendezvous with her. After the rendezvous, back to Lambert. He almost unveils his secret. But then he decides to go ahead without

* This word is underlined twice.

Lambert. Here (through Versilov), the flight of the old Prince (both Lambert and everything else). The Youth straightens everything out again. He is also the one who, for all the good he has done, must suffer humiliation and <being taken to> the police station. N.B. (Having seen through His vileness, the Youth still refuses to leave his side!) He goes to see Him and communicates to Him his own idea of exposing <her>. But as he is leaving Him, he is already cursing Him. N.B. (Shouldn't it be done this way: He advises the Youth not to use violence, but rather advises him to overwhelm her with his magnanimity: spare her.) The Youth leaves, and night. He is wavering: (he is now definitively and cynically criticizing Versilov) decides in favor of disorder. In the morning, Lambert and Versilov. The notion that He has joined forces with Lambert in such a villainy lies heavy on the Youth's mind. And so on.

At the time Makar was discussing Elias and Enoch. About how the Antichrist-to-come will capture people by <his> beauty. The springs of morality will grow turbid in the hearts of men, the green grass will be dried out.

"*He* used to talk (there's a thicket in his heart),* while I was marveling at Him," ~~think said~~ writes the Youth. And later, to Him:

"Do you really believe?"

He to him: "Maybe, no. Yet we were still capable of getting carried away and deceiving ourselves, thinking that (*we believed in the beautiful*) we believed in something, while you aren't capable of this either."

"Well, this may be all to the good," says the Youth.

"It is all very bad," He replies, "and what is worst of all is that you've got nothing with which to replace these daydreams." And this is where he tells him about communism and Christianity.

And later, after Makar's death, they decide <to perform some> feats, and He delivers his confession before him.

THE MOST IMPORTANT OF ALL THE IMPORTANT ADJUSTMENTS IN THE PLAN.

Prior to the "charity" <incident>, the Youth hasn't been discussing *her* with Him at all, nor was there any *confession on His part*. The only thing they discussed were *Elias* and *Enoch,* communism, Christianity, and Makar, and that's the extent of it. (Also about the feats.)

But after the "charity" <incident>, the first thing the Youth does is

---

* See n. (*), p. 461, above.

to go to see Him and tell Him the whole thing. That's where he gets his impression, Makar's death, and only after that (immediately after Makar's death) He approaches the Youth and says:

"We wanted to perform a feat; here's one for you: a confession," and he tells him everything, communicating it with energy, fervor, animation, sadness, bitterness, and <self->accusations. The Youth, while he is listening, contradicts Him. The latter defends himself, refutes the other's arguments, gets angry, but finally says:

"When *She* was attacking me, you were probably contradicting her, just as you are contradicting me now; now, you do not believe me, and are taking my* side."

At this point there takes place, between Him and the Youth, a most ardent and irrepressible declaration of love: "I understand everything. You love me, and I love you; you are dear to me; now I am yours forever. I understand everything, all your actions. Your simpleheartedness fascinates me. I had thought that there was more of a mystery about you." About Mother, about Liza, "Let us lead an orderly life, devoted to self-perfection." About *the idea* and *even* about Lambert.

About Mother: a few anecdotes about her. Encounter with Lambert. An agreeable impression. Suddenly, the marriage proposal (from Anna Andreevna). Mother's birthday: the bouquet and the chopping up of the icons. ~~He joins Lambert.~~ Almost. He is looking for Versilov. His** meeting with her. Then, on to Lambert ("I felt insulted"). Almost a plan. Flight of the old Prince—the insult, the police station. The Youth goes to see Versilov, to offer him the document. (Magnanimity.) And suddenly He is with Lambert (*traître,*[7] couldn't stand it through the night). The conflagration. Then, the Prince. He shoots himself. Death of the old Prince. Versilov. And *she,* her image. And then, THE IDEA.

One ought to give some thought to a *definitive* and *most detailed* plan.

*Minute.****

I was understanding only too well what could happen... <?> I think that we were both feeling that we owed each other many ex-

---

* Apparently an error; should be "her."

** Capitalized, therefore Versilov is meant.

*** In French.

[7] French: "Traitor."

planations... or, perhaps, none at all. Though I was looking him in the eye, but his eyes were telling me nothing on this score. Yes, there were some scores to be settled between us... But I like this kind of people: "Let begones be bygones, and let's start a new score." He explained this and that to me... "No, they weren't questioning me about everything." "Very good." I remained silent. Lambert. Alas, they already knew, while I was still afraid of mentioning Lambert. I had forgotten where he lived. [I was worried by one thought.]

He, to Makar: "I like the harmony you carry."

Bending over <to me>, in a whisper: "They lack order and harmony; I don't like them."

"What are you saying there?"

"Keep quiet, I'll come to see you."

<I> returned, and regeneration to a new life. But initially, simply a ray <of light>. I returned with great curiosity.

After Makar tells about his wanderings, Tatiana Pavlovna, who had been afraid that the Youth might make some boorish remarks, or chuckle <disrespectfully>, suddenly says to him: "Good boy, good boy."

For the first time, a feeling of "moral disorder."

...Regenerate, but not reformed. My feelings were not of the best, I'll admit that.

A feeling of vengefulness. Against whom? Oh, I knew even then against whom, i.e., I had picked out the person on whom I would vent my feelings, but I am not going to name that person right now. A lot of it was quite wrong, but some of it was right. Some of it.

And she, the poor dear, thought <. . .>

Incidentally, this thing: I always did love Mother.

"You are my enemy, but one can do business with you."

I decided to think it over as far as Lambert was concerned.

The venerable old man must die away.* It is more splendid that way. "Thank you, you have edified me. They both teach: the old man the old <wisdom>, the young man the new." "You are a wanderer, what is a hermit going to teach you? He doesn't know life."

After his first meeting with Makar, his mother says, in passing: "Our dear and welcome guest." "Darling, dear mother," and I was stroking her cheeks... No matter what moral disorder you may be liv-

---

* *Ugasat',* a verb used mainly of a fire or of a candle.

ing in, but as long as there is such a thing as motherly love, that is, so long as there is still moral beauty in this world. <. . .> "Don't tell them, mother." "Very well, my dear, but why are you angry with Liza?"... and she left. I was not angry with her.

[Here] Makar about the hermit, about the fact that he is not alone... "There's the grass growing."

[2d chapter] Liza. Not enough honor to the Prince. To Vasin. (My anger.) I decided to go and see the Prince immediately after rising. (Stebelkov has been arrested.) Versilov, Mother revered Versilov for his behavior. The doctor. (In narrative form.)

[3d chapter] Makar's stories. He is contradicting himself. Versilov's opinion (of Makar).

Minute. 1) The tone of the narrative (after Makar, suddenly *ex abrupto*).

I adjusted my clothes and left, and this is what I decided: "I am free. Turn over the document, the Prince, etc. Arrange things for them. As for Versilov, either save him, or abandon him, but act energetically at any rate." Nastasia Egorovna and Anna Andreevna.

Minute. 2)

[4th chapter] I adjusted my clothes and left. Here's what my plan of action was like: hand over the document, meet my obligation, and leave Versilov without saying a word, without asking any questions, which is going to surprise him, and also be his punishment. (N.B. Prior to this, <I> had been in love with Versilov, for the way he was treating Makar. N.B. Versilov's opinion of Makar, and the Youth delivers his tirade on "moral deformity." ~~Ideas~~ Versilov remains silent and, up to this point, does not offer to join the pilgrimage. Then, the Youth cuts their conversation short, and leaves.)

And then, I've got: 300 rubles which is enough. I left. The Prince, Liza, Vasin, Nastasia Egorovna, Anna Andreevna. No, leave everything, everybody, everybody. [Only that last thing remains.] In a hurry. I haven't mentioned it yet: The other day, Tatiana had told me in a whisper that I should come to her place. Charity: I hadn't expected it. At first I was talking to Tatiana; then the other woman suddenly opened the door. Yet I did not hand over the document. How many-sided man is: I did not hand over the document! Return. Mood. "There's a thicket inside him."* Devoted to Versilov, a scene, night and hatred for her.

---

* See n. (*), p. 461, above.

And on the following day, another event: Liza's story with Vasin. The Prince is jealous (the day of the wedding had been set before, in narrative form). The denunciation. News about Bioring, excitement. Appeal to action, rather than to solitude. Lambert (an unexpected encounter), a feverish conversation, first mention of the document. As he is leaving Lambert, this psychology: "Why did I mention the document?" (he explains his soul to the reader). [The sadness of terrible moral disorder.] [6th chapter] To Makar. Makar's sudden death.

Versilov's idea. Rule over mankind. A better man cannot possibly escape solitude. <His> spiritualism comes to the fore. An image of Russia. To perfect oneself. ["Are you a party to that conspiracy?"] "This is no conspiracy." Freemasonry. "I'll explain it to you later, let's walk together. She's got me confused" (with boundless mockery of himself as well as of her). "Let's walk together." The Youth tells him about her, and gives him the details of his meeting with her. *Naïvely* admits his hatred for her.

And so Versilov's idea has remained unexpressed. Marriage to <the Youth's> mother. And then, on the following day, the news of His sally against Bioring and about his proposal *to her*. Mother is crying. Anna Andreevna. I was running around looking for him. At his mother's party. Chopping up the icons.

"Our best people are lost, many men, many minds. Samarin, Fadeev, communism."

"The best people of Russia must unite."

But everything feverishly, fervently, and sincerely.

Liza was rude <to Makar.>

"I mean my legs."

He began to laugh, to my surprise.

Liza flushed.

Versilov with a radiant smile. (A radiance emanating from his face.) I felt like embracing them all. "What a rogue I am, yet I want to 'remain silent'!" "NO, THIS IS NOT WHAT HE WAS LIKE," SAYS VERSILOV OF MAKAR: "HE IS ABOUT TO EXPIRE."

"Even from my grave, I still love you, my dear ones."

I staggered back, quite delirious. Suddenly my mother came in.

Mother: "He is quite delirious."

"Our dear guest."

I: "Shine, oh beautiful ray of light, sing, <of> God's green grass."

July 23.

He announces to Versilov that there isn't anything viler than those lives of theirs—his mother's and his, Liza's with the Prince—as far as he can tell, and that his own life is the worst of them all... Moral deformity.

Versilov says outright that he is ready to go on a pilgrimage. *About Christ.*

About Christ. About how He discovered Christ while he was working as a District Commissioner <during the Land Reform>.

"Don't wish to be better than other people; rather, make it your first concern to be yourself."

"And so he never did express his idea."

"Why, isn't it all the same what your idea is?"

Aren't all Russians obsessed with ideas? Wisdom, a capability of sacrificing oneself, both in one's youth and in one's old age, a thirst for the common good, a passionate civic concern—all this the Russians have, but they lack one thing: *something in common,* concord. They don't have three men who could agree about anything.

Isn't an immediate and frighteningly powerful feeling for *her* to be preferred? Happiness with her. This is given once.

[Insert this into chapter one.] [Here chapter two] "When is a man morally beautiful?" I suddenly asked Versilov three or four days later, without any preliminary remarks, right in the middle of some trival and unimportant conversation.

"When he firmly knows what he has to do ~~and what he is always going to do~~," he answered, also quite suddenly and ~~without~~ without giving the matter any thought, ~~and~~ as if he had had the answer ready for a long time, and as if he had been doing nothing all this time but continually thinking about this question. But about this, later.

(A bright spot. Mother.)

A spiritual program.

A yearning for harmony. Harmony is in its apogee after Versilov's *Confession.* Moral disorder (jealousy) is in its apogee after the conversation between Him and her, which the Youth overheard.

He gets drunk at Lambert's. Revenge. (Little boy, little boy. Alphonsine's lullaby.)

Flight of the old Prince. Work, the insult. A night at the police station.

A thirst to break <with everything> and escape to a harmonious life. An anguished feeling for Him, because He has taken another, decisive, fall in accepting the Youth's plan of revenge with the aid of the document.

The conflagration.

Epilogue: An explanation, a ~~quiet~~ thirst for a harmonious life, yet *wordly life* and all the instincts, *she!*

All this was very well, but it was now time, to prove.*

Chapter ix. 9th chapter.

I woke up rather refreshed. My ideas were now clearer. I was understanding him. I was struck by the notion that it was so simple, and felt a little sorry that it was so simple. To be sure, <the truth> about <his> love was more complex, but even that I was understanding better than the day before. He didn't want *fatum* <to take its course>. She. I am for him. Mother won't fill the want. That's how it should be. Their destiny. An avenger, but more than anything else—the golden age. But then, there is Lambert, what about that? The document. Fallen out of love. Oh, I believed <it>, precisely on account of the senselessness of that last explosion. However, restlessness. Nastasia Egorovna. [The spy.] Call <her in?>. "Tell me ~~I'm not going to come~~ this very important thing." "Allright, allright." I'm not going there. I'm going to tell Him! Now, briefly. Went to see him, not in. Went to see my mother, sadness, tears, Liza, interrogated by Tatiana Pavlovna (tenderness). "Let me know if you should see <him?>." Again back to His place, in anxiety, not in. "Why won't you run over to Anna Andreevna's?" Over to my own place. Lambert: "Your lies are too plain." "Did you tell Him about the document?" "No." "Anna Andreevna has been telling me <this>." "There's ~~again~~ something fishy about this, come to my place" (that's Lambert). Lambert was asking me: "How was that thing you said about Anna Andreevna?" ~~The Landlord~~ The Landlord furnishes a room (for the old Prince). Strange inquiries. I was lying there, suddenly jumped up, tapped my forehead, "Could it be that he went to Tsarskoe Selo?" Alphonsine—asking me to come over to Lambert's place, right away. *She,* she is promising me some news about *her. I:* ("Go to hell, *à la porte!*")[8] Trishatov. "I shall never come to your place!" Before Alphonsine's visit: "Never see Lambert!" (before Lambert). Fell asleep. The following day, to his place: "No, nor has he been in." To the funeral. To Anna Andreevna's place, not at home, to Tsarskoe Selo. Mother, at home. Name day party. Daydreams. He arrives with a bouquet of flowers—in the evening, at teatime. Makar had willed the icon to Him. Irritation. Grabbed the icon and broke it to pieces, then left. "Say farewell!"

---

* Unclear in the original.

[8] French: Literally "To the door," but idiomatically, "Get the hell out."

x. Ran over to Anna Andreevna's place. "I've been telling you."* Over to his place. At the door, Tatiana Pavlovna. Nastasia won't let <him?> in. But they bring the Youth back. He is yelling. Tatiana Pavlovna: "Will you give me your word that you won't go in?" "I do, I do." They enter. *She* and *He*. A showdown. I run over to Lambert's. Lambert is not in. *"Je vous cherche."*[9] Alphonsine with her guitar. Asked for some wine. Pawn something. Champagne. About *vieux prince*. Drunk. Lambert. Got drunk—in the morning: they cut out <the letter>.

"They'll get *her* entangled also."

"How do you mean, entangled, in what?"

"Well, you can be sure, they'll get her entangled."

Une rose.

This is more important than pride.

The double burst out laughing at the funeral.

Passion and fame.

Fell asleep: All this high society is frivolous.

I was in that tavern on Canal <Street>. Had something to eat. Lambert came in several times.

1st chapter: Went to see Anna Andreevna—left. That night the Junior Chamberlain was there. Don't get involved with Lambert. Trishatov. Fell asleep. A frightful intrigue.

xi. Came home. The old Prince. *Carême,*[10] the Landlord. Anna Andreevna. The Junior Chamberlain. I went to see Tatiana, made an appointment with her, returned. The Junior <Chamberlain> had withdrawn, the Landlord too. Bioring: an insult. The Prince flings himself into <my> embrace, sobbing. To the police station. ("I love her.") ["<My> head, and I'll go out of my mind."]

xii. A night at the police station. In the morning, went out to see Tatiana. Now, all <the rest> in a few words. A hellish machination. And how the whole thing happened. The conflagration.

xiii. Conclusion.

9th chapter. Lambert: "Well, let's go, let's go and have dinner, let's have a drink, I'm going to get her for you, you fool, you." But I still believed in <his> sincerity. That wench had me fooled.

Here, the programme.

---

* The gender of the verb suggests that this is said by Anna Andreevna.

[9] French: "I am looking for you."

[10] French: "Lent."

A sheetful of cute expressions.

After the chopping of the icons: Mother shouting after Him: "Andrei Petrovich, at least say farewell to me, before we part forever."

"I am afraid of Him; I knew that He was going to start laughing."

IN <HIS> CONFESSION, prior to this, He is talking to the Youth about <the latter's> mother, as if he were driven by something.

The Youth, after "he has not forgiven": "Why, you are arguing against yourself by saying this."

He was telling how that mother lost all of her children, and how the last one, a consumptive boy, was at the factory, and how that merchant grew fond of him: "I'll spend my whole capital, but I'll have him cured!" He died. The little one was left after him (he married her).

Makar: "No one can say how the word enters a man's heart, or by what routes it travels. Nor does anyone know how God is going to exact a return <of our debts>. The seed in the ground."

Makar: "If each were helping the other, do you think that we would have famine and plague? We'd have paradise. But now you'll rake together a lot of gold, all by yourself—and you're bored to death. But if this other thing happened, it would all be such fun. (Description of how it would be fun.) We don't need to have any property of our own. Take mine."

And suddenly (at Lizaveta's). Well now, what do you think happened? The merchant died and left *seventy thousand* to the blessed Lizaveta in his will. She gave away everything. Asked to accept the money and sign for it, she signed everything (they'd have put it in trust, but she screamed, "I don't want that!"), took the money, signed for all of it, brought it home. She started handing it out to people, ["you better look out."] So they sent a policeman to guard her, <and> she took fright. Everything to children, to orphans.

I am thinking in my mind that often, when a man laughs, it is quite repulsive to watch ~~him~~. And altogether, there is something banal, base about laughter. ~~To be sure~~ An extraordinarily large number of people don't know how to laugh ~~at all~~. ~~Even~~ So that those thousands of people who ~~to be sure~~ not only don't know how to laugh but don't laugh at all are actually enjoying an advantage. Many a man will altogether give himself away by his laughter, and all of a sudden you'll know him inside and out. What is most important about laughter is sincerity, and how many people have sincerity? It would seem that laughter asks for good nature, while most people laugh maliciously. Sincere and good-natured laughter means gaiety, but ~~really~~ where do you find gaiety in people; in fact, do ~~they~~ people still know how to be gay? I am saying one thing: If you want to examine a man and learn something about his soul, [observe him carefully, not when he is silent, nor when he is talking, nor when he is weeping, nor even when he is full of the noblest indignation, borne by the loftiest of ideas, but] rather observe him when he is laughing: if his is a good laughter, ingenuous and gay, he is a good man.

Note, however, that neither should a man's laughter appear stupid; you may be stimulated to feel amused, and cheerful, and communicative, by a man's laughter; yet it is also important that the man himself shouldn't appear funny ~~to you~~. In a word, laughter is the most reliable test of the soul.

The old man was laughing. I am recommending this especially to women, and in particular to brides who are about to pick out ~~their bridegroom or prospective husband~~. There are some characters whom it takes a long time to crack—you might not be understanding a person, but there, suddenly, he'll become gay, or think that now is the time to be gay, and he'll be spread before your eyes, as if on the palm of your hand. Only a man who has gone through a superior and a most felicitous mental development knows how to be gay in a communicative, that is, in a perfectly good-natured way.

"My legs, I'm very much afraid, still don't carry me."

Makar admires him: "He is bright, really bright." There's another trait that reveals a man's character, that thing about his hands and feet.

July 25.

BASIC IDEAS

In the *Finale.* Though I have been warning my reader many times, in the course of these "Notes," that now, as I am writing them, I am no longer the person I was at the time <it all happened>, it sems to me, after having studied all the pro's and con's, that I am really entirely the same person. The person I used to be, the person I am now, and the person ~~when I was and lived~~ I was when all this happened, and later, when I was writing about it, and now, when I've quit it. I was merely saying it for my own consolation.

By smashing the icons he was, perhaps, renouncing all of his ideas.

July 26/27.

The Prince betrays Dergachev, but Stebelkov had almost at the same time betrayed them both. The Prince could have kept it to himself, but he revealed it <to the authorities>. [Here]

His rendezvous with *her* must be sincere in the highest degree on His part, as well as REVEALING.

"You used to have your idea; weren't you pursuing some kind of an idea?" *she* says to Him (N.B. She must also be speaking with the greatest sincerity and ~~as if~~ *timidly,* which also *completely* explains the plausibility of this last meeting and a personal showdown between these two people. For she is hoping that she may talk Him into leaving her alone: which is also based on her continued and unimpaired respect for his high calling).

"Yes, I do have an 'idea,' " He answers, "an idea which tells me what we all ought to be doing right now and which might save all of us, but what does it matter to you what this idea might be—in fact, what does it matter to anybody? Aren't there thousands of people each of whom has his own idea and, along with it, a belief that it is precisely his little idea that is going to save everybody? I belong to those thousand or so people who cannot remain indifferent to all this confusion and nonsense, but who would rather die than pass by it apathetically. Rather than give up one's search for a solid foundation, and remain content with *some kind* of a compromise. We, i.e., a thousand or so people, are each of us suffering sincerely, and this is all that is worthwhile about us. However, it goes without saying that among those thousand people you wouldn't find as many as two who would agree with each other (irony)." When

"You see, people in Russia have been doing a lot of thinking, but they haven't been living at all. And therefore, it really does not matter what my idea is all about, this or some other thing. When I was dislodged from my rut (perhaps because there really wasn't any rut, or because the rut came to an end), I went mad and wanted to take my own life. That's when I escaped abroad. But I did not destroy myself: I conceived, at that time, my original idea: seek to perfect yourself, try to break your own resistance as your conscience, and your faith will tell you, to the best of your ability, and, once having conquered yourself, you may perhaps also find that ultimate idea, your own solution 'what to do?' and 'what to preach?' I passionately clung to this idea. You were all laughing at my chains. Why? I was actually wearing them, but you didn't know what was going on in my *soul.* Yes, it may be that, finally, I did persuade myself that mine was the right way, but then you appeared before me, and I suddenly realized that without you I am nothing, and my idea is unrealizable. What kind of an "idea" is this <, you ask,> which suddenly turns into nothing only because you appear on the scene? I don't know if I love you, I only know that I need you. In my pride, I came to hate you. I convinced myself that you have all the vices... I swear, I was capable of persecuting you with slander. Perhaps, capable of poisoning you."

[She: "That is, capable right now."]

["You know what, I actually could have poisoned you. Do you know that there already was a day and an hour when your life was hanging by a thread?"]

"You repulsed me. I sought salvation in Lidiia, finally thinking that I had forgotten you. Oh, how I laughed at my own 'self-perfection.' Here then, I decided I would devote myself to food and family life, later join some little conspiracy, some kind of socialist propaganda or something, picking out the most stupid and insignificant, so I'd be tried and deported. Oh, believe me, I know how to loathe myself, and how to hate myself. What is most stupid about this thing is the fact that, eventually, I forgot about you altogether, and found myself laughing at that silly little passion of mine. And here now, the nadir of my humiliation: so long as I was hearing of you, knowing that you were single, I was quite indifferent, but when I heard the first report about your getting married, I was thrown into a frenzy. [Oh, what do I care about that man?] ~~Forgive me that I have proposed marriage to you, it's an absurdity, but how could you come to this rendezvous?~~ I have proposed marriage to you. I need you. Let us go on together. You know, I still believe that, though I may not save mankind, I may *still* do a lot of good. So let us go on together. I am yielding. All right, let it be an act of charity on your part. I'll accept charity from you..." And later: "Tell me outright (for I can see from your face that you are not deceiving me, and that you are ready to tell me everything): did you ever love me at all, even a little bit?"

She flushed.

"I did." ("That's what I expected," says the Youth.)

"And now?"

"No, maybe, I don't. I don't love you. I don't want you..."

In the finale of the scene, He says: "I am going to destroy you."

[At mother's side] "Perhaps there is a lot of faith in me even now. Let us go on together. I have been saving <for it>, like a miser, while you are spending it, gathering nothing. I have been suffering, while you have been getting it for nothing. Would you believe that I hated you? Of course, I am insulting you. This must be what is called a passion. So far I have never known passion, though I have had a number of affairs. I could hardly define this fire even now, not knowing what it is, or what it is that I want of you. What I do know is that, without you, I am finished. I also know that he who experiences such passion can also hate ~~love and hate~~ at the same time. Hate as much as love. Have mercy on me, I can't go on this way."

At the rendezvous, She (standing there, wavering): "I do not know, I can't. You are going to take revenge on me, if I should hand out some charity to you."

He: "Do you remember Abishai in the Bible, remember, I read it to you. Perhaps you are right. Having accepted your charity I may, perhaps, get to hate you, remembering: 'Why did I injure this woman?' " (pointing at the portrait of the Youth's mother).

She: "If this is so, what am I to do?"

He: "Why, of course, you are going to leave me" (lost in thought).

[Here.] And, as he leaves: "Don't love me, don't live with me, let's never meet. I shall be your slave, if you should call for me, [I am not going to harm you.] And I ~~shall be that~~ I shall disappear, if you want me to, so you won't see me, or hear of me. I shan't bother you, nor shall I do you any harm. I shall disappear, only, only... only don't marry any other man!" (This is his very last word, as He is already leaving, and after the words: "I will destroy you!") "I SHALL DESTROY."

She, to Him (incidentally, about the Youth's mother), later: "You believe in God, you were preaching Him so ardently and so sincerely. You loved God."

"Is this what you think? Yes, I believe, but I have quit thinking of Him, ever since you appeared and all my thoughts were stopped. I cannot ~~now~~ think of Him, I haven't been thinking about anything at all in a long time. I am finished... I... I don't care. I—I—I am going to destroy you, that's what I'm going to do" (he got up from his seat, pale).

Bello vu <sic>

"I am giving you a deadline, think it over. You see, I—I'll try to kill myself first, so I wouldn't kill you."

"But if I should be unable to restrain myself, I might kill you first, and only then, myself."

In the very finale of the novel: and so, His "idea" has remained unexpressed. "Why, what does it really matter?" as He himself once said.

N.B. In Versilov's Confession: the most sympathetic, the most sincere, and the most naïve words about <Russian> youth.

She: "And this is Versilov? A man of honor, spiritual strength... I have always believed in you!"

She: "What am I to do then?"

And later, immediately: "No, for nothing in the world. You are threatening me with death—for nothing in the world."

He: "I am not threatening, just understand..."

"No, I don't love you. I can't. Better kill me."

?("I'll kill you") (and suddenly, some affectionate word, some kind question: "Tell me, didn't you then... where have you put my portrait?"). ("And do you remember..." And so on, about Abishai, about the Bible. "Tell me, what does your 'idea' consist of?")

"I don't want *this kind* of a Versilov."

He: "Would you take any other kind?"

"Where were you later? In Paris?" (Private conversation. This is before the very finale.)

She to Him: "I can't wish you any evil. I have always wished you well."

He to her: "You were laughing at me."

She: "I never did. What I always valued so highly about you was your sincerity. My poor father, you drove him right out of his mind then. I saw in you a man..." etc. (Affectionate, kind, warm words.) "You were one of those few *sincere* people whose minds are never at rest. You are the noble bearer of an idea. Believe me, I shall love you, <but> leave me alone."

He, in passing: "The world must be refashioned, so let us start with ourselves."

She: "Listen, you were never a spiritualist, were you?"

"No."

"Are you a Mason?"

"No."

He, in passing: "It is my idea that the world must be refashioned, but that the first step ought to consist of definitely starting with oneself."

"How does one start?"

"Get honest."

"Aren't there any honest people?"

"Not one" (silence). "However, what do you care for my idea!" (Irony.)

She: "No, no, listen, you said—honest, what about her, <the Youth's> mother?"

(He: irony.)

?("But with Lidiia, was it honest?")

(He: "Yes, it was.").

July 27.

Schedule.

3d part, *1st half*. Makar's death. "Let's go to my place. I'm going to show you my child. You must absolutely come. Go! go!"

2d half. Versilov makes a confession even before the rendezvous with her.

4th part, 1st half. From the rendezvous (at Lambert's, right after the rendezvous) up to and including the conflagration.

<4th part>. 2d half. Epilogue.

In the Confession, not a word about her: "Let's forget about her."

And, in the Confession, at first life with <the Youth's> mother. Memories. Makar—on the harmonious life.

All about the subject of the harmonious life. Marrying <the Youth's> mother, etc.

At the time of the funeral, a most complete report about Bioring. So that Versilov had sent the letter on the day of the bouquet, and after chopping up <the icons>. Anna Andreevna brings <the news about> the letter.

About zoology. However, also about Stebelkov's arrest, about her, about the existence of the document in His letter to her.

<July> 27/28.

~~About Liza. Not a word about the document.~~ *Minute.** Filigrane.

2<d chapter>. Everything about Liza. Can't renounce them; yet they are my own. It wasn't I who divided them. Where did <he?> learn about Liza and Vasin? Yet I could not flee. Nastasia. Nastasia's report about the old Prince, to Anna Andreevna (in narrative form, and in scenes) about the infant ("I should also like to tell you: This is about Lambert," *after her*).** About her, about Bioring, he has fallen behind. The effect of Versilov's letter, about those words in the letter which suggest that the document has not been burned. My excitement (about the young Prince, Liza). The absence of harmony. I got up and went down to see Makar. As if on purpose, Liza and Versilov were with him. (How Versilov treated Makar.) The story of Tatiana's trial. Makar's tale. He gets up: "What is harmony?" An excited night, in love. An explanation of *my* love. Isn't this where the conflagration comes in?

3d chapter. ~~Makar~~ *Recidive* of his illness. A few days. I shall not be describing my sufferings. Makar's tales, his influence. Versilov's opinion of Makar, Versilov has forgotten to add <something>. I suddenly came up with a tirade on the harmonious life. Versilov [abruptly] agreed. Suddenly, Liza's affair with Vasin.

4th chapter. My sudden departure. Everybody... Anna Andreevna with something new (perhaps about Lambert?). The young Prince. (In his excitement, he has just made his denunciation, is jealous, mar-

---

* In French.

** The gender of the verb suggests that the remark is made by a female speaker.

riage.) Full of excitement about the news concerning Lambert. To Tatiana. Charity.

5th <chapter.> Came home. Liza has been insulted. Makar about the closet <?>. To go on a pilgrimage. Versilov. Couldn't stand it. To Lambert, blackmail, about the document. Got me confused. ~~Strange feeling.~~ From Lambert, he learns of her <planned> wedding with Bioring. (Bioring's affairs have picked up.) Home. A terrible night of <inner> struggle. The image of a conflagration.

On the following morning, the news of everybody's arrest. (A strange note from the Prince.) Suddenly, I felt like fleeing. Flee, but then there is Makar. I've got 300 rubles. Rent a flat. To Makar, or to Lambert, and that's it. Makar's sudden death. [Versilov embraces my mother. "Come to my place, I'll show you <my> child." At home, the confession. The Youth is deeply moved, and reconciled <to Versilov>: "I shall return the document to her." Frightful pangs of conscience on account of the conflagration. A horror of Lambert. I shall never forget these moments of gratitude which I felt toward Versilov for this purification.]

Versilov's confession. On the day of the funeral, he chops up those icons. [And then, already after the chopping, the letter.]

[*Here:* Anna Andreevna had actually been sending <me?> there on account of Lambert. She had also been trying to find out some things about Lambert herself (not necessary to mention the fact that Lambert had been previously acquainted with Versilov). Then, when the Youth is at Lambert's, the latter is talking mostly about the document, and mysteriously in a general way. There seems to be a mystery everywhere. The Youth lets <the reader?> know that, although he had inadvertently let out the secret of the document before Lambert, he also realized that this was really all that Lambert was after. Lambert arranges for the Youth to come and see him, then later goes to look for him himself. The Youth wants to rent a flat. Dreams of a conflagration. Again, he meets Lambert. They quarrel in the street. He goes home. Makar's death. Versilov embraces <the Youth's> mother, and says to him: "To me, to me."]

10) At Lambert's, drunk, they cut open <his pocket>. The old Prince, the police station, struggle. Conflagration, etc.

27 July.

Final *minute.**

---

* In French.

2d chapter. About Liza. Briefly and completely, yet in a business-like manner, and abruptly. "I decided to get busy as soon as I got up. I decided not to do any thinking. Imagined myself <in such-and-such situations>. <Decided> not to discuss her with Versilov." (A flashing thought: What is Versilov's attitude toward Makar Ivanovich?) A propos: about His letter to Bioring. Nastasia's visit. News, in great excitement. Went to see Makar. Tatiana's story, about Liza, form an alliance with her. "We have both been insulted." One of Makar Ivanovich's stories, "Makar Ivanovich, have you ever seen anything of this kind?" (Tatiana's question), and here then, Makar's story.

I got up and left. This time, I liked the old man very much. Versilov's opinion of Makar. Suddenly asked Versilov about the harmonious life.

That night, excitement. About the document (was I really jealous?) ~~in the form of a nightmare~~ A nightmare. Lured her <to his flat> in order to rape her, and Lambert.

3d <chapter>. As a result of such anguish, a relapse. ("I'll return the document!") Evenings. Stories. Versilov on communism. Mother. ["There's a thicket inside him."]* Tatiana would join us on those nights. [At this point, all of a sudden, Liza's episode with Vasin, the Prince is jealous.] [I am going to step out tomorrow.] Suddenly I gave Versilov my opinion regarding the harmonious life.

And, 4th <chapter>. I was going to surprise them the following day—by leaving the house. I stepped out and visited everybody. The Prince. The Prince wants to get married. To Tatiana.

5th <chapter>. I came in— Makar. Shouldn't Liza's episode ~~with Vasin~~ take place earlier, and now the Prince is jealous, and only then, Makar about that little closet** and about Liza. The thicket. Let's go on a pilgrimage. I am delighted. Versilov. At night, mental anguish. ~~But I was diverted.~~ On the following day, Vasin's arrest ~~The story of Liza and Vasin. Vasin's arrest. The Prince's marriage.~~ Confused. ~~Went out.~~ Encounter with Lambert. A conversation. Acquainted with Versilov. Blackmail. About the document.

Then: a feeling of moral deformity. On to Makar. Makar's sudden death. While Makar is laid out—Versilov comes in—the Confession.

On the following day, at Anna Andreevna's. A letter containing a

---

* See n. (*), p. 461, above.

** Could also be "cage."

marriage proposal. Makar's funeral. Mother's name day. Chopping up the icons.

Minute (2d chapter). The Prince is a nonentity... However, she was partly right (partly), because, actually, and everything considered, the Prince never really was altogether worthless, and indeed, presented me with a problem [by his person] for a long time to come... However, I wanted to keep aloof from the Prince's affairs, as if none of it were any of my business, and I even tried to pretend that I wasn't a bit worried about what was going on, and if I really had started a conversation, I'd have [purposely] talked about zoology or the Roman empire, just to show that I had no desire to participate in any current affairs, and *theirs* least of all.

I am talking merely about the act I was putting on, but then, Nastasia Egorovna's visit brought back the pain... [About the document. Take revenge on her.] I had everything ready—and I was anxious to get up as soon as possible. My heart began to palpitate, and I went to see Makar. Liza. "We have both been disgraced." "I am too goodnatured." Here, all of a sudden, Versilov. His attitude toward Makar. He relates Tatiana's trial. Liza's quarrel with Makar. Which means that we had been gathering around him even before. Versilov's opinion of him. "Tell us the end of that story about the merchant," said Tatiana. [About how Stebelkov has been arrested.]

3d chapter. *Recidive* of <my> illness. Evenings. The document. About how Makar Ivanovich had many stories to tell. Lizaveta, etc. How Versilov would meddle in the conversation. Here, Versilov's opinion about him. My opinion, stated to Versilov, concerning the "moral disorder" of their life.

4th chapter. (Yet Versilov had achieved his goal. By writing that letter he had stopped Bioring from marrying <her>.) I passed by everybody as I was leaving. I was in a hurry. The Prince (Liza is there), Vasin. The Prince is jealous of Vasin. To Anna Andreevna. About her. At Tatiana's—charity.

5th chapter. I returned, Versilov and everybody else at Makar's. About communism, "There's a thicket inside him." Vasin proposes marriage to Liza. Went to see Lambert, then back home. Excitement, and hatred for *her*.

6th <chapter>. Rapid narrative about how Dergachev and Vasin were arrested. The Prince gets married. News of Bioring's success, and about his encounter with Versilov, or *something like that*. A feeling of "moral disorder," restlessness. Back to Makar. Makar's sudden death.

[psychology] 7th <chapter>. On the day of Makar's ~~death~~ funeral ~~he~~ I went to see him. Confession. Everything is said, and nothing is made clear.* Regeneration. About Lambert and Versilov.

8th <chapter>. ~~On the following day, Anna Andreevna.~~ Three days later, a lot of fuss and excitement around the house: Versilov is gone. Anna Andreevna, His letter to her. Lambert with Anna Andreevna. Mother's name day, chopping up the icons.

9<th chapter>. A depressed feeling. His rendezvous with Her. (Occasioned by her engagement to Bioring.)

Vasin to Liza: "It is unwise to love the Prince. You are mistaken in your feelings."

The Prince to the Youth: "I want you to be my witness." He tells the Prince about Makar.

Like an *entrefilet*[11] in a newspaper.

"What did I know? Me, I knew *the dream*."

"So you denounced these people *solely* to get rid of your enemy, Vasin?"

Stebelkov. He denounced <those other people> in order to ease his own position.**

The finger. Calmed him down, talked about Zershchikov; he had forgotten, refreshed his memory. "All right then, and how are you now, my dear Arkady Makarovich? Let us now pass on to the main point." Vinegar. God knows what about the main point—live in Northern parts,*** with Liza. "And Liza, Liza—are you taking her

---

* Difficult to translate: the original has the verb *govorit'*, "to speak," with two different prefixes: *Vse vyskazano i nichego ne doskazano.*

** There follow some entries in chaotic disorder: "they want to organize a latrine," "this is as clear as day," "the whole value of the document," "The sordidness ~~Stebelkov~~ of these crooks and, perhaps, a whole gang of crooks, better together with me. This is why she was calling me so. But on the day I left the house he did not try to contact *her*. Regarding this particular thing he had ~~he did not have~~ his own *plan*. But, first of all <?>, let me repeat, this is an *entrefilet*. I knew nothing—But I had a premonition on account of that *dream*. Now I shall begin right where it all started. It started from a distance. I had not left the house yet. ~~Liza, Vasin~~ Mother's name day. When he could already see that I could be talked to in clear terms, then Anna Andreevna, too. Why should I be listening—if he's a scoundrel as you say. This is quite intolerable, to insult a person in this fashion. Oh, I was then talking as if in a delirium, saying that I felt insulted by Bioring, and what's more, at Lambert's, I was in a state of ecstasy. Then, I could have never imagined it, but now I know for sure that he had gotten on the tracks of this thing even while I was still ill. But even after the good French fashion, your surname; it is so important that you did not tell it."

*** Euphemistic for "Siberia."

11 French: "Newspaper item."

along, to ruin?" He got up without a word, turned around, grabbed his head, sat down again. ~~you're not so~~ "I'm dreaming of spiders all the time. You wouldn't believe how much she means to me."

"You are all excited." "No, allow me, we must reach a decision." Again about Zershchikov. Stebelkov is a pig, but about Makar. "Oh yes, let it be; well, you know, it's just I am that way."

I got up. "Spare Liza, and good-bye, I find it painful to look at *you.*" Vasin.

"Have you made out the main thing—my son?" Bioring and the Akhmakov woman. Nastasia Egorovna. "Do you remember Nastasia Egorovna?" "Oh yes. I'm quite sure. I also used to know a certain old man. Oh yes, right here, a guard."

Vasin. The insult. I was getting ready to leave. Liza was lying there. ~~On the following day, Liza.~~ Makar Ivanovich about Mother. Mother's name day. (Versilov and Mother.) The end of my life is at hand. ~~On the following day~~ Liza. An impression on Liza. She began to cry, went upstairs. On the following day, insulted by *the Prince.* On <her?> knees before Makar. Doesn't know life. Heard that Vasin has been arrested.

Liza: "Be at his place tomorrow."

Night, *She,* am I in love? Evil spirits. The plot, a struggle. The day I left the house ~~the plot~~. The young Prince. He betrayed <them?> ~~Anna Andreevna a woman's influence scenes~~ The Youth is told about their intrigues, i.e., Versilov <tells him>. About "that business," contemptuously about Anna Andreevna. Stebelkov had told <him?> about Bioring. At ~~Before~~ Anna Andreevna's, a woman. Explanation of their plot (BY THE NARRATOR). (About Bioring)? About Lambert.

5th chapter. Lambert. Blackmail. An affair.

"What is *she* thinking of me?" A student.

I am now embarking upon the catastrophe. It started at a distance. Vasin, etc. ... (learned from Mother). Then, at Makar's. Mother. Liza on her knees before Makar. Liza leaves, greatly shaken.

N.B. *And this is where it happens!* Night. An evil spirit. She leaves, etc.

On the following day (more rapidly). News of <his> arrest. On <her> knees before Makar. They have been arrested. (He does not know people.) Makar orders her to get married. "Give me your blessings for my many sufferings." An oration, admonitions to me, to her, about Liza. "Dear Sir," etc. "The end of my life is at hand." "You know, they have been arrested."

Through my dream, I understood Lambert's role. Through my dream about the document, I both knew, and didn't.

An idea: Should I start with an explanation of Lambert's scheme, when I was at Lambert's? (I had a premonition. Through that dream.) And that's it. Now let me start. It all started at a distance, Vasin, etc. But the dream before I left the house, and evil spirits. "What, in particular, is she thinking of me?" The catastrophe. However, I must anticipate a part of my explanation, otherwise I won't manage to tell it properly. At the time, of course, I knew nothing at all, but I am going to explain that which I know now. (More briefly.) Lambert. Blackmail. (More briefly.) All frozen stiff, he lets out the secret.

About *her*. "Now, now," he shouted, "really, what am I doing? There, read this!" he threw the letter to me. "Nastasia Egorovna!" he shouted and left the room.

I say, he has forgiven my mother. *She* has put a stop to my wanderings, to my anguish. Tatiana. This is a nice woman. *She* loves the poet in me. "I love you for your whimsical traits." To write, grammar, she began to cry. In creatures such as Makar you will find the kingdom of Heaven. I am lower than anything, lower than anybody. I love children. Laughter, she is cheerful. "I'll go in," and the other woman <. . .>

THE WHOLE IDEA.

A passion for Mother.

"I must make at least one person happy. And suddenly—passion."

"At times, a cerebral and a generous love, and at times, very real love. You, generous and cerebral person that you are, couldn't go through with this thing."

"I do not think so, my boy." Sunken cheeks. "I realized that Mother's return was the best thing about all my wanderings. I'll do away with Mother's fear, I'll show myself with all my shortcomings. I'll explain to her how, in a sense, she stands above me. I barely made it to Königsberg. All the time, I loved her while away from her. All of a sudden I felt that I needed her."

"She is in my way ~~yet this was a love at one time~~. But this is not love. Was at least one person ever happy? <?> No, it began all of a sudden, from love. Memories of a kiss. He shudders.

I was looking at him, enraptured.

He was telling me anecdotes; he wasn't going to let me go. Accompany me. "Stay for a while, why won't you stay!" ~~About Lambert~~ About *Lambert*.

"Oh, let it be blessed, and even though other things may have happened thereafter, that evening will remain."

Perhaps all this is merely the portrait of a bookish man, but why is it that only these bookish, these "paper" people go through so much real suffering, and why do some very real tragedies occur among these people? Chastity and pride.

Finis. Most of all, his humility before me, his sincerity before such a boy.

8th chapter. Now I shall try to finish my account by way of a very concise narrative.

This is how everything happened. She knew through Lambert. The whole fact of <her?> perfection is colossal. His face darkened. "But how is that?" However, he revealed it to me. ~~He~~ met her. Told <me?> about Lidiia, etc., the chains, the slap in the face. Now Bioring. "You think so" *(bis)*. He jumped up from his chair: "There, read it, read it!" (her letter). "And so what, a story, <I> felt nothing. Went to see Mother. Death. "Oh, I sent her my blessings." (About life.) "Oh you did?" Not yet, though."

The historical <aspect>.

Levin.

Look at Versilov and his family. And therefore, if the novelist is a youth, an *accidental* family. "You there, you are an accidental family."

1st embryo of a plan.

10 days of illness.

[3 weeks] 1st half of part three. (Enumeration of events.) Makar and Versilov. Liza and her sallies. Vasin and the news of Kolosov and the other people arrested. Tatiana and her maid. Anna Andreevna (Bioring, news about *her*). A fatal heart attack. Lambert. (A scene with *her,* at Tatiana's. A bit of charity, in passing.) [a week] (Chopping up the icons. Versilov is gone.) A letter to her, containing a marriage proposal. Hatred. To Lambert. Telling <him?> of the plan. Lambert about Anna Andreevna. Almost an agreement. ~~Antics~~ Versilov's antics at the old Prince's (they want to lock him up). ~~At Bioring's.~~ [a week] The old Prince flees to the Youth's place of his own accord, so that Anna Andreevna does not have to do a thing. Bioring and *she* tear the Prince away from the Youth by giving him a promise that the old Prince will get married. Versilov goes to see Bioring and unsettles him. ~~Versilov, the letter with the marriage proposal. Rendezvous. The young Prince on trial.~~ The Youth's agreement regarding the letter. With Lambert, but finally he decides to go it

alone. (Liza, etc. Mother.) Versilov, a meeting with her. The Youth witnesses it [2 weeks] He withdraws into himself, gives up his <former> intentions. He goes to see Tatiana. ~~The young Prince on trial.~~ (Alphonsine's treachery. All the scenes of the conflagration.) The young Prince on trial, and he shoots himself.

<July> 27/28.

Last *minute.**

But Lambert! Lambert! Who is Lambert? The conflagration, a dream, at the end of chapter two, a relapse. Makar's tales. He puts his dream aside.

3d chapter. Liza, suddenly, to him: "~~He~~ The Prince is calling you (tomorrow)." To Versilov, on the harmonious life, a tirade. But on the following day, the Prince has made his denunciation. Anna Andreevna. Lambert. Goes to see Lambert. The document, conflagration. He leaves—horror. Find a flat. To Makar. Comes there. Makar. "My little closet."** Makar's sudden death. Sundown. Versilov embracing Mother. Liza her brother. Suddenly, Tatiana. Sternly. "Come here, come here (to me)." *He:* "Why, everybody here is worrying..." Went <there>, and "charity." He is crying about "the harmonious life." Failed to hand over the document. Leaves, runs into Versilov—"Come to me, to me." All this, the first day he leaves the house. See *Basic ideas.* Versilov's role in chapter three, see *Basic ideas.*

August 1.

3d part, 2d chapter. Before he leaves he gives Versilov a tirade on the harmonious life in no uncertain terms, even though he had promised *not to say a word.* Versilov's *"you are right"* leaves him stunned. The dream.

3d part. In chapter three. Now I shall leave my own inner life. I'll say just one thing: I had already been stung by the serpent, and I was guarding *my wound* from everybody, as if it were a precious treasure. The impact of *the dream* was still present. What she meant to me: I was in love, every bit of news about her would take my breath away, yet at the same time I—I was *yearning* for Lambert. There was that *dream.*

[3d chapter] [Evenings and relationships] But I'll leave this for later, until the proper time. I shall now proceed to my description of those two men who have had the greatest impact on me in my life

---

* In French.

** Or: "cage."

so far: Makar and Versilov. As for Versilov, my studies and observations are surprising indeed; as for Makar, this is what happened: in the beginning, and so long as he was hanging around right in front of me, it was as if I couldn't make him out. Even if I wasn't actually treating him with condescension, I was indifferent to him, and this in spite of the fact that during that particular period my heart was, imperceptibly to me, opening itself to many and immense <impressions>: for my whole life, through Makar. However, I began to feel this, and became aware of it, only much later, and for the time being I was behaving, as already said, with a certain condescension and without the proper attention, so much so that if there hadn't been Versilov's example, who was surprising me by his respectful attitude toward Makar, I might have failed to observe, and missed forever, many things. Right here, at this spot, Versilov's opinion of Makar Ivanovich. So then, what did actually happen? Nothing special, it would seem. We got into the habit of getting together in the evening. Incidentally: if somebody should ask how it was possible that I should, after what I had stated about my relations with Versilov, and *to him,* too, and after the things I had come up with before my family, still participate in these evening gatherings, I will answer him as follows: Anything would be possible with Versilov. He was asking no questions, nor was he angry with me; he treated me exactly as before. This was his manner of being above things, and his permanent attitude. But I was also getting to see some other attitudes toward me. (N.B. Magnanimity toward the world, not getting angry with people, <is> one of his most captivating traits.) As for Mother and the others, they were, of course, feeling some compassion for a sick <member of the family>, as well as something else they must have agreed on concerning me. But for the time being I didn't really care. I was feeling drawn to something entirely new—something very firm, but something that I was postponing for the time being, so that I wouldn't even be thinking of it before I recovered from my illness. And so in the meantime I began to participate in their gatherings with undivided attention and without giving myself any airs; on the contrary, quite amiably and in friendly fashion. We used to get together. Even the doctor. It started with some stories... Versilov. Liza and Vasin. How he used to teach Mother how to walk. "Our dear Andrei Petrovich, Sir."

Liza: "Come to his place tomorrow." ?(From Tatiana: "Tomorrow at 7 o'clock P.M. be at my place ~~will I be there?~~." "Liza, I'll be there, only don't tell anybody that I am going out.") The Prince left the house. Anna Andreevna (striking news and riddles, not a word about Lambert). To Lambert: at Lambert's, a terrible outburst of emotion, with eyes flashing, Mother. As <I> left, remorse over this fall, crossed <myself>, on the boulevard. ("Oh, there were many such moments of remorse in my life." The little beetle.) Oh, it is not frivolity on my part that makes transgression and remorse appear in such rapid succession: the punishment was already in my heart, even while it was still full of criminal intent, even as I was entering the door to Lambert's flat. It was just that my emotions had caught up with me after a hot pursuit; and when I *developed* this emotion before Lambert, punishment followed quite automatically, to counterbalance it. [MOST IMPORTANT]

The old Prince dies without having <re>married. Versilov an idiot. Finale.

Bioring, while taking the old Prince away from the Youth's flat, terribly insults the Youth.

"C'est le carême,"[12] says the old Prince.

I was very much irritated by their pity for me, and once when Mother gave me something to drink, I began to cry. Night, light. The idea of being resurrected to a new life.

Silently; we must be silent now, never say a word, never.

Makar: "An old man must be satisfied with just being alive. Enough!—Everything is good. An old man must die in the full flower of his wisdom, like a magnificent ripe fruit which has fulfilled its mystery."

"What is a mystery?"

"What is a mystery? Everything is a mystery."

And Makar: "You are a youth, you are having it wonderful. But it is also wonderful that I have gotten up—I, an old man. I would like to live again. Life is ahead of you. An old man blesses sunset, but to live again would be good also. Perhaps this is a sinful thought."

The Youth: "Why sinful?"

"I don't know, my friend, In my own opinion it is not. If someone were to raise a murmur, saying that life is too short, well, that would be sinful; but if it is without a murmur, while blessing the ray, the bounties of the Lord <. . .>"

Now about something entirely different. By the way, I'll say a word or two about myself (i.e., about the state of my mind). Now about

---

[12] French: "It is Lent."

something entirely different: a whisper, <I> came down—and later, after the scene with Makar—about the state of my mind.

August 2.

Final division.

1st half of part three. Makar's death, and *she* steps out of the door.

2d half of part three: Prior to that night at Lambert's and about how they cut out the document. I.e., *she*. His confession—the funeral, chopping up the icons, at Tatiana's, Lambert, Anna Andreevna lets <me> eavesdrop on <their> ~~confession~~ rendezvous. A night at Lambert's.

4th part, 1st half. The Prince at his place. The scene with Bioring. The police station, and in the morning, at Tatiana's. Conflagration.

2d half: Everything that's in the epilogue.

See sheet 4. Silence and distrustfulness. Makar and accessories. ~~(The rendezvous.)~~ Versilov, the confession. Link up Tatiana and her cook <to the plot> better. Justice of the Peace. I am saying nothing about Liza. Narrative—Liza, sallies, Vasin, I went to see the Prince, Vasin. Meeting with Anna Andreevna (she herself calls me to her place). Took a letter containing his marriage proposal over there.* At this meeting, Anna Andreevna expresses herself unclearly. However, the Youth assures her that He hates Katerina Nikolaevna, and expounds his own theory about him to Anna Andreevna. I am excited. Makar's sudden death. First encounter with Lambert. Mother's birthday, the bouquet, chopping up the icons.

After having left there, a sudden scene with Tatiana. *Rendezvous* and *charity,* Tatiana's confession. An old maid. Sheds tears. Discussion about: Is He, or isn't He in love? (As a result of <his> conversation with Anna Andreevna, he is under <her> influence. Tatiana's true character is revealed.) Makar's sudden death. A decisive conversation with him—1st half of part three—more rapidly and sticking to the main subject. Anna Andreevna calls him quickly, tells him about the letter containing a marriage proposal. He goes to see Lambert. Mother's birthday, the bouquet, chopping up the icons. Versilov is gone. Anna Andreevna, a *rendezvous* at Nastasia Egorovna's (the flat is being rented in Nastasia Egorovna's name, but by Versilov). Again, a meeting with Lambert. *Almost an agreement.* Suddenly,

---

* The gender of the verb suggests that Anna Andreevna is the subject of this sentence.

flight of the old Prince. (Versilov has given him a scare.) Anna Andreevna says: *"I don't want it this way."* Lambert. The Youth swears to save her. Bioring insults the Youth. The police station. (A lively scene.) Liza's wedding. End of part three.

Makar, after the first scene, simply anecdotes, then about Liza and her relations. Tatiana and her cook. With Versilov, about things connected with Mother. Then, it was on that day that I left the house. Makar about Elias, Enoch—with Versilov about communism, with Lambert. On disorder and order. The Youth declares his love for Him to Him. *Makar's death,* a confession about feats.

The Youth in the midst of a deep and decisive inner struggle: should he take his revenge, or should he persist in virtue. An awareness of *disorder. A decision in favor of withdrawing from people.* (Makar and Versilov.) Order and disorder. The Youth has a hunch that all this disorder and mess has something to do with the <present> generation. *He makes a generalization,* integrates it, reducing it to our society and its laws. This is the most important page of the novel.

He is, of course, struggling against the idea that Versilov is only an exception, an ideal. However, he suspects and then actually *concludes in his own mind* that, in Russia, these ideals do in reality exist, that it is they who have such influence, that it is they who are playing *a decisive role,* for they are <Russia's> thermometer and barometer, and not any railwaymen or shyster lawyers, nor that old society of Levins (Count Tolstoi); also, that you won't get very far with these ideals.

The good wins the upper hand. He goes to see Tatiana. He tells Tatiana about the document. A rendezvous with her. Lambert makes him drunk. An argument about <his> idea. He falls into Lambert's hands, drunk. He regains his senses, having lost the letter, but without being aware of this. Rapid narrative about how they succeed in luring her to the flat, having tricked Tatiana into leaving it. The cook plays a role <in this>. The conflagration scene. 1st half of part four.

Dénouement. The young Prince is released. Death of the old Prince. Her illness and her meeting with him. The image of Versilov-the-idiot. The idea lies in the future. Tatiana's role. Liza's role. 2d half of part four (see 3d sheet).

"Why then, are angels sent down to Earth, if this is really so? You are an angel, consequently you haven't the power to do as you please, consequently you have an obligation by virtue of this very fact. You had an obligation." *She to Him:* "I am an ordinary woman. It is you who elevated me to being an angel. Why, besides, there aren't any angels."

"How much pride there is in these words."

She: "Leave me alone, leave me alone! I find it hard to stand your presence."

He: "Beware!"

She: "I know that you are capable of everything; but I am not afraid. I can't be afraid. I am in the right."

Most important. The Youth observes, on his own part: "All these declarations of his, the whole impatience of his declarations—all this was so naïve and ingenuous that I felt charmed and full of compassion for him." And later: "It was truly a strange man who was showing himself there: naïve like a child, ingenuously impatient, with a deep content inside, and the most childlike external form, so that even I could understand him."

Extraordinarily important:

I wanted to put him to the test: "Let's go and perform some feats."

"Let's go."

"Are you really serious?"

Toward the very end, the Youth finds out that (contrary to Lambert's banal view) she isn't really too afraid of the document. But he is begging Tatiana to arrange for a rendezvous between him and *her* at Tatiana's flat, solely so that he can explain things to her, tell her the whole truth, and return the document to her, after having *pleaded guilty* before her. And not at all with the idea of frightening her.

6th chapter. "But you are good children..." *Makar Ivanov (about his wife).* "It is all my fault, for it was I who allowed this to happen. (His wife with Versilov.) Should have used the rod. But I felt sorry for you. Forgive me, my children, forgive me, my dear ones. And forgive me, too, Sir, for the rod should have been applied to you, too, for even though I should not have used it in a bodily way, I could have spiritually. And why not even in a bodily way? Even that would have been possible, for, though gracious, and given to new ideas, <you> still would have sent <me> to Siberia."

"As she threw herself on the ground before me ~~in~~, in the storeroom, kissing my feet... the Lord will forgive! (Giving her a tender look) Listen, Sofiia, don't blame yourself. The sin was mine. The husband is head: understand that."

"And she (Stinking Elizaveta) heard a voice: 'Keep silent, wild one.' " During his confession there suddenly became apparent about Versilov something which he wasn't aware of himself—something frightfully small, whereas I had always thought that there would be something great.

Anna Andreevna. "I am motivated by the most sacred of feelings."

"He is compromising us too much."

"You are having an extraordinary influence on him."

~~"He is compromising us too much."~~

"You are his favorite child."

Nastasia Egorovna joined Anna Andreevna's household, i.e., to nurse the infant.

"*Maximum!* I have sworn to protect her!"

N.B. Versilov had explained to Lambert ~~the importance~~ the meaning of the document, and Lambert knew where the document was.

Regarding the confession. The Youth is telling the story of Versilov and *her* from his own point of view, but interspersed with His words.

Order: First the letter with the marriage proposal. Then, Anna Andreevna summons the Youth and shows him the letter. (End of conversation *ex abrupto.*) Then, Anna Andreevna let him eavesdrop on the rendezvous. Then, when the old Prince has run away, Anna Andreevna takes fright: "*I* don't want it to be that way."

To Makar. Only at this minute is this old man (dear to us). His death. Tatiana is not present. Went to see Tatiana. "Listen, you, stay here," and *she* left. I was crying.

That night, at Versilov's (during the Confession), I finally found out who Makar really was, and, also from Versilov, a complete understanding of him, one might say.

IMPORTANT.

Start the 2d half of part three this way: Now only the facts, and there couldn't be a more suitable matter to begin with than an exposition of that momentous event, an exposition which has been prepared without my heart having any part in it, as if I weren't actually reporting it either, but as if it were some *entrefilet*[13] from a newspaper. And here then, the news of Bioring and a positive announcement of their wedding. I shall add nothing more. I knew nothing of all this just a few days earlier, but Mother was sad. Versilov is not there. A strange welcome. Lambert. A quarrel with Lambert. The funeral and the bouquet: factual description à la Shakespeare. On the

---

[13] French: "Newspaper item."

following day, from Anna Andreevna, the secret about Bioring. The harmonious life exemplified by Makar, disorder exemplified by Versilov. The Youth wants to escape from disorder.

Psychological arrangement. At first, the Youth is under the influence of an evil emotion (revenge) and so becomes involved with Lambert, actually communicating his project to him. But after his meeting with her (charity), after that scene with Versilov, after Makar's death, and finally, after the breaking of the icons and the flight of the old Prince—THE YOUTH IS SUDDENLY STUNNED BY THE MORAL DEFORMITY OF THIS MILLIEU, he becomes devoted to her, swears that he will protect her honor, and this in spite of the fact that he was insulted by Bioring and <had spent a night> at the police station. However, *he* sees in this only *order,* that is, in returning good for evil. But after that night at the police station, very much excited, he spends a night at Lambert's place, and it is there that the latter cuts open his pocket. N.B. That same night he learns from Lambert that the latter is acquainted with Versilov. Lambert had made VERSILOV'S ACQUAINTANCE much earlier, while <the Youth> was sick in bed: Lambert used to come and see <him>.) The Youth tells, from his own point of view, how Lambert and the others got it all set up.

In the end, the Youth feels insulted, but withdraws into himself. <His> idea, more than ever before. SOLITUDE. The child. He becomes attached to the child.

Versilov, *an idiot,* kissing Mother's hands and praying.

Maximum. Contacts with Tatiana, and an explanation from Tatiana. The old maid (cries). Tatiana used to be in love with Versilov.

2d chapter. N.B. Versilov has one principal point, which is: Her marriage to Bioring. This he cannot stand. *He* would have left her alone, if she had remained single.

"How is it that you are the permanent guardian of my conscience and of my morals," *she* says to Him, "who gave you this assignment? And why is it that it is I whom you must absolutely save?"

~~Yes~~ The Youth to Makar: "Say, you are wrong here, you are misquoting the text."

Makar: "Why, you may be right. I am not a learned man. There you have it, he's set me straight. Smart boy."

What purpose do Vasin and Dergachev serve in this novel?

Answer: As an accessory which sets off the figure of the Youth so much more clearly, and as a motive for that *definitive discussion* between the Youth and HIM.

[4th chapter] It is now time to admit something: why did I write these notes? I was struck by that *disorder.* Oh yes, I was very angry even at school; yet, before I came to Petersburg I really knew nothing. I imagined some things to be even worse, I did imagine villains, but I was thinking that all men, villains and good men alike, have something in common, something which they respect, something which they hold sacred and about which they have no arguments. Versilov's moral *disorder,* that absence of principles. Makar alone is in order, but is he possible <as a contemporary man>? My mother alone is a saint, but how does she live? I came to have great faith in *her,* but how does she live, what goals does she have? She'll be at my feet on account of that document. *Most important.* N.B. The reason why he is so glad to have <his> idea is that *she* does not fear the document. To *her,* Bioring means strict order, while "the world is disorganized and depraved" (*she* says that herself) "and everything in it is in ferment, and nothing is really there in it." "I am thirsting for order," she says (to Versilov), "And I, too, am thirsting for order." It develops that the Youth has picked up the word *disorder* from *her.* *She* had already talked about it to Versilov during their rendezvous, which the Youth had secretly witnessed. She has this to say about Bioring (to Versilov): "He is honest, a man of strict, old-fashioned principles, even educated, definitely no fool, and what's most important, a German, not a Russian. For with a Russian, things are always in disorder, Russians know no order." Though she is saying this in a half-mocking tone, the Youth later thinks to himself, it sounded a lot as if she actually felt that way.

[2d chapter] Versilov himself, guiding the Youth, imperceptibly, to the conclusion that Makar is "impossible," suddenly has this to say about Makar: "WHY, HE ACTUALLY DOES NOT KNOW LIFE AT ALL." What he has failed to mention, though, is the fact that, although Makar may not know life, the very possibility of his appearance among people is incomparably more useful than He, Versilov, with all his "knowledge of life," and with his desperation, directly emanating from such knowledge.

~~*Versilov*~~ *The Youth* to Anna Andreevna (when the old Prince has just run away): "I don't know, Anna Andreevna, but I am constantly struck by the disorder of our society. As long as everything remains within an official and prescribed framework, Russian man and the Russian family retain the semblance of some kind of order. But the moment a misfortune befalls them, all this will immediately become apparent—that total absence of any moral foundation—and disorder will set in..." This, he says to Versilov, and CONTINUALLY after Makar <begins to exert an influence on him>.

Versilov, in his confession: "*She* was watching me with a mocking smile, and the closer I looked at her, the more I saw that laughter in her face."

During his meeting with *her,* Versilov tells her that she is perfection itself (he had been telling the Youth that she had all the vices). *She* tells Him that *she* is a very sinful woman, but that he would very much like to find some particular vice in her, so as to smother *her* reputation with it.

"Let's rather be friends," *she* tells Him (Irkutsk), "I am going to respect you. It's a lot better this way, than living in disorder. I am not getting married just to settle down; I am looking for some order, I don't love Bioring at all."

As he is leaving her, Versilov accuses her of being ready, for the sake of acquiring a position in society, to come up with a vile action and to betray her conscience (i.e., let herself be raped by Lambert just to get that document, all the vices), *which is also why* he incites Lambert to give it a try.

To the very end, the Youth is possessed by the somber idea of taking revenge on someone (he has picked her to be his victim). ~~But~~ He communicates his entire plan to Versilov ~~but Versilov prefers Lambert to him~~, at white heat (to which end he goes to see Him and finds Him in some dive, especially after having been insulted by Bioring). Versilov, it seems, is ready to go along with him, but then he prefers Lambert to him. This leaves the Youth *badly shaken.* Even before Alphonsine<'s visit>, he had been struggling with himself all night (i.e., should he, or shouldn't he start that *conflagration?*), and suddenly, Alphonsine. He runs over to Tatiana, etc. The whole scheme. Having communicated his plan to Versilov for the first time, the Youth leaves him in a sad mood: Why did He agree? "All right, let me be vile, but not Him," and here, a night of vacillation; he [finally] decides to go it alone, without Him. Sneering at the world. And then, suddenly, Alphonsine.

In his confession, Versilov makes this important admission: "Makar has had an impact on me during my entire life. Let's go on together. I am renouncing the demon *(she)!*"

[2d part] "Demon, demon! Minutes of happiness, life be blessed, let's drink to this." Makar: "To Mother."*

At the end of the 2d chapter of part three, and throughout the third chapter: "Lambert, Lambert, what is Lambert? (N.B. Why should I

---

* Or: "Let's drink to this, Makar, to Mother."

be afraid of Lambert? I am stronger than he!)." Suppositions, dreams, and convulsions, along with being deeply moved by Makar.

In the 3d chapter. Every time I returned deeply moved by Makar's stories, but at night, dreams, voluptuous dreams, finally (return the document!) a decision, evil spirits, and good ones. With Versilov, about communism. But he does not discuss Makar with Him prior to his confession. On the day he leaves the house. "Do not visit Lambert!" But he did go, and he *dirtied himself.* To Makar! Sunset.

The Youth, as he is quarreling with Lambert: "Look, friend, I am now stronger than you."

At Lambert's, during his first visit. His friends, a breakfast with champagne, then the lure: "You'll get your revenge, and I'll get my money. You'll get the higher, and I the lower, thing."

N.B. Here. "No, you're just a youth, you are still little. We had that one—such virtue—and the same kind as this one of yours, too; yet she began to tremble all over when we threatened to make everything public. She was quite docile. We took both one thing, and the other, and money. Now she is a society lady, inaccessible, all virtue. Fie, the devil, if you had only seen what barn it was, where it all happened. What barns they wouldn't shun, these ladies! [Alphonsine occasionally goes to Tsarskoe Selo, bringing <her> some toys.]"

("We've got a gang-leader—a whole story ") "I am leaving for America. They are depraved to the core. I've been thinking of that!" the Youth keeps exclaiming.

N.B. *Lambert:* "Is she pretty?"

The Youth: "She is."

Lambert: "I have seen her."

The Youth: "I know that you have seen her."

And again, and again: "I've been thinking of that, I've been thinking of that!" And later, as he is leaving, desperate about having soiled himself, he keeps exclaiming: "Yes, I have already become depraved myself, I've been thinking of this, and when? When Makar was telling his touching stories! I've been thinking of it every night" (good and evil spirits). Remorse: "To Makar! to Makar!" Sunset.

With Lambert. Lambert simply takes him under his wing and it turns out that *he already knows everything.* "I've been expecting you." *A sensation:* "~~Though~~ It was giving me great pleasure to work hand in hand with him. This pleasure was being enhanced by the thought that, so far, I was still independent, and that I was doing everything of my own free will."

Lambert is in possession of some details about *her,* he shines <with his knowledge>; Lambert has got everything arranged; he has spread his nets everywhere—he even knows Bioring.

Lambert: "(You could even marry her.) Doesn't she love you? Doesn't she? Haven't you been telling me that she does?"

"That was then, when I was delirious."

"You could marry her, but then you really ought to rule her with an iron rod. These noble ladies must be treated despotically." The idea of marrying her pierced my heart with a voluptuous feeling. Oh, I was stupid. Let me note here this terrible stupidity of mine: I was dreaming of marriage even when I was only 16. This bit of information really ought to be crossed out. But all right, let it stand. [Very important.] I gave Lambert a look; <he?> was serious. "Versilov hates her. Hates her."

The Youth to Lambert, about him and about *her:* "There is an animosity between them, animosity, such animosity, that I have actually lost track. I've been watching them, but quit. ~~From~~ Only it is a terrible enmity, of that old-fashioned kind, on account of something exalted, some kind of nonsense, in the Romantic style of the forties."

"We shall save her from his revenge."

"But what if I have such a document?" I shouted, with my eyes flashing.

Lambert: "Do you really think I don't know that you've got it? You told me yourself, didn't you?"

"When? While I was delirious?"

"Yes."

Lambert: "You are very kind, ~~you are generous~~."

The Youth: "Yes, I am kind."

Lambert: "You are generous."

The Youth: "Oh, I am generous."

Lambert: "I saw her, but she didn't see me. It is important that she shouldn't see me."

"Only you're stupid, Lambert, that's what; really, you don't understand a thing of what I'm saying."

Lambert does not argue the point.

In chapter three, Versilov's role, communism, inevitability, economic overcrowdedness in the world. Suffocation (a fantastic picture, with brilliance).

"The Lord will save us, He will send us something."

Political ideas. Talked about the future of Russia, about wealth. Versilov about the Chinese.

N.B. All this together<is> two chapters. Lambert, also a separate chapter.

AFTER THE RENDEZVOUS SCENE, and so to the very end, the Youth is tormented by the thought that he loves the woman with whom his father is also in love. That drunken night at Lambert's he hated <Him?> for this. But he has a change of heart and loathes himself for it the next day.

In the beginning of chapter three. Versilov came to my place and timidly said: "Makar Ivanovich is asking for you. We have decided to keep it secret from your mother. Be patient, my friend, if you can. And if you can, please come down and join <them>."

I was moved... I'll say nothing about myself.

And then, throughout the chapter: And later: he returns, and a dream, a dream, a different, bestial dream, how could hell get on with paradise so well?

[3d part. More briefly] For the first time I was observing myself with some puzzlement.

I should have placed some value on Versilov's feelings toward my mother, but even then I didn't know everything, and the rest was a part of me.*

AFTER THE CONFESSION. "Oh, blessed be this minute, Versilov. ~~The memory~~ The memory of those great moments. No matter what would happen later... I regret that I started these notes in this tone of a raw youth. Yet, I do have some things to remember, too!"

~~GENERAL THOUGHTS~~

IN HIS CONFESSION Versilov speaks with enthusiasm of the sincerity of a youth (about Diakov, etc.), about Mother, about her purity. "Long live everything great!" "What is great?" "Sincerity."

3d CHAPTER. Not a word about myself. I was well again after three days. A feeling of convalescence. Versilov came to my room: "Makar Ivanovich is asking for you. Be careful." I am not describing it in consecutive order. I was feeling attracted by the old man. Versilov's opinion. I would have liked to ask him: "Aren't you envious?" But I found it impossible: obvious sincerity. I was surprised by his deference. Stories. Tatiana. Stinking Lizaveta. "There is understanding in you." N.B. These few days, oh, blessed be... A different Versilov, evenings, Mother. This old man. Versilov's opinions. We did a lot of talking. But I no longer was afraid to talk. All this was only about

---

* Unclear in the original.

Roman emperors, and such things. Not a word about her, and I was feeling at ease. Arguments. Politics. Mother. Versilov about socialism. Soon, Mother's name day; Makar about Mother's childhood. The episode with Vasin. Thereupon, their arrest. Liza insulted, the marriage. Versilov: "He can't tell her a thing, he does not know life." Liza at Makar's, tears, Liza. "All kinds of grief will pass, Job had children," Versilov ("I'll get married"). I to Liza: "Tomorrow I shall go out, only don't tell anyone." Good spirits and evil. Lambert, the crime, and this immediately after the scene at Makar's.

THE CHILDREN OF JOB. 4<th chapter>. Going out.

After the meeting with Lambert in chapter four. Dirtied myself. But something was pulling me toward that snake pit with a furious vehemence, with a voluptuous feeling, and a sinking heart. I wanted to escape from that moral deformity and ended up by outdoing all the others. I was frightened. I got scared. To Makar.

BASIC IDEAS.

In chapter three: "What could *she* have been thinking of me?" (Ever since that first letter to Bioring).

In chapter four, after Lambert, returning to Makar. "They've got a scheme, a scheme! Run."

[HERE] IN THE FINALE. When did the old Prince flee? his flight takes place in the morning. Lambert, together with Anna Andreevna, but he cheats her right there: He had promised her that, upon the old Prince's flight, he would confirm him in his ideas by showing him the document. But what actually happened was that the night before, having gained possession of the document, Lambert decided to wait and not show it to the old Prince, ~~for~~ figuring that Anna Andreevna might not marry <him> after all, for some reason or other; so that, in that case, he couldn't collect on her I.O.U. But having the document in hand, he decided to better wait another *day* or so and try to sell the document to *her:* collecting on an I.O.U. of hers would be a much surer thing. In the meantime Anna Andreevna has already given the old Prince a bad scare by telling him ~~that~~ orally that the document exists and that she is going to show it to him, as soon as he runs away. But the document never is produced. And then, Bioring appears on the scene, and the Prince leaves, angry at Anna Andreevna because he thinks that she has deceived him. However, the Prince had been frightened more than one might have expected beforehand. When Bioring appeared, he embraced him with tears of remorse, telling him about the document, and that he had been deceived. All this day Anna Andreevna was pestering Lambert, urging him to let her have the document as promised. But Lambert failed to show up, giving as an excuse that it was the Youth who had the document. The Youth, in turn, proudly declares to Anna Andreevna that he's got the document in his pocket and that he is not going to give it to anybody. Yet it is he again who is insulted by Bioring, after having acted in this fashion.

3d chapter. *One more programme.*

[I've gotten up and I'm not going back to bed again. I am putting this down because everything that happened then meant the formation of something new, the formation of a <new> life.]

Convalescence. Strength. Versilov comes to see me: "Makar Ivanovich is asking for you." Makar Ivanovich. *His health.* I was touched by their common sympathy. That time, of the evening.

[Tales about saints. Few images. <Illegible> a dreamer.]

As I recall it, this old man was treating <me> with a strange condescension. I'm afraid to say that it is perhaps the brightest <memory in my life>.

Arguments—about the hermit, about the reign of Christ. This is communism. Not entirely so. "You are a great dreamer." Enthusiasm. Tales about saints. Mary of Egypt.

[A few days of convalescence. Even the doctor.]

[I forgave the doctor a lot. Of course, this was one of those ~~rather~~ most ordinary people. But I liked his affection for our family. Medical arrogance.]

[Versilov's respect for Makar, Versilov. Mother is grateful. But I noticed that even Versilov himself used to pay visits to Makar. I was very anxious to hear what they might be talking about. They are interpreting <the Book of> Job.[14] A thicket.] I was surprised at Versilov's respect for Makar.

Only after a long time did I understand who Makar was. Evenings. Used to tell stories, inconsistency. For example, how they beat up that monk. "You are contradicting yourself." About the merchant. About Stinking Lizaveta. About Job. Satan, etc. About the future of our world. (All exalted ideas.) "There is a thicket inside him." Once, about politics. Mother stands up for Russia. By the way, about Mother, her childhood. (Here, Tatiana.) N.B. Polish this.

Back to bed. An evil spirit bit me. A wound. "I wonder what *she* thinks of me?" (Bioring). Shines. *A dream* (briefly, forcefully and

---

[14] See note 2 of this section.

through hints, the document). Evil spirits. Liza. Vasin. She feels insulted, in brief, <her> story. Liza. They've been arrested. "He is calling you."

My heart was palpitating ("Go, go! "Should I see Lambert, or shouldn't I?"). Absolutely, absolutely! I am stronger than Lambert.

N.B. "That's what it means to live in sin: the tale about that soldier, a soldier is a muzhik gone rotten. A lawyer is a hired conscience."

In <his> confession—Versilov about the harmonious life.

"When you pronounced that word 'the harmonious life,' I thought to myself, why really, this is my own idea, and you are mine, you are my son."

A first, gasping for breath.

Later, communism, the idea contained in atheism.

Makar: "My dear children, it isn't that I'm <praising?> dead nature, and they shall see the sign of the Son of man, and they will prostrate themselves."

"Most probably you are right, Makar Ivanovich."

N.B. N.B. N.B.

About politics, after the stories.

This is what he told <us>—Mother is a patriot. Then about Job, about Mother. I'll never forget it ~~the story~~, <that> night, about atheism, and gasping for breath.

In the morning, Liza. The arrest. Liza with Makar. Liza. "What is he going to tell her? He does not know ~~anything about people~~ people." About the arrest. "He isn't as he used to be before; he is dying, he is going to die soon, he is going to die much sooner than we think, we must be ready."

I shall not try to formulate <my> mental condition. If my reader were to find out he wouldn't believe it. Rather, I'll tell about it later, in a factual way that will allow me to express myself better. Let my reader only keep in mind the soul of a spider, and this in a person who was going to leave them all, and forsake the world in the name of "the harmonious life." A thirst for the harmonious life coupled with God only knows what other thirsts, and all of it in perfect consciousness.

"Is it a breadth of character that one finds in Russian people, or is it simply baseness?" said Andrei Petrovich, "here is what I have to say: I didn't know myself at that moment whether I ought to be proud, or ought to despise myself."

"As for them, they've all condescendingly forgiven it." Versilov. <?>

"So then, tomorrow I am leaving the house: I wonder what *she* thinks of me? Here, here is my most important line..." Leaving the house.

A few days passed. How one thing could exist right next to the other. A calm with stormy intentions. A rich man.

But before <beginning to realize> my stormy intentions, I decided I was going to get completely well again, and in the meantime take advantage of the calm.

See BASIC IDEAS.

"Why pamper them? If I did, they'd ~~talk~~ raise an even louder howl against me. Why feel sorry for them? All this will be to no avail—people will talk even more."

Could it be that anybody would refuse to accept such great luck? Finally, he says to her: "Here's what, my honest widow..."

Again, there's a lot of stealing going on.

These people are like little children; whatever they see they grab.

To take upon oneself such eternal torments.

I also used to ~~execute~~ administer similar beatings to the one I had before.

Learn something, don't fool around.

All this is to no avail. People will talk even more.

This man has turned into a brute.

The Abbot. Whispered something in her ear. She agreed.

The livelong day. As was your pleasure.

Any good thing takes time. Keep still, don't fuss around.

Not exactly aunts, just distant relations.

Comfort in my grief, which has afflicted me gravely.*

This arrow has pierced my heart.

As Thou didst, at one time, oh Lord, accept Paul, so accept me, oh Lord, me the cursed, me the outcast.**

If I spend my time without profit to my soul, I won't be able to return it.

There was an unhypocritical love between them, and like a single soul in two bodies.

---

* Entirely in Church Slavonic; perhaps a biblical quotation.

** Entirely in Church Slavonic.

You have turned me over to all <these> people to be trod upon.

One does not communicate with a stranger (not communicating).

Nor will the Lord leave my sorrow unrewarded, nor my wanderings.

And to leave all this is no mean cross, nor a light sorrow.

And for a woman to remain alone, like a swallow that has lost her nest.

He was tossing about and grieving, like a fish on dry land.

And he lost some of his own capital.

These people are worn out. And you are more worn out than they are.

Even God's angels are imperfect; only our Lord Jesus Christ is perfect and without sin, which is why the angels serve him.

The words of a desperate man are spoken to the wind.

He hath cast me into the mire, so that my very garments loathe me.

My glory hath been dispersed, like the wind, and my happiness hath passed, like a cloud.*

Inescapable grief.

"I was hard and cruel, I imposed heavy burdens and was demanding of people."

"What does a man live by, but good examples."

"My life is coming to an end."

Whosoever does not want to work, let him not eat either.

A man is being stubborn: "I'm not going to forgive you," for perhaps that man doesn't even know what makes him stick to his own <position>.

These are worn-out people in these parts, people here can't take much.

Little children, little troubles.**

Live off you for a while.

Do us a favor, show us your favor.

"So that's what you thought."

"I have been administering similar beatings to the others as well, so what does he <illegible>."

To get married.

---

* Apparently these last two or three phrases are quotations from memory from the Book of Job.

** The Russian editor has *detki malen'kie, tak i vedki malen'kie,* where *vedki* (which makes no sense) is clearly misread, or misprinted, for *bedki,* 'troubles.'

I was in profound agreement with him. The doctor: prescribed some drops, left, took 800 rubles.

He had committed many sins, without giving it any thought at all, but now this one little sinless soul had him caught. He could not stand it. This is how miraculously things happen at times.

"You, my honest widow, you are still young and lovely, I know what you need, you need a husband," he was saying that in a frenzy.

There is such cough; whooping cough it is called.

And so they got that cough.

The girls.

Little children, in the sunshine, in their bare feet... they see no evil, sense no danger, sunshine—they are so happy, sleep at night like little angels.

She gave all her money to her monastery, to be distributed among widows and homeless orphans. As for Afimevsk, things went a lot worse than before after he had given up the factory.

So he is sitting there, in the tavern, naked, not a thread on his body. He'll leave the tavern—these are worn-out people, they'll get drunk themselves, then wail over their own misfortunes...

"You can't deal with these people in any different way," says the merchant ~~what are they complaining about, what~~, for he would pay them at his own pleasure, "I know," he would say, "when it is the right time to pay a man."

About the boy: He isn't this, nor is he that, he's just looking at him in wonder. He's got him scared, that's what it is. Only he doesn't know that. "Why doesn't he love me?"

"The boy is not going to forgive us." She shakes all over, makes a bow before him, and so each goes his own way. Having mourned her children and her husband, for she had, in those three years, come to love him in her heart.

But it hasn't the right foundation; all this can't overcome, in his heart—those things that had happened before.

He summoned a painter.

2 little fists, God, the river, got himself all worn out.

"The child has not forgiven us."

"I am going to build a church for him."

They went.

They called in doctors from the capital.

A good deal of incoherence about these stories, i.e., sometimes it remained completely unclear with what aim the story was being told. I repeat, from tender emotion.

Not too mystical.

Not too interested in current secular events.

His pleasure at hearing certain political news sometimes would reach the level of pure bliss.

"This is what the communists believe," he would add every minute. "However, I do not know whether this is what the communists believe in, for I am not sufficiently familiar with this matter." There remained a terrible suspicion in my mind: "Don't you believe in these very things yourself?" I was avidly listening to him.

Versilov: "No, this is what the communists believe in, at least this is what they ought to believe in, because otherwise they won't get anywhere at all."

I: "This is still dead nature" (Oh, I didn't understand, then).

"Dead, my friend," exclaimed Makar, "but suddenly there is Christ who says: 'Here I am.' "

Mother is a patriot, Mother's childhood, on the occasion of Mother's name day.

After the stinking one: Mother's name day was approaching, *if I'd only stay alive until then.*

Incidentally, Mother is a patriot.

Recollections of Mother.

"Allow me to shake hands with you and to declare that, sometimes, you are still an honest man."

Versilov and I: I'm feeling uneasy.

For there are instances where even the victor is sometimes ashamed before the man he has defeated, for having gotten the better of him.

We both seemed to be embarrassed. Though there were frequent outbursts of irrepressible emotions, we were still seeking to restrain ourselves, as if we were both ashamed of each other ~~because~~ and, to tell the truth, it apparently made the whole thing more pleasurable. ~~For there are instances~~

Communism. Oh yes, this is so—but he was greatly interested, was asking questions very eagerly, but then Versilov *cut us short.*

There are many diversions; you may easily forget all about mankind. Money isn't a god, it is a demigod. I learned this from his stories. They didn't have the slightest moralizing tendency; all that seemed to matter was that they should be very moving. A house serf, a passion for ideas, for news, a respect for education, because he doesn't mind being close to his masters. ~~Politics~~ "You know, he actually likes politics. A muzhik couldn't care less about such things, not excluding, perhaps, even the bible-reading sectarian."

Communism: Economic power will never tie people together, only moral power will. Where, then, do we get this integrating moral power? Versilov was claiming that the most advanced among the communists were seeking it in atheism. The love of God and God divert man from his love of mankind. But then, everybody will move up closer to everyone else, like orphans, and man will begin to love his own solitary majesty. In the beginning, a man will sacrifice everything for the sake of another man. Later, all of mankind <will do the same> for the sake of nature.

If we believe in God, our respect for human reason must needs disappear, and from <a disappearance of> respect for human reason, also our respect for the image of man, which gave birth to reason, and consequently, also <our respect> for human dignity <must disappear>, and so our respect for one another.

But all this he would repeat only in a casual manner: most of all he liked that mood of tender emotionality, which is why he was often telling us his stories.

Job—new children.

Old evil vanishes, and changes into tender emotion. Here, Makar switches from his own stormy <?> life to recollections of my mother—how she used to sanctify his soul even while still a child.

Children don't stand <on the same spot very long>. This is how God will sometimes find a human soul. "I am going to make a man out of him, he does not love me. Why doesn't he love me? He is not devoted to me."

He took him from the factory. "Maybe I will make him the heir of my entire fortune." He pressed his two little fists to his heart.

Finale. 1st, starting with a new chapter.

I verified these words on my own part: I remember, that morning I was struck by a feeling of sympathy. Without Versilov, I would have missed a lot about this old man, who has left some momentous memories in my heart. He had little education, didn't know any <?> broader ideas.

Versilov: "He wasn't that <bad>. He is approaching his end." "Come on, he'll live some more, but is it true that he is really that bad?"

N.B. Made up with the doctor. I ascribe this also to <my> convalescence.

In the *Finale.* Yet Lambert found out something that was of great value to him. He realized what the document was really worth, seeing and deducing it from the scare it gave the Prince—a scare which he hadn't at all expected to be that strong. This is why he got the idea that some people who had an interest in this matter might really pay a lot for that document.

Liza: "So you know? You really know?" We embraced on the stairs.

Lambert, during our very first meeting, began to talk about how one might shake <her> down for some money. I decided that I was going to be *broad-minded,* so I sat there and listened to him. "Lambert, but this is called blackmail!" "They are pigs themselves."

AT ANNA ANDREEVNA'S. I felt that she was lying, and that she was a wicked woman, but it is a strange thing with women: this semblance of integrity, these manners, this impregnability of high society eminence and proud chastity, this show of virtuousness—all this got me confused, and I began to find myself in agreement with her, that is, so long as I was sitting there with her. At least I wouldn't have dared to contradict her, not for anything in the world. A man is decidedly, in a moral sense, a woman's slave. Such a woman can persuade an inexperienced and generous man of almost anything. I was actually feeling sorry for her, by the way, for only recently I had still loved her and, as far as her scheme with the old Prince was concerned, I still did not entirely understand the whole extent of it.

N.B. Anna Andreevna would have preferred to be dealing with me, rather than with Lambert (N.B. Absolutely include an explanation on the part of the Youth). I was sitting there, thinking to myself: "How could she join Lambert?"

Anna Andreevna: "I am too proud to deal with persons unknown to me." And, during our second meeting: "But you have got the document?" Nastasia Egorovna: "And you aren't going to run off, Sir?"

[Anna Andreevna is hoping that the old Prince will send for Prince Platon and some other people to whom he will then show the ~~letter~~ document, to prove that he is not insane.]

Paid no attention to broad-mindedness. Is this broad-mindedness, or simply baseness? (After the Prince's confession) I always asked myself this question: Is this <a sign of> broad-mindedness in the Russian character, or is it simply baseness?

The Youth to Lambert: "I've got *an idea.*"

At the police station. The police officer. On the next day.

"I am told that you've come up with something."

"I haven't done a thing, I was at my own home."

He used to kiss her (Mother), he used to call her his *wife.* Never would I have suspected such powerful feeling in him. Before me, there was standing a different person.

The Youth to Lambert, regarding His love for *her:* "I was believing it, but only *for one moment,* but now I don't, now I know what the situation really is like." (It is pride.)

[Chapter, beginning.] I must explain directly something I still did not know then, though I did of course have my suspicions, or, to put it better, I was suspecting *the worst, without being properly afraid of it:* Lambert was the ringleader of a so-called blackmail ring. He had heard about the document from me. But, after his own fashion, he was extremely smart. His further *plans will be explained later.* Oh, he would have betrayed me. He wanted to join Anna Andreevna, but the thing was that the document was then still in my hands.

Lambert and I, for the first time.

All the things which we had been talking about were, so it appeared to me, completely implausible, unrealizable, and fantastic, yet I was discarding, one by one (as if I were reading an implausible, yet enticing novel) all of these improbabilities, as I kept on talking solely to enjoy my own fantasies, and something else yet, something that was swarming all over my heart, like some predatory beast, like some vile serpent. Before leaving the house: "Now I must myself piece together this whole plot." Did I really love her?

AT THE POLICE STATION: PRINCE DOLGORUKY?

The Youth lets Anna Andreevna know that *she* has treated him so very badly (giving in). Anna Andreevna is enthusiastic in her sympathy for him.

With Anna Andreevna: that Katerina Nikolaevna has again begun to show herself in society, about Bioring ("Maybe I've got Bioring"). Anna Andreevna was feeling that things were again going smoothly between <*her* and> Bioring, and was worried that there might be another sally on the part of Versilov, which is why she was seeking the Youth's help. This the Youth explains, as he is leaving Anna Andreevna, already *from his own point of view* (i.e., that thing about Bioring).

Lambert has two plans: if the document does exist (as he has told Anna Andreevna), then either sell it to Anna Andreevna for *money,* after she has gotten married, or sell it *to her?* [or to Bioring?] What would be the most profitable? That's why he is informing himself through the Youth: where would he have a better chance? And what's most important, he would very much like to become the sole holder of the document, by cheating the Youth, which is also why he is needling the Youth with such questions as: Did it hurt a lot when Bioring gave him that licking?

Or to Bioring, or to Versilov? But he never does approach Versilov.

The Youth, *from his own point-of-view,* to the reader about how Lambert succeeded in "filtering himself through" to Anna Andreevna. "How did they do it? And what could they have said to each other? I couldn't have done it."

A project to kidnap the Prince and bring him to my flat, and to show him the document right there.

[Lambert's simplicity.]

It is Anna Andreevna who asks the Youth that definitive question:* i.e., "Can I count on you if the Prince seeks refuge at your flat? That is, that you are going to show him the document."

[Here.] WHAT'S MOST IMPORTANT, all this is told *from* the Youth's *own point of view,* though, at their first meeting, Anna Andreevna says next to nothing directly, only in obscure allusions, which goes for Bioring, and the flat, and the document. Instead, she sends him to Lambert. She tells him that Lambert had come to see her to inquire about the Youth's health, while he was ill, asks him about that night and about how he was insulted by Bioring; in a word, she is *excessively* solicitous.

[He is greatly pained by those rumors about Bioring.]

In theory, it didn't bother me.

That demon, that demon, and life be blessed; that shame; I swear it was all so innocent. Just an urge to live, to live. No, I think that I'll accomplish a good deal in my lifetime. So far I have never once lost hope.

Alphonsine to Tsarskoe Selo. But about this, later. The small pictures in the stethoscope. *Alphonsine, là voila.* Ah-ah-ah, tooboe.**

Further idea of parts three and four.

Versilov lays himself bare entirely. He speaks of humility as of the greatest power, which has conquered the world, and of independence through self-restraint; chains (he is rather cool toward Makar), and only occasionally does he allude to the letter, in a strange, fitful way. (The Youth suddenly learns that he ~~has been~~ is looking for that letter.) Finally, he decides to marry Sofiia Andreevna. The Youth is begging him to do it. (A pathetic scene.) Suddenly, chopping up the icons and, the day before, a marriage proposal to the Akhmakov woman who, in turn, is already engaged. Then, he disappears until

---

* In the original, a *lapsus calami:* "answer."

** For *tout beau.*

the Youth finally finds him. (This is pride and passion in the highest degree, to the point of madness.)

And then the conflagration.

[In part four] When the Youth told him about the document he said: "I always suspected it, in fact I was convinced of it."

In part three, the Youth is wondering why Versilov seems to have forgotten all about the document. But, having chopped up the icons, and disappeared out of sight, Versilov did make an attempt to make a deal with Lambert and with Stebelkov. But then he left them in a hurry. When the Youth has finally found him, he lets him have the document. He does not take it. They go on together.

The ideal, its presence in one's soul, a thirst, a need to believe in [something... to worship something] and the absence of any kind of faith. This gives birth to two feelings in <the soul of> a high type of contemporary man: boundless pride and boundless self-contempt. Observe his hellish sufferings, watch him trying to convince himself that he is actually a believer... And then, his clashes with reality, where he invariably shows up so ridiculous, so ridiculous and so petty... and so insignificant. *He* suspects that what one must do is work on oneself, restrain oneself, and that this would cost an endless effort. And so he does tax himself with the duty of self-perfection, does it gladly, enthusiastically... [choosing for himself nothing but chains all along.] Occasionally, he would be bothered by a feeling of tormenting unbelief and skepticism, but He stands, and, finally, it appears that he has come close to his goal... And there, as he clashes head-on with reality, he takes a terrible fall, showing himself feeble and nerveless. Why? <Because> He is uprooted from the soil, a child of his age...

[Makar the Wanderer, the one who just died, gave me this idea.]

You are angry because there are such people. In order to get a really close look at them, in order to discover what is innermost in them, one must have a love of people. Then, you'll also have the eye for it, and you will see that there are many of them.

N.B. *August 11*. [this, in the confession <scene>]

It is Versilov who makes this revelation to *her,* and *she* suddenly says to him: "You are going to seek a terrible revenge for the humiliation of this confession."

"We are among those who are unable to remain at rest in a vacuum. And so, finally, I acquired a faith in self-perfection and in my chains. Let it be that I believe in nothing, but this is because I am a<moral> cripple, a child of my age, [Russian] and have to bear the curse of my age, because I am depraved and was born depraved, for Russians, for these last two centuries, have been born depraved. But I am going to break myself, and then my vision will be purified. Then I shall believe, and here *You* are!"

The underground man is the principal type of this Russian world. I have discussed him more often than any other writer, though others have discussed him too, for it was impossible not to see him.

My story about the merchant. Such complexity, along with such immediacy, you won't find in any other writer today.

Versilov (on the day before <the Youth> leaves the house) about the Prince (they have been arrested), and furthermore: "My friend, I'd wish *to warn* you of some scoundrels and... (here we looked at each other, and both of us blushed) However, what am I... how silly!" He grinned, and left.

Ohé, Lambert, où est Lambert, as-tu vu Lambert?[15]

Lambert.

"I've got an *idea.*"

"Why, you always used to have ideas, you were the most clever of all of us in school." (This coarse flattery had its effect.)

"Versilov is clever, he is deceiving you."

"You know nothing, you... dog (why was I calling him a dog?). Now I'm stronger than you are, I can beat you up."

"I'd deserve it."

"But remember, Lanz, the Catholic?" (he's a good fellow, I thought).

I left, drunk. Having left drunk, I remembered on the boulevard: "*She,* a student, what would she be thinking of me!"

It was the Prince who denounced <them>. Of course, he knew nothing very substantial himself, and his denunciation was made on a random guess; yet it turned out that he had known a thing or two after all. With Liza. Oh, how we embraced. And I still went to see Anna Andreevna.

Dinner: The fat-arsed little Prince was crying. Kept pestering some officer. The pock-marked fellow was sulking and remained silent. While the taciturn tall fellow suddenly began to shout *Ohé, Lambert!*

THE NIGHT THE DOCUMENT WAS CUT OUT, the Youth, in a frenzy (at Lambert's): "He is the purest of men, and He must not know about this, but I shall show Him what kind of a woman she is. She is in His

---

[15] French: "Oh, Lambert, where is Lambert? Have you seen Lambert?"

way. She has ruined His life. She has received so much for nothing, while He has had to pay for it with his own suffering, and *she* triumphs, while He is lost. I want to save Him. I want to smash His idol. Let me have Him back. I want to restore him to the state which He was in three days [nights] ago. I will show Him what she is capable of. "You take the money, and I... and when she hands over the ransom money, I'll fling that document in her face! Let Him see all this filth, and come to his senses. You, Lambert, are a scoundrel," etc.

On the next day ~~at the Akhmakov woman's~~ at the old Prince's (i.e., at my own place). Won't release the document. What was I waiting for? But how could one smash His ideal? Which is the better: not smash it, or smash it? Not knowing which was better: <I> refused to let anyone see the document. Thereupon, <my> arrest, and a night at the police station. Unequivocal decision to clear myself, and then <pursue> my idea, my idea!

The day before, at the time of the old Prince's flight, Lambert had learned from the Youth that the latter had agreed to let *her* have the document, *on the following day* and through Tatiana, at Tatiana's flat. They arrive. Makar Ivanovich: "Leave it, forget it." Versilov's son, <his> role.

Finale. And how could I stand the fact that Versilov was right there, with him, with Lambert, involved in a blackmail plot, robbers, my ideal trampled underfoot.

In the last chapter: A letter to *her,* about the document. Must be from Tatiana.

The Youth made an arrangement with Tatiana the day before, still on the day of <the scene with> Anna Andreevna, according to which Tatiana would write her that the Youth would like to hand over the document to her. Tatiana did write that letter. [The first meeting does take place at Tatiana's.] A night at the police station, but the document is already gone for a long time. Went to see Tatiana. He reaches into his pocket—no document! At Lambert's. Alphonsine comes running (or the Youth): *"C'est chez nous!"*[16] Tatiana then over to *her,* to tell her that she shouldn't come. The Youth to Lambert, along the way he learns that it isn't Lambert who has it <now>, but Tatiana. He returns and catches her. *"Il n'est plus temps."*[17] To my flat. Alphonsine, on the contrary, tells the Youth,

---

16 French: "It's our place."
17 French: "There's no more time."

"C'est chez nous,"[18] Tatiana has been tricked. Let Tatiana know so that she can warn *her* not to come. Tatiana.sends word to her, and she comes to see Tatiana, and so they are both at Tatiana's, which *the Youth* has found out, so that he stays at Tatiana's.*

At Lambert's, *le grand dadais* and *le petit vilain,*[19] at three roubles each. *Le grand dadais* had been kicked out of Dussot's <restaurant> for pestering some officer. He was standing there, waiting, at the windows for a long time.

Dies irae, dies illa solvet saeclum in favilla. I love Margaret, crying.[20]

Something more delightful.

About Efim.

!Lambert! There is a priest there.

[Here.] in the finae. The Youth: "I let a certain person read my notes, and here is what he told me" (and here, quote the author's opinion, that is, my own).

And instead of the traditional family (the Rostovs), an emerging family, an ephemeral family, and new, searching for the harmonious life, seeking to find its own level, and even (new) forms.

Versilov's confession. A pattern of universal self-conceit, a pattern of universal searching for the cause of our <present> misfortunes, and of seeking to find a remedy for them in certain external causes, <all this> has made me turn to the inner man, and to ask myself: "Could it be that I myself am guilty?" And therefore—self-improvement.

"Why, you are yourself a crook. Why do you think people ought to be honest?" I said to Lambert.

"Doesn't one need honest people in a crooked business? Much more so than anywhere else, ha-ha-ha!"

As the Youth is walking over to Tatiana Pavlovna's immediately after Makar's death, to inform her of it, he thinks to himself: "How is this? Only the other day Makar Ivanovich was prophesying his own death, and on the very next day he actually died."

The Youth and Lambert, in their second meeting, prior to the chopping up <of those icons>.

---

* Not quite clear in the original.

[18] French: "It's at our place."

[19] French: "The big clown." "The petty villain."

[20] Latin: "Day of wrath, the day that will turn the world into ashes." From scene xx of Goethe's *Faust.*

"Because this is so simple and so banal."

["It can't be that simple."]

"Because you are hidebound. You are obtuse. [I've got you caught."]

In the *Finale* (the Youth is seeking <his own level>, the lost level of the Rostovs). [*They go and join the people.*] The Russian family as such is seeking <its own> level.

But in Russian youth, there is a good deal of instinctive striving for the good, for light... Versilov in <his> confession... This is touching, this is naïve. His whole irrepressible love for you has come to the fore <here>."

His was a great idea—but he had none of the means to transform it into action. There aren't any bad people in Russia, there aren't any at all.

Lambert, during their encounter: "You know, *they* (Mikhailov, Trishatov) have gone over to his side (i.e., to the pock-marked man's)."

Lambert: "I am no criminal, but he (the pock-marked man) is. He would drive nails into a box containing a corpse to <the accompaniment of> a piano, and he will corrupt them."

I to Lambert: "You are getting all excited about that pock-marked man. It seems that I am the only one left with you."

N.B. MAKAR'S DEATH and <Versilov's> decision regarding Mother (i.e., his decision to leave *her* for good)—such is the effect of Makar's death upon Versilov.

N.B. THE LIFE of that old man was tying ME down, I couldn't decide my own fate.

THE GIST OF THE CONFESSION. What *she* meant to Him. "Now I am leaving her with a feeling of reverence. I am free. I have a feeling that I can leave her. Let's go. I love you, my boy. Your mother has allowed me to marry her. Do you know this? An ecstatic image of youth, of everything, of a new life, which has begun for Versilov. Blessings, "I am drinking to her. This is what *she* has meant to me" (story). Then the story of my mother, in a few lines. "I was noticing the thoughts she was having, as I looked at her surprised face, when she (Mother) and I were setting out to meet life together, and she was getting involved deeper and deeper. (The difference in our backgrounds, in our education, all this she did see, she *the ignorant peasant woman!*) Oh, if you only knew what a human being she is." ("The little beetle." A feat for her sake. About Lidiia.)

About Mother and Makar. The little beetle. Self-perfection. SHE.

Got it for nothing. Mother has allowed me to marry her. He about about *her*—badly. "Now again, just as an ordinary mortal, as your Mother's husband and your father." About Tatiana Pavlovna. The boy on the harmonious life.

You've been looking for it. The Rostov family, going out to join the people. "Let's drink!"

In the confession, THE MOST IMPORTANT THING.

Versilov: "All *she* has given me is torture, so let us drink to torture! Now away with this, I am renouncing it, I love only you! Why, do you really think that you'll escape from me? You have defeated me, boy!"

Sitting in a corner... (A tender and ecstatic declaration of love. Princess Katia.)

Now I was suddenly feeling as if all this were only a mirage. The harmonious life. I was looking for it. Living to become like the Rostovs. "And so you escaped into your *idea.* You are dear to me. You have defeated me, boy."

"Everything is good, all life is good, merge with the universe." Atheists. Christ on the White Sea.[21]

"(Are you a Freemason? Are you in on some plot?)"

"No, my dear."

"I was, my dear. Could there be a Russian who was not, at one time, involved in a conspiracy?"

Finale... Isn't it Tatiana who writes a letter about the document, so that the rendezvous will take place at Tatiana's flat?

Versilov's criticism.

Makar: "Love had grown in her heart." He'd come up with such colossal pronouncements with the greatest of ease, yet at the same time he'd be talking about the rod.

Makar. I was struck by his humane attitude. He thought in terms of the rod, yet "love was growing in her heart."

From Versilov's confession it becomes apparent how much Mother means to him (that He had loved her 1,000 times more and *had been taking this liaison much more seriously* than the Youth would have ever thought. "The little beetle," and suddenly, a meeting with *her.* Königsberg and Mother.)

---

21 Reference to Heine's poem "Frieden" from his cycle *Das Buch der Lieder.* Heine narrates the return of Christ to earth and the regeneration of the people under Christ's love. Heine's poem, as well as Versilov's dream, must be counted as precursor of "The Legend of the Grand Inquisitor."

[Recalled Makar.]

After "the little beetle"—about Mother, her surprise. Wrote for Mother to come, and there she suddenly was.

A thirst for the harmonious life. "You, my dear, were enthralling me; the same was happening to me as was then happening to you. After that outburst with Bioring, a reaction took place: I felt that this had been my last insane act and that I was, like you, thirsting for a harmonious life. And who was it that planted these feelings inside me? He and no one else, Makar, 'innocent infant, grow, God's green grass.' "

"Today is the day of <my> great triumph. I feel that my madness has ended. Let us drink to *her*. This has been a captivity of beauty. A powerful feeling, here on Earth. She got it for nothing. She is actually evil.* She is a most ordinary woman. She is virtuous enough to feel sorry for Mother. If I were to abandon *her* too lightly, she'd poison me after your own fashion. Oh, if *she* only were to hear me, she'd forgive understand me. But let nobody know about it." "*She* is going to know," the Youth shouts. "And you love her"; passionate words.

[Here] Also, in the beginning of the confession—a critique of society, of degenerate Russian thought.

N.B. Take *from the Little Beetle:* about responsibility to oneself, once one has become conscious, and about the golden age.

He to her at the rendezvous: "I would like you to understand *my innocent one,* in what state you are leaving me here."

He: "I would like to know that you have understood in what state you are leaving me here."

"I am going to destroy you."

She: "And you won't feel sorry for my youth, aren't you going to feel sorry for what has been before?" (She is afraid).

"Say yes, submit."

She (proudly): "No... Let it stay the way it is. I am myself a little like you."

He: "That's better. A little more, and I might have forgiven you and left—now you are beautiful that way."

She: "Let's both forgive everything to each other and—go our separate ways."

He: "~~What if I can't?~~ I can*not*... because everything is finished. Nor does it really matter."

---

* *Durna:* ambiguous in Russian, since the adjective means "evil" and "ugly."

He: "No, as for revenge, blood—that's, too, a sort of possession."

<His?> blood all clotted in bruises.

She: "Why, this is all from books."

She: "Why won't you kill me right away?"

He: "I can't right now."

She: "Oh yes, your word of honor."

"No, it isn't that; rather, I'll be thinking about you tonight yet."

She: "Torment yourself as you did that time?"

"Let us part: and I shall be thinking of you as of a most precious person, as of a great heart, as of something truly great for me to respect and to love. You are going to be a great and a most serious thought in my life."

(She laughed at debauchery among children. N.B. Some kind of graceful confession to him, à la Princess Katia.)[22]

She to Him: "Yes, I used to love you; but not enough. I quit loving you very soon, seeing that here... *I hadn't found what I needed."*

"What is it you need? Please do condescend to my insignificance. Tell me what is it you need?"

(She advances the ideal of a simple and clean-cut man.) (*"I like cheerful people."*)

She to Him: "I am not worthy of you. I am a blockhead."

"Well, I'm going to tell you the whole truth: There is something funny about you."

She to Him: "Be virtuous, marry Mother."

About Mother—"Don't you dare to mention her."

"You're inhuman," Bioring.

"Now I believe that you are telling the truth." Here, the *Finale.*

"Because you have been taking such great risks, I may actually forgive you. Leave me alone, spare me this."

After having chopped up the icons: "No, this isn't so simple. [Remember forever.]"

Lambert and He agree that Lambert is going to rape her.

She to Him: "If that's what you want, I'll marry you, just don't kill me."

After the confession chapter: Now I shall proceed in simple narrative style so far as this is possible. At Mother's. Body. Tears, etc.

The Youth explains, from his own point of view, His character prior to the concluding scene of the *conflagration,* i.e., of the *fatum* of

---

[22] A reference to a character in Dostoevsky's *Netochka Nezvanova* (1849).

love. That is, how he had hoped, having become convinced of *her* high society vileness (with Lambert), to fall out of love with *her,* and become cured. N.B. *"But, having failed to fall out of love, he quite naturally went out of his mind,"* the Youth notes ON HIS OWN PART.

She: "Maybe I'll marry <you>, I'm very much afraid."

He: "I keep imagining you, and I do nothing all the time but talk to you. You are laughing all the time (during these nocturnal conversations)." A double. Madness.

One man burst into laughter over the grave.

I broke the icon.

The night before, Alphonsine, *"chez qui, chez qui?"* Later, Alphonsine saw the Youth entering Tatiana's flat. Later, the Youth <tells> Lambert, both the day before as well as after he is released from the police station, that he is going to see Tatiana. Then, when he shows up at Tatiana's: Alphonsine: *"C'est chez nous,"*[23] he cuts open the pocket and finds... a piece of paper. Alphonsine shows some remorse. So Alphonsine runs over to Tatiana's place. Tatiana, having received word from Alphonsine, runs over to *her* place; meanwhile, the Youth has just left and sees Versilov and Lambert. He pushes Alphonsine aside and enters through *Maria* <'s room?>.

A BIG QUESTION: Why does Lambert need Versilov?

Versilov may have had an agreement with *Maria,* and has thought it all up.

N.B. It's the idealist, more than anyone else, who is inclined to believe anything vile <of someone else>.

The Youth relates: He was convinced that *she* would fall with Lambert.

This is how Lambert begins <his interview> with *her:* "I am a friend of the Youth's, he has asked me to hand this to you, here's the letter."

It might have been assumed that Katerina Nikolaevna would come by our place first, to clarify the matter, but it could have happened otherwise, too; she could have proceeded to the other location directly, and in that case she would have been lost. Versilov <illegible> the double, <illegible>—"That's precisely it, the double, that's it," Tatiana Pavlovna drawled.

Lambert was exaggerating the importance <of the document?>, nor did he realize with whom he was dealing.

---

[23] French: "It's at our place."

7) "My friend, if I were a Russian writer of talent, I would definitely take my heroes from among the Russian hereditary nobility, for it is only among this particular type of Russian people that there is a possibility of finding, if not order, <so> at least a semblance of beautiful order and of that very "harmonious life" which you and I have been looking for. You are laughing. Yet I'm [almost not talking nonsense,] really, and I'm almost not joking either. Already Pushkin, [our dear Pushkin] gave an outline of the plots of his future novels in "Onegin," at least some appointments,* and believe me that this is all that we've got ~~beautiful~~** that's beautiful ~~not beautiful So beautiful~~, at least as a whole, this ~~social class is~~ is everything we've got that's at least to some extent perfect. I am not saying this because I am Versilov and [so myself a nobleman] ~~it turns out~~, being the descendant of Suzdal' princes of the twelfth century, and very fond of being a nobleman, but rather because there is, at the foundation of this highest class of people, something that is without any doubt, immovable and incontestable. I am saying this because here ~~there are already existent, have been created~~ there already exist certain finished forms of honor and of duty, ~~and consequently, both the touching and the pathetic are open to the novelist. There is nothing in Russia that nothing, save the nobility, exists in Russia!~~ [that nowhere, except here in Russia, has ever been begun, much less completed] [that nowhere in Russia not only was never completed] which is the thing you find rarest of all in Russia. ~~There~~ Whether that honor is good, or whether the nobleman is true to his duty is a different question. What is important is the completeness ~~acquired~~ of these forms and, whatever kind of order it may be, an order ~~acquired over the centuries, saved by successive generations~~ not established by decree from above, but rather developed by the Russian people themselves ~~by the people themselves~~. My God, why, the most important thing for Russia is to have at least ~~some sort of stability and even the least~~ something stable, and an order which has not been decreed from above. ~~And what kind of a noble theme for a writer Oh, having lamented.~~ So then, if I were a novelist, I could be a realist ~~in the highest~~ to the highest degree. [and so my novelist said to himself, having no apprehensions whatsoever.] [Old-timers at the Club. Moscow gossips.] I might make no effort whatsoever ~~at realism~~ to conceal the

---

* Unclear in the original.

** Here Dostoevsky is vacillating between *prekrasny* and *krasivy*.

fact that my heroes are most frequently the most ordinary people, that there are some very funny people among them ~~not being afraid to touch upon the highest born~~. I shall actually show [even] the most monstrous cripples, such as Silvio and the Hero of our time. I can trace the whole transformation of European ideas in the persons of the Russian nobility ~~there are going to show up in my work and among them also Freemasons and Decembrists~~, and each of these individuals may emerge from my pen ~~my side really very funny~~ as a most entertaining personage, and with amazing humor, and still ~~he is firm as a whole, and beautiful~~ present an integral whole—all this is going to be <a portrait?> poetic <?> of [extremely] <?> ~~as a whole, whereas it is dear to us even as a mere hope and more firmly in the picture as a whole,~~ beautiful and even sweet ~~willy nilly as in a picture and even hope.~~

Here there is hope, and you can rest your eyes: at least something that is ~~complete~~. Here you've got a family, here you've got ties and traditions, and in fact faith, ~~but~~ not a wrecking job, no debris or rubbish, from which nothing has come during those past two hundred years. Wherever it may be hidden, but still, some genuine faith.

My dear, ~~But there is still another type of cultured individual which I have never failed to observe and which I have noticed even while I was still in school~~ I know that we have some children who even in their childhood think about their families, who even in their childhood are ~~already~~ hurt by the unharmonious life of their fathers and of their whole environment. ~~My friend, I have known this for a long time, since my earliest childhood, known that even in our schools, that we've had we've developed for a long time some strange~~ [We've got many underground men]. [But what about the people, what about the Makar Ivanovich's?]

"Now. Now there are more of them. There aren't any established forms in existence here. I've been thinking about you and, incidentally, I've been very much afraid that you might <decide to> 'join the people.' "

"I shall follow you."

"<I have> finished <my> wanderings. I was very much afraid for you, my dear. Thousands of times did I see you before me, at night, under your blanket. These are attested <?> When I went abroad—this you must know—I severed my ties. I was leaving forever. *I emigrated.*"

"To join Herzen?"

"No, my friend."

"A condition of serfage. Didn't we emancipate the peasants? Wasn't I a District Commissioner myself? But suddenly it began (the backslide); do you think I was afraid of those feuilletonists, or of that disorder which is now becoming the perdition of Russian youth? Peter the Great made us citizens of Europe, and we became the bearers of that universal union of ideas. Europe has been dear to us for 200 years. A Russian nobleman cannot live without Weltschmerz, and so I, too, had to suffer from it. Beppo."[24]

"Isn't it true that, before these men, you <. . .>

Claude Lorrain. The setting sun <. . .>

"What about the chains?"

"I was saying farewell to Europe. I knew that everything was doomed. Claude Lorrain.[25] Oh, if I could only believe <in> barricades! Too late. It couldn't be. I didn't believe either over there, or here. (A shoemaker.) Because I was feeling very sad. A Russian nobleman. Whims of a Russian nobleman."

"Let it be that our bones are rotten and tired. [As a Russian nobleman I was an atheist. The sun setting over the Tuileries. I want to embrace you."]

[I was a melancholy wanderer/Beppo a Russian nobleman cannot/ The attempt/Tuileries <twice>/You won't understand/chains/ Then they burned/Atheism/After atheism, Beppo/Claude Lorrain/ Before these men/Claude Lorrain/Atheism/Mother, and <his> passion for her.]

"As a Russian nobleman, I was an atheist. But in Europe, I would have been alone even as an atheist. I had the feeling that the sun was setting, only for the last time."

"What then saved you?"

"Mother, Mother. Blessed be the day she appeared <before me>."

Slippery ground (atheism). "I am telling you these things because I want to embrace you."

---

[24] Comic narrative poem by Lord Byron written in 1817 and published in 1818.

[25] Dostoevsky saw Claude Lorrain's painting "Acis and Galatea" in Dresden in 1867, and it served as inspiration for Stavrogin's dream of the golden age in the suppressed chapter of *The Possessed* and for Versilov's dream in *A Raw Youth,* which appears in Part III, Chapter 7:2 of the final version. Claude Lorrain (1600–1682) was a painter of idyllic landscapes, often depicting, as in this painting, the happiness of primitive peoples. Dostoevsky extended the meaning, in all probability, beyond Lorrain's intention. There is explicit reference in the novel itself to Lorrain's painting in Part III, Chapter 7:2.

"But what then saved you?"

"Mother, <her> sunken cheeks. Love."

"Don't I know that this is what's going to happen, everything is going to perish in this conflagration (the Tuileries). But I don't want this to happen. I love my past. And if there are any conservatives at all in Europe, it is we, the Russians. Claude Lorrain, and a description of melancholy. I knew that this had to perish. Europe has become our home. I exchanged Beppo[26] for Venice—Prince Vronsky's Venice.[27] But it is still Venice. And I am still proud of Proudhon. The French never liked us, but we really were their kin."

HERE.

N.B. "How did it happen that we have developed this curious type of a universally suffering man, from Peter the Great's nobility? [And why say that he is good for nothing but wandering from place to place? Why, could it not be true that Weltschmerz is also a great thing? Have all of them really suffered thusly? They have been the leaders, and they still are."

"Really, and the serf-owners, too?"]

"Sure, exactly the serf-owners. Beginning with Chatsky[28] the serf-owner; but isn't one out of a 1,000 enough—thousands and tens <of thousands> have passed on without leaving a trace, but this Chatsky is the one who is remembered. Oh yes, there were many braggarts among them, many ridiculous people; why, I'm not praising everything."

The Youth: "I've seen her. She said... regards to you."

"Do you love her?"

"O, blessed be" (*the tone of these notes*).

Music.

The Boy about *Dadais:* "He has wasted his sister's dowry on food and drink, left her as good as penniless, I can see that he is suffering, he quit washing himself. Oh, how he can sometimes sing! I feel so very sorry for him—both of us; everybody wants to be honest. I want to save him... yet I am myself such a worthless, confused boy. Will you let me stay with you?"

---

[26] See note 24 of this section.

[27] Prince Vronsky and Anna spend some time in Italy at the beginning of their cohabitation.

[28] See note 1 of Part IV.

Finish it at Miliutin's store, with a quarrel with Lambert. "The trouble is you're so stupid, Lambert, that's what you are, why, you don't understand a thing of what I'm saying."

The Youth to Lambert: "I am stronger than you are." [he is a modest man; he'll meet you.]

The Youth to Lambert: "I am listening to you only because I am broad-minded."

The Youth to Lambert: "I've got an idea. You know what: if this whole business is going to flop I'll still have my 'idea,' into which I'll then withdraw."

"You were acting odd only because you were unhappy about 'having become a victim of your environment.' "

"Oh, my friend, what's the difference! Let's drink."

"I am like Herzen."

Out into the street: "What is it makes *her* so excited?" *Everything else aside,* I am stunned by this question. What is their relationship? Why is *she* thinking that now *something* has happened so that he is going to leave *her* in peace? Of course, the fact that he is going to marry Mother. Oh yes, he is going to. For sure. Yes! So then, what about *her?* ~~Why~~ Is *she* glad that He is getting married [and, having gotten married, is going to leave her in peace,] or is she unhappy about it? Why was she so excited?

Yes, this thought did flash through my mind. I remember. I am mentioning it, since it is important for me. ["This thought, which flashed through my mind then, as a memento."] I shall not try to describe [But actually] my own excitement, ~~but~~ a painful emotion was gnawing at my heart. It was a chaos—not just a painful feeling. Yet I was ecstatic <also>.

An encounter on a sidewalk. "Is this you? This must be providence. You know, I already was at your place, and you were not in [your government clerk said, as if this was what I needed.] Where should I be looking for him, I thought. So I went along, and I swear, I was firmly convinced that I was going to run into you, my dear boy; so I'm going to be sitting with you all night, talking. Let's go to my place."

Excitement. The flat. Superficial description. The Prince's child. "There's <her> portrait. A madwoman. I was going to marry her. Your mother had assented to it. (Definitely a madwoman.)"

Nobody ever comes to this place, except Liza. Even Tatiana Pavlovna doesn't.

"I have been thinking, even since before your arrival from Moscow, that you and I might live here together."

"So you did love me?" (à la Princess Kitty).[29]

"What could I tell you, my dear boy? You are looking for the harmonious life, and so am I. Which means simply to persist in one's disorderly ways. This is most remarkable. You belong to the same type as I. I have noticed that you have a need for the harmonious life. Who are you? We are *a thousand old-timers,* we are glad to have reached our conclusions—that's what we've got *en lieu*[30] of life. (So the more you love me, the more you will be my judge.) You've got *an idea?* To be the sovereign king of an island. I knew it, Freemasonry is waiting for you."

"*The Rostovs* and you, the new <generation>—which has always existed—*you* are looking for the harmonious life. (You've condemned serfage.) (A Jewish officer—something one's got to get used to.) You've got purity. (Nihilistics. Thirst of glory, of harmonious new forms.) You are good. Of course, there are awfully many beefy ones among you—but you are the ones that count. Why, it's the one in a thousand who is in command. Oh, I've been depressed for those past 10 years. Right after I quit as District Commissioner I rushed abroad. Makar being the reason. I couldn't stand your mother. Surprise. A close look. Abroad, Venice. Then, the Tuileries were taken. I also want to take a firm stand, to believe, <yet> I believe in nothing. I was saying farewell to Europe. A picture. The golden age. Mother. To be honest. Let it be true that the environment is at fault, but so am I. (I've come to this conclusion through experience.) At least I have gone through everything. Something of that sort. Then things got to where I began to wear chains (in a humorous vein). I sent for your mother. She had stopped in Königsberg. Meeting *her.*"

"She's an ordinary woman. *She* is the average woman. *She* took everything. She chased me away; yet at the same time she would have resented it, had I left her. But what does it matter anyway, say what you want: it became *a passion.* I abandoned everything: that consumptive girl, Liza—I talked myself into believing that I actually loved the consumptive girl, trying to save myself. I abandoned everything, returned <to Russia?>. That slap in the face made me so glad;

---

[29] Reference to Kitty of *Anna Karenina.*

[30] French: "In place of."

that I could bear it. I lived on, having lost my respect for myself. Now you've come—the last outburst, let's drink to life—champagne! Today I've found out that life has started <again>, that N'ovra <?> has been strangled. Here is <her> letter: she is going to marry Bioring, and I have come <here> with the idea of resurrection. I've embraced your mother. Now I am her husband and your father. Let's drink to life! Let's drink to it! I am like a convict whose chains have just been removed! I have been waiting for you, my boy. Praised be my boy and his mother. Now leave me, I'll be walking around all night. Save yourself from Lambert. There's this letter—tear it up. We are happy. Let's become *pilgrims,* good-bye!"

(N.B. Where is the pakage. HERE.)

He refused the inheritance. This was sincere. Which means that he was capable of anything, provided (yet He) <. . .>

"Let's dring to madness, too. Maybe that's what life really is."

"Really?"

"Then what is the harmonious life? How should I know?"

"Don't you love her? of course you do!" (The dear.) (Some funny, cheerful stories.) About those 1,000 who are not indifferent. N.B. (basic ideas) N.B. and (HERE)

"Are you involved in a secret society?"

"I love children. I've come to love this child."

"I realized that I wasn't *the same* anymore, which is not to say that I had fallen behind the times, it's just that I wasn't the same man anymore. There were other times when it appeared to me that I wasn't standing on the sidelines at all, but on the contrary, that I might have been at the head of a movement, and become a leader. But look here, I must admit that I haven't even to this day made up my mind."

"A Freemason? You might find consolation in being a Mason, or a leader. I don't. This isn't what I need. I don't even need *life.* What I need is the harmonious life—truth, peace with myself—and if I had to be a bad man, so solely by my own fault, so that I could always set it straight myself, for there would be something perfect outside me. Oh, if this were so, I'd fear no chains in thc world."

I: "I don't understand you."

["My dear, this is a long story—for example, what should one be: universal man or Russian? I still don't know. I can't be either the one or the other, because there isn't such a thing as the first, and I myself don't want to be the second. With my friends, these things usually end in a joke or some witty remark, but those 1,000 of us, we suffer from each of these trifles."]

"How sad it is, as a somnolent shadow—*

"But this is not my case. Show me the sun, and I shall die with joy, I'll be glad, even if I were left behind."

"Now I shall simply be a father, a husband, and a humane man. This is entirely sufficient and, what is most important, I'm glad I have the chance. The chains have fallen!"

Underground man is the most important type <today>.

A man of culture?

Melancholy Levin.[31]

"I am convinced, my dear, that you won't understand even half of what I'm saying, but I really needed you today."

The golden age. Makar Ivanovich and Mary of Egypt. "Join the people; it's better, after all, than butchery.** Let the Minister of Public Education say of me, too, that it happened 'by permission of his parents,' though, let me say this, if all our fathers were like me, things wouldn't be in such vile shape. We <were> sincere, my dear, that's what we were. Oh, we were little liars, too, but we loved truth."

"Let my bones be weary, but show me the sun, and some movement, and I'll welcome it, every bit of it, including the fact that I've myself fallen behind; grow, God's green grass, even from the grave, my love."

"We have the right to be irreconcilable, for we haven't forgiven anything to ourselves either."

"Those who are born with a snotty nose" (Versilov used to say.)

The deputies Nàquet and Màdier de Mòntjau. <Sic!>

A fine country across the Altai
Flung an Elbow over to China.
Tra-ta-ta, ta-ta-ta,
The cat married the tomcat.

---

* A quotation from F. I. Tiutchev's poem "Kak ptichka ranneiu zarioi" (1836).

** Used apparently without the connotation of the English word, but as a metaphor for "a coarse, animal existence."

[31] Levin of *Anna Karenina*.

He is much more educated than I am, but he has decided to concern himself with nothing anymore. He is a cynic.

"Good-bye!" (abruptly and gloomily).

He knows what *Butte aux Cailles* is.

"I am a citizen of the town of Butte aux Cailles."

"Słońce, panie? Butte aux Cailles,* that's where you will observe that a pair of trousers is worn for 15 years, without taking them off once, and no shirts are worn at all. *Mlle Alphonsine,* will you fix my tie (*le vilain,* he bought it for his own money)."

"Allons prendre un verre de l'absenthe vert et[32] <illegible>. You are dressed like a dandy. A jacket, have you got another jacket? I can give you some money, come to my place."

*"Nous avons un rouble d'argent de parier** jaune que nous avons prêté chez notre ami."*[33]

He was talking in sections between two commas, and it might have been funny, if it hadn't been so long.

"He knows his business. *Vous vous répétez.*[34] (He knows his business.) *Je voudrais vous pleurer, quand vous mourrez... Où est donc votre montre?*[35]—Spent it on food—*Le petit vilain, n'as pas son montre,*[36] gilded, 8 rubles."

"Si vous ne rendez pas 10 roubles je parlerai de mon nouvel ami Dolgorouky de grosse voix."[37]

Lambert got mad.

They cost more than there is use in them.

Walking home drunk, about le vilain: "A dear boy, an unfortunate boy! Why, I'll be exactly like him, I am, too, a *vilain, 'File petit vilain!'*[38] Why does she have an aversion to him?"

Lambert goes with him, he is talking about them and, apparently, cannot restrain his anger; only from time to time he says to the Youth:

---

* Polish: "The Sun, Sir?"

** Apparently a misprint for *"papier."*

[32] French: "Let's have a glass of green absinth."

[33] French: "We have a ruble of yellow paper money that we borrowed from our friend."

[34] French: "You are repeating yourself."

[35] French: "I would like to cry, when you die... Where then is your watch?"

[36] French: "The petty villain does not have his watch." Dostoevsky uses the wrong gender for "watch." He says "son montre" instead of "sa montre."

[37] French: "If you do not give back the ten rubles, I will speak of my new friend Dolgoruky in a loud voice."

[38] French: "Run off, petty villain."

"Well, how glad I am, how glad I am!" And then again: "These skunks," etc. "I'm finding it so annoying, I wasn't expecting you—there will be another fellow, a real bore, please do put up with it, and after dinner you and I will <really talk things over>."

"Oh, I'm going to break with them!"

And right there, with the oysters, he virtually forced him to have one drink after another and tried to take him over to his own place, but he didn't want to drink.

?About Anna Andreevna? A question. Shouldn't it be told so that both Lambert and the Youth fail to mention her on purpose, and that later, when drunk, the Youth says: "Isn't it true that we both purposely refused to mention Anna Andreevna?"

The tall fellow knocked down Lambert's hat. Lambert: "This is <just> a kopek's worth, but you could really deliver me (your friend) <from these people>. If we could make 3,000 I'd send them all away to the thieves' den where they belong."

Astonished eyes. "And we are strangers, always strangers to each other."

"Your sincerity has won me over: ~~let us~~ I thought that there was more of a mystery about you. I am glad that this *was all so simple*. Let's live together, in order and in self-perfection. I am yours, yours forever. Let us go."

Or: "So then, what's the matter with you is merely that she got in your way, when you and she met, that you were already about to start a harmonious life when she came along and destroyed everything?"

"Almost like this, my dear boy," he smiled.

His idea, formerly: could it be that self-perfection, *the* <moral> *feat,* would *lead* one to everything else as well? Be a man—this before everything else. All right, let there be some hitch—it can't be helped. So you suffer some—that's what life is for; but to make up for it, you've done everything you could do.

"You haven't achieved it even after all those sufferings, while She's got it for nothing!" shouts the Youth.

N.B. Envious of Makar (<who is> harmonious and calm), he went abroad. Thoroughly investigated the idea with those chains. He wrote to her asking her to join him, [Mother ("thinking that I was condescending to her. <Actually> I was being arrogant, just as with Makar. She could teach me many things").] (Turn all the goods over to her.) And there, that meeting with *her*—and everything collapsed.

"Yes, fasting, genuflections. The longer I watched myself the more thralldom I saw in myself."

N.B. "My story is a comical one," he begins his narrative. "I discovered the slave in a free and perky man. Only they (those who practice self-perfection) have a right to judge society and to make demands on it. Yet they won't judge it either, they'd much rather help."

The Youth: "I understand. The servitude of the nobility."

He: "Not at all."

Moving abroad; a complete rift between one's life and one's convictions. At every step. People have one balsam—self-esteem (the last of the passions, which does not desert the wise man, according to Tacitus).

"What should I be, what should I do? Be content with the role of a humble shoemaker (as our new people have prescribed us)—a man of the caliber of those who die on the cross couldn't stand for this."

"Did you ever join a secret society?"

"No, my friend."

["I am a nobleman—to serve the nobility is not enough."]

"This animal idea of love is torturing me to death, so humiliating it is. I was aspiring to perfection... This was very funny. But that's the way I am. The most important fact here is that I was capable of believing in perfection. I'm believing in it even now... there are 1,000 of us. There must be many of us, some pulling one way, and the others pulling the other way, in these times of transition."

N.B. "Why, she isn't perfect at all," *He* says, giving the Youth a strange look. "But she must be perfection itself."

"Why?" The Youth is giving him an astonished look.

"But if she has *such power* over a man, she must be perfect."

HE HAS AGREED WITH LAMBERT THAT LAMBERT should rape *her*. *He believed* that *she* would consent. (A psychological trait of his character.) Besides, he hoped that if *she* consented, he might be cured of his love for *her*. But having realized that he couldn't be cured, he went out of his mind.

She to Him: "Please, I shall marry you, <but> don't kill me."

His IDEA*: She* is not worth his love; such torture and a whole life broken for her sake, "<your> mother is worth incomparably more."

[THE YOUTH EXPLAINS, FROM HIS OWN POINT OF VIEW, HIS <Versilov's> CHARACTER, PRIOR TO THE CONCLUDING SCENE OF THE CONFLAGRATION, I.E., THE FATUM OF LOVE.]

And now HE HIMSELF, in his *confession,* explains to the Youth what precisely has been so tormenting Him, what precisely has been *hurting* Him so much. Why this *fatum,* which has broken [all his life to pieces,] a blind love for an unworthy creature, whom he rejects, for he has begun to love Mother. As for that, he had begun to love Mother abroad, after "the little beetle." (N.B. There is, however, the curious fact that every time he got together with Mother, he always grew indifferent and developed a contempt for Her. "Could it be that I have not found my ideal in *Her?* I couldn't help despising her as I would any vile society woman.")

"And now I am *cured.*"

DELIGHTED WITH MOTHER. That night, enthusiastic words of praise TO HER.

"Oh, don't be scared, we are still the same old liars, yet we love truth."

"I used to love suffering, those sunken cheeks, that beauty spent on me; Russian women lose their beauty early. And still... The Beauty—of other forms—and everything is finished."

"I left <Russia> to get away from <its?> movement, and I was a wanderer out of pride, not from remorse, without anger."

"Were you regenerated by Europe?"

"Europe was those very same noblemen who'd run away from their nobility."

"Serfdom. Why, weren't we the emancipators, didn't we abolish serfage, Anton Goremyka: [39] I left Russia out of pride, and actually not because I had not received enough in return for my liberalism. On the other hand, I was repulsed (1) by those self-satisfied fools, those brazen-faced fellows, those opinionated feuilletonists, (2) by the crooks who were using those new ideas to enrich themselves, and (3) by those poor souls who are now 'joining the people,' and <finally,> by the fact that I could see [everywhere] the slave behind that mask of insolence. I simply asked myself what my role was and what I had to do, whether I ought to become a humble shoemaker," etc.

[I am searching for the harmonious life.] Breaking up one's own self (Makar, envy of Makar. "Grow, God's green grass.")

"For us, foreign countries are <like> stones; why, before these men you are—the Tuileries—the golden age."

"Just be a loving <husband?>, she, she."

In the meantime, <my> *idea* was growing.

"We could not help developing into propagandists and promoters

---

[39] See note 16 of Part III.

right away. No one knows where to draw a limit. Not to himself, nor to his epoch."

"I made a start with my chains. But there *She* appeared."

The Youth comes out running to his own place. His character. He has passion. (He found that out.) And in such passion—the insult. *Resurrection.*

"Byron, Beppo, Venice, the Tuileries, a Point of rest. I was sad during my wanderings. I was saying farewell to Europe. I believe in nothing new. [In nothing at all. Oh yes, I believe in an economic breakup, in the hearth, but in nothing else."]

"I am the last of the Mohicans. The Tuileries. Really, before these men you <. . .> We, the Russians of former times, used to wander around and pray; like Makar Ivanovich, we were pilgrims."

Claude Lorrain.[40] The beginning of European humanity.

Mother. You. *She.*

Specialists, etc.

The Youth: "You are hostile to specialists. I am noticing a certain amount of hostility about you."

He: "Perhaps this is so, my dear, and I am altogether grateful to you for your remarks. I like your remarks very much."

"Russian man would acquiesce in being no good himself, as long as, outside himself, there remained something which was inaccessibly holy. But when everything *that is outside* has been destroyed and he has been left alone, Russian man will refuse to go on. [That's why we've got the type of the nobleman to help us recover our identity at a <time> like this.]"

Self-satisfaction comes with contempt <for others>. (Atheism is love for mankind.) I was having a feeling of hatred. I had a need for what had been before. To adore the past. I was seeing nothing at all in those new people save traits that were deserving of contempt. Became a misanthrope. Was saying farewell to Europe. Claude Lorrain. Mother.

N.B. Up to this point, not a word about Mother.

Sunken cheeks.

Breaking oneself.

"Were you a believer?"

"No, my friend, I believed in nothing."

An image of atheism. Belong to them, the whole immediacy of

---

40 See note 25 of this section.

life through this love for *her.* I did not want to participate in life in this fashion. I had been preaching something different, I wanted to fight, and there, *fatum.* She was bound to be perfection itself.

"Let's drink to Mother and to her. (N.B. The fact that I am drinking *to her,* proves that I am cured.)"

Atheism is the love of mankind.

The Youth: "If you understood it that way, why then, could you be unhappy? Why didn't you join them?"

He: "I was having a ~~contempt~~ feeling of contempt for them. OURS, too, i.e., I, for my part, could tell them what their philosophy was. Whereas they could do nothing of the kind. Besides, I had remained true to the past."

"Is this how you believe in Christ?"

"Yes, this is how I believe in Christ," he said (alas, he did not believe).

"Eh, no, my dear, I believed in nothing!"

[My friend. I have never believed in Christ."]

"Is that really so? But what about your chains?"

"My friend, you are my judge. I have been expecting you. What would I have told you right now, as you are my son, and she is my wife..."

"I am an idealist. Yes! I couldn't stand their coarse, positivistic* atheism."

About food, a cult of blood, for the sake of blood, even before anger.

The burning of the Tuileries. In order to prove that we dare do it.

Oh, these phrase-mongers.

"Oh, we were understanding it differently. Atheism."

"Yes, to be sure, it is scary without God, but we can *nestle up* to mankind and to all the universes—"

"This is a deity, too."

"No, my friend. This is antitheism."

"But what are you doing to me!" (exclaims the Youth).

He describes the picture to Rostov.

"Why didn't you call for me?" (I put my hand on him).

"What should I have told you?"

"This very thing."

---

* Sapozhnogo ateizma, literally, "boot atheism," alluding to the positivist slogan that "boots were more important than the Dresden Madonna."

"I was thinking of that. I was thinking right now, as I was waiting for you. I've always been thinking. But who was I myself?"

"Oh, I need you tonight, hear my confession. People aren't this cruel, you are wondering what it may be that I love so much. Yet I have quit it. After <my tenure as> District Commissioner <I went> to Europe."

IN PASSING: About the Russians who were then in Europe, after having abolished the old order based on serfdom (he touches all this *in passing*).

Russia is so strong, still <we have> no fatherland.

But better let it be not me, but the new <generation>.

I'd let the people in on everything (exhaustion of authority), and <even> those rampaging seminarians who have replaced the nobility.*

The Youth: "It seems to me that you are so much an idealist that you could not stand real, immediate life."

("Your remarks are amazingly original.")

He: "I know that communism will fail, and that it is going to come."

The little beetle. "This is where I wrote to your mother that she should join me. Note that she didn't actually get there, but got stuck in Königsberg. I've seen her, she has allowed me to marry."**

[Here.] "Why didn't you call me?"

"What could I have told you? Do you think that it has been very often that I have been in a position so close to an integral and perfect completion of my affairs, as I am today? *What could I* have told you?"

"Well, this very same thing," etc.

That sunset in Claude Lorrain's picture is a riddle and a mystery.

But I dreamed that the mystery had already been realized; why, really, before these men... <. . .>

"Mother, you."

Atheism is a state of deep orphanhood, there is *no* God to nestle up to...

If they took away God and all gods

Deification of mankind in place of God.

The great mystery was accomplished, the appearance of Christ.

---

* This as well as several of the preceding phrases are unclear in the original.

** Might also be: "I saw her, and she gave me permission to marry <Lidiia>."

~~Everybody worshipped~~ What is it I have been teaching you? Everybody worshipped.

Eternal life.

[Makar (One cannot help worshipping).]

The Youth: "This is atheism—this is pure atheism! Which comes with God on your lips."

In the beginning, Claude Lorrain—everything will pass, but instead of pictures [of blood, or freezing to death,] dreams, ideals were created. Later, atheism.

"Idealist! Idealist!"

But at this point, the idea of the chains. Then, the idea of Mother, sunken cheeks, *amazing views.*

He didn't come for a long time, chains. At this point, he meets *Her.*

Resurrection, *She* had written me a letter.

I read it, got up, and instead of hatred, sent her my blessings.

"I understand that you have respect for it. Yet in the meantime you are telling a mere youth, such as myself, about it."

"Why, no one is forcing me to say a thing. I'm doing it to embrace you. Today I have a son, and, consequently, a new life is beginning for me."

"For us, we together," says the Youth.

"They become attached to the civilized type, but to some of them with hatred; I always imagined leaving you as such."

The Youth: "But Mother and her tranquillity won't give you your peace. You will be again tormented by pictures and the fate of man kind."

"And let it be, such is our life! In Russia, there seems to have developed a strange cultural type of <people who feel> Weltschmerz for the whole world... Let it be suffering, we wouldn't have accepted happiness anyway. It is a ridiculous type, but let it be. I want nothing good and new, I love the old, my own."

The sun, and movement.

"But playing the fine gentleman is a good thing, my dear."

Venice, Beppo, Laura. I loved Venice more than Russia.

"You again, with that serfage of yours."

"What good is this life to me, once I have seen that I can be a criminal (poison her)."

[A task for 1,000 people] It's enough if there is one in a 1,000, but there are more of them.

Later, join the people. [make <her> a cripple]

The Youth: "But I am satisfied with you alone. I shall follow you!"

"Me? Oh, my friend, what did you just say? My wanderings are over. The last act took place several years ago when I went abroad. To call you then, to take you with me, I wasn't able at the time, I really wasn't able. I cursed everything, abandoned everything, and left in a terribly depressed state of mind. [Yet I <even then> believed more in you and in your mother, than in all] of my wanderings. My dear, I am telling you all of these things in some kind of a strange hope that you may understand all this balderdash. I have called you here (in the end) because I felt a need to embrace you and to call you *my son*." (N.B. Here, a picture of Europe.) +

(Atheism.) "This is where I never knew how to bring things to an end. Here, I always ran into some kind of mystery. I <never> managed to end it simply."

"Perhaps it is really so that there is no simple ending to it."

He: "Entirely possible, my dear. I like your remarks, my dear."

The funny thing was that I never got the idea (that I should love Mother). But I was all too happy when I <finally> got the idea. [What is of the essence here is a bit more serfdom, <somebody to tell you> what to love, what to believe in, and what to *be*.]

A cadet—a Jew—why did I take offense?

Venice—why do I love Venice more than Russia?

The Rostovs changing into the new <generation>. Oh, I am not talking about the fact that <Russian> fathers are welcoming dishonor, or the fact that they have become mortgagers, or feuilletonists gloating about the latter fact. But rather, about the fact that all this is, say what you want, simply a mirage.

He must himself define beauty.

Restless and skeptical even in their childhood.

Yet it is impossible to show mercy to them, for already their ranks have been swelled by prodigious masses of noblemen as well.

Abroad, we have noblemen who have fled the nobility.

I am not feeling sorry about that; much rather, I am for these new ideals. However, I do want to establish the fact that our country is now in ferment, and that it is impossible not to register this in a chronicle of our time.

"My boy, I've said this about you only right now. This is how I used to see you at the time I was dreaming of you."

Love for Mother and her sunken cheeks would not atone for anything, however...

As far as I was concerned, atheism would not lead to bloodshed, but to every man embracing and welcoming the other.

A Russian nobleman cannot help suffering from Weltschmerz, and Peter implanted an idea <. . .>

Could it really be that my yearning (abroad) was only a whim?

I am saying that there are 5,000 of us—

Why, before these *men* <. . .>

*This crude positivism** was getting me confused. By the way, there is a secret hidden here ~~the ideal~~.

[A task, there are 1,000 of us.] Reality always smacks of boots, even in the presence of a most vivid and pronounced striving for an ideal. The Tuileries shouldn't have disturbed me. But I didn't want to submit. This thing was repulsive to me, and I turned away. I don't want any part of the new, I want my own queer ways.

Atheism.

Bone-tired.

"But who knows: perhaps I was really grieving over the ruin of the nobility."

But that a nobleman and a man of culture <. . .>

"I am a young swell. I am a District Commissioner. I am disenchanted. I am suffering from Weltschmerz. My friend, all this may perhaps sound funny to some people, but please do show some regard for the fact that I have saved this for you, that I have decided to make this confession before you. For this is the most important thing in the life of a cultured Russian."

"What is perhaps the strangest thing about this confession of mine is the fact that I want to make it so clear." ~~and that I am trying~~

A most honest young girl.

She is working for a living, for she finds it too much of a burden to eat her father's bread.

This is true in 1,000 exceptional cases, but ~~in general~~ as a ~~rule~~ general rule it presents a frightful distortion of human feeling.

"Really, what are you doing to me," exclaimed (the Youth). I was all rapt attention. In a frenzy.

"That was affected 'love of mankind,' while this is, on the contrary, immediate, genuine love. Being the idealist you are, you are frightened by such immediacy right away."

---

* See n. (*), p. 535, above.

"I like your remarks, my dear."

"Atheism—I have felt universal love, but I don't love Mother."

"Mon cher, je suis gentilhomme avant tout et je mourrais gentilhomme."[41]

"My dear, I am a little overcome by my ridiculous enthusiasm, and I keep digressing into extraneous details."

"You won't understand it, but still I'm going to plant some seeds [in your mind]."

Then they burnt the Tuileries. A Russian nobleman could not approve of that.

The Russian nobleman as a herald of world (and of the union of all mankind) citizenship and of universal love. He has received this mission from ~~his~~ the course of history. These vistas were opened to him by Peter, and formulated by Catherine the Great. Let it be the mission of all Russian people. Yet the Russian nobleman was a pioneer, a leader of this <movement>. I stand for it, and this is how I have understood its calling. [To be the pioneer of a great idea in Europe, and perhaps for all of mankind.] [Nastasia Egorovna, get us some wine. Two hours before Makar <?>. I needed you.] ["Looks like boots."] And indeed, what else could he be but a pioneer, since he alone was the bearer of enlightenment and of honor.

"But what about Makar Ivanovich?" I was embracing him.

"The truth of our people will be fused with ours, and we shall go on together. The time is near."

"Society must be built upon moral foundations; nothing can be founded upon the flesh, upon an economic idea, upon making stones into bread, and so far our politicians are fooling only the gullible. The moral ideas of a nation are derived from religion, or are formulated by popular religion. Anyone who wants to reject and *break up* the old foundations, such as private property, family, etc., must break up the old faith. So they have announced that they are atheists. The Russian *gentilhomme* could not agree with this, or cure himself, being himself an atheist—I've been seeking to reconcile—<and> sought to reconcile many <of these conflicting tendencies>. I could not, of course, but admit that atheism was on the ascent in this world. Yet I was viewing the setting of our old sun with sadness. Even if it passes, a great <new age> will begin. This is actually what I wanted to express. But so far no one has been able to understand me. And

---

41 French: "My dear, I am a nobleman first of all and I shall die a nobleman.

I have been wandering alone. For only a Russian heart can divine the future of this world, that is, a Russian of the advanced, civilized type. You are laughing. I am not a madman. Then they burned the Tuileries. And after the Tuileries, a universal reconciliation of ideas. For a Russian nobleman is the universal reconciliation of ideas. For, in our time, educated Russian thought is the universal reconciliation of ideas. The educated Russian type is a universal human type, and up to now it has been only the Russian nobleman. A Frenchman is only a Frenchman, but a Russian... a Russian is a progressive; his thinking is very much ahead of everyone else's. The bearer of a universal ideal. You are surprised, my boy. My soul is outraged. They burned the Tuileries, they fought. Only the nobleman is waiting, biding his time. You are surprised. How this amuses me. We have developed a type. The Russian land is demanding an ideal of me. Universal reconciliation of ideas. But this you haven't got in Europe. Except for our 1,000 people. We are the bearers of an idea. Acis and Galatea."[42]

"What are you doing to me?"

"My dear, I have called you in, so you might understand one-hundredth <of my ideas>. The Russian nobleman, a universal idea. I am little bit in a state of enthusiasm," and here, the mission of the Russian nobleman. "A pioneer." "I did not cease calling myself a Russian when I realized that I loved Venice more than Russia."

"But weren't you in the government service prior to that?"

"Such was the legacy of Peter and Catherine. A pioneer, though much of it might have never happened."

"Yet I was sad. The Tuileries."

Solomon—everything will pass away.

"EVERYTHING WILL PASS AWAY?" "Everything, my friend, and perhaps nothing of what you have loved will remain, because a new order will begin."

"As a nobleman I cannot allow this to happen—as a nobleman."

The sun, and movement.

"What utter weariness, while I do have faith, and an idea. I want no part of the new. What is left to me is my dream that perhaps things may turn out my way after all."

Atheism. Makar: "I love even from the grave."

---

[42] The title of Claude Lorrain's painting. See note 25 of this section.

Every Frenchman and German. Only a Russian can be more French than a Frenchman.

Universal reconciliation of ideas. Beppo, stones. Why, before these men, you are.* Atheism. They were persecuting God. Crude positivism.** I have a sad feeling. For it is my idea, after all, that is right. Oh, it seemed to me, the gold<en age>.

Fatum. "Why did I have to insult her? But I did insult her. She was sitting there, in Königsberg, and I didn't even send her any money. [Incidentally, note that I was taking her (Mother) <abroad> to tear her away from her native land, since I wasn't intending to return to Russia.]"

"I was beginning to feel tied down, and I wanted to kill her."

Makar's idea. Asceticism.

"<You> simply could not stand an immediate love."

THE COMING OF CHRIST. Why, this is it. The very thing.

(There it is, the dream of a Russian nobleman.)

About Mother, about Tatiana. Her love. [Made her happy with a kiss.]

Well really, how could she understand a nobleman's melancholy.

Tatiana understands it.

To be an honest man. Support her and make her happy.

"Je suis barinet gentilhomme."[43]

Makar Ivanovich, [being part of the people,] belongs to the nobility.

"This is how I understand it, my dear, our role. And this is my final conclusion."

"*She* has broken the flow of my thoughts."

"We [Russian] nobles are now concentrating on a new universal union of ideas. And in the meantime—in the meantime it represents all that is positive about the future, ad what is really going to happen."

Russian self-restriction is neither cynicism nor shamelessness, as is the the case with those people who are thirsting for their right to be dishonorable, but merely sincerity with a striving for improvement. The ideal. To bow before something outside one's own self (see page 5).

---

* Apparently an incomplete phrase, though it might be translated: "Why, you are before these men."

** *Sapozhnost'*. See n. (*), p. 535, above.

[43] French: "I am a noble lord." "Barinet" is probably a misprint for "barine."

"Yet you were happy."

"Who told you that I was unhappy? I've been happy all my life, but I was sad, and... and... ~~there was~~ there came a moment when I was perfectly happy. Mother."

"Oh, my dear, how often does love meet hatred, or even look altogether like hatred."

?To develop such a beautiful type—it cost dearly. Mine, a nobleman's happiness, and mine, a nobleman's idea.

The muzhik and Mother, sunken cheeks. For me, it all started with her sunken cheeks. Her photograph. I wrote to her, asking her to join me, but in the interval I fell in love. About Mother. She didn't even make it to Königsberg.

A letter from her.

Oh, it didn't happen suddenly, that I fell out of love with her. Even to the very last outburst... I was reproaching myself that I was acting that way toward Mother.

I was feeling, and had felt for a long time, that I was *free*. This outburst was... probably some sort of recollection, the dregs, something external and incongruous—yet I myself was already free.

What then, was the meaning of those recent events, of that last outburst and, last but not least, of Lambert? He and Lambert. Hadn't Lambert been offering him something?

And later, when I met Lambert, he lied to me: "No, I haven't been telling him a thing."

Misérables,[44] and Mother in Königsberg. All the same, a man's life is like a book read to the end.*

"Mother, allow me to read to you from the Gospels."

"Ah, how well you read, my dear. Read this Epistle, he used to love this one particularly."

I at Lambert's. "<Meet> her in some dive. Invite Him. Let ~~her~~ him see, let him!" "This can be done," says Lambert.

When the old Prince has come to stay at his place, he goes to see Tatiana and tells her about the letter. They agree that Tatiana should write to her the next morning. But upon leaving Tatiana he runs into Lambert and tells him that he will be at Tatiana's on the follow-

---

* This phrase is quite unclear in the original. The translation is a mere conjecture.

[44] Reference to Victor Hugo's *Les Misérables,* which Dostoevsky ranked above his *Crime and Punishment*. The novel is referred to in the final version in Part III, Chapter 8:1.

ing day, that he is going to return the letter to her, thus putting an end to the whole affair. As for his visit to Tatiana, he had come to tell her the news about the old Prince, and she informed Bioring of it.

The question of that letter written [by Tatiana]: How did Lambert and He find out that Tatiana had written that letter? (Perhaps <through> Maria?) Think over and find out.

N.B. Solution of the problem: The day before, the Youth had left the old Prince <at his flat> and visited Tatiana, to tell her that she should write to her. Tatiana had given him a tongue-lashing, but she had written the letter, sent Maria to deliver it. [Here N.B.]

?They started begging Maria not to deliver the letter. But Maria, once she had received the letter, delivered it, and he and she quickly sent her over to her place, and Alphonsine to ours. In Tatiana's letter not a word was said specifically about the flat.

YOU ARE THE TYPE OF AN ACCIDENTAL FAMILY, AS OPPOSED TO A TRADITIONAL FAMILY. THE TRADITIONS OF A RUSSIAN FAMILY—THAT'S BY PUSHKIN.

There was no better way to use your leisure or, so-to-speak, your day of rest.

BUT THERE IS THIS QUESTION: ARE THERE MANY TRADITIONAL FAMILIES LEFT, AND AREN'T EVEN THE TRADITIONAL FAMILIES TURNING INTO ACCIDENTAL ONES (as a result of our ideological chaos). Versilov has a lawful family. Just see if the family unit is intact here! The Junior Chamberlain and Mitrofaniia. A personage showing the dimensions of the Very Reverend Mother Superior, Mitrofaniia,[45] of course, without meaning to suggest anything criminal.

The Professor: "You were concealing your document—this is most characteristic."

"Look at the persuasions of your father: he is a nobleman, of ancient lineage, and yet at the same time a Communard, and simultaneously, a true poet without any faith at all, yet one who is ready to die for something quite indefinite, in which he believes, following the example of countless civilized and Europeanized Russians of the Petersburg period of Russian history. Leo Tolstoi did not spare even his own Pierre, whom he had been leading with such a firm hand throughout his novel, even in spite of <his> Freemasonry. He loves Russia, yet rejects her altogether; he tortures the members of his family, and considers this to be his right, his responsibility (Makar

---

[45] She was accused of forgery. Dostoevsky was acquainted with the trial.

Ivanovich, Mother, guilt, illegitimacy, Liza is pregnant). What could be more perverted, more disorganized?"

["You are a youth from an accidental family. God save you."]

N. Nik. About Versilov. No signs of ~~education~~ strict scientific discipline. All these people were living in terms of inspiration and prophecy. Even public figures, even scholars—the whole thing being <a lot> like the practices of the Khlysts:[46] spinning around in a circle, and prophecy. Just as the system of serfdom placed the nobleman under an obligation to get an education (ever since Peter), so a merchant's inherited millions present an absolute obstacle to his getting educated. What do you care about scholarship when, at twenty years of age, you've got millions on your hands? And as for our Seminarians, though they are the most educated of us all, they have the quality of taking everybody else, i.e., all Russia—simply everybody—for the very kind of Seminarians they themselves are, which is also why they are so much bolder than anyone else in their conclusions and in their views.

A history of the Russian [noble] family.

... In the form of a magnificent historical picture (War and Peace) which will be handed down to posterity, and without which posterity could not carry on.

The accidental family is a much more difficult project.

N. P. : "If you were to publish this manuscript (your sincerity would be against you), ~~but~~ your strong sincerity would harm your belletristic success..."

N. M. : "All the old has been destroyed rather thoroughly and accurately; what's ahead of us—one can only speculate on what's ahead: it's almost frightening."

[Letter of Nik. Semen.] "Our youth is 'joining the people,' yet it is full of self-sacrifice, some fine feelings have remained even from our past history, though the future is altogether problematic. You are from an accidental family... [God save you]." These are the last lines of the letter, and suddenly a *postscriptum*. About an abandoned infant and Nikolai Petrovich's role (three or four lines with a nuance of touchiness).

---

[46] A religious sect that arose in the middle of the seventeenth century. By the middle of the nineteenth century they had disintegrated and no longer functioned as a group. They were distinguished by the belief in eternal rebirth, and the materialization of the holy spirit. They whipped themselves (Russian word *Khlyst* means "whip") to drive demons from their bodies.

The career of a lawyer. I myself have been thinking of one—the satisfaction derived from money, fame coupled with dignity and even some of that *breadth* to which you devote a good deal of attention in your notes as well as in your fantasies.

(The old Prince keeps closing his ears and waving everybody aside.) "Don't say that! Don't say that!" If somebody enters his room, he gives him those pained glances. They put him to bed, then dinner. I had stuffed Katerina Nikolaevna's photograph into the bag.

About young Versilov. "*Ce jeune homme, il est charmant, mais je ne l'aime,*[47] don't let him into my room, don't let him." Nasty little photographs. He looks, laughs with affectation, and then suddenly bursts into tears precisely [because] they are making him laugh.

Oh, people are very nice. Yes, but this is not going to be part of my plan.

[It's the flat that matter, she about the little dog.]

"My friend, I am in a very immediate way convinced of my <imminent> death," an old man with an icon, with an icon split in half.

[It seemed to me all the time that this was merely an allegory and that, though he did love Mother, he was still in a state of frenzy and had the absolute desire to bring something to an end, just as he had <finished off> this icon.]

Versilov went out of his mind; I had been predicting it.

A shirt. What shall be put into <his> grave? "If you know something, better not tell anybody. Let them do what they want. Is it true that they want to put me in an insane asylum?" (and he burst into tears).

The conflagration. "He is going to kill her!" I shouted. "Quite likely!" said Tatiana.

[Anna Andreevna, to the Youth, about the old Prince: "No, on the contrary, I sent you to him ~~perhaps~~ also so He couldn't kill her."]

The old Prince to Anna Andreevna: "Why can't I see both of you together? Why won't the two of you make up, *et voilà tout*."[48]

About von Sohn. "*Mais, mon cher, je suis libre, n'est-ce pas?*"[49]

The Junior Chamberlain. Split the fortune.

After the funeral Liza whispered to him that they were expecting him, that He might actually come.

---

[47] French: "This young man; he is charming, but I don't like him."

[48] French: "And that's all."

[49] French: "But, my dear, I am free, am I not?"

[N.B. important.] Lambert needed Versilov to get her out of the way, for his influence, for his familiarity with the circumstances—and, in the case of a commotion, so he could blame the whole conspiracy on Versilov; this is what I think—the more so, since Versilov did not need the money and Lambert was getting all of it, as much as he could extort <from her>.

AT THE RENDEZVOUS. *She* tells Him about the *document,* about Mother, what a wonderful woman she is, "You—how I *respect* you" —(feverish!). He was all flushed.

N.B. (More than anything else, she *fears* the document), [and nothing else.]

She: "Compared to you, I am <like> a stone."

He, pointing at Mother's portrait: "I know that you know her. There she is."

"The dear."

"My angel, be my angel."

"I shall be your angel, certainly. I shall make a point of becoming worthy of you; I shall respect and esteem you immeasurably."

"Perhaps I shall destroy you. I gave you my word. Go."

Folding <her> hands: "Don't ever threaten me again, ~~spare~~ forgive me."

And VERSILOV entered the room: here now is the whole terrible scene, as things happened, one after another.

Feebly <?>: "This, however, is not why I have come... This is not what I wanted to tell you... Sonia, have pity on me, poor wretch that I am!"

"Really, wouldn't you at least say farewell to her?"

The old Prince: *"Le carême—Dites, dites, y-avait-il quelque chose,"*[50] and he went down on his knees (toward the end, after this the Youth goes to see Tatiana Pavlovna).

A panegyric to Katerina Nikolaevna [by the old Prince,] memories of her.

"ANNA ANDREEVNA, YOU MADE THIS RENDEZVOUS POSSIBLE, counting on a scandal; even while admitting me, you counted on him" (at Lambert's, on that drunken night).

At Lambert's: "I'll see to it that Bioring won't get her!" (i.e., he is himself in love with her).

---

[50] French: "Lent—say, say, wasn't there something?"

Lambert: "She reveres him something terrible."

"You know, Lambert, she may really be in love with him."

ANNA ANDREEVNA: "Lambert has disappeared. He has promised me an awful lot, but now he is gone."

I'll admit that I was feeling sorry for her.

Chistov's house. His wife. The Junior Chamberlain, an incident, to Anna Andreevna.

Current affairs. At the tavern. About the pock-marked man. Lambert has been imprudent, he has done a foolish thing.

At the tavern on Canal street. He *was* there. I ate, then just sat there waiting, about Mother. The Junior Chamberlain. Came home. Alphonsine, at the government clerk's, steal the document, steal, [perhaps even kill the landlord.]

What made me mad was the fact that Alphonsine was in my room.

Asked to send the pock-marked roomer out.

"I gave her my word of honor, I vouched for him."* And altogether, watch her very carefully, don't leave her out of sight, (and the landlord), and, one must give her credit, she did take care of her commission, though dishonestly, then,**

"Was she really so much afraid?"

"Yes, he had threatened to kill her before."

Little Trishatov. Ran over to his place once more and fell asleep.

Asleep, Mother's face. These are the high society people who have offended <me?>. The golden age. But be he blessed!

In the morning, among other things, back to Anna Andreevna, told that she'd be in at five o'clock.

N.B. In the morning, the Youth is even more strongly convinced that He loves his mother, and didn't he actually start to console <him?> along these lines, while reading the Gospel (warm words). *"I know for sure."* And after the chopping up of the icons he learns about the letter from Anna Andreevna (about Bioring)—and (?) that he had also conveyed the letter to her through Anna Andreevna. The latter had promised. Nastasia Egorovna. "Go and tell Nastasia Egorovna from me that she should let you in, and don't you forget that I did this for you. Only <for you?>."

When the Youth comes to Tatiana to deliver the document: "I'll hand it over myself."

---

* The gender of the verb suggests that this is a woman speaking.

** The whole paragraph is quite unclear in the original.

"He wants to show off."

"Well no, I'll give it to her myself."

N.B. The effect of the document on the Prince and on Katerina Nikolaevna was stronger than I had ever expected.

The assistant to the officer in charge of the Police Station. At the Police Station. "My, what a strange young man you are; I haven't ever seen one like you."

The old Prince: "*Chèr enfant,* if you have something you want to tell me, better leave it unsaid."

Anna Andreevna, having told the Youth of the rendezvous she had granted him upon his entreaties (under her guarantee), gave it some thought, then allowed me to listen in. <N.B. "Oh no, oh no, I won't eavesdrop under any circumstances!"). For the sake of clarity, let me make a preliminary remark. In allowing me to overhear <their rendezvous>, she had her own, strong reasons. Knowing Katerina Nikolaevna and *their* relationship, she was firmly convinced that the rendezvous would lead to nothing at all (i.e., regarding acceptance of his marriage proposal), but then again, I might rush in and create a most beneficial scandal, and secondly, my presence would still be a guarantee that he wouldn't kill her (which possibility Anna Andreevna may have been considering), and finally, the last reason, she was hoping that after it was over I might release the document. And, finally, that I would retell everything to her. Anna Andreevna always hoped that <one day> I would lose my temper and present the document—to the old Prince, of course.

It wasn't Anna Andreevna who gave him permission, but Nastasia Egorovna.

A new version of the CONFLAGRATION. The night before, prior to Bioring's raid, Tatiana had been to *her* place to tell her that I would come at 11 o'clock of the following day to hand over the document to her. And so it would have actually passed, and they would never have found out about it, but then, late that night, Katerina Nikolaevna heard of my arrest, and, in the morning (before she had had a chance to see Bioring, at 8 o'clock, when it was still dark), she showed up at Tatiana Pavlovna's to find out what had happened to me, ~~what is it~~ "Is it really true that he has been arrested?" They then hurriedly agreed that *she* would come at 11 o'clock as scheduled before, while Tatiana Pavlovna would run over to the Police Station to get in touch with me. But it happened that I met Tatiana while already on my way and that, upon entering the house, we didn't find Maria at home (she had been bribed). In the meantime, Maria rushed over to let them know, and an hour later, while we were still warming ourselves, suddenly, Alphonsine... *"Mais s'est chez nous..."*[51] <sic!> Then, etc., FINALE.

The rose. I was crying *about something,* melting into tears and kissing the rose (I had forgotten about all of them)—I am reporting this as a strange psychological fact. Since I had forgotten them all, I was merely kissing <the rose>.

"The other day I sent <for him?>, and he seemed not to have paid any attention to *her* letter."*

Delivery by the pock-marked man,

"Really, at times I am trying to imagine: How is man going to live without God, and will this be ever possible, and I must admit, my dear, I invariably reach the conclusion that it is impossible, that people will still end up going back to Him! But for a certain period, conceivably... as a consequence of the principle.** I am imagining, my dear," he went on, smiling, "that the battle has ceased and the struggle has subsided. ~~And there I~~ I imagine that, after the battle, after curses, ~~blood~~ clods of dirt, and whistling, and when ~~everybody~~ the struggle has subsided, people will suddenly sense that they are alone on this earth. This would be just as in Claude Lorrain's painting, also with the sun setting, majestically and with a strong call, yet setting as it were on the last day of mankind, That great source of strength, which had until then fed and given warmth to mankind, was passing away, just as that sun, and people would suddenly have a deep sense of their orphanhood. ~~Oh~~ My dear boy, I could never imagine people as being thankless and having grown stupid. Alone and orphaned, they would immediately nestle up to each other so much more closely and lovingly; they would grasp each other's hands, understanding that now ~~merely~~ only they alone ~~only~~ are everything there is to one another. That great idea of immortality would have disappeared, and it would have to be replaced, and the entire great surplus of former love for Him, whom they had left, would now be turned, in their hearts, toward nature, the world, people, any little blade of grass. They would begin to love the earth and life with a special, no longer with their former, love; they would observe and discover in nature

---

* Quite unclear in the original. The gender of the verb suggests that the speaker is a woman.

** Unclear in the original.

[51] French: "But it's at our place."

such phenomena and mysteries as no one would have even suspected to exist before, for they would now be viewing ~~her~~ nature as a lover views his beloved, and not just with a knife in hand ~~before, the former utility~~ as before, not just for gain, utilitarianism, and ~~greed~~ mere curiosity. They would awaken in the morning and ~~caress~~ kiss each other, hastening to love each other, each of them knowing that his days are short, and that this <life> would be all that he'd get. They'd be working to help each other, and each would be happy to give his own to everyone else. Every child would know and feel that any person ~~he'd meet around~~ he'd chance to meet was his mother and his father. 'Let tomorrow be my last day,' each of them would think, looking at the setting sun, 'but all the same, I shall die, yet all the others will still be there, and after them, their children,' and the very thought that they would still be there, still loving each other, their hearts still throbbing for each other, would replace the idea of a reunion in a life beyond the grave. 'Let me die without leaving a trace, but there will remain in their hearts the memory that I have lived and loved them, and when they, too, have passed on, and an entirely new generation has arrived, even then, thousands of years later, those new people will remember us all, all of us who lived before, that we were once alive and loved them before they ever came to life on this earth, and that we would have liked to see their happiness. And let it be true that in the end the earth will come to its end, and the sun will be extinguished, and yet somewhere ~~in the harmony of the universe~~ there will remain the thought that all this did once exist and *in some way served* ~~universal harmony~~ the all—and people will come to love this thought. Oh, they'll hasten to start loving each other, yet the longer, I think, the sadder ~~they~~ will all be. They will be proud and strong each for himself, yet they'll become they will become timid for each other. They'll become tender toward each other, nor will they be ashamed of this, but will caress each other, like children. ~~They~~ When meeting each other, they'll look at each other deeply and meaningfully, and in their glances there will be love and sadness. And each will tremble for the life and happiness of every other. ~~And then, a great vision will arise before the eyes of all men~~—oh, I cannot ~~imagine anymore~~ imagine people *without Him,* my dear! He was here once, and He cannot leave <us>. And even if He leaves, they will have found Him themselves. I imagine that He will stand up among all those people, hold out his hands, and say: ~~'Children, angels~~ but ~~you~~ how could you forget Him? And He will lead them to Him. And it will be as if the scales have fallen from the eyes of all men, and shouts of delight and happiness will ring out everywhere on earth, and everybody will be resurrected to a new, now already a boundless, love. Forgive me, my friend, but I couldn't help concluding my little picture of the future of the human race in this, and in no other fashion. I am a philosopher and a deist, but being a Russian I am also a dreamer who just can't help dreaming. Of course I have always ended up leading them to Him, and here is my *profession de foi:* My dear, this is a fantasy, and really an unlikely one. But ~~I swear~~ I want to confess just one secret to you: it is only too often that I am imagining it ~~as I think about the future of this world~~ —but how? Even now I frequently imagine it, for I just can't help thinking of it. Oh, I can't, I just can't help thinking about it, or something of this kind. But I have always concluded my picture with a vision, like Heine's, on the Baltic Sea: He was coming. He was coming, and they were all recognizing Him. What are these chains of mine?—All nonsense! But I'll confess just this one thing before you: I could never imagine people without Him. I always ended up by leading them to Him."

"What <were you doing?> before you no longer cared, and how did you treat her?"

"I sneaked up to her and kissed her."

"Suddenly I remembered this and fell in love <with her>."

She didn't even get as far as Königsberg.

I sensed, however, that there was in it all, something that had been prepared beforehand, something like an earlier involuntary daydream about how he was going to relate this dream to me. Yet there was nothing unnatural about it; it was all pure feeling. I thought a little and told him so.

About her. This was a mood, I don't know how I fell in love with her. N.B. And frowning from time to time, and even angrily.

Mother. The photograph. A saintly Russian woman. Lidiia—don't be jealous. An idealist's remark. "I was waiting for you here" (the child, tea). "Why didn't you call me?" "But what could I have told you?"

Rostov. "Joining the people." "Are you a Freemason?" "Why, why didn't you call me?" "You are stingy." The confession. I was a wanderer. Everything will pass. I didn't believe and wanted nothing better. I didn't want anything new, even if it were better <than the present>. "That's serfdom," the feuilletonist is going to say. Really, so help me God, he may perhaps be right. An old type. A Jewish officer. Atheism. Why, before these men, you... Venice. Fell asleep. Claude

Lorrain. Mother. About love for Mother ("Grow, God's green grass!"), with love grown infinitely great. My idea (later, in the form of madness caused by <his?> love for *her*). Makar: "God's grass is to grow." Chains. Meeting with her. *She, fatum.* The cure. About Makar. Today is Sunday. Let's drink. Let's go on a pilgrimage together, enthusiasm (Princess Katia). Order: Venice. Men. Claude Lorrain. A mystery solved, or atheism. The coming of Christ. The idea of chains. Mother's sudden idea. *She.*

Order. "My God, what is most important here in Russia is stability and order... Fathers and mothers, who are not in the least ideal, but who represent something complete; there's something both touching and pathetic <about it?>, there's something stable at the foundation."

"The abolition of serfdom."

"Look at our seminarians."

"They've got no traditions, no faith, and no form. And yet they have taken root."

"The likes of Shevchenko."

"They've got no traditions. Up to now they used to take root. But now, perhaps as a result of their condition of servitude, they've become rickety. Yet they, too, will become a part of the people."*

"But having found you, I am beginning to take root." "Why, fathers don't fall from the moon, or do they?" And while still in the nursery, <my> soul was seeking its proper place, and order. Such searching may cause one great mental anguish. Oh yes, of course, some would take root in a slavish way, still others with envy and bitterness. Only recently one could hardly notice them, though there were enough of them.

"This was the anguish of a Russian nobleman."

"Je suis gentilhomme avant tout."[52] About His nobleman's anguish.

"We emancipated our serfs just so, there are 1,000 of us. A part remains. Out of 1,000 or so people there is one stelite."

"I was dear to you, wasn't I?"

"Oh, I shall follow you."

N.B. References in *Otechestvennye zapiski.***

N.B. References in *books* about the Rostovs, etc.

---

* The whole paragraph is quite unclear in the original.

** *Fatherland Notes,* the journal in which *A Raw Youth* appeared.

52 French: "I am a nobleman first of all."

Name and Topic Index